The Ambitious Life of
an American Icon

TED SCHWARZ

TAYLOR TRADE PUBLISHING
LANHAM • NEW YORK • BOULDER • TORONTO • PLYMOUTH, UK

Published by Taylor Trade Publishing
An imprint of The Rowman & Littlefield Publishing Group, Inc.
4501 Forbes Boulevard, Suite 200, Lanham, Maryland 20706
www.rlpgtrade.com

Estover Road, Plymouth PL6 7PY, United Kingdom

Distributed by NATIONAL BOOK NETWORK

Library of Congress Cataloging-in-Publication Data

Schwarz, Ted, 1945–
Marilyn revealed : the ambitious life of an American icon /
Ted Schwarz.
p.   cm.
Includes bibliographical references and index.
ISBN-13: 978-1-58979-342-2 (cloth : alk. paper)
ISBN-10: 1-58979-342-0 (cloth : alk. paper)
ISBN-13: 978-1-58979-413-9 (ebook)
ISBN-10: 1-58979-413-3 (ebook)
1. Monroe, Marilyn, 1926–1962.   2. Motion picture actors
and actresses—United States—Biography.   I. Title.
PN2287.M69S39 2009
791.4302′8092—dc22
[B]
2008041645

Manufactured in the United States of America.

CONTENTS

INTRODUCTION

Norma Jean Mortenson wanted to be famous. It was a goal not much different from that of many other young girls growing into womanhood in Los Angeles and elsewhere.

Not that Norma Jean had a specific profession in mind. The adults she knew worked almost exclusively in the motion picture industry, but so did many of the parents and family friends of the boys and girls with whom she went to school. Hollywood was a company town, just as much as the parts of the country in which the economy was focused on coal mining or manufacturing. The studio moguls were like the mine owners. The support personnel—film cutters and editors like her mother, seamstresses, carpenters, electricians—rode the same trolley cars, shopped in the same drugstores, bought food in the same grocery stores, and purchased their casual clothes in the same specialty shops as movie stars making a thousand dollars a week per picture.

To a kid like Norma Jean, movie stars were neighbors as they went about their daily lives, exciting to see only when there was a disconnect and they were projected on a giant screen, their names in marquee lights.

Even in Los Angeles, where women had been writing scenarios from the start of the movie industry and many were well-paid employees of the studios, there was little talk of women doing more than marrying and raising families while their men earned the family income. Throughout the nation there was a small but growing number of women entering the medical field, including such "male" specialties as surgery. Women were reading for the law, an apprentice system considered the equivalent of going to law school, as well as taking university classes when they could gain admittance. And there were entrepreneurs, such as San Francisco resident Sarah Breedlove who died in 1919, just seven years before Norma Jean was born. Using the name Madame C. J. Walker, this woman, the daughter of former slaves, became the first black millionaire businesswoman in the nation.

Despite the realities of the changing times, despite the impact of the Great Depression—which saw women as well as men seeking jobs in any field to help their families—the 1930s, when Norma Jean was growing into a teenager, was a time in which no one talked about female role models, self-esteem, and achievement outside of motherhood. Norma Jean became infatuated with the older boy down the street, marrying him just before he felt the need to enlist in what had become World War II. Then, lonely and resentful over the lack of her young husband's companionship, Norma Jean, with her mother-in-law's help, got a job working in a defense plant. There she found other young women her age and slightly older: all of them lonely; some married; some despairing the fact that they were not; and all gradually becoming friends in the manner of those who share the same experiences.

Norma Jean forgot about being famous. Her goal, and that of the other young women, was to try to add style and sensuality to the coveralls they had to wear. They might be faceless individuals on an assembly line, but with some adjustments to the coveralls, they could at least pretend to be sexy.

And then David Conover came by. He was a photographer on assignment to boost morale by taking pictures of pretty young women in wartime jobs, then having them printed in the various publications for the soldiers. Officially, the captions would show how everyone was working together, the people at home supporting the boys overseas. Unofficially the images were as close to pin-ups as the boys would see in *Yank* and the other publications created for their entertainment.

Conover delightedly photographed several of the assembly line women, noticing that Norma Jean's expressions seemed especially responsive to the lens. All the women he used were pretty, but there was something in the one young woman that would make a reader linger a bit longer over her face. He had permission to take extra images for personal freelancing, both to military and civilian publications, so when he was done with his assignment, he arranged for Norma Jean to put on a sweater she kept in her locker and join him outside during a work break.

The photographs were what he desired—a pretty girl, young, fresh, enjoying the moment. Norma Jean was paid for her time. Conover was paid by the image. And enough magazine editors responded to the assembly line worker the way he did that he found it profitable to return to the girl for further posing. He also recommended her to other professionals and, eventually, to a local modeling agency.

Once again, Norma Jean wanted to be famous, an ambition no longer a mere fantasy—if she limited her thinking to modeling. A few months after meeting Conover, having obtained so much work that she quit her defense industry job, Norma Jean's face could be found on magazine covers sold throughout the United States. It was an achievement most young women would have considered an ultimate goal in itself. But this was Los Angeles, and fame meant something greater than being a pretty face on what was often a pulp magazine cover. Too many other young women had achieved the same success. Norma Jean wanted more, and Los Angeles being the heart of the movie industry, she asked the modeling agency director to help her get even a small role in a film.

The problem with becoming an actress was that Norma Jean could not act. She was beautiful. She came alive for the camera. She was a delight to behold. But so were hundreds of other young women who had flocked to Hollywood with the same goal.

Some, like Norma Jean, had grown up with the film industry, their families or their friends' families working behind the scenes or paid as extras. Many had first been models. Others came by train or bus from small towns and big cities having first tasted show business by starring in a high school play where they received standing ovations from siblings, parents, grandparents, and assorted friends. A few had real professional experience as paid actresses on the stage or entertainers in nightclubs. All thought they were at least as good as the stars of the various studios, and all were fiercely competitive.

Fortunately studio contracts were relatively easy to obtain, even for a young woman like Norma Jean who had only worked in front of a still camera. Such contracts, though officially for seven years and seeming to promise fame and fortune, were misleading. Numerous escape clauses inserted by the studio lawyers allowed the studios to hire an actor at their minimum rate, use the person as little or as much as they liked for six months, then fire the individual. This was why early musicals often had dozens of beautiful girls, always in the background. They were inexpensive, they worked hard to keep their contracts in force, and they delighted young men who might otherwise take their girlfriends to some other form of entertainment.

Norma Jean was like almost every other starlet with no experience other than putting a smile on her face and sticking out her chest for the camera. She looked beautiful in scenes that mostly were left on the cutting room floor. She was just one of many pretty girls in the scenes an audience got to see. And when she was fired after the first six months, no one wrote to the studio to ask what her next picture would be. She had reached the pinnacle of the success about which she had fantasized, or at least the pinnacle for her abilities, and she was on the way back downhill before she realized it was over.

But Norma Jean had started to master the game of becoming famous. She had learned where to compromise and where to object. That was why she fought altering her hair color, accepting what eventually became platinum blond when she learned that the change made it easier to light her face when the background was dark, resulting in more work. And for some of the same reasons she eagerly agreed to go on multiple-day photo shoots, during which she traveled with and shared a motel room with the photographer.

As a starlet there had been a number of changes beginning with her name and continuing into a social life that involved looking pretty at poker games and other males-only parties held in the homes of powerful producers. Wives were never present, but starlets acted as room decorations available for "borrowing" when one of the men decided to take a break in one of the guest bedrooms.

ℬ

In Hollywood a girl's virtue is much less important than her hairdo. You're judged by how you look, not by what you are. Hollywood's a place where they'll pay you a thousand dollars for a kiss, and fifty cents for your soul. I know, because I turned down the first offer enough and held out for the fifty cents.

The actress known as (but not yet legally named)
Marilyn Monroe, as quoted by her ghostwriter,
Ben Hecht.

Introduction

࿎

Norma Jean would later talk about how much she hated this period of her life; but Norma Jean wanted to be famous, and when she found herself represented by one of the most powerful agents in Hollywood, she realized she could achieve that goal in the show business in which she was barely competent. Norma Jean could become a star.

There was other help coming from unlikely vessels, including a Hollywood columnist who cadged a free office above the pharmacy department of Schwab's Drug Store. He told Norma Jean that her childhood was too normal, too boring for anyone to want to write about her. The only dramatic upbringing she knew was the harrowing tale of orphanages, foster homes, molestation, and rape endured by her foster sister, Beebe Goddard, during the years before they met one another. Soon she related the tales as she remembered them, generating compassion and fascination from the media for a life she never experienced.

The men Norma Jean bedded and/or wedded were often coldly chosen for how they could help her achieve her dreams. The first was a boy barely out of high school, scared about going to war, filled with raging hormones that blinded him to the difference between lust and love, and willing to do a neighbor a favor in exchange for what he thought was "forever." Instead, he was Norma Jean's "starter husband," providing little but a chance to escape into the world at large.

Then there were the producers and directors who said "thank you" with movie parts, casting influence, and contract guidance. There was the baseball player who, along with Norma Jean, became part of the most glamorous entertainment couple of the day, their fans mobbing them throughout the world. Yet privately he preferred television and comic books to sex, and showed his resentment over Norma Jean pursuing a film career instead of just caring for him by physically beating her.

Then there was the adulterous playwright who was simultaneously sating his physical lust while keeping adequate intellectual distance so he could make notes as though his wife were a case study in preparation for a new play that became a reality after her untimely death.

And there was the final lover, the politician in competition with the long-ago actions of his adulterous father. The affair was known to a handful of West Coast–based newspaper reporters. But the affair was also part of the politician's private life, and in those days such privacy was respected.

The fame came at a price, one she could not have anticipated. The major motion pictures studios had long been supplying their employees, from the talent to the assistants to the tech people, with pills meant to enable them to work more effectively during the long hours of a production. There were pills to take at bedtime since sleep, when in the midst of filming demands, was limited at best. The medicine rendered the user unconscious almost immediately, no matter how unsettling the day might have been. Stimulants were provided for morning use so everyone could arise before daylight to prepare for the day's shoot. The fact that they were highly addictive and that some studio employees would find their effectiveness waning with time led to abuse that would eventually destroy such famous lives as Judy Garland and Peter Lawford.

Norma Jean was too weak to resist the allure of the drugs. She had the money to buy anything she wanted. She had doctors willing to prescribe medications without learning what else she was taking through the largesse of other medical professionals. And her friends were simply bemused by the fact that, when she stayed with them, if she felt she had reached the maximum safe amount of her own prescription drugs she could take to sleep, she would go to the friend's medicine cabinet. There she would take whatever looked helpful, washing it down with champagne, the alcohol contained therein another depressant.

In 1956, with her body ravaged by drugs that were slowly eroding her health and endangering her life, her appearance on movie sets erratic at best, *Time* magazine sent one of their West Coast staff reporters, Ezra Goodman, to prepare a cover story on the woman who had legally changed her name to the one she had used for a decade of work—Marilyn Monroe. She was thirty years old and had been living a series of often-contradictory lies that other journalists had accepted. This time Goodman went deeper, checking her statements, traveling to find family members, former teachers, fellow actors, and anyone else who could either confirm or correct the history of Norma Jean as she grew to womanhood and fought her way to the top of the film industry.

Goodman discovered that Marilyn Monroe knew the father she claimed had disappeared or been killed, that her mother was alive and not dead as she claimed, and that the loving way in which she was actually raised was in sharp contrast to the studio biographies. He prepared a lengthy article that told the true story of Marilyn Monroe and sent it to the magazine's editorial department in New York. There the staff was horrified. They were fans like the rest of America. By the time they finished altering Goodman's work, placing Norma Jean's Marilyn Monroe picture on the cover, the ultimate imprimatur of fame in that era, the lies had become truth for the American public.

It is with this history that every biographer must approach the subject of Marilyn Monroe and the times of the woman who created her. Sometimes the lies are outrageous; yet there are also times when the truth rings false because so many myths have so long overshadowed reality. Always there are those who want to add their own bias based on something read, common gossip, an Internet site, or some other unchecked or uncheckable resource. They talk of Marilyn working for the CIA, seducing heads of state and others with knowledge needed by our government. They say she was murdered or committed suicide. They turn her into a Barbie doll, dressing her in elaborate costumes, and then have her act out imaginative stories about the life she never led, creating a world that becomes their unshakable truth.

And beyond the conspiracy theories related to Monroe's death are the fringe true believers who will not let Marilyn Monroe (or Norma Jean) die: such as Sherrie Lea, a woman whose psychiatrist convinced her (as she has, in turn, convinced other past-life enthusiasts) that she is the reincarnation of the actress. As proof, she has "memories" of events involving Monroe and either one other person, such as the late Jack Kennedy, or several people, also all now dead.

Even vengeance and greed have come into play since Marilyn Monroe's (first?) death. Norma Jean stole the story of Beebe Goddard's life. She also left an estate in excess of a million dollars, with none of it going directly to her foster sister. Hurting for money, and because it was known that occasionally Marilyn had sent Beebe presents over the years, Goddard began selling and auctioning Marilyn Monroe possessions she had been given. The income proved substantial enough so that Beebe could live out her days without wanting. It was also based on a false premise. Not only did she sell items Monroe had never provided, many of them were not even made until after Marilyn's death (though within the lifetime of Sherrie Lea—but apparently the "reincarnated Marilyn" never reunited with Goddard).

Ultimately the question remains, what caused the film industry and the nation to be so taken with one actress whose skills, roles, and performances showed less ability than other actresses from the same era who are long forgotten?

๛

Time magazine writer Ezra Goodman said, "There are any number of top-notch Hollywood directors whom she has driven to professional distraction and who will tell you firmly that Monroe cannot act her way out of an old brassiere."

๛

Other actresses married prominent men. Other actresses led lives of questionable morality. And other actresses manipulated the media with whatever "truth" suited the moment. Yet only Marilyn lives on in the hearts and minds of generations not yet born when she died.

To understand who she was and how she continues to impact popular culture is the purpose of this book. So fasten your seat belt. It is going to be a wild ride.

ACT I

Norma Jean

One

~

Meeting the Constant Lover

They were the Celluloid Commandos, the daring young men of make-believe for whom no mission was too dangerous, no enemy too strong, and all acts of derring-do were selfless in their spontaneity and heroism. The Celluloid Commandos were America's elite unit of noncombatants. They bore their weapons—typewriters and still and movie cameras—as they recorded ceaseless triumphs over the enemy in fake newsreels, propaganda posters, placed articles, and training aids for real soldiers, sailors, and airmen such as actor Jimmy Stewart who put the phoniness of Hollywood behind him when he became a bomber pilot, truly risking his life for his country.

Ronald Reagan, the extremely nearsighted B-movie actor, was an Army Air Force captain in service as one of the stateside Celluloid Commandos. He took to the air with some frequency, braving regular small plane flights to Catalina Island during which he was repeatedly challenged by the scourge of airsickness. Fortunately, he was able to have his fevered brow soothed by his then-wife, Jane Wyman, with whom he slept almost every night of his active duty. The rest of the time he was on his nearby base—the former Hal Roach Studios—shared with such fellow physically unfit actors as Alan Ladd and Clark Gable. Long known for its production of comedy shorts and features, it was appropriately renamed Fort Wacky when it was drafted into wartime duty as the headquarters for the West Coast–based Celluloid Commandos.

The work of Fort Wacky had a more illustrious history and more serious technical challenge than the conglomeration of physically unfit Hollywood misfits and its nickname implied. The simplest work was the propaganda film, designed to give Americans the idea that our fighting forces were doing better in combat against the Axis powers than they actually were.

The training film was quite another matter. This was a sophisticated version of work done by the Taos, New Mexico, Society of Artists during World War I. That earlier work involved the painting of murals that matched the terrain American soldiers would encounter as they fought throughout Europe. The murals were positioned on a firing range used for practicing cannon fire at the approximate distance that the large guns would be used in actual combat. Then, as round after round was fired in simulated battle conditions, the men hopefully learned skills that would result in the enemy taking more casualties than would be possible if the allied forces were seeing the land for the first time.

Technology, both for weapons and training, advanced quickly. World War I bombers dropped the explosives by hand, leaning over the side of the open planes, estimating the angle at which the bomb would be dropping, hoping it hit an enemy target. Everything was guesswork and only experience improved the limited accuracy.

By the start of World War II, sophisticated sighting equipment inside an enclosed cockpit was used to determine when to release the bombs carried in the belly of each plane. The bombers flew faster and higher than in the past. New gun sights showed the terrain, but the view was quite different from what might be seen from the older, lower-flying aircraft.

The new equipment required new simulation training aids. It was no longer possible to send a camera crew over enemy territory to record the view for insertion in a bombsight simulator. Instead, the technicians at Hal Roach Studios gathered stock footage from past motion pictures, travelogues, and documentaries that showed Japanese cities and factories targeted for future bombing. These would be edited and rigged so a new pilot could practice bombing runs looking at a movie that matched the view he would have in real life.

Another aspect of the propaganda effort (coordinated from, among other locations, Fort Wacky) was to show the American people that Hollywood stars were involved with the fight. The problem was that straight (openly gay and lesbian volunteers were rejected), physically fit males were enlisting in the military. The seemingly virile men available for roles were either homosexual, disabled in a manner that might not be obvious on the screen (Peter Lawford's mostly useless right hand, for example), or too old. This reality frequently meant that an actor stationed at Fort Wacky would be shown in print ads and placed articles as being active military, presumably going back and forth to the front.

The nearsighted Captain Reagan, for example, had been inducted into the active military on April 14, 1942, training at San Francisco's Fort Dixon before being transferred to the army air corps and stationed at the Hal Roach Studio, then called the Army Air Force First Motion Picture Unit. He would not have been able to safely handle combat, his poor vision making him a danger to anyone around him. But as a real soldier in a pretend war, or a pretend soldier in a real war, he felt so comfortable wearing a uniform and making movies that supposedly simulated what active duty soldiers were accomplishing that they became a part of his mental résumé. Over time he seemed to forget that his films from that era—*This Is the Army, Secret Service of the Air, Mr. Gardenia Jones, International Journey, Murder in the Air, Rear Gunner,* and *Desperate Journey* were fantasies, and that his other films, made for training, also were not experiences he had lived. By the time he was president of the United States approximately four decades later, he occasionally presented himself as an eyewitness to a history that never happened.

The truth was that during World War II, Jane Wyman Reagan was frequently in more danger than was her husband because she regularly traveled the country with other civilians, selling war bonds and encouraging support for the Red Cross. Captain Reagan had the equivalent of a nine-to-five job, sleeping in his own bed almost every night. When the couple was apart, it was usually because of Jane's war work, not her husband's. However, the fan magazines were read by teens and young women who had boyfriends, husbands, sons, and fathers in combat. The editors, working with Fort Wacky personnel and others, devised stories about Captain Reagan's "sacrifices" so that men would relate to him and women would relate to his wife.

The July 1942 issue of *Modern Screen* was typical of the planted stories meant to boost the morale of the readers whose loved ones were likely to be in the midst of battle. The article told how Jane Wyman had ". . . seen

Ronnie's sick face bent over a picture of the small swollen bodies of children starved to death in Poland. 'This,' said the war-hating Reagan between set lips, 'would make it a pleasure to kill.' "

Whenever Reagan made public appearances in the Los Angeles area, the stories always said he was "on leave." Both the studio and the military wanted him to have the image of a man fighting for his country while helping out at home whenever possible. And he came to believe his own press.

For example, President Reagan gave one talk in which he mentioned seeing heroism during his service in World War II. The incident he described involved a B-17 pilot whose aircraft had been hopelessly damaged by enemy fire. The plane was going to crash and there was nothing to do but order the crew to parachute to safety, which most did. The exception was the belly gunner, a youth who had been badly wounded when fighting the enemy aircraft. He couldn't jump, and even if he could leave the plane, it was obvious he was dying in excruciating pain.

The brave pilot, unhurt and able to escape, was unwilling to leave the weeping, terrified youth to suffer alone during those last few minutes of life. Instead the pilot sat on the floor of the plane and cradled the man in his arms. " 'Never mind, son,' " President Reagan quoted the heroic pilot as saying. " 'We'll ride it down together.' "

Usually President Reagan told the story as though Captain Reagan had been a witness. His eyes would seem to glaze over as he remembered the scene of selflessness. Tears would often be present, and his voice would choke as he quoted the heroic pilot.

The only problem was that he had not been there, could not have been there. Any witness would have died in the plane crash. President Reagan was simply remembering a war movie Captain Reagan had made. Thus, in hindsight, he was the perfect person to set in motion another fantasy life, this time that of a young defense plant worker he did not know existed.

The incident occurred when Captain Reagan was asked to arrange for photography inside a war plant. Still photographs of the home front were provided by Fort Wacky and other military base photographers who went into their communities to record bond drives, scrap metal collection drives, the use of ration stamps, United Service Organization activities, and other efforts to support the armed forces. The pictures were then sent to newspapers and magazines read by servicemen and -women throughout the world.

The other area of coverage, one popular with both the servicemen and the photographers, was what was generically known as Rosie the Riveter. Prior to World War II, the United States had been more rural than urban. Life primarily revolved around agriculture communities where the roles of men and women were clearly defined. Even in the city, women raised the children, cared for the home, and supported their husbands when they went to work each day.

The aftermath of Pearl Harbor and the declaration of war against Germany was that the men who formerly worked in manufacturing plants were drafted into uniform. Women flocked to shipyards, aircraft plants, munitions factories, and the like, taking the jobs that once were restricted to males only. They received the same pay as men. They began living on their own. And they experienced an instant social shift no one had anticipated. They also made assembly lines look sexy.

There was more to Captain Reagan's work with the Army Air Force First Motion Picture Unit than just being a vehicle for home front support. He was serious about his job and worked to find ways to build troop morale. One of his ideas was to supply the weekly magazine *Yank* and the newspaper *Stars and Stripes* with pictures of pretty girls working on the assembly lines of defense plants.

Yank, which sold for five cents a copy to assure that the members of the army, navy, and army air force respected the publication, was available only to the military. Published from seventeen different countries, 2.6 million copies sold each week in twenty-one different editions. New York was the editorial headquarters for the articles, photographs, and comic strips that were used in every copy worldwide. To this material was added regional interest items provided by staff members in the seventeen different countries. Then each issue was printed regionally and distributed to the buyers. The publication only existed through the end of 1945, but that was long enough for Captain Reagan's idea to be adopted and for him to be given permission to dispatch PFC David Conover to a war plant to shoot young women to be featured in all copies of the August 2, 1945, edition. *Stars and Stripes* and nonmilitary publications also used some of the photos though not to the degree of *Yank*.

Captain Reagan's choice of a defense plant to photograph was the model airplane factory owned by actor and friend Reginald Denny. The British actor working in the United States was best known for the stock comic caricature of the "silly ass Englishman" in many movies of the era. He was seen most frequently in the Bulldog Drummond series of detective mysteries.

Model airplane enthusiasts and the military knew a different side to Denny. For years he had been developing sophisticated radio-controlled model airplanes that could be operated in a manner exactly duplicating the fighter tactics American pilots and ground crew gunners would be facing in Europe and Asia. Instead of movies, Denny's catapult-launched aircraft were flown at a height that made them appear identical to the larger aircraft flying at higher altitudes against American ground forces. Anti-aircraft gunners in training were able to hone their skills with weapons as large as 40mm. Prior to Denny's work, cloth sleeves would be attached to the rear of a manned airplane. Then the pilot would fly through the sky while the anti-aircraft gunners fired at the large billowing sleeve. Sometimes they missed. Sometimes they hit the sleeve but could not tell they had done so until the aircraft landed. And sometimes their inexperience resulted in the accidental death of the pilot and/or the loss of the plane.

Denny's aircraft, which returned to earth with a twenty-four-foot parachute, provided the first meaningful and safe training tool for anti-aircraft gunners.

Conover, a Sunset Boulevard studio photographer before the war, was part of a public relations camera crew that descended on the various plants to photograph the women at work. Reagan's staff, among others scattered around the country, would go through the photos taken by the various PR photographers, selecting illustrations for publication. This meant that all the photographers were on the lookout for pretty girls whose faces would attract reader attention.

The assignment given to Conover and the other photographers was one that provided an unspoken but frequently achieved bonus. The men were allowed to make arrangements with the women they recorded to take additional pictures for freelance sales to magazines and newspapers when they were on their own time. The photographers paid the women whatever way they wished (professionals received a minimum of five dollars an hour; amateurs sometimes received free prints and no money).

The market for pictures of pretty girls was just beginning to increase beyond anyone's expectations. They were sought for a growing number of men's magazines. They were sought for women's magazines. They were eventually sought for "true" romance and confession magazines, general interest magazines such as *Pageant*, true crime publications, and even magazines devoted to photography such as *U.S. Camera*, in which Norma Jean would eventually appear. Perhaps the most unusual were the magazines such as *Laff*, a seemingly less literate version of college humor magazines such as *Life* and *Judge* that were popular two decades earlier.

Laff combined photographs of models wearing form-fitting, one-piece bathing suits, short shorts, and tight blouses, with cartoons and short humor, the latter often dealing with dating and marriage. Different poses and different locations were used when taking the photographs, and each image of the same girl in a different outfit and/or setting would often have a different name provided for the caption. A girl leaning against a ranch fence would have one name; the same girl in a bathing suit running into the ocean would have a second name, and the same girl curled sensually in a hanging chair would have a third name. The model was routinely paid by the hour, but the photographers were paid by the published image, making them eager to have a model in as many outfits and locations in as short a shooting time as possible.

The possibility of freelancing to such publications was frequently in the minds of the photographers who were handling the public relations pictures when, in early 1945, PFC Conover arrived at Radio Plane with his cameras. There he found Norma Jean Dougherty working in the "dope room" spraying chemicals ("dope") on fuselages. The job, one of the relatively skilled positions, was a promotion she had received following her earlier work as a parachute inspector. The higher-paying position brought her twenty dollars for what was usually a fifty-hour week.

Years later, when Norma Jean was asked about her work, she proudly explained what she had done before her promotion. "I first had a job inspecting parachutes," she told some reporters. ". . . not the kind a life depends on; the little parachutes they use to float down the targets after the gunners are through with them." For reasons never understood, several newspaper reporters twisted what she said, creating the idea that she was both callous and stupid. They created a quote that read, in part, ". . . her first job was packing parachutes but she was fired because she kept making mistakes and two men died. . . ."

The Radio Plane factory work was tedious yet important, the training from the use of the models making the gunners more effective in the field. The women who worked there were freeing men for combat, praying that their brothers, boyfriends, husbands, and former classmates would return home. Yet though they rarely saw a man of dating age who was out of uniform, though their work could be dirty, they still wanted to look as much like available young women proud to show off their bodies as they had before the war. Toward this end they would request coveralls one size smaller than they should have worn, so that every curve and contour of their bodies would be enhanced. They also kept sweaters in their lockers, changing before they left for home each day.

The photographers were often drawn to one worker or another, arranging to photograph them for nonmilitary publications during breaks, before and after shifts. David Conover was no different, zeroing in on Norma Jean Dougherty, a young woman whose husband had enlisted in the merchant marine. He photographed her and the others in the plant with both a 4x5 and a roll film camera, using black-and-white film extremely sensitive to light. Then he asked her to put on the sweater she kept in her locker and go outside during a break so he could photograph her in color with a 35mm camera and Kodachrome Film.

Norma Jean was flattered, not so much by the prospect of appearing in a magazine as by the fact that a stranger, a man who had owned a photo studio in civilian life, found her to be photogenic. She did not hesitate to give him her home telephone number when he said he might wish to hire her for more sessions during her free time if the images were as successful as he thought they would be.

Conover and the other photographers processed the film they used for black-and-white images, but Kodachrome was a slide film that required special equipment and handling available only from an area Eastman Kodak processing lab. Each roll of transparencies was then checked for quality control, in this case by an inspector who called Conover to learn more about the model. She seemed so spontaneous and natural, as though she were on the most enjoyable date of her life, the camera lens a surrogate lover, that he was curious where the photographer had found her.

David was delighted to learn that his impressions of the woman were validated by someone else in the business. He not only was able to sell some of the images to a publication called *Laff* that combined cartoons and jokes with pictures of pretty girls, he also introduced Norma Jean to Potter Hueth, a civilian photographer friend with a studio on Pico Boulevard. Conover would have continued working with the young woman but he was being reassigned to the Philippines and would have no more time.

Norma Jean was delighted. Hueth was less so. The freelance work done by both the photographers connected with the Celluloid Commandos and by men who were not in the service required their spending money in advance. They had to hire the model for her time even when it was not certain that her looks would please an editor. They had to buy the film, pay for the processing, pay for the printing, and only then begin offering the material to the magazines, most of which were headquartered in New York, Chicago, and Toronto. This meant mailing expenses that would not be reimbursed even when a sale was made.

Once a photographer was known to the publication's editor, the photographer knew which images would sell and which would not, reducing the cost of waste. But when Hueth met the young woman Conover had been photographing, he both recognized her salability and the fact that he could not afford to hire her for a session. He was too new in the commercial photography business to take any work for which payment was uncertain, and while young women who wanted to model professionally routinely paid for the photographer's time creating her portfolio, Norma Jean had not expressed such interest. She was asked to pose. She had not requested such an experience.

Conover and his friend Hueth both photographed Norma Jean prior to Conover's going overseas, though apparently only David paid her up front for her time. This was enough money so that she decided to quit Radio Plane to explore whether she could actually become a professional model.

For reasons never discussed, Norma Jean decided to not tell her husband what was taking place. The job at Radio Plane had been taken out of boredom, not patriotism. Jim Dougherty was in the merchant marine, and without his coming home each day from a regular job, life was boring. The assembly line work brought in extra money, provided a social life, and enabled her to meet other young women her age who were experiencing many of the same emotions.

Modeling was not a type of work the couple had discussed, because neither of them knew anyone who modeled and Norma Jean did not fantasize herself on a magazine's cover. Even the initial photography that David Conover shot seemed somehow apart from the world the couple had known. She did not realize that her picture would soon be on the cover of *Yank*, a publication seen by her husband and countless other servicemen throughout the world. Her only interest was in learning how to improve her posing techniques, not where and when the images taken for the military might appear.

Hueth was especially impressed with Norma Jean's professionalism. She asked to see all the photographs taken of her, not just the ones culled as best. She studied how the light could sculpt her face, affect her hair, set her apart from the background, or seem to engulf her so unflattering features disappeared. She asked about makeup, clothing, and hairstyles. She questioned body positions in different types of light. Then, each time she gained a better understanding of what was taking place, she tried correcting the pose, the clothing, or whatever other feature was going to be a factor in the image the photographer was trying to achieve. She obviously had a hunger to learn, and Hueth decided to get her representation from a modeling agency. The one he chose, Emmeline Snively's Blue Book Modeling Agency, was in the posh Ambassador Hotel and was considered one of the finest agencies of the day.

Snively reviewed the pictures Hueth had taken, interviewed Norma Jean, and agreed to sign her for representation. The arrangements were finalized on August 2, 1945. It was the same day that Norma Jean's husband, Jim Dougherty, had his first hint of what was happening with his wife. He, and everyone else in the military who picked up a copy of the current edition of *Yank*, saw Norma Jean's defense plant photo on the cover.

Emmeline Snively had first entered the beauty business when she and her mother, Emma, opened the Village School in 1937. It was part finishing school, part modeling school, and part charm school. The students learned everything from poise and charm in daily relationships to posing for the camera. They were mostly the daughters of wealthy families whose future was more likely to be that of wife than someone with a career. Their knowledge would be used to look beautiful at catered parties and business events involving their husbands.

Emmeline realized that she was more interested in the work-a-day world of glamour. She and her mother closed the Village School in 1943 and Emmeline began the serious representation of professional models. Her timing was excellent, because the publishing and advertising businesses had changed. There was growing demand for young women who could pose for advertising, appear on covers, and make personal appearances at trade shows, conventions, and the like as the representative of one or another company's products. There was also a demand for attractive young women to work as extras and bit players in the movies, and the pay for such roles had risen to a level where a booking agent's percentage could mean a substantial income.

The Blue Book Modeling Agency had approximately twenty reasonably experienced models at any given time. She also had young women like Norma Jean, experienced enough to be considered embarking on a professional career but lacking the extra training needed to handle any assignment. For them she developed a side course costing her one hundred dollars (which she quickly earned back because she only enrolled young women she was certain would succeed). Maria Smith taught makeup and grooming, Emmeline Snively taught posing for the camera, and Mrs. Gavin Beardsley provided instruction in fashion modeling.

Another twenty-five dollars had to be spent to have their photographs and basic information of height, hair color, body measurements, and the like printed in a catalog used to gain new clients. By the time the model was trained and in the agency book, she would need to work twenty-five hours to meet the up-front expenses.

Rather than discourage the young women, Snively let them pay her from their modeling assignments. This made the training seem free, especially since they were working in ways they had previously only dreamed about. Equally important, Snively made certain the women she represented were types that, once trained, would be in demand, so none ever felt the school portion was a scam.

The publishing and advertising businesses were increasingly in need of models, and Los Angeles area photographers supplied images to editors and account executives throughout the country. However, the East Coast and Midwest had the greatest concentration of publishing companies, corporate headquarters, and advertising agencies. Young women on the West Coast often wanted to work in the film industry, and Snively had neither knowledge nor connections with the studio casting directors. To be certain she benefited from all possible work, she utilized Helen Ainsworth, the West Coast chief of the National Concert Association, who placed appropriate models with the film studios, splitting her commission with Snively.

Norma Jean Dougherty had never thought of herself having a modeling career until David Conover photographed her in the defense plant. She never thought of herself working in the movie industry until she got to know some of the established models who were making the move to studio contract players. These were women who often had great looks rather than talent or experience, and though they signed long-term contracts, escape clauses assured that most would work no more than six months. They attended classes at the studios, and they were placed in films that needed a lot of people who had few, if any lines. They might be in a beach scene one day, a ballroom scene another, and strolling among the townspeople in a period Western in another. Those who showed talent, ability, and a screen presence would continue working. Others would go back to still photography posing, perhaps with another studio giving them a chance a few months later. Even the chance to work a few months was intriguing, but while Norma Jean fantasized about a possible future, Emmeline Snively was far more realistic.

A critical analysis of the young Mrs. Dougherty showed that she was extremely limited in what she could offer clients. The cheesecake photos were fine. They weren't close-ups. They weren't meant to sell clothing or a product the model was holding. They were pretty-girl shots and she did fine with them. She also would likely be able to handle "face in the crowd" jobs with the movie studios. Everything else was likely to present a problem, the reason she insisted she focus on the more obtainable still photography work.

The problem Emmeline Snively faced was that Norma Jean was double jointed and had hyperextension of the knees. A fashion client looking at her portfolio would see the perfect girl-next-door type for a line of dresses.

However, once hired, Norma Jean would be expected to do a graceful runway walk in which one foot was placed in a direct line in front of the other as she moved smoothly, acting like a hanger for the clothing. Norma Jean's walk dipped slightly, making the clothing look as though it had been placed askew on a hanger, bunching together folds of fabric that should have hung loosely. Since all clothing models were viewed by the potential fashion buyer as having the perfect look for the outfit, it would likely be assumed that the dress was unattractive, not that the model was unable to wear it effectively.

The best work, other than posing for still photographs, was trade show and convention jobs, in which personality mattered and the client had the model interact with potential customers. This often meant memorizing general information about a company and its product, then talking with potential customers who were drawn to the exhibit by the young woman's beauty. When the questions went past the flirtatious and the basic, the customer would be turned over to a full-time technical expert to provide details and perhaps make a sale. The pay was just ten dollars a day, less than Norma Jean could make for cheesecake-type modeling but more than double what she had been paid at Radio Plane.

Norma Jean's first trade show job was during a September industrial show at the Pan-Pacific Auditorium. She represented the Holga Steel Company for ten days, and then went on to another six days of work for clients of Emmeline Snively. Part of the time was posing with products for a Montgomery Ward catalog, and part of the time involved a fashion show with too low a budget to hire competent runway models.

Norma Jean was certain that her decision to quit her defense job was the right one when she met the cost of her training and was making more money than with her past full-time job and all within less than three weeks after finishing her classes. She also discovered a talent that remains evident to this day, more than six decades later. The person looking at her photographs has the impression that she is delightedly, sensually, erotically focused on the viewer of the images, not a camera and photographer. She learned to seduce the lens in such a way that when the finished image was used as the cover of a magazine, a casual buyer perusing a newsstand would feel compelled to pause and look at the picture even though it was a different magazine than normally purchased. Often this led to a noticeable boost in newsstand sales, a fact that could lead to higher advertising rates and/or the sale of more advertising pages.

Emmeline Snively showed photographers the impact of Norma Jean's look and they responded by taking their own pictures of her for their clients. By the end of her first full year of agency modeling, Norma Jean Dougherty had appeared on thirty-three magazine covers. She knew she could never go back to being just a housewife or another teenage girl on the factory assembly line, and if she and Jim ever seriously talked about the changes in her life, she knew that, if he objected, the marriage would be over. The camera had become her primary lover of choice, and when she began to think about it, the motion picture camera was nothing more than a more sophisticated lover. She was mastering magazine modeling. It was time to turn to the movies. What she did not realize was the full price she would have to pay for that decision. In order to become the most famous star of her era, Norma Jean Mortenson Dougherty would have to carefully evaluate every last vestige of the life she had led, the people she had known, and the experiences she had had. Some would be discarded, lies and deceptions piled so high atop reality that when journalists uncovered the truth, their editors refused to run the story, certain the reporter, not Norma Jean, was making up falsehoods. Others would simply be hidden from view, living in the dark fringe of shadows from a life glowing so brightly from its artificial light that few bothered to see what else was close at hand.

As for the real Norma Jean Mortenson Dougherty, she would be "killed" in the office above the Schwab's Drug Store pharmacy that was provided without charge to entertainment columnist Sid Skolsky. It was a "murder" her ancestors would probably have applauded because it was a crime of passion based on a dream that glowed brighter than reality, and the one thing her ancestors shared was the uncontrollable desire to pursue dreams and schemes and imaginings.

Two

The Real Norma Jean

They were an odd mix of people, Norma Jean's ancestors. They were dreamers and schemers, of course, but they were also sexual libertines and self-righteous conservatives, self-taught scholars and illiterates proud of their lack of knowledge, religious zealots and ardent nonbelievers. Several experienced ill health that affected their ability to think clearly—neurosyphilis, cardiovascular disease, multiple mini-strokes—that would lead to a misguided belief in the family that mental illness was rampant. Others were simply young moderns in rebellion against the strictures of the Victorian era, men and women who would eventually be classed as part of the Roaring Twenties.

Tilford Marion Hogan was typical of Norma Jean's ancestors. He was an uneducated Missouri day laborer who supported his family with a strong back and muscular arms, working the land, taking whatever jobs he could find, and using his spare time to pursue the dream of a life of scholarly reflection and good works. He and his wife, Jennie Nance Hogan, could barely feed their three children, yet Tilford prided himself on inviting passing strangers to share a meal with them. He was a self-taught reader who laboriously struggled with the complexities of poetry and literature. He bought books whenever possible, his constantly growing library staying with the family as a mix of hard and flush times caused them to seek new living quarters every few weeks or months. Sometimes this meant a log cabin; other times they stayed in a portion of someone's barn or found other makeshift shelter. Wherever they moved, he eagerly worked to master the ideas in his books, especially poetic concepts he would share with anyone who would join in a discussion with him.

Della May Hogan, the couple's middle child, was as dedicated to mischief as her father was to learning. She avoided school whenever possible, led her siblings on adventures that invariably got them in trouble, and reached her teen years as one of the girls known for her willingness to take a favored boy out behind the barn or into the woods for some serious kissing. She was one of the subjects of her parents' constant bickering over who was at fault and what to do about it, though much of the stress on Jennie came from Tilford's indifference to their intermittent poverty and his irrational pursuit of a scholar's life.

Tilford and Jennie realized that they needed to divorce, but at the same time that they were dealing with the disintegration of their marriage, they wanted to find a husband for Della May. She seemed destined for pregnancy from one boy or another, and they wanted to make certain she was married before that was a reality.

Della May proved to be more unconventional than they realized. She did not get pregnant, nor did she find a husband like other teenage girls. Instead she managed to reach what was then the age of early spinsterhood—twenty-two years old—before falling passionately in love with a dreamer of her own, a man named Otis Elmer Monroe.

The physical appearance of Otis Elmer Monroe was strikingly in contrast with his physical labor of choice—house and office painting. He believed that a man should always dress in the manner of the person he wished to become. There was no reason a laborer should not utilize the services of a custom tailor even when the only money left after the tailor's fee was for the cheapest available fabric. He could then walk proudly into a room filled with men of privilege and breeding and have his clothes fit as perfectly as theirs. The fact that the other men always looked at the fabric more than the tailoring and then dismissed him as a servant with pretensions did not matter. He had set himself apart and would use the same skilled custom work when he had the money for the finest material.

The image of sophistication Otis tried to convey was enhanced, in his mind, by a pseudo dueling scar on his left cheek. The years prior to World War I were a time when members of the German aristocracy sent their sons to expensive dueling schools. A man bearing the mark of a saber slash had a scar that announced to the world that he was from an elite family. Otis had simply had an accident while working the land, yet he was certain that in his best clothes, the scar denoted how special he would one day be perceived, when he and his wife were living in Paris—the other portion of his fantasy.

Otis might paint buildings for his living, but in his mind, he painted canvases of such sophistication that the work was hanging in museums, supported by wealthy patrons, and approved for display in the salons. He regularly spoke of art and artists, reading magazines filled with pictures and stories about the lives of those whose work truly was acclaimed.

The fact that Otis owned neither canvas, nor paints, nor brushes for painting, and that he never so much as lifted a pencil to sketch a scene of beauty was easily explained away, both by himself and by his beloved new bride, Della May. A true artist lived for his or her heart. A true artist did not work in any other business. A true artist either lived on inherited wealth, savings from long years at toiling in other jobs, or the largesse of a wealthy patron from among the Parisian elite. He could not begin to achieve his dreams until he could pursue it full time, and toward that end he and Della May decided to move to Mexico.

The Mexican National Railway was hiring laborers with no experience for far more money than Otis had been making as a painter. The couple could live cheaply in the border town of Porfirio Diaz while saving money for traveling to Europe.

There were two difficulties with Otis's plan. The first was the more obvious of the two. Della May gave birth to two children, Gladys Pearl and Marion Otis. It was easy for a childless couple to save money with Otis's pay. It was almost impossible to get ahead when they became a family of four. Worse, sanitation in the area was poor and food was often unclean. Della May wanted to live in a better place for the children while she and Otis worked toward their move to Paris.

The second difficulty was invisible, slow-acting, and far more insidious. Otis had contracted one or more viruses in the area without realizing he was sick. Such diseases were fairly common and at least some of the locals had developed an immune system that could fight them. But an American who had never before lived in Mexico was susceptible. By the time the couple returned to Los Angeles where Otis used the skills he had gained working on the Mexican National Railway to get a higher-paying job with the Pacific Electric Railway in Los Angeles, he was seriously ill. However, because the diseases were not common, the symptoms were misunderstood and Della May thought that Otis was drinking too much, perhaps becoming an alcoholic.

Otis started becoming forgetful. There were mornings he returned home, confused about where he had been the previous night. Della May knew he would never have an affair, so she did not worry about his cheating on her. What did concern her was his breath and clothing. She should have been able to smell the alcohol on him if he had been drinking even moderate amounts. The odor would have been impossible to miss if he drank himself into a stupor where he could not come home. Instead, there was nothing.

The idea that he could be alcoholic pleased Otis because it was an explanation for his otherwise inexplicable behavior. He had enjoyed socializing with the other railroad men in the past, going to bars, and occasionally drinking a little too much. He had set aside such ways for the most part, rarely taking a drink anymore, but perhaps he was fooling himself. Perhaps he was taking more than was healthy for a man who loved his family. He decided to stop drinking entirely; yet the forgetfulness and confusion continued. He also gradually became irrationally belligerent, to the point where Della May had to have him placed in the Southern California State Hospital at Patton for diagnosis and treatment. There they found a doctor who was familiar with the viruses endemic in some of the Mexican border towns, and his diagnosis was devastating. Otis was dying from neurosyphilis—a form of syphilis that was believed at the time to be unrelated to the sexually transmitted disease. Today it is known that neurosyphilis can develop from untreated syphilis. However, it takes ten to twenty years to develop, a fact that led the sufferers and many of their caregivers to believe that it was a separate problem, not related to syphilis whose symptoms appear quickly after sexual activity with an infected partner. Otis's increasing confusion and seeming madness was the result of the brain being destroyed from the viruses he had encountered in Mexico. There was no hope.

Otis was diagnosed in 1908. He died July 22, 1909. The story of the neurosyphilis was rarely shared by the family. Instead, the children and grandchildren were told that Otis died in the state mental hospital, and they assumed he was mentally ill.

Della May Monroe was the next member of the family to be considered mentally ill. She had developed the early stages of cardiovascular disease. She began to have a series of tiny strokes as her arteries became clogged.

There were no obvious problems at first. Her speech never changed. She seemed to continue to be capable of caring for her children. It was a situation that was initially almost unnoticeable, as if a light switch had been flashed off and then on: something had happened, but it did not seem to make a difference.

The most obvious sign of the strokes was a growing paranoia she had never shown before. She began to distrust others, including those on whom she had relied for years. Since she was unexpectedly a widow with young children to raise, the friends assumed the mistrust was a normal result of what she had been through. Wariness toward strangers and even well mean-ing friends seemed logical. They did not look beyond her immediate cir-cumstances.

Della May's paranoia did not prevent her from turning her attention in a somewhat different direction—men who might be interested in romanc-ing a widow with children. She had loved not only Otis, but also their sex life. She wanted to put aside the enforced celibacy of the last few months as her dying husband was unable to be intimate with her. Now that he was dead, she wanted to find the same happiness with a new man that she had known with Otis.

Della May was a woman of high standards for commitment—the man had to be loving, faithful, hardworking, and willing to raise her children as his own. When such a man did not appear quickly enough, she began "road testing" those individuals who were at least erotically appealing. Some would be declared fiancés, and these men would have overnight privileges. Others she declared to be her "boyfriends" and these men would be guests during the day. The children would be told to leave them alone so the adults could go into Della May's bedroom to "talk."

Young Gladys was aware of what was happening. It was not unusual for a girl of fourteen or fifteen to marry a boy a year or two older. There were enough good-paying, unskilled laboring jobs for the young that a boy of sixteen could earn a man's pay and support a family without finishing his high school education. However, while Gladys and her friends talked seriously about their own budding relationships with boys, she was still too young to be comfortable with her mother dating; and the blatant sexual activity, though kept behind closed doors, was still obvious. It was all quite disturbing for a pre-teenager.

The solution to the problems of both mother and daughter came in the form of Lyle Arthur Graves, a friend of Otis's from the time they both worked for the Pacific Electric Railroad. The shy Lyle had been immediately taken by the outgoing personality of Della May when Otis introduced them. He never said anything, never made any inappropriate overtures. But with his friend's death, Lyle began watching Della May to see if she might be a part of his future. He was six years older than his friend's widow and understood that eventually she would be ready to settle down again. He simply remained a constant presence until Della May began looking at Lyle as a potential lover and husband, not just Otis's friend. The two started dating, and on March 7, 1912, they were married.

Della May's undiagnosed cardiovascular disease was getting worse and it soon affected her new marriage. Lyle was faithful, loving, and spent most of his time away from work with Della May and the children.

Della May gradually decided that Lyle was drinking too much, though it was based on twisted logic. Otis had been an alcoholic. Lyle was Otis's friend. Therefore Lyle must also be a drunk. The fact that he did not drink, had never been seen drinking, and never came home smelling of alcohol did not change her twisted belief.

Lyle thought he had to court Della May anew. He began buying his new wife presents to try and prove his love. He also arranged for his entire pay to be given to her to handle so she would know that he could not possibly be involved with another woman. Still her concerns worsened, neither recognizing the source of the problem, and she finally decided that she had to leave her second husband. They had been married just eight months.

Lyle loved Della May and had no intention of letting her leave him because of false suspicions. He spent as much time as possible with her. He took her dancing. He spent hours talking with her. He did everything possible to show her his love, and though she was growing increasingly irrational, she decided that her "alcoholic" husband had changed his ways. That Christmas—their first and, as it turned out, their last together—he was allowed to return to their home.

The strokes were getting worse, yet there were no symptoms that would cause her or Lyle to think she needed medical help. She was seriously ill, her paranoia growing, and her reconciliation short lived. Five months after Lyle returned home, Della May filed for divorce based on "failure to provide, dissipation and habitual intemperance." The divorce was granted on January 17, 1914.

In the years to come, both when Della May was completely lucid and after her death, stories about problems with Lyle became part of the family lore, an oral pseudo-history meant to make sense of what none of them understood at the time. The retellings painted Lyle as the bad guy, the one with the odd behavior that had caused Della May such grief. He must have been mentally ill, just like Otis, the reasoning went. And the incorrect saga of the family's "history" of mental illness continued to build.

Della May decided to pursue a new husband almost four years after her divorce from Lyle. This time she decided that a new location would help, so she chose Venice, California, a community just south of Santa Monica where a boarding house owner welcomed her and her two children.

Venice was the type of eccentric planned community for which Southern California would eventually become known. The developer, millionaire Abbott Kinney, wanted to re-create Venice, Italy, along a stretch of the Pacific Ocean just twelve miles from downtown Los Angeles. There were to be canals and streets, arched bridges and small shops, cottages, restaurants, and even two dozen gondoliers. The latter were personally hired by Kinney who relocated the men to Los Angeles in order for them to ply their trade in the artificially created waterways.

Venice, California, quickly became known as the "Playland of the Pacific" and was so successful in drawing tourists and pleasure-seekers that Los Angeles would annex the community in 1925. By then oil had also been discovered in the area, the chance for wealth attracting wildcatters who shared development efforts with concessionaires, restaurants, cheap housing, modest bungalows, hotels, and prostitutes. There were dance halls and places to gamble. The location was neither prestigious, as Beverly Hills would become, nor disreputable in the manner of East Los Angeles many years later. Its inclusiveness drew people from all walks of life.

Couples found it the ideal place to date, and lovers learned the best trysting spots. Families could take their children, and the elderly could have an adventure unlike anything then available to them.

Gladys was just fourteen years old when she and her mother moved to Venice, and the young woman seemed to have inherited her mother's lusty temperament. Like most teens, she could not comprehend that her twice-married mother might still be interested in sex. It was one thing for Gladys to pursue the older teen boys who spent their days at the beach. It was quite a different situation to have her mother bring home yet another man, then go into the bedroom "to talk." Fortunately for both of them, the hunt for the third husband was over quickly. This time the man was Charles Grainger, a professional in the oil industry, the business that had become one of the most important in the Los Angeles area.

Unlike the other men in Della May's life, Grainger had a maturity and a worldliness that came from working internationally, not just pursuing a dream. He had lived and worked in India and Southeast Asia, holding jobs with the Burma Oil and Shell Oil Companies. He was lean, powerful, handsome, and intelligent. He had moved to Venice because of a series of oil industry strikes. His job—both in Venice where he was to be based for the immediate future, and around the country when he was needed for short-term special assignments lasting only days or weeks—left him financially comfortable but intensely lonely.

Grainger had been married before but his first wife could not adapt to a man who had an unconventional lifestyle, having to leave her to travel to one country or another, one oil strike or another, for days or weeks at a time. The divorce was amicable, his ex-wife and two sons living in Northern California which he visited periodically. However, there was no chance the two would ever reconcile. Charles could not provide the day-to-day presence she needed from a husband.

It was the loneliness that took Charles from his two-room bungalow at 410 Carroll Canal Court to one of the beachfront dance halls on December 31, 1917. The New Year's Eve dance attracted both couples and lonely singles who wanted to dance in the new year.

Della May was Charles's last dance partner that night. She was more enthusiastic than graceful, and when she started to fall, he caught her and lifted her as naturally as if they had deliberately been dipping to the music. They left the floor, began talking, and apparently never dated anyone else until they decided they would move in together.

Gladys was horrified by her mother's bedding yet another man. Della May always kept the rooms they rented on nearby Westminster Street before Charles entered their lives, though she would take Gladys to live in Charles' home for days and weeks at a time. The two residences were concessions to Gladys's emotional state. Della May and Charles were not to be denied their pleasure, but they wanted to be certain Gladys did not feel she was permanently uprooted while the adults were lovers, not yet husband and wife.

Della May, loving both her daughter and Charles, began calling herself "Mrs. Grainger" so Gladys would not be embarrassed and Charles would know of her emotional commitment. What she did not realize was that she had inadvertently established a de facto marriage under California's common law marriage statute.

Gladys was fourteen when she fell madly in love with a tall, lean, sophisticated businessman of twenty-six. John Newton "Jasper" Baker was raised in small town Kentucky, joined the army's cavalry unit to travel the country at government expense, mastered trick riding, saved as much of his pay as possible, and when mustered out in Southern California, began looking for businesses to buy in the Venice area.

There were two steady sources of reliable income in the Venice area: the concession stands and apartment rentals. The concession stands were permanent versions of the type used by carnivals traveling from small town to small town throughout the summer months. There were shooting galleries, dice games, dart throwing games, ring toss games, and the like. There were also penny arcades and similar, larger diversions; all kept open the year around. As with all such enterprises, enough people won the (supposed) games of chance to keep the interest of passers by, and enough people lost to assure good incomes for the owners.

As for real estate, Jasper Baker realized that if he bought apartments and filled them with tenants paying market value rent, he could hire a manager to oversee the holdings and still make a profit. He decided to combine the two businesses, devoting his attention to the concession stand while an employee handled the apartment rentals and maintenance. The apartments would also be a ready source of cash if he decided to sell them and go into another business.

As Jasper planned his civilian entrepreneur career, Charles Grainger, who had spent his first year in Venice studying the amusement business of the Pickering Pleasure Pier on Ocean Park Drive, decided to temporarily quit the oil business and take a job as supervisor. Soon Della May was coming by the amusement area to see Charles; and Gladys, who had developed the face and figure of a young woman of legal marrying age, also delighted in the activities and the people. It was at some point during this period that Jasper Baker, already having invested in his first apartments, came into all their lives.

It is not known exactly when Jasper met Della May or why he offered her a job, but she was soon working as manager of Baker's apartments. He was also intensely attracted to the lusty Gladys, who found Jasper the perfect "cure" for her virginity. The couple decided that it would be wise to approach Della May about marriage when they learned that Gladys was two months pregnant.

It is doubtful that Jasper knew Gladys's age when he dated her. Even if he did, Della May and Charles had no interest in raising prickly legal issues with a man who could help them finally be rid of the girl. If the worst fate that ever befell Gladys was an early marriage and family, that was fine with them. Della May was happy to create a story that would assure a legal marriage for her underage daughter.

On May 17, 1917, Della May declared that Gladys was an adult—eighteen years old—who had just moved from Oregon to be with her mother. She then witnessed the marriage, delighted to give the newlyweds the Westminster Street rooms she had been renting to Jasper and Gladys so she could move permanently into Charles's home.

Jasper and Gladys Baker's first child, a son named Robert Jackie, was born that November; and a daughter, Berneice, was born in July 1919. The problem was that Gladys was little more than a child herself. She had no experience taking care of anyone, including herself. She had no idea how to cook. She had no interest in cleaning house. And she had no sense of the helplessness and needs of babies. She thought that if diapers were clean, stomachs were full, and they were in the home, the babies could be left with whatever neighbor said she would look out for them. Then Gladys felt justified in going down to the pier to dance the day away with whatever men showed an interest. She was not being unfaithful. She would never cheat on her husband. She just wanted to have a good time when he was busy with his work. The fact that the children were in the care of a neighbor convinced her that she was being mature about the arrangement.

Jasper always expected more from Gladys than she was capable of giving. She had the body and the face of a woman, but she was twelve years younger than Jasper, still in her teens, of limited education, and no sense of life outside the Bohemian existence of her mother and her mother's friends. Jasper, by contrast, was from a small Kentucky community. It was here he had developed his work ethic. He had been raised to think that his role in life, once he decided to become an entrepreneur, was to build his business, using the profits to expand in any way he thought might benefit the family. Long hours on the job were considered normal.

Gladys lacked the maturity to understand Jasper's extensive time away from home. He was always tired when she wanted to have fun. And Jasper was drinking—or Gladys thought he was drinking. Or Gladys thought that any man who drank was an alcoholic, the scourge her mother thought she had endured.

Much about this relationship is uncertain. Gladys also alleged domestic violence, though this was another questionable charge without witnesses except to a cultural phenomenon she had not experienced.

Jasper took Gladys and the children to the isolated small town of Flat Lick, Kentucky, a wooded mountain community so isolated in 1920 that many Kentucky residents did not know it existed. The town was where Jasper had been raised, and he wanted his family to meet the people he had known all his life.

The first problem that confronted the couple when they reached Flat Lick was Gladys's personality. She was a flirtatious young woman who had teased numerous men, all of whom knew that she was not promiscuous, would not violate her marriage vows. But this was the type of behavior possible in an urban community filled with young people comfortable with casual relationships. Flat Lick was a no-nonsense small town where the children gained an education, worked in whatever way would keep a roof over their heads and food in their stomachs, and let them save to support a family. They married whenever it was appropriate, but their roles were clearly defined. The women did not cheat on the men. They did not run around to some carnival because they were bored. And any reliance on a neighbor was mutual interdependence.

Gladys knew none of this, and when she met Jasper's younger brother, Audrey Baker, she found that she enjoyed his company. He was taller, handsomer, and long competitive with Jasper, the latter something she had not known and which Audrey enjoyed exploiting on those rare occasions when it was possible.

Audrey, recognizing that his brother's wife was unfamiliar with mountain ways, told Gladys that he would show her the sights from a nearby mountaintop so she could experience the great beauty of the land. There was a trail through the woods leading to the lookout area and he assured Gladys that the walk would be enjoyable. What he did not say was that the trail was a long established location for courting couples. They would walk together, find the clearing, and enjoy a "make-out" session as a pre-engagement ritual. A married woman accompanying a man other than her husband on such a walk was closely akin to adultery. And even if the locals understood that Gladys was being misled by Audrey, the walk was a vicious slap in the face to Jasper, even though Audrey had no intention of taking advantage of his sister-in-law's naiveté.

Jasper's perception of what was taking place when Gladys went for the walk with Audrey was undoubtedly clouded by drinking and brooding while they were gone. He could not bring himself to criticize Audrey. Instead, even knowing that Gladys had never been to Flat Lick and never heard of the pre-engagement hiking trail ritual, he still felt that his wife should be physically punished when she returned.

The moment Jasper saw Gladys returning with Audrey, he picked up a bridle and began chasing her. Each time he got close he struck her across the back, hurting her enough to send her running faster.

Gladys had never been struck before, neither by any man she had known, nor, so far as she could remember, by her parents. She was scared, but not seriously hurt, even though she was bleeding, and was determined to get Jasper in trouble with the locals. She was certain that if she ran into what passed for the business district—a cluster of small businesses—men and women would see Jasper chasing and physically abusing her. She did not realize that his actions were the appropriate responses for a man whose wife had engaged in improper behavior in Flat Lick. To do less would have made him seem less of a man to the community.

The first local person Gladys encountered was Maggie Mills, a widow who owned the grocery store. She was thirteen years older than Jasper, a full generation older than Gladys. She was also even more conservative than Jasper and felt that, if anything, he was being too gentle with a wife who would so misbehave.

Worse for Gladys, Maggie was so supportive of the young wife's punishment that Jasper fell in love with her maturity. It would be Maggie who supported Jasper's assertion that Gladys was an unfit mother when Gladys filed for divorce on June 20, 1921.

The culture clash was clear. Gladys felt that so long as she never had an affair, her going dancing while a neighbor kept an eye on the children was not inappropriate for a married woman. Jasper, having been raised with the conservative culture of Flat Lick, not the liberal Venice Beach area, felt he had to protect the children by gaining legal custody.

The divorce arrangements would not be settled until May 1923. The interim arrangements forced Gladys and the children to remain in Los Angeles, while Jasper, though no longer living in the same home, would have regular visitation rights.

Gladys was more upset with the divorce than Jasper. He had skills, a job, and a support system back in Flat Lick. Gladys had made no preparation to ever have to live on her own. She had never held a job, never been responsible to an employer or anyone else. She was more adolescent than adult, and she did the only thing she knew to do. She went to see her mother, who had begun to markedly deteriorate from her currently undiagnosed heart condition, the vascular damage from which was increasing her paranoia.

Della May was frequently fighting with Charles, accusing him of drinking too much, cheating on her, and anything else that struck her fancy. There was never any proof; she never felt there needed to be. They would fight. He would leave. They would reconcile. And then the cycle started anew.

Finally, in March 1922, Della May decided that she would live with her daughter, Gladys, and her two grandchildren, not her husband. They would move together to a four-bedroom bungalow at 46 Rose Avenue. The women would share one bedroom, the children a second, and the remaining two bedrooms would be rented out. Della May would act as housekeeper, Gladys would work outside the home, and if everything worked as planned, they would be able to pay the hundred dollars a month rent as well as cover their extended family's needs. For reasons never explained, "Mrs. Grainger" leased the house in the name of "Della Monroe" even though Charles continued to provide her with money for some of the bills.

Della May suddenly had the income to be independent, though not the maturity. She set the cash aside for rent, then decided that she and Gladys should go partying, taking a little of the cash at a time. When she could not afford the rent, she refused to admit her actions; instead, each accused the other of stealing the money they both were spending.

The owners of the bungalow had no patience for their new tenants. The women and children were evicted in July 1922, Della moving into a home Charles owned in Hawthorne.

The Bakers were officially divorced in May 1923. There have been stories that Jasper took the children to Flat Lick, leaving them in the care of his mother while the divorce proceedings were underway. This is doubtful, because the divorce arrangement established that Jasper would be with the children on weekends and that they would be with their mother during the week. Instead, after the divorce was finalized, Jasper loaded them in his car one weekend and drove them to Flat Lick, Kentucky, where his mother and the widow Maggie Mills were waiting. His mother agreed to watch the children until Jasper and Maggie married. The only question about what was taking place was the legality of it all.

There were a number of different stories about the trip. The first was the story of Jackie's health, the child allegedly being seriously ill. Jasper immediately placed his son in a Louisville hospital to which the child was returned with some frequency. For reasons never explained—Jasper believed that Gladys would steal the boy? Or that she had caused his health problems?—the hospital staff was warned by Jasper to not let his ex-wife into the building to see their son.

Some biographers claim that Jasper was abusive to the children, his violence condoned by his family in Kentucky where such abuse was common. The fact that he had attacked Gladys with the bridle is used as further proof. However, child abuse was more common in high-density population areas such as the Midwest. The community of Flat Lick acted together to help families, and child abuse, unlike the punishment of a supposedly cheating bride, would not be tolerated.

Berneice, just two years old at the time, later recalled family stories she had heard about her brother's problems. He was supposedly careless, one time accidentally cutting himself severely enough to need medical attention when he played with broken glass from a trash can. Another time he supposedly fell from an open car. But she was not a direct witness to any of this.

It is possible there was some genetic damage. Jackie had one leg shorter than the other, and at fourteen he was diagnosed with tuberculosis of the bone. He was always sickly, and whatever was wrong, it is almost certain that Jasper did not physically abuse the boy. He certainly was never hesitant to get medical help for his son.

Jasper was eventually able to gain full rights to the children, taking them and his new wife to Middlesboro, Kentucky, where he felt it would be easier to care for his son. He was later quoted by his daughter, Berneice, as saying of Gladys, "Your mother was a beautiful woman. But she was also very young, too young to know how to take care of children. That's why I brought you and Jackie to your grandmother—so you'd be taken care of. That's why I married an older lady next time."

With all Jasper's caring, the idea that Jackie was accident-prone was proven over and over again. Berneice remembered a Fourth of July when Jackie lit a large firecracker and placed it in a Coca-Cola bottle, then ran to join the other kids a safe distance away. The fuse was both longer and slower than Jackie anticipated, and when the firecracker did not explode immediately, he figured it was a dud and went back to replace it. The firecracker exploded, shards of glass striking him in the face and destroying one of his eyes.

Eventually Jackie entered the hospital for a long-term stay related to whatever caused the leg problems. Berneice remembered the illness moved into his kidneys. He was so severely ill that a tutor was brought to the hospital to help him keep up with schoolwork, since it was unknown when he would return to his classes. Eventually, when there was nothing more the doctors could do to help him, he was sent home. His condition would not improve, and Jasper was willing to provide whatever care his son needed at home.

Gladys Baker may have been immature and unable to fully care for her children, but she did love them and wanted to be near them. She briefly relocated to Louisville where she took a job as a housekeeper. She was desperate to see her children, though what she did and when she did it is uncertain. It is known that when Jackie was terminal, the hospital's doctors explaining to Jasper that it was just a matter of time before he died, Gladys apparently visited the boy at least once without any opposition from her ex-husband or the hospital staff.

Gladys also went to see her daughter, though apparently there was no "visit" as such. She watched Maggie, Jasper's new wife, interacting with Berneice. She saw that their relationship was a good one and accepted that her ex-husband and his new wife could provide more for the children than she was able to do. She returned to Southern California in May 1923.

Jackie continued to deteriorate. Emergency catheterization equipment had been sent home with the family along with instructions for its immediate use during a crisis, the Louisville hospital that treated him being too far away to handle the crisis. The problem was that no one had thought to train Jasper in sterilization. He successfully catheterized his son, but the tubing was inadequately clean. The boy's kidney became infected and he died on August 16, 1933. He had not yet reached his sixteenth birthday.

Gladys returned permanently to Venice Beach, determined to get on with her life. Still more child than woman, she threw herself into all the nightlife the entertainment district had to offer. Prohibition was in effect, so there were speakeasies and jazz joints, prostitutes selling their bodies, and movie stars using the illegal card rooms for high-stakes gambling. There were also the "bad boys," men who delighted in drugs, women, and living for the moment. They were just the type of individuals Gladys found appealing.

Charles Stanley "Stan" Gifford was the bad boy who thought the wild Gladys might be right for him. He was recently divorced for his myriad affairs, as well as for what his ex-wife Lillian believed was his fondness for heroin.

Whatever his faults, Gifford was holding a steady job as foreman of the day shift at Consolidated Film Industries, a Melrose Avenue motion picture film processing lab. He knew that Gladys needed a job and he thought that if he hired her, she might show her gratitude in private. There was an opening as a film cutter, and he arranged for her to work under the direction of the experienced Grace Atchinson McKee, a twenty-nine-year-old multiple divorcee with a wild streak of her own.

Three

~

Even Norma Jean Had a Daddy

Stan Gifford read the erotic potential of his new hire correctly. Gladys Baker liked her times wild and her men sexy. She was a beautiful woman with reddish brown hair, green eyes, and a figure she dressed to ensure men's notice. She worked hard on the job so that no one would think she traded sex for money, but away from work she both dated and bedded Gifford often enough that, when she eventually became pregnant with Norma Jean, many assumed Stan was the father.

Gladys was young but she was not inexperienced. She had gotten pregnant and given birth, but she also knew well how to avoid pregnancy. She and her lovers took adequate precautions because she was not about to let any man's passion override her common sense. Guys like Gifford were for fun. More serious men were for marriage and pregnancy, and the most serious of all in her life was Ed Mortensen.

Mortensen was boring by comparison with other men she met at Venice Beach during her time off. He was a meterman for the gas company who thrived on routine. He liked the music, the dancing, and the excitement of the Venice area, but he was a homebody at heart. He was certain that one day he would marry and settle into a life of work and family until whatever children he might have were grown and on their own, and he and his wife could enjoy a quiet retirement.

Ed Mortensen did not want to go to Paris, France. He did not fancy himself an intellectual. He was an ordinary guy, ironically as dull as baseball

42

great Joe DiMaggio would prove to be for Gladys's daughter a generation later. But initially Gladys and Ed were intensely taken with each other, fancied themselves to be in love, and impulsively married on October 11, 1924. By February of the following year, Gladys realized that either she was not a one-man woman, or good old reliable Ed—who would eventually achieve what he considered success by having a career with Southern California Gas—was too dull for a lifetime. She did enjoy him in bed, though, and until their divorce was final, she welcomed him with some regularity despite an official separation pending the final legal decree.

Gladys did not mourn the end of her marriage, nor did she waste time filling the nighttime with companionship when Ed was not present. She again shared her favors with Stan Gifford, as well as a local developer named Raymond Guthrie and a fellow motion picture film cutter named Harold Rooney. In the end, though, it was Ed Mortensen who left Gladys with the most lasting souvenir of their time together: a daughter, Norma Jean, who was born on June 1, 1926. He had nothing to do with raising the child, though that may have been the result of Gladys's desires. Ed kept all documentation related to the marriage, the 1927 divorce decree, and the birth of his daughter, and he did so from the child's infancy. In addition, either he, Gladys, or one of Gladys's friends made certain that Norma Jean always knew where her father was living so she could contact him. However, when she one day became famous, Ed refused to have anything to do with her. Some acquaintances felt that because he had a steady job, a savings account, his own home that he shared with his wife, and a pension, he was afraid that his daughter would sue for back payment of what today would be child support. Others thought he feared that people would think he was trying to use the relationship for personal gain. The former was probably the more accurate account, because one of the documented contacts had him telling his daughter to call his lawyer. Twentieth Century-Fox publicist Roy Croft also recounted a time when Norma Jean called her father, reached his wife instead, and was told that Ed did not want to speak with her. Either way, father and daughter, though they occasionally saw or talked with one another, were estranged their entire lives.

For reasons that were never explained, Gladys decided to change the history of her life so far as her most immediate family members were concerned.

43

She filed false paperwork at the time of her third child's birth. Berneice and Jackie, her two children then living in Kentucky, were acknowledged but declared "deceased." Ed Mortensen's name was changed to "Mortenson" and he was listed as a baker whose current address was "unknown."

So adding to the confusion for later biographers of Norma Jean was yet another supposed husband of the lusty Gladys Baker: Twenty-six-year-old Martin Edward Mortenson, a man with a wife and three children in Haugesund, Norway, who had come to the United States to work as a baker. Somewhere, presumably in the Venice area, he was alleged to have met and married Gladys Baker. Whether or not he divorced his first wife is problematic; in any case, he quickly abandoned Gladys and moved to Ohio. There, on June 18, 1929, he was "killed" while riding his motorcycle. Or such was the story. It also was not true.

Even Norma Jean's name was soon in confusion. The child was Norma Jean, but Gladys periodically signed legal documents for the child as Norma "Jeane." Then, years later, Norma Jean herself would add the "e" to the spelling because she felt it made the name seem sexy.

Gladys Baker Mortensen chose to twist the truth, but her daughter Norma Jean preferred a good story to the more mundane truth. Years after her birth there would be many Hollywood tales of friends going with Norma Jean to one location or another where there was housing obscured by foliage, other buildings, or whatever. She would have the person wait in the car, then she would get out and go to see her father. She would return deeply saddened because he wanted nothing to do with her. However, when acquaintances who had gone on these journeys compared stories, they realized that she always went to different locations. They assumed the father was a fantasy, not knowing that she created a myth because Ed Mortensen just did not care.

(Some biographers claim that Stan Gifford was Norma Jean's father. For reasons never clearly explained, friends of Gladys and biographers liked the idea that Stan had gotten Gladys pregnant. Not only is the idea almost certainly inaccurate—only DNA testing, nonexistent at the time, could prove the allegations to be false or true—there is no question that Gladys was frequently intimate with Mortensen at the time she became pregnant. In addition, given his concerns about any involvement with his daughter, it seems certain that Mortensen would have firmly denied fatherhood if that had been the case.)

The last time Ed Mortensen was known to have discussed Norma Jean was in December 1980, long after her death, when he mentioned his daughter to his physician, Dr. Victor Herlacher. It was a time when Ed felt he would not be embarrassed. Celebrity gossip and personal tell-all books by movie and television stars were being promoted in bookstores and on television talk shows. Many actors discussed their estrangement from their parents, sometimes because of their own wild, inappropriate behavior; sometimes because of drug abuse in the family, and sometimes because the parents felt that a career in film was beneath the family dignity. Whatever the case, to be the parent of a star with whom he had little or no contact was no longer considered disgraceful or evidence of bad parenting. Ed did not feel he had to explain why he never spent time with his daughter while she was still alive.

On February 10, 1981, Ed Mortensen, then eighty-five, suffered a heart attack while out driving. His car went out of control, crashing into another vehicle. He was dead at the scene. Three days later, writer Vernon Scott of the *Star-Ledger* broke the story of Ed's identity. The story received almost no attention. The myths surrounding Norma Jean Mortenson were too well established and far more interesting. Truth would have just been an unwanted intrusion.

As to why Gladys periodically changed the spelling she used, no one knows. It only served to add more speculation about the "unknown" father who was actually well known to Norma Jean.

Four

~

In Hollywood, All Things Were Becoming Possible

The idea that Norma Jean Mortenson could be born and raised as almost the afterthought in the lives of all the adults who interacted with her, then transform herself into the international star Marilyn Monroe, seems less unlikely when her life is viewed as part of the early movie industry itself. The year of her birth, 1926, was also the year of radical changes in Hollywood.

The origins of the motion picture studios had initially not been so much the creation of an industry as it had been the pursuit of separate but interrelated businesses. Some people liked writing scenarios, the story outlines from which films were made before talking pictures forced the necessity of full dialogue scripts. Some people liked acting in films, including the physical challenges of stunt work, since everyone cast in a picture performed every acting task required. Some people were fascinated with working the cameras and planning the lighting. Some people wanted to own theaters where they could show films. Some people liked marketing films to theater owners and theater chains. Each business was separate: an inefficient way to run an industry.

It was the advent of sound and the pursuit of greater corporate profits that led to men such as Joseph P. Kennedy Sr. bringing business manufacturing and distribution methods to a Hollywood that formerly was run by men who were more entrepreneurial gamblers than savvy business professionals.

The vertical merger concept was introduced, sound production companies joining with theater chains, motion picture studio facilities, and even costume shops and construction facilities. A screenwriter could take his or her ideas to a producer, and if there was interest, all facets of creating, distributing, and showing a film would be utilized from one location. The logical interactions of related businesses that came to create MGM, Twentieth Century-Fox, Warner Brothers, and the other names that now seem to have existed from the onset of the film industry actually shared their infancy with Norma Jean.

1926 was also the year that Hollywood became a real community where men and women set down roots and started careers, either in the film industry or in serving the people who worked on stage and behind the scenes. Prior to that time, housing was a haphazard mix of residential hotels, rooming houses, small housing enclaves, and the like, all served by businesses located wherever there happened to be space. But by the mid-1920s, there was a real community with businesses that would become synonymous with what was then looked upon as the new Hollywood. And among the ones that opened in 1926, the best known would prove to be Schwab's Drug Store, a joint venture of Jack Schwab and his three younger brothers, Leon, Bernard, and Martin.

The location of Schwab's did not seem to portend success. The previous drugstore on the same site had failed. However, Jack Schwab thought there was a way to make the brothers' business indispensable. They would not only offer food, medicine, and a wide variety of personal and luxury items; they would provide a quality of service never before seen in the area.

Quality service was an unusual entity in those days, and not just on the West Coast. The economy was booming throughout the nation. The stock market was rising, and money could be made with seemingly little effort. The public had accepted the idea of going into a store, buying what they wanted, and leaving, the owner never worrying about how the customers were treated. The attitude was that if one unhappy customer failed to return, two more customers would take his place. The Great Depression, just three years away, was not considered a possibility by any of the financial "experts."

The Schwabs were not fortune-tellers in creating a business that was run differently from the retail establishments of the day; rather, they understood

47

what others overlooked. A drugstore would be successful in a city prone to excess if the products and the service could attract everyone from an apprentice carpenter, to a starry-eyed, would-be actress fresh off the Greyhound Bus from the tiny Illinois town where she last appeared as the star of her high school musical, to the wealthiest producer in the area.

The Schwabs also recognized that they could gain free advertising with a little creative use of space. For example, there were some steps behind the pharmacy section and they led to a small room that could easily serve as an office or be adapted for storage. They decided to give the room, rent-free, to former New York theater columnist Sid Skolsky who arrived in Hollywood on October 12, 1933, to begin reporting on the world of motion pictures. In return, Skolsky frequently mentioned the drugstore in his column.

Almost everyone who aspired to a movie career hung out at the drugstore. This eventually included Norma Jean Mortenson, when she first began appearing in movies. She befriended Sid Skolsky, and he traded publicity for her fledgling career and guidance concerning how to get attention from the studios and the public for rides whenever she was driving a car. He never learned to drive—becoming perhaps Hollywood's only hitchhiking newsman—and the actors who helped him could count on positive mentions in his syndicated column.

Leon Schwab, during an interview shortly before his death, said that the main attraction of Schwab's was actually their food, not their pharmacy. Lunch counters traditionally served whatever could be quickly grilled or simply made: burgers, fries, ham-and-cheese sandwiches, and the like. Instead, Jack and his brothers hired the finest chef they could locate, paid him well, and gave him a free hand to create whatever he desired. The freshest ingredients were to be used, and the mark-up over cost was to be minimal.

For example, Leon remembered that expensive restaurants offered a quality roast beef sandwich for between four and five dollars in 1926. The drugstore lunch counter chef purchased the identical quality beef, then prepared a same-size sandwich with identical ingredients, and sold it for no more than seventy cents. There was profit built in, but it was so minimal that it was often lost when customers did not pay their tabs: another Schwab's innovation.

The Schwab brothers never let anyone go hungry or go without the opportunity to get an acting job. If you were an actor who could barely find a place to stay and certainly had no money for food, you could use Schwab's as your office. The pay telephone number was routinely given to agents, managers, producers, directors, and anyone else who might offer an actor a part. Then the men and women would sit around the drugstore, lingering over coffee and cigarettes while waiting for the telephone to ring. And if anyone waiting was hungry, Leon would get the person a meal, then explain that he was putting the cost "on the tab."

There were actually two forms of the "tab," and unless someone admitted to the arrangement being made, no one knew who was flush and who was broke.

The first type of tab had the potential to be charity, though the brothers always hoped their customers had the integrity to repay when they could. This was the tab provided to actors who had no savings, were not working regularly, and might never be successful enough to pay what they owed. Some repaid eventually. Others did the minimum work outside of acting that they needed to keep a roof over their heads, then spent the rest of their time in Schwab's, waiting for the phone to ring, no one ever mentioning the debt or the futility of the actor's nonexistent career.

The second form of the tab was for service personnel such as police officers and firemen. They used the drugstore like a no interest credit card loan, meeting their bill every two weeks when they got paid. On those rare occasions when someone who had a regular job could not pay the bill in its entirety on payday, Leon would sit down with the person and ask how much he or she made. Then Leon would go over the customer's debts, helping the person to understand how much money had to be set aside for other expenses. Whatever was left went toward the tab, and it was rare that anyone failed to get current in the next few weeks. The service benefited the drugstore, but it had the added value of providing meaningful debt counseling information to people who otherwise might lose everything from careless spending.

Leon Schwab talked about the other customer services, such as the times when a customer called about getting a two-cent stamp and Leon had it delivered to the person's home without additional charge.

Large items outside of those carried in the store were also tracked down for customers. During World War II, actor Charles Laughton complained to Leon that he needed a car, but because of the shortages, it was "impossible" to get the Cadillac he desired. Leon told him it would be no trouble, and then arranged with an acquaintance to get Laughton the vehicle he cherished. There were no tacked-on fees and no profit for the Schwabs. The brothers understood that such a courtesy from a business that had nothing to do with automobiles would assure Laughton's being a loyal, long-term, and high spending customer.

There was more to the story than the service side, however. "The first question Laughton asked after taking possession of his new car," said Leon Schwab, "was 'Now where do I learn to drive?'"

The Schwab brothers made certain that the store was stocked not only with the necessities of everyday life routinely available from a drugstore, but also luxury items. Leon would make regular buying trips to Europe to seek exotic items of all types. He also created custom items for the richest among his customers. For example, when he discovered that the most luxurious specialty store in the Los Angeles area had perfume selling for as much as $250 an ounce, he decided to create a demand for something greater. He went to a perfumery and had a unique fragrance developed. It was viewed as so exotic, from the aroma to the packaging, that he did a brisk market at five hundred dollars an ounce.

By the time Norma Jean Mortenson was a young adult, Schwab's had so fine a reputation as a purveyor of both fairly priced items and luxury goods that no one dared challenge their market. That was why there were no objections when Leon Schwab convinced producer Louis B. Mayer to let him open what amounted to a branch store on a soundstage at MGM every November.

Mayer at first thought Leon's request was an outrage. He wasn't about to close down one of his soundstages, even one not in use at the moment, so a retailer could profit handsomely from the Christmas selling season. He felt that the actors and technicians should shop on their own time.

Leon pointed out that he knew where and when the MGM employees were shopping. They would each take two or three days when they would call in sick or claim a family emergency was keeping them from work. Production would either have to be delayed or scenes would be shot out of sequence, also causing unexpected expense. This meant that while Louis B. Mayer was cursing his bad luck, Leon Schwab would see the same "sick" actors and technicians come into the drugstore for shopping and lunch. MGM would save thousands of dollars in lost production time by letting Schwab's come to the soundstage.

Mayer reluctantly agreed, and from then on production costs drastically declined for studio films made late in the year. The delighted Schwabs continued their pretense that they were only interested in serving the community.

And all of this began the year of Norma Jean's birth.

Five

~

Meanwhile, on the Other
Side of the Continent . . .

If Norma Jean could be said to have been born at a time and in a place experiencing the adolescence of a burgeoning billion-dollar industry that would impact the world, other men and women who would have remarkable impact on her life had reached young adulthood with a passion for theater as it had existed for centuries. They were born a generation earlier in Europe, the Midwest, and the East, and many of them gravitated to New York, the center of American theater.

The movies were mostly employers for the young, especially where actresses were concerned. Someone larger-than-life on the screen had only to look riveting, a combination of personal style, makeup, lighting, and luck. Not even talent had to be involved. The most popular film actors of the day were often able to do little more than memorize a few minutes of dialogue for use in a single scene, since filming was done scene by scene and often out of sequence. Broadway, Off-Broadway, and regional professional theaters, by contrast, cast based on whatever age, race, and type actor was needed. The stage actors had to enter the reality of the roles they were creating, then carry that character through from one to two hours of a play, during which the audience served as the fourth wall. They knew they were seated in a theater, yet so real was the acting that the technical side—the lighting, the set design, and the like—was banished from conscious awareness. Whether Shakespeare or the latest musical, the audience needed to feel itself in a corner of the world in which the acting was taking place, hidden, silent, yet very much present—the fourth wall.

The theater also brought with it a different type of actor in those days. The stage drew on a lengthy history of approaches to acting, directing, lighting, costuming, and the like. Some producers liked to have their casts receive minimal direction, the actors discovering how they viewed the characters they were playing, then interacting in a manner that seemed like scripted improvisation. The words were the same from performance to performance, yet the flow of the story and character interaction could be quite different. Other directors were dictatorial. Some actors spoke naturally, learning to project their voices to the back rows of the theater without seeming to be shouting or even raising their voices. Other actors "honored" the words with exaggerated pronunciation, creating a theatrical speech that would have seemed pompous if used off the stage.

And always there were questions concerning preparedness. How did an actor who had been raised in an ethnic, economic, and social situation that infused his or her being create a character from a totally different environment, sufficient that any audience member raised in that environment would assume the actor must have been a neighbor?

Intermingled with all this were political concerns that had not previously been a part of American theater. Actors from throughout Europe had come to America to perform almost since the founding of the nation. Some had been horrified by the experience, such as when Enrico Caruso, beloved as a pop singer by Italian immigrants, fled in terror after finding himself in the midst of the San Francisco earthquake. Others routinely toured a number of cities, especially New York, Chicago, San Francisco, and Bellingham, Washington. And still others fell in love with the relatively young country and chose to stay. However, immediately following World War I ("the war to end all wars") and the Russian revolution, the nature of the actors, writers, producers, and directors began to change. Many had experienced censorship or condemnation, either for past work or because they did not share the politics of those entering power. Many were Jewish at a time when growing anti-Semitism limited the jobs they could hold, where they could live, and other quality-of-life issues. The true danger would not be understood until after Adolf Hitler took power in Germany, but it was clear that there would be overwhelming restrictions on creativity.

As the fascists began dominating Italy, Germany, Austria, and the like, actors, writers, and others in the theater started looking toward what they perceived was the opposite of such oppression: the Communist Party. Communism in its evolving form under both philosophical thinkers and early rulers, from Karl Marx to Joseph Stalin, seemed to embrace the working man. It also seemed to be providing the only opposition to fascism, the United States being a country in both physical and intellectual isolation. Because of this, immigrants to the world of New York theater and, to a lesser degree, the Los Angeles film world, brought with them strong political views, most of them left-wing in nature.

The Europeans also brought with them ideas about how actors should perform, some of which they taught and others of which became corrupted by early proponents. The one approach that would affect both Norma Jean when she became an adult and theater people a generation older would come to be called "The Method." And its strongest, most autocratic proponent was Lee Strasberg, who completely misunderstood it and never tried to learn what he claimed to be teaching.

The Method was actually the Stanislavsky Method, or so it was claimed. The name, but not the technique, was based on Konstantin Stanislavsky, a Russian born in 1863 and trained at the Paris Conservatory where actors learned a style of performing that, to today's theatergoer, made them seem like caricatures of the characters they were playing. Overacting, overly precise enunciation, emotions so exaggerated as to be artificial, and the assigning of parts based on a star system, not the ability to most effectively deliver a performance, were all part of Stanislavsky's training. He found it ridiculous. He felt there should be a naturalness to acting so that the audience felt it was watching real people living out their lives, rather than constantly reminded that what was taking place was make-believe.

Lee Strasberg never met Stanislavsky, though he was alive, well, and teaching such Americans as Stella Adler, a friend and theatrical partner. Strasberg's knowledge came from studying with Russian director Richard Boleslavski, who had studied with Stanislavsky. However, it is not known if Boleslavski presented Stanislavsky's methods or if Strasberg assumed that was what he was learning. Truth did not matter, though, because Strasberg was working primarily with young actors who were intensely insecure and had less experience than Lee, who first performed on the stage in 1925 when he was twenty-four years old. Seven years later, when Norma Jean was six, he had created the Group Theatre that used a summer camp to help very young, impressionable, and often insecure actors with little experience.

Typical was Elia Kazan, who eventually became arguably both the most celebrated and most vilified director of both film and the Broadway stage in the last half of the twentieth century.

Kazan, born in 1909, had long viewed himself an outcast and a loner. By the time he was twenty-two, he had rejected a position in the family carpet business and the family rug cleaning business. He rejected the dark-haired Jewish girls whose parents, like his own, were immigrants to the United States. And he was, in turn, rejected by his Williams College classmates who were mostly WASP, mostly third-, fourth-, or older-generation Americans, and mostly committed to business careers. His love was theater, a world where he would gain fame, controversy, great financial rewards, two Academy Awards and the position of director of choice for the Pulitzer Prize-winning plays of Tennessee Williams, Arthur Miller, and others. He also came to have a fondness for bedding blondes, eventually including Norma Jean. But what was noticeable for Kazan was the pain he carried from this period, pain he first addressed when he was the requested speaker for the fiftieth anniversary of his graduating class.

As he explained to the surviving members:

> Do some of you really have a memory so bright that you can recall me in those murky years, 1926 to 1930? Because I spent most every hour of our time locked in my room or in the stacks of the library. I carried no varsity letter, played no role in Cap and Bells, didn't make Gargoyle. An obvious neurotic, apparently without the faculty of speech, I was known to be completely silent for days at a time. Naturally I was not "rushed" into a fraternity; that would have been like inviting a ghost to haunt a house. Socially I struck out; through four years of holidays and celebrations, I didn't dance, not once. At your house parties, I stood behind a table in a white coat splotched with grenadine pink, my heart rotten with envy, and served spiked punch to your dates. Don't feel sorry for me: I did that for myself.

The Williams experience formed Kazan's initial understanding that directing was more than just telling the actors where to go onstage and how to effectively deliver their lines. He learned to think of the stage as a canvas and to plan the movements of the actors, as well as the stage positions, to suggest emotions, dramatic conflict, and the like. He was taught about rhythm and pace, strong movements and weak movements, and the fact that the actor could *not* be relied upon to carry a play. Instead the actor was one element of a picture viewed from the audience. The positions of the actors, their movement, the lighting, the utilization of areas of the stage that were either strong or weak, the costumes, and the set design all were interwoven to make a tapestry of experience that fully expressed the playwright's creation.

At the same time, the way in which Kazan was treated by his classmates made him keenly aware of class differences in America. He came from a financially successful family, but that was not enough to win him respect. He eventually felt himself emotionally aligned with European immigrants who were being forced into ghettos, denied the right to live and work in many areas of their own countries. It was an experience that also brought him into left-wing politics for a brief period of his young life.

The actual academic experience was not as hurtful as the social. The Williams style was typical of the training of many schools whose professors realized that their students would likely be either teaching themselves or directing amateur actors in the years to come. But as much as Kazan was preparing for the future, he was troubled by what was happening in the country at large. Immigrants were fleeing oppression and poverty abroad. Once-wealthy families were suddenly poverty stricken from the Great Depression. Those who had money seemed to hold in disdain those who did not. And those who had Eastern European accents or whose parents had such accents were viewed with less respect, regardless of income or career achievements, than those who had been in the United States at least through the third generation.

For many of the young actors who had worked their way through school while studying the theater, childhood had been filled with taunts, something to which Kazan could not directly relate but for which he had compassion. He listened to their stories of being ridiculed by classmates because of the thick accents of their parents. He heard how they were mocked because they lacked quality clothing. Even the intense work ethic that drove them to take any available job in order to pay their way through college was considered further proof of their lower-class origins.

The taunting spawned anger they wanted to express through the plays they wrote or the characters they played. When the rich and poor were forced onto a level playing field by the ravages of the Great Depression, they delighted in the humbling of the elite. They wanted to prove their worth, prove that they had a better way to live, to act, and to be.

Actors whose families had not had to struggle, whose education had been assured as a birthright, also wanted to be radicals. They were desperate to learn about the world from which they were far removed. They wanted to relate to the masses, the working class, so they could broaden themselves and be more sensitive.

For a few months Elia Kazan, ashamed that he had not suffered enough, felt great discomfort that his chosen profession could be viewed as elitist. It was a profession where only the stagehands and lighting techs got dirty, where he did not know the hard work of the masses. He felt he had to immerse himself in the other side of America, not certain what that meant but determined to end his naiveté.

It seems silly now and was certainly an embarrassment to Kazan as he matured, but Elia began taking periodic pilgrimages South to sit in the homes of Negroes. His girlfriend, Molly Thacher, was both a playwright and a social worker. He was impressed with her knowledge of "real" working people since he was raised by a man who ran a successful import business and let him enjoy an elitist childhood.

Kazan also began working with actors, directors, and playwrights who told him they were members of the Communist Party. He was thrilled to be associated with theater people who were teaching that the real heroes in America were not the bohemians, outcasts, or other independent spirits, such as he often felt himself to be, but rather "workers." This was a somewhat nebulous term that would include all physical laborers, the more underpaid the better. Beyond that, the precise definition of the term varied with the person using it.

Kazan wanted to know these workers firsthand. After graduating from Williams College and taking graduate classes at the Yale Drama School, as well as trying to find his rightful place as a self-proclaimed Communist in the theater, Kazan decided to see workers' America. He traveled from New York to Washington to meet the musician Huddie Ledbetter. Ledbetter wrote and sang about the poor and downtrodden so effectively that some of his songs, such as "Irene," became major commercial successes.

The commercial success of Ledbetter—known professionally as "Leadbelly"—created a conflict for many of the young Communists. They understood that Leadbelly richly deserved the rewards his talent had earned him. At the same time, commercial success meant an end to suffering and deprivation; and without such suffering, could the person still be a real worker?

Kazan ignored such political, existential nonsense. What mattered to Kazan was that Leadbelly had served time in prison for having killed a man during a fight.

Having been in prison was important for a hero of the workers' struggle as Kazan was taught it. Even better was to have been wrongfully accused and convicted. The suffering ex-con innocent of the crime for which he was sent to prison was a major part of the mythos of such working-class heroes.

To make the meeting with Leadbelly even more exciting, the musician had shared a meal with the young Kazan. The simple fare consisted of beans and rice—good workers' food in the thinking of the day. The fact that Leadbelly might have been happier if Kazan had taken him to a restaurant and picked up the tab was ignored. There was solidarity in the beans and rice that apparently would not have existed with steak and potatoes.

After talking and eating with Leadbelly, Kazan went to Chattanooga, Tennessee, to spend some time with a Communist organizer whose real name he never knew. On that trip, the man was called Ted Benson. At other times he might be Sid Benson or Ted Wellman or Sid Wellman. The pseudonyms, used even among the party faithful, did not bother Kazan. The truth of the man's importance could be read in his face. Bones had been broken and the flesh heavily scarred over the years. He looked like a boxer whose sole purpose in the ring was to be the punching bag for one opponent or another. The battered look delighted Kazan, who thought a man was leading a glamorous existence if he had been beaten on behalf of workers' causes.

On that same trip Kazan tried to sound like every "real worker" he met. He tried to use the same speech accents typical of the South and Southwest of his travels. He also took odd jobs along the way, including working three days for a rancher in Texas. When he went to restaurants, he proudly ate in low-cost greasy spoons chosen solely because truckers ate there.

No one watching Elia Kazan during this period would think he had real political understanding, any interest in changing the government, or even recognized that only the middle class and the wealthy found glamour in poverty. He could not imagine that someone who was eking out a living from the land—from intense physical labor, or from doing whatever menial jobs others did not desire—might wish to trade places with him, the college kid who had three meals a day, decent clothing, and a consistent place to live.

Part rebel, part seeker of "truth" (as truth was defined by seemingly anyone charismatic and counterculture, even if that was the culture of the theater), and part full of himself as only a late adolescent can be, Kazan decided to try to join a much-talked-about summer camp for new people in the theater. This was the Group Theatre's summer work camp at Sterling Farms, Dover Furnace, New York. He was accepted as an apprentice, paying twenty dollars a week to cover room and board, and he arrived on June 19, 1932.

The Group Theatre with whose summer camp program Kazan was first involved was headquartered in the Forty-Eighth Street Theater in Manhattan. It was led by Lee Strasberg, Harold Clurman, and Cheryl Crawford. Although Lee and Harold, at thirty, were only eight years older than Kazan, they had an arrogance and a sense of purpose that put him in awe of them.

In the years that have passed since Lee Strasberg began teaching his version of the Method, he has been credited with being the source of greatness for numerous Academy Award–winning actors, including Marlon Brando, who became one of the most famous of Lee's alleged students. The problem is that most of what has become "history" was never true.

As Brando explained in his autobiography, he studied with Stella Adler of the New School's Dramatic Workshop directed by Erwin Piscator. Adler did work with Lee as one of the original teachers at the Group Theatre starting in 1931. She and the others wanted to "mount an alternative to the commercial Broadway theater, staging productions they felt were the cutting edge of social change," according to Brando. However, in 1934 Stella Adler traveled to Paris for five weeks of study directly with Konstantin

Stanislavsky of the Moscow Art Theater. There she found that Lee knew nothing of Stanislavsky's "Method," at least as it had evolved. Stanislavsky taught actors to create the characters they were playing by using their imaginations rather than their memories of their past.

"What Stella taught her students was how to discover the nature of their own emotional mechanics and therefore those of others. She taught me to be real and not to try to act out an emotion I didn't personally experience during a performance," said Brando, two years older than Monroe. Always this came through observation and imagination. Brando was successful because he was always observing how people react when alone and with one another in any situation he encountered, from a coffee shop to a party to buying clothing in a store. Then, as he read a script, he was gradually able to develop the character through actions that seemed appropriate for the character and the story. It was a simple method for an actor to learn and seemingly always successful. It was not the Strasberg "Method," though that did not stop Lee from claiming greater influence than he had.

Brando later said,

> After I had some success, Lee Strasberg tried to take credit for teaching me how to act. He never taught me anything. He would have claimed credit for the sun and the moon if he believed he could get away with it. He was an ambitious, selfish man who exploited the people who attended the Actors Studio, and he tried to project himself as an acting oracle and guru. Some people worshiped him, but I never knew why. To me he was a tasteless and untalented person whom I didn't like very much. I sometimes went to the Actors Studio on Saturday morning because Elia Kazan was teaching, and there were usually a lot of good-looking girls. But Strasberg never taught me acting. Stella did—and later Kazan.

Kazan discovered that there was a power to Lee Strasberg's presence that kept those who studied with him completely intimidated. As Kazan would later explain,

> [Lee] had a gift for anger and a taste for the power it brought him. No one questioned his dominance—he spoke holy writ—his leading role in that summer's activities, and his right to all power. To win his favor became everyone's goal. His explosions of temper maintained the discipline of this

camp of high-strung people. I came to believe that without their fear of this man, the Group would fly apart, everyone going in different directions instead of to where he was pointing. I was afraid of him too.

Lee taught his actors to launch their work on every scene by taking a minute to remember the details surrounding the emotional experience in their lives that would correspond to the emotion of the scene they were about to play. "Take a minute!" became the watchword of that summer, the phrase heard most often, just as his particular kind of inner concentration became the trademark of Lee's own work when he directed a production. His actors often appeared to be in a state of self-hypnosis. When he directed a love scene, the "lovers" would seem to be not altogether aware of whom they were with but, instead, involved with their own inner state. There'd be no hint of how they proposed to consummate their love.

Kazan found that most of the young actors of the day were as mixed up as he was. None of them seemed to respect their own world of the theater. They saw the people who were involved with any other type of job as having the glamour the average fan ascribed to actors. To the members of the Group, all outsiders were "really in life." When that fantasy was added to the personal insecurity many of them felt about themselves, they were ripe for dominance by the leaders of the Communist groups. It was the thinking that had led to Kazan's wanderings, and it was reinforced by being in the midst of equally misguided youths.

Some of the members of the Group, including Paula Strasberg, became members of a Communist cell that neither Lee Strasberg nor the other two director/founders knew anything about. The cell members received periodic instruction from Communist leaders who often traveled from Detroit where they were trying to infiltrate the autoworkers' unions.

The instruction was called "Democratic Centralism," a concept Kazan later looked on with bemusement. He felt that it was such nonsense that only the young and insecure would believe it. Since he fit into both those categories, as did the members of the Communist cell within the Group Theatre, he was affected by the approach to thinking as well.

As Kazan later explained it, a member of the "hard-core" of "leading Comrades" would visit the Communist cell within the Group Theatre, coming from his base in Detroit, Michigan. Each visit would involve a lecture on what Kazan called the "true dope," the facts of life as they should have been thinking of them instead of wasting their time playacting.

The political concepts were often unrealistic, yet most of the actor/ members participated to learn as much as possible, stimulated by the growing horror stories about Jews and intellectuals, concentration camps, rumors of mass deaths, and eyewitness accounts of families disappearing from their homes. The immigrants did not know the full scale of what was happening, but enough of the horrors they did know were confirmed that they were desperate to have the U.S. government intercede, a desire shared by the shocked young members of the Group Theatre. They became Communists because they were convinced that what some of the immigrants said was true—without the United States doing more immediately, Russia was the only hope for stopping the Nazis. A Communist Party in the United States might lead to a more responsive government.

Over time, the idealistic members realized that there was a reality disconnect between helping those in danger and the methods theater people were to use to help. For example, the various speakers made clear that the role of theater and film was never to entertain but always to inform with such force that the viewer went home changed, converted to their political cause. Scripts should be like lectures at a university, always with directed purpose, always providing a critical lesson, and always changing the hearer. It was not only nonsense, implementing such concepts would have been impossible.

The "teachers" from the Communist groups in Detroit did not understand the role of the arts in hard times. The 1930s was a period when the Great Depression and looming war in Europe made the theater successful as an emotional escape, a place to go to be entertained. Yet the Communist speaker ordered the actor members to create only plays that would force the audience to gain revolutionary insight, ignoring the market reality that there was no way to fill the seats if people had to face propaganda drivel. The actors might write and put on such a play, but it would open and close on the same night. The theater and the movies were for escape, not haranguing by actors parroting concepts even they did not fully understand.

The one-sided lectures always told the members what to think, then ordered them to briefly reflect on what had just been said, after which they were expected to decide that they agreed with everything they had just heard from the speaker. Finally they were to go home and implement what they had learned when planning future productions.

Discussion was unnecessary because dissent was meaningless. It was an attitude so outrageous that Kazan was later embarrassed that he had ever been impressed with such nonsense. He and most of the others participated as long as they did only because they thought they were hearing the authentic views of real working people and that those views would somehow help them as actors, writers, directors, and producers. But real working people were home working. Their lives were not going to be revealed by a political speaker whose goal was ultimately to help overthrow the government or at least radically change the social system of America.

It was "cool" to join such a countercultural organization when Kazan was barely in his twenties. It was exciting to also be working with the Theatre of Action Communist group, another so-called cell, though his interest was in having extra time to work on stage. But within eighteen months of membership, Kazan saw a fallacy in the way the writers and actors were being treated. For example, there was an exercise meant to create unity through emotional violence. The visiting leader would select one of the members of the company, a youth he had never met, and berate him for not acting appropriately during times when the leader had not been present. Everyone else knew that what was being said was not true. They knew the selected member, how he lived, and what he did, and the "chosen" victim had never seen the speaker before. Yet as time passed during the lengthy meeting, the group fell under the spell of the leader, who was as charismatic as Lee Strasberg. They soon mimicked the leader's hostility toward the innocent emotional victim of the evening. It was bullying on a scale that exceeded even Lee Strasberg's and a disgusted Kazan soon left the group. He was no more than twenty-five years old, barely at the end of adolescence, yet his actions, then and subsequently, would ultimately have a profound impact on Norma Jean when she was nearing the height of her greatest fame.

Kazan's break with the members did not change his thinking at first. He was taught the Communist line of the 1930s. The theatre was to serve as a weapon, with each play meant to teach the audience some lesson. This sweeping revolutionary insight would fill the audience with hope and courage, emotions they would take home with them after the evening's entertainment.

Among the messages Kazan was taught that the audience should be given was that society was hostile, repressive, and corrupt beyond peaceful change because it was run by money men. Change had to be complete; but fortunately change would happen because the working men would demand that it take place.

The theater was to help the audience learn the "right way" and lead them down the "right path." This also meant defending the U.S.S.R. despite its faults, because it was a better system than was in place in the United States.

It took Kazan only eighteen months to become thoroughly disenchanted with Communism and the Communist cells he had experienced. He began studying more mainstream politics, becoming a follower of Franklin Delano Roosevelt. He later wrote that he felt Roosevelt embodied the changes society needed without having to change the government. He came to feel that every speech the president made was reinforcing the idea that "this society can be made to work. Our people are good. Our problems can be solved—our way. Democracy must be preserved. We'll overcome all obstacles."

Six

Norma Jean Grows Up

Gladys Mortenson, unaware—and, like most film studio employees, uncaring—of the world of the East Coast theaters, was part of a different radical movement when she gave birth to her third child. The creation of the studio system meant that what had been a haphazard industry was suddenly big business, offering career options that brought thousands of new residents to Los Angeles. Carpenters who previously might have entered the building trades found work creating sets for motion pictures. There were jobs for makeup artists and hair stylists, costume designers and seamstresses, lighting technicians and cinematographers, writers, directors, actors, and even studio physicians. The cumulative payroll for men and women employed by the Hollywood film industry reached twenty-five million dollars the year Norma Jean was born, and ticket sales throughout the world brought several times that amount in profits for the studios.

Studio related jobs paid extremely well for all skill levels. Only a handful of movie stars earned the three-thousand-dollar-a-week figure mentioned in many newspaper and fan magazine articles, but almost every job paid better than the eighteen-dollar-a-week average pay for semi-skilled workers in the East and Midwest. However, the population growth in the Los Angeles area meant that most jobs were being filled by existing workers and their family members. The greatest need for outsiders was for lawyers, accountants, seamstresses, and other critical skills held by people who would never appear on camera. These were also usually not skills held by starry-eyed young men and women who took the bus, the train, or their cars to reach the city, expecting to find instant success in front of the camera or, if necessary, behind it.

The Hollywood Chamber of Commerce, upset by the influx of jobless teenagers from throughout the country, placed advertisements in eastern newspapers telling people *not* to come. For example, one advertisement showed a photograph of a street jammed with men. The caption read: "Thousands buck the line on every call issued for a few movie picture extras. This is a sample of the customary massed assault on the employment bureaus resulting from an ad for a very few men and women to work in an insignificant scene. The wage is meager for a day or night of hard work."

Then, in bold type, the ad warned, "Don't Try To Break Into The Movies In Hollywood Until You Have Obtained Full, Frank and Dependable Information from the Hollywood Chamber of Commerce." It continued, "It May Save Disappointments. Out of 100,000 Persons Who Started at the Bottom of the Screen's Ladder of Fame ONLY FIVE REACHED THE TOP."

The chamber of commerce may not have wanted an influx of unemployed young people, but the owners of hotels, restaurants, amusement area concession stands, and the like delighted in the publicity the community was receiving, because the stories also generated increased tourism. It was an ironic situation for what was becoming a community suddenly dominated by a single industry, a very different situation from when Gladys was a child and oil and agriculture were the economic mainstays.

Among the unexpected realities of the movie colony for people who resettled there was the fact that the stars were not distant figures living lives apart from the average person. If Gladys took a trolley to work, she might ride with one or another of the major stars of the day. This was a blue-collar industry founded largely by immigrants who often became filmmakers after earning their living with pushcarts, retail sales, and nickelodeon ownership. The actors were often good-looking kids who never went past high school, if they even had that much education. They had drive, sometimes talent, and a willingness to do whatever the studios demanded to have their chance to be on the screen.

In addition to the interaction of all social classes, there was a lack of nightlife for people who worked so hard and earned such good money.

The film industry was daylight-dependent. Actors and all studio personnel working on films had to be in the studios before sunrise to take advantage of the maximum amount of daylight for shooting. This meant that most area residents were in bed by nine o'clock, the time when businesses, including bars and restaurants, were closed for the night. Tourists were more accustomed to the twenty-four-hour nightlife of cities such as New York and Chicago, and many visiting writers wrote unflattering comments about the lack of anything to do other than go to the movies, go out to eat, and go to bed.

Gladys, her daughter, and her friends were not affected by the changes in the studio business structure other than to suddenly have greater job stability. However, during this same period there was a radical new way to see the movies, and though it was adopted in other parts of the country, it was especially popular in Hollywood where there were so few after-hours entertainment options. This was the design and construction of movie theaters so large and ornate that entering them was considered an event in itself. Even the smallest of these new theaters would hold a minimum of a thousand people in a facility so luxurious that a patron could imagine being in the midst of a party both hosted and attended by royalty. Larger facilities included the Hollywood Pantages, named for founder Alexander Pantages, which held 2,812 people; and the Warner Brothers Theater, which had 2,700 seats when it opened on April 26, 1928. These were all single-screen theaters, not contemporary multiplexes, and the shows were frequently sold out.

Teenagers and adults living outside Southern California fantasized about what it would be like to see their images projected many times larger than life as they had an adventure, a romance, or filled the house with laughter with their comic sensibilities. Children growing up in Hollywood were looking at familiar faces when they watched the screen. Many had parents in the industry. For them, the idea that they could one day be the person everyone admired, the one strangers looked upon with envy and called a star, was very real. It was often their neighbors or their parents' co-workers who were on that giant screen.

Gladys Mortenson was enough in love with the movies that she named her daughter after actress Norma Talmadge, who was twenty-one when she became a star back in 1914. Her daughter's middle name of Jean was simply one Gladys liked. However, when nineteen-year-old Harlean Carpenter became a star in 1928 and her name changed to Jean Harlow, both Gladys and her best friend and co-worker, Grace McKee, fantasized that Norma Jean might one day be just like the young actress.

It was shortly after her second daughter's birth that Gladys decided having a newborn would cramp her style and her income. She was well liked at both Columbia Pictures, where she was working full time as a film-cutter when she gave birth, and RKO-Radio Pictures where she soon took a second, similar, part-time job. Her co-workers at Columbia took up a collection to help defray the expense of the doctor and her recovery, though exactly how much money Gladys made, or what other resources she may have had from family and friends, is unknown. What is known is that twelve days after giving birth, Gladys arranged to pay twenty dollars a month for full-time foster care for her new daughter. Gladys fantasized about having a daughter who might one day become an actress on the big screen, and she would share this dream with her daughter when the child was older. However, there was a difference between dreaming about an adult and the realities of day-to-day care of an infant. Grace McKee and some of Gladys's other friends were delighted with the newborn and anxious to help with the care. Gladys not only had no maternal feelings; she seemed delighted that Jasper and his new wife had taken her first two children off her hands.

Gladys knew she did not want to lose custody of her newborn to the baby's father or any of the social service agencies, but she also had no intention of quitting her job or cutting back to part time. The only answer seemed to be the foster care system, a quite different arrangement than exists today.

Children were resilient creatures, according to the thinking of the 1920s. They needed to be protected, fed, clothed, and safely housed, but the presence of a parent was no better or worse than if the child was raised by a surrogate. Equally important, there were adults who enjoyed parenting, or at least were willing to turn it into a business, and adults who thought parenting was best left to those who specialized in it.

Ida and Albert Wayne Bolender were professional parents recommended to Gladys when it was obvious she did not want regular responsibility for Norma Jean. Gladys was simply a biological mother who retained a mother's rights while paying another couple to take on all the responsibilities. In 1926, this was a socially acceptable arrangement.

Ida and Wayne (as Albert was called) provided foster care from their four-room bungalow at 459 Rhode Island Street in Hawthorne, just down the street from where Della May Grainger lived with her lover. The couple was everything Della May's daughter was not: hardworking religious conservatives with one child of their own and one or more foster children for whom the parents paid twenty dollars a month. Della May recommended them, though it is hard to know if she actually knew them as more than neighbors in the child care business. She had personally been so uninterested in her granddaughter's birth that she went on a cruise with her lover during the latter weeks of her daughter's third pregnancy.

Hawthorne was approximately sixteen miles from where Gladys was living in Los Angeles. It was close enough that she and/or her best friend, Grace McKee, could go to see the child and take her on outings. It was far enough that when she did not wish to be bothered with even this token attempt at mothering she could use the "lengthy" trip as her excuse.

In hindsight, the placement of Norma Jean on June 13, 1926, seems to have been acceptable to Gladys not only because her mother recommended the couple but also because their lifestyle was everything Gladys's was not. Wayne Bolender was a postman whose steady government job enabled the family to get through the Great Depression with few problems. He also had a small printing press and liked to print his own religious tracts. Ida was a housewife who believed in the strict raising of children. Both were part of a radical new religious movement, Pentecostalism, that had started on Los Angeles's Azusa Street in 1906. The movement featured ecstatic speaking in tongues—the language of angels harking back to the tongues of fire mentioned in Acts 2 of the New Testament. There were strict rules of behavior and often a rigidity of thought about what was right and wrong. Going to the movies was for the most part considered sinful; not because of the nature of the films but rather because the time spent in a theater was better spent in other pursuits.

Della May was caught up in the excitement of Pentecostalism and the flamboyance of some of the preachers. Among these was the soon-to-be-infamous Aimee Semple McPherson, whom Della May felt should baptize Norma Jean.

Aimee Semple McPherson was a moral contradiction. She was part minister, part showman, and part vamp. Twice married—once widowed, once divorced—McPherson founded the International Church of the Foursquare Gospel. Along the way, she never let her unusual marital history interfere with her evangelical Christian healing ministry. She began preaching in 1907 at the age of seventeen. When radio became a communication medium, she learned to be a broadcaster, the first woman preacher on the air working from a radio station whose powerful signal reached across much of the United States and up into Canada.

There would be a third marriage, a series of affairs including one with actor Charlie Chaplin, and a time of national concern when she was "kidnapped." When she finally "escaped" from her captors, fleeing the desert where she claimed to have been held, she entered a hospital looking remarkably unharmed and unmarked for a woman who was supposedly hungry, thirsty, and had been tied hand and foot during her captivity. The truth was that she had simply run off with her lover of the moment, a fact she dared not admit.

The hope Sister Aimee offered to her blue-collar audience, especially those who were ailing, worked for many reasons including the joyous fervor of the services. First there was the reality of Los Angeles in that era, something described by H. L. Mencken, who wrote:

> The osteopaths, chiropractors and other such quacks had long marked and occupied it [Southern California]. It swarmed with swamis, spiritualists, Christian Scientists, crystal-grazers and the allied necromancers. It offered brilliant pickings for the real estate speculators, oil-stock brokers, wiretappers, and so on. But the town pastors were not up to its opportunities. They ranged from melancholy High Church Episcopalians, laboriously trying to interest retired Iowa alfalfa kings in ritualism, down to struggling Methodists and Baptists, as earnestly seeking to inflame the wives of the same monarchs with the crimes of the Pope. All this was over the heads of the trade. They [Iowans] longed for something that they could get their teeth into. They wanted magic and noise. They wanted an excuse to whoop.

Sister Aimee understood the challenge she was facing. She arrived in Los Angeles with a broken-down car, one hundred dollars in cash, a mother, and two small children. Her mother had been part of the Salvation Army, and her first husband, Robert Semple, had been a part-time Pentecostal minister who died from malaria after a mission to Hong Kong. It was through Semple that Sister Aimee got her interest in preaching.

Sister Aimee's second husband was a grocery clerk named Harold McPherson. Their son, Rolf, joined her daughter, Roberta Star, by her first marriage. Sister Aimee was just twenty-eight when she reached Los Angeles in 1918, rapidly finding success.

Sister Aimee combined expressions of the new Pentecostal faith in which jubilant, ecstatic responses and speaking in tongues were combined with show business. The Angelus Temple, large enough to frequently be filled with a congregation of five thousand, had reminders of her success. There was a Miracle Room, in which crutches and braces from the people who had been healed were kept for anyone who wanted to see them. "Jesus is the healer," Sister Aimee stressed. "I am only the little office girl who opens the door and says, 'Come in.'" To the faithful, however, that little office girl was all-powerful. In their minds, she was the person chosen by God to open that "office" door, a feat no one else could equal. The fact that the building she had constructed cost $1.5 million was further proof of her ability to influence the masses.

Sister Aimee, whose looks and vanity resulted in her never arguing with her description as "The World's Most Pulchritudinous Evangelist," loved to put on a show. She was usually photographed in a flowing white gown with a cross on her chest, but her services could be stage shows. One time she dressed as a traffic policeman and rode a motorcycle down the aisle. Stepping off the bike, she raised her hand to the congregation and shouted, "Stop! You're speeding to Hell!" It was outrageous, unlike anything even the most extreme Pentecostals and evangelicals in the area were doing, and the people loved it.

In 1926, McPherson represented the height of spiritual leadership to Della and Gladys, yet by the time Norma Jean was born, Sister Aimee was embroiled in the controversy that caused her to lose a bit of her saintly image. She and Kenneth G. Ormiston, the radio operator for Sister Aimee's broadcasts, decided to run off together for a few weeks of uninterrupted sex and fun.

The ruse was elaborate. On May 18, 1926, Sister Aimee and her secretary, Emma Schaeffer, went to Venice Beach for a working one-day vacation. Emma was sent on an errand while Sister Aimee settled in a tent near the water. As soon as Emma was out of sight, Sister Aimee met with Ormiston and the two began moving among a series of hotels where they would have their affair for the next thirty-seven days.

Sister Aimee's mother apparently was not in on the ruse. She seemed genuinely concerned, offering both a twenty-five-thousand-dollar reward and establishing a thirty-six-thousand-dollar memorial fund while exhorting the followers to pray for her daughter. None of the money came from either her pocket or her daughter's. Instead it came from the followers—and when Aimee was found safe, it was not returned.

Because the nation assumed Sister Aimee had drowned, the return had to be dramatic. Ormiston had been reported missing by his wife, a fact overlooked by everyone but the sheriff, who took him in for questioning when he went to the beach where it all started. Prior to that, he had taken Sister Aimee to Aqua Prieta, Mexico, just across the border from Douglas, Arizona, so she could pretend to have made her escape. She was seemingly exhausted at 3:00 A.M. when she aroused a slaughterhouse keeper seeking help.

As the story unfolded, Sister Aimee said she had been approached by a woman who needed help for a dying infant resting in a car. But when Sister Aimee rushed to aid the baby, she was grabbed by two men, Steve and Jake, who kidnapped her for a half million dollars. Then she was taken away to a desert hideout where she was usually kept tied hand and foot. It was only when they relaxed their vigil that she was able to walk across the desert to safety.

Sister Aimee talked of being tortured with a lit cigar, of having bruises on her wrists and ankles, of having her feet blistered by the hot desert. The trouble was that her clothing was too clean for the ordeal she claimed, and her injuries did not match the treatment she allegedly endured. Still, thirty thousand followers met her at the train station when she arrived back home, and one hundred thousand came to see her triumphal return to the pulpit. She insisted that witnesses who had seen her with Ormiston had actually seen some other woman made up to look like her. And it was at the height of the emotional furor over Sister Aimee's triumphant return that Norma

Jean was baptized. It would be the newborn's first experience with media hype and what might be called good public relations helping bad people.

Not long after the baptism, the attitude of the public toward Sister Aimee changed radically. She was put on trial for fraud, and Ormiston agreed to testify for the prosecution. However, the prosecutor suddenly dropped his charges and moved for a directed verdict of acquittal. The judge complied, not understanding why the prosecutor would discontinue what obviously would have been a winning case.

The truth concerning the prosecutor's decision will probably never be known. Two years later that same prosecutor was sent to prison for taking a one-hundred-thousand-dollar bribe to walk away from a stock fraud case. The prosecutor was proven to be a man who would enforce the law according to whoever paid him the most money. As a result, it has been assumed by many that at least some of the money Sister Aimee's mother retained from the reward and memorial may have found its way into the prosecutor's pockets.

It is presumed that the Bolenders, who were originally as impressed with Angelus Temple as Della May and Gladys, joined those who became disillusioned with Aimee Semple McPherson. The scandal was also likely to increase their resolve to discern and follow, along with the children in their care, what they saw as God's laws for salvation. They felt there were only limited means for earning extra money without sacrificing their souls. For them this meant becoming professional foster care parents, a designation that enabled them to care for both orphans and parent-placed children like Norma Jean. The fee was always the same—five dollars per week. Sometimes the money came from the state of California. Sometimes, as in the case of Norma Jean, it came from one or both parents.

The Bolenders kept books and toys for the children. They took them to church and had them participate in church pageants and plays. They also enjoyed listening to the radio as it became available. It was only attending the movies they considered a waste of time. They knew that Gladys and Grace worked in the film industry yet never criticized the ways the two earned their living.

Later Norma Jean would claim that the Bolenders made clear to her that if the Lord came for you when you were in the movie theater, you would burn along with all the bad souls since you were not out and about and doing good work. (Other taboos, beside movie theaters, included smoking, drinking, and taking the name of the Lord in vain. However, the truth of Norma Jean's allegations has been questionable.)

It was in the first few months following Norma Jean's placement with the Bolenders, a time when Grace lived near the studios and Gladys temporarily moved into her mother's home, that Grace and Gladys developed a ritual for Norma Jean. They would take her on Sunday outings to the homes of the stars, looking at how they lived and excitedly telling the stories of the men and women they spotted out on their grounds, going shopping, and otherwise handling the chores they had to do on what was also their only day off.

Gladys's arrangement with her mother had been planned when the older woman was increasingly frail from the heart condition. Gladys would make sure her mother was able to get through the day and then would board a trolley and travel to the studio where she worked. What neither woman understood was that Della May's myocarditis, the general term for her heart condition, was affecting her ability to think. The more severe the heart problem, the less rational she became. That was why, on August 4, 1927, Della May spontaneously decided to get out of bed and go see her granddaughter down the street.

Della May was not expected. She knocked politely but there was no answer. Instead of realizing that no one was home at the Bolenders, she felt they were avoiding her. She began pounding on the door, becoming increasingly frustrated by the lack of response. Finally she covered her elbow with her blouse sleeve, then smashed the glass in the door and walked away. Apparently, rather than trying to use the opening she had made to get inside, she felt herself sending some sort of message that she had been there.

Someone in the neighborhood witnessed the vandalism, called the police, and Della May was taken to Norwalk State Hospital. There it was found that her heart and the surrounding tissues were inflamed. She was in a manic state when interviewed, but her disturbed thinking was the result of the myocarditis. It was also found that she was so seriously ill, she had to be admitted immediately.

There was little the doctors of that day could do other than keep Della May comfortable. Her body was too weakened and the medication available relatively ineffective. She died on August 23, Gladys never coming to understand her mother's real condition. She always assumed that the problem was mental illness, not abnormal thinking caused by a physical condition.

ℰ

There would be many stories about this period of Norma Jean's life, each seemingly more sordid and twisted than the previous. The primary thread was the idea that she had been in more than a dozen foster homes, horribly mistreated, and estranged from her mother. Fortunately everyone mentioned the Bolenders, and so, in 1955, when *Time* magazine assigned journalist Ezra Goodman to investigate Norma Jean's life, he decided to talk directly with the people who had been involved with her childhood. Among those with whom he spoke were Mr. and Mrs. Albert Bolender of Hawthorne. Albert had retired from the post office by then and they lived in an aging six-room house where Goodman found them. Not only did they tell Goodman that they had never before been interviewed; he learned that they did not speak of their connection with Norma Jean who had become the successful movie actress Marilyn Monroe.

Goodman wrote in his book *The Fifty-Year Decline and Fall of Hollywood*,

> In the living room were an old piano, a red print rug, a wooden rocker, and a copy of *The Letters of Edna St. Vincent Millay* on the coffee table. Ida Bolender, a gray-haired woman with horn-rimmed glasses who took in homeless children for boarding from time to time, told me that Gladys Baker, Marilyn's mother, had lived on the same street as they did and that they were friendly. Norma Jeane, or Marilyn, lived with the Bolenders from the time she was born until she was eight years old. Most of the time, Mrs. Bolender said, "Mrs. Baker was with me. She stayed in Hollywood when working nights, as a negative cutter, and stayed with me while working days."

Reinforcing the story were photographs and such documents as "dated receipts to prove that Marilyn's mother had footed the bills for her daughter's upkeep." In his book, Goodman quoted Ida Bolender further:

> Her mother paid her board all the time until her breakdown from overwork, when she was put into Norwalk hospital and Norma Jean went into

75

the children's home. Before that her mother supported her all the time and bought all her clothes and she had beautiful clothes. She went to Washington school in Hawthorne until she was about eight. She always made good grades in school. Lots of folks here in Hawthorne remember her.

After the orphan home . . . Norma Jean stayed with Aunt Ana and with Grace McKee Goddard until she got married. We went to see her lots of times. I don't know where those stories come from about her staying in twelve foster homes.

⅋ล

With her mother's death, and trusting in the Bolenders' care, Gladys made no further effort to stay near where Norma Jean was living, nor was she concerned with participating in the daily care of her daughter. She returned to Los Angeles where she worked six days a week for two separate film studios, and returned to her active nightlife. The Sunday outings with Norma Jean would continue, but only with some reluctance while Norma Jean was still a toddler. They rode the Pacific Electric trolley, going to glass factories, having picnics, and visiting various tourist attractions. The Venice Beach area had a variety of street entertainers, from mimes to musicians, a miniature railroad, jugglers, and other delightful distractions.

The relationship among the two friends and Norma Jean changed gradually as the child grew old enough to be aware of the movies and the movie stars. For example, Grauman's Chinese Theater had been built in 1927 and the publicity-minded owner was already having the ceremonial placing of stars' hands and feet in wet cement so tourists and locals could see the names and see how their hands and feet compared (Norma Jean eventually had the same size feet as Rudolph Valentino). Gladys and Grace usually stopped by to see which stars were there, and they tried to get to any film premieres being held there for the same reason.

The two women were awe struck by the stars, though only "Aunt Grace" fantasized that little Norma Jean might one day be among them. Gladys saw them as people apart, and though she did not fixate on her daughter having a future in the industry, she indirectly glamorized it by telling her stories of the actors' lives, at least as created by the publicists, in much the manner that other parents tell their children fairy tales. For example, Norma Jean heard about Jean Harlow when other children might have been hearing about Cinderella.

76

Gladys and Grace were in the business, working on the movies in which some of the stars were also their neighbors, a situation that eventually made the idea of a film career seem possible for Norma Jean. The interaction of stars and laborers on the streets, in the grocery stores, and even on the trolleys created a blend of fantasy and reality in which any future seemed possible.

By the time Norma Jean was able to read, fan magazines regularly told the stories of the stars, allegedly in their own words. The fact that all the information, the quotes, and even the illustrations were carefully planned and written by the studios, the photo shoots choreographed like a production number, was irrelevant. Gladys had Norma Jean read the stories aloud, then told her additional "facts" she had learned in years past.

Norma Jean led a show business fantasy life with her mother and "Aunt Grace," but the Bolenders introduced her to her first experience in show business. This occurred during the annual Easter pageant held in the Hollywood Bowl.

Seven

~

Never Work with Children or Dogs

Two decades before Norma Jean's birth and baptism by the Pentecostal evangelical Aimee Semple McPherson, the city of Los Angeles was shocked by a story in the *Times* that told of what was then a new religious sect meeting on Azusa Street, a mostly industrial part of the city. On April 18, 1906, the *Los Angeles Daily Times* reported that, "Colored people and a sprinkling of whites compose the congregation, and night is made hideous in the neighborhood by the howlings of the worshippers who spend hours swaying forth and back in a nerve-racking attitude of prayer and supplications." The reporter explained that the people told them they had been given the "gift of tongues" and that they could both speak and "comprehend the babel."

The evangelical and Pentecostal theologies that emerged from the Azusa Street Revival influenced not only conservative, blue-collar religious seekers like the Bolenders but also wealthy individuals who relocated from the East. Among these was Mrs. Christine Witherill Stevenson, heiress to the Pittsburgh Paint fortune. She actively supported the new movements, though she was not one to preach to others and try to save souls by direct intervention in their lives. Instead she sought to enlighten them through the arts.

Mrs. Stevenson arrived in California in 1918, delighting in the weather that made outdoor activities possible the entire year. But as much as she enjoyed the climate, she was horrified to discover that there was no place for the production of religious theater.

Mrs. Stevenson was not one to embrace the nickelodeons and the silent movies of the day, including those that had religious themes. She did not feel that the new medium was a waste of time, as the Bolenders allegedly believed, but she did feel that biblical stories were most uplifting, enlightening, and emotionally absorbing when acted out by stage performers. It was also a medium to which everyone then living in Southern California—Indians, Spanish, and Anglos—could relate. She had the money to pay for the creation of anything she desired, so in 1919 she established the Theater Arts Alliance. She arranged for like-minded locals to help with the operation, but she made certain that none were so well endowed financially as to be able to disagree with whatever she wished to purchase, build, and perform.

In September 1919, the Theater Arts Alliance spent forty-nine thousand dollars to purchase vacant ranchland, then called Daisy Dell, on which to build the performance center that would eventually be called the Hollywood Bowl. It was a decision not reached hastily.

The first concern prior to purchase was the acoustics. The group found that you could hear a coyote howling from one hundred yards away but they were uncertain if you could as easily hear a voice lifted in musical praise of the Lord. The answer was determined by taking boards out to the sagebrush and setting them on the ground in the approximate place where a stage might be built. Then they hauled in a grand piano and asked a local contralto to sing.

As the opera music filled the air, mice scurried, and prairie dogs bobbed up and down in their holes to alert one another to the strangers, members of the alliance walked about the area where they planned to have seating. No matter where they went, they could hear perfectly.

Mrs. Stevenson was so impressed that she moved ahead with the construction of a full outdoor theater without first seeking the agreement of the other members of the alliance. She hired the San Francisco architect Louis Mullgardt to design a million-dollar theater, approving plans the others disliked. Then, to fund the dream, she demanded that the alliance immediately raise two hundred thousand dollars.

The leadership balked at Mrs. Stevenson's arrogance and grandiose plans. They wanted a theater as much as she did, but they resented her using the fact of her greater wealth to act like a spoiled brat. They saw her as being like the rich little boy who owns the only decent baseball and bat on the playground, demanding that he be made team captain or he will take his toys and go home. They were correct in their assessment.

Mrs. Stevenson informed the group that she had paid for the initial land. She had planned the location to allow the production of those plays she knew were right for the community. If they didn't agree, she would sell the land, abandon the theater group, and busy herself with other good work. After all, she and the good Lord knew how much there was to do to appropriately bring the Word to people living in so morally backward an area.

The alliance members were delighted by the possibility of ridding themselves of Mrs. Stevenson. Five of the eight board members, the simple majority necessary, decided that selling the land was a fine idea, but when they started to put it on the market, they were informed by the attorney that it had been purchased specifically for civic and cultural use. They could only sell it to a group much like themselves.

The answer to the problem came in the form of the Community Park and Art Association, which took over Daisy Dell in 1920. Artie Mason Carter was hired to develop such theatrical works as *The Landing of the Pilgrims* as performed by Lionel Barrymore, and the Hollywood Community Chorus under the direction of conductor Hugo Kirchhofer.

The program was a community diversion that was neither Broadway professional nor little-theater awful. No one had anything better to do than attend the performance, so the townspeople willingly turned out, walking up a hill to an area in which the weeds and grass were up to their knees. There they stood, nibbled on by bugs, unable to comfortably sit down, applauding the break from daily boredom as much as the quality of the performance.

Hugo Kirchhofer was enthusiastic about the site of that first musical. He loved the sound quality, envisioned the potential, and recognized that the physical layout was just like a giant bowl. Inadvertently he had given the location its new name. The former Daisy Dell would now be known as the "Hollywood Bowl."

The annual pageant in which Norma Jean would participate was started five years before her birth, on Easter Sunday, March 21, 1921. A platform of boards was built in the center of the Hollywood Bowl. Then the Community Park and Art Association, which had grown to one thousand members, sold thirty-six thousand tickets to see a sunrise pageant. This time W. A. Clark Jr.'s Philharmonic Orchestra performed, and the audience was delighted to learn that, in addition to the pageant, a full concert season was planned beginning in August.

Professor Antonio Sarsi and his Los Angeles Municipal Symphonic Band were featured at that first concert, and by then the Association had made a few improvements in the Hollywood Bowl. The grass and tall brush had been cleared. The access had been graded, and members of the audience could sit without feeling as though they were being attacked by an army of insects. However, the ground was still dusty when the weather was dry, and muddy whenever it rained.

The first year's season raised nine thousand dollars. By 1923 there were eight full concerts ("Symphonies under the Stars") including the Easter performance. And by 1924, with admission remaining at twenty-five cents—slightly less than an hour's pay for film industry workers—the Hollywood Bowl was owned free and clear.

The year Norma Jean was born was the year that the Hollywood Bowl first became a serious tourist attraction. The Hollywood Bowl Association, organized to manage and develop the operation, brought in workers who used one hundred kegs of blasting powder and four thousand sticks of dynamite to alter the land into a symmetrical bowl for performances. Thirty-six thousand yards of dirt were graded by mule teams, and three acres of land were prepared for the seating of seventeen thousand people. Then a concrete stage 138 feet by 90 feet was built, along with storage space and dressing rooms underneath and a parking area in back. A shell for performances was later added, the design work done by architect Frank Lloyd Wright.

The Bolenders were among the families who attended the Easter Pageants, and they were delighted when Norma Jean was selected by her second grade teacher to be one of the fifty children who would participate in the creation of what was called a living cross. The children all wore white garments covered with black robes. As Norma Jean later explained, "We all had on white tunics under the black robes and at a given signal we were supposed to throw off the robes, changing the cross from black to white. But I got so interested in looking at the people, the orchestra, the hills, and the stars in the sky that I forgot to watch the conductor for the signal. And there I was—the only black mark on a white cross. The family I was living with never forgave me."

Norma Jean may have embarrassed herself in front of thousands at the Hollywood Bowl, but her early elementary school years were happy ones. From the time she was enrolled in Hawthorne's Washington Street School the year before, she experienced a freedom in which she reveled. She walked to and from the building with two other children. She could play in the schoolyard, and she began creating her own games, often re-creating the stories of the radio detectives she heard with the Bolenders, such radio shows being accepted entertainment in ways movies were not.

Eight

Growing Up Too Happy

Marilyn knew how to sell herself. She instinctively understood the value of publicity. If she hit upon a story about herself that was colorful, she was the first one to realize its publicity value. The next time she told the story, it was embellished to gain her even more publicity.

How much of the story about her bleak childhood is actually true, I really can't say. But she was not quite the poor waif she later claimed to have been. When I first met her, she was supposed to have lived in three foster homes. As time went on it became five, eight, ten, because she knew it was a good selling point.

—Sidney Skolsky, columnist and friend, writing
in *Don't Get Me Wrong—I Love Hollywood*

❦

Norma Jean Mortenson had a nontraditional early childhood, though it was not all that unusual by the standards of the day. The Bolenders were professional foster parents who saw the children in their care as a business and a responsibility. They never let the children call them "Mom" and "Dad," or any variation of that. These were children who had at least one parent, and the moment the parent did not or could not pay the next month's twenty dollars, the child was returned.

Prior to the Great Depression, people like the Bolenders were the long-term, "sleepaway" equivalent of quality day care. Their role broadened when the economy began to fail, providing a safe location for the children while their parents worked as many full- and part-time jobs as possible to rebuild the family finances. For some this meant months or years with the children in continuous care and the parents moving among tents, barns, and other makeshift housing.

The problem for Norma Jean, and probably all the other children, was how to define the foster parents in their lives. These were the adults who helped them with school, took them out to play, gave them chores, celebrated their birthdays, and nursed them through the myriad illnesses all children get. In Norma Jean's case, these were also the people who changed her diapers and taught her to walk.

The longer Norma Jean and the other foster children lived with the Bolenders, their primary caretakers, the easier it was for the children to view them as their "real" parents. The Bolenders were her parents six days a week, and only on Sunday would the nice near-strangers, Gladys and/or Grace, appear in her life. It was easy to call Grace McKee "Aunt Grace." But calling Gladys "Mother" seemed an insult to Ida, whom Norma Jean looked upon as her real mother.

It was in 1932 that Gladys decided she had to stop having the Bolenders raise her daughter. She had written "deceased" for Berneice and Jackie when Norma Jean was born, and she had essentially erased them from her life. Jasper had not wanted her to come to Louisville to visit them, but she had gone there during one of Jackie's hospital stays, assuring herself he was cared for. She stayed away from her ex-husband's new family after that, but she apparently maintained contact with someone from Flat Lick because she learned that Jackie had died. It is not known if she knew the cause of death was the infection caused by Jasper's attempt at catheterization, or if she just thought the death was the natural result of Jackie's increasing weakness from all his body had endured. Whatever the case, she seemed to be reevaluating her role as a mother when seven-year-old Norma Jean experienced a personal tragedy and Ida Bolender felt her real mother should handle the aftermath.

Norma Jean had found a stray puppy she named Tippy. She asked to keep it, knowing nothing about how to care for a dog, and the Bolenders agreed, though their knowledge was no greater than that of the child.

The stray bonded to Norma Jean to such a degree that there were days when Tippy would follow her to school, then hang around the schoolyard until she emerged at the end of classes. The trouble was that Tippy went untrained in any way, frequently disturbing the neighbors with constant barking.

An angry neighbor of the Bolenders said that Tippy needed to be kept quiet. He could not be allowed to roam the neighborhood, chasing and barking at birds and squirrels. The noise disturbed the neighbor's sleep, and if it continued, he would take matters into his own hands.

The Bolenders thought nothing of the threat, and Norma Jean had no sense that there was a problem. Then, in late June 1933, shortly after the child's seventh birthday, Tippy was again allowed to roam outside. He saw a squirrel, delightedly barking at it as he chased it about the yard. Inside the house the Bolenders heard the dog, then the sound of a shotgun blast, and then silence. Tippy was dead. Norma Jean was inconsolable.

Gladys, summoned by Ida Bolender immediately after the murder of the dog, decided she could no longer avoid her responsibilities as a parent. She brought the last twenty-dollar payment for the Bolenders, and with the help of Grace who drove her to Hawthorne, helped Norma Jean bury her dog and pack her possessions before returning to Hollywood. Gladys had rented an apartment at 6012 Afton Place in Hollywood, but her real goal was to buy a house. Toward this end she had become a freelance film splicer, working six days and nights at both Columbia and Twentieth Century-Fox. She was able to pay the rent, save $750 toward a house, and still go to bars, nightclubs, and movies with her friend Grace. She had little sleep, drank too much, and was increasingly exhausted. Despite that, it seemed as though her dreams were going to be possible to achieve.

Gladys turned to the Home Owner Loan Corporation (HOLC) for a five-thousand-dollar loan which, when added to her savings, allowed her to buy a six-room house at 6812 Arbol Drive. The Corporation had been created under Franklin Roosevelt's administration to help people buy homes, and the money was provided by the Mortgage Guarantee Company of California. Gladys was afraid a single parent would be rejected even though she more than met the requirements so she listed herself as Gladys Baker, a married woman.

The house Gladys purchased was three bedrooms and fully furnished, including having a white Franklin baby grand piano. Gladys did not play, though Grace McKee would see that Norma Jean took lessons. However, white pianos were being used in a number of current movie musicals on which Gladys had worked and she seemed to think that the piano was a positive omen, assuring a happy ending to her story.

Gladys knew that she was overtired, that she could not continue working and playing at the same pace as before she became fully responsible for her younger daughter. She made plans to rent out the entire two-story house to people who would not need all the space but could afford the monthly payments. Then she would use a small portion of the money to sublet just the rooms she and Norma Jean would utilize. The kitchen, living room, and bathroom would be shared space.

Gladys's emotional stress was compounded when President Franklin Roosevelt closed every bank in the United States to stop the panic removal of depositor funds. The action, which came to be known as a bank holiday, only lasted from Friday, March 3, 1933, through the following March 9. However, while it was in effect, businesses, including the movie studios, could not pay their employees.

Roosevelt was successful in staving off the run on the banks, and depositors used better judgment when they reopened. Businesses, including the studios, also changed their ways. The studio heads figured that, since everyone had a taste of what it would be like to be out of a job, they would be happy just to be working for a paycheck, even if that paycheck was smaller than in the past. The studio box-office income was not yet being seriously affected by the Great Depression, but the bank holiday seemed a perfect time to cut costs. What they had not expected was for all the technical workers, including film cutters, to be asked by the unions to go out on strike.

Gladys and Grace agreed that the arbitrary cutting of their pay by up to fifty percent was wrong. Grace felt she should honor the strike. She also had adequate savings to meet her needs if the walkout did not last very long.

Gladys agreed with her friend and with the union leaders. She did not feel that she could join them, however. She had the expense of her new home and the full-time responsibility of her daughter.

Gladys went to the RKO lot where she and Grace had been working before the strike. She knew that she could not cross the picket line or be seen by her co-workers entering the building. The strikers were periodically violent, smashing cars and attacking people who tried to enter the studio. She also knew that once she got inside, she would be paid for the work she did as though there was no strike.

The RKO lot was massive and surrounded by fencing, much of which was not visible from the entrance. Gladys walked around the perimeter until she found a place where her friends and co-workers would not see her, then climbed the fence and returned to the cutting room. There was no backlash against her, implying that either she was never caught by the strikers or they understood her desperation. They may also have had sympathy for a single mother, especially since many of them had met little Norma Jean when her mother had to take the child to work with her, Norma Jean playing quietly while Gladys and Grace worked nearby. Whatever the case, Gladys worked and was paid during the strike.

Gladys had other problems beyond assuring a paycheck. Most of her time was spent inside in the dark, a fact that led to depression in a form similar to the now-understood seasonal affect disorder. She ate little, exercised less, and further depressed herself when she used alcohol to try to relax. She was also beginning to sleep erratically and that was affecting her ability to think clearly. Her behavior was increasingly erratic, though consistent with someone who was affected by poor diet and lack of sleep.

Grace McKee worried about her friend and tried to ease the burden of motherhood. She began taking Norma Jean to as many different places as she could, supplementing the time Gladys could spend with her child.

Grace, in all probability, had the more maternal feelings toward Norma Jean, but what neither she nor Gladys's daughter realized was that Grace was not committed to caring for her the way they might have thought. Grace was single, paying her own way, and with no other distractions. She would soon meet a man, fall in love, and pursue her own life. But that was in the future. Her concerns for the moment were for Gladys and the child.

Gladys found further help when she was able to rent the house she was purchasing to an acting family she and Grace knew as casual friends. George Atkinson, originally from Liverpool, England, was a character actor who was in numerous movies in the 1920s, including the George Arliss film

Disraeli. He worked steadily, usually in small parts, and occasionally without credit. His wife was an extra and his daughter was the stand-in for actress Madeleine Carroll. By the time the family rented from Gladys Baker, he had mostly dropped out of the movies and planned to return to England, either at the end of 1934 or early in 1935. He had an offer to work as an editor for British-based movie magazines, something he wanted to try to see if he would enjoy the work. As it turned out, he didn't, and would return to the United States in 1939 so he could resume his acting career. It was then that he gained greater fame for roles in such movies as *Raffles*, *A Guy Named Joe*, and *I Remember Mama*, though they never returned to the Arbol Drive address.

It was in October 1933 that Gladys was notified about a man who had been out of her life for many years. Tilford Hogan, her grandfather who had abandoned both her grandmother, Jennie Nance Hogan, and her mother, Della May, was dead. A distant cousin had taken it upon herself to locate and notify as many of the estranged family members as possible. She found where Gladys was living approximately five months after the death.

Tilford was seventy-seven when he fell in love with Emma Wyatt, a widow who saw him as a handsome, strong, and decent man. She seemingly did not mind when he told her that his kidneys were bad and his lungs were weak, nor was he overly concerned about what apparently was Emma's recent heart attack. Both had worked hard all their lives, and they planned to lease a small farm to provide adequate income for their old age.

Tilford did not think about the Great Depression and its impact on the prices of farm goods. His lease was based on an economy that was quickly changing, and he soon realized he could not produce and sell enough of the goods declining in retail price to pay the rent. The landowner explained that he and Emma would have to leave, a fact he could not bear to share with her. On May 29, 1933, Tilford watched as Emma left to do some shopping. Then he walked into the barn, threw a rope over a high beam, fastened a noose around his neck, and killed himself. He was eighty-two years old and did not have the courage to admit he was a failure to the one person in his life who would not have cared.

For reasons that will never be known, Gladys decided that Tilford was neither emotionally weak, as almost everyone else considered him to be, nor severely depressed by life circumstances he did not wish to endure. He had left her grandmother and her mother. He had left Emma. He was cowardly and pathetic to almost everyone else, but Gladys refused to believe the truth about the sick old man. Instead she convinced herself that he was mentally ill and that this mental illness—not heart disease nor any of the other conditions that afflicted her relatives—was the family curse. She also was certain that she was next in line, and she justified her self-concerns by noting that she was frequently overtired, depressed, and unable to spend evenings partying as she had in the past.

Gladys's thought process was an outrageous distortion of her life, and the tragedy was that it was never countered, either while she and Norma Jean were alive or in the years that followed both their deaths. She was already suffering environmentally related depression when Tilford committed suicide; and it was his action that seemed to be the ultimate stress to overwhelm her, even though she had never known the old man, never talked with him, never seen him. Neither his life nor his death had affected her directly, yet the way he died was emotionally shattering. She stopped eating regularly and began losing weight and becoming malnourished. She slept little, eventually developing sleep psychosis where rest was almost impossible.

Grace became frightened of the radical changes in her friend. She knew something had to be done to help Gladys, but she had no idea what might be best. Finally she convinced Gladys to go with her to see a neurologist who prescribed inadequately tested and understood mood-altering medication.

There was little comprehension of mood disorders in 1933 when Gladys went to see the doctor. Conditions such as Post-Traumatic Stress Disorder resulting from experiencing an overwhelming trauma had yet to be fully identified, much less understood. Doctors still referred to traumatized World War I veterans as having "shell shock." Straitjackets were still a common tool for behavior modification, and most of the medications available were stimulants and depressants, neither well understood nor with predictable results.

The neurologist put Gladys on a medication regimen not unlike what many of the movie studio physicians were prescribing at the behest of the producers who were also using such drugs. There were sedatives to help everyone sleep and stimulants to bring them fully alert each morning. Side effects, often serious in nature, were relatively common.

Appropriate dosages were seldom known. The addictive nature of the drugs, and the reactions to them, which could include an increase in the symptoms they were supposed to alleviate, were all still being discovered.

Grace and Gladys may have known about some of the drugs from their work at the studio. Certainly they would have thought them harmless even as Gladys began having adverse reactions to the dangerous and unneeded medication. However, this was not a time when even the most educated people questioned doctors. The medical community was held in unwarranted esteem, and drug abuse would eventually prove a problem for numerous stars, including Judy Garland, Peter Lawford, Robert Walker, and Gladys's daughter, Norma Jean.

Gladys was one of the people who never should have been given the medication, and her health deteriorated more rapidly. Her heart condition worsened, her mood swings became more intense, and the doctor assumed that she simply needed more medication, never understanding that she was having an adverse reaction. The medicine should either have been switched or eliminated.

Trusting the doctors to know what was wrong, Gladys assumed in her lucid moments that she was becoming mentally ill, and that the medicine was keeping her from getting worse. Mental illness was her family's curse, or so she incorrectly believed, and it was now her turn in life.

Gladys tried to continue the same work and recreation schedule that she had maintained before seeing the neurologist, but it was not possible. She needed full-time care, and so Grace helped her go to a Santa Monica rest home early in 1934. Unfortunately, because psychiatry and psychopharmacology were in their infancy, rest homes were literally places to rest. Medications were not tested or adjusted. Psychologists did not work with the residents. The only drugs encountered other than what the patient brought from the doctor who was treating the person before admittance would be sedatives to assure the person rested. The fact that the sedatives were unnecessary and might dangerously interact with other medicine was not understood. Gladys and many others often left in worse health than when they entered, conventional wisdom blaming the patient rather than the care.

In Gladys's case, after several months without improvement she was transferred to Los Angeles General Hospital for intense, long-term care. Still, there was no effort to look beyond medication and relative isolation. She was warehoused in the hospital, no effort being made to help her leave and be productive again.

Grace McKee and the Atkinsons took over the full care of Norma Jean. Gladys was again a stranger who rarely saw her daughter and certainly was incapable of meaningful parenting.

Nine

The Better the Story, the Greater the Publicity

There are many questions about how the young Norma Jean perceived herself in relation to Gladys. The interviews she gave as the years passed provided insights into a series of foster homes and often-tragic experiences that were so richly detailed that many interviewers believed them. Sometimes they were outright lies; other times the events were real but had been experienced by another child who had related them to Norma Jean.

For example, when detailing the various foster care experiences, Norma Jean—by then living as Marilyn Monroe—related a story of sexual molestation to both her "ghost" autobiographer, Ben Hecht, in 1953 and, later, to George Barris, a photographer for *Cosmopolitan*:

I was almost nine, and I lived with a family that rented a room to a man named Kimmell. He was a stern-looking man, and everybody respected him and called him *Mister* Kimmell. I was passing his room when his door opened and he said quietly, "Please come in here, Norma." I thought he wanted me to run an errand.

"Where do you want me to go, Mr. Kimmell?" I asked.

"No place," he said and closed the door behind me. He smiled at me and turned the key in the lock.

"Now you can't get out," he said, as if we were playing a game.

I stood staring at him. I was frightened, but I didn't dare yell . . . When he put his arms around me I kicked and fought as hard as I could, but I didn't make a sound. He was stronger than I was and wouldn't let me go. He kept whispering to me to be a good girl.

When he unlocked the door and let me out, I ran to tell my "aunt" what Mr. Kimmell had done.

"I want to tell you something," I stammered, "about Mr. Kimmell. He . . . he . . ."

My "aunt" interrupted.

"Don't you dare say anything against Mr. Kimmell," she said, angrily. "Mr. Kimmell's a fine man. He's my star boarder!"

Mr. Kimmell came out of his room and stood in the doorway smiling.

"Shame on you!" My "aunt" glared at me. "Complaining about people."

"This is different," I began. "This is something I have to tell . . . Mr. Kimmell . . . he . . . he . . ."

I started stammering again and couldn't finish. Mr. Kimmell came up to me and handed me a nickel.

"Go buy yourself some ice cream," he said.

I threw the nickel in Mr. Kimmell's face and ran out.

I cried in bed that night and wanted to die. I thought, "If there's nobody ever on my side that I can talk to I'll start screaming." But I didn't scream.

There was a slight variation in the story when she related it to George Barris. Instead of referring to her "aunt," she talked about her "foster mother."

There are several problems with this. The first is that the time related was almost certainly a period when Norma Jean was still living with either her mother or the Atkinsons and Grace McKee. The "star boarder" statement made no sense, since this was not a facility with multiple boarders but a couple with a grown daughter. Most important of all in revealing the nonsense of her stories of sexual molestation, told when she was giving what was supposed to be an intimate personal interview, was the fact that there was one person who knew the truth and had nothing to gain by countering what she said. This was her first husband, Jim Dougherty, who wrote in his book, *To Norma Jean with Love, Jimmie.*—

Norma Jean Mortenson (sic) had known absolutely nothing about sex when she married me. Truly nothing at all, except what her girlfriends had told

93

her, what they'd giggled about, looked up in books and magazines. My mother had cautioned me about her, telling me she was a virgin and that I should be very careful of her on our first night together. I remember that sweet night. We were both gentle with each other, and it was very obvious that Norma Jean's "delicate threshold" had never been crossed over before. There was some pain, but I was aware of it and sensitive to her, and after that small discomfort, Norma Jean just fell crazily in love with sex. I was one lucky man.

In addition to Dougherty's statement was the question Norma Jean allegedly put to Grace Goddard. She said, "Jim's such a wonderful person. I want to marry him, but I don't know anything about sex. Can we get married without having sex?"

The trouble was that real life—a teenager marrying while young and naïve—did not make for a good background for a movie star "sold" as a sexual being. Marilyn Monroe "deflowered" young, either by force, desire, or both, meant far greater fan interest than the truth.

What is certain is that Norma Jean originally looked upon the Bolenders as her parents, no matter how much they tried to dissuade her from such thinking. They were her primary caretakers for the first several years of her life, the people who were always at hand when she was happy or sad, having new experiences, or seeking an adult with whom to talk. The couple also kept in touch after she left their care, attending her wedding to Jim Dougherty almost nine years after she left their home.

The horror of having her dog murdered, then immediately being forced to leave the Bolenders to go live with her mother was undoubtedly traumatic. Her being shuffled from caretaker to caretaker was also difficult, but she had the consistent love of Grace McKee and the involvement of the show business friends of Grace and Gladys. She also delightedly mocked the lies she had been telling when she was just beginning to be known as Marilyn Monroe and the studio was working to publicize a group of eight starlets newly under contract, including herself.

The incident occurred in September 1949. *Life* magazine photographer Philippe Halsman was sent to photograph the new "talent" for the October 10 issue of the magazine. Each of the actresses was asked to act out four situations—meeting a frightening monster, laughing at a hilarious joke, being embraced by a lover, and tasting a delicious drink.

The newly minted Marilyn Monroe was bored with the exercise. A studio contract had not made her a star. It assured she was another pretty face available for crowd scenes and, occasionally, to be the playmate of an important producer or director if she wanted that contract renewed. She had changed her name, changed her look, and while *Life* was the most important picture magazine of her time, this was just a fun photo shoot, a novelty item for the magazine. The primary appeal was no different from when she posed for cheesecake images, and she decided she would tease the photographer.

Halsman, apparently trying to get the actress to relax, asked Marilyn how old she was the first time she had had sex.

"Seven," she replied softly, demurely lowering her eyes as though embarrassed by her confession.

"And how old was the man?" the shocked photographer asked.

"Younger."

The one lingering trauma, different from many other children growing up in Depression-era Los Angeles, was her mother's health. Norma Jean, Grace, and others close to Gladys all assumed that the rest home was a place of rehabilitation. They were under the misguided impression that she was being treated, that the medication would make her well. In truth she was warehoused, the medication meant to control her behavior for the convenience of the staff. There was no effort to treat her physical conditions—her lungs, cardiovascular system, inappropriate eating habits, and the like. However, it was Norma Jean's belief, apparently shared by Grace, that when Gladys did not leave the institutions, it was because she was either severely mentally ill or rejecting her daughter once again. Fortunately Grace McKee was determined to help the child in whom she had so much faith as one of the Hollywood children who would grow up to be a star.

Gladys and Grace had different attitudes toward the film industry and the possibility that Norma Jean might one day be on the screen.

Gladys was what might be called a fan with illusions. She read all the movie magazines and followed the gossip columns, accepting everything she read as factual. She knew that the industry had a publicity machine that made certain that a star's image on the screen carried over in whatever way was appropriate for daily life. She and Grace also knew many of the stars on a casual basis, since Hollywood residents shopped in the same stores, took the same trolleys, attended the same events, and relaxed at the same beaches. She also worked at a job where she spliced together the raw material that would eventually comprise the unfolding story they would see on the screen.

Despite Gladys's intellectual awareness, she shared the often-created stories of the men and women profiled in the fan magazines with her daughter the way other mothers might tell the stories of Cinderella, Snow White, and other fairy tales.

Grace McKee, by contrast, was an industry pragmatist. She loved the created fantasy that Gladys accepted as "truth," but she understood the practical side of how a child could grow up to be in films. She recognized that women did not magically step off a bus and become successful. They had to learn their craft in addition to having a certain style, a certain look, and a unique way with the camera. Many had been on the stage, sometimes in their home towns, sometimes in a major city such as New York, and sometimes they had traveled with a touring company. The successful ones were aggressive and willing to do anything requested of them in order to gain a role.

Norma Jean was still living with the Bolenders when Grace began talking with her about becoming a movie actress. She talked about clothing, hair, and makeup, and as Norma Jean became old enough to be interested in such matters, Grace paid for the lessons necessary to teach the child the proper way to sing, how to dance, and how to play the white piano that delighted Gladys when the Arbol Drive home was purchased. It was Grace's way of not only helping the child but having her see that acting was work, real work, for which even the most beautiful of women needed to prepare.

The role model for Grace's plans for Norma Jean was the daughter of a Kansas City, Missouri, dentist who was the original platinum blond. Prior to Harlean Carpenter (Jean Harlow), brunettes were the symbols of all that was dangerously sensual and intensely sexual. In fact, Carpenter was born around the time when Theodosia Burr Goodman became the most infamous actress of her day, assuming the persona of Theda Bara and dying her hair brunette because there were no meaningful roles for blondes.

The truth about Goodman was that she was raised in Cincinnati, Ohio, the daughter of a Jewish tailor and his wife. She became interested in the theater and moved to New York where she found minor success in a play called *The Devil*, eventually touring with the show. She turned to films at the same time that studio publicity departments began creating promotable lives for stars whose real backgrounds were as mundane as those of ordinary fans.

Goodman, renamed Theda Bara, an anagram for Arab (Bara) Death (Theda) became "The Vamp" when she starred in a movie called *A Fool There Was*. She was thirty years old, "ancient" for an actress in a medium where teenage girls played older women, but her life story was crafted to be like no other. With her dyed black hair, heavy-lidded eyes, and costumes that often included snakes and skulls, she was turned into an actress whose studio bio said that she was born in the Sahara to a French artiste and his Egyptian concubine. She was supposedly possessed of supernatural powers that enabled her to seduce and destroy any man, no matter how devoted he had previously been to the woman he loved.

Goodman had a sense of humor about the roles she played and the medium itself. Years later, looking back on the times when she was achieving her greatest fame, she said, "To understand those days, you must consider that people believed what they saw on the screen. . . . Audiences thought the stars were the way they saw them. Why, women kicked my photographs as they went into the theaters where my pictures were playing, and once on the streets of New York a woman called the police because her child spoke to me."

Harlean Carpenter, a generation younger than Theodosia Goodman, made as radical a change as had "The Vamp." She bleached her hair platinum blond, creating a new type of sex symbol. Dark-haired women, once considered the most sensual and dangerous of predators, raced to the store to buy peroxide in order to achieve the new look.

Carpenter was afflicted with a combination of ill health—meningitis at age five and scarlet fever at age fifteen—and a mother with personal ambitions to be a star. Her mother divorced her dentist husband and remarried a man connected with both the film industry and organized crime, and the family relocated, first to Chicago and then to Los Angeles.

Carpenter, legally renamed Jean Harlow in 1935 when Norma Jean was most influenced by Grace McKee, starred in such movies as *Hell's Angels* and *Platinum Blonde*. It was her life and her rise to stardom at age eighteen that inspired Grace and led her to take Norma Jean to as many Harlow films as she could. Unlike Gladys, Grace saw that if an actress had the right screen presence, she could be a star, regardless of her background. She added peroxide to her own hair to look more like Harlow, and she persuaded her best friend's daughter to add color to her face with a little rouge, in the same manner as Harlow.

The interactions of Grace McKee and Norma Jean Mortenson were much like that of mother and daughter. Grace recognized that no one else cared for the child as she did, and she decided to gain legal custody. Once again, an action meant to help Norma Jean would also add to the myth of her childhood experiences.

The California state requirements for an adult seeking full guardianship of a child to whom she was not related required a period of time during which they would live apart. Grace would be investigated, including reports concerning her involvement with Norma Jean while the child was being cared for by the agency with which she would temporarily be placed. In addition, Gladys would either have to willingly give up parental rights to her daughter or be declared legally incompetent to care for the child. As it turned out, her condition deteriorated, she was moved to Norwalk State Hospital where Della May had died from her heart condition; and on January 15, 1935, Gladys was declared legally incompetent. Grace McKee was to handle her affairs, managing what little money and few possessions remained.

Grace never attempted to personally profit from the estate other than to get reimbursed for expenses incurred for such matters as the fee paid to the Santa Monica Rest Home on Gladys's behalf. Gladys's car was returned to the original owner rather than trying to pay off the $250 still owed on it. The piano was sold for a $35 profit over what was still owed, the extra money going properly into the estate. And there was cash and a check totaling $150, among other minor holdings. The approval for the final dispersion of all assets was completed on June 1, 1935, Norma Jean's ninth birthday. The British boarders had returned to England and the house was repossessed.

Grace filed for the custody of her best friend's daughter. She obtained statements from the doctors treating Gladys attesting to the "fact" that Norma Jean's mother was irrevocably mentally ill. The state of psychiatric treatment at the time was such that among the "proofs" supplied by the medical professionals was the fact that, when isolated in a state hospital and regularly tranquilized, she became depressed, agitated, and could be seen praying a lot. The religious fervor and the desire to be active as she had been before being institutionalized would seem to most people the normal result of being locked away from all that she enjoyed. But the doctors saw it as madness.

Grace did not argue on her friend's behalf. She was given permission to take over Gladys's affairs, and she applied to be Norma Jean's legal guardian based on the incompetence of the only living parent Gladys acknowledged. Ed Mortensen was never sought by Grace or the authorities.

The guardian arrangements for Norma Jean and her "aunt" Grace were rather odd. As the child was not allowed to live with Grace during the period when the state investigated her fitness to have custody, this meant she had to go to any approved foster care facility—such as an institution or a private home—while Grace filled out paperwork and was investigated as a fit guardian.

The logical place for Norma Jean was the Los Angeles Orphans Home, a large institution providing care for orphans as well as children whose parent(s) paid for the type of care the Bolenders provided. Norma Jean was not an orphan, and though her mother was in the hospital, her "aunt" had been caring for her and would be getting her permanently. As a result, the Orphans Home put her on a list for September admission for foster care during the investigation. This meant an interim arrangement was necessary, and that proved to be the Harvey Giffen family in West Los Angeles, neighbors of Grace.

The Giffens were either kindhearted or needed extra money. Harvey worked as a sound engineer for the Radio Corporation of America. They had three children of their own, several foster children, and a house so small that it was barely adequate. They explained that they could not keep Norma

Jean for long, but the child was happy with the arrangement. She was uncomfortable with the idea of living in an institution, no matter for how short a time. She had known only home-like settings all her life and did not want to go anywhere different.

The investigation into Grace McKee took many weeks, but the court investigator recognized that "Aunt Grace" would ultimately be approved. The Giffens, from New Orleans, had warned Grace that they were leaving the film business; but during the time they cared for Norma Jean, they decided they wanted to adopt her. They went to see Gladys, who refused to give up her parental rights, a fact that made them tell the court they could not continue with the child because they were returning to New Orleans.

This time permission was given for Norma Jean to live with Grace's aunt, Edith Ana Atchinson Lower, in the older woman's apartment on Lodi Place in Hollywood. Grace, in control of Gladys's estate, applied for twenty-five dollars for her mother in payment for caring for Norma Jean.

Grace also sought other funds during this time. These were reimbursements for out-of-pocket expenses, including $49.30 still owed to the Santa Monica Rest Home in which Gladys had first been placed, and $24 for Julia Bennett, apparently a private duty nurse. There was also a $43.16 request to reimburse Grace for clothing she bought for Norma Jean.

Grace's ward was not well received by anyone in her family other than her mother. Some had met Norma Jean before, a few when she was still a baby. They had heard about her mother and grandparents. They were certain that Gladys's problems were genetic, the same "mental illnesses" that had affected Della May, Otis, and Tilford. None of them were aware of the history of heart problems or the other conditions that had impacted on the family. They were certain that the child would prove to be as unstable as they perceived the rest of her relatives to be.

Grace would hear none of it. Gladys had long been her friend, and while she knew little about her physical problems, she saw the stress, the overwork, the lack of sleep, the poor diet, and the other factors that truly mattered in her deteriorating condition. As for the child, Norma Jean was like a daughter to her. She was convinced that nothing could stop her from raising the child to adulthood.

What she did not consider was that she might unexpectedly meet a man for whom she would experience head-over-heels lust.

Ten

Grace Finds Her Man

Erwin "Doc" Goddard, the unexpected man of Grace's dreams, was 6 feet 5 inches tall, handsome, rugged, and ten years younger than Grace. He was a sometime movie actor, a stand-in for Joel McCrea, and had nonspeaking extra parts in a number of movies. He was someone who seemed to like everyone. He was also, some allege, a periodic drunk who, after one drinking bout, kissed Norma Jean in an inappropriate manner, forcing Grace to choose him over the child she loved. The story is dramatic, the source uncertain, and the reliability doubtful. Grace McGee would never have married a man who acted so inappropriately with the child.

Doc Goddard was the son of a physician and an amateur inventor who had a "day job" as an engineer at the Adel Precision Products Company. He also had either two or three children by a previous marriage. The two children who are known for certain were Josephine (called Nona) who became a film actress using the name Jody Lawrance, and Eleanor (called Beebe) who was the same age as Norma Jean. Beebe had lived in a series of foster homes where she was brutally treated.

The story of Grace's romance is not known. What is certain is that Doc delighted in the energetic older woman who constantly worked to make herself look more attractive, and she lusted after the rugged younger man who was intensely affectionate. Finally, in August 1935, the two traveled to Las Vegas for a wild weekend that ended with Grace's Aunt Ana Lower witnessing their marriage.

Edith Ana Atchinson Lower was both a real estate investor, a practice she made when still married to Edmund H. "Will" Lower in the 1920s, and a paid practitioner of the Christian Science faith (Church of Christ, Scientist), a small group that had been founded in Boston in 1866 by Mary Baker Eddy. The Lowers had divorced in 1933, dividing the investment property they previously jointly owned. Each bungalow or cottage had rental tenants until the Depression became severe enough that some tenants sneaked out without paying. Still, there was enough money so she never wanted, and her work as a paid practitioner—the equivalent of a doctor in her new faith—enabled her to live comfortably, though not extravagantly.

The theology of Christian Science follows Mary Baker Eddy's understanding of the Bible as explained in her book *Science and Health with Key to the Scriptures*. It included spiritual healing rather than the use of, or even study of, medicine as traditionally practiced.

Eddy believed that when a member of the faith fully understood Jesus' teaching and healings as noted in the Bible, sickness, sin, and even death would be destroyed. Toward this end, there were practitioners of spiritual healing who would often be summoned to a member's bedside in much the same manner as a physician might make a house call. Ana Lower was an ardent believer and student of the faith that had an estimated 270,000 believers spread among a thousand congregations in 1938 when Grace's aunt became a professional healer. She was paid in the same manner as a doctor, though prayer, rather than medicine, was the treatment of choice.

Unlike Aimee Semple McPherson's approach to religion, the followers of Mary Baker Eddy were comfortable with the entertainment business and the ways of the world. The group's newspaper, *The Christian Science Monitor*, remains a respected journal. Thus Aunt Ana, as Norma Jean would come to know her, was comfortable with Grace's work in the film industry and with her enthusiasm to make the child a star.

After their August 1935 marriage, Doc, Grace, Norma Jean, and Doc's older daughter, Nona, moved into a bungalow on Odessa Avenue in Van Nuys, a property owned by Ana Lower. The two girls were not particularly close, but they were of similar temperament. Each was extremely shy, observers of life who, as future actresses, seemed most comfortable when pretending to be other people.

Doc was doing more tinkering and occasional acting than full-time engineering back then. Grace was working, but not steadily employed. The couple had little money, and though Doc would eventually find moderate success as a research engineer, the marriage came when money was tight.

There is again some confusion about the guardianship arrangement Grace was establishing. Norma Jean had happily lived with Aunt Ana Lower for a while, and she had lived briefly with the couple involved with professional foster care.

Gladys had been approached by past acquaintances who were talking of adopting Norma Jean if she would allow it to happen. Presumably Grace McKee had been one such person, though that is uncertain. Gladys was not only adamantly against giving up her daughter; she also spiraled into depression each time the idea was broached with her.

The guardianship was a different matter, though even here the stories abound. What is certain is that there was a period when Norma Jean lived with Nona, Grace, and Doc, a later period when she lived with Beebe (also spelled Bebe), Grace, and Doc, and an almost two-year period beginning on September 13, 1935, when she was placed in the so-called orphans home.

Eleven

Not Quite an Orphan

The Los Angeles Orphans Home Society was located in Hollywood on El Centro Avenue. It had been built in 1880 as a place where parents experiencing hard times could take one or more of their children and leave them for whatever period of time they desired. Actual orphans were rare, though the county used the home for placement of children whose parents either were dead already or had died while a child was being cared for in the home.

The Orphans Home could not be used like daycare. Each child with a parent or guardian who could legally remove the child was classed as a "transient." A transient lived in the home for an indefinite period of time based on the stated need of the family. When matters changed and the parent who placed the child could prove that he or she could again properly care for the transient, the child would leave. This might mean days, weeks, or years. It was a service rather than a true orphanage.

Grace paid fifteen dollars a month to have Norma Jean be a "guest." She came regularly to take her to movies and for ice cream, bringing her presents and explaining how far along the custody efforts had progressed. She began showing the child how to use makeup and how to dress. There was a stability to the relationship that Norma Jean could count on.

The tales of Norma Jean's stay have grown taller over the years, the possible result of her becoming fascinated by the life of her foster sister, Eleanor "Beebe" Goddard, with whom she lived with "Aunt Grace" and her new husband after the Orphans Home. The fact, based on the administration record, was that she was there for nine months. This would match Grace and Doc's needs, though most biographies stress her presence from September 19, 1935, the time everyone agrees she entered the place, to June 26, 1937—an unlikely length.

Norma Jean's history, as told to Ben Hecht, included the comment "I lived in the orphanage only off and on." Then she added a variation of the story she created at the suggestion of Sid Skolsky when she was first gaining success as an actress. "Most of the time I was placed with a family, who were given five dollars a week for keeping me. I was placed in nine different families before I was able to quit being a legal orphan." (The fee structure, at least, seems illogical at best. It was the cost of a foster care facility such as the Bolenders. Since Grace was paying five dollars a month *less* to the Orphans Home while Norma Jean lived there, and since there was no state money paying for her care as there would have been had she been an orphan, it is doubtful that the home contributed the difference.)

The time in the Orphans Home was difficult for Norma Jean, though not because she was exposed to horrible hardships. Like all the residents, she shared a room with three to five other girls. Boys and girls lived in separate wings, but the design was more like that of a slightly overcrowded college dormitory than the barracks-like arrangement she would later pretend had been the case. (She claimed to have had Bed 27, but even if the beds had been numbered, they were not all together in row after row like an army barracks as the bed number designation seems to imply.)

The "official" story of the Orphans Home stay, which Norma Jean developed in conjunction with studio publicists and her friend, gossip columnist Sid Skolsky, had her taking cold-water baths, experiencing low-quality food, and working as little more than a maid, forced to do everything from scrubbing toilets to washing endless dishes. She was paid five cents a month, with one cent withheld for Sunday school—or so she claimed. The work was always done after the children were awakened at 6:00 A.M. so that chores would be finished before school.

Eventually details were added. Norma Jean washed one hundred each of knives, forks, spoons, plates, and cups. She did this work three times a day, seven days a week, even though the staff, upon hearing this nonsense years later, noted that such work would have taken the child at least four hours. She would not have had time for school, sports, games, and the other activities.

The food was also supposed to be terrible, a real-life version of food in an institution in which the inmates had to riot for change. The truth was that it was typical of hospital food: perhaps a little bland, but varied and always well received. "She sleeps well and eats well," read one of the reports in Norma Jean's file. "She is bright and sunshiny."

Real life for Norma Jean was not interesting enough for studio bios and interviews with the actress known as Marilyn Monroe. She explained to one *Time* magazine writer that the five cents per month allowance was all taken from her except for the occasional penny she used to buy a hair ribbon. Another writer learned that all the pennies were saved in a Christmas fund so that each child could buy school supplies such as notebooks and pencils: the only permissible expenditure. Except for the Sunday school contribution. Except for the hair ribbon. Except. . . .

Rather than putting the Orphans Home into perspective as she got older, Marilyn changed the stories to be ever more dramatic. In reality, she did get an allowance of five cents—but it was per week, not per month. The chores were not endless, and no one was assigned to do the same task over and over again. Instead, they were handled in turns in the same way they might be in a regular family. She dried dishes for one hour a week, rotating with the other children. She was responsible for keeping her section of her room clean and tidy, but the orphanage had a staff of twenty-one who took care of most of the work. There were sports, games, a swimming pool, toys, a radio, and a phonograph, as well as a chance to perform in plays and musicals on a stage. With a housemother for every ten children, the children were loved and cared for. It was a large-scale version of the professional foster care world of people like the Bolenders.

The circumstances were not easy, however, and the home was obviously another rejection for Norma Jean, who had expected to remain with Grace or at least her aunt Ida. And she was undoubtedly lonely. She probably was telling the truth when she said that her escape was the ability to sit by the window in her bedroom and look toward Melrose and Gower, where one of Hollywood's many film studios was located. Ironically, what she could see was the then-famous logo featuring a massive globe topped by a brightly lit radio tower and the letters RKO.

RKO was created through the 1928 merger of the Keith-Albee-Orpheum vaudeville circuit with Radio Corporation of America in order to create a motion picture production company where both Gladys and Grace worked as film cutters. Businessman Joe Kennedy, who began amassing a fortune as a bootlegger working with Al Capone and then moved to Wall Street and Hollywood, had negotiated the merger. Neither he nor young Norma Jean had any idea that one day she would be having an affair with at least one of Joe's sons in the manner of Joe's affair with actress Gloria Swanson.

Norma Jean did have a difficult time in the public school she attended while in the Orphans Home. She was a good student according to the home's records, but the kids from the Home were known to their classmates at the Vine Street Elementary School they attended. Though they did not wear uniforms, they did walk to school together and were readily identified that way. She also was troubled by both teasing (since she was not living with a family) and the idea that she might be a real orphan. She was not an orphan, and did not want what she considered the stigma of being known as such. Grace made certain that Norma Jean knew Gladys was alive in the hospital; that, though mother and child were by then essentially strangers, she did have a mother.

Grace filed the formal papers for full guardianship on February 26, 1939, another detail that brings the accuracy of claiming Norma Jean spending almost two years in the Orphans Home into question. The nine months between the request and the time when Norma Jean could be fully with Grace was logical. There had to be full investigations into the mental stability of Gladys, Grace's living conditions and the way she planned to care for the child, and related documentation. So why has the "almost two years" story somehow become accepted as the truth, when there appears to be nothing to substantiate it? It all has to do with what else happened the same month.

Once Norma Jean had become Marilyn Monroe, studio publicists most often compared her with that other "unnatural blond" actress, Jean Harlow, who died on June 7, 1937. Harlow had suffered from acute respiratory infection, acute nephritis, and a cerebral edema while suffering from uremic poisoning resulting from kidney failure, none of which had to do with

Norma Jean. In fact, Harlow had been in declining health since having scarlet fever as a child, and without dialysis—not available until long after her death—there was no hope of saving her.

The movie studios tried to find or create a blonde successor to Harlow, but no one captivated the public at the time. It was only several years later, with the creation of Marilyn Monroe, that Harlow's mother, Mrs. Jean Bellow, thought the right woman to star in a movie called *The Jean Harlow Story* had been found. It was only then that the studios publicly fought for the rights to make the film. Additional hype involving Marilyn would come through the cooperation of syndicated columnist Earl Wilson, who wrote about asking Monroe if she would play the role. She says she would if the script was right, though ultimately it was not made because of the objections of her then-husband, Arthur Miller. And all of this related back to yet another myth the studios wanted to create, that of what might be considered reincarnation. If Norma Jean left the Orphans Home on June 7, 1937, instead of the real day, then that just might mean that when the Platinum Blonde died, she was also reborn in the child Norma Jean.

Other research indicates a date of June 26, 1937, for Norma Jean to have left the Orphans Home. If that is accurate, and it still seems out of line for when the background investigation was begun, then a bright publicist may have suggested she move the date back a few days to correspond with Harlow's death and let the press come to its own conclusions.

Grace nurtured her own Harlow fantasy in Norma Jean. She was convinced that the child could be as successful as Harlean Carpenter, a woman who, to Grace, was the epitome of a movie star.

Grace also fostered a second fantasy for Norma Jean. This concerned Clark Gable, whose movies the two always enjoyed. Gable looked much like Grace and Gladys's old supervisor and Gladys's occasional lover, Charles Gifford. Gladys had kept a framed photograph of Gifford that Norma Jean had often looked at. He was one of the men she claimed to have been her father, and there were stories of her calling him on the telephone, explaining that she was Gladys's daughter, and then being hurt when he hung up on her. There was no documentation of his possible paternity, as there was for Ed Mortensen; but because of his physical similarity to Gable it made for nice press when the story was occasionally leaked.

Whatever the date Norma Jean left the Orphans Home, she had changed, becoming more emotionally withdrawn than she had been in the past. She was a good athlete, and playing baseball and other sports at the home gave her a social outlet as she enjoyed developing her natural athletic ability. But the pleasure she found in the home was shattered when she went to school, where she was either teased or worried the other kids would again make fun of where she was living. Her immune system was down, probably as a result of her emotional depression, and it was noted that she had an unusual number of colds.

The staff of the Orphans Home understood Norma Jean's problems. They recognized her need for regular reassurance that she was okay, that they knew she had a real mother as well as an "aunt" who loved her and would be bringing her home. But they were also keenly aware of the depths of her feelings, especially when she sent herself a postcard "signed" by her mother and father. The card was part of her pretending that her parents were on a long trip and would return for her one day.

Despite the low self-esteem, fear of being sent to yet another home, and lack of friends, Norma Jean was intrigued by Grace's idea that she could be the next Jean Harlow. Certainly, as Grace pointed out, Harlow and Norma Jean had similar facial features—the same blue eyes, the same chin in need of fixing. And eerily, the date often quoted as that on which Norma Jean went home with Grace "forever" from the orphanage, a day after which she felt free to pursue any future she wanted, was the day the radio announced that Jean Harlow had died.

Returning to the custody of Grace and Doc Goddard was difficult for Norma Jean. The weekend outings with Grace had always been personal ones. The relationship was much like a mother with an only child who was pampered emotionally in a way not possible with other siblings clamoring for attention. Upon moving to the Goddard home, though, she found she now had to contend with Doc's three children—Beebe, who was nine, John (called Fritz) who was seven, and five-year-old Josephine (called Nona before entering the film industry as Jody Lawrance). There were also Persian cats and a spaniel, though the animals were probably comforting to her.

Norma Jean was enrolled in Sawtell Elementary School, eventually attending Emerson Junior High. Grace was relieved that the child's life would become more conventional, and let Gladys, then living in Agnews State Hospital in Van Nuys, know exactly what was happening. Gladys, in turn, wrote to her older daughter, Berneice Baker, who was then nineteen years old and recently married to Paris Miracle. She gave the young woman Norma Jean's address so she would know where her twelve-and-a-half-year-old half sister was living. What Gladys had in mind is unknown. As for Grace, in July 1939 she and Doc Goddard had to go to West Virginia where Doc had a short-term engineering job. Grace took it upon herself to have the two of them pass through Pineville where Berneice, now twenty and in her ninth month of pregnancy, was living with Paris.

The visit was a surprise one for Berneice, who was not at home when Doc and Grace stopped by, leaving word that they were on their way to West Virginia and had just wanted to say hello. Norma Jean was not along, having been left in the care of Grace's aunt, Ana Lower, and her absence made Berneice and Paris suspicious that Grace thought she might get them to take in Berneice's half sister. That idea ended when Grace, though not finding the couple, did see that they were living in a two-room apartment.

Norma Jean apparently did not mind the absence, having grown close to the woman she, too, called "Aunt Ana." In the years that followed, including after her marriage, she would regularly spend frequent periods of time with the older woman. Sometimes she would spend all day Sunday; sometimes she would spend several days.

Aunt Ana was also a supporter of Norma Jean's ambitions to become an actress. Grace worked to make Norma Jean follow in Harlow's footsteps, but Ana Lower just encouraged her to pursue her dream. It was the unconditional support of an older adult, who felt that whatever brought the child happiness in adulthood was all right with her. As Norma Jean explained to Clarice Evans, with whom she was sharing an apartment in the Studio Club in the mid to late 1940s, "There's only one person in the world that I've ever really loved. That was Aunt Ana . . . Aunt Ana was sure—surer than I am now—that I was right in my ambition to be an actress and that I'd be a success. But she'll never know whether she was right or wrong. She died [March 14, 1948] before my first bit part."

While Aunt Ana filled one need for Norma Jean, a neighbor of the Goddards would soon fill another. This was Jim Dougherty, a youth who had known his own childhood pain. His parents never placed him in one of the homes, but they had five children at the height of the Depression and often lived in a tent, working as farm laborers. Jim was six when he was taught to herd cows, and the entire family picked fruit during harvest season. Eventually the family's fortunes improved, they were able to live in a real house situated directly in front of the bungalow in which Doc, Grace, and the girls lived. It was there that he came to know Eleanor "Beebe" Goddard and Norma Jean Mortenson, two kids five years younger than he was and in whom he had no interest while in he was in high school and they had yet to reach puberty.

Twelve

Steal a Life, Be a Star

In the years since the death of the woman who came to be known as Marilyn Monroe, the name Eleanor "Beebe" Goddard has come to be used with both respect and disgust. Beebe's ultimate importance in the creation of the movie star Marilyn Monroe has often been overlooked. This is because Norma Jean Mortenson realized her childhood was not dramatic enough for the media and the press agents for the motion picture studios publicizing Marilyn Monroe. She had lived with the Bollender family until she was seven, moving back with her mother when Gladys was able to buy a house. Grace McKee cared for her until arrangements could be made to have her full time, a period when she was either in the Orphans Home or with Grace's aunt Ana, though still being with Grace at least weekly. Finally Grace, who married Doc Goddard, blended her into what amounted to an extended family since he had custody of his three children by a prior marriage.

The constant changes and fairly frequent losses undoubtedly were strong factors in Norma Jean's inability to commit to any long-term relationship, but they were not all that unusual during Depression-era Los Angeles. She never wanted for food, clothing, and shelter. She was never raped, molested, or in any way abused. In a sense, her life was rather boring.

Beebe Goddard was six months younger than her foster sister, Norma Jean. She was also the same height, weight, and hair color, allowing them to share clothes and makeup. They roomed together and became close friends,

Beebe revealing her own childhood that had genuinely been filled with abuse. She was eighteen months old when her parents divorced, the three children staying with their mother at first, and unlike Norma Jean, her mother had proven to be hopelessly mentally ill. The woman was a sociopath with no sense of right or wrong. She did whatever she wished, often becoming violent, especially when anyone, her children included, dared to object.

There were no agencies involved with the family, probably none in existence in the Texas communities where they lived. The violence was such that the children ultimately were simply moved among family members, foster care homes, and strangers. Their father had little or no contact with them until he married Grace McKee, at which time he brought them to live with his new bride and her ward, Norma Jean. But that was several years after Beebe had been enduring a nightmare existence.

Beebe Goddard had been sexually molested, forced to work in the same manner as adults, and often ill fed, ill housed, and ill cared for. Her life was filled with abuse and loneliness, if not in one foster care situation, then in the next, and there were many. All the stories were shared with her new best friend, Norma Jean, who not only remembered the horrors, she incorporated them into her answers when Marilyn Monroe was interviewed by various writers. Beebe's childhood became Marilyn's childhood.

࿔

Note: Official studio biographies are quoted at the end of this book. Most of the use of Beebe's life seems to have come during interviews when Monroe sought to shock or gain sympathy. However, it is impossible to know what Beebe endured and what Marilyn added. For example, it is known that Norma Jean was a virgin at the time of her marriage, but over the years she claimed to have been raped for the *first* time at six by a family friend. An adult boarder named Litman—according to Norma Jean/Marilyn Monroe—penetrated her at seven when both lived in a foster home. There were two molestations and a full rape when she was eight, one by an unnamed foster home boarder and the other two by a Mr. Kimmel. She was also raped by a foster parent, becoming pregnant prior to living with Grace and Doc Goddard. Finally, there was a rape by a foster home boarder when she was eleven, forced oral sex with a grocer who caught her stealing fruit, and a rape with a beating at twelve when she was with an artist. None of this happened to Norma Jean. Presumably some or all of it happened to Beebe Goddard, and whatever had not been Beebe's misfortune, Norma Jean created from her fertile imagination.

ƕ

Beebe Goddard and Norma Jean Mortenson had a choice between two high schools: University High in West Los Angeles and Van Nuys High School near the Goddard home. The Goddards chose the closer Van Nuys High, a fact that seemed only to matter because it gave them something in common with the young man who lived in the house directly in front of where Doc, Grace, and the girls were living.

Jim Dougherty was a bright, aggressive youth who was made strong by his family's hardships during the Depression. Born on April 12, 1921, he seemed to blossom when he had a real home and the chance to go to Van Nuys High School in the same way as other boys who had never known his poverty. He was a handsome youth, strong, a star football player and a skilled amateur actor who appeared in several school plays, including one called *Shirt Sleeves*. That play has been long forgotten but not the girl who played his daughter in the production. Her name was Jane Russell and she would go on to greater and longer-lasting fame than Norma Jean, albeit with less scandal in her private life. His football skills were such that he was offered a scholarship to the University of California in Santa Barbara. Instead he took a job at Lockheed Aircraft so he could financially help his parents. Working as a metal cutter on the night shift actually brought him more money than he would earn in any of the professions for which he might have trained at the university, or so he justified his actions.

(Jim Dougherty's poverty helped him in an unexpected way when he became older. The family's meals were often dependent upon the food they grew and the animals they hunted. Bullets were expensive when Jim, his parents, and his siblings were still living in a tent. The family had a gun, and when Jim was assigned the task of killing wild game for his mother to fix for dinner, he quickly learned that bullets were so expensive, if he missed the shot, the family would have no meat that night. Eventually he was the top shot with a handgun on the Los Angeles Police Department, creating among other things one of the first Special Weapons and Tactics—SWAT—teams in the country.)

It was 1940 when Jim graduated from high school. The girls at the Goddards were just fourteen, and though his parents were friends with Doc and Grace, Jim thought nothing of the kids. He obtained a job at Lockheed, earned enough to buy himself a car, and began dating several girls.

It was the fall of that year when the Goddards moved to Odessa Street, approximately a mile away. The new house they rented was in poor condition but larger than the one on the property shared with the Doughertys, and with two teenage girls at home, everyone was happier. The only problem was that the girls had further to go to school.

Jim Dougherty's mother, Ethel, suggested to Grace that her son could give the girls a ride home. He was on the late shift at Lockheed, and the route he had to take made it easy for him to pick up Norma Jean and Beebe, dropping them off at their home on his way in to work.

What happened next is uncertain. Norma Jean had reached an age in which she was interested in boys, and Jim was something special. He was older, handsome, yet someone she knew from the neighborhood. She began practicing flirting with him, or so it seemed as she daily climbed into the front seat before Beebe, making certain she was in the middle of the three as they made their way home from Van Nuys High School. As he would later write, ". . . it was impossible for me to not notice she was pressing close to me, and when she laughed her musical, light laughter, I also couldn't help but notice that her hand would gently touch my knee. And, our daily conversations were becoming more familiar, kind of just for us, to a point where poor Beebe was being left out altogether."

It was in December 1941 that everything changed for Jim and Norma Jean. She was physically maturing and had a look older than her years. Jim was keenly aware of her body, a longtime friend, but still thought of himself (probably rightfully) as too old for her. That did not matter to Grace and his mother. Doc Goddard was working for Adel Precision Products, a company that was holding its annual Christmas Dance despite the recent bombing of Pearl Harbor and the knowledge that the nation was going to war. Dougherty remembered that everyone was trying to maintain some sense of normalcy, following the routines of the past, as though such actions might help make everything all right. Thus he was not totally surprised when he was asked if he would take Norma Jean to the dance. She and a date were welcome as part of an employee's family.

Norma Jean thought of the dance as her first real date. Jim thought he would "show the kid a nice time. I mean after all, it was the least I could do, it being Christmas and all."

Years later Jim was able to put the dance and the growing relationship with Norma Jean into perspective. He learned that she was always in awe of anyone who was famous enough for their acting ability to be remembered by others. This was probably the result of Grace and Gladys's constant talk about movie stars, looking through the fan magazines, and showing her photographs of the stars. The fact that he was older, drove a car, and was somewhat a man of the world, if only in his mind, had not impressed her in the slightest. Instead it was the fact that his photograph was hanging just outside the drama classroom in Van Nuys High School. To a high school kid who never really knew any actors despite the weekly prowling of wealthier neighborhoods when Grace or Gladys took her to Hollywood for the day while she lived with the Bolenders, Jim Dougherty was as good as it got. Every student in Van Nuys High School saw his picture on the wall every day they had classes, but only Norma Jean was dancing up close with him at Doc's company dance.

What happened next is uncertain. Doc Goddard was interviewed years later and became extremely angry when it was suggested that he, Grace, and or Ethel Dougherty arranged for Jim and Norma Jean to get married when the Goddards had to move out of state for Doc's company. Certainly the relationship was encouraged to intensify, especially following the dance where Grace and Doc watched the children together, noting that Norma Jean moved as close as she could and Jim responded in ways that assured he no longer thought of the teen as a nuisance neighbor kid.

But why the encouragement? Did Grace know they would be moving to West Virginia and had no intention of bringing Norma Jean along? Beebe would be coming, though Beebe needed more nurturing than Norma Jean. Her life had been harder. Her rejections quite real. Her pain a form of child abuse.

Most likely the relationship was simply another of Grace's romantic notions. The actresses she admired had often been teen stars and teen brides. Grace had had several husbands, enjoyed sex, and had no illusions about "forever" in any relationship. It is quite possible that she simply saw a romance with Jim, wherever it led, as the next step in building Norma Jean's life and eventual career. Whatever the case, she gave Norma Jean enough money to take Jim to the movies, encouraged their going for long hikes in romantic wooded acreage, and had them take canoe rides together. She often packed a picnic lunch for the two of them so they would stay away longer. She even encouraged their rides along Mulholland Drive, knowing they would stop at Taylor Walk in order to make out. It was as though she wanted them to live out the scenes from a movie, knowing it would lead to the happy ending

It was spring 1942 when Ethel Dougherty, having talked daily with her friend Grace, explained to Jim that the Goddards were moving to West Virginia. Although Doc had been going back and forth to that state on temporary assignment for quite a while, this was something new, a full-time job for more money. However, for whatever reasons, he was only allowed to take his wife and any dependent child living at home. Beebe was fine. Norma Jean was neither his daughter nor his wife's. The guardianship did not matter. She could not relocate with them. (Note: It is likely that this was a financial concern as well. This was the height of the Great Depression, and if Doc's company was paying a relocation allowance based on family size, it was in the company's interest to only move blood relatives living in the home.)

Norma Jean was not quite sixteen and needed to be cared for. Ana Lower was aging too rapidly to look after the girl, and there was no one else for her. Grace had explained that she would have to return to the orphanage until legally an adult.

The story did not impress Jim. Norma Jean's problems had nothing to do with his life, or so he thought until his mother explained that Grace thought it might be nice if Jim married Norma Jean.

Ethel Dougherty pressured her son, making clear that he would not want Norma Jean to endure the "awful" orphanage. He would be doing her a favor, saving her from suffering that was unavoidable.

Jim Dougherty was just immature enough himself to think of his role as that of a knight in shining armor saving a hapless heroine. He reluctantly agreed that he would do it, only to be told that the wedding was set for June. Ethel and Grace had worked out all the details before telling their children. They probably both realized the marriage was doomed to be brief, though presumably sexually enjoyable. But Grace, at least, had never had a problem with either marriage or sex, seeing them both as so enjoyable when she was young that she went through several men. If Norma Jean and Jim had a lifetime together, so be it. And if this was simply a "starter marriage," that was okay with the older woman as well.

Not everyone in Norma Jean's life thought she was making a sensible decision. She had switched to University High School, and being the new girl, she delighted in getting attention by talking about her planned marriage to Jim Dougherty. Among those who listened was her social studies teacher who recognized the decision as a major mistake. He took the teenager aside and tried to explain that at not quite sixteen, she was not ready for marriage and all the responsibilities it entailed.

The Bolenders agreed with the social studies teacher but they were no longer in a position where they felt they should express themselves. They had not spent time with the child they had raised for seven years, and it seemed inappropriate to speak their opposition to a marriage Norma Jean could not possibly comprehend. They would attend the wedding. They would show their love and support for Norma Jean. But they would not be happy about it.

Norma Jean, by contrast, fancied herself in love. Jim was a man, not a high school boy, and he was obviously devoted to her. She was in love with love, a not unusual circumstance for an adolescent.

Jim Dougherty recognized that he was far more experienced than his bride. He spoke with Ana Lower about the fact that Norma Jean had never been able to trust others who spoke of their love for her. Her biological mother was gone, and Ida Bolender, the woman who had raised her, sent her away at the age of seven. Grace McKee had promised to care for her into adulthood, yet even though it was a temporary move, suddenly Grace, Doc, and Beebe were traveling to West Virginia. Doc considered it an opportunity. Norma Jean considered it a betrayal.

The relationship with Jim was probably not love either, though it was also more than raging hormones. Jim found Norma Jean to be beautiful, especially in the moonlight. He liked her, liked the idea that she wanted him, liked the idea that he could help her develop into full womanhood.

Norma Jean seemed to just like being wanted. Here was a boy who had been so popular in high school that his picture remained on the school wall even after he graduated and entered the working world. This was a boy who had dated the most popular girls in high school and was old enough to be able to date grown women, yet he wanted her. And when Jim told her he loved her, it was all a new experience, a wonderful experience. It would also mark the last few years that Norma Jean would exist.

Photographs of the couple show that they look close in age, a fact that may have made Jim more comfortable. Yet the truth was that he seemed so much older to Norma Jean, before they started dating, back when she and Beebe were just getting rides in his blue Ford, she would call him "Mr. Dougherty."

The Goddards left for West Virginia in March 1942 and Norma Jean stopped attending high school. It is unknown if she was troubled by adults who had criticized her decision, such as her social studies teacher, or if she made the decision that she was a woman, not a kid, and only kids went to school. Whatever the case, the lack of education would always haunt her. She felt inferior and the studios were uncomfortable with the truth about her past. The publicists gradually gave her more credit than she had earned so the public would not think she was dumb.

There was an ironic side to Jim Dougherty's decision to marry Norma Jean. He, too, was a product of the movies, but he was a product of the ideal reel world. He had been a country boy much of his life, learning about how to behave from the big screen.

Grace wanted Jean Harlow to be Norma Jean's image, but she was talking about the creation of a star, not a moral code practiced in the world of the movie script. Jim went to see Andy Hardy pictures, and it was in the stories in which young Mickey Rooney was starring that he learned what he thought was the right, good, and noble way to behave. Ironically those lessons were carefully crafted by Louis B. Mayer, head of MGM Studios for which Rooney worked and who had a less than noble personal life.

Mayer produced fourteen Andy Hardy pictures as starring vehicles for Mickey from 1937 through 1943. These were enormously popular, returning no less than a half million dollars per release, a remarkable sum in those days. Their success was because they created the same "feel good" family situations that would translate to television in a few years with such programs as *Father Knows Best*, *Leave It to Beaver*, *The Life of Riley*, and *The Trouble with Father*.

Mayer was so pleased with the image he was creating with the Andy Hardy series that he went so far as to go on the set to show Mickey how to act for maximum pathos. Mayer showed Rooney how to fall on his knees, clasp his hands together, and look to heaven, begging, his face obviously close to tears as he passionately said such lines as, "Dear God, please don't let my mom die, because she's the best mom in the world. Thank you, God." And among those in the audience watching it all and viewing it as something to emulate was Jim Dougherty.

Norma Jean might have been guided to see only the glamour of being an actress, but youths like Jim Dougherty were focused on the story lines. Norma Jean had an understanding that came in part from having her mother and "aunt" Grace work as technicians in the industry, and to have lived for a while among actors. Jim and many of his friends had no such understanding or experience. They also did not know that Mickey Rooney, the star of the Andy Hardy pictures, was notorious for constantly chasing after girls when he wasn't working. It was a "hobby" he would pursue throughout his life. And Judy Garland, his frequent co-star, was both a heavy user of drugs and delighted in using sex as a recreational pleasure with friends. This might not seem upsetting today, but at the start of World War II, having such information become public knowledge would have ruined them both.

The end result was that Jim Dougherty, living out the ideals of young manhood as learned from the movie screen and reinforced by his mother and Grace Goddard, nobly married Norma Jean Dougherty to save her from the orphanage. The date was June 19, 1942, two weeks after Norma Jean's sixteenth birthday. She was a virgin counseled by both Ethel, who also explained to her experienced son how to be appropriately gentle the first time, and her "aunt" Ana Lower who provided her with a book filled with so many euphemisms and ways of avoiding describing the act or the body parts involved, that most of the information was about cleaning, cooking, and maintaining the bridal home.

Attorney Chester Howell, a friend of the Goddards, had the couple marry in his home. The Doughertys supplied their friend, the Reverend Charles Lingenfelder who ran a nondenominational Christian church, to officiate. He was the person who had taught young Jim to hunt, fish, and enjoy the outdoors. And Marion Dougherty, Jim's brother, served as best man and personal bartender, slipping Jim two shots of whiskey to calm him enough to say "I do" in all the right places.

(A few years later, the wedding dress would become just another prop for a cover photo. Photographer Richard Miller saw the wedding photo when he picked up Norma Jean at her aunt Ana's house. He was just taking her to a movie that day, but when he arranged to photograph her for the June 1947 issue of *Personal Romances* magazine, the wedding dress was worn for the cover shot. And among the stories promoted on the magazine's cover was "Marriage Without Kisses.")

Long after Norma Jean and Jim were divorced, she was asked what she thought of her first marriage. The answer, probably an accurate one, was "our marriage was a sort of friendship with sexual privileges." It was also closer to child's play than an adult relationship.

The Doughertys rented a studio apartment at 4524 Vista Del Monte Street in Sherman Oaks for the first six months of their marriage. The apartment was little more than a big room with a bathroom, cooking area, and Murphy bed. The latter was meant to provide additional space. Lowered, it was a normal bed. However, when the night was over, the bed could be raised so it went flush into a box against the wall that took only three or four inches of space. Furniture could be placed in front of it, then moved aside at night when the bed was lowered. They did not live together prior to marriage but moved their possessions into the building so they could spend their first night in their new home as Mr. and Mrs. Dougherty.

Jim later commented that Marilyn "began our married life knowing nothing, but absolutely nothing, about sex. But Norma Jean loved sex. It was as natural to her as breakfast in the morning. There were never any problems with it." Neither then nor in her talks with Ana Lower and Ethel Dougherty did she ever hint at the idea of rape, molestation, or pregnancy. Those were not mentioned until she was climbing to stardom and co-opted Beebe's childhood to make for more dramatic answers to reporters' questions.

❧

After Marilyn Monroe's death, the auction house Christie's sold many items that were part of her estate. The collector interest, both for that auction and for often lesser items sold individually, was and is so great that Beebe Goddard began selling items she had been given. Then she began offering other items as Marilyn's, and experts in the field soon realized that Beebe was living out her last days on money gained from items that not only were never owned by Marilyn, they may have been made after the death. A rumor in the field was that all Beebe Goddard items were banned from Christie's. A check with the auction house revealed the following:

> As a matter of policy, Christie's will not sell any lot that we know or have reason to believe is inauthentic or counterfeit. This applies to all property that we offer for sale around the world, from fine art to motor cars, from furniture to wine. We take all appropriate steps to establish authenticity and work with the leading experts, authorities and institutions in the relevant field to research the property that we sell. Regarding Marilyn Monroe memorabilia, the market has generally lost faith in the Beebe Goddard provenance and we are mindful of this when any Marilyn Monroe memorabilia is presented to us for potential consignment. We rely on our experts and their knowledge of the marketplace, however, not an arbitrary policy, to establish the authenticity and provenance of each lot that is presented to us. – Sara Fox, Public Relations, Christie's, 20 Rockefeller Plaza, New York, New York.

Marilyn "stole" her foster sister's life. Beebe Goddard sold whatever she could, using her foster sister's name with her own as what proved to be a disreputable provenance.

❧

Jim delighted in sex with Norma Jean, but the maturity of her body did not match the emotional needs of the teenager she actually was. She liked to go outside and play with the other kids on the street. She kept dolls and stuffed toys on top of their chest of drawers so that "they can see what's going on." She put love notes in her husband's lunch box (calling him "Daddy" and referring to herself as "Your Baby"). And she was anxious to have a baby and become a mother, primarily because pregnancy would create a family that she had never really known. Fortunately Jim recognized that she wanted a child for all the wrong reasons and was not ready to be a mother. He convinced her to practice birth control.

Dougherty later claimed that Norma Jean's sexual appetite became increasingly intense, in part, he realized later, from her insecurity. Sex seemed to be a way of reminding herself that she was loved and wanted. It also was a physically obvious way of seeing the man's desire. She would be deeply hurt by any failure on his part to show what she thought was appropriate passion, including when they were driving out in the country and she would place her hand on his crotch. He preferred the more conventional approach of going home to their bed, but she would have him pull over and park, looking upon the countryside as more romantic for their sexual trysting.

As for the "Daddy" and "Baby" references, in the 1940s men were often viewed in a paternal role in the household. The wife was considered not just physically weaker but less emotionally and mentally developed in every way. The man ran the house, caring for his wife while she did what she could to make his world run smoother. Terms like "Daddy" and "Baby" were not considered to have deeper significance than appropriate terms of affection. And the attitude was seen earlier when she referred to her neighbor as "Mr. Dougherty," a term of address it is doubtful a contemporary fourteen-year-old would use when talking about a twenty-year-old today.

It is impossible to say what would have happened between Jim and Norma Jean had the nation not been at war. Dougherty later felt Norma Jean was seduced by the movie industry but would have preferred the type of home life he could have provided had everyone's lives not been turned upside down by Pearl Harbor and its aftermath. He was doing valuable war work on his job and was exempt from the draft, but he was troubled by watching friends and acquaintances going into the military. However, Jim was aware that the war was not going well for the allied forces in 1942. Fighting was often intense, men were dying or being taken prisoner, and to Jim, not being in the midst of battle seemed somehow unpatriotic. Someone else could take his position at the aircraft factory, perhaps someone too old for the military. Jim, without telling Norma Jean, went to see the navy recruiter, filling out the papers needed to enlist. He knew there were many war brides who were alone as Norma Jean would be, knew they would help her as would his family. He felt compelled to go to war.

Norma Jean was outraged. She thought she was being abandoned once again because Jim didn't have to go. He was making a choice to leave her alone. If he wanted to go to war, he should have consulted with her first. She angrily confronted Jim, who proved to be more sensitive to his wife's thinking than other adults in Norma Jean's life. He understood that she was viewing his action in a manner quite different from what it really was and he understood why. He could not change how she saw the world because it was too deeply rooted in her past. He returned to the navy recruiter and had him tear up his enlistment papers. Then he went to the fire department to apply for a job. The factory work was too distant from the war effort. As a fireman, he would at least be actively involved in helping others and saving lives.

Once again there was a problem. Jim would have a schedule he thought was ideal—several days off where he and Norma Jean could engage in love-making, go fishing, drive in the countryside, and otherwise indulge themselves. As a trade-off, though, he would also have several days on duty, sleeping in the firehouse, ready to answer any emergency call that came in.

Norma Jean still could not see Jim's actions from any viewpoint other than her own. In her mind the fire department work meant extended time when he would not be with her. She ignored the lengthy time they would be together when he was not on duty. Once again he returned and had his application destroyed.

The needfulness and possessiveness Norma Jean was showing would become obsessive as the years progressed. She had been so hurt by the perceived constant abandonment of people she thought loved her that she was becoming self-centered and self-absorbed. She would eventually expect a type of love that was both possessive and obsessive from the men with whom she would have long-term affairs, always trying to end the relationship before they could do so themselves. She came to revel in the attention of men who were icons in their fields: athlete Joe DiMaggio, playwright Arthur Miller, and politician Jack Kennedy, among others. Yet at the height of their adoration, she was usually on the prowl for her next lover, her next intense relationship.

The only strain Dougherty noticed in the marriage came because of his own jealousy. Norma Jean was extremely shy and introverted, often sitting with her husband and his friends, listening rather than talking. However, when they had a chance to dance with friends in their home, she came alive. She moved sensuously, erotically, delighting in the attention she received. Then she added to the reaction by moving from one man to another, making certain she danced with all the male guests.

It was during these early months of their marriage that Jim and Norma Jean began moving to ever-bigger places so they could have more room for entertaining. First they moved to Jim's family home on Archwood Avenue when his parents had to leave the area for a while and wanted a house-sitter. Then they moved into a house on Bessemer Street where they stayed until Jim felt the need to more actively serve his country.

The Bessemer Street house was in an area where a neighbor owned a cow that was left outside, regardless of the weather. The animal had access to shelter from storms, but in Norma Jean's mind, there was something inherently cruel about the way the cow was being treated. One day, during a rainstorm, she tried to coax the cow into their home so she could dry her off. She fantasized that it would behave little differently from a big dog once the animal realized Norma Jean was trying to help her. Fortunately for the interior, Jim was able to stop her before she got the animal through the door.

Emotionally unable to accept deferment from the service when other able-bodied men were in uniform, Jim decided that he had to enlist in the merchant marine. He would be based near home, and though he would be at sea for several months at a time, the absences would be predictable. Norma Jean would know when he would return, limiting her possible anxiety.

It was shortly after the Doughertys' first year of marriage that Jim told his wife of his plans. She became hysterical, terrified of losing him, terrified of losing the normalcy she had achieved as a wife. She had forced herself to learn to fish, to cook, to prepare wild game they both hunted in a manner that both enjoyed, and even to utilize vegetables that she did not like to eat.

She had done everything she could to be the way she perceived every other new bride in America behaved, and it still wasn't enough.

Norma Jean begged Jim to get her pregnant so she would always have a part of him if anything happened to him. He knew he would probably serve close to home, and his first assignment was Catalina Island, where she was able to accompany him. But there was still the risk he would go overseas or on an assignment where his ship became a target. "I explained to her that if anything did happen, the child might end up like she did—with a mother who couldn't support it because of the pressures, and it would wind up in an institution. But she wouldn't agree, and she cried and wept all night."

Years later, in the manuscript published posthumously as *My Story*, Monroe wrote a totally contradictory account. It is also probably false, another Monroe twist that became truth only after she was a star. She said,

> Jim was a nice husband. He never hurt me or upset me—except on one subject. He wanted a baby.
>
> The thought of having a baby stood my hair on end. I could see it only as myself, another Norma Jean in an orphanage. Something would happen to me. Jim would wander off, and there would be this little girl in the blue dress and white blouse living in her "aunt's" home, washing dishes, being last in the bath water on Saturday night.

Whatever the truth, there would be no pregnancy.

Norma Jean was seventeen years old and in the throes of adolescent emotional upheaval when Jim left for basic training. He called home every few days, and his mother, Ethel Dougherty, tried to help her.

Jim Dougherty was made the physical instructor for new recruits, and he and Norma Jean took an apartment on Avalon. He worked much as he would in a civilian job, returning to his home each evening. It was the same type of arrangement that was enjoyed by actor Ronald Reagan and his wife, actress Jane Wyman.

Dougherty grew restless and was not comfortable training others who would go on to overseas duty while he returned home most nights. He volunteered for an overseas assignment, knowing it would be dangerous but wanting to share the risks of so many other men in uniform. The only action he felt he could not take was to lie to Norma Jean, telling her he had no choice. He did not want her to think he was leaving her as so many others had done. Besides, she would be living with her mother-in-law, providing some degree of stability.

Doc Goddard knew his friend Ethel Dougherty needed a job, so before he and Grace left for West Virginia, Doc helped Ethel get work in the infirmary of the Radio Plane Company. Norma Jean realized she would be bored staying at home all the time so she had Ethel help her find a job there as well. She later explained,

> I first had a job inspecting parachutes—not the kind of parachutes a life depends on, the little parachutes they use to float down the targets after the gunners are through with them. That was before I worked in the "dope" room, the hardest work I've ever done. The fuselage and various parts of the ship were made of cloth at that time—they use metal now—and we used to paint the cloth with stiffening preparation. It wasn't sprayed on; it was worked in with brushes, and it was very tiring and difficult. We used a quick-drying preparation—a type of lacquer, I guess, but heavier—the smell was overpowering, very hard to take for eight hours a day. It was actually a twelve-hour day for the other workers, but I only did eight because I was underage. After the cloth dried, we sanded it down to glossy smoothness.

Norma Jean also wrote to Jim, a letter going out almost daily. This was important for his ego, not just to ease the loneliness. His idea of marriage, common among men of his age and background, was that the woman's place was in the home and the man's place was where he wanted to be. So long as he was sexually faithful, it did not matter what he did. It was common for Jim to go to pool halls to play games with his friends. He would be late getting home, feeding her insecurity and endless fear of abandonment. Even their arguments left her needing to find a way to please him because, when mad, Jim would frequently leave their bed to sleep on the couch. She desperately sought a way to feel a sense of self-worth, and the devotion of the men in her life (or who were about to be seduced into it as in her later years) was something she needed. Since Jim seemed to thrive on her dependence, considering such an attitude proper for a faithful wife, the constant letter writing kept them close during this period, albeit in a seemingly neurotic way.

Just as Norma Jean would one day create Marilyn Monroe, so men who met her occasionally indulged in their own creation of a history that did not exist. One of the more blatant was a man named Ted Jordan who eventually wrote a book that included his wild sexual escapades with the insatiable Norma Jean, a new model for Emmeline Snively's agency with whom he had his affair in 1943. The problem, beyond the fact that there has never been documentation for many of his claims, is that Norma Jean did not sign with the Blue Book Modeling Agency until 1945. Other writers have enjoyed creating sexual histories with the actress that never took place. Most blatant was a famous syndicated Hollywood columnist who knew her well. He was aware of her high-profile affairs and many of her off-screen antics. He regaled this author on tape concerning incidents regarding Monroe, but when asked if he ever went to bed with her, he laughed and explained that he hadn't. He said he would have loved to do so but had never had the opportunity. The famous columnist became old and increasingly known for his imbibing prodigious amounts of alcohol as the years passed. Then he started writing about his personal history, and suddenly he, too, claimed to have been a physical intimate of the by then late actress.

There was no hint of the stress or change in their marriage during Dougherty's first shore leave after being overseas. He and Norma Jean spent the entire time in the La Fonda Motel on Ventura Boulevard. She brought a black net nightgown. Jim brought the lust that comes from being faithful while apart. Most of their meals were brought to them by room service, and when it was time for Jim to return to sea, he had no reason to believe the future would hold problems.

The only tension during Jim's shore leave came from his discovery that Norma Jean was trying alcoholic beverages. She ordered a Tom Collins at the motel, something she would not have considered before he shipped out. Given her age, her sudden independence, and her making friends among her co-workers, the idea that she might start drinking was not unusual. She was not overindulging; nor was the incident foreshadowing a future of drug addiction. Norma Jean was no different from other girls her age just beginning to taste the formerly forbidden choices in life.

Jim may have worried a bit about whether Norma Jean was drinking very often when he was gone, but the reality for both of them was that the real problem she would face was the dirty little secret of the motion picture studios. It was 1938 when Louis B. Mayer and other top executives at MGM discovered that the ideal way to maximize the work of the actors, technicians, and even themselves was through the use of two new wonder drugs—Benzedrine and phenobarbital.

The beauty of Benzedrine and phenobarbital was that they were the modern equivalent of the all-purpose elixir sold by traveling salesmen and other itinerant vendors. Take the two together in the right dose and you could maintain your weight, an important concern for actors. Come to work tired and the right combination would make you wide-eyed and fully alert. And feel a little hyper at bedtime and you could again use what was needed to sleep. Best of all, the drugs were absolutely harmless—according to the MGM doctor who doled out the medication to everyone from the lowest technicians to Mayer himself. The drugs were often used in addition to alcohol (wine, beer, and liquor) raising the possibility of cross-addiction and/or severe depression. Only in hindsight would actors recognize that it was the cause of the deaths of so many of their generation—Peter Lawford, Robert Walker, Judy Garland, Richard Burton, and numerous others. One of the rare survivors would be Elizabeth Taylor, a woman whose stays in hospitals trying to fight either the drugs or the physical damage they caused her body became legendary.

Norma Jean would soon enter that same world of destructive behavior, but at the time she and Jim were still newlyweds, her drinking was typical of a late adolescent trying to be as grown up as her friends. She was exploring the larger world around her, and when David Conover showed up at Radio Plane, asking to take more photos than he needed for the magazine, her life changed forever. As Jim Dougherty would write many years later:

"How seductive it must have been for this young, lonely child-woman, Norma Jeane (sic) Dougherty, to have suddenly been offered a glamorous, exciting new life as a model, an actress, to have enough money to never have to worry again. How bewitching to have these promises made to her. She would be taken to these glorious places, they told her, by the use of a simple, everyday device—the camera."

Thirteen

Becoming a Model

You'd better learn secretarial work or else get married.

—Emmeline Snively, Blue Book Modeling
Agency, on Norma Jeane Dougherty's long-term
potential as a model in 1944.

Norma Jean Dougherty was an odd success for Emmeline Snively. The booker's appraisal of the woman who was coming to her after limited experience with David Conover and his friends was not good, especially for the bulk of her clients—department stores needing occasional clothing models, product advertisers and the like. "There isn't enough upper lip between the end of your nose and your mouth," Snively explained.

Norma Jean listened and would eventually have corrective surgery for perceived flaws, though for the moment she chose to use a trick she was shown to better handle the lighting. She posed with her head angled slightly downward and worked her upper lip lower. The result was what some critics and fans considered a sexy pout. She just saw herself correcting a flaw, and the photographers who booked her for magazine work loved the result.

The years following World War II were a magazine golden age for freelance photographers and young women with pretty faces and attractive figures, especially those who lived and worked in Southern California. Sunny skies meant that much of the year a photographer with little money could use the outdoors as a studio. Sandy beaches and warm temperatures justified clothing that fit every type of pretty-girl cliché—form-fitting sweaters, short skirts, tight slacks, two-piece bathing suits, and the like. Sometimes the images were shot on location, the clothing appropriate for a day at the beach, enjoying a sailboat ride, or hiking in a wooded park. Sometimes they were made in the studio with seamless backdrop paper and props such as chairs, hammocks, or even step ladders and ski poles.

The models were all pretty girls, some of whom earned their living with posing and some of whom were under studio contracts for which their work was little more than being a face in the crowd. The credits varied, though once a girl was under studio contract, the movie name was used exclusively.

The publications ranged from *Laff: The Humorous Picture Magazine* that had stories such as "Change Your Love Life" and "Can Nite Clubs Cure Insomnia?" along with slightly risqué cartoons and cheesecake photos, to *True Experiences, Cheesecake: An American Phenomenon, Sir: A Magazine For Males*, and, once Norma Jean was under movie studio contract, various film magazines. There were also foreign publications that frequently had Los Angeles and New York editorial offices, advertisers who sold products with bathing suit-clad models, and men's magazines such as *Man to Man: The Stag Magazine, Male*, and even *Cartoon Cuties*, a periodical that combined cartoons, pin-ups, and models who were promoting movies in which their major contribution might be to look pretty as they walked through the background. What made Norma Jean different was that she insisted upon learning how to improve herself, to be able to position herself so the photographer would need to do less work to get an effective picture.

I would take home photographs of myself to study how I looked and if I could improve myself posing in front of a mirror for hours.

The next day I would see the photographer who took those pictures and ask, What did I do wrong in this photo? or Why didn't this photo come out better? When they told me, I would never make that mistake again. I believed in myself. I just had to make it. I was determined to make it. Nothing was going to get in my way.

Then they started to put me in bathing suits, and all of a sudden I became popular.

—Marilyn Monroe, as quoted in *Marilyn: Her Life in Her Own Words*.

❧

Norma Jean had appeared on approximately thirty magazine covers when she convinced Emmeline Snively that she had learned enough to give movies a try. She understood how to pose for maximum bust line and minimum viewing of her facial flaws. She also had come to understand that she would have to make one other cosmetic change. She could no longer continue with her natural hair color—brunette.

Miss Snively explained to Norma Jean that the nature of the lighting, the film, and the most frequently used backdrops in the studio and on location were such that brunettes were limited in the work they could do. Too often the hair color seemed to blend into the background of a photograph. Even with techniques such as separately lighting the backdrop and adding an additional highlight to the model's hair when posing in the studio did not always work. Admittedly this was the fault of the photographer who was not skilled in lighting, but the model would get blamed and, by association, the modeling agency that had supplied the young woman.

Blondes, by contrast, reacted well to everything from floodlights to flash bulbs to sunlight. Sometimes their hair shone like the unnatural platinum of Jean Harlow. Sometimes it seemed to darken against the backdrop. Even variations in daylight, from the cold, gray light of early morning, to the harsh overhead light at noon, to the extremely warm-toned late afternoon sun, all enhanced blonde hair. A brunette often required supplemental lighting to work as effectively.

Photographer Raphael Wolff was the photographer who was responsible for Norma Jean's becoming a blonde. He had several magazine editors and advertisers for clients who all wanted to use a face and figure like that of Norma Jean, but the hair had to be blonde. He explained to Emmeline Snively that he would pay for the bleaching and for different, more effective styling. She later told George Barris her reaction: "When I saw myself in the mirror, it just wasn't the real me. They had converted me to a golden blonde. At first I couldn't get used to myself.

"But then I saw it worked. Miss Snively sure knew what she was telling me. I began to get more modeling assignments in photography for glamour poses, and especially cheesecake pictures."

The opportunities afforded Norma Jean Dougherty came because of changes in advertising, popular culture, the new independence of young women, and numerous other factors created during and immediately after World War II. There had been a time when a young woman was considered to be behaving properly when she lived at home until her marriage. Her parents, especially her father, established the parameters of her daily activities, from the type of work she did (ideally in a secondary position when compared with a man, such as secretary, clerk, nurse, elevator operator, schoolteacher, or something similar, rather than a business executive, doctor, school principal, or other "male" roles), to when she would date, where she would go, and with whom. She was no longer seen as property to be exchanged from an older man (her father) to a younger man (her betrothed) for social, political, or monetary reasons, at least in the pre–World War II United States; but she was also not seen as fully capable of independence. Even after society began to change, housewives (though not unmarried women) bore the brunt of humor in everything from cartoons—including in family publications such as *Look*, *Collier's*, and *The Saturday Evening Post*—to radio comedy shows such as *Easy Aces* with Goodman and Jane Ace.

The idea of a woman holding a "man's" job, earning a man's pay, and moving from her parents' home into her own apartment, not only before marriage but often before she was dating anyone steadily, was a radical social change. Young men had gone to war thinking they would return to a world that still had a small house, a garden, two or more children, a picket fence to keep in the dog, and a woman in an apron waiting lovingly for their return from whatever work paid the bills. Young women had endured the war by taking jobs in defense plants, driving trucks, becoming pilots of transport planes, learning to run businesses, and otherwise establishing themselves in ways previously not possible. They demanded the right to attend nightclubs, bars, restaurants, and theaters, all either on their own or with female friends. Businesses that tried to stay with an "escorted women only" policy found themselves going out of business.

Apartment owners also found that it was good business to rent to women. Sometimes entire buildings existed for young ladies, as did the Hollywood Studio Club, a specialized holding of the YWCA that was an apartment solely for women in, or trying to break into, the movie industry. Other times landlords accepted the inevitable, renting to both single women and groups of female friends, when in the past they would have presumed the tenant to be a prostitute or other undesirable to be excluded.

Jim Dougherty was a traditionalist, a man who married to protect a neighbor girl in trouble, went off to war because serving one's country in time of crisis was the right thing to do, and planned to return to his wife to live an idealized version of an Andy Hardy movie. In truth, he was married to an adolescent just beginning to discover herself, the reality of her past, and the chance to escape based on a combination of physical appearance and hard work. More important, she did so at a time and in a place where literally any pretty girl who could walk, smile, and not trip over her feet could become a cover girl, runway model, and/or studio employee with an occasional line in a film. The circumstances were such that the emotional relationship with Jim was over the moment Norma Jean realized that David Conover was just one of many photographers interested in her. She wanted to model, to feel the constant approval of the camera, an acceptance inadequate in any other form.

To say that there was something special about the way Norma Jean's photographs looked when compared with other still images of models used by the same photographers and same publications in 1945 is to deny reality. She was special in only two ways. The first was her willingness to work on her body and her posing when she realized she was flawed. For example, her light brown hair that had to be changed because it was too hard for the photographer to separate it from a dark background and her upper lip that had to be pulled down; additionally, Norma Jean had been told by experts that her teeth needed fixing and that her nose was less than perfect. Even Grace McKee Goddard, her most ardent cheerleader for a career in films, was often telling her what needed to be corrected in order for her to become the next Harlow.

It was insecurity about her appearance led Norma Jean to request to see all the photographs taken of her when she was modeling, wanting to know how she looked with the light at different angles, how her clothing appeared, and what needed to be done to improve the next images to be taken. She had learned the basics in Emmeline Snively's required course. She also knew that the agency representing her would not let her do fashion work because her one experience showed that her appearance was not a neutral one. The ideal fashion model was a hanger for the clothes. Norma Jean's expressions seemed to beg others to look at her. As a result, she was being booked for print—clothing, cheesecake, and the like, no different from dozens of other young women with the exception of her determination to grow within the limited field in which she was working.

The other attribute that made Norma Jean popular was her willingness to do anything that the job entailed. Standard posing techniques for many of the publications in which she eventually appeared required her figure to be shown. Sometimes this involved her bending over so her body was partially away from the camera and she was looking back at the photographer. The image that resulted was always playful, hinting at sexuality and of a more intense relationship to come. It also was painfully awkward, yet she repeated it for take after take without losing the sense of spontaneity. At other times she might be kneeling with her shoulders back to exaggerate her bust line—again, an awkward position to maintain.

To see the covers (for the Swedish publication *Hemmets Veckotidning*, the American *Laff*, the Italian *Mascotte*, and numerous others) is to see what looks like a happy moment in time. She has seen a friend and partially risen to wave. She is leaning back into the sun. She is on a mountainside, her shoulders back, her head turned toward the camera. She is always happy, always welcoming the person who seemingly has just come upon her. But try to duplicate the pose and you realize that holding such a position while the photographer clicks away is extremely uncomfortable. Then, when you learn that numerous variations of the same image exist, the photographer looking for the perfect angle, you realize that Norma Jean willingly endured sometimes intense discomfort during the sessions, always working with the photographer for the perfect shot. It was her work ethic and willingness to do whatever the photographer asked, rather than any unusual beauty, that made her the favorite of so many studio owners.

Norma Jean's work ethic was even more evident in the less-well-known side of her modeling career. For four years, starting in 1946, she worked for pin-up artist Earl Moran.

Moran was a magazine cover artist, illustrator, and photographer in Chicago in the 1930s, and it was there that he eventually had an exclusive contract with Brown and Bigelow, a company that used his images for everything from calendars and prints to marketing products such as boxed chocolates. When he moved to Hollywood after the war, he added the painting of movie actresses to his calendar work for Brown and Bigelow. Norma Jean posed for him and became his favorite model. Again, this was the result of her willingness to assume any position and hold it for prolonged periods without complaint. She respected the fact that such patience was necessary to provide the artist with what he needed, and he respected her willingness to help him achieve the end he had in mind. The result was a long-term friendship extending after he went into semi-retirement, painting primarily fine art subjects until his sight started to fail.

The decision to do whatever was necessary for the photographer was more than a career move; it was a decision that would have an impact on what was left of her marriage. And the man who was as influential on this decision as David Conover had been in introducing her to the camera was a Transylvania native named Andor Ikafalvi "André" de Dienes.

André was one of the most brilliant and innovative photographers of the 1940s and 1950s. He was also a man whose childhood had far more horrors than that of Norma Jean.

Inflation in Hungary had destroyed the currency system and over-whelmed his family. He had been eleven when his mother committed sui-cide by throwing herself down a well on the family property. De Dienes blamed the devalued currency, though the family otherwise survived, his father traveling to Budapest for reasons never explained. André followed him there when he was fourteen, hoping to live with the man. When he could not locate him, he got a job working in a fabric store during the day and another working as a stagehand at night so he could enjoy the operas and musicals he could not otherwise afford to see.

De Dienes left Budapest at eighteen, traveling Europe and Africa, learn-ing to paint and make photographs. In 1934, at age twenty-one, he was photographing statues in a Paris park when he met British clothing designer Captain Edward Molyneux. That meeting led to his being given a contract to do fashion photography exclusively for Molyneux for enough money to pursue a series of photojournalism-type self-assignments.

Picture magazines such as *Life* had yet to be created and the idea of using a camera to tell a story was not a familiar one. De Dienes was one of the first, starting with street scenes throughout Paris and later traveling to areas as diverse as New York's Harlem and the various American Indian reservations. He recorded without bias, fascinated by the various cultures and the different lives, and shocked by the way members of mainstream society deliberately marginalized people who were as intelligent and sophisticated as they.

De Dienes tried to sell the work he self-assigned, but the periodicals he contacted were only interested in his fashion work, his art studies, and his cheesecake style. Despite this, he made several thousand images, a body of work that preceded such better-known and more widely published practitioners as Arthur "Weegee" Fellig, Gordon Parks, Henri Cartier-Bresson, and W. Eugene Smith. He also developed a reputation for falling in love with his favorite models during the period he worked with them.

De Dienes was primarily based in New York when he first went to Los Angeles for fashion, glamour, and figure assignments. He used the Blue Book Modeling Agency and came to rely on Emmeline Snively to pick appropriate young women. Then, in 1945, he moved his base of operations west to the Garden of Allah Hotel, a Hollywood landmark known for the various stars who had lived there at one time or another. He later wrote that shortly after moving there,

> I phoned Emmeline Snively, who had the Blue Book Model Agency at the Ambassador Hotel, and I explained to her that I was back in Hollywood again and that I needed models for photos of nudes, artistic nudes, for a new project I had in mind. Miss Snively said there was a very pretty girl in her office, waiting for her first modeling assignment, a model who just started in the profession, and perhaps she would pose for nudes. Miss Snively said she would send the young lady to see me right away and that her name was Norma Jeane Baker. (Norma Jean[e] frequently used the Baker name, including when she married, rather than the Mortenson name on her birth certificate.)

What happened next would speed the change in Norma Jean's life, though it was not as dramatic as the photographer's words. He was young and lusty. She was making a major decision about her life and her immediate future. He wanted to take Norma Jean to bed. She wanted the freedom to be a model and see how successful she could be. He was a romantic. She wanted to have fun. He controlled the camera, who was her one constant lover. She learned from the other models that sex with a photographer was no big deal, that it assured the girl would get more work—a trade-off Norma Jean eventually felt was worth the effort.

"Norma Jeane seemed to be like an angel," André would later write. "I could hardly believe it for a few moments. An earthly, sexy-looking angel! Sent expressly for me! . . . As minutes passed, I fell more and more in love with Norma Jeane."

Love at first sight is doubtful, but the desire to bed Norma Jean was intense and a subject of some amusement for her. She was married, and though she and Jim were estranged, the divorce she saw as inevitable was still in the future. That was why, in the first few days of working together, the only intimacy Norma Jean allowed was with the camera.

Fourteen

André and Gladys and Jim

Johnny Meyer and Emmeline Snively had much in common when it came to the beautiful young model and actress "wannabes" of Hollywood. Emmeline hustled women in a manner so sophisticated that no one thought of her as a procurer. She was a respectable business owner working openly from the Ambassador Hotel, arguably the grandest hotel in Los Angeles. There were luxuriously appointed rooms, individual bungalows offering privacy for the affairs of the rich and powerful, a swimming pool surrounded by an artificial sandy beach, a miniature golf course where Katherine Hepburn and Howard Hughes passed many an hour, and even a famed nightclub, the Cocoanut Grove, located on the grounds.

In the 1920s, before Emmeline Snively opened her agency, William Randolph Hearst found the Ambassador the ideal location in which to live with his mistress, Marion Davies, before they moved north to San Francisco. And numerous other movie stars either engaged in outrageous behavior or attempted to do so.

One story, for example, concerned the time when actor John Barrymore was living in an Ambassador Hotel bungalow. Actress Tallulah Bankhead, encouraged by drink and friends, decided to surprise Barrymore, even drunker than Bankhead, with her willing—albeit unexpected—presence in his bed. Barrymore, perhaps to both their regrets, had imbibed even more than the actress when he at last crawled into the bed where she was waiting.

He allegedly told her, "Another time, Tallu. I'm too drunk and you're too awkward."

Not that Emmeline was ever so blatant as the movie stars whose antics delighted gossip columnists and staff. She was a woman of dignity, and she made certain the young ladies she booked were properly trained and properly presented. However, she knew, like everyone else in Hollywood, that a model determined to rise to the top either posing for covers or moving to a studio basic acting contract would enhance the skills taught by Snively. She might take singing, acting, or dancing lessons, though these would be provided to new hires in the larger film studio schools. She also might practice saying "yes" to every request to spend private time showing producers, directors, and other power players her erotic skills.

Emmeline Snively never openly discussed the reality of the world in which she made her fortune. She would have been horrified if a photographer requested a model both skilled in posing and adept in the bedroom. Such a request would have been crude and unprofessional. However, all of her girls knew that photographers often liked to have sex with their models, especially when they worked together regularly. And while models who were willing to pose in the nude—as Emmeline thought Norma Jean might do for André—were not assured bedmates, they obviously had fewer inhibitions about many aspects of life than those who would not. The same was true for the lingerie models, an acceptable source of income for a young woman seeking to reach the height of her profession, but only on the West Coast. In advertising centers such as New York, Cleveland, Detroit, and Chicago, lingerie models were considered the lowest level of the business and often were not asked to pose for more sophisticated work. (On a national level, it was not until almost two decades later that actress Jane Russell broke such taboos by modeling the Cross Your Heart Bra for a national television advertisement. However, even then the only way she avoided being scandalous was to appear fully dressed in the commercial, the bra worn *over* her sweater.)

Johnny Meyer, by contrast, fulfilled fantasies by bringing together beautiful models and actresses with men of power and influence. Each understood the unspoken rules. The women were not prostitutes though they had to be paid well for their time. The men were not cheating on their wives, just spending the evening (and often the night) with representatives of the businesses with which they were involved. And everyone had to be discreet, conveying a fantasy of mature sophistication when everyone knew that many a business deal was determined more by the frequency and intensity of a man's orgasm in the privacy of his hotel room than the dollars-and-cents reality of a proffered corporate business plan.

Johnny Meyer had nothing to do with Emmeline Snively, though he undoubtedly knew of her agency. By the time he came into the life of one of her models, Norma Jean Dougherty, she had established herself in the public eye, if only as the good-looking woman in a skimpy two-piece bathing suit on the cover of a magazine.

The transition of Norma Jean Dougherty, frustrated but monogamous housewife, into a woman of such ambition that she would routinely accept sex as either a perquisite or a requirement of employment began when Emmeline Snively sent her to work with André de Dienes because his assignments were legitimate and his skills fully professional. His first efforts with his new model were experimental, using locations within a short driving distance.

For example, Norma Jean was dressed in an apron and holding a new-born lamb in a field for an image that eventually was the cover of the April 1946 *Family Circle*. For another photo she climbed on a fence wearing a red blouse knotted under her breasts, a pair of blue jeans, and her hair tied back for classic cheesecake. She was photographed along Route 101 near North Hollywood, by the beach, in the woods, and other locations, sometimes as the innocent girl next door at play; sometimes as a young woman whose emerging sensuality gave a subtle eroticism to the images. De Dienes was more than pleased with the versatility of his model; he was sexually aroused, and convinced himself that he was in love.

De Dienes did not tell Norma Jean of his feelings, but he was certain he had found his muse, his lover, and, as matters worked out, someone he could exploit. He decided to offer her a flat fee of two hundred dollars to travel with him and be his exclusive model in locations in multiple states. He would pay for her hotel room, provide transportation in his Buick Roadmaster, supply the clothing, and supply her with all the food she wanted, a serious consideration for a young woman who was still a teenager with a typical teen's appetite.

Emmeline thought the payment was fair. Norma Jean was delighted with so much money for what would almost be a working vacation. And de Dienes knew that the value of so many images, when sold to the magazines to which he had long contributed photographs, would provide him with income well beyond all expenses. He told himself he was in love, but the deal seemed to imply the love was more for the money than for Norma Jean.

Jim Dougherty knew nothing of de Dienes's plans for his wife, though he saw how excited Norma Jean was when she showed him the photographs from her early work with the photographer. She was proud to be on magazine covers, and she delighted in everyone who photographed her both from when she was still at Radio Plane to after she joined the Blue Book agency.

Dougherty did not seem to think that the photographs were immoral, nor did he think his wife was unfaithful (she had yet to be, despite later stories by self-proclaimed lovers of the "young Marilyn Monroe," none of whom could justify their claims). Instead, he was troubled by seeing the dependent young woman he had married and expected to nurture into the role of supportive housewife developing a drive for a career of her own. The fact that she quit her job at Radio Plane without discussing it with him and had been earning relatively sizeable sums on her own added to his awareness that their lives would never be the same. He was the most important man in Norma Jean's life when they married. Now that she was modeling, he was simply the man she lived with. Neither realized that their unspoken emotional reactions to each other marked the end of their marriage. Divorce was a future that would only confirm what had already taken place.

De Dienes was unaware of the personal drama in his model's life when they began traveling among adjacent states so André could photograph her in a wide variety of clothing and terrain. They started with bathing suit images and volleyball play at Zuma Beach, then gradually made their way north. They had separate rooms at each overnight stop, frustrating the photographer but making Norma Jean feel more comfortable about what she was doing.

Everything changed for Norma Jean when she and the photographer approached Oregon and she took the time to call her "aunt" Grace. There was news of her mother, who Grace explained was living in an inexpensive Portland hotel.

The tragedy of Gladys's life was not that she was mentally ill—she wasn't—but that she was forced to live in a treatment facility for the mentally ill. The staff had certain behavior expectations for the men and women who were there, rewarding those who were docile. The "best" patient, often heavily medicated, kept him- or herself clean, spent much of the day sitting quietly, and kept to whatever routine was expected. The patient rarely initiated a conversation with either the staff or the fellow patients. For the severely mentally ill, this situation might have been acceptable for the era, but for those such as Gladys who arrived exhausted, perhaps depressed, but not severely mentally ill, to fit in meant to become institutionalized.

The staff finally admitted there was nothing wrong with Gladys and no reason she needed to stay in the facility where she had been living. They gave her two hundred dollars and two dresses when she left. They did not prepare her for the fact that she had forgotten how to behave in order to blend in to the outside world that she had long forgotten.

It had been six years since Gladys had seen her daughter. She knew of Norma Jean's adult life, her marriage, and her modeling, through letters from Grace who always kept in contact with her. She did not try to contact her daughter when she left the institution, moving among shelters built by the Salvation Army before getting a permanent place in the Portland, Oregon, hotel. However, Grace wanted Norma Jean to see her mother, and since the young woman was coming to Oregon with de Dienes, Grace told her where to find Gladys.

De Dienes later wrote of the moment,

> Norma Jeane's mother lived in an old hotel in the center of Portland, in a depressing bedroom on the top floor. The reunion between mother and daughter lacked warmth. They had nothing to say to each other. Mrs. Baker was a woman of uncertain age, emaciated and apathetic, making no effort to put us at our ease. Norma Jeane put on a cheerful front. She had unpacked the presents we had brought: a scarf, scent, chocolates. They

stayed where they were on the table. A silence ensued. Then Mrs. Baker buried her face in her hands and seemed to forget all about us. It was distressing.

What he did not say when he wrote that passage for his book *Marilyn Mon Amour* was that Gladys whispered to Norma Jean that she would like to come and live with her daughter.

When Norma Jean returned to Los Angeles, many aspects of her life had changed. Her marriage, ended in theory when she started the modeling trip, was over in reality after she bedded de Dienes in Mt. Hood, Oregon's Timberline Lodge following the emotional shock of meeting her mother again and his relentless sexual pursuit. She also planned to move into a two-room apartment owned by Ana Lower, using the modeling money to pay the bills. Then she had her mother return to Hollywood.

Gladys seemed to respond quite well to the new relationship with her daughter despite the small space and the need to share a bed. Gladys understood that her daughter was becoming famous as a magazine cover model: Thanks to de Dienes's work, she was being seen around the world. Though Norma Jean was thrilled, other photographers realized the truth. The two-hundred-dollar flat fee the photographer paid for Norma Jean's time seemed like a lot of money in the day, and certainly satisfied Emmeline Snively, whose agency took a percentage. What went unsaid was the fact that de Dienes made far more money as he sold the images, and it was felt at the time that a more reputable photographer would have either paid based on sales or given her a percentage of his profits. He eventually proposed marriage to Norma Jean, the ceremony to take place after the divorce. She initially agreed, then made clear that she had no interest in following through on her statement. Her career was too important.

Gladys tried to be useful. She answered the telephone as though she were her daughter's secretary, learned the time Norma Jean would be needed to get to a job, pose, and leave, then booked appointments accordingly. During quiet times she went out for groceries and ran errands for both of them. She also took the streetcar to the Ambassador Hotel so that she could meet Emmeline Snively and personally thank her for the opportunity she had afforded her daughter.

Unspoken was the subtle message to Jim Dougherty, the man who was still Norma Jean's husband and in whose bed his mother-in-law was sleeping. There was no room at home; there was no room in his wife's life.

The Dougherty marriage might have lasted somewhat longer had Norma Jean told her husband that she had visited Gladys and that her mother had asked to join her back in Los Angeles. He might have helped her rent a slightly larger place that the three could have shared. However, even if Jim had been open to such an arrangement, she not only had had sex with de Dienes, she seemed to want to have sex with each of the photographers who used her on a regular basis over time. And always it was the camera, not the man, that seduced her.

Some of the photographers recognized the reality. Scottish photographer William Burnside who allegedly had a brief sexual relationship with Norma Jean after a number of sessions explained that there were two stages to the model's "love." First came the love of the camera, the one constant in her life. Then came love, or at least a willingness and desire for intimacy, with the man who operated the camera. However, no one was ever assured of an intimate relationship; nor did everyone want to bed Norma Jean. The men were professionals interested in satisfying their clients' needs before they considered personal desires. And among the men for whom she posed extensively, neither illustrator Earl Moran nor celebrity photographer Joseph Jasgur ever attempted to bed her. Yet both gave her the "love" of having her pose for them.

Perhaps most telling in this period of transition from housewife Norma Jean Dougherty to cover girl Norma Jean Dougherty to soon-to-be actress Marilyn Monroe was the song lyric segment she sent Burnside when their photographic and intimate sessions were over:

> I could have loved you once, and even said it
> But you went away,
> A long way away.
> When you came back it was too late
> And love was a forgotten word.
> Remember?

Norma Jean, who wrote down the lyric before Burnside "abandoned" her by taking an out-of-town assignment, was likely speaking of Jim Dougherty's merchant marine enlistment and every other man in her life who would disappoint her because of her fear of rejection.

Try as they might, Gladys and Norma Jean could never get along. The living arrangement was too close in a pair of undersized rooms, and their lives in recent years too radically different. Like a bad marriage, Norma Jean left her mother and moved into the YWCA's Studio Club apartments, whose suites were reserved for young women entering show business. The building was dubbed "the pussy palace" by older male actors who knew that some of the residents would "audition" for them when they went on "dates" that often ended with cash "presents" to help with their career. (Among the famous actors who tipped his dates from the Studio Club was Milton Berle, a washed-up comic who gained fame and wealth when he became the king of television. Both he and Norma Jean later talked of their having "dates," though Berle's friends knew it was strictly a business relationship.) Gladys returned to the hospital, not happy but comfortable with the familiar. Although there would be endless suspicion about her condition by members of the press who discovered her existence, she was never shown to be mentally ill. It was as though she had committed herself to a medical rest home where all her needs were met and her life, though lacking in pleasure, also lacked emotional pain.

Norma Jean was still under legal age for signing contracts, however, and when Johnny Meyer entered her life during this period, it would be Grace who was her legal guardian, signing the papers that would start her ward to stardom.

Fifteen

~

Howard Hughes Sends His "Pimp"

André de Dienes had the façade of sophistication and the patience to be gentle in his determination to exploit Norma Jean, both personally and professionally. He may have even believed he was in love and that the exposure she received meant more than the large sums of money he made from cover sales of her image.

By contrast, Johnny Meyer, whose involvement with Norma Jean was the result of her work as a cheesecake cover girl, had no such façade of nicety. He worked quietly, anonymous to anyone with whom he did not do business. He also never put himself directly into situations where he could get arrested. Some clients came to him for recreational drugs and he put them in touch with the appropriate dealers. Other clients, allegedly including Errol Flynn and Charlie Chaplin, had Meyer arrange for sexual trysts with willing partners whose ages might be below the legal minimum under California law. He was alleged to have bragged, apparently with reason, "There is no human desire that I can't satisfy through some of my connections." Apparently there was also no level of wealth or power he could not influence, including Elliott Roosevelt, President Franklin D. Roosevelt's son.

The Roosevelt connection was made on behalf of multimillionaire Howard Hughes, from whom he began receiving cash payments in 1938 while working from San Francisco. The date remains controversial, some biographers placing it between 1939 and 1943, though Hughes's personal assistant, Noah Dietrich, provided the off-the-books money and he said the payments for services began in the earlier year.

Howard Hughes was the perfect employer for Johnny Meyer because Hughes indulged in life with all the enthusiasm of an omnivorous glutton feasting with abandon in an exotic foods emporium. His father, Howard Hughes Sr., was the perfect role model, a man who married the former Allene Gano in 1903, a time when he had fifty thousand dollars in the bank. The sum made him wealthy at the time, but he allegedly ran through $49,100 of his savings enjoying what may have been the most expensive honeymoon of his day. The loss never worried him because he was in the oil business and had a wildcatter's optimistic mentality, always certain the next strike would bring him wealth beyond imagination.

Howard Sr. lost the search for oil but discovered a new drill bit created by Mississippi millwright Granville A. Humanson, bought all rights to it for $150, modified it, and patented the end result. The bit was the start of Hughes Tool Company and a product so far superior to all else on the market that Howard Sr. became rich enough to indulge in the periodic pleasures of Hollywood when away from his Houston home.

Howard Jr. was born in September or very early October 1905. His mother fantasized about her beloved child and decided she wanted to create a special history for him. She declared that his birth was December 24 of that year, noting that another special child, Jesus of Nazareth, shared the birthdate. While no documents survive for any date, records do exist of Houston, Texas, hotel owner James Lawlow, a friend of Howard and Allene, having dinner with the couple in his Rice Hotel dining room. He noted that Howard Jr. was three months old and a nanny gave the parents a respite so they could enjoy their meal with their friend.

There are myriad stories about the odd relationships among the family members. Howard Sr., who spent more time away from home than with his family, had one bedroom, and Allene and Howard Jr., called Sonny, shared another. Allene was germ-obsessed, a phobia her son would share at the end of his life, and had daily health checks that included everything from making certain he washed properly to careful inspection of his penis, his anus, and even his stool before he was allowed to flush. She also liked dressing him in lingerie as a substitute for nightclothes. The abusive perversions of Howard's childhood and the mental and physical degeneration he would experience in the last years of his life were not in evidence in 1938. Howard had inherited his father's tool company and created or purchased numerous businesses, most of which would add to his great wealth. (Howard Hughes Jr. became America's first billionaire.) These ranged from an aircraft company, to the financing of early silent motion pictures, to the purchase of RKO-Radio Pictures. But always, no matter what business occupied his workday, he liked to bed both established movie stars and models willing to do anything to get ahead. It was this outrageous lifestyle that also brought him to the attention of the gossip columnists and, through them, to the United States as a whole.

The Hughes/Meyer/Roosevelt relationship began with the desire of Hughes Aircraft to gain a contract to produce new planes for the army. The year was 1939, and though the United States was not yet at war, everyone involved with the military knew that it would only be a matter of months before what would be called World War II brought a mix of blood and profits to the country.

Hughes Aircraft was counting on the success of what it called Duramold, a mix of wood and resin that Hughes believed could be shaped into the D-2 fighter plane. The attempt to develop the lightweight aircraft led to the hiring of five hundred scientists, engineers, and designers, the expansion of his aircraft company into Culver City near MGM, and the investment of several million dollars.

The problem for Hughes, one he never admitted, was that the plane was a bad idea, poorly engineered, and ineffectually designed. It was touted as being able to fly 433 miles an hour at 28,000 feet with a range of two thousand miles. The materials used were of questionable value, and the testing of the plane, including a flight Hughes himself made on June 20, 1943, showed that the plane did not handle effectively. The plane was a waste of time and money for the military, but Hughes was unable to face reality.

Matters seemed to change when the army realized it needed a reconnaissance aircraft. This would be a plane that could fly over strategic terrain, photographing the land, the entrenched enemy positions, and all other details needed to effectively prepare for combat. The existing aircraft in use for these missions were converted from other uses and were slower and flew at a lower altitude than enemy aircraft that were shooting them down.

If the D-2 would not succeed as a fighter aircraft, Hughes decided he could sell it for reconnaissance, even if that meant changing the construction material to more conventional metal. In August 1943 Hughes gave Johnny Meyer authorization to take two hundred thousand dollars and prepare the most seductive reception possible for Colonel Elliott Roosevelt, son of the president, and other army officials who would be touring companies that might provide the new plane.

Elliott Roosevelt was selected to lead the group investigating reconnaissance aircraft because he had previously been head of the Mediterranean Allied Photo Reconnaissance Command. In that position he had seen how inferior the American planes had been and how easily they could be destroyed by the enemy. Hughes Aircraft was added to the list of such better known and more experienced companies as Boeing, the result of pressure in Washington. But everyone knew that the Hughes aircraft was a work in progress. That was why Hughes needed Johnny Meyer's special skills at corruption. That was also why Hughes personally flew Elliott to the Lake Harper test site for the D-2 as well as using his yacht for visiting Catalina Island.

In addition to the personal tour, Hughes had Meyer lease a mansion on Doheny Boulevard as the base of operations. Johnny was ordered to supply it with beautiful young women who either were under studio contracts or were models whose faces and figures had been seen in various magazines. Each understood she had a job to do: for example, dancing with the officers, or moving among them (unless one of the men seemed particularly interested in a specific woman, in which case she was to focus solely on him, and respond to his attention in any way she felt was appropriate). No one was told to have sex with any of the men. None of the men was told the women would be willing bedmates. However, each girl was told that her pay would range from one hundred dollars for the night—the base rate for each—to four hundred for providing whatever entertainment was requested.

The house was stocked with champagne and caviar prior to August 8 when the men arrived (the men stayed three days, leaving on August 10). In addition to the escorts, there was entertainment in the form of Judy Cook, the beautiful star of swimming shows, who did a water ballet while clad in a sequin-covered, flesh-colored bathing suit. And the meals included lobster, beef Wellington, and squab, all delivered during a period of wartime shortages and rationing.

There was also an arrangement to assure that Elliott in particular was exposed to those of his favorite male actors who were not in the service, such as Cary Grant, as well as to a vast array of actresses chosen for their super-structures (allegedly the introductions were called, by Johnny, the "boob ballet"). Among these was a Warner Brothers contract actress named Faye Emerson.

Emerson, a blonde from Louisiana, was a competent actress with the requisite beauty—and, allegedly, sexual skills—needed to gain and retain studio contracts. Her greatest success would come in a few years when she became the darling of early television talk shows. She also fell madly in love with young Roosevelt, and he with her. (Johnny Meyer was given a five-thousand-dollar bonus by the delighted Hughes when he realized how thoroughly Elliot was compromised.) The couple spent the evening together, then adjourned to his luxury hotel suite, ignoring all else. They were married four months after their meeting. No one could connect him with the "professional" escorts because of his chance intoxication with and subsequent marriage to Emerson: a good thing because there was one part of what amounted to a three-day bribe that Meyer had neglected. He let others arrange for the hiring of waiters, cleaning personnel, and the technicians needed for the makeshift set used by Judy Cook, and among those hired were a number of undercover FBI special agents making note of all that went on.

Hughes and Meyer planned well, but Hughes was greedy enough to want to deduct the payment to the actresses and models as a legitimate entertainment expense. He also understood that the men, no matter how happy during their trip, still had to return home to wives who were possibly feeling neglected. Nylon stockings, almost impossible to get, were provided to each man for his wife. (Faye Emerson was personally given $132 in nylons when she joined Elliott in New York following their meeting in Los Angeles. The gift was meant to impress Roosevelt. Emerson had her prize in gaining the colonel's love.)

The D-2 was a lousy plane no matter what faith Hughes had in it. However, the military brass, including Colonel Roosevelt, were so sated through Johnny Meyer's ministrations that it was clear they were leaning toward approval. When Colonel Roosevelt and the others returned to the East Coast, and before they could make their recommendations, Johnny Meyer joined them, treating the group to such nightclubs as the Copacabana and the El Morocco. By August 20, 1943, Howard Hughes's D-2, its name changed to the XF-11, was a reconnaissance plane preferred over the Lockheed P-58. The latter was considered the only competition, though the experts who had not enjoyed Johnny Meyer's company were convinced it was the far better plane. Truth did not matter, though, and Hughes won a $43 million contract for one hundred of his substandard aircraft. The order was issued on September 1, despite extensive paperwork showing the decision was a bad one.

The end result was that Hughes could not fulfill the contract or even stay on schedule. He tried to charge the army air force an additional $3.6 million for the development of the D-2 *prior* to any name change, and *prior* to the army contract for one hundred XF-11 aircraft. Then there were labor problems with the United Steelworkers over the Hughes Tool Company employment conditions in Houston, a valid though potentially destructive strike that was averted only because the plant made products vital to the war. The War Labor Board ordered the employees back to work while management negotiated with the union.

The war ended before Hughes could be fully called to account. The XF-11s were no longer needed after the bombing of Hiroshima and Nagasaki and the subsequent surrender of the Japanese. This was fortunate because they were never delivered, though ironically Hughes Aviation and another of his companies, Toolco, became major suppliers of airplane parts.

Eventually there was a congressional investigation because, to the delight of the Republicans, the president's son was involved. Johnny Meyer was someone who could never be disgraced. He had accomplished what the Hughes corporations needed done and advanced to a new role, procurer. It was he who would help Hughes inadvertently change Norma Jean's life and career.

The magazine was *Laff*, and the specific issue is uncertain. Howard Hughes was living in Cary Grant's villa while recovering from the near-fatal crash of one of his XF-11 reconnaissance planes. The crash occurred on July 7, 1946, several months after World War II was over and several months before the aircraft would finally perform in a way that would have warranted its quantity purchase, had the war continued longer than it did. The day of the crash he was making tests to assure the army the plane was still worth purchasing, though the order had been reduced to just three aircraft since more were no longer needed.

The XF-11 required two pilots to handle the radically new design but Hughes was adamant about handling it himself. At 9:30 A.M. he and flight engineer Gene Blandford, also a pilot, ran through a series of limited safety tests. Then after a break from the work, he had the plane loaded with twelve hundred gallons of fuel and told his assistant he would fly for at least two hours. That was double the fuel and almost three times the maximum time that was supposed to be used while testing the plane for the army. His flight plan was also improper: the army wanted him to use the army test base later called Edwards Air Force Base, which was safely located in the sparsely populated desert.

Hughes took off alone, ignoring abnormal sounds and an instrument light glowing red as a warning. He assumed the plane was fine, just new, and that the light was a malfunction. He was determined to travel at four hundred miles an hour, passing over Venice Beach and Beverly Hills before returning to Culver City. The craft began pitching violently; the airspeed dropped, and the plane pulled right as it lost altitude. Wind currents shook the falling craft, the right wing dropped under some unknown pressure, and the plane plummeted to an estimated five hundred feet above busy Santa Monica Boulevard.

The dropping plane sheared the roof from the North Linden Drive home of Jules Zimmerman, DDS, known in Beverly Hills as the "dentist to the stars." Then it cut through the bedroom of municipal justice John Ashton Shidler and his wife, the movie actress Rosemary DeCamp, finally coming to rest when it crashed into the rear brick wall of the North Whittier home of Lieutenant Colonel Charles A. Meyer.

Hughes, burning, bloody, and vomiting, managed to get out of the plane, where he was rescued by Marine Sergeant William Lloyd Durkin who was visiting a friend on whose lawn one of the XF-11's engines, still on fire, had landed.

After a prolonged hospitalization, Hughes retreated to Cary Grant's villa. Grant, knowing that Hughes was bored and had no interest in books, brought his friend copies of the various magazines of the day, including *Laff*. The exact issue is uncertain, but of the two possibilities—June 1946 and August 1946—the June issue listed the model as Norma Jean Dougherty and the August issue listed her as Jean Norman. Though the stories differ, Hughes apparently gave the Norma Jean Dougherty name to Johnny Meyer.

The photo used in June shows Norma Jean in a two-piece bathing suit, sitting on a balcony rail overlooking the ocean. The cover stories were "Billion Dollar Babes" and "Life and Love at a Summer Theatre." The August issue shows Norma Jean with lighter hair posed in front of a red seamless paper studio background.

The earlier photograph was one of those taken by David Conover, the person Johnny Meyer contacted to locate Norma Jean. Hughes wanted to put her under a seven-year movie contract, certain that if she had any talent—the one unknown about the young woman—he could use her as a minor player. And if she didn't, he would pay her for six months, probably try to bed her, use her as a beautiful extra in the background, then cancel her contract.

(All motion picture studio contracts ran for no more than seven years at that time. Contracts longer than seven years were considered indentured servitude under California law. However, regardless of the way the contract was worded, two factors were common. The first was the initial pay—seventy-five dollars per week when Norma Jean planned to enter the business, twenty-five dollars more than the average salary of the reporters who covered show business and other Los Angeles news. The second was a six-month escape clause. The studios could fire an actor after six months, then rehire the actor at the same pay rate. If the contract was allowed to roll into the second six months, the pay had to be raised. Actors who did not become stars were regularly fired and rehired to keep their costs down. In addition, the six-month firing possibility was an added incentive for an ambitious actress to go along with the sexual demands of producers and directors.)

Sixteen

The End of Norma Jean Dougherty

Norma Jean had talked with Emmeline Snively about the possibility of getting a movie studio contract when the request for contact came from Johnny Meyer. Later there would be variations on the story, including one where Hughes was still recovering in Cedars of Lebanon Hospital and had a staff person contact Miss Snively about a screen test at Hughes's RKO-Radio Pictures.

Emmeline Snively was thrilled. The Hughes interest meant that Norma Jean could achieve the dream most of the girls had: to gain a screen test and, hopefully, the initial contract. She also understood that she was in no position to ever negotiate with someone like Hughes. Whatever he wanted from Norma Jean, or any young woman for that matter, was out of her league. She immediately turned to a friend, Helen Ainsworth, the West Coast representative of the National Concert Artists Corporation. Ainsworth was to the movie industry what Snively was to print, and the two women immediately plotted a way to take advantage of the Meyer contact.

Norma Jean signed with Ainsworth's agency on March 11, 1946, Grace Goddard co-signing as her guardian since her ward was not yet twenty-one.

Again matters have become mythological with the passage of time. The two friends, with nothing to gain but Helen Ainsworth's 10 percent commission from any work that resulted, made the moves that led to the creation of Marilyn Monroe. That much is fact. Also fact is that eventually Ainsworth used one of her employees, a Harry Lipton, for some of the work. And all of this took place while Norma Jean's divorce proceedings were moving forward.

The sequence of events that turned Norma Jean Dougherty into Marilyn Monroe began when Grace helped Norma Jean travel to Las Vegas to stay with Minnie Willette, the sixty-nine-year-old aunt of Grace McKee Goddard. A lawyer named C. Norman Cornwall was obtained to file the divorce papers (on the grounds of "extreme mental cruelty that has impaired the plaintiff's health," a catch-all used before someone created the generic "irreconcilable differences") and Norma Jean was to stay in the city without leaving from her arrival on May 14, 1946, until the judge's decision would be rendered on September 13.

The divorce itself, when it occurred, was a simple matter before Judge A. S. Henderson in Las Vegas. He asked if Norma Jean intended to stay in Nevada as her permanent place of residence and if she had already been there continuously since her arrival. When asked to explain the problems with her husband who, she said, had been unjustly treating her, she said, ". . . my husband didn't support me and he objected to my working, criticized me for it and he also had a bad temper and would fly into rages and he left me on three different occasions and criticized me and embarrassed me in front of my friends and he didn't try to make a home for me."

The testimony was Norma Jean's first acting job, and some critics might say it was her best. Certainly she was given a reward that, for her, would matter more than an Oscar: Approximately five minutes in court won her a divorce. Jim Dougherty, innocent of all the accusations, counter-signed upon receiving the papers two weeks later. Norma Jean kept their 1935 Ford Coupe, the only meaningful property they owned together.

The car, which Norma Jean delayed registering in her name, was used for trips to the photography studios where she was regularly working. Heedless of where she parked, she got ticket after ticket. Eventually there were so many that an arrest warrant was issued for the owner of the car: Jim Dougherty. Then, before the hearing could be held, Norma Jean had an accident, wrecking a car owned by a priest. Although he wasn't injured, he sued the listed owner of the car: again, Jim Dougherty.

The matter was resolved, though the law was ambiguous. Jim was the registered owner of Norma Jean's car, but the divorce settlement cleared him of any obligations related to her actions following the divorce. Eventually the matter was dropped. Norma Jean had no money and few prospects of earning enough to make good on the damage she had caused. Jim Dougherty was no longer legally involved with his by-then-ex-wife or her actions.

℘

> My marriage brought me neither happiness nor pain. My husband and I hardly spoke to each other. This wasn't because we were angry. We had nothing to say.
>
> —Marilyn Monroe, concerning the divorce from Jim Dougherty. (This could more accurately have been said about her second divorce, that one from Joe DiMaggio with whom she spent far more time. The Dougherty marriage was primarily a victim of their youth and the separation during wartime, a not uncommon occurrence in the 1940s.)

ACT II

Welcome to Hollywood Whoever You Are

Seventeen

Enter Hedda and Louella, the Wicked Witches of Show Business

They were the wicked witches of the west, at least to those who felt their typewritten ire or those who desperately needed a positive reference to their work. Gossip columnists Hedda Hopper and Louella Parsons were arguably the most powerful women, and among the most powerful people, in Hollywood. They could save a career with positive mentions of an actor the studios had wanted to destroy, and they could destroy a career no matter how hard the studio publicists worked to ensure an actor had a positive reputation. The only controls the studio heads maintained involved access, but even then, a rising star knew that it was better to defy one of the moguls than to become inaccessible to Hedda and Louella.

The columnists themselves had quite different backgrounds. Louella Parsons was the better educated and more sophisticated of the two rivals, a woman who gave the appearance of being someone's Midwest-reared, churchgoing aunt beloved for her baking at the annual county fair. Her work, by contrast, was something quite different. However, the newspaper industry was a cutthroat business when she started as a writer, a place where reporters would lie, bribe, steal, or intimidate in order to gain a story.

A story was told about a person who had recently met Louella being shocked by the radical contrast between her work as a columnist and her genteel appearance. The questioner supposedly asked, "Isn't it possible she

161

is a nice lady who happens to be involved in a dirty business?" And the reply was, "Yes, except that she happened to invent the business."

Louella and Hedda created the style of journalism eventually imitated by all the supermarket tabloids, though their columns appeared in mainstream newspapers throughout the nation. They sought sources everywhere they could, sometimes paying regular amounts to keep someone alert and sometimes paying strictly for information provided. An actor never thought about the number of people involved in his or her private life, but Hedda and Louella (as well as many who followed them) certainly did. The columnists befriended not only the obvious, such as waiters in upscale restaurants who would report on who was doing what with whom in private seating areas, but also the less obvious: for example, garbage collectors. Maids, hairdressers, janitors, medical lab technicians, receptionists in medical offices, security guards, parking attendants, and anyone else who regularly encountered the famous and powerful soon learned that observations were rewarded with cash because the brilliance of Hedda and Louella was that they had such people on their payrolls.

The best example of how the two rival columnists worked came from Louella Parsons, the older, more experienced columnist; and though she was not averse to mixing fact with fiction, this particular story was true. Actress Teresa Wright and her then-husband writer Niven Busch were a popular item in the Hearst chain of newspapers for which Louella wrote her column. Among the people on the Parsons's payroll was the employee of a medical testing lab who watched for prominent names attached to whatever lab work came in the office. The lab worker saw a pregnancy test for Wright, checked to see the results, then called Louella Parsons.

Louella was delighted to get a scoop on every other columnist in the city (there were four hundred reporters of all types assigned to exclusively cover Hollywood at the time, more than covered any other community except Washington, DC) and she called Wright to get a quote. However, when Parsons offered her congratulations, Wright indignantly replied that she was not pregnant.

The actress was so adamant that Louella was taken aback. After all, she had heard the news directly from the technician who ran the pregnancy test—though she could not tell that fact to Teresa, or her source would be fired. As Louella later recounted, Teresa then said angrily, "I think I'm the best authority."

However, before Parsons, now thoroughly embarrassed and confused, could hang up the receiver, Teresa Wright's other telephone rang. She excused herself for a moment, then returned to the columnist's call, bemused. As Parsons related, Wright said, "I'll never doubt you again, Louella. You were right. I am going to have a baby. I'm glad you told me first. That was my doctor on the phone. He just got the lab report."

It was doubtful that Teresa Wright, her husband, or her doctor were pleased that the powerful columnist was the first to know. But it was a sign of Louella's power that no one criticized the outrageous invasion of privacy.

Parsons was in many ways as interesting a fraud as the men and women she eventually targeted for her column. She was born Louella Oettinger on August 6, 1881, then lopped twelve years off her age by writing in her 1943 autobiography *The Gay Illiterate* that she was born in 1893. She was ten years old when, certain she had become a writer of professional quality, she presented her story *The Flower Girl of New York* (a city she had never visited) to the editor of her hometown paper, the Freeport, Illinois, *Journal Standard*. Success was not instantaneous, though. He explained that he would not publish it until she was dead, implying at the same time that he hoped she would have a long life. However, she handled the rejection well enough to continue writing, and by the time she reached high school, she had a five-dollar-a-week job as drama editor for the *Dixon* (Illinois) *Morning Star*.

Louella's personal life was filled with men, none of whom seemed to last if they were "appropriate" (single during her affair). Real estate agent John Parsons was first, an unhappy affair during which he cheated on his bride, then was killed on a transport ship in World War I. She moved to Chicago and married riverboat captain Jack McCaffrey, from whom she was soon divorced.

About that time Louella apparently decided that having a philandering spouse was painful, but being the love object of such a man could be delightful. That was when she took up with married New York labor leader Peter Brady.

A conversion to Catholicism apparently ended Louella's wandering ways, and in 1930, long before she had heard of Norma Jean or Howard

Hughes, Louella married Dr. Harry "Docky" Martin, the most popular urologist in Hollywood. In his early years of practice, he developed the always-in-demand skill of curing venereal disease among the rich and famous. Later he was hired to be the Twentieth Century-Fox doctor in charge of giving actors and crew whatever drugs would keep them alert and active throughout each day's shooting schedule. He performed abortions as needed, yet had the integrity such that, when cheating on his wife (as he often did during trips to New York where he enjoyed Broadway actresses) he would pay the women for their time and talent. This made him enormously popular with the women who were accustomed to men of such power and influence simply using them and walking away.

Martin was also a drunk, and Louella's acceptance of his weakness led to such delightful stories as the night of a party when the good doctor went to sleep under the couple's piano instead of going to their bedroom. A guest pointed him out to Louella who allegedly said, "Let Docky sleep. He has surgery at seven tomorrow morning."

Louella's literary career began in 1910 when she started working as a reporter for the *Chicago Tribune* and a writer for Essanay Studios. She created film scenarios, the rather simple plot lines for the early silent pictures. The money was excellent, paying twenty-five dollars for a story created and filmed by the studio, but the *Tribune* money was steadier and Louella was perpetually broke.

Louella's writing for Essanay was competent, but no better than dozens of other would-be scenario writers, and as she made sales she began asking for more money than the studio could afford. Suddenly out of her part-time job, she wrote the book *How to Write for the Movies*, a surprisingly popular handbook about the new industry. She also developed an idea for a new type of newspaper column. The *Tribune* was not interested, but the *Chicago Record-Herald* was intrigued.

The column was a simple idea. Actors regularly had to travel between the movie studios of Los Angeles and both the movie studios and live theaters of New York City. The trains they took always had a two-hour layover in Chicago. She proposed, and had approved, a column in which she would interview the actors during the layovers, then publish whatever story she was given.

Parsons moved to New York in 1923, going to work for William Randolph Hearst's *New York American*, and two years later she was the movie editor of his syndicate, the Universal News Service. Three years later she was sent to Hollywood where she would write a column that would soon reach four hundred newspapers and, in 1929, pay her five hundred dollars a week—far more than many of the "famous" actors on whom she was reporting.

Louella not only invented the gossip column, she also found a way to use it to wield power greater than that of the studios themselves. It was all well and good for the Hollywood moguls to have police on their payrolls, to have publicists, and to have doctors and lawyers who could hide or eliminate any indiscretion. Louella invented the art of making the public believe that the real Hollywood was whatever her columns said it was. She revealed the private lives, joys, and indelicacies. She told of romances starting and romances ending. She told of dramatic childhoods, scandals, and triumphs on the movie sets, and any other stories her millions of readers wanted to hear. And when an actor, producer, or director did not appreciate her style of journalism, Louella wielded the ultimate power: she stopped writing about the person or the film, and the career or the picture was history. That was why she had an ironclad rule when accepting tips: "You tell it to Louella first!"

Louella could also be bought by the studios. She was aware that the married Spencer Tracy was having an affair with the single Katherine Hepburn, a violation of the morals clauses in the studio contracts; yet she never wrote about the relationship. However, the actors all knew that the studios were not above destroying an actor by leaking negative information to Louella and Hedda Hopper themselves.

There was also indirect bribery. Louella wrote *The Gay Illiterate* and Twentieth Century-Fox informed her that the book would make a fabulous motion picture. They did not want anyone else to have such delightful stories so they paid her seventy-five thousand dollars for the film rights, an unheard-of amount for the day. The book was then placed on the shelf, presumably never to be looked at again, but Louella was apparently satisfied.

In addition, both Louella and Hedda received Christmas presents from everyone whose career they could influence. These were not simple tokens of esteem. One year, a Rolls-Royce was delivered to Louella. It was understood that none of the extremely expensive gifts should be personalized in any way. The vast majority were returned to the stores for cash.

૪ર

Did I mention that Louella was a power-mad, nasty, destructive, vengeful bitch?

—Actress Mamie Van Doren, whose run-ins with Louella Parsons included Van Doren's being rejected for a Paramount Pictures contract she had with her interpretation of a scene from Clifford Odets's *The Big Knife*. As soon as word reached Parsons, then dating Van Doren's manager, songwriter, and agent Jimmy McHugh, she told Paramount to cancel the signing or she would stop reviewing Paramount pictures.

૪ર

Louella may have always known she wanted to be a writer, but Hedda Hopper started her theatrical career as an entertainer who, for some unknown reason, sought attention through the wearing of outrageous hats. The daughter of a Pennsylvania butcher, Elda—who later changed her name to Hedda—lived with her family until she was twenty-two, when she moved to New York to audition for musical comedies. She was hired for the choruses and earned her way into starring roles. She also managed to shed at least five years in age, eventually claiming she had left Pennsylvania after the eighth grade.

Hedda married actor DeWolf Hopper, a Broadway music star of sorts who was older than her father and seemed to have married every woman with whom he ever acted (Hedda was actually his fifth wife). The relationship was strained almost from the start because, though neither was particularly memorable in their roles, she was better than he, and was considered the better box-office draw. She also photographed better than he did, another sore point, especially as both attempted to move into films. When her pay exceeded his, despite his many more years in the business, his ego overwhelmed him and their marriage was over. Altogether, Hedda appeared in an estimated 140 films credited as either Mrs. DeWolf Hopper or as Hedda Hopper before deciding she needed a different business.

166

Hedda and Louella became friendly and Louella introduced her to publisher William Randolph Hearst. He mentioned to the editor of the *Washington Times-Herald* that the actress was interested in a career change, though Hedda not only lacked a background in journalism; she also was unable to type.

The *Times-Herald* was a quirky paper owned by Eleanor "Cissy" Patterson. It was an outspoken journal to which almost no one in power listened. It hired many a DC area socialite, though beauty, rather than journalistic skills, seemed to be the reference that mattered. As World War II approached, for example, the paper employed both Kathleen "Kick" Kennedy, the daughter of Joe and Rose Kennedy, and Inga Arvad, a Dutch emigrant believed to be a Nazi sympathizer and the lover of Kick's brother, Jack Kennedy. (Jack and Inga were recorded enjoying one another in a hotel room when a former Harvard classmate of Kennedy's joined the FBI and was assigned to get whatever information he could about Inga. The matter was top secret for years, though the type of gossip column item both Hedda and Louella would have loved.)

Hedda Hopper, glamorous if only because of her show business past, was first assigned to write a weekly fashion column. Soon she, too, was sent to Hollywood where her column, changed to "Hedda Hopper's Hollywood," was published in the *Los Angeles Times*, along with the *New York Daily News* and the *Chicago Tribune*. Ultimately her readers were approximately the same as those of Parsons, but in the early days, when Louella was beginning to regret helping her former friend, Hedda Hopper did not understand the competitive nature of both Parsons and the newspaper business. She knew that Louella was the far superior journalist, so she joked, "Louella Parsons is a newspaperwoman trying to be a ham. I'm a ham trying to be a columnist."

The dirty little secret of the two women, one not known by Hopper but understood by Parsons, was that Hedda was hired as a way of reducing Louella's influence. There was a dramatic announcement, a party greeting her arrival, and immediate access to the stars as a way of stopping some of Louella's power and vindictiveness. They had not counted on Hedda, who had also briefly worked unsuccessfully as a real estate agent and talent manager during her transition from the stage and screen, having the aggressive nature to rise to the challenge. When the two women reached the peak of their careers, they shared an estimated seventy million readers and could make or break any movie, any actor, any Hollywood legend.

By the time Howard Hughes was looking at *Laff* and Norma Jean was planning her move into films, Hedda and Louella were at war. They fought one another for scoops and were vicious to anyone who tried to alert both women to the same gossip item at the same time. Hedda, the gentler of the two when on the attack, stressed that "no one is interested in sweetness and light." She referred to one man who wanted to be an actor, then changed his mind and left the business, by saying, "He had certain qualifications, including no money and a total lack of responsibility."

Emmeline Snively knew that the name Howard Hughes in relation to any woman would get the attention of both columnists and warrant an item in each of their columns. She also knew that she had to choose carefully. Louella, if she liked an actor, would champion that person to the point of suppressing scandalous information that she alone in the industry discovered. (However, when racing a rival columnist for a scoop, she did not care which entertainer was bloodied by the revelations. That was the game and that was understood by misbehaving stars. The willingness to suppress came only when no rival had the information.) By contrast, if Louella felt she had been betrayed by an actor because he or she mentioned an item to Hedda first, she would do everything in her power to ruin that person's career.

Years later, comic George Burns was speaking at a tribute to Louella Parsons. He jokingly brought up the most famous feud in the world of newspapers. "I'll never forget one time Hedda Hopper—if you'll excuse the expression—caught me in a picture and in her review, she said, 'George Burns is the lousiest actor I've ever seen.' Louella got very sore. She called me up and said, 'George, we've been dear friends for years. If you've got an item like that, why didn't you give it to me?'"

In the viciousness of her attacks, Louella was much like her mentor and employer, William Randolph Hearst. Orson Welles claimed that his highly acclaimed movie *Citizen Kane* was not about Hearst, for example. However, one of the dirty little secrets of the movie and of Hearst's life was that he referred to the genitalia of his lifelong mistress, Marion Davies, as "Rosebud." Welles deliberately appropriated the name for the mystery of the movie, though in the film it was found on a sled. The public assumed that there was nothing more to the images than what they saw on the screen. Hearst got the message that Welles was mocking him. In retaliation, no newspaper, in any way controlled by Hearst, anywhere in the world, reviewed Welles's work or wrote about his career. Parsons likewise could turn a celebrity into a nonperson.

Biographers of Monroe unfamiliar with the gossip columnist wars have often said that both Hopper and Parsons were alerted to the supposed interest of Howard Hughes. What is certain is that Hedda Hopper's column for July 29, 1946, had an item that read: "Howard Hughes is on the mend. Picking up a magazine, he was attracted by the cover girl and promptly instructed an aide to sign her for pictures. She's Norma Jean Dougherty, a model." The item that ran was a variation of the release that was sent by Snively: "Howard Hughes must be on the road to recovery. He turned over in his iron lung and wanted to know more about Jean Norman, this month's cover girl on *Laff* magazine."

The story, as Norma Jean later told writer/photographer George Barris, was that "when Howard Hughes saw my picture on a magazine cover, the mere fact that word got out to the Fox studio talent agent Ben Lyon that [Hughes was interested in me] was enough for Fox to take notice and then want to give me that screen test in color. The interesting thing was [Lyon] didn't even ask me if I had any acting experience. He did not ask me to read any scripts. Nothing."

There are several stories about what happened next. In some, Norma Jean went to Twentieth Century-Fox on her own. In others she was taken there by Helen Ainsworth, whose agency would be handling all film work in the same manner that Emmeline Snively handled the still photography bookings. And in the third variation, Harry Lipton, an agent who worked under Ainsworth and would be assigned the day-to-day management, claimed credit for taking her there. Given how the next few weeks unfolded, it is likely that Helen Ainsworth took Norma Jean to see Ben Lyon, a casting director and recruiter for Twentieth Century-Fox.

Ben Lyon was a longtime British actor married to actress Beebe Daniels. The couple had a radio show, *At Home with the Lyons*, and in recent years Lyon—who ironically was credited with discovering Jean Harlow when both actors were in a 1930 Howard Hughes film called *Hell's Angels*—had become the head talent scout for Twentieth Century-Fox. More important, he was a friend of Helen Ainsworth, and his wife was a close friend of Louella Parsons. Hedda Hopper may have broken the Hughes story, but by going to Ben Lyon, Helen Ainsworth ensured that Louella Parsons would essentially handle the young actress in a nurturing, positive way.

(Looking at the Parsons/Hopper rivalry—and the hatred each woman had for the other was genuine—it seems odd at first to know that Hedda Hopper ran the Norma Jean/Howard Hughes item, yet Louella would champion the actress she later called "Cinderella." The change was a subtle one, seemingly justified by the fact that Hedda Hopper wrote about Norma Jean Dougherty/Jean Norman and Louella only wrote about Marilyn Monroe.)

Lyon, according to what he later told Louella, found that Norma Jean was physically perfect for film. She quoted him as saying of the would-be actress, "She had a good face. . . . You can tell with some faces, the way the flesh sits on the bones; the planes and angles—that they'll photograph well. And she was real blond, a rarity. In addition, there was the way she moved."

Curious as to how Norma Jean would handle a script, Lyon handed her a copy of *Winged Victory* he had on his desk. The movie, released in 1944, had starred Judy Holliday, and it was a few lines of her role that he wanted to hear. There was no record of what he thought about Norma Jean's reading, though she could not have been terrible since he asked her to return for a screen test.

Norma Jean was thrilled with the proposed screen test. She saw the opportunity as the high point of her career to date and the achievement of a dream. Lyon was less than enthusiastic. He did not think he was discovering a star, something he had done earlier in his career with the actress Jean Harlow. Instead, he saw himself as potentially hiring a beautiful young woman to be another of the approximately forty young, beautiful white women who had the same seven-year studio contract at any given time. Most were dropped at six months. Some were offered a raise as low as another twenty-five dollars a week and renewed for another six months. But most would be fired before they could request serious money from the studio budgets, a handful rehired if they would return to the original beginner's salary. In theory, so long as an actress either retained her youthful looks or developed an appearance unique enough to be a character actress, she could spend twenty years or more working for the same beginner's salary.

Helen Ainsworth understood the game and recognized that Norma Jean Dougherty had a better chance at lasting more than six months at Fox than at RKO. She knew that there was even a chance that Hughes was not serious, that he was hoping the appeal of a rich man's interest would lead the model—whatever name in *Laff* was real—to go to bed with him. There might be no screen test or signing. But such information was not known by Lyon.

Once Ben Lyon recognized that Norma Jean had the facial bone structure that would record well on camera, Ainsworth immediately demanded a screen test for the next day. Lyon reminded her that studio head Darryl Zanuck was out of town. This was a period in the making of motion pictures when the studios were beginning to use color film. Prior to this time almost all the movies were in black-and-white. Just as the coming of sound pictures cost some enormously successful silent movie actors their jobs because their grating voices sounded terrible, so color was changing the way actors were viewed. There were those who made the transition easily. There were others whose flesh tones, regardless of makeup used, lost the appeal they had had in black-and-white.

All new hires that might have a future in films needed to be tested in color, and such tests were expensive. Studio head Darryl Zanuck had given Lyon the authorization to test anyone he wanted in black-and-white. However, if Ben thought that there was longer-term potential color needed to be used and Zanuck had to approve such tests. The autocratic Zanuck was often quoted as ordering his staff, "Don't agree with me until I'm finished talking!" Whether true or not, he was the type of man who seemingly never met a good idea except as it came out of his mouth.

Helen Ainsworth understood her bargaining position. There was almost as much rivalry between studios as there was between gossip columnists. She knew that, not only was Norma Jean potentially a woman who could succeed to some degree in films; there was the added bonus of Fox being able to brag that they "stole" the actress from Howard Hughes.

Lyon told Ainsworth that he could only arrange for a black-and-white test the next day. He would need to wait until Zanuck returned for color.

Helen Ainsworth played hardball. She told her friend that he would test Norma Jean or she would take her to RKO. Reluctantly Lyon asked for two days to make arrangements. Helen agreed.

There was a standard studio test given to an actor being considered for hiring. The color test would run approximately twelve minutes in length, the duration based on the container of film used in the motion picture camera. A script would be chosen either at random or because the person giving the test happened to like it. Usually it was drama, comedy being so specialized that not even an actor who had achieved great success was likely to be able to handle it without more work than circumstances allowed. And there would be a second actor during the test, someone experienced so that the person being tested could play off another person, as would be expected in a real movie. The script would be provided a few days in advance, the novice learning his or her lines and deciding how to play the role.

Everything possible was done to ensure that the color screen test approximated the real experience of making a movie. A person from wardrobe would fit the actor with an appropriate costume. There would be someone handling makeup, someone else handling hair. There would be a set and props, though sometimes, if the schedule permitted, an existing set for a movie in progress would be used. Finally, the lighting would be set so that the conditions would be identical to what would affect the actor prior to being projected on the screen.

To authorize a color screen test without Zanuck's permission would be to risk his job, yet Lyon decided to go ahead with one. He knew that if Norma Jean was competent in the test, Zanuck would approve the hiring. However, in case she wasn't, he decided to take the least risk possible, using minimum personnel and equipment and having the test literally before sunrise.

Actress Betty Grable was starring in the film *Mother Wore Tights*, which was currently under production, and there was a set for the film that would not be in use at 5:30 A.M. Grable, at $208,000 a year, was believed to be the highest-paid woman in the country at the time, and some of the support people, including her makeup artist, had to be available before she arrived. This was the reason Lyon would be able to use them. He confirmed his plans with the film's director, Walter Lang, and Lang also agreed to help with the screen test. As it turned out, eight years after the screen test, Lang would direct the movie *There's No Business Like Show Business*, which would be filmed by Leon Shamroy, who was working the camera for the unauthorized screen test of the future star, Marilyn Monroe.

Shamroy, who had three Academy Awards prior to the test and would later earn a fourth, as well as a total of twenty nominations, was a huge man who delighted in conspiracies, knew he was one of the best in the business, and did not care about Zanuck's rules. He was also comfortable setting the lighting himself, planning the shot, and then loading the camera so there would be no assistants who might reveal what was being done.

Ben Lyon asked Charles LeMaire, head of wardrobe for Fox, to prepare Norma Jean in the sequin evening gown that some say LeMaire personally selected and others say Ben sneaked from where the costumes were stored.

Makeup artist Allan "Whitey" Snyder, who would be working with Grable for the authorized filming on the same set later in the day, agreed to apply Norma Jean's makeup. He also knew there would be trouble others had not anticipated.

Color photography in 1946 was still an evolving chemistry problem, and each manufacturer, as well as each different color film by the same manufacturer, responded uniquely to the lighting and reproduction medium—print or projection. Use the wrong combination of makeup, lighting, and color film, and a model would look like the makeup had been layered onto her face: very obviously not her natural look.

Norma Jean stepped from her makeshift dressing area having ordered Whitey to make up her face as she had done hundreds of times for the still camera, its film, and the lighting conditions familiar in the magazine field. She might as well have slapped on painted clay.

Shamroy noticed the problem immediately and raised hell with Whitey, who had been professional enough to respect Norma Jean's wishes, even knowing she was wrong. The makeup artist was told to whisk Norma Jean to the makeup area, where he could quickly and thoroughly wash her face. Then he was to apply makeup properly for the Technicolor test.

Norma Jean understood that everyone was being kind to her by getting angry with Whitey, since they also knew that he knew better. Nothing further was said, though, and when she returned she had trouble talking.

Fortunately there was not going to be an actor working with her. The test would be a silent one.

> We rehearsed my first big scene and then I began the scene and prayed silently that this was my start, the beginning of becoming a motion picture actress. This is what my big scene consisted of: I walked across the set; I had to light a cigarette, inhale, then blow the smoke out, get up, then go upstage, cross, look out a window, sit down, come downstage, and then exit the set. Those bright lights were blinding me, and for some strange reason—instead of being nervous and scared as I thought I'd be—I just did the best I could.
>
> —Marilyn Monroe, as quoted by George Barris

The screen test was made quickly, and as was the nature of making movies, none of the men who observed the action had any sense of how Norma Jean fared. Each was concerned with a specific aspect of the filming, not how well Norma Jean was doing. It was only when the film was processed and viewed that the men realized Norma Jean was special.

No one knew if Norma Jean could act. None of them had any idea if she could play off other actors, speak in a way that was believable, or otherwise become a quality actress. What they recognized is what still photographers had seen when working with the young woman. She knew how to project a smoldering sexuality. When she was viewed on film, she was larger than life and yet lifeless, a creation of light and shadows, of color and form, projected onto a screen. Yet somehow she was riveting. Men felt her presence as palpably as if she were coming on to them in a bar, a predator who had settled on her prey and was moving in to take full control. She was both naïve and dangerous, a cauldron of barely contained emotions. She was the type of woman who, if she could be developed into an actress, not just a screen presence, would definitely become a star.

> Early in her career, an assignment called for a blonde. After much persuasion, Norma Jean consented to bleach her hair the platinum shade that it still is. (I recalled this at one time to Ben Lyon who

had told me of her natural "blondness." His answer was, "She *is* a natural blonde. I didn't make the mistake. Nature did.")

—Louella Parsons writing about the woman
who came to be known as Marilyn Monroe

ഇൗ

Leon Shamroy later discussed that as he watched the processed film, focusing on Norma Jean rather than the technical side of the work that had engrossed him during the test, that he was seeing someone special. He related that he felt he was looking at a beauty like Gloria Swanson who also had the sexual radiance of Harlow. This Norma Jean Dougherty was able to sell emotions with silence.

In the next few days, possibly over the weekend, possibly that following Monday, Darryl Zanuck, a man who loved brunettes and had little tolerance for blondes, was underwhelmed by the Norma Jean Dougherty screen test. Unlike other beautiful women, she had never had an acting lesson, never appeared in little theater or any other type of theatrical setting. She was not someone who had sung in clubs, danced, or otherwise done anything that would help her with this changed career. And though Shamroy and Lyon obviously were excited by her, he was not. Still, six months at seventy-five dollars a week would make everyone happy, and she would look good in backgrounds. He told Lyon to sign her.

Years later, Norma Jean found it more exciting to have had instant success. She created her own version of the Zanuck review of her screen test for George Barris, ending her story by having Zanuck say, "That's a damn fine test. Who is the girl? I hope you signed her."

On July 23, 1946, Helen Ainsworth, having accomplished her goal with Norma Jean Dougherty, assigned agent Harry Lipton to handle the new client on behalf of the National Concert Artists Corporation. Grace Goddard signed the contract on behalf of her legal ward, and Norma Jean Dougherty was part of the Fox stable.

All that was left to create Marilyn Monroe was to find a name that looked better on a marquee than "Dougherty" and also was easier to pronounce. Again, there are many "factual" stories about what happened, though the truth seems to be fairly straightforward.

Ben Lyon explained the problem to Norma Jean, and she thought it might be nice to use her mother's maiden name as her new last name: Monroe. It was easy to say, simple to spell, but there was an awkwardness to it with either of the first names she was using as a still photo model— Norma Jeane Monroe or Jeane Norman Monroe. (During this period Norma Jean was using the "e" at the end of her middle name because she thought the spelling looked sexier than just "Jean.") Finally Lyon decided to go for something totally different: "Carol Lind."

The name was still being decided when Norma Jean started attending acting classes with Jean Peters, also just starting in her career and a future with Howard Hughes. Peters later commented that she disliked the name Carol Lind. "I was arguing with her that she should call herself Meredith something," Peters explained in an interview many years later.

Finally Ben Lyon had another idea. He had once been engaged to a Broadway singer/dancer/actress named Marilyn Miller who had died young. He liked the name Marilyn, and it fit nicely with the last name of Monroe. Norma Jean agreed for the sake of her career. However, though her public would know her from then on as Marilyn Monroe, she so hated the name that she refused to legally change her name in the manner of other renamed actors until March 12, 1956.

�

It is understandable why, long after her death, some men decided to claim they had once had a sexual relationship with Marilyn Monroe. Even if the lie was discovered, the alleged bedroom romp would have been recorded somewhere and possibly retrieved by the naïve and impressionable. It is less understandable why someone would misrepresent how Norma Jean got her name. However, in May 1998, Pete Hamill of the New York *Daily News* related what occurred during an interview with Mickey Rooney: "He [Rooney] talks of another old friend named Marilyn Monroe, a screen name Rooney claims he invented. ('I told Norma Jeane Baker she needed someone she could trust, an agent, because there was gonna be a line of people trying to jump her bones. I told her she also needed a new name. At the time, there was a great stage actress named Marilyn Miller. So I told Norma Jeane she should be a Marilyn. Then I got a call from a screenwriter named Monroe Manning. And it clicked.')"

176

Was Mickey lying? In his own book, *Life Is Too Short,* published seven years earlier in 1991, he had a different story:

> I wanted to do this particular friend a favor, so I took Norma Jean out for drinks early one night to see for myself. Wow! She wasn't wearing a bra, or stockings, or panties, either. Her skimpy little frock left nothing to the imagination. She was all there, right in plain sight. And the way she looked at me—with her moist, half-opened eyes and her moist, half-opened mouth! And the way she talked! Every word she uttered seemed to have a sexy subtext. "But Mickey," she said in her precious little voice, "I'm more than just a pretty girl. I can do—*any*thing!" She reached over and touched my knee.
>
> So I helped Norma Jean Baker get a bit part in *The Fireball.* I remember her having one line: "Honey, I'll be here when you want me." Oh yes, she soon changed her name—to Marilyn Monroe, and became one of Hollywood's legendary sexpots, one of the best cocksuckers in Hollywood, according to my friends, Richard Quine and Blake Edwards.

Rooney may have viciously defined the Monroe sexual persona, but in his own book he makes no claim to providing Norma Jean with the name by which she would be known to the public.

§a

Ben Lyon was impressed with Norma Jean's sincerity. There was no question that she wanted to be an actress and was willing to work toward that end. He knew when she mentioned that she lived in the Studio Club (with fifteen dollars in rent that was past due) that she was not trying to be kept by a wealthy man who would help her, at least financially, as she tried to get in the movies. Some of the young women who lived in the Studio Club were comfortable accepting pay for "dates," but they were full-time actresses (or "wannabes") who put their careers ahead of all else. There were serious beginning actresses being kept throughout Hollywood, but they were as much in the minority as the part-time hustlers in the Studio Club.

Lyon explained that under the standard studio contract she would be making seventy-five dollars per week for the first six months of the standard seven-year contract, and fifteen hundred dollars per week during the last six months of the same contract. She would be given a raise of twenty-five dollars per week every six months if she was not let go. Everything would go through her agent's office, no different from the way she worked with Emmeline Snively. However, though Helen Ainsworth had gotten the interview and unauthorized color screen test for her, Norma Jean would be assigned a lesser staff member named Harry Lipton to handle her needs and future negotiations.

Later Lipton would become one of the legions of men and women who knew Marilyn Monroe, worked with or for Marilyn Monroe, and felt they had to take far more credit for her career than they deserved. In the later telling of the creation of Marilyn Monroe, Lipton claimed to be the agent that took her to see Ben Lyon. He claimed that he had gone to Fox before Hughes, though an employee named Fred Schussler sought to give her an RKO contract. He said that he told Schussler that it was too late, that Fox had an option for the Technicolor test. He also claimed to have been present with Lyon and Norma Jean when she was given the name Marilyn Monroe.

What mattered to Norma Jean was that, whether or not she liked the name by which she would be known to all but her closest friends in Hollywood in the years to come, she was in the movies. Or Marilyn Monroe was in the movies. Or Marilyn Monroe *would* be in the movies if she ever got past the endless array of acting classes, makeup training, dance lessons, voice lessons, and the myriad other offerings the studios provided their "talent" during the first six months. She had no history in theater, not even in a high school play while growing up. Her skills were so limited she might ruin even a bit part, but her looks were so fresh and attractive that she was given a new biography and a series of appearances meant to promote movies in which she had no part.

> That very evening I was in a parade when some kids asked me for my autograph. I didn't know how to spell Marilyn, and I had to ask a stranger how to spell it.
>
> —Marilyn Monroe talking to *Saturday Evening Post* associate editor and author Pete Martin

Eighteen

The First Six Months of Marilyn Monroe

The problem with the early creation of Marilyn Monroe is that no one seemed able to get the story straight. Norma Jean had one childhood that she lived, another that Beebe Goddard lived, and a third that Harry Brand of the Twentieth Century-Fox publicity department had her live in his press releases. Even then, there was inconsistency—as can be seen below, where Norma Jean supposedly wanted to be a secretary early in the telling of the story, but wanted to be a photographer in the later part of the same release.

December 30, 1946. 20th Century-Fox Biography of Marilyn Monroe as issued by Harry Brand, Publicity Department, based on an interview by Roy Craft of that same department:

Eighteen-year-old Marilyn Monroe, 20th Century-Fox discovery, is being ballyhooed as sort of a junior Lana Turner, and like the famous star, she's a Hollywood-born-and-bred youngster who didn't have to leave town to attract the attention of the talent scouts.

Once named as the "Oomph" girl of Emerson Junior High School, Marilyn nevertheless had no screen ambitions. She wanted instead to be a secretary, went to work for a defense industry owned by Reginald Denny after her graduation from Van Nuys High School who asked her to do some army motion pictures.

As a result of that, she went to work as a photographer's model, worked for some of the biggest agencies in the Los Angeles area, and appeared on some of the fanciest magazine covers.

A short time later Miss Monroe, to add to her income, went to the home of a 20th Century-Fox talent scout to sit with the baby. He was so impressed with her beauty he arranged for her to have a screen test in black-and-white film. This was so good she was then tested in Technicolor and signed to a long-term contract.

That's fast action in Hollywood, where such behavior is usually considered "impulsive," but the studio execs didn't want to take a chance on a youngster they consider a terrific bet for stardom.

To date, Marilyn has no picture assignments; she's down for six months of intensive grooming before she faces a camera, with dramatic lessons, dancing lessons, and voice training.

She was born on June 1st. Her father died in an automobile accident a year later, and as her mother was too ill to take care of her, she was adopted by Mr. and Mrs. E. S. Goddard, family friends in the manufacturing business. Her real name is Norma Jean Dougherty [sic], which the studio changed because it's too long for a marquee; and they expect her name to land on a lot of them.

Personal data: Loves swimming, horseback riding, yachting, but has a tendency to get seasick . . . writes poetry, but won't show it to anyone . . . loves music, from the classics to boogie-woogie . . . hobby is photography, until her movie career hoped to become a woman photographer of baby animals, kittens, puppies, et cetera . . . hates untidiness, careless drivers, closed places, and cowboy music.

And she loves movies.

Vital Statistics
Real Name: Norma Jean Dougherty [sic]
Birthplace: Los Angeles, California
Birthday: June 1st
Foster Mother: Mrs. E. S. Goddard
Foster Father: E. S. Goddard
Height: 5 feet 5½ inches
Weight: 118 pounds
Hair: Blonde
Eyes: Blue
Education: Emerson Jr. High, Los Angeles
Van Nuys High, Van Nuys, California

૪૭

Publicity made up a story about how I was a babysitter who'd been babysitting for the casting director and that's how I was discovered. They told me to say that, although it strictly wasn't true. You'd think that they would have used a little more imagination and that they would have had me at least a daddy-sitter.

—Marilyn Monroe, as quoted by *Saturday Evening Post* associate editor Pete Martin

૪૭

Norma Jean's Marilyn biography, one told to reporters, did not include any dreams of working in an office or photographing puppies, kittens, and small children. As she was quoted in the Ben Hecht book, "I used to think as I looked out on the Hollywood night, 'There must be thousands of girls sitting alone like me dreaming of becoming a movie star. But I'm not going to worry about them. I'm dreaming the hardest.'"

Later, in the same book, she explained,

There was this secret in me—acting. It was like being in jail and looking at a door that said "This Way Out."

Acting was something golden and beautiful. It was like the bright colors Norma Jean used to see in her daydreams. It wasn't an art. It was like a game you played that enabled you to step out of the dull world you knew into worlds so bright they made your heart leap just to think of them.

That's the way it was when I sat alone in my Hollywood room . . . I thought all actors and actresses were geniuses sitting on the front porch of Paradise—the movies.

Norma Jean thought she was at the start of her career. The support staff of Twentieth Century-Fox knew her for what she really was—a beginner with no proven talent other than looking pretty on the screen. Every year young men and women signed their seven-year contracts with one or another studio. Every year the studios sent their relatively inexperienced newer members of their publicity departments to interview the new hire to get whatever facts they were going to retain in the studio biography. They asked numerous questions about their education, experience in the entertainment world, husbands, boyfriends, favorite foods, hobbies, and every-thing else that might interest someone. The notes might be used or embellished. They might be filed away and a biography created in the same manner as her name—whatever sounded good.

The Marilyn Monroe biography would be regularly updated and altered over the years. For the first one she decided to play the part of the orphan though her mother, doing better outside the hospital, had married once again. Eventually Marilyn would steal most of "her" life from Beebe and the studio would delight in playing up the tragedy of her past so her audi-ence would be regularly coming to see her triumphs over early sadness.

The official title for girls like Marilyn was "starlet," a term that delighted them because it sounded like "star." They were given a free education in the skills needed for the film industry. There were voice lessons, makeup lessons, singing lessons, acting lessons, and depending upon the films being made at the studio, some of the starlets, as well as the young males receiving the same treatment, might learn sword fighting, horseback riding, and the like.

Despite the fantasy story in her first studio biography, Marilyn had once spent a portion of her childhood going to see every movie she could and then trying to remember the dialogue and speak it in her room. The habit of imitating what had been filmed was carried over to the studios. Marilyn would stay late when she could, going to an empty soundstage to practice reciting lines. She also took home screenplays to study.

The publicity department considered the starlets to be a low-budget resource for attention-getting images that would sell one movie or another, even though it was rare for the starlets to actually be in any of them. Instead, they would be costumed and ride floats. They would be sent on location to pose for still photographers in a manner no different than was begun with David Conover. Their images would appear in newspapers and magazines, though as starlets they were more likely to grace the inside pages of one of the tabloids—such as the *New York Daily News*—than *Laff* and *Titter*.

Starlets were cheap publicity for the studios. They were told they would be used in movies as background, walking down the street, dancing in nightclubs, passing by in cars, and otherwise becoming a part of the set. They were also told that they would be doing more as soon as the right part was found. During that first six months the right part was rarely found, and when it was, it was almost always for a girl with a meaningful background.

Betty Grable, for example, was also a twenty-year-old when she was given her first contract at the studio where she was starring when Marilyn arrived. However, Grable had toured on the Wheeler and Woolsey vaudeville show. She had also been on the professional stage with a small part in the musical *Follow the Fleet*, originally starring Fred Astaire. Her part was small but it gave her professional experience Marilyn lacked.

The one "new girl" who was about to star was actress June Haver who, at the end of Marilyn's first six months, was given the lead in the film *Scudda Hoo! Scudda Hay!* (The original story was called *Summer Lightning*, but apparently the change for the U.S. release was meant to stress the real stars: a pair of mules whose lives were the focal point for all the action. *Summer Lightning* was used abroad, but the better title did not improve the quality of the picture.)

The movie would also be Marilyn Monroe's first film but the second one to be released, and her part left almost everything to be desired. There was no credit for the part and no name in the cast list, just "girl friend." However, in the film, either because of the script or an ad lib, she is called "Betty."

Marilyn's one and only appearance at the end of her six months was in a low-budget film that was part of a series that each of the major studios seemed to create in the 1940s whenever a low-budget concept did well with the public. In the case of *Scudda Hoo! Scudda Hey!* there had been adequately successful stories about country people to warrant one more; in this case, the fight of a brother and sister to save a pair of mules critical for the family farm when their father dies and their wicked stepmother and stepbrother try to steal the inheritance. Later the studios would switch from low-budget farm stories to low-budget stories about juvenile delinquents, and then to movies about monsters released because of radiation, and then to. . . . This was not great cinematography by any means, but it was Marilyn's first film and she was excited.

The longest stretch of film containing Marilyn, the one that ended up being cut from the movie, had her sitting in a rowboat with Colleen Townsend, who was also an uncredited girlfriend, in this case one called June in the movie. The two girls are seen rowing up a creek past Stretch, the rotten stepbrother. They want to stop at the dock on which he's sitting so they can go swimming. He tells them, "You're too young. Come back in a couple of years' time." Then they giggle and row out of the picture.

Although this bit of motion picture mediocrity was excised before the audience could see it, Marilyn was mistaken when she later said that her part was removed. Just short of an hour into the movie Marilyn is walking down a church's steps and says, "Hi, Rad," to June Haver who plays the star, Rad McGill. Haver replies, "Oh, hi Betty." And that was the culmination of six months' work.

The film was generally damned with faint praise, such as the *New York World-Telegram*'s review which noted that the film, which cost $1,685,000 and went on to actually make a modest profit in its first theatrical release, was "made for people who like good shots of honestly sweaty farm activity with sentimental tears dripping as heavily as the perspiration."

It was not an auspicious beginning.

The second movie in which Marilyn was cast was *Dangerous Years*, a melodrama without redeeming social value, designed to tell the "true" story of teenagers on the loose. Her part—this time a credited one—was that of Evie, a waitress at The Gopher Hole, a teen hangout where you could get soft drinks, ice cream, and one of the girls who worked there if you got lucky.

The story is about Danny Jones, the new kid dropping into a social club run by schoolteacher Jeff Carter, who is determined to get the teenagers he sees every day through the dangerous years just prior to adulthood. Danny has more appeal to the other teens than does Jeff, and when Danny decides to rob a perfume company warehouse, Jeff interferes and is killed.

The story leads to a murder trial in which Danny is revealed to be the previously unknown son of the prosecutor, District Attorney Edgar Burns. There were two special children in the orphanage as a result of their parents' divorce, ironically a place identical to the one in which Norma Jean spent time. One, a girl named Connie, was so depressed to not know either of her parents that a staff member told the DA that she was his daughter. Delighted to find his child, Burns raised her as his own. The other child, Danny, was the DA's real child but boys supposedly did better in those circumstances than did girls. The staff person let things be, Danny leaving the orphanage as a teenager, then turning to making trouble and, previously, petty crime.

There is no question that Danny is guilty of the accidental killing of schoolteacher Jeff Carter, but he accepts responsibility and is reunited with his father. He is sentenced to life in prison, but a portion of his life is finally resolved.

And if it is not obvious from the description, the fifty-nine-minute movie neither won nor was nominated for any awards. In fact, by the time it was released on January 16, 1948, Marilyn had been out of work more than four months. The filming ended just before her second six months, and when her contract was to go into the second year, Marilyn was told her "talents" were no longer necessary. She had proven valid Darryl Zanuck's concerns that her lack of stage experience meant she would be of no more value to Fox than any other starlet. In her case, it was probably luck, or Ben Lyon fighting to prove he had not made a mistake, that led to her getting a second six months' renewal. There would not be a third, a fact that was emotionally shattering.

ℰ∂

> I knew then [when under her first film contract] what I had known when I was thirteen and walked along the sea edge in a bathing suit for the first time. I knew I belonged to the public and to the world—not because I was talented, or even beautiful, but because I had never belonged to anyone else. The public was the only family, the only Prince Charming, the only home I had ever dreamed about. I didn't go into the movies to make money. I wanted to become famous so that everyone would like me and I'd be surrounded by love and affection.
>
> —Marilyn Monroe

Being fired was never a possibility in her mind.

ℰ∂

There may have been a more serious reason for Marilyn's being fired from Fox than just her relative incompetence as an actor. Research done by author Tony Summers, but not corroborated elsewhere, indicates that she had a brief love affair with a young actor named Tommy Zahn, another one of Twentieth Century-Fox's contract actors who was fired at the same time as Marilyn. The difference between them was that Zahn was allegedly hired to be groomed to marry Zanuck's daughter. The problem for researchers is confirming that Zahn and the Zanuck girl even dated. But if the story is true, it does not change the fact that Marilyn was not yet competent enough to warrant a raise and continuation into the third six months of the seven-year contract.

Nineteen

~

702 North Crescent Drive, Beverly Hills

Norma Jean had to have help spelling Marilyn Monroe the first time she had to write it for what may have been her first fan. Sam Spiegel created a non-Semitic alias—S. P. Eagle—and then used it only after he had so much power that no one cared about his ethnic heritage or his religion. Yet each was hungry for success, and each would do whatever it took to achieve the desired end. Thus it seems only appropriate that their relationship would lead to Hollywood's most unlikely romance: between one of its most powerful agents and one of its less successful starlets.

The real Sam Spiegel, born in Jaroslaw, Poland, in 1901, was a rather amoral hustler, despite having a family of devout Orthodox Jews. Simon Spiegel, Sam's father, was a tobacco wholesaler more concerned with studying the Talmud than selling smoking products. His older brother, Shalom Spiegel, became a noted rabbi, theologian, and college professor.

Sam preferred getting his education in the streets. He loved to go to the marketplace and listen to the traders hustle both legitimate products and pipedreams from which only they would profit. He learned the languages— German, Polish, and Russian—and tried to find his own cons to make some illegitimate money. Then, with change in his pocket, he went to the nickelodeons to see the new one- and two-reel silent movies.

It was not the street cons that upset the Spiegel family. It was the time spent in nickelodeons, for the escapism that delighted Sam prevented him from adhering to the 613 laws of the Torah, which his parents believed was required of an Orthodox Jewish male.

Sam Spiegel was not a true rebel in those early years. He did not want to displease God or dishonor his mother, Regina. He knew that under Orthodox teachings, the work done by women was so godly that they were excused from many of the laws men were expected to follow. However, a woman's honor was determined by how devout the men in the family tried to be, and Sam simply could not stay away from the movies.

Simon and Regina Spiegel realized that with the coming of World War I and the Russian Revolution, emigration might be the only chance of survival for a Russian Jewish family with two sons. They joined thousands of other émigrés, in their case moving first to Vienna, then to Palestine, and finally to the United States. Sam added English to his language skills and also took a wife.

Sam's young bride was an idealistic Palestinian Jew who thought that Sam would want to join her and her friends in building a Jewish homeland. Instead, he just wanted a job where he would not have to sweat. Once the couple had been together long enough for her to realize that Sam had no intention of laboring side-by-side with his bride and her friends, finding joy in deprivation and hard work to build the new land, she wanted a divorce. He agreed, walking away from the marriage and his six-month-old daughter, whom he would never see again.

Sam decided to return to the street skills he had learned in Poland. He became a cotton broker and stock promoter, traveling throughout Europe and eventually mastering nine languages to help him with his work.

By 1927, the year after Norma Jean's birth, Spiegel's travels included the United States, where he planned to go to San Francisco to sell cotton futures. The movies had fueled Sam's belief that America was the place to get rich. He saw the elaborate estates and assumed that everyone lived that way. However, once on the East Coast, he quickly ran out of money. He was certain that if he could get to the West Coast he would find the success that so far had eluded him. All he needed was a stake.

Sam's answer was to contact the son of a wealthy Kansas banker he had met in a Jerusalem hotel catering, among others, to wealthy Americans. He had befriended several guests, kept contact information about them, and figured the Kansas youth would be willing and able to cash a personal check for $150, trusting in Spiegel's presumed honesty. By the time the youth learned that Sam had no money in his account, the $150 had taken Spiegel to the West Coast, where he became even more adept at writing bad checks.

It is difficult to understand why Spiegel felt he needed to continue his bad-check scam after he arrived on the West Coast, where he had proven skills in great demand. The movie industry was in a period of change. Sound pictures had been released for the first time the year before Sam reached Los Angeles, and no one was certain how to maintain the European market. Silent films were a universal language. With the talkies, the appeal of films became more specialized. The studios needed someone with language skills and a knowledge of film who could help decide what stories would play well abroad. Spiegel's background made him the ideal man to hire.

Spiegel delighted in Hollywood, where he took a variety of jobs, including that of translator. He also found enjoyment in the favors of actresses seeking either sex for pleasure or sex as a way of ingratiating themselves with men like Sam who they thought could help their careers.

Unfortunately for Sam, he seemed unable to stop writing bad checks. Hollywood was too small a town for such endeavors, and he was becoming too high profile. He was caught, arrested, and returned to Poland. From there he moved to Berlin, taking a job in their film industry just as Joseph Goebbels was imposing Nazi censorship of imported films. Spiegel tried to work with the Nazi censors until March 3, 1933, the Saturday of the Reichstag fire that set the stage for the anti-Jewish violence to come. He later related:

> I got up late that day, and went around the corner to my barber to get a shave. While he was shaving me, the barber whispered, "Don't go home tonight." That was sufficient warning. Without a hat, and with only a few marks in my pocket, I walked out of the barbershop and went directly to the station without returning home. The banks were closed that day, so I couldn't stop to get money. The train for Vienna crossed the Austrian border at 2:00 A.M. of the following morning. At 6:00 A.M. the borders were closed forever—and thereafter nobody left Germany without the permission and knowledge of the Gestapo.

At 1:00 A.M., while my train was still inside Germany, my house was surrounded by fifty Nazis. They broke in and smashed everything I owned. They wouldn't believe my aged Catholic housekeeper when she said she didn't know where I was, and so they beat her so badly that she spent months thereafter in the hospital. My barber had been a member of that troop.

Spiegel, along with other Jewish refugees, including director Otto Preminger, tried to find work in the French film industry. After getting a job, he began a pattern that would continue through the years. He would befriend the wealthy men in the movies, from producers to financial backers, then use them for his own ends. Frequently this meant having a party where he hired expensive prostitutes and served the finest food, all at his personal expense. Then he would engage his wealthy guests in a game of gin rummy, a game at which he was an expert. He would usually win back the cost of the food and entertainment, sometimes making a small profit on the day. When he lost, he was rarely asked to pay the gambling debt because his guests had enjoyed such a pleasurable evening. Expenses were further reduced when he did not bother to pay the women, the caterers, and anyone else who had serviced the party where the gin rummy winnings went to others.

Ultimately Spiegel returned to the United States as a seasoned professional in the business of making movies, a bad check artist with outstanding warrants for his arrest he chose to ignore, and a love for corrupting the wealthy. He was rightfully convinced that if he could find ways to make many people in positions of power and wealth feel indebted to him, they would do what he asked to return his favors. They would back his pictures, indulge his past (and sometimes current) dishonesty, and give him a status that would otherwise be impossible. (Sam did learn from the past, though. He always kept two stacks of traveler's checks ready for a fast escape if it was ever necessary.) The only question was how to create such an arrangement, and this resolved itself in 1941 when he decided to model his home life after the lifestyles of Hollywood producer Mack Sennett and a New York woman named Polly Adler.

Mack Sennett's parties were legendary among the male power brokers who preceded Spiegel to Hollywood. As Walter Wanger, production manager for producer Adolf Zukor, recalled: "He'd give a dinner party, and if you didn't take the young lady on your right upstairs between the soup and the entree, you were considered a homosexual."

Spiegel decided that his own home would always have similarly classy women available to delight his frequent dinner and card playing guests. They would be there as part of the decor—interior design by Eros. And all of them would be connected to the studios, starlets who understood that by becoming a regular at the parties, contacts could be made, relationships forged, and careers assured. Or not. But the price of admission was a willingness to say "yes," and among those who felt they had nothing to lose and everything to gain was Marilyn Monroe, gamely moving ahead despite her contract being canceled after the first year with Fox.

Sam really knew how to play on other people's weaknesses. He was an inspired pimp. He could create those very high-class mush pits. Women were looking for acting jobs and it was a knee up the ladder.

—Writer Budd Schulberg, as quoted by Spiegel biographer Natasha Fraser-Cavassoni

The decision to enjoy Spiegel's Crescent Drive mansion was a good one for Marilyn's career, such as it was. Among other benefits, she would eventually be introduced to one of the most powerful agents in show business, a dying man who thought he had found the love of his life, despite already having a wife and children. This was Johnny Hyde, and during the time he had left to live, he would become as important in helping Marilyn transition into movies that mattered as Emmeline Snively had been in helping her gain success as a photographer's model.

You can't sleep your way into being a star, though. It takes much, much more. But it helps. A lot of actresses get their first chance that way.

—Marilyn Monroe in a reflective mood

ACT III

Politics Pollutes the Film Industry

Twenty

HUAC

Norma Jean wanted stardom, and sex was as important as talent. She was determined to attend the right producers' parties, to participate in the studio's publicity stunts, to make herself available in whatever way was requested so she could move ahead. But while she saw the hedonistic side of the film industry, powerful men in Washington had been gradually combining fact, fantasy, and the misinterpretation of the events of the day to start an assault on Hollywood.

It is doubtful that Norma Jean had any understanding of the congressional investigating committee known as HUAC, which was a government creation that followed the intense publicity late nineteenth- and early twentieth-century investigative reporters brought to bear on national scandals. Child labor, filthy food processing plants, the spread of disease through sweatshop-manufactured clothing created by women and children, often in ill health, who had to work long hours for low pay, and similar concerns were the subject of exposés that created a national social conscience. Monopolistic practices, the Teapot Dome Scandal, potentially violent political social groups (Bolsheviks, the Ku Klux Klan, German Bunds, anarchists, Communists, and the like), were all threatening the country.

In addition, there were the social conditions that were unique in American history. As World War I veteran, writer, and editor Edmund Wilson wrote of what was taking place in the early 1930s: "There are today in the United States, according to the census director, something like nine million men out of work; our cities are scenes of privation and misery on a scale which sickens the imagination; our agricultural life is bankrupt; our industry in shifting to the South, has reverted almost to the horrible conditions before the Factory Acts, of the England of a hundred years ago, and the fight of the unions there for recognition is all to begin again; so many banks are failing that the newspapers do not dare to print the truth about them. And when we look to South America or to the European countries west of Russia, we see only the same economic chaos, the same lack of capacity or will to deal with it, and the same resultant suffering. May we not well fear that what has broken down, in the course of one catastrophic year, is not simply the machinery of representative government but the capitalist system itself?"

The members of Congress were aware of the problems, including the violent hate groups that were terrorizing parts of the country. Some were outraged at the violence affecting the neighborhoods in their districts. Others were supportive when the group's hatred matched their own, a not infrequent problem with the anti-black, anti-immigrant, anti-Catholic, anti-Semitic members of the Ku Klux Klan.

Legislation to outlaw the hate groups or stop some of the violence was often outside the constitutional mandate of the House of Representatives. Instead, starting after World War I, Congress began making use of the investigative committee to expose regional and national problems. Sometimes the investigations were preliminary to legislation. Other times they were an end in themselves.

The committee that would ultimately impact most heavily on the motion picture industry, pulling Marilyn, her onetime lover, Elia Kazan, her soon-to-be-husband, Arthur Miller, and others of her acquaintance into its vortex, was the House Un-American Activities Committee, generally known as HUAC. It was established in 1937 under the chairmanship of Representative Martin Dies of Texas' Second Congressional District. Dies, an attorney, was a New Deal Democrat who supported Franklin Roosevelt when he won his first election in 1931. However, he was also a racist whose morality seemed to extend only to his biases.

The idea behind HUAC was simple and seemingly laudable. Numerous hate groups were operating on both ends of the political spectrum. Some were engaged in violence against their neighbors. Some were attempting to change the political system. Some were hostile to religious groups whose theologies differed from their own. Stories of lynchings, fire bombings, beatings, and groups living in fear while trying to go about their daily business abounded in the country. Often what passed for law enforcement in a community actually had the police and sheriff's departments complicit in the crimes. And because of constitutional freedoms, such groups could operate with impunity, facing only a local investigation into each individual crime that was committed, or nothing at all. There was no way to expose an entire organization on a local level, and no way to ban a violent organization on a national basis. The congressional committee, by contrast, could investigate at will, bringing light into the darkness.

On August 10, 1938, the *New York Times* quoted Martin Dies, stressing that HUAC would not smear the innocent or engage in character assassination. "It is easy to smear someone's name or reputation by unsupported charges or an unjustified attack, but it is difficult to repair the damage that has been done. When any individual or organization is involved in any charge or attack made in the course of the hearings, that individual or organization will be accorded an opportunity to refute such charge or attack."

In the approximately one year that this noble enterprise had existed, a number of truths became evident despite the rhetoric. First, American right-wing extremism was to be ignored if the extremists supported Dies or his friends. Most blatant was the deliberate disregard of the Ku Klux Klan and similar hate groups. Representatives John S. Wood and John Rankin, both members of HUAC who shared the Dies shift away from Roosevelt, stated: "The threats and intimidations of the Klan are an old American custom, like illegal whisky-making." They were just fun-loving boys from hell, though extremely appreciative of the de facto support of the members of the new committee of Congress. As the Klan's leaders wrote in a telegram to Dies, "Every true American, and that includes every [Ku Klux] Klansman, is behind you and your committee in its effort to turn the country back to the honest, freedom-loving, God-fearing American to whom it belongs."

Seven years later, Representative Emanuel Celler noted that a study of the early years of the Dies committee, undertaken by more than one hundred of the top attorneys in the nation, found that "while giving lip service to impartiality and fair play and proclaiming its devotion to Americanism and American institutions, it used its hearings, the forum provided by Congress, for the dissemination of irresponsible slanders against honest public servants and private individuals and against public-spirited organizations, on testimony consisting of surmise conjecture, unfounded opinion, unsupported conclusions, which no self-respecting, fact-finding agency anywhere would consider—a proceeding wholly unworthy of the committee of the legislative body of a great and free Republic.''

The concern of Representative Celler and the attorneys who evaluated the work of HUAC actually meant nothing. Even as the committee members changed with the years, the targets were almost always men and women guilty of real or imagined slights toward the committee and its values. The number of "bad guys"—individuals who had violated the law or could legitimately be charged with some offense—was laughably small. By contrast, a large number of Americans would have their reputations smeared and their careers horribly altered or ended.

Theater and motion pictures were the focus of the early investigations, sometimes with malice and sometimes without logic. In theory, the two industries could reach and influence millions, a fact that made Dies and his supporters quite wary. The result, among other actions, was an assault on the Federal Theatre Project, a government agency that was part of Roosevelt's New Deal.

In 1938, Dies ordered Hallie Flanagan, chosen in 1935 to head the Federal Theatre Project of the New Deal's Works Progress Administration, to appear before his committee. The plays they produced were ultimately seen by twenty-five million Americans, a fact that led Dies to feel he must question Mrs. Flanagan, an action that served only to reveal the ridiculous bias of the chairman. Among his questions to Mrs. Flanagan was:

Do you not also think that since the Federal Theatre Project is an agency of the Government and that all of our people support it through their tax money, people of different classes, different races, different religions, some who are workers, some who are businessmen, don't you think that that being true that no play should ever be produced which undertakes to portray the interests of one class to the disadvantage of another class, *even though that might be accurate, even though factually there may be justification normally for that,* yet because of the very fact that we are using taxpayer's money to produce plays, do you not think it is questionable whether it is right to produce plays that are biased in favor of one class against another? [emphasis added]

Among those outraged by the reports of what was taking place was a young playwright named Arthur Miller who, along with a friend, Norman Rosten, expressed his feelings through a heavy-handed play so immaturely laden with anger that it is rarely remembered even by Miller buffs. However, while it was an impotent cry against an increasingly powerful body, it would be located years later and used against him. Given the egos and attitudes of Martin Dies and the members of HUAC, only the opening needs to be seen to understand why Miller was facing an unexpectedly hostile future.

The play *Listen, My Children*, was written for the Federal Writers Project and opens with the scene meant as an attack on Dies and HUAC's assault on the nation's artists and writers:

"In the center of the room, in a rocker, sits a man. He is securely tied to a chair, with a gag in his mouth and a bandage tied over his mouth. Water, coming from a pipe near ceiling, trickles on his head. Nearby is a charcoal stove holding branding irons. Two bloodhounds are tied in the corner of room."

Adding to the concerns was FBI director J. Edgar Hoover, who explained his fears of a Communist menace in the film industry during testimony before HUAC on March 26, 1947:

The American communists launched a furtive attack on Hollywood in 1935 by the issuance of a directive calling for concentration in Hollywood. The orders called for action on two fronts: One, an effort to infiltrate the labor unions; two, infiltrate the so-called intellectual and creative fields.

In movie circles, communists developed an effective defense a few years ago in meeting criticism. They would counter with the question, "After all, what is the matter with communism?" It was effective because many persons did not possess adequate knowledge of the subject to give an intelligent answer.

Hoover listed fourteen points that show the "real character" of Communist organizations. Even at the height of interest in left-wing causes fifteen years earlier, the list looks ridiculous when considering the Hollywood writers, producers, directors, and actors who were criticized.

1. Does the group espouse the cause of Americanism or the cause of Soviet Russia?
2. Does the organization feature as speakers at its meeting known Communists, sympathizers, or fellow travelers?
3. Does the organization shift when the party line shifts?
4. Does the organization sponsor causes, campaigns, literature petitions, or other activities sponsored by the party or other front organizations?
5. Is the organization used as a sounding board by or is it endorsed by Communist-controlled labor unions?
6. Does its literature follow the Communist line or is it printed by the Communist press?
7. Does the organization receive consistent favorable mention in the Communist publications?
8. Does the organization present itself to be nonpartisan yet engage in political activities and consistently advocate causes favored by the Communists?
9. Does the organization denounce American and British foreign policy while always lauding Soviet policy?
10. Does the organization utilize Communist "double talk" by referring to Soviet dominated countries as democracies, complaining that the United States is imperialistic and constantly denouncing monopoly-capital?
11. Have outstanding leaders in public life openly renounced affiliation with the organization?
12. Does the organization, if espousing liberal progressive causes, attract well-known honest patriotic liberals or does it denounce well-known liberals?
13. Does the organization have a consistent record of supporting the American viewpoint over the years?
14. Does the organization consider matters now directly related to its avowed purposes and objectives?

And none of the criteria—all of which would add to the committee's assault on Hollywood—had anything to do with breaking federal or state laws. Character would be smeared regardless, as Norma Jean would gradually discover.

Twenty-one

~

The Cheviot Hills Country Club,
August 1947

A decade had passed since Director Hoover and Chairman Dies first focused their attention on the question of the politics of Hollywood. Their concerns were increasing, and many in the film industry were aware that their lives were going to be changed over the legal but currently unpopular activities in which they had engaged when young.

Norma Jean was not among those concerned with Washington, DC committees and the efforts of politicians to gain headlines. On that afternoon in August 1947, she was hot, tired, and hungry—mostly hungry—as she walked the eighteen holes of the Cheviot Hills Country Club golf course. More than fame, fortune, and the attention of the photographers for whom she would smile and pose each time they asked, the newly minted Marilyn Monroe wanted a hamburger.

The celebrity golf tournament was an event that occurred with some frequency in warm, sunny Southern California. The golfers were the established young stars of the day: Duke Wayne, Jimmy Stewart, Johnny Weissmuller, and John Carroll, among others. It was for Carroll that she was pretending to caddy while hoping he didn't hear her rumbling stomach.

Carroll did not expect the starlet to do any real work. At 5 feet 5½ inches tall and just 118 pounds, she was almost a foot shorter than John Carroll, and his oversized clubs weighed nearly as much as she did. Both the actor and the "caddy" understood that the tournament was a way for the studio to generate publicity during the slow summer period. So long as she was cooperative and looked pretty, Carroll would handle the real work of moving his bag of clubs around the course.

Norma Jean's willingness to do anything to get attention was caused in large measure by fear. Marilyn Monroe was about to become a former starlet and show business trivia question unless her agent, Harry Lipton, could hustle another contract for her. In the meantime, she had been placed in the hands of a studio "planter," the member of the publicity department whose job it was to get as many of the new starlets as possible involved in high-profile activities. The attractive young women were provided without charge to conventions involved with some of the same activities to which she had been sent when working with Emmeline Snively. Instead of working for a company displaying at the convention, the starlets might act as greeters and guides, moving about the convention floor, mingling with the attendees and getting their pictures taken with people deemed important by hometown newspapers that would run their photographs in the days that followed. There were starlets at supermarket openings and ground-breaking ceremonies. And that day at the country club, there were starlets serving as caddies who also happily posed for cheesecake images that would be run with a credit including both the starlet's name—e.g., Marilyn Monroe—and studio, such as Twentieth Century-Fox.

Marilyn had been working with a planter for much of the previous year. However, she had more reason than the other starlet "volunteer" caddies—approximately thirty in all at that particular tournament—to do what she could to be noticed. She had two weeks before Fox dropped her contract at the six-month escape clause.

"There were dozens of us on the set," she would later recall of the time when she was first under contract. "Bit players, with a gesture to make and a line or two to recite. A few were young and had nice bosoms; but I knew they were different from me. They didn't have my illusions. My illusions didn't have anything to do with being a fine actress. I knew how third-rate I was. I could actually feel my lack of talent, as if it were cheap clothes I was wearing inside. But my God, how I wanted to learn, to change, to improve! I didn't want anything else. Not men, not money, not love, but the ability to act."

Marilyn viewed her golf tournament appearance as her one chance to connect with someone, anyone, who would give her another break, either with Fox or some other studio. Starlets were hired and fired, rehired and fired all the time. It was a way of keeping costs down for roles that required a pretty face and figure, not skills in acting, and because the money was good even at the low end, many women willingly endured the emotional roller-coaster. That was why she wore a too-tight sweater to the golf tournament, her breasts so cantilevered by her tissue-stuffed bra that no one could miss noticing what she assumed were her most saleable assets.

Marilyn's dress was excessive even by studio publicist standards and they were met with bemusement by John Carroll. He, like the other established stars, had seen such girls before. They were always more determined than talented, frequently allowing themselves to be repeatedly "auditioned" on their backs or on their knees. Even her figure did not impress him. She was the same size 12 as his wife, Lucille Ryman Carroll, a talent coordinator for MGM. Besides, Marilyn had a high, grating voice that made the afternoon a little less pleasant than it might otherwise have been.

Lucille Ryman Carroll saw Marilyn as appealing only in the manner of a pathetic waif. On the one hand, she seemed like a kitten caught in a rainstorm with no place to go for shelter. On the other, she knew how to attract attention, something she obviously desperately wanted.

The pathetic waif image was enhanced when she quietly talked with the Carrolls at the end of the tournament. She and the other starlets joined the actors for drinks and hors d'ouevres, then she confessed to John that she was both hungry and needed a ride home. She had come with another starlet who could not take her back. The actor decided to offer her a ride, never realizing that the obsessive Marilyn Monroe would become a calculating leech until Johnny Hyde entered her life two years later. He also told her he would stop by Musso and Frank's Grill on Hollywood Boulevard where he would buy her the hamburger she craved.

The moment John Carroll bought Marilyn dinner, she thought she understood what was expected. Lucille Ryman Carroll had left the golf tournament in a separate car, a sure sign to Marilyn that the marriage was in trouble and John was looking for action on the side.

Because of the publicity Marilyn Monroe created, the image the various studios projected for her in their biographies and media coordination, and the support of a variety of columnists, it is easy to think of Norma Jean as a victim of sleazy Hollywood. Men used her, both as a child and as an adult, according to what she told reporters. They were callous, manipulative, and determined to get what they could from her before discarding her for the next young, naïve, beautiful woman trying to be a star.

The truth was that Norma Jean committed herself to not only creating Marilyn Monroe but also to doing anything that would help her to survive as she was fighting to get ahead. She stole her foster sister's early childhood to gain sympathy. She lied about her mother. And she decided that sex, for pleasure or payment, was a small price to pay for anything.

Marilyn needed bras and boxes of tissues to better shape the fabric. She needed clothing. And she needed to eat. It was how she handled the latter that was most surprising for the people who interacted with her at the studios.

Each morning, according to some former friends and acquaintances, or several times a week, according to others, Marilyn went out and stood along Hollywood or Santa Monica Boulevard. Within a few minutes, a man would come along and take her to a restaurant to buy her breakfast. Then she would have him come back to her apartment just long enough to give him oral sex as a "thank you." No money was ever exchanged, though men like Milton Berle would give her cash as a "present" when she lived in the Studio Club and went on "dates." Instead, she exchanged sex for breakfast and assumed that any man who wanted to buy her something would expect such a payback.

What Marilyn did not understand was Lucille Ryan's position with MGM. Her job was not to discover new actors. That was the casting director's concern. Instead, she was to locate stars, people who had a unique quality to them and, ideally, were already beginning to make names for themselves in the entertainment world. Then she would sign them to a meaningful MGM contract, becoming their mother confessor, career adviser, and advocate within the studio system.

Lucille was paid big money to assure MGM obtained and regularly used the best talent available. At MGM, and earlier at Warner Brothers, she had handled Janet Leigh, Katherine Hepburn, June Allyson, Lana Turner, and many other stars. The Norma Jean–type studio contract actresses were a dime a dozen. In fact, the only reaction she had to Marilyn that day was to think, "she's a cute little trick."

Lucille Ryman Carroll could not stay long after the tournament because part of her job required her attending plays, nightclub acts, and other events where MGM stars or potential stars were appearing. It was a priority of her life that occupied up to several nights a week.

John was a working actor as well as a successful investor, and together the couple owned a ranch where they raised and trained horses. He was frequently tired in the evening and chose to stay home. Lucille either attended events alone or had a male escort, a common situation in those days. Their marriage was strong and neither needed an affair to compensate for any perceived lack of desirability.

The intensity of Marilyn's appetite in the restaurant caused John to gently question her about her life. She had obviously been having trouble making ends meet, though he did not realize that she was recklessly buying cosmetics, tight sweaters, and other items that had little to do with necessity. All he knew was that even at the seventy-five dollars a week starting pay for starlets, someone like Marilyn was doing extremely well. Starting pay for contract actors was still twenty-five dollars more than the pay provided to journalists on the area papers, and they could afford to feed, clothe, house, and educate a family of four. This young actress who claimed she was living from paycheck to paycheck should not have had problems. But instead of living more frugally and setting aside part of her income, everything went to buy her fantasy. She had nothing for when the paychecks stopped.

When John took Marilyn home from the restaurant, she invited him to come inside. "How can I thank you if you don't come in?" she asked John.

"You're thanking me now," he told her.

Marilyn did not realize that John Carroll was happily married and had no interest in taking advantage of her. Instead he gave her twenty dollars, all the money he had left in his wallet, and went home to discuss Monroe with his wife. Making a decision they would both regret, they decided to treat her a little like a daughter, eventually letting her use Lucille's in-town apartment.

As the Carrolls would later discover, Norma Jean never liked the idea of ruining a good story with the truth. She was an orphan, she told them. She was the victim of incest. She was raped at the age of nine. She was having sex daily by the time she was eleven years old. She was in a dozen or more foster homes.

The stories were all tragic and used whenever she needed sympathy. Rarely was there truth to them.

Marilyn, desperate to stay in the industry, began to use her new contacts without their permission. She went uninvited to see Lucille at MGM, trying to gain sympathy by saying she was an orphan. She was forced to admit that she did have Harry Lipton as an agent for her film work, and Lucille explained to her that Lipton was the person who should be looking after her. Lucille told her to ask Lipton to contact the casting department personnel who worked with new talent. If there was work with MGM, that was the way to get it.

Marilyn was frustrated with the response, though at that point Lucille was not trying to get rid of Monroe. She simply was the wrong person at MGM and she had no influence over how the studio structured its talent acquisition. Marilyn needed to use an agent, either Lipton or someone else, because the personal touch would not work.

John Carroll was working at Republic Pictures when Marilyn approached Lucille, and when Lucille would not help her at MGM, she thought John might be more amenable. He was kinder than his wife, or perhaps not as busy. In any case, he agreed to have lunch with her at the Lakeside Yacht Club. They talked through lunch and lingered after the meal while Marilyn again tried to get the help she wanted, still not realizing he was the wrong person.

Fortunately for Marilyn, there were other men around the yacht club, and she thought at least one of them might play "rescuer" to her "damsel in distress." She talked with them when she finished with John, explaining that she was being forced from where she was living and would need a place to stay in the valley where she could be near both Warner Brothers Studios and Universal Pictures.

One of the men told Marilyn that he knew a woman who had a home in the area who would be returning to the East soon and wanted a housesitter to look after her plants and generally take care of the place. There would be no rent charged.

The situation should have been ideal. Marilyn still needed to get back in the film business, but with free rent she could be a model for still photographers to earn enough money for food. What she didn't expect was that a modeling fee of fifteen dollars would put her in physical jeopardy.

Banking was different in the 1940s than it is today. Checks could only be cashed in the bank that issued them or in a bank where the recipient had an account. There were no check guarantee cards, and a stranger to a bank, offering a check on a different bank, had to have a depositor vouch for him or her.

At the same time, department stores were quite lax. The Los Angeles stores kept blank checks from every bank in the area as a convenience for their customers. Anyone could walk in, make a purchase, then request a check from whatever bank they desired. The person would fill out the check for the amount owed, it would be accepted, and the customer would leave with the merchandise. No identification of any sort was necessary. The checks were always honored by the stores.

When Marilyn wanted clothing and was short of cash, she would go into a department store, name any bank she could think of, fill out the check, and go home with the clothing. The fact that she had no checking accounts in any of the banks did not matter to her. The stores gave her the checks, she filled them out, and took home the clothing. It was theft, but Marilyn knew she would not be remembered; furthermore, the stores did not share information about customers who had cheated them in that way, which enabled her to go elsewhere when she felt she might be discovered.

The fifteen-dollar check was for a modeling job, and though Marilyn lacked a bank account, she thought cashing it should be easy. She was walking along Hollywood Boulevard and entered the first bank she saw, surprised when the teller refused to honor it.

Marilyn went to a second bank, and a third. Each time the story was the same. She had no account. She had no one with an account to vouch for her. The bank would not cash the check.

Frustrated and desperate, Marilyn tearfully approached a police officer walking a beat in the area. She told him her plight and he gallantly agreed to help. In exchange for full personal information about her (name, address, telephone number) he walked her into a bank where he had an account. He agreed to be responsible if the check bounced and the bank accepted it, giving Marilyn her fifteen dollars.

There are two different stories of what happened later that night. What is certain is that the police officer was a serial rapist and Marilyn Monroe was targeted as his next victim. What is uncertain are the details.

The *Hollywood Citizen-News* reported that while Marilyn attended a late-night party, the off-duty police officer had staked out her home and was waiting for her. She went inside, closing and locking the screen door. After a few moments, he cut through the screen, stepped inside, and attempted to rape her. Marilyn, screaming, fled to the street, alerting neighbors, who called the police.

The other story, probably the more accurate, had her in bed when the man broke inside. Either way, Marilyn had to flee and never again felt safe in the house.

The attempted rape and the aftermath were true. What is uncertain (since, again, there are two stories) is exactly what happened next.

In one story, Marilyn called the compassionate Carrolls, who offered to move her into a little-used apartment Lucille maintained on the northeast corner of La Cienega and Fountain boulevards. It was one Lucille rented when John was in the service and in which they lived together while building their ranch house. They no longer needed the apartment but Lucille found it convenient to keep it. The drive to the ranch was relatively long and there were nights when going home meant getting little sleep. That was why, when she was up late in the city scouting nightclub acts and attending theater performances by MGM stars, she would go to the nearby apartment to sleep. The apartment seemed an ideal place for Marilyn to stay until she felt safe returning to where she had been living.

In the second story, one John Carroll told friends, he spotted Marilyn at a drive-in restaurant following the attempted rape. Her car was obviously filled with her possessions and she told him she was giving up on acting and moving to San Francisco. She hadn't found work, was deeply depressed, and did not want to go back to the place where she was housesitting.

Whatever the truth, John and Lucille Ryman Carroll were about to endure several months of Good Samaritan nightmares after inviting her to live with them at their ranch. In the end they would spend much of their time plotting to rid themselves of what they came to call the Marilyn Monroe problem. Their hostility, along with Sam Spiegel's parties, Johnny Hyde's obsessive love, and John Huston's gambling would eventually bring her to the most important audition of her life.

Twenty-two

The Ryman/Carroll Ranch

Marilyn Monroe was the guest from hell. She seemed to have her own personal agenda and was determined to have the Carrolls adapt to her desires, fantasies, and eccentricities.

At first Marilyn was given a room in what might be considered the business side of the ranch house. John Carroll used one of the bedrooms as his office, maintaining a desk, telephone, dictation equipment, and male secretary during the day. The section of the house was the center of his business outside of his work as an actor, and Marilyn's room was across from John's work area.

The first night John and Marilyn were in the house together, the Carrolls got a glimpse of Marilyn's unconventional lifestyle. She took off her clothes and began working in her room. Lucille closed the door, Marilyn claiming embarrassment because she had not thought about the fact that John was not only in the house but directly across from her. However, when she thought Lucille was in a different part of the house, she again opened the bedroom door. She was still naked.

"John, I think our stray kitten is an alley cat," Lucille told her husband.

Friends of the Carrolls were amused by the stories John and Lucille were telling about Marilyn, the seeming sexual predator in starving waif clothes. They were especially amused by the fact that John was her target. His success in films came because he was a song-and-dance man who looked like Clark Gable without having to be paid the salary of Clark Gable. His eventual decline in films, after his one "famous" picture, *The Dancing Pirate*, was introduced in the new Technicolor process, came because he had none of Gable's talent.

It was during the period when he had acting success, with its accompanying female adulation, that John became uncomfortable with aggressive women. He did not like being approached because he knew the woman always had a hidden agenda, planning to use him and anyone else she thought could help her, in order to gain a role in a picture. As a result, John only became sexually aroused when he felt himself in control of the relationship. He had to be the pursuer, the seducer, the taker. A naked Marilyn desperately trying to get a new studio contract was exactly the behavior he hated in women.

Not that John would be totally immune to her actions. Police officer (and later private investigator) Fred Otash, a close friend of John Carroll's, said that John admitted to going to bed with Marilyn at least once. However, Otash was certain that the stories of anything more—and there were rumors of a long-term affair in Hollywood after Norma Jean became famous—were nonsense. John was not always faithful to Lucille, but he loved and respected her. So far as those closest to him were aware, there was no way the rumors of anything more than a one-night stand could be true.

The problems weren't just sexual. Marilyn needed to be close to potential jobs and was delighted to spend weeknights in Lucille's two-bedroom, two-bath apartment during the week, driving out to the ranch only on weekends. She quickly learned, in part from private, intense talks with Lucille, that the sexual aggression was not appreciated, and she had enough of a survival sense to back off John. Instead, she became a user in other ways.

Marilyn's car was frequently in the repair shop, a problem she had had the day of the golf tournament and the reason she needed a ride. The cost of completed repairs was close to eighty dollars—two weeks' take-home pay for many workers at the time and more than Norma Jean had earned from posing for still photographers while trying to get back in films.

Lucille knew that the sooner Marilyn was working full time, the sooner she and John could get rid of her. She gave Marilyn eighty dollars, telling her to pay for her car and pay off cleaning bills and other small debts she had.

Shortly after giving Marilyn the money, Lucille needed to use the apartment for a day or two. This should have been no problem, because Marilyn had been told that she could have exclusive use of only one bedroom and bath, as well as shared use of the kitchen and living room. The other bedroom and bath were to be left exclusively for the Carrolls.

When Lucille walked into the apartment, she found brassieres hanging throughout both bathrooms. Marilyn, she learned, had taken the eighty dollars, walked to Hollywood Boulevard, and bought twenty-five brassieres for three dollars each. Not knowing they were clean and ready to wear, she washed them, making it impossible for Lucille to force their return to the store.

Marilyn also had extensive tissue paper, though this was a common sight. Bras were shapeless in the 1940s. It was common for women to stuff them with paper, regardless of the size of their breasts. The paper added stiffness to the bras, which in turn made the woman's chest more shapely.

"This is the only thing anyone ever looks at," Marilyn told Lucille. "If I didn't have my tight sweaters. . . . These [the paper-stuffed bras] will push them out. I can walk down Hollywood Boulevard and everyone will look at me."

Lucille later recalled, "I said, 'Honey, you don't want to do that.'"

"And she said, 'Yes, I do. I want everybody to look at me.'"

Marilyn was not the only troublesome actress in the Carrolls' life together over the years. They had had problems with other actors they had tried to help. Just the year before Marilyn came into their lives, an actress from Chicago arrived in Hollywood to be the lead in the MGM production of *Madame Bovary*. The Carrolls tried to assist her, especially when she became extremely nervous about the wardrobe tests she was about to take. To their dismay, a friend of the actress came from Chicago to "help" by bringing her drugs to calm her down. The actress took the drugs and could not function at all the morning of her test. The studio had to let her go.

At least Marilyn seemed serious about acting during this period, and Lucille helped her enroll in a drama program held at MGM. The young actors all learned by doing. The idea was to experience the full range of a production. If there was a play with very small parts and lead roles, one night a student might do the lead, and another perform what might be little more than a walk-on. Each student played every role to get the full experience of both the play and the parts as they came together during the performance.

Marilyn would have nothing to do with the program as it was presented. She arrived late so she could make an entrance. She constantly complained when asked to do any small parts. She only wanted to be the lead, something specifically not allowed within the program. The staff wanted to throw her out, especially since she usually failed to memorize her lines regardless of the part. They did not need to take action, though, for she only lasted a month.

During this same period Marilyn enrolled in the Actors Lab, one of many Los Angeles acting schools, this one "stealing" the same name as a famous school in New York. She seemed to accept the fact that the Carrolls would help her meet her bills, constantly "borrowing" money she had no real thought of returning.

The Carrolls realized that they had taken Marilyn into their home and their lives to keep her off the streets. They also began to realize that she did not care. Marilyn was out of their control and, if they were honest with themselves, was taking control of their lives. Marilyn was acting like an irresponsible adolescent daughter over whom they had no influence. For her part, Marilyn seemed to view the Carrolls as overly indulgent parents who might bluster about her habits but would ultimately give in to her requests.

Marilyn pushed the relationship with the Carrolls beyond appropriate limits. She began calling John and Lucille four times a day, even though they specifically told her not to bother them at work. She ate at the Lakeside Yacht Club because either John or some other member would pay the tab. She upset John's mother, an elderly devout Catholic who also lived with them, with her exaggerated sexuality around the house. Then she pretended not to understand when the older woman complained about her deliberate sexual acting out.

Weekends could provide a respite from Marilyn since she frequently would spend the time with still photographers. They took hundreds of photographs of her, and her face and figure ended up on the covers and inside pages of numerous magazines of the day. These were usually pulp magazines—low-cost niche market magazines printed on cheap paper. These included true detective stories, confession magazines, men's interest and humor magazines, and the like. Marilyn was mostly used for the humor publications which combined "naughty" jokes with risqué cartoons and cheesecake photos. The pay per photo was low, both for the photographer and the model, but the volume used was high, and young Los Angeles photographers trying to gain publication credits frequently sold to them. Marilyn was both an enthusiastic model and a willing sex partner when the sessions stretched overnight.

The Carrolls solved part of their problems with Marilyn by moving her to a different room, away from John's office. They couldn't change her behavior, but they at least could prevent her constantly exposing herself to John.

The move seemed to be solely for Marilyn's benefit. She was given what others might consider a suite—a living room, bedroom, and bath. In truth, it kept her more isolated. Unfortunately, it also seemed to fuel her imagination.

Years later, both in conversations related by John Carroll's friend, private investigator Fred Otash, and in a series of interviews Lucille taped with author Donald Spoto for his biography of Marilyn and preserved in the archives in the Margaret Herrick Library, Lucille related an odd conversation. Marilyn said she had a personal question to ask, one apparently based on her reading of the household and not on an incident that preceded it. Marilyn wanted to know if Lucille would give John a divorce—presumably so he could marry her.

Marilyn explained that she didn't think Lucille loved John. Her idea of a loving marriage was what Jim Dougherty had discussed with her in terms of their relationship. Lucille was frequently not at home when John was there, especially in the evenings when, in Marilyn's view, a wife would be fixing her husband dinner and otherwise caring for him. By contrast, Lucille was frequently out in the evening, going to theaters and nightclubs, often with a male escort (though this was because either a single woman alone was not allowed into a club or it might call attention to her position with MGM).

Lucille tried to explain to Marilyn, a woman of experiences that nurtured cynicism, not sophistication, that having an escort as part of her job did not mean that she was involved with them. She explained that John had his own life and had no interest in trying to go out with her every night to watch acts that mattered only to her studio. Then Marilyn made a telling remark about how she understood love.

A man was in love with Marilyn when he focused his time and attention on her. John Carroll was patient with her. John Carroll tried to advise her concerning personal matters for which she needed help. That must mean he was in love with her, just as the photographers who gave her attention and support by their pictures advancing her fledgling career must have been in love with her.

Marilyn told Lucille that she was going to ask John to marry her, still not understanding the reality of the situation. She had planned the proposal for a while but wanted to talk with Lucille first.

The reality of the Ryman/Carroll marriage was that it was still rather fresh—the couple having first met in 1945—but John was no saint. He admitted to Fred Otash that he had cheated one time with Marilyn, though he was insistent it had never happened again. Apparently he thought she was like so many other starlets: willing to give someone higher up on the studio ladder a sexual experience with no strings attached other than the understanding that the man would help when and where he could. Instead, to Marilyn, marriage was the next logical step.

In later years, Jim Dougherty discussed his surprise at Norma Jean's suggestion that they live together after their divorce. She had thought it would be nice to be with a friend, have sex, and generally behave as a married couple when it suited her and have no constraints on her activities when she went with others. Marriage was not a long-term commitment. Marriage was a stepping stone, and John Carroll seemed just fine as the next step. Fortunately, she said none of this to Lucille Ryman, nor did she mention that she had had sex with John.

Lucille recognized that it was her husband's job to talk sense to Marilyn. She knew that John had no interest in leaving her, and certainly not for a predatory starlet. However, she told Marilyn that if her husband asked for a divorce, she would give it to him. Then she called her husband down from his office and asked him to talk with Marilyn privately. When they were finished, John said, "Lucille, I want you to help me with this little girl. I've explained to her that I want to help her get started, to fulfill her dream. And that she wants to be a star, and we all hope that she becomes a star. But very few people do, and if there is any way we can help her, we will. But my interest in her and her interest in me should be strictly a fatherly one. And if she has misinterpreted my feelings, I want her to know."

The incident was one of those dramatic moments the film industry love. You could almost imagine Marilyn with a slightly red nose, puffy eyes, and tear-stained cheeks, her expression a brave one as the music, probably supplied by violins, swelled in the background.

This was not a Technicolor moment, however. This was real life, and in real life, Marilyn was a user who discovered she had one less man to service. So long as she got the Carrolls' continued help, she was happy. To not have to consider marrying John Carroll as a career move was actually a great relief.

Marilyn was becoming increasingly costly for the Carrolls, financially as well as emotionally. Lucille decided to help Marilyn get on her feet by establishing for her what was, at the time, considered a management agreement. In Lucille's mind, it was probably more an allowance to give Marilyn the income to stay out of their lives as much as possible.

The contract was an odd one because Marilyn, never a fan of her real name, Norma Jean, decided to change her name to Journey Evers. The management contract she signed—in September 1947 according to some sources; early in December 1947, according to others—was between John Carroll (Lucille was not a legal party to the matter, presumably to avoid any hint of conflict of interest with her job at MGM) and Norma Jeane Dougherty, also known as Journey Evers. The Carrolls arranged for Marilyn to receive one hundred dollars a week. The money was from the Carrolls' considerable resources and was paid from Lucille's MGM office. Marilyn's agent was to receive 10 percent of the money as it was repaid, and it was to begin to be repaid when Marilyn was again working. Harry Lipton would lose nothing he might earn, but at no time did the Carrolls think they were backing a future star. They were just creating a situation that would enable Marilyn to support herself.

The money, and Lucille's paying six months' rent (three hundred dollars) in advance, enabled Marilyn to move out of the Carrolls' homes.

There was further help for Marilyn, and it would reveal the reality of her acting ability. Harry Hayden and Lila Bliss conducted acting classes for the stage and operated the Bliss-Hayden Miniature Theater. It was there that the students could practice their newly learned skills. Some would go on to professional stage work. Some would go into the movies. Lucille had helped her friends by having an occasional exceptional actor come over to MGM to audition, as well as to learn how the studio operated. She asked their help with Marilyn and they willingly cast her in a production of one of the least known of Broadway productions, *Glamour Preferred*, written by Florence Ryerson and Colin Clements. It was an odd choice by most standards: a comedy so weak that the professionals on Broadway could only sustain it for eleven performances before being forced to close. However, there is a chance that the rights were cheap and the theater owners may have felt it was a good play for unskilled amateurs and semi-professionals. (Marilyn had been fired, after all.)

Marilyn and an actress named Jane Weeks were both cast as the second leads, scheduled to appear on alternating nights. The play opened on October 12, 1947, and ran through November 2. Marilyn stayed with the company for eight months and appeared again from mid-August 1948 through September 12, 1948, in the George S. Kaufman/Edna Ferber play *Stage Door*.

There are some factual issues that have been challenged with discussion of the time on stage. One story has her failing miserably after just two performances in *Glamour Preferred*. Another has her doing well enough that it was hoped talent scouts would be in the audience and return her to the movies. Instead, multimillionaire Huntington Hartford (A&P Tea Company heir) came backstage to ask her out.

Ignoring the issue of when she appeared and how often, the stage experience taught Marilyn and others who observed her an important lesson. Marilyn was not an actress in the manner of those who learn on the stage, then transition to films. She could learn her lines with no trouble at this early stage in her career. She could memorize the entire script and have a feel for how the story could be conveyed to the audience. But Marilyn was intensely insecure.

Part of the insecurity was legendary. Marilyn would spend hours making changes in her personal appearance before she left home, invariably showing up late, and frequently going immediately to where she could check and fix her appearance. She frequently put on makeup, removed it, then started fresh. This deep insecurity carried over into her acting. Not only did she arrive late enough that the start of the play might have to be delayed several minutes, upsetting the rest of the cast; she also sometimes stammered and appeared uncertain of her lines. When lines were not delivered as rehearsed, the rest of the cast was thrown and even the best plays suffered. A bad play, like *Glamour Preferred*, could be ruined.

The theater work revealed to Marilyn and the professionals around her that she could only handle film work. She could memorize a script but she could only sustain character for a few minutes at most. She knew how to handle the dialogue, a skill that, as with all actors, improved over time. She knew how to project a searing sexuality to the camera and thus to the audience; and at her best, it seemed impossible to look at anyone else in the scene. But Marilyn's talents were never transferable to live theater. She could not continually sustain a character throughout an entire act on the stage. Her future would solely be in films.

Twenty-three

Joe Schenck

Joe Schenck was something of a hero and something of an embarrassment in 1947 when he first met the twenty-one-year-old Norma Jean on the lot of his studio, Twentieth Century-Fox. Schenck had been born in Rybinsk, Russia, in 1878, two generations before the actress he first noticed from his limousine. He was a man who, along with his brother Nicholas, had worked in various businesses before settling on the entertainment field to make their fortune. They were barely in their twenties when they owned and operated New Jersey's Palisades Amusement Park, promoting it in the then new way of having a motion picture placement deal when the pioneering serial *The Perils of Pauline* included footage of the park. That business also brought them into association with Marcus Loew who owned a chain of theaters before moving to Los Angeles and helping to create what became MGM studios.

Joe Schenck married into early show business royalty. His wife was Norma Talmadge, the actress Norma Jean's mother so admired, and his brother-in-law was Buster Keaton. He became an independent producer, then grew rich running United Artists, Twentieth Century Productions, and in 1935, after a two-studio merger, Twentieth Century-Fox.

Schenck's career was tainted in the early 1940s when he essentially took the fall for a number of studio executives who had been paying bribes to the stagehands' union leadership of Willie Bioff and George Browne. The two thugs from Chicago, working with leaders of organized crime, had created an extortion racket that began with the theater chain owners. The theaters paid "protection" or found themselves with stink bombs rolled into the aisles during the showing of popular films. Cans of film were also "lost" and/or mysterious fires would take place in the projection booths.

Eventually two illegal rackets were being practiced simultaneously in Hollywood. The union extorted money for labor peace, Joe Schenck and his Twentieth Century-Fox paying fifty thousand dollars a year, for example. And the studio heads bribed the union leadership, paying the union leaders to dissuade the rank and file from striking even when the issues with which the laborers and technicians were concerned were valid ones. Both actions were illegal, and everyone was careful to arrange bookkeeping and special accounts to avoid the Internal Revenue Service.

Joe Schenck's actions were not covered as well as he hoped, and he was eventually forced to serve four months and five days in the U.S. Correction Institute in Danbury, Connecticut, the federal prison. However, because of the outrageous actions of all involved, and because Schenck had obviously taken the fall for all the large studio heads who were equally guilty though not charged, President Truman eventually pardoned him two years before he met Norma Jean.

Back, free, in Hollywood, Joe Schenck again lived the lifestyle of the Hollywood moguls who enjoyed good food, good cigars, gambling, and women, all in the privacy of one of their mansions. He held regular Saturday-night poker games that had expensive food, fine cigars, and starlets who could be counted on for their beauty and friendliness. The starlets served the executives but were also expected to adjourn with them to one of the bedrooms when requested. There was no coercion. The women understood when invited that their futures would get a boost up if they pleased the men.

Some stories have Schenck becoming friendly with Norma Jean prior to her attending one of his parties. Other stories say that Pat De Cicco, the creator of Bon Bons (a chocolate-covered ice cream ball that was sold through movie theaters), introduced Norma Jean to Schenck after meeting her through his friend John Carroll. This story placed the meeting in February 1948, after which she attended one of the Schenck parties.

However the original meeting took place, Norma Jean became a friend of Schenck's, frequently being seen at his house during the card parties as well as dining with him in restaurants and occasionally back in his mansion. They were never lovers, but friends knew that Norma Jean occasionally had sex with him, her typical way of thanking men who helped her.

Joe Schenck apparently grew genuinely fond of Norma Jean and wanted to help her career. There was never a love affair, but since Norma Jean was no longer wanted by Zanuck, and Columbia Pictures head Harry Cohn was one of the regular poker players at Schenck's house, the producer called his friend about Norma Jean. Cohn agreed to give her six months—not seven years—but at $125 a week. She would start March 9, 1948, though only after further changing her hair. The hairline was made higher through electrolysis, and then the color was stripped from her naturally brown/blonde dyed hair. A combination of ammonia and hydrogen peroxide created the platinum blonde look that would be hers the rest of her life.

There were no parts for Norma Jean, no pictures just waiting for a failed Fox starlet, but that was normal for the new hires. What mattered most, in hindsight, were the two relationships that resulted from the change in studio—vocal coach Fred Karger and acting coach Natasha Lytess.

Columbia Pictures was headed by the notorious Harry Cohn. His skills as a businessman in the film industry were without question. He and his brother Jack founded the studio in 1924, and though it was always smaller than some of the other major companies, it became a major force, both with the success of its films and with Harry Cohn's skill at discovering new talent.

Cohn's abuse of both male and female actors and his use of the casting couch were legendary. Hedda Hopper commented that you had to stand in line to hate him. When he died, comedian Red Skelton went to the funeral with actress Amanda Blake and both were shocked to see an estimated five thousand people present for the service. Skelton looked around and said, "It just goes to show you that when you give the public what it wants, they all turn out."

In 1948 Cohn was at the peak of his power but saw no future in Norma Jean/Marilyn Monroe, even though he went along with Joe Schenck and gave her a contract. Allegedly one of the reasons, besides doing a favor for a friend, was that Norma Jean considered herself a Christian Scientist at the time, the same faith as Cohn's wife. Ultimately, after casting the actress who would be credited from then on as Marilyn Monroe in one picture during her six months, a film called *Ladies of the Chorus*, he referred to the actress as a "fat pig," and questioned whether the director had bedded her, the only reason Cohn could see for giving her a part. He bluntly assessed her acting skills as essentially nonexistent and refused to extend her contract past the first six months.

Cohn may have hated Monroe but her training at Columbia assured the further development of her skills, such as they were at the time. This was the result of vocal coach Fred Karger and acting coach Natasha Lytess. The first provided her with real skills and a romantic interlude. The latter changed how she approached a character, instilled in her a work ethic, and ultimately was a nuisance to every director with whom Marilyn worked in the next few years.

It is easy to stereotype Fred Karger, the man Marilyn claimed was her first love despite having been married to Jim Dougherty. He was thirty-two, more than a decade older than she, well established, and living a life that was partially public—he had a band that played many area society functions, and was a musician, composer, and occasional vocal coach for Columbia Pictures—and partially private. The latter included an extended family living together on Harper Avenue. There was Fred and his younger sister Mary Karger Short, both divorced, both with children (he had a young daughter named Terry; she had a boy and a girl named Bennett and Anne), and their widowed mother, Anne. Fred and Mary's father, Max, had been one of the founders of Metro (MGM after mergers) but had died when Fred was five.

For a time, Max and Anne Karger had raised their children in the Hollywood Hotel before they had the home on Harper. The widowed Anne delighted in having her children and grandchildren with her, and Fred knew that any of his or Mary's friends were always welcome. That was why, when he learned the tragic personal life of the new starlet whose voice he was to train, Fred felt comfortable inviting her to his house.

Marilyn understood Fred's importance to her career with Columbia since she had no intention of being fired from this, her second contract in the industry. She wanted him to feel sorry for her, so she pulled her usual "broke waif" routine, despite an income that would have been the envy of almost every blue-collar family in America. He met her one day buying raw hamburger and she led him to believe that her diet consisted of raw hamburger and black coffee for dinner, and grapefruit, coffee, and cottage cheese for the other meals. It was a way of saving on expenses while keeping her figure—or so she lied. She did not explain about the meals purchased for her by men who picked her up on the streets, a way of stretching her income that had not fully stopped when John Carroll and Lucille Ryman took her in to their home.

Fred was concerned enough about Marilyn's circumstances that he drove her home—or so he thought. Marilyn was living in the Studio Club, and everyone knew its cost, the quality of the living arrangements, and its safety for young woman. She did not tell him to go to the Studio Club, though. One of the other starlets had been living in a vermin-infested apartment building that the landlord never bothered repairing, knowing that actors with almost no money would tolerate the surroundings if their living quarters were cheap enough. She had shown Monroe the building and, like Beebe Goddard's troubled childhood, Marilyn adopted it as her own when Fred wanted to drive her home. She gave him the address, watched his shock as he let her off, then went inside the lobby until he drove off, after which she walked to her apartment in the Studio Club.

ℬ

Note: Just as Marilyn Monroe was a created entity, her history often changing at the drop of a publicist's pen, so were her living/loving circumstances at various times early in her movie career. Different books and magazine articles, by reputable authors striving for accuracy, have come up with different versions of Marilyn's life, each believed by its author to be factual. This is one of the aspects of her biography that makes her life so interesting. It is also why Internet junkies find what seem to be dueling web logs, each purporting to have *the answer*, whatever that is.

The Fred Karger relationship falls into this category. One story has Marilyn living in the disreputable apartment where Fred stopped by when she called in sick. He was upset with the place, and after beginning to have an affair with her, had her move into a better building near his family's home.

Another story has Fred telling Marilyn that he could never marry her because if anything happened to him, she would be left to raise his *son* and Karger did not feel she would be a good influence on him. But Terry was a girl, and this story further errs in saying that he was still married to his previous wife, Patti, though all other sources indicate he was divorced when he met Marilyn.

It is also possible that some of the confusion came because Marilyn lied, a not uncommon occurrence, as has been noted. Between meeting Fred Karger and falling passionately in love with him, and her moving on to other men, Karger suddenly became a heinous villain in the retelling. Among those to whom she spoke about him was director Elia Kazan, who met Marilyn in 1950 and had a brief affair with her. In his memoirs *A Life*, he wrote of the Monroe/Karger relationship as she told it to him:

> Fred was a musician, scrawny but able in love. She came as many as three times with him in one go. He was vulgar and coarse and scornful with her. He said she was no good for anything except fucking. He found her dress "cheap." He told her her breasts were too big. He didn't like to sleep in the same bed with her. He thought her beneath conversation, said she was stupid and only good for one thing, which he didn't regard too highly. He boasted that he never had to make a pass at a woman—they all came after him.

When examining the retelling of incidents in Marilyn Monroe's early years for which she was the initial source, the truth will always be a challengeable judgment call.

ॐ

Fred would not learn about the deception until he had been dating Marilyn and she decided that she was in love with him. However, he was mature enough and had enough experience with aggressive studio starlets to know that Marilyn was not someone about whom he could get serious, even as he brought her into his family. The others did not care, though: Mary saw in Marilyn the sister she never had, since they were the same age and shared some of the same experiences; and Anne accepted her almost as a daughter. Well after Fred Karger moved on to dating others, Anne and Marilyn retained a friendship.

But that was later. In these early days Marilyn made the mistake with Fred that she had with John Carroll. Any man who helps her without demanding sex in return must be in love with her.

Fred Karger may have personally been interested in Marilyn, but his primary involvement was as her vocal coach under contract for Columbia Pictures. His job was to teach her how to improve her abilities as a singer, a skill she hoped would lead to renewal of her contract. He also was both sufficiently professional and personally circumspect that he never allowed physical intimacy to be a part of his work at Columbia, and he never admitted to or even hinted at sex being a part of their frequent dates. The fact that they spent two- and three-day weekends in each other's company meant they had enjoyed sex together, but unlike men such as director Elia Kazan, Karger felt that intimacy was a totally private matter.

Marilyn seemed to ignore the fact that Karger would be intensely involved with her voice work, an area of great need, and have an intense, helping relationship with her so long as they both worked for Columbia. There was no question that he was personally interested in her, perhaps to the point of considering her as a wife, and that reality was reinforced in Marilyn's mind when he intervened with Dr. Walter Taylor, a Los Angeles orthodontist. Taylor was an alcoholic whose drinking was destroying his kidneys and liver, but he had worked with many of the both young and established actors. He understood their need to be attractive before the camera, especially if they were new in their contract. They could not be using any unnecessary oral correction devices, since these might prevent their taking a role or even appearing in the background. That was why he fashioned a readily removable retainer for Marilyn that would gradually eliminate her slight overbite. The device easily slipped in and out of her mouth, and she was to wear it except when going on the soundstage.

It is unclear if Fred was going to pay for the orthodontia. He bought her no special gifts that she ever mentioned, so it is presumed that he knew the doctor would be sympathetic to a starlet who had recently been out of work for six months. And in the end, the work was apparently done at no cost. Certainly Taylor and Monroe became friends, the actress visiting him in the hospital when he finally was dying from his alcoholism. But even that introduction by Karger would have been an act of love, in Marilyn's mind.

Columbia's contract required Marilyn to work on her singing with Karger. She had a pleasant voice, could adequately carry a tune, but she was unable to properly project her voice, to deliver a song in a way that would capture the audience. As with John Carroll, Marilyn seemed to feel that the attention she received from Karger reflected more of an interest in her than just a working relationship.

What Marilyn seemed unable to recognize was the type of man Fred Karger had become during his first marriage. The fact that Karger had custody of his young daughter should have warned Marilyn that he would not be committing to a relationship with an actress on the make. It was rare for a judge to award the father the custody of his child. The presumption of the day was that only a mother could properly raise a child, and only a mother *should* raise a daughter. Yet there was Fred's child, living happily with Fred, his sister Mary and her children, and their mother, Anne. Marilyn would never fit in that mix other than as a visitor and a friend.

Marilyn and Fred continued to date, and Marilyn held out hope that he might change his mind about marrying her when she let it be known that her home really was at the Studio Club. For a divorced man with custody of a young daughter, a studio employee who had watched his share of over-the-top ambitious actresses do anything to get ahead, and a bandleader who was regularly approached by women who ignored their marriages for a chance to bed a celebrity, knowledge of the lie was too much. He would never trust Marilyn as a potential spouse. Instead, when actress Jane Wyman ended her studio-arranged marriage to actor Ronald Reagan, she and Karger married, then divorced, remarried, and divorced. He was on his third (or fourth, depending upon how you count) wife when he died in 1979, seventeen years to the day after Marilyn.

Note: There are facts concerning the Studio Club, and there are facts concerning Marilyn Monroe. Author Maurice Zolotow was one of the first of the truly serious biographers who worked with Marilyn while she was alive. His was what might be called an authorized biography—a book he wrote about her, but with regular access for interviews. He assumed that whatever she had to say about her life was true, and some of the details were verifiable. Others . . .

Zolotow has Fred Karger telephoning Florence Williams, who managed the Studio Club, to arrange for Marilyn to live there for twelve dollars a week. She had a roommate, Clarice Evans, who was then an opera student, and it is unclear what financial arrangements Evans made. In this telling, Marilyn moved in on June 3, 1948.

Lucille Ryman explained in interviews after Marilyn's death that it was she who had provided the money for Marilyn to go to the Studio Club on June 9, 1948. However, almost two years earlier, in July 1946, Marilyn, still living as Norma Jean, had left her mother in Ana Lower's apartment and given herself the freedom of her own place in the Studio Club. The 1946 move seems to have been her first stay and the confusion may have been the use of first one name and then the other, much as there are references to Norma Jean(e) Mortenson(sen) and Baker in the years prior to the name change.

Perhaps part of Marilyn's confusion about Fred's interest in her life came because everyone at Columbia treated her differently than she had experienced at Twentieth Century-Fox. Each starlet seemed to matter, and the studio executives kept in contact with them on the lot. That was why there were individual lessons more often than the group classes common with many of the other studios. And among the individual lessons were those Marilyn received from the arrogant, autocratic, intensely insecure Natasha Lytess, a German immigrant who liked to claim she was Russian.

The seemingly interdependent relationship that developed between Natasha Lytess and Marilyn Monroe has led to all manner of speculation about the women, their sexual orientation, and who manipulated whom. The truth has not always been easy to discover, in large part because, in the 1940s, it was shockingly embarrassing.

The 1930s was a time when a number of European men and women active in the arts fled their countries of origin because of the impending war and the growing violence against Jews and other minorities. Among these were Bruno and Liesl Frank, Bertolt Brecht, Heinrich Mann, Bruno Walter, Thomas Mann, Lion Feuchtwanger (whose writing was among the first to be burned by the Nazis in the 1930s), and Natasha Lytess.

The signal that it was time to flee Germany came in March 1933. On February 27 of that year, an arsonist burned the Reichstag building in Berlin. The arson, a crime whose perpetrator was unknown, enabled Adolf Hitler to claim that it was part of a Communist plot. The fire was actually a signal that would trigger a workers' revolution against President Hindenburg and his government.

Hitler was persuasive enough that President Hindenburg declared a state of emergency during which all civil liberties were suspended. This allowed Hitler to send his elite forces to stop all opposition through the destruction of their writing, political campaign materials, and other items, as well as to order mass arrests of those who opposed him or were perceived to oppose him. Among those who fled as a result were Bruno and Liesl Frank, actor, director, and producer Max (Goldman) Reinhardt, and various actors, writers, and others in the arts who formed a loose association devoted to Reinhardt's ideas about theater and motion pictures.

Natasha Lytess filled an awkward position among the German immigrants (by the end of World War II she often claimed to be Russian so she would not be faced with anti-German bias). She was an ardent advocate of Reinhardt's concept that the actor was the most important person in a play. Everyone and everything else—writer, director, composer, set designer, technicians, and others—had to focus on the actor. This was in radical contrast to the American film industry, where the actors re-created the director's vision of the story being told.

In addition to her work, Natasha was an embarrassment to some because of her personal life. References to her life often mention her "marriage" to Bruno Frank or the fact that they were lovers. They had a daughter, Barbara, whom she raised alone when her lover died in 1945, but his obituaries—and there were many because he worked in film, as a novelist, and in other areas of the arts—spoke only of his wife, Liesl. His affair and his daughter by Natasha Lytess, with whom he apparently was living at the end of his life, was a dirty little secret.

The issue of Natasha Lytess's sex life was not yet of interest when she was first working at Columbia. Instead, it was her methods. They followed a style that pleased Reinhardt and the Austro-German audiences who came to see his work, but they were inappropriate for much of American film. As a result, some of the actors who were exposed to Lytess's training at Columbia had the sense to ignore her words when they were in conflict with those of the film director. Marilyn, by contrast, lacked the judgment and experience, never having acted prior to her time at Twentieth Century-Fox. She was impressed by the seeming self-assuredness and forceful attitude of the acting coach, and her early films at Columbia showed the problem.

First, there was the Monroe dialogue. Watching her early films, especially her first movie for Columbia when she had just started working with

Lytess and was determined to do whatever the coach said was best, is a painful experience. Her words are exaggerated, overenunciated, and it is only with the comedy that it inadvertently works. The careful speech seems like what one might hear from a woman of limited education and experience trying to sound as though she had been born into high society. It could have been deemed a cute affectation or part of a deliberately created comic character had she not used the same exaggerated pronunciations for every role, serious or humorous.

Almost as bad were Marilyn's gestures. They were often exaggerated, almost like poses, the result of constant practice on her own, with Lytess, and with anyone else who would work with her. She was determined to improve her skills, to not lose the Columbia contract, to become successful. Unfortunately, she came to use Lytess instead of the film director, demanding retakes when Lytess said she was not doing as well as the coach felt she should be doing, or not acting as the director desired.

The relationship with Natasha Lytess began at a difficult time for Marilyn. "Aunt" Ana Lower died during the summer of 1948, and it was not long after the funeral that Marilyn was going to be cast in what would prove to be her only film at Columbia: *Ladies of the Chorus*. Producer Harry Romm did not feel she had the skill to handle the role, that of a burlesque star named Peggy. In addition to acting and dancing, she had to sing two songs, "Anyone Can Tell I Love You" and "Every Baby Needs a Da-Da-Daddy." Fred Karger would handle the singing. Natasha Lytess was assigned to make her an actor.

The first meeting of the two women seemed to establish the emotional relationship they would have for the next several years. Marilyn was extremely insecure and very much aware that the small role she had in the rather short B-movie Columbia would be shooting would also make or break her career with the studio. She had been lucky to run a year with her previous contract. She knew she was being looked at by Harry Cohn as someone who would go six months and then be out.

Marilyn was twenty-five minutes late to her first appointment with the acting coach. She arrived dressed in a manner that might have pleased some of the men—white shirt tied around the middle and white slacks—but

Lytess saw the outfit as cheaply provocative. She was convinced that Marilyn Monroe was just another starlet who was to be transformed into an actress long enough to appear in a movie before fading into oblivion. The fact that she was disrespectful by her lateness did not help.

It is not known how Marilyn viewed Natasha other than as a critical player in her life's drama as she fought to stay at the studio. Lytess has often been described as volatile and tense, her hair graying and somewhat unkempt, and her demeanor autocratic. In truth, if unposed photographs of her are to be believed, she was an attractive woman whose appearance would be enjoyable to watch on the stage or screen. She did not have the in-your-face look and attitude of Marilyn on the make, but was more like the attractive girl next door who is transformed as the years pass from one of the neighborhood kids to a desirable young woman.

Disappointed in the look Marilyn apparently thought was appropriate for the first meeting, Natasha decided to see how she handled herself with a cold script reading. Marilyn was handed pages of a part in which Rita Hayworth had acted. Marilyn spoke with her mouth nearly closed, her voice described as almost a squeak by both Lytess and by a number of other people who heard her early reading. But it was Lytess she wanted to impress, to please, and it was Lytess, Marilyn later explained, who "made me feel so shallow and without talent."

> My illusions didn't have anything to do with being a fine actress. I knew how third rate I was. I could actually feel my lack of talent, as if it were cheap clothes I was wearing inside. But, my God, how I wanted to learn, to change, to improve! I didn't want anything else. Not men, not money, not love, but the ability to act.
>
> —Marilyn Monroe

Immediately Lytess began showing Marilyn what to do. She was to open her mouth wide and speak much louder than she had been. She was to not just memorize her lines but know them cold. Because the actor was the center of everything, Marilyn needed to be so comfortable with the script that she could ignore it and express the soul of the character.

The concept Natasha tried to convey might have worked for European drama on a stage where the director let the actor control the play, but it was exaggerating the importance of the film in which Monroe was to be featured. *Ladies of the Chorus* was a low-budget movie with a trite script and an eleven-day shooting schedule.

The show was simple. Marilyn was cast as Peggy Martin, a burlesque dancer like her mother, May (played by Adele Jergens). May had been a star, but her time in the spotlight was over. She and Peggy—young, ambitious, and wanting to emulate her mother's success—dance in the chorus until the day May has a fight with Bubbles LaRue (Marjorie Hoshelle), one of the featured dancers. Bubble walks out and, of course, Peggy is tapped to take her place and becomes a big success.

(The story requires a little historic understanding today. This was an era when burlesque was still a bawdy type of show that included social satire, beautiful women, and far less clothing than many thought proper. The young women were not prostitutes and certainly not as sexually active as Monroe and many of the other starlets. They were hardworking professionals on one of the lower rungs of show business, and they often learned with difficulty that it was best to fall in love within the industry. Many of the burlesque houses were frequented by wealthy, young, college-educated men who fell in love with the beautiful, friendly dancers. They would date and, occasionally, decide to marry. However, social snobbery was such that the young women, no matter how intelligent, sophisticated, and proper they might be, were still condemned for their work.)

In the movie, May had been hurt when she was young by such a love affair and marriage, and she does not want to see Peggy hurt the same way by wealthy Randy Carroll (Rand Brooks) who claims to be in love with her. This concern comes to a head when May and Peggy are invited to Randy's home by his mother (played by Nana Bryant). She has learned of the love affair, knows nothing of Peggy's life, and wants to celebrate her son's engagement. The lavish affair includes a band, and the bandleader recognizes Peggy, is delighted to see her, and reveals what seems to be an embarrassing secret that will end the engagement.

Randy's mother is more mature than May's fears. She has recognized that, regardless of Peggy's past, the young woman truly loves her son as he loves her, and that the couple is right for one another. She decides to prevent any future problems by lying about her own life. Although she has never been involved with theater, she invents a secret past for herself that she reveals that night to her friends: she, too, was in show business before her marriage and she is delighted that she has that in common with her future daughter-in-law.

May, relieved, also decides to get married. However, this time she chooses a comic in the show with whom she has been close for years, and mother and daughter each find happiness.

Lytess helped Marilyn with the limited acting and Fred Karger handled the singing. Marilyn had a limited range, a soft voice, and phrasing that spoke the words but conveyed neither personality nor emotion. Marilyn met with Karger daily during this period and practiced her two songs every night. The effort improved her work but not enough for Karger to relax. He coordinated her appearance with the sound recording engineer so her voice would be enhanced wherever that was necessary.

Ladies of the Chorus received mostly tepid reviews at best, when critics even bothered with the trite concept presented by weak actors. However, the *Motion Picture Herald*, essentially an industry trade paper, had a reviewer named Tibor Krekes who took the film for what it was: a job for a new hire in the industry. He said that Marilyn's singing was "one of the bright spots," and noted that she was pretty, had a pleasing voice, and showed promise. It was the type of review that is often used with phrases out of context to promote a show. In a weak movie, even a "bright spot" can be rather dim. However, Marilyn ignored all reality and clung to the hope she took from the Krekes review. She was certain Columbia would keep her for another six months. Instead, barely having improved and not liked by Harry Cohn, Marilyn was fired.

Twenty-four

Johnny Hyde, *Love Happy*, and Oh That Wiggle When She Walked

The publicity about her is far in excess of her talents, but not in excess of her sexual impact.

—Cary Grant

It was television that almost cost Norma Jean Mortenson her career as Marilyn Monroe. Had she been born even five years later than she was, her effort to move from successful photographer's model to screen actress probably would have left her with only stag films greeting her with open arms (and naked bodies). This was because Marilyn's contracts with Twentieth Century-Fox and Columbia came at the end of the era of the B-movie as it was then known.

The B-movie was to a major motion picture what a group of top college senior basketball players is to the rookies of the National Basketball Association. The college players may be as good as or better than the NBA rookies, but they are getting the experience they need to be most effective in professional play.

The B-movie actors were often those who were quite competent and soon to be major stars. They also included actors like Marilyn, handsome men and beautiful women who had mastered memorizing their lines, walking and talking at the same time, and not upstaging the stars. However, no one knew if they could perform well enough for a serious career, and they were often placed in roles where they were part of crowd scenes, chorus lines, and the like.

Ladies of the Chorus was a typical B-movie. The audience enjoyed a confection they would likely soon forget. The songs were pleasant but unmemorable. The costumes and dancing were adequately revealing to rivet a man's attention on those areas either uncovered or encased in a manner that enhanced every curve. And the story had enough romance—the working girl triumphing over the bigotry of class consciousness—to delight the women in the audience. The brilliance, or lack thereof, of the actors was not a concern. It was a date movie, not too heavy for a couple in the early stages of romance and not so enthralling that a more committed couple couldn't go up to the theater balcony, sit in the seats below the projection booth, and "make out."

The problem for such pictures was that television was quickly replacing the B-movie as entertainment. A couple seeking intimacy would still go to a heavily promoted film, but it was easier and cheaper to sit on a living room couch and watch television when the receivers became reasonable enough to purchase. There would be a brief renewed life for B-movies to be shown at drive-in theaters, but these were usually genre films—science fiction, horror, Westerns—and not the musicals that had dominated past low-budget production.

The next two films in which Marilyn appeared revealed the reality of the changing movie business. In one she thrived, despite a role of almost meaningless proportions; and in the other . . . she gained a screen credit. But first Marilyn met Johnny Hyde.

It was New Year's Eve 1948, and 1949 would be starting without a contract. Marilyn could do nothing about the latter, but she could relax with Sam Spiegel and the powerful men and often-willing women who attended his lavish year-end party.

Spiegel's home wasn't a castle, and the former Russian immigrant acrobat Ivan Haidabura was an unlikely visiting Prince Charming. He had come to America to work the vaudeville circuit at the urging of promoter William Morris. Haidabura was part of a family of acrobats, but he was tired of the travel and the hard work, and in 1926, the year Marilyn was born, Morris mentioned to Ivan that he needed to expand his booking agency office staff. The acrobat knew all sides of the business, had observed the many touring acts, and was a natural for the job at a time when he was tired of performing.

Ivan changed his name to Johnny Hyde, and he was astute enough to stay ahead of the changing entertainment industry. He was booking talent for the new radio shows that featured live music in the broadcast studios and productions similar to the mysteries, soap operas, and comedies that would later dominate television. He was also active in the movie industry as it passed from silent to sound, and as the actors began looking to not only be a part of the contract player system but also to challenge it when their success brought large sums of money to the box office.

Hyde was physically small—just five feet tall—with a passion for promotion and a lust for women. He had become vice-president of the William Morris Agency by 1948, and he represented the giants of the era—Bob Hope, Rita Hayworth, Betty Hutton, Lana Turner, Esther Williams, and numerous others. He was the first agent to break the seven-year studio contract system and get clients who were proven top box-office draws both higher pay and a piece of the action. He followed the example of the mother of child actress Shirley Temple in insisting the contract assured a client would get paid every time a movie was shown in any way. The studios agreed because they were thinking movie theater showing only. Hyde had no idea what the future might hold for electronics and film reproduction, but his prescience assured that when the actors he represented had their movies shown on television, and later on video and DVD, they would be paid once again. Today the residuals, as they are called, unrelated to the initial movie might exceed the pay the actor first received.

Hyde, fifty-three years old, a regular guest of Sam Spiegel and partaker in Sam's women, was long emotionally estranged from his wife, Mozelle, and seemed to be seeking one last "romance" before he died. His heart was bad, his body deteriorating, and he knew it might only be a matter of weeks or months before he died. New Year's Eve 1948 he thought he might have found the woman who would be his final bedmate in life.

Marilyn understood Johnny Hyde and men like him. He was lean, balding, and, though vibrant, obviously ailing. Even those who did not know he had to see his doctor weekly for constant medical adjustments to keep him alive could see that he was sick. He also was an ardent, aggressive lover who was not as well equipped as he fantasized. He could perform as admirably as a younger man with a good heart, but he often came up "short" in his ability to give as much satisfaction as he gained from a woman. This was why Marilyn admitted to friends that, when they had sex, she often complained that he was hurting her, that he was just too big. And Hyde, not recognizing her effort to please him emotionally, was both proud and concerned lest he cause her long-term discomfort.

Oddly, like seemingly every other man who had a long-term interest in her life, Marilyn was verbally abused by Johnny. In hindsight, though, he seems to have been less interested in controlling Marilyn than in being brutally honest. She was a lousy actress. She sounded more like she was reading a script than being a character. But there was something about her appearance on the screen that was visually exciting, a fact that could make her a Hollywood star.

(This concept of the difference between an actor and a star would soon become more apparent as television programming expanded. Television is a close, intimate medium, especially in the early days when a 10-inch or 12-inch screen was considered "large." A skilled actor could become a believable character in a television movie or series, and that actor could become equally popular and believable when projected in a theater. But a star who was riveting when viewed larger-than-life could seem an incompetent joke when viewed on television. This is even more obvious today when the early films, all made specifically for viewing projected in a theater, are seen on a tape or DVD on a television set or similar size monitor. Marilyn's work, viewed in a theater at the time it was originally filmed, hinted at star quality. That same work, viewed on television, shows how lacking she really was at that stage in her career.)

Marilyn knew that Johnny believed in her star quality, that he looked at her dream and was convinced it could be, and would be, a reality. But as an actress . . . she was a "chump."

Perhaps it was because he first met Marilyn at a Sam Spiegel party that Johnny thought of her as empty-headed and loose-moraled. She had a limited education, was focused on acting over any other interests, and was one of the girls Spiegel's regulars liked to joke about. Whatever the case, when

Johnny called a young woman a "chump"—and he made clear to Marilyn that this was what she was in his mind—it meant she was just another actress who would do anything to get ahead. The fact that Marilyn never sold her body in exchange for a part did not change the fact that she rarely said no to a man's request.

It is doubtful that Johnny Hyde took Marilyn to one of the available Spiegel guest bedrooms that New Year's Eve, but his attraction to her was obvious. Mozelle was not at the party and would soon be filing for a divorce. Johnny was going to Palm Springs for a few days' rest at the start of the new year and asked Marilyn to join him. She agreed.

Marilyn soon became Johnny Hyde's "devoted companion," director Elia Kazan mentioned years later, commenting on his first meeting with Marilyn and Johnny Hyde. She was "a fair-haired young woman, not blond, not straw, not platinum as she later would be, but a lovely natural light brown. She had the classic good looks of the all-American small-town girl, and when she looked at Johnny, she gave him that dazed starlet look of unqualified adoration and utter dependence. Clearly she lived by his protection and was sure of his devotion . . ."

Johnny was also devoted to Marilyn and to helping her achieve success as a star because she was not what he considered an actress. As he explained to Marilyn, "It's hard for a star to get an eating job. A star is only good as a star. You don't fit into anything less. Yes, it's there. I can feel it. I see a hundred actresses a week. They haven't got what you have. Do you know what I'm talking about?"

Marilyn probably didn't understand what Johnny meant, but she did understand that he was a man who could benefit her in ways no one else could. He was willing to leave his wife for her, and when she repeatedly refused to marry him, he made the ultimate Hollywood sacrifice. He allowed himself no other mistresses until the day he died.

"Prince Charming" took Marilyn to live in a North Palm Drive home he rented to give his adultery a respectable touch. And from there, Johnny Hyde became Marilyn's personal cheerleader, her agent, mentor, teacher, lover, friend, and confidant. He bought her contract from Harry Lipton and began knocking on doors. He was one of the highest-powered agents in Hollywood and the majority of his clients did extremely well. No one wanted Marilyn other than Johnny, however, and when he wasn't around, friends derisively called the couple the Beauty and the Beast.

It was at this time, when Marilyn was not yet on her way to success, that another actor was leaving the types of films that had made him and his brothers famous. Groucho Marx, whose career would soar when he switched to television, was making one last Marx Brothers movie. It was their thirteenth, and if anything made it unlucky as per the superstition, it was that it was made at all. The script was weak, as was the humor; the music was adequate, and Harpo, Chico, and Groucho Marx did as little as possible to provoke interest or laughter.

The story starts with Groucho as private investigator Sam Grunion, who has spent the previous several years trying to find the million-dollar Roman-off diamonds. Ilona Massey plays bad girl Madama Egelichi, who had the jewels sealed in a sardine can marked with a black cross and smuggled into the United States. Harpo Marx, the always-silent comic, steals the can along with other food needed for a group of starving entertainers rehearsing the show *Love Happy*, which is also the film's title.

The movie is ultimately a series of slapstick chase scenes following Harpo's feeding the sardines to a cat, then discovering and taking the jewels. The can is found and Madama Egelichi's gang is out to find the jewels.

Harpo gives the diamond necklace to leading lady Vera-Ellen, whose character, Maggie Phillips, had had a fight with her boyfriend. Harpo, convinced that the necklace is beautiful but worthless, thinks it will make her happy. Maggie is delighted, but certain it is fake, places it on the theater piano where Chico, who is playing, pockets it. Madama Egelichi spots what is happening and sends more bad guys into the fray. Everyone ends up on the roof of the building; Harpo steals the jewels from Groucho's pocket, and Groucho's character, Sam Grunion, marries Madama Egelichi.

At their madcap best, the Marx Brothers did not need a good script to get laughs. *Love Happy* had a bad script and bored stars. Groucho acted as narrator and often did his part alone, as did Chico and Harpo, their scenes edited together to look as though they were performing at the same time.

The money paid the actors was according to the quality of the film. Groucho routinely received $70,000 a movie, an enormous sum at the time. For *Love Happy* he accepted $35,000. His only perquisite was that one scene, later cut to thirty-eight seconds' duration, would involve sexual slapstick. The person chosen for this scene was Marilyn, and the limited involvement provided unexpected benefits far exceeding the length and importance of her role.

As Marilyn related to Ben Hecht,

Someone I met at a lunch counter told me they were making retakes on a movie called *Love Happy* and needed a girl for a bit part. Harpo and Groucho Marx were in the movie.

I went on the set and found the producer Lester Cowan in charge. He was a small man with dark, sad eyes. He introduced me to Groucho and Harpo Marx. It was like meeting familiar characters out of Mother Goose. There they were with the same happy, crazy look I had seen on the screen. They both smiled at me as if I were a piece of French pastry.

"This is the young lady for the office bit," said Mr. Cowan. Groucho stared thoughtfully at me.

"Can you walk?" he demanded.

I nodded.

"I am not referring to the type of walking my Tante Zippa has mastered," said Groucho. "This role calls for a young lady who can walk by me in such a manner as to arouse my elderly libido [he was 58 at the time] and cause smoke to issue from my ears."

Harpo honked a horn at the end of his cane and grinned at me.

I walked the way Groucho wanted.

"Exceedingly well done," he beamed.

Harpo's horn honked three times, and he stuck his fingers in his mouth and blew a piercing whistle.

"Walk again," said Mr. Cowan.

I walked up and down in front of the three men. They stood grinning.

"It's Mae West, Theda Bara, and Bo Peep all rolled into one," said Groucho. "We shoot the scene tomorrow morning. Come early."

"And don't do any walking in any unpoliced areas," said Harpo.

Groucho told much the same story as Marilyn concerning her audition, but not the unspoken (at the time) decision for choosing her. According to Groucho's biographer, Richard Anobile, Groucho related, "Boy, did I want to fuck her. She wore this dress with bare tits. . . . She was goddam beautiful.

I may have tried to lay her once, but I didn't get anywhere with her . . . She was the most beautiful girl I ever saw in my life."

Columnist Earl Wilson told a slightly different story, though whether it came from Marilyn, the studio publicists, or a combination thereof is unknown. Wilson said:

> One day she met Louis Shurr, the Hollywood agent who keeps a lot of mink coats for emergencies, and without so much as offering her a coat he suggested she go to see producer Lester Cowan.
>
> Groucho Marx was there, too.
>
> Groucho said, "You get behind me and walk like I do."
>
> Groucho did a girlish swagger, very much exaggerated. She did it, and they said, "You start tomorrow."

And then there was the second story Marilyn told years later. "There were three girls there and Groucho had us each walk away from him. I was the only one he asked to do it twice. Then he whispered in my ear, 'You have the prettiest ass in the business.' I'm sure he meant it in the nicest way."

Groucho, knowing the script was the weakest of all the movies the brothers had made, improvised dialogue and arranged a camera angle that he thought showed the young actress's only asset. As played on the screen, Marilyn walks into Detective Grunion's office, her hips in motion, her cleavage well exposed. "Is there anything I can do for you?" asks Groucho. Then, leering at her, he adds, "What a ridiculous statement."

"Mr. Grunion, I want you to help me . . ." says Marilyn. "Some men are following me."

Groucho works his eyebrows and says, "Really? I can't understand why."

Since Marilyn was the best reason to see the film, Groucho knew to take advantage of her. Her part had nothing to do with the plot. It was a sight gag inserted to get a laugh at the expense of a pretty girl. The fee was five hundred dollars and the credits state, "Introducing Marilyn Monroe," even though she had had bit parts in three previous pictures and only thirty-eight seconds in *Love Happy*.

What made *Love Happy* different was that it was a film of desperation. Chico was in over his head with gambling debts and needed the money from a movie to pay off his creditors, presumably organized criminals who would cripple or kill him as an example to others. The money to pay for the film ran out, so the producers used product placements to meet their financial needs. That is why, at the end of the movie, the scene shot on the roof of a building has lingering moments on signs advertising the companies that paid to get such attention—Bulova watches, Kool cigarettes, Baby Ruth candy bars, Fisk, Mobil Oil, and Wheaties.

In addition, producer Lester Cowan paid Marilyn another three hundred dollars to pose for publicity photos (none of which had to do with her scene), and another hundred dollars a week to go on a promotional tour. The weather in much of the country was expected to be cold, and both Johnny Hyde and Natasha Lytess had Marilyn take high-necked blouses, sweaters, wool suits, and a jacket, none of them expecting to have her arrive in New York City during a major heat wave. The publicist, upon seeing Marilyn sweating profusely in her inappropriate but form-fitting clothing, arranged for her to be photographed eating three ice cream cones. The publicity shot, sent to papers throughout the country, had a caption reading, "Marilyn Monroe: the hottest thing in Hollywood, cooling off." Similar pictures were taken in such major release cities as Cleveland and Chicago before she finished the publicity tour.

Marilyn was also nicknamed the "Woo Woo Girl" and the "Mmmmm Girl."

It was unusual hype in Hollywood for so limited an actress in so short a scene in so weak a movie, but Johnny Hyde, who had attended an advance showing of the movie, knew she was being used to distract potential viewers from the generally poor reviews. No one thought she was anything more than a body to be exploited, like dozens of other equally attractive, frequently more talented young women.

Ironically, the sexploitation of the *Love Happy* role was a time that revealed a very different image of Monroe. Marilyn understood that when she was sent on tour, she would arrive with an entourage, be greeted by reporters and photographers, and be expected to act as an imperious beauty. Photo opportunities were deliberately planned in advance. They ranged from cheesecake to showing the star appearing briefly at a hospital, orphanage, or similar location.

Marilyn was given the star treatment to gain publicity for the film, but she did not follow the script. In at least two cities—Newark, New Jersey, and Oak Park, Illinois—Marilyn was taken to facilities that touched her heart. One was an orphanage, the other a clinic for the low-income sick and disabled. Instead of taking a few pictures, then rushing on to meet her schedule, Marilyn would not leave. She asked the photographers to stop shooting pictures, then began talking with and shaking the hands of every child in each place. They were sick, hurting, and lonely, all emotions she understood well from her own childhood in turmoil. She felt a closeness to them, a genuine compassion from when, as Norma Jean, she had been shuffled among various living arrangements. She had grown intensely bitter about the way she was treated as a child and wanted to be certain that the children she encountered knew at least one glamorous adult understood and cared.

Years later there would be many stories about Marilyn's lateness on the set. She always had one excuse or another for why she would make interviewers, cast, crew, and anyone else wait as long as two hours for her. Often these were jokes, such as explaining that she was not too late; the entire film crew was too early. At other times co-workers and friends would claim that she was extremely insecure and perhaps showing the early stages of some serious emotional disorder.

The truth was quite different. In her early years as a model and actress, Marilyn had been grateful for any part, generally treated with respect by her fellow cast members, and often nurtured by older actors who remembered their own struggles early in their careers. She also was personally treated as an object to be used, attending lavish parties where she made important contacts, yet knowing that, though the truth was unspoken, her continued presence was based on her willingness to provide men with oral sex. They were aroused by her body. They respected the fact that she never traded sexual favors for a role in a film, a not-uncommon situation for starlets. But they also knew that anyone could bed her given the right circumstances, and in any given week the right circumstances seemed to fall into place with some frequency.

Marilyn never complained about what was happening. She accepted it as the reality for a woman trying to succeed in a business ruled by powerful, amoral men. But she was inwardly bitter and sought revenge in a way that could hurt the film industry power brokers almost as much as castration:

she deliberately cost them money by wasting the expensive time of fellow cast members and the crew. In a moment of bitter confession she commented, "I feel a queer satisfaction in punishing the people who are wanting me now. But it's not them I'm really punishing. It's the long-ago people who didn't want Norma Jeane . . . the later I am, the happier Norma Jeane grows."

Twenty-five

She Got Naked and Almost Nobody Noticed

I don't want to tell everybody who interviews me the same thing.
I want them all to have something new and different and exclusive.

—Marilyn Monroe speaking to Pete Martin for
his book *Will Acting Spoil Marilyn Monroe?*

The story was pure Monroe, which meant it changed with the telling. Always she was the victim of circumstances: rent problems, car problems, no studio job, etc. Always she was out of control because of some special need, some special circumstance. And always the revelation would shatter what was still a nonexistent career.

First, the facts: Marilyn Monroe had been a nude model for Earl Moran. The illustrator made extensive photographs of her posing without clothes, as he apparently did with other models. Then, when he needed to paint the human figure, he could go to his collection of images and not have to pay someone to pose again and again. He might paint the woman's face. He might create a face from his imagination. But he maintained files of images, including nudes, as did many other illustrators.

Moran was a true professional, which meant that he did not try to sell the photos for extra money. Even if that had been a consideration, he was too well paid for his paintings to lose credibility with his models. However, because neither Norma Jean nor Earl Moran ever talked about the posing she did during their approximately four years of working together, knowledge of the images came forty years later. It was 1987, and *Playboy* was able to publish them from the estate of the late artist. But until then, Marilyn's biographers followed her lead and told the story of the damsel in distress who exposed her body for a photograph that became the image known around the world. They did not know about Earl Moran's pictures, and they did not realize that Marilyn had talked about her posing when almost no one had previously noticed.

For Ben Hecht, Marilyn said that her car was repossessed when she was out of work. Suddenly she could not get to the studios for casting calls. She contacted the sheriff and the company that did the repossessing, neither able to help her. She thought of calling millionaires she had met, then rejected the idea. Sad and frustrated, she said, ". . . all I could do was throw myself on the bed and start crying. I would cry and yell and beat the wall with my fists as if I were trying to break out of someplace." She talked of going hungry, of wishing she was dead. And then the phone rang.

Tom Kelley, a studio owner for whom she had posed in the past, told her that he had a job for her and it paid fifty dollars. She explained what had happened and said, "For fifty dollars, I am ready to jump off a roof."

Kelley explained that the photos would be nudes for a calendar. He told her ". . . they will not be vulgar. You're ideal for the job not only because you have a fine shape but you're unknown. Nobody'll recognize you."

Marilyn went to the studio and posed for the photographs. Her only concern, she claimed, was what would happen when she became an actress, a star, and somebody recognized her on the calendar.

For Pete Martin, Marilyn said, "I was behind in my rent at the Hollywood Studio Club where girls live who hope to crash the movies. You're only supposed to get one week behind in your rent at the club, but they must have felt sorry for me because they'd given me three warnings. A lot of photographers had asked me to pose in the nude, but I'd always said, 'No.' I was getting five dollars an hour for plain modeling, but the price for nude modeling was fifty an hour. So I called Tom Kelley, a photographer I knew, and said, 'They're kicking me out of here. How soon can we do it?' He said, 'We can do it tomorrow.'"

There were two poses, according to this story, both made in the presence of Tom's assistant, Natalie. One photo had her sitting up and the other had her lying down. She preferred the latter.

For George Barris, the story Marilyn told was one of desperation. She was nearly broke, she said, not mentioning either being behind in her rent or the repossession of her car. "I posed for Mr. Kelley two hours and signed the model release, 'Mona Monroe.' I don't know why, except I may have wanted to protect myself. I was nervous, embarrassed, even ashamed of what I had done, and I did not want my name to appear on that model release."

Tom Kelley, speaking for the first time in 1964, had a very different story of his relationship with Marilyn. He explained that he first met her by and in an accident. It was autumn of 1947 and he was driving east on the Sunset Strip when he saw two smashed cars and several people standing around at Sunset Plaza Drive near the LaRue restaurant. He was formerly a news photographer for the Associated Press and even though he had a commercial studio, he still routinely pulled over to look at any accident, fire, or similar occurrence.

Kelley saw that there had been an accident with rather severe damage to the car of the driver who was at fault. This turned out to be Marilyn, and she was standing with the irate owner of the vehicle she had struck and a police officer who had arrived at the scene.

Kelley hung around the crash scene, then talked with the frustrated Marilyn. She told him that she had been on her way to audition for a play, and he saw that she was dressed like every other actress just starting her career. Her dress was too tight and matched with unusually high heels, the combination meant to show off her body. She was also broke, another common trait of beginners.

Kelley gave Monroe five dollars and his business card. He told her to take a cab to where she had to go, then return his money whenever she could.

Two years passed. Kelley's studio was hired to photograph a billboard for Pabst beer. He told the modeling agency with which he worked the type of model he needed and he was sent Marilyn for consideration. He had no recollection that they had ever met, and even if he remembered the incident, she looked different: her hair was now dyed a reddish-blond, then had been curled and fluffed around her face in a style popular at the time.

Marilyn did remember Kelley, remembered that she had never repaid his kindness, but said nothing about either fact. She was also not ready for the image he needed. She had put on makeup that was too heavy, much as she had done for her first screen test.

Natalie, Kelley's assistant, took Marilyn into the dressing room, helped her to get ready, changed her makeup and fixed her hair. She wore a bathing suit and posed with a beach ball as though she was outdoors. The session lasted an hour, and though Marilyn was offered periodic chances to rest, she kept working, kept holding the ball at an angle that Kelley knew had to be tiring. However, each time he suggested she rest, Marilyn insisted she was fine, an unusual act of professionalism on the part of a model. Her willingness to give him maximum effort so impressed him that he talked with her about an assignment he had from a calendar company that needed nude images of beautiful women.

Marilyn well knew from her work with Earl Moran that there was a market for artistic nudes. He and many other illustrators maintained photo files to help them with magazine, calendar, and similar assignments. During the approximately four years she worked for him, Marilyn was one of several models who were photographed nude, the images filed and used for reference. The photos were never published. The paintings based on the photos usually had the appearance so changed that no one would recognize the model(s). And always the work was tasteful, in contrast with the deliberate sexual imagery of pornography. For models like Marilyn, the nude sessions were a way of earning at least double the usual posing rates. For illustrators like Moran, having nude sessions reduced costs, since he could work from a file instead of having to hire a model each time he received a new assignment calling for a nude image.

Marilyn never mentioned the nude sessions. She knew that they were a part of the business, nothing to be ashamed of, and nothing others would ever see unless she deliberately asked for a print or had Moran give her a copy of the illustration based on her body. In fact, it was not until 1987, well after both Monroe and Moran were dead, that the estate sold some of the images to *Playboy* magazine, which ran a spread of the reference nudes Moran had maintained.

When Marilyn agreed to pose nude for Tom Kelley, she knew he was on specific assignment for calendar images to be published by John Baumgarth of John Baumgarth & Son, a lithography and art calendar print shop located in the Chicago suburb of Melrose Park. The calendar, like numerous others, was usually a simple affair. There would be a photograph at the top—nudes for male businesses such as auto repair shops, gasoline stations, manufacturing plants, construction site shacks, and the like, and other images, such as pets, landscapes, and urban scenes for homes and business offices. Below the photograph would be a pad of tear-off pieces of paper, each with a full month on it. The single photo and the simple tear-off pad kept costs to a minimum and let the calendars sell for from fifty cents to a dollar, including those custom printed with the name and address of a business that wanted to advertise itself by giving the calendar to customers at Christmastime.

The calendar images never showed pubic hair, a critical concern. Nudes that were deemed artistic by a committee working for the U.S. Postal Service could be sent through the mail. Such matters as form, light and shadow, and symmetry were all considered in the same manner as a painting. The nudes Tom Kelley had been hired to take had to be sent by mail. Both he and Natalie were careful to check the angle from which Marilyn would be recorded by the camera, but also constantly checking with both their eyes and the image framed in the tripod mounted 8 × 10 Deardorf View Camera he was using for his client.

It was 7:00 P.M. Friday, May 27, 1948, when Marilyn arrived at Tom Kelley's studio for the two-hour session. She was wearing red high heels, a low-cut blouse, and rolled-up blue jeans. Her only nervousness came from not wanting to hurt her acting career—if she ever had one truly develop—and from wanting to be paid that night. She was reassured on both counts. Kelley was legitimate and had both the model release and the check in hand for when the session was over. He also knew that no one recognized the models used on the calendars unless someone specifically talked about the work.

Natalie took Marilyn into the dressing room where Monroe changed into a robe that was loosely tied so she could maintain modesty without leaving any marks on her skin when she slipped it off. Natalie handled her makeup and hair, then Marilyn and Tom each had a cup of coffee while discussing the shots. Some would be taken sitting up and others lying down. All were to be shot on a red velvet cloth.

A record player sat in a corner, Artie Shaw's *Begin the Beguine* playing to set the mood. Kelley later said that he always found that particular recording effective in helping when a model needed to feel sexual before the camera. The large studio lights were turned on and carefully positioned to effectively record Marilyn. The exposures were slow—1/5th second each with the lens set at F:18 for maximum sharpness. Twenty of the large transparencies were taken for the client and then Kelley switched to a more versatile 2-1/4 × 2-1/4 inch Rolleiflex for four 12-exposure rolls. The film used absorbed light slowly so Marilyn had to hold her poses longer than normal. The work took approximately two hours, and when he had met his client's needs, he exposed four twelve-exposure rolls of film in his Rolleiflex. The prints from the latter eventually would become a wedding present for Marilyn's second marriage. The former, except for the two images bought by his client, were stolen from Kelley's file and never recovered.

Later that evening Kelley, Natalie, and Marilyn went to Barney's Beanery for chili and coffee. There Marilyn said that the reason she posed for Tom and not the others (choosing to ignore the work for Earl Moran) was that he had been so kind when she had her car accident on Sunset. At the end of the evening, Marilyn, "in a playful mood," signed the release "Mona Monroe" and took her check for the fifty dollars. The three did not work together again but they remained friends, Marilyn dropping by for coffee and conversation in the years that followed.

Oddly, the disposition of the images has been in question with biographers. Maurice Zolotow, in his authorized biography of Marilyn, quotes Kelley as saying, "A lot of the companies I showed the pictures to didn't think they were so hot." He explained that ultimately the Western Lithograph Company bought one of the pictures for $250. It was called *A New Wrinkle*. The second image, *Golden Dreams*, was the calendar pose and showed her breasts. It was the one that would become famous through its use in the December 1953 first issue of *Playboy*. Zolotow said it sold to John Baumgarth for five hundred dollars for all rights. (Kelley, when interviewed before his death, stated that it was only three hundred dollars for the Baumgarth image, a picture that made the calendar maker a millionaire.) It is not known if Marilyn's fifty dollars came from the three hundred Kelley was paid or was billed to the client. Although the dollar amounts seem small today, it must be remembered that Marilyn's share represented a good week's pay for the average married worker supporting a family of four. Even when all expenses are taken off the total, Kelley also did well for the day.

The Aftermath

The calendar with Marilyn Monroe's nude photo was available in 1949 and did as well as any other calendar with a basic nude figure. No one got rich. It simply went into the pipeline of calendars aimed toward the men's market.

Years passed, and as will become apparent, Marilyn began attracting attention for her films: fourteen in all. Sometimes this was because of her acting; sometimes it was because of heavy studio promotion that created excitement about the woman even when her skills in whatever movie was being hyped were adequate at best. Then, in 1952, came her fifteenth release, the forgettable *Don't Bother to Knock*, a Twentieth Century-Fox release in which Marilyn plays Nell, a former mental patient with a "hotel-sitting" job—babysitting for the children of hotel guests—arranged by her uncle Eddie (Elisha Cook Jr.).

The plot has Monroe attempting to have an affair with a traveling salesman whom she has never previously met but believes to be her fiancé, while the child for whom she is sitting seems to get in the way of her desired romance. The child ends up bound and gagged, presumably to be murdered; Marilyn is found and arrested, and the salesman stays true to his real love, a singer in the hotel. The film has a better script than it sounds, the only problem being Marilyn. As the *New York Times'* Bosley Crowther put it, "It requires a good deal to play a person who is strangely jangled in the head. And, unfortunately, all the equipment that Miss Monroe has to handle the job is a childishly blank expression and a provokingly feeble, hollow voice."

The original planning began May 17, 1950, when Darryl Zanuck asked screenwriter Daniel Taradash to adapt the novel *Mischief* (by Charlotte Armstrong) to the screen. The story would take place in one day within a hotel, limiting costumes, set, and scenery needs.

The only concern, other than budget, was the growing unionization not only of the film industry but of the country at large. In a humorous memo, Zanuck's secretary Molly Mandaville insisted that Marilyn's character never be called a "babysitter." She said that there was too great a risk that babysitters might be organized and have a backlash against the film. (The critics offered the real backlash, including the *Los Angeles Times* mentioning that Marilyn's "portrayal is reinforced by virtually no acting resources whatsoever.")

The problem for everyone involved was that William Randolph Hearst was supporting the film, and how his newspapers promoted the movie and Marilyn would have huge impact at the box office. Not that the movie was a big money venture. The total cost proved to be $555,000, and though the box-office gross was not particularly impressive, it was $1.5 million—meaning that the film made almost a million dollars.

This was an era when movies needed to be profitable for everyone to keep working, but the degree of profitability was not important. A million dollars made everyone happy. Bad press did not.

The timing for the public becoming aware of the calendar was manipulated by Marilyn, Hugh Hefner, and Sid Skolsky, the latter a man who liked to give actors media relation advice when he wanted to boost their careers. This also made him privy to backstage gossip that might be fodder for his columns or for making money from *Confidential* magazine. *Confidential*, best described as the forerunner to a cross between *People* and the *National Enquirer* with organized crime coverage in the mix, had a staff of aggressive journalists, a private investigator fact-checker, and a secret payroll that included all the major columnists—Hedda Hopper, Louella Parsons, Sid Skolsky, and others—who were primarily Los Angeles–based and could feed the publication factual material that was too salacious for their columns. (Years later the *National Enquirer*, then owned by Generoso Pope, followed much of the same concept. Geraldine Barr, sister of comic Roseanne, told how her onetime brother-in-law, Tom Arnold, was paid to alert the *Enquirer* to his dates with Roseanne so they could be ready to photograph the couple prior to their marriage. And the author of this book stayed in the Beverly Hills home of a prominent entertainment lawyer who bragged that she was paid by the *Enquirer* to provide them with the dirty little secrets of her famous clients. Attorney-client privilege, like so many other areas of morals and ethics, was a rule to be ignored in Hollywood.) Sid knew how to sell a story, what stories to sell, and when to sell them, and he advised Marilyn when her name was at last connected with the long ago session in Tom Kelley's studio.

Monroe was getting extensive press, especially from the Hearst newspapers whose founder, William Randolph Hearst, allegedly was an investor in the Fox film. The question was whether her limited acting ability, as noted by most of the reviewers, would cause the studio to invoke the morals clause to cancel her contract. There is also, in hindsight, a question of whether Marilyn understood that any publicity she might obtain would help her, since, as Johnny Hyde discovered, Norma Jean was constantly refining the character named Marilyn Monroe.

What is known is that Twentieth Century-Fox executives were livid when they learned of the calendar and the subsequent interview. They felt that it might be better to shelve *Don't Bother to Knock*. They could take a write-off on the cost and just leave it in the can, unreleased. So serious were they that Harry Brand, the studio's director of publicity, alerted Sid Skolsky to the problem.

Marilyn went to Schwab's Drug Store to meet with Sid Skolsky and discuss how she should handle the growing rumors about the nude pictures. She had been advised by the studio to shut up and say nothing, but this angered her, because she believed she had done nothing wrong. "I needed a job badly to pay the rent," she told Skolsky. "Lots of other girls were doing it. There's no law against it."

Skolsky advised Marilyn to tell others the truth: that she had desperately needed the money and that's why she had posed. Marilyn knew there was no reason to admit that the nudity was a lark, a way of thanking Kelley for his kindnesses.

Skolsky said that Marilyn needed to make a preemptive strike on behalf of her current film. Toward this end, he arranged for her to have lunch with Aline Mosby, the West Coast correspondent for United Press International (UPI).

The use of Mosby was a recognition of the competitiveness and cattiness of the Hollywood columnists. Marilyn could easily have gone to either Hedda Hopper or Louella Parsons, but choosing either of the women would have meant she would be targeted for attack by the other. Their competitiveness was too great.

Skolsky could not use himself, not only because Parsons and Hopper would both have been angry, but also because the public might not believe an innocent woman had confided in a man. This was an era where intimate secrets were shared only with women friends. The East Coast reporter was as close to being an acceptable neutral party as could be found.

Skolsky later wrote of the incident, "I told Marilyn not to say a word about the nude calendar until the interview was over and Aline closed her little notebook and said, 'Well, I think I've got enough. You've been very nice, and it'll make a good story.' At that point, I instructed Marilyn, 'You'll be familiar enough with Aline to say to her, "I like you very much. I've got a problem I want to ask your advice about. Something confidential."'" Skolsky told Marilyn to then quietly explain about the calendar. He knew that Mosby would scrap her original story and focus her writing solely on the nude image. It would be big news in 1952 and she delighted in what she was certain was an inadvertent exclusive.

Soon Mosby and others were running the story of Marilyn's moment of desperation and the public was deeply moved. They sided with the actress, though no one ever checked to see if the stories she gave out ever matched. They didn't. For example, Aline's March 13, 1952, story as carried in the Hearst paper, the *Los Angeles Herald Express*, included the following quotes:

Oh, the calendar's hanging in garages all over town. Why deny it? You can get one any place.

Besides, I'm not ashamed of it. I've done nothing wrong.

I was a week behind on my rent. I had to have the money. A photographer, Tom Kelley, had asked me before to pose but I'd never do it. This time I called him and said I would as soon as possible, to get it over with.

His wife was there. They're both very nice. We did two poses, one standing up with my head turned profile, and another lying on some red velvet.

Tom didn't think anyone would recognize me. My hair was long then. But when the picture came out, everybody knew me. I'd never have done it if I'd known things would happen in Hollywood so fast for me . . .

I was told [that January, when Fox executives first learned what had taken place] I should deny I'd posed . . . but I'd rather be honest about it.

I've gotten a lot of fan letters on it. The men like the picture and want copies. The women, well . . .

One gossip columnist said I autographed the pictures and handed them out and said "Art for Art's Sake." I never said that.

Why, I only gave two away.

Marilyn had planned her comments carefully and some of the quotes appeared in other publications. *Newsweek* for February 24, 1952, had the quote before the Mosby follow-up story broke.

On March 7, 1952, *Life* magazine declared the story to be news. The publication released a small copy of the photograph as an inset.

The *Life* article showed Marilyn's carefully orchestrated wit. She mentioned that she was using dumbbells for exercise. "I'm fighting gravity. If you don't fight gravity, you sag," she said.

During this interview, Marilyn said, "Once this fellow says, 'Marilyn, what do you wear to bed?' So I said I only wear Chanel No. 5 and he groans, 'Oh no, I can't use that.'" (Marilyn used the same line with Sid Skolsky when he interviewed her on the set of *Niagara* and he did use it in his column.)

A variation of this occurred in an interview when she was asked about posing for the calendar photos. "What did you have on?" she was asked.

Marilyn smiled and said, "The radio."

The wit was a delight to the public. What no one realized was that little was original and even less was as spontaneous as it seemed. The jokes were staples of vaudeville and had probably been rehearsed with her by the studio's publicity department. What mattered was her brilliant sense of comic timing that enabled her to sound as though she was spontaneously funny.

Perhaps the most dramatically fanciful tale concerning the calendar was woven by Marilyn in an interview with Liza Wilson of the *American Weekly* magazine insert available through Sunday newspapers around the country. In the November 23, 1952, issue, Marilyn was quoted as saying:

I got four weeks behind in my rent at the Studio Club (in Hollywood) and the manager—she had been most kind and patient—finally had to tell me to pay up or move on.

Nearly every photographer I had ever worked with had asked me to pose in the nude. But I had always refused.

One photographer, Tom Kelley, I liked very much. I had done some beer ads for Tom and his wife, Natalie, and they asked me if I would like to do a nude for a calendar firm. They said no one would recognize me. I refused at first.

But the day I received my eviction notice I called Natalie and said, "When and how much?"

They arranged for me to pose at the studio that night. I received fifty dollars. The next day I paid my rent and treated myself to a quiet dinner at home.

There would be other stories as well, including one where she desperately needed her car to get to auditions and studio jobs. The car was in the shop. The repair bill was fifty dollars. The rest was history.

Whatever story a reader believed, the results were the same. Marilyn's career would be boosted beyond her talent.

Twenty-six

Truth Can Be a Real Nuisance

She wears the expression of a racy woman who has just been hit on the head by a sash weight.

—David Hempstead, Twentieth Century-Fox producer, speaking of Marilyn Monroe in the June 1952 issue of *Redbook* magazine

The crisis began with an article entitled "So Far to Go Alone" written by Jim Henaghan for the June 1952 *Redbook* magazine. The publication was a critical one for Marilyn's career because the readers were the type of people Fox wanted as fans. They were mostly intelligent women with no more than high school educations, married to men who were blue-collar workers, and mothers of at least one child. They were also intensely interested in learning about issues in medicine, education, and other areas that could affect their families. Often complicated stories, such as the latest information on heart disease, a major killer of blue-collar men in their forties at the time, were presented in ways that could easily be understood despite the sophistication of the subject.

Redbook did not seek movie stars as cover or inside article subjects for the sake of gossip or sensationalism. They wanted celebrities with a serious story to tell, and that was the way Marilyn was presented to them by the studio publicity department. What they could not imagine was that after their deadline, after the article was set in type, after it was too late to change because the issue was reaching the stands, they would learn she had lied.

The article in the June 1952 issue discussed Marilyn's being an orphan in the care of Los Angeles County. It told how she was often boarded out, never loved, always alone.

Some of the story she told had truth to it. When speaking of her time in the Los Angeles Orphan Home Society when she was nine, she said,

> We went to school at a public school a couple of blocks away. We all wore gingham dresses—of different colors, but all the same style. Probably the hardest thing I ever had to do in my life was go to that school, because once in a while I'd hear another kid say, "She's from the Home," and I knew I was different—and I didn't want to be different.
>
> I was always shy and scared. At one time, just after school started in the fall, three boys in my class liked me. And then they found out I was from the Home—and it was terrible.

Marilyn claimed to have worked in the Home pantry for five cents a month, explaining that when she was promoted to kitchen dishwasher, her pay was raised to ten cents a month. But the worst experience, according to the partial fantasy she weaved for the writer, was when she was farmed out to local families.

> I don't think any of the people I lived with ever were knowingly unkind to me. It's just that there was never any love or affection for me. They never hugged or kissed me. They'd . . . just pat me on the head, like a puppy. And they *kissed* their own children.
>
> And when Christmas came, it was always different for me. The families would buy us all dresses, maybe, but I'd get the brown one or the cheapest one. And one year all the other kids in the family I lived with got wonderful presents and I got a ten-cent manicure outfit. And while the rest of the kids sat around the floor and admired their loot, I sat in a corner pushing back my cuticle. Yes, the Christmases were the hardest.

The story was so deeply moving, the sympathy for Marilyn so great, that when reporters learned that her mother was alive, there was intense anger. The knowledge of the nude calendar photo further upset the media, not because it had been taken but because there was suddenly so much thrown into question.

The response by Monroe was swift. Acting almost certainly with the assistance of Sid Skolsky, who was far more sophisticated in these matters than the studio publicists, a letter went immediately to the editors of *Redbook*. It appeared in the July Letters to the Editor column and was signed "Marilyn Monroe, Beverly Hills, Calif." The letter read,

> I am so grateful for the wonderful story Jim Henaghan wrote about me for *Redbook*, but I want to explain why I withheld certain facts about my life.
>
> I can understand your insistence on editorial accuracy, but I frankly did not feel wrong in withholding from you the fact that my mother is still alive but from my earliest childhood was hopelessly invalided for many years in a state hospital.
>
> I have told the story the way I knew it as a child, and even since knowing of her existence, I have tried to respect my mother's wish to remain anonymous . . .
>
> Since we have never known each other intimately and have never enjoyed the normal relationship of mother and daughter, I have been content to accept the orphan's life which your article describes.
>
> If I have erred in concealing one fact, please accept my deepest apology and please believe that my motive was one of consideration for a person for whom I feel a great obligation.

Marilyn's letter to *Redbook* helped her gain sympathy in much the same manner as the story Sid helped her concoct about why she was so desperate for money that she would pose in the nude for the first and only time. No one wanted to think of her or any other starlet as being so aggressive and determined that she would lie about her life and experiences. It was easier to believe a well-told falsehood than an uncomfortable truth.

During this same period, an extremely difficult one for Monroe, yet another problem emerged, though this time she was innocent and deserving of the sympathy she received. The name Marilyn Monroe was being used in a scam perpetrated by Jerry Karpman, age forty-six, and Morrie Kaplan, thirty-two, whose arrests made headlines in Los Angeles on June 26, 1952.

Karpman and Kaplan were selling photographs of women in a direct-mail scam. Each letter was the same as the one that follows, but there were thirty-nine different names used, the majority of which had "Marilyn" in it. Some were supposedly pictures of Marilyn Monroe. Others were signed Marilyn Miller, Marilyn Marsh, and numerous variations. None of the women whose pictures were being sold were aware of what was happening until the fraud was brought to their attention. In Monroe's case, the letter read:

> Hello there!
>
> My name is Marilyn Monroe . . . I hope you don't think me too bold for writing, but it is out of necessity that I do . . . I'm out of a job and have to raise money quickly, therefore I have had to do something that I never would have done under ordinary conditions.
>
> A short time ago, two friends of mine and myself got together and took some pictures in almost every pose imaginable. They got a lot more enjoyment out of it than I did but of course that is only natural. Due to the nature of these pictures it is very important that you keep this matter very confidential as I am not too happy about the whole thing.
>
> I feel that these pictures, which are not easily obtained, are worth more than the price I have found ordinary pictures are selling for. I will send you eight pictures (absolutely unretouched) for $4 or all 16 that we took plus two very unusual shots given by a friend for just $7.

Always a mailing service address, similar to a contemporary private post office box, was used to hide the real location of the men. The police staked out the address they thought was most current—7960 Beverly Boulevard—and quickly caught Karpman when he was checking to see what orders had arrived.

The police discovered that all the photographs were nude and indecent under the law. These were not the art-type poses of the calendar models. These were lewd images and none of them was actually Marilyn Monroe or any other woman ever identified by Jerry Karpman, the photographer. They may have been custom-made for the scam or they may have been stock images he had taken before his friend suggested the sale. There was no evidence that the men who offered them for sale were the ones who had originally taken the images.

The use of Monroe's name was seemingly inspired. Her popularity was such that the letters allegedly coming from her resulted in orders of a thousand dollars per day. And that volume did not include any of the other names used, to which men were responding, although in lesser numbers.

Marilyn was subpoenaed to testify against the men who were charged with selling without a license, misrepresentation, and other violations. Deputy Los Angeles City Attorney William Still put Monroe on the stand, handed her a copy of one of the letters signed with her name, and had her answer four questions: Is this handwriting yours? Is the signature yours? Did you write this letter? Did you authorize anyone else to write it?

The answer in each instance was "no." There were no further questions from the prosecution or the defense. On June 27, 1952, the jury found Karpman, who had taken the pictures of some unknown model, and Kaplan, the salesman, guilty of five misdemeanor charges each.

Twenty-seven

I'm Going to Make You a Star

Everything changed in the entertainment business as the 1940s were coming to a close. In 1946, one year after the war had ended, eighty million Americans went to the movies every week. Then came radical changes. World War II was over. Returning service personnel received unprecedented benefits, including fifty-two weeks of twenty dollars a week, enough money to buy one of the newly available automobiles and see the country. Many married the girls who had waited for them. Many decided to get a higher education, using their money for student housing. Babies were born in record numbers and low-cost tract housing was built on land within commuting distance of major cities to provide a place for the young families.

There was money for necessities but little else. GI benefits might cover much of the initial costs, but the rest came from jobs, and this was an era when women stayed at home, the family living on the man's paycheck, usually from an entry-level work position. Luxuries had to be put off, and among these was the regular attendance at the movies. Thus by 1948 only 67 million Americans went to movies each week, and in 1949 that number was dropping even faster.

Starlets who had been around for a while were either released from their contracts or ignored for new material because they did not lend themselves to the new business of promotion. Men and women who had worked in propaganda during the war—for example, organizations such as the OSS (forerunner to the Central Intelligence Agency) or other government agencies—were becoming part of the lucrative advertising industry. They understood how to sell a product, whether the war that was just fought, a single movie, or a single star. But there was no question that the industry was in crisis, as were actors who had been around for a few years but had not become stars.

The business side was evident to everyone. Infusions of cash, desperately needed, came from spinning off businesses that had once made production companies more profitable. Paramount Pictures sold its chain of movie theaters, calling the business they dumped United Paramount Theaters. This was in imitation of a similar move by Howard Hughes, who separated his motion picture production company from RKO Theaters, once the home of vaudeville when it was still the Keith-Albee-Orpheum chain.

Television was still an unknown, but the introduction of "big-screen" sets—12 and 16 inches, up from the 7-inch screens that first created a market—created a new demand for product without anyone knowing what that meant. Radio shows were converted for television. Variety shows of a type popular with vaudeville were converted to television. And the work was live, a hybrid of stage and screen that made many professionals uncomfortable.

The motion picture producers realized that the B-movie as a training ground was probably finished. Worse, with television a starlet actually had to do something. For example, Johnny Hyde approached one of the new children's variety shows hosted by an old vaudeville and burlesque comic named Pinky Lee. Hyde wanted twenty-five dollars for Marilyn to make an appearance: not an exorbitant request. Lee refused, though. Neither he nor Johnny could figure out just what Marilyn would do to earn the twenty-five dollars.

Hyde had no illusions about Marilyn. He seemed to feel that he was the only person working on her behalf who believed she could be a star, and if she didn't work on her skills outside the bedroom, there would be no future. He kept reminding her that she was a chump, and when it came to sex, "You're not an expert, baby." He berated her for not spending more time with him because, if she didn't, when he was gone, she'd "fall on her ass like the others." He added, "so don't try to get by on your fucking. Take it from me, I know. I've had experts."

Marilyn said nothing about Hyde's viciousness or health, even though each time they had sex, Johnny had to start with a pill to ease the pain from one of his arteries. Doctors were uncertain whether it was defective or blocked, but in those days all they could offer was relief from the pain while the patient slowly died. But Hyde stayed active in bed, and Marilyn found a subtle way to rebel. Just as she would frequently complain that Johnny was hurting her during intercourse, implying his male organ was bigger than it was, she also would make an exaggerated effort to have an orgasm when she was aroused and not fulfilled. Many a night she would sadly tell Johnny that she was glad he had enjoyed an orgasm, because one of them should leave the bed fulfilled. It was never a direct criticism, just an undermining of his fantasies about himself.

Sometimes the talk between them was viciously inappropriate. For example, there was the night when they were in a club watching some black entertainers, Hyde told Marilyn, "You have a behind like a nigger." Marilyn, fuming, quietly convinced Johnny that she had "colored blood." Oddly, this false confession to being of mixed race, which in 1950 would have made her a social outcast had it been known, seemed to bolster Hyde.

He occasionally saw Marilyn as being too perfect a physical woman, either in his own mind or in the minds of others. He stopped being so verbally abusive, helping her keep her secret. It was only after his death that she told friends what had happened and what she had done.

Always there was an understanding between Hyde and Monroe. He knew the "chump" would probably continue to go to bed with men who meant little to her other than a chance to be photographed, get a role, or otherwise help her career. Certainly she had stressed to him that while she loved him, she was not "in love" with him. She also refused to marry him during those early months when he had left his wife and children to be available to her at all times. The proposal was repeated with increasing frequency as his health declined. He wanted to leave her a wealthy widow, someone able to enjoy a good life while building a career. She knew Hyde was ridiculed for his affair, hated by members of his family, and scorned by some industry executives (though others considered him a "real man" for slowly dying in the company of a sexy, willing young actress). She felt that if she married him, she would be seen as someone who only wanted his money and the backlash against her would end her career.

Johnny was desperate to find Marilyn parts in films, to prove to her both his abilities and his love. He decided to try to get her more press, and, toward this end, he arranged for an interview with Earl Wilson, a self-described New York saloon columnist.

Wilson was as competitive as the other columnists but he had a sense of humor, keen observation of the entertainment scene beyond his column, and a wariness of aggressive women who would do literally anything to get a mention in his column if they thought it would boost their careers. He periodically had his wife accompany him to interviews where he suspected the subject might otherwise create a problem for him. He also understood that beauty, brains, and the ability to communicate did not necessarily go hand in hand. However, instead of savaging the subject, Wilson would find a way to combine an almost meaningless interview, press releases from the studio, and whatever else he could cobble together for a column that was both fun to read and revealing without being hurtful. This was definitely true with Monroe.

Johnny Hyde quietly alerted friends to the fact that Marilyn was a work in progress. Norma Jean wanted to be a star and was determined that nothing would get in her way. Marilyn Monroe was the vehicle for that success, and though she had the sex part down perfectly, the walk, the smile, there was much about Marilyn she had yet to figure out. That was why she was regularly seen with books on everything from anatomy to philosophy to acting technique. She knew the writing would have value to her, though her husbands and lovers found that she felt she did not have to read in depth. She could skim through the work and gather what she felt was an understanding of the key points. Some lauded the effort. Some thought she was a self-delusional twit, or worse—such as Johnny Hyde at once loving her and considering her a "chump." Earl Wilson took what he got and had fun with it.

ℰ

Earl Wilson's column as carried in the *Los Angeles Daily News* on July 30, 1949.

> Over the years, Hollywood has joyously given us its "It Girl," its "Oomph Girl," its "Sweater Girl," and even "The Body"—and they've all become big movie names.

Now we get the "Mmmm Girl."

Miss Marilyn Monroe still wasn't quite sure what an "Mmmm Girl" has to do when I talked to her.

"But I'm sure none of the girls ever got hurt by being called such names," she said.

Miss Monroe is probably right. They don't get hurt, but they get mighty tired, even sick, of the tags. Miss Monroe, who is practically an unknown, is a twenty-one-year-old, long-haired blonde from Van Nuys, California. She has a nice flat waist that rises to an (mmmm!) 36-1/2-inch bra line. She also has long, pretty legs.

"But why do they call you the 'Mmmm Girl?'" I asked her.

"Well," she said, "it seems it started in Detroit where they were having a sneak preview of my picture."

But why?

"Well," she said, doubtless remembering it just like the press agent told her to, "it seems some people couldn't whistle so they went, 'Mmmm.'"

"Why couldn't they whistle?" I said.

"Well," she said, "some people just can't whistle."

Maybe they couldn't whistle because they had their mouths full of popcorn, I suggested.

Personally, we think the whole thing was dreamed up by the publicist— but the fact remains that these appellations (get HIM) have helped make a few girls pretty famous.

Annie Pie Sheridan, the "Oomph Girl," told me once she was sick to death of oomph, and she was a good enough actress to make people forget she ever was the Oomph Girl.

❧

The 'Mmmm Girl' starts out, candidly, without any claim to acting genius. She was working as a typist in a factory in California a couple of years ago when The Big Thing Happened.

Wilson told about how Marilyn got into modeling and then acting: "'They gave me a bit part in a picture but cut it out.' she says. So she left there.

"One day she met Louis Shurr, the Hollywood agent who keeps a lot of mink coats for emergencies, and without so much as offering her a coat he suggested she go to see producer Lester Cowan."

He then told the story of Marilyn's imitating Groucho's walk.

"That's how she got into the picture *Love Happy*, and got acquainted with the press agent who insists there are people in Detroit who can't whistle but say 'Mmmm' instead. . . ."

℘

And so Marilyn became nationally known, when the truth about her appearance in the movie was that it was just thirty-eight seconds, and not a particularly memorable thirty-eight seconds at that.

A Ticket to Tomahawk was Marilyn's next film, a picture for which she was chosen to play her standard role—pretty girl. This was a period film, the story taking place in September 1876 on the train the *Emma Sweeney*, taking its maiden trip on the Tomahawk and Western Railroad traveling through the Colorado Rockies. The dramatic tension results from an evil stagecoach line owner who hires the Overland Gang to drop a boulder on the tracks and disrupt service. The stagecoach owner knows that the train's license is good only if, in the immediate future, it transports at least one passenger to Tomahawk by September 5. The fact that forty miles of track were lost on the way from England, leaving a gap between Epitaph and Dead Horse Point, adds another element to the story because some other form of transportation must be used. All that matters is that the train starts with at least the single passenger and ends with that passenger reaching what eventually will be the train's destination by the deadline.

Naturally, there is a hero (Johnny Jameson, traveling salesman) and a heroine (Kit Dodge Jr.). Kit is the granddaughter of elderly Marshall Dodge, who deputizes the girl to see that the train makes its destination. The train also has a second passenger, a mysterious individual who proves to be a bad guy infiltrating the train, as well as a showgirl troupe. Marilyn, as one of the girls, appears in four scenes. In three, she just has to look pretty. In the fourth, she and the others, along with Dan Dailey (the actor playing Johnny Jameson), do a song-and-dance number.

The original script was played more for laughs, the showgirls described by writers Mary Loos and Richard Sale as being six in number and all of them "homely as mud fences." Their costumes would range from camisoles to old-fashioned nightgowns, some unattractive, others actually representing what was considered appropriate fashion for the era. Twentieth Century-Fox head Darryl Zanuck, whose studio was making the film, changed the concept, insisting upon just four showgirls, all beautiful, and all chosen from the stock company of starlets. Thanks to the Earl Wilson piece, Marilyn made it, though she was so insecure that she mostly kept to herself, calling Johnny Hyde long-distance to talk almost daily for the five weeks of location work.

The movie is not bad for a B-film and contains fight scenes, cowboys, Indians, and a love story in which the girl is the "tough guy." It was filmed in Durango, Colorado, then mostly a wilderness area with the nearest "big city," Silverton, accessible only by narrow-gauge railroad. The work was done in July and August, and the film eventually cost $1.91 million. It earned back $600,000 less on its first showing, a serious problem but not one that concerned the supporting cast such as Marilyn.

What did matter for Marilyn was a last-ditch effort to save the movie through a promotion, the impetus of which was a later campaign that would help make her one of the most popular actresses in the country. The problem the production company faced was actually with a 1949 movie called *The Beautiful Blonde from Bashful Bend* that starred such A-list actors as Betty Grable and Cesar Romero. The movie had also been a Western, and it did so poorly at the box office, Zanuck did not want to throw much promotion money at *A Ticket to Tomahawk* in case it also did poorly. The fact that the film could not succeed without the promotion was seemingly ignored.

Finally, in July and August 1950, some regional theater owners in Tulsa, Oklahoma, decided to see if they could boost attendance through effective advertising of the movie. They believed that the title was in no way commercial. Eunice McDaniel, the publicist for the Ralph Talbot Theater chain, came up with the idea of calling the movie *The Sheriff's Daughter*. Then, with the approval of the company's top executives, she launched a series of advertisements with different headers and different body copy, but with the same idea. The writer of the ad was frustrated that a lousy title was keeping people away from a great film. The ads all started with either "I Didn't Like the Title Either!" or "I Like Terrific Pictures to Have the Right Title!"

The body of one ad read: "Twentieth Century-Fox made a very funny burlesque about cowboys and Indians, a traveling salesman and a gorgeous, gun-crazy gal—but it's called 'A Ticket to Tomahawk'—and nobody knows what it means! So, I'm calling it 'The Sheriff's Daughter.' After you see it, tell me which title you like best!'' The ad was signed by the theater manager, as was a second, similar ad with slightly different copy.

The take at the box office soared. Whether or not the public thought the movie was great, the advertising challenge was effective and noted in the trade journals. The Fox publicity department quickly adopted the ads and sent them to other theater owners. Unfortunately, almost every theater that was going to show the movie had already done so, always to disappointing numbers, and could not bring it back to try again. But where the film was still fresh, the ad campaign boosted attendance compared with comparable cities that did not have the ads.

It would be two years later, when Marilyn made the equally forgettable *We're Not Married*, that the advertising approach learned through the regional marketing of *A Ticket to Tomahawk*, would truly be effective. But for the moment, the concern was getting Monroe a part which, if not great, would at least be memorable.

Twenty-eight

Milton Greene—The First Time

There was more publicity for Marilyn as Johnny Hyde, Lucille Ryman, and John Carroll all worked to move her career forward, albeit for radically different reasons. Her extensive experience as a still photography model assured her use in studio promotions connected with the important national magazines of the day. For example, in September 1949, Marilyn became involved with Rupert Allan, a writer and editor for *Look* magazine, a publication that specialized in photo features (in contrast to *Life*, which was conceived as a news magazine using photographs to illuminate stories told in great depth in the sister publication, *Time*). *Look*'s strength was feature stories, and these sometimes included "soft" material on the stars.

Allan, who was based in Hollywood, lived on Seabright Place in one of the canyons of Beverly Hills. He planned to bring several photographers from New York to do a photo essay on starlets. His only concern was how they would look in the magazine, and he agreed with Johnny Hyde that Marilyn would work well in the group. She also surprised him by being interested in the past images taken by the photographers who were handling the assignment. It was while reviewing them that she discovered the work of Milton Greene, one of the men who had come west for the project.

Greene was twenty-seven, divorced, and totally devoted to his profession. He looked so boyish that Marilyn was amazed that so young a photographer could be so skilled. She wanted to be photographed by him the first night they met, though it is believed that they ended up in the more intimate setting of his hotel room at the Chateau Marmont Hotel on Sunset Boulevard.

Later there would be claims of a romance between the two. Certainly they developed both a close friendship and a business partnership that would continue through the rest of her life. However, when Marilyn was linked romantically with a photographer, the reality often was different from what even the photographer might believe. Two years before her death, in a conversation with a writer and longtime friend named Jaik Rosenstein, Marilyn said, "When I started modeling, it was like part of the job. All the girls did. They weren't shooting all those sexy pictures just to sell peanut butter in an ad, or get a layout in some picture magazine. They wanted to sample the merchandise, and if you didn't go along, there were twenty-five girls who would. It wasn't any big dramatic tragedy. Nobody ever got cancer from sex."

The photo essay, the contacts with the photographers, and the new relationship with Greene were all important, but the next major achievement in Marilyn's career resulted from a director's profligate ways.

Twenty-nine

The Asphalt Jungle

John and Lucille Ryman Carroll, like so many successful people in the entertainment industry, owned horse property that they used as a small business. Their San Fernando Valley ranch had the facilities for boarding and training horses, frequently for other show business personalities. And among their customers was the director John Huston.

That John Huston was one of the greatest minds in the film industry was never in question. His work as both a writer and a director was internationally acclaimed. He was paid extremely well, though not yet well enough for his lifestyle. Between extensive gambling and living beyond his means, he was always broke, always in debt. In the case of the Carrolls, he was eighteen thousand dollars behind in paying them for handling his horses on their ranch. While he assumed they would eventually press him for the money, he also knew they were wealthy enough to let the debt remain without doing anything to collect if they chose. What he did not expect was blackmail.

John Huston was preparing for a new movie to be called *The Asphalt Jungle*. It was the story of professional criminals planning a million-dollar jewel theft. Although Huston originally wanted to use people who were not actors in the film, he eventually cast Sam Jaffe as the head of the gang planning to steal the jewels, Louis Calhern as a corrupt lawyer financing the theft, and Sterling Hayden as an alcoholic, small-time gangster who would be part of the theft. Angela, the part for which Marilyn was testing, would be Calhern's "niece." As soon as the scripts were printed, Lucille began looking for people under contract to MGM to use in the cast. The studio system demanded that anyone making a film for the studio use as many contract actors as possible. Only when the appropriate people could not be found would the director go outside the system. Lucille had to coordinate the top roles.

Lucille realized that there was a perfect part for Marilyn. She could not fluff her lines. She could not really be bad in it because it was not that big. It was so minor that no one was likely to mind if she went outside MGM to hire the actress, yet it was a part that would get some notice.

Lucille called Johnny Hyde and told him that the script was perfect for Marilyn. She had already done enough in-house casting so he could feel safe that if he brought her to audition, Marilyn would be given a serious chance at the part.

Normally Lucille would have sent the scene in question to an actor's agent. Knowing Marilyn, she sent the entire script. She also explained that Hyde should talk directly to both Huston and Arthur Hornblow, who was producing the movie, concerning the audition. The fact that the script had been written by Huston and Ben Maddow, based on the novel by W. R. Burnett, added to Huston's concern that the actors be up to the challenge.

Arthur Hornblow knew Marilyn from Sam Spiegel's parties and similar places, and wanted nothing to do with her. He said Johnny should talk with John Huston, knowing full well Huston wanted Lola Albright or an actress similarly known for her ladylike manners.

Lucille reminded both Huston and Hornblow that Lola Albright was earning $1,500 a week for every picture, and she was in such demand that she was making one picture right after another. The role of the mistress in *The Asphalt Jungle* was worth no more than $500 a week. (Marilyn was eventually paid $350 per week to do her part in the film.) Lola, who was being groomed to become a major star, would not take a cut in pay and the budget would not allow a $1,000-per-week indulgence. Lola was out.

Besides, Lucille reminded John, the part really called for a sexy young woman, not the "lady" that Albright came across as being. Frustrated that he couldn't have his way, Huston angrily growled at Lucille, "Don't tell me what I have in the script. I wrote the part."

One Friday, Lucille learned that Huston had arranged for eight girls to be at the casting office the following Monday to test for the role of Angela, the lawyer's mistress. One was Lola Albright. None of them were Marilyn.

Upset at being thus thwarted, Lucille complained to her husband that evening. Huston was totally convinced that Marilyn was wrong for the part and wanted nothing to do with her. However, John thought he knew how to solve the problem.

John casually called Huston, who mentioned that he and his fourth wife, Soma, would be in Malibu on Sunday. John arranged to go for a private walk with him along the beach. Then they would return to the ranch where Lucille and Soma would be waiting.

Huston was angry when he arrived back at the ranch with John Carroll after their walk. He gave Lucille a nasty look, then went to the ranch telephone and called MGM's central casting department. It was 4:00 P.M. on Sunday and he wanted them to send Marilyn the scene that would be rehearsed. Then he called Johnny Hyde to let him know she was to be tested.

Lucille Carroll knew that Huston was going to be paid fifty thousand dollars to direct *The Asphalt Jungle*. She also let John know that Huston had taken the money in advance, then spent it. The man was broke.

Knowing full well that Huston could not pay the eighteen thousand dollars, John had demanded the money on their walk. He told Huston that financial matters were not good. They could not continue underwriting Huston's horses. The animals were good ones; they might even develop into fine racing stock one day. It was a pity the Carrolls would have to sell them in order to get back the money they had spent.

Huston had been extremely upset. He loved his lifestyle, his possessions, his horses. The fact that he could not afford any of them at the moment meant nothing to him. He could not bear to part with any of them—as John well knew.

When Huston had finally fallen silent, John Carroll had told him that matters might be different if Huston would do the Carrolls a favor. John had said that he knew Huston was testing the next day. He had said that there was only one person who could do the role, and that was Marilyn Monroe. Carroll had asked Huston to make a test.

John Carroll had stressed that he was not using blackmail to assure Marilyn got the part. He was not asking Huston to *cast* Monroe. He just wanted her tested, and if she didn't pass the test, it would not matter. His obligation would be met and Huston would not be pushed for the money he owed for another six months.

Huston had angrily agreed. The Carrolls did not tell him that Marilyn already had the script, had gotten it right after Lucille had received her copies. Huston was not told that she had been practicing with Natasha Lytess. He assumed that whatever he was going to see during the test was the result of the work Marilyn did late that afternoon.

Marilyn Monroe was frightened as she prepared to enter the Culver City office of writer/director John Huston. She knew he had become legendary for such earlier films as *The Maltese Falcon* and *The Treasure of Sierra Madre*. She understood that her greatest personal fame had been a thirty-eight-second part in *Love Happy*, and that was only because the studio had used her for an ultimately less-than-successful promotion tour.

Worse for her sense of comfort, Marilyn was a terrible actress and knew it. She had appeared in five movies where casting depended solely upon being a young, attractive studio employee who took direction and didn't call attention to herself.

The eccentric Huston wanted a cast of unknowns. He talked of men such as John Reed and Ludwig Bemelmans for the leads even though his staff had never heard of them. This was because they weren't actors but journalists Huston knew and admired. Presumably Lola Albright was either the exception or Huston considered her to be someone so new in her career that she might as well be an unknown.

Marilyn Monroe was also a name unfamiliar to Huston's staff, though she was at least in show business. When producer Arthur Hornblow Jr. demanded that Huston stop his fantasies and cast real actors, not journalists, Monroe was the only person originally considered who would get a role. However, this was not because of an impressive audition—despite Huston's comments to the contrary when he sought to control how he was viewed in film history.

Marilyn was unaware that she was a pawn in a chess game orchestrated by the Carrolls. She did not know that Huston's involvement with high-stakes gambling, an outrageous lifestyle, and mob-connected friends all made him vulnerable to blackmail. She was also oblivious to the fact that she had become such a nuisance to many of those closest to her that they would do anything legal to get rid of her. They had already convinced themselves that she had little future in the film industry. They regretted that they had fueled the illusions that kept her walking the streets, knocking on doors, and doing whatever she could to get noticed.

Only Johnny Hyde truly believed in her, and for most actresses that would have been enough to assure a jump-start to a major career. He held a position of power and influence as a partner in the prestigious William Morris Agency. In the past, when he recommended a talent, producers and directors were eager to sign the person to a contract. But Marilyn was different, and the fact that everyone in the industry knew she was Johnny Hyde's lover did not help her credibility. There had to be some other pressure on Huston, though neither Johnny nor Marilyn ever learned the truth of why she was being seen that day.

To add to Marilyn's nervousness, she had earlier watched Huston at work with his partner, Sam Spiegel, on the Cuban war movie *We Were Strangers*, which they filmed in 1949 when they were all at Columbia Pictures. Evelyn Keyes, Huston's wife at the time, noted that Marilyn was just "one more little blonde with the preferred size tits and a funny walk": the "tits" and the "funny walk" were enough for a few of the Columbia executives to consider asking Monroe to join them on the casting couch, a fact that had upset Huston. To head off such action, he had planned to offer the starlet a real screen test. There was a small part in *We Were Strangers* that an actress of limited ability could carry off, and the picture's star, John Garfield, agreed to see if Monroe could handle it.

Sam Spiegel pointed out to his partner in the film that there were known young actresses who could take the role in *We Were Strangers* without going to the expense of a screen test. "Are you prepared to pay for this?" Spiegel demanded to know, and neither Garfield nor Huston would go that far to help Monroe.

Marilyn approached the meeting with Huston knowing that if she did well in front of the director, Hornblow, and Huston's assistant, Albert Band, she would have the first meaningful role of her career. If she failed once again . . . well, as she would later comment, "When you're a failure in Hollywood, that's like starving to death outside a banquet hall, with smells of filet mignon driving you crazy."

What Marilyn could not know was that, though she would once again fail, with the unlikely fairy godparents of Sam Spiegel, John and Lucille Carroll, and Johnny Hyde on her side, Huston would be the answer to her every prayer.

Before going for the test, producer Arthur Hornblow Jr., who considered Marilyn coarse and vulgar in both her appearance and her actions, arranged for her to get makeup and styling from MGM's Sydney Guilaroff. More than forty-five years later, he wrote about that day, making clear that he recognized she could be a star, seemingly the same future that Johnny Hyde believed would be hers. Or so he said, with the benefit of hindsight. However, his reasons made sense: "During my years at MGM, I had developed a good sense about what kind of an impression someone made on movie audiences. In the silent era, it was called flesh impact. Studying the planes of her face, the way she carried herself and the way she radiated her feelings, I became convinced that Marilyn had it. After reading the screenplay, I knew she was born for the role."

Guilaroff also took credit for Monroe's success in the audition when he wrote his memoirs, *Crowning Glory*. This story is a little less credible. As he told it, Marilyn was wearing a white shirt and sweater, and Guilaroff stood off camera, directing her every move of the screen test. This was separate from the reading she did for John Huston, the film viewed later to see how her image transferred to the screen.

According to Guilaroff, Marilyn was guided through a series of emotions. He first asked her if she would smile if he told her a joke.

"Yes," she answered, breaking into a smile. Just above her, peering through the lens, the cinematographer also smiled. Her emotions registered beautifully.

"Now think a little seriously," I continued. "Think about something bad in your life, something that happened to you." Her look broke your heart. Of course, I couldn't know then about the indignities and abuse this girl had already endured. I knew only that she was a natural, that she could convey all that sadness and vulnerability to an audience.

"Try to appear sensuous, Marilyn," I called softly. "I know you have that sensuality, and so do you. But show it now in a very quiet way." I put her in a swivel chair and told her to twirl around, to gaze back at me standing next to the camera. "Just look over your shoulder," I whispered.

"Now, lean forward on your crossed leg. Then smile at me." She did, and the effect was unsettling in its erotic impact.

Guilaroff was convinced Monroe got the part because of the screen test. Huston wanted to claim it was the quality of her reading that got her the part. As he later wrote in his self-serving autobiography:

> I was testing for *The Asphalt Jungle* when little Johnny Hyde of the William Morris Agency called and said he had a girl just right for the part of Angela—might she read for me? Arthur Hornblow, the producer of *The Asphalt Jungle*, was with me a few days later when Johnny brought the girl around. I recognized her as the girl I'd saved from the casting couch. The scene she was to read called for Angela to be stretched out on a divan; there was no divan in my office, so Marilyn said, "I'd like to do the scene on the floor."
>
> "Of course, my dear, any way it feels right to you."
>
> And that's the way she did it. She kicked off her shoes, lay down on the floor and read for us. When she finished, Arthur and I looked at each other and nodded. She was Angela to a "T." I later discovered that Johnny Hyde was in love with her. Johnny was a very fine, very reliable agent, and we were friends, but Marilyn didn't get the part because of Johnny. She got it because she was damned good.

Or so he said. The truth was a combination of the blackmail and sexual attraction, something revealed in interviews given by Lucille Ryman and stored in the Margaret Herrick Library, as well as through Albert Band speaking to not only the author of this book but also to other authors writing about the incident.

Band, who has had a long career as a Hollywood director, was just starting in the business by working as an assistant to the legendary John Huston when Marilyn was brought in to audition by Johnny Hyde. Monroe arrived in what Band considered typical bimbo fashion—her blouse cut low and her skirt cut high.

To Band, seeing the way Monroe was dressed that day, the role of Angela, the bimbo mistress, seemed like typecasting. However, as Jack Lemmon would later comment about actress Judy Holliday, "It takes a brilliant woman to play a bimbo." Monroe did not seem to have that genius, nor did she seem to have any talent. She was a "little-known," seemingly a slut, and someone who would be dismissed in contemporary times as a "wannabe."

As Band later explained,

There was a standard procedure John Huston followed when casting a picture. First there was a reading. His assistant, me, would go into a room of his suite of offices and work with the actor auditioning. We would read from the script together so the actor could become familiar with the lines and the style. Then we would go before John and his producer, in this case Arthur Hornblow Jr., so the actor could read the now familiar part. Read well and you got called back for a screen test. Read poorly and you were told how well you did, how great you were, and you knew you'd rot in hell before you'd hear from Huston.

That was the way it was for everyone, big name or unknown. That was the way it was supposed to be for Marilyn.

She was very nervous when she walked into the room and John graciously tried to put her at ease. Then we went into the other room and rehearsed the part a couple of times. She was terrible, the reading unimaginative, unexciting, barely competent.

"Well," she sighed. "I'm as ready as I'll ever be, I guess."

We both sat at John's desk and started doing the scene. Hornblow was to one side, though I paid no attention to him. He was a millionaire, the man who controlled the finances, but the power was with Huston, a fact which even Hornblow recognized. Instead of saying anything, Hornblow nervously used his fingers to comb and shape the nonexistent hair on his bald head. He was like the cliché of the old war movies, the man who loses his leg, then feels phantom pain in the area where he had his, now missing, limb. Hornblow seemed to remember the texture and appearance of the thick, wavy hair which must have once adorned his scalp. Unable to accept his loss, he almost constantly rearranged the fantasy strands he seemed to believe might still exist.

After a couple of beats, John picked up a pencil and started doodling—a sign of death. Doodling was John's unconscious signal to those around him that he was no longer listening. The reading was terrible, and he barely looked at the hapless girl, his mind undoubtedly considering who else might be auditioned.

The reading was mercifully brief. When it was over, John looked up, beamed at her, and seemed to want his expression to make her feel there was still hope for someone who would undoubtedly become the most beautiful waitress or hooker in Hollywood. She had no future in films.

"That was just *fine*, dear! Just *fine*! We'll let you know."

Marilyn was being dismissed, something she would not stand for. Blushing, her voice registering her despair, she said, "Oh, Mr. Huston, that was just *awful*! Please! Please can I do it again?"

The reaction caught Huston off guard. No one had ever refused to leave before. No one had ever asked for a second chance. Probably uncertain what else to do, John said, "Why, sure, dear . . . Go right ahead." The shocked Hornblow began rubbing his head so rapidly, I thought the friction might cause it to burst into flames.

In films of the day there would probably have been slightly ominous background music with just enough of a happy lilt hinted by the score that you knew everything was about to change. The actress would stiffen her back, square her shoulders, clear her throat, and deliver the most brilliant reading anyone had ever heard. Immediately she would be clad in a thousand-dollar gown, whisked by limousine to a posh Hollywood gathering, and handed an Oscar as the most brilliant new star in America.

But this wasn't a movie. This was real life and Marilyn Monroe was a no-talent bimbo. The second reading was as bad as the first. The only difference was that John wasn't doodling any more. He was looking at her, really looking.

John, Arthur, and I all told her how well she had done, each of us lying through our teeth. I escorted her outside, knowing I would probably never see her again. Then, rather impulsively, she turned, thanked me for my kindness and assistance with the reading, and kissed me.

It was a long kiss, friendly but with enough open-mouthed lip movement on her part to reveal the reason Johnny Hyde was interested in her. The only problem was that she wore that thick red lipstick so popular with bimbos of the day and I hated the feel and taste of it. Even worse, I knew that no matter how I tried to wipe my mouth, some of it would linger on my lips and the rest would forever stain my handkerchief. There would be no way to adequately explain what happened when I went home to my wife, Jackie. Just another hard day with the no-talent bimbos, my dear . . .

"She's stunning, isn't she?" I said when I returned a moment later. There was nothing else you could say that was positive after a terrible reading like that.

Hornblow, finally relaxed, blew his nose and said, "She's terrible. Forget it."

"No, wait a minute. She's got spunk," said John, a glint in his eye as he rushed to the window and parted the Venetian blinds. She was leaving the Thalberg Building on the MGM lot where John had his offices. He watched her wiggling down the steps, then turned, smiled and said, "Look at the ass on that little lady! Spunk. Just what the role calls for."

She got the part.

Johnny Hyde understood the importance of Marilyn's part in *The Asphalt Jungle*, not because of its size but because it was a John Huston picture. The director's work was always studied closely both by the critics and people within the industry. He carefully crafted each script, planned each shot, then let the cameras roll through an entire scene even when mistakes were made, lines dropped forcing the other actors to improvise, and similar mishaps occurred. Other directors would stop the filming with the first mistake, then shoot the scene again. Huston realized that, while often the footage was not worth keeping, sometimes the way the actors adapted to the mishap created a stronger scene than he originally envisioned. This combination of brilliance, planning, and flexibility were unique among major directors of the day, the reason the critics often referred to "the Huston touch."

Marilyn's part in the film was of limited duration, yet one was guaranteed to be noticed. In the conservative 1950s, her character, Angela, was the type of woman parents warned their children against. A girl who didn't listen to her mother and father, who chose to pursue selfish desires instead of proper marriage and family, and could become the play-toy of an evil man. Such characters on the screen were at once compelling and revolting to the audience, the reason they lingered in the mind disproportionately to the time the character appeared in the film.

Johnny Hyde did not expect Marilyn to become an overnight star in Huston's latest film. Instead he hoped that it would lift her out of the anonymous roles that had so far defined her career.

Hyde was not the only person in Marilyn's life who had hopes for the role. Natasha Lytess had left Columbia Pictures and become not only Marilyn's private drama coach but also her closest female friend and mentor. She was asked by Marilyn to stay on Huston's set with her, standing just out of camera range. Marilyn wanted to be perfect, and was convinced that only Natasha could help her achieve such success. She was unaware that Huston and Lytess worked in such radically different ways that the drama coach was hated. The only reason Huston tolerated the intrusion was because he so feared the wrath of Ryman and Carroll, the calling-in of his debt, and the loss of his horses that he would say nothing. Whatever Marilyn wanted, Marilyn was allowed. There was too much at stake to challenge Lytess, in case she had Lucille and John's tacit approval.

In hindsight, neither Marilyn nor Natasha could clearly define their roles in each other's lives. They seemed to have a love/hate relationship. At first, Monroe did whatever Natasha told her, so cowed by the older, more experienced, more sophisticated acting coach that she once said, "There were days when I couldn't figure out why she kept me on as a student, because she made me feel so shallow and without talent. Very often it seemed that to her I was one of the hundred neediest cases."

Lytess, who seemed jealous of her protégé's looks and sparking personality, eventually came to think that Marilyn was a manipulator. She used everyone, even going so far as to periodically move in with Natasha and her young daughter in their one-bedroom apartment when she did not want to stay with Johnny Hyde. Yet Marilyn's actions during the filming of *The Asphalt Jungle* seemed to reflect her insecurity and, at least at the time, total reliance on her acting coach to the exclusion of others more directly connected with the picture.

It was Marilyn's idea to have Lytess work as her acting coach for her small part in *The Asphalt Jungle*. Marilyn's willingness to stand up to Huston impressed Natasha, who did not realize that it was the director's debts and the blackmail he was enduring that made him acquiesce and that kept him silent when he would have preferred to have Natasha banned from the set.

Huston's problem was that each time there was a scene with Marilyn, she would look over at Natasha for approval. If Natasha did not like the way something was done, Marilyn wanted to repeat it. Worse, Natasha made Marilyn self-conscious. She became so concerned with her appearance and movement that many takes failed to capture the character she was playing. Fortunately for Hyde's plans and Marilyn's career, the approximately five minutes of Monroe that made it to the screen (culled from many times that much film taken for each of the scenes) were brilliant.

As finally edited, *Marilyn* is introduced approximately a fifth of the way into the picture. She is resting on a couch, the "niece" of the elderly lawyer. (The term "niece" was used to protect the film from censorship.) The two embrace, kiss, and he sends her off to bed. Everyone seeing the film understood the subtext when Marilyn called the man "uncle," but to actually use the word "mistress" would have created a censorship problem for Huston.

The second appearance in the film brings depth to her character. She is seen in a black strapless gown and is upset that she may be abandoned by the man who is keeping her. She is going to be sent on a cruise to get her out of town, and the more she thinks about it, the more she suppresses her anger and starts fantasizing about how she'll look. She says, "Imagine me on this beach with my green bathing suit. Yipes! I almost bought a white one, but it wasn't quite extreme enough. Don't get me wrong. If I'd gone in for the *extreme* extreme, I'd have bought a French one! Run for your life, girls, the fleet's in!"

The third scene is the most complex, though again it lasts only a very short time—approximately two-and-a-half minutes, about the same as a popular song heard on the radio in that era. This is the start of the dramatic downfall of the men who were trying to execute the jewel robbery. Marilyn's character, Angela, has been caught telling lies to help the lawyer's alibi. She is both terrified of what is going to happen and angry with the police officer putting her in so uncomfortable position with the man who has been keeping her.

There was one ironic aspect to the film when it premiered at Grauman's Egyptian Theater. The movie had been publicly previewed at the Picwood Theater in West Los Angeles on February 16, 1950, in order to gain audience reaction when they filled out review cards at the end of the film. To Huston's delight, only one person out of the audience of 282 disliked it, and almost 200 in the audience described it as either "Excellent" or "Very Good." The hype he built from that initial showing led to a star-studded formal premiere with members of the movie industry coming to see the film and a large number of fans crammed against barricades as they shouted for autographs. The Los Angeles Police Department dispatched several officers to work that evening—and among them was Patrol Officer Jim Dougherty.

In the aftermath of the successful launch of the movie, there was no question that a portion of Hyde's strategy had been successful. Marilyn was noticed both by some of the critics and by various studio executives, but almost entirely for her beauty. Unfortunately the success of the film came mostly from the fact that it was an effective ensemble company. No "star" stood out, because the characters and their relationships with one another came across as real to the audience. It was the fact that her character blended so well with the others that showed her improvement as an actress, which did not translate into the type of work Hyde hoped. Instead, Marilyn obtained an uncredited cameo in the MGM film *Right Cross*, playing a character similar to Angela. She also had a brief role in a film called *Home Town Story*.

As much as Hyde was against Marilyn returning to playing little-noticed cameos in often second-rate movies, he arranged for her to take the two small parts as a way to keep her working. Marilyn wanted and needed the adulation that came from being on the screen, if only for a brief time, and Johnny was a dying man desperate to prove his love to the end.

There were studio executives at MGM who would have placed Marilyn under contract after her work with Huston, but they could not override studio head Dore Schary, a man who might be described as a pragmatic moralist. He had both seen the competence of Marilyn's work in *The Asphalt Jungle* and was aware of her personal reputation off screen. Hiring her to act in a single film was fine since presumably she had earned the right through a screen test and a reading (he did not know about the blackmail by John Carroll and Lucille Ryman).

Dore Schary was a pragmatic moralist. He would authorize the hiring of seemingly anyone in Hollywood to appear in a movie for which he or she was appropriate. Marilyn certainly fit this category when she was hired for *The Asphalt Jungle* following both a reading and a screen test that John Huston used to justify the one-picture contract. But the moralist in Schary made him believe that a long-term contract should only go to an actor of high standards. Marilyn was known in the industry for her willingness to please men. Schary had heard the comments of young men like Mickey

Rooney who bluntly called her a cocksucker. He personally saw her as little more than a prostitute, despite how well she handled the part of Angela. He would not hear of giving her a job other than on a per-picture basis.

Johnny kept looking for the next "Angela" type of role that would enhance what Marilyn had accomplished with John Huston. He was convinced she just needed time on screen with the right director and technical people. He knew that being a star meant electrifying the screen with your presence, not having acting skills such as those expected on the stage. Besides, her soft voice was death in the theater but readily enhanced for film. Her tendency to forget lines or stumble through a scene mattered not at all because there could be a second try and a third if necessary, a luxury not possible when a show had to be performed from beginning to end without the audience losing the suspension of disbelief.

Adding to Hyde's belief was the fact that, when photographed for magazines, Marilyn's image was one of simmering sensuality, of sex waiting to explode. She was the virgin next door, the neighbor girl grown to womanhood, emotionally barely contained as she looked for the right man with whom to share a lifetime of sexual activity. When Marilyn appeared on the screen, every male in the audience knew instantly that, given just a little luck, he would be that right man.

With such an on-camera persona, acting was secondary to camera angles, lighting, makeup, and wardrobe. Hyde supported the acting lessons Marilyn took and the ways in which she wanted to better herself, but he also saw them as secondary. You either had the right screen persona or you didn't. *The Asphalt Jungle* had proven she had it.

Natasha either saw none of what Hyde saw, or she saw it all too clearly and feared losing the woman with whom she was so emotionally intertwined. That was why she continued working with Marilyn after the actress had finished her one picture for MGM.

Natasha Lytess trained young actors, including Marilyn, as though they were the serious acting students with whom she had worked in the European theater. There were diction lessons, for example, in which she stressed perfect pronunciation that came across as artificial on the screen when Marilyn followed her directions. Lytess also stressed mastering a role over spontaneity, though the latter was critical for comedy and Marilyn, if at all competent in her early years, seemed to do well with comedy. She had the right combination of observation of the absurd in everyday life, timing, and an understated way of delivery that was unique to only a handful of actors. Had she lived past the years when almost everyone from casting directors to Marilyn herself felt that sex was her primary selling point, she might have become a successful character actor.

Marilyn was also taught understated movement, an important part of film since the camera is much closer than with stage. Stage actors learned to make sweeping gestures and broad pronouncements, since the audience was some distance away. With film, a tear drop making its way slowly down a cheek could be filmed many times larger than life. Yet on stage, no one would ever see the person cry.

No matter what problems Marilyn caused herself, either with her relationships or her ongoing work arrangement with Lytess, her obsession with improvement was impressive. She seemed uninterested in money except for survival and eventually began living in three places based on what she could afford and the people helping her. She rented a one-room efficiency apartment with cinder-block walls in the Beverly Carlton Hotel, where she lived alone. She stayed for days or weeks with Natasha Lytess and her daughter in their one-bedroom apartment. And she lived in the home Johnny Hyde had rented.

Marilyn also actively pursued physical fitness, lifting weights and jogging each day, neither practice common for women or even most men in that pre-physical fitness era. However, she not only enjoyed it, she felt she had to do everything possible to be ready for the next opportunity, regardless of what Johnny was trying to do on her behalf.

Marilyn never fully trusted anyone else to get her work; when someone did, she had no illusions about what it meant. She had gained the role in the Huston film, yet was not suddenly a star. She knew Johnny had done his best and was grateful, yet there were other powerful men who might exchange favors with her and not with Johnny.

Marilyn recognized that Natasha was a little like a stage mother. She seemed to be living a part of her life through Marilyn's achievements. It was a relationship that would always be filled with tension for both women. However, Marilyn recognized that by living independently from Natasha and Johnny for periods of time, she was in control of both relationships. She accepted the verbal abusiveness of both of them, recognizing that always they wanted her with greater intensity than she needed their approval for her acting skills.

Monroe also understood her power position. Johnny wanted her to marry him and inherit his wealth, something he would not give to her unless she was his wife. Natasha Lytess was paid for her acting lessons, and, even with Marilyn's payments and the money Natasha earned from her other students, she was barely getting by. She had quit her studio job in anticipation of the private students she imagined she would have, and which would allow her to meet all her financial needs; then she discovered she needed the income the studio had paid her. As a private coach, she could not afford to lose the income from even a single student.

Just as the multiple living arrangements worked to keep Hyde and Lytess emotionally off balance, so her messy, one-room efficiency apartment had its purpose. Marilyn used it in the manner of a studio set. She would occasionally bring a friend there to see her limited circumstances and cramped lifestyle. Like the Carrolls, they would feel she needed help, giving her money to help her get by. They never knew that others paid her rent and she had seemingly unlimited resources for survival if she chose to use them.

But most important of all, Marilyn felt that maintaining the small Beverly Carlton Hotel apartment would enable her to use someone she felt was more powerful than Johnny Hyde. She wanted to use Joe Schenck.

Joseph Schenck had a reputation among Hollywood insiders for training women to accomplish things they might not be able to achieve themselves. Sometimes this was moving a limited talent starlet into a successful marriage. Sometimes he helped them advance their careers by arranging for parts, auditions with men who owed him favors, or other forms of pressure. And all he asked in return was an occasional expression of carnal gratitude.

Marilyn knew she could not be living with Johnny Hyde and having regular sex with Joe Schenck. Each man might understand what was happening with the other, yet with Marilyn staying in the small apartment, both their actions were acceptable. She put her emotions on hold, seeking nothing in the present but a way to achieve her ultimate plans for the future.

Johnny Hyde did not like the fact that Marilyn was not living with him, and even Natasha kept encouraging her to have more contact with the agent, to spend more intimate time with him. However, he was aware of the Schenck relationship, had long called Marilyn a "chump," and since he knew he wouldn't change her sexual promiscuity, he was willing to use Schenck's connections to help Marilyn gain a part that would give her at least as much attention as her five minutes in *The Asphalt Jungle*.

Hyde may have been willing to not fight Marilyn's relationship with Schenck for another reason. Johnny wanted only one thing from Marilyn—to be Mrs. Johnny Hyde, so she would be a rich woman when he died. He did not understand the intensity of Marilyn's desire to be a star. Money was not important to her (and as it turned out, poor advice and iron-clad contracts assured that she never financially benefited from her popularity in the manner of other actors).

Marilyn understood that the moment she became Mrs. Johnny Hyde she would never again be taken as seriously as she was at that moment, and that was not very serious at all. She had grown from a weak to a mediocre actress. She had an adequate singing voice and style of presentation. She was an acknowledged hard worker both on and off the set, but she herself admitted her other skill when she learned that her success in *All About Eve* meant that future roles would be larger and her pay greater than in the past. She commented about her changing relations with producers and directors, "Now I won't have to suck cock anymore."

※

Actress Zsa Zsa Gabor was married to actor George Sanders, one of the stars of *All About Eve*. George and Zsa Zsa had a chance to watch a portion of Monroe's personal life during hours when they weren't on the set, and George was rumored to have had sex with Marilyn when his wife was away. Whatever the truth about the sexual relationship, Zsa Zsa later recalled for *Playboy Video Magazine* that Marilyn "was a very dull girl. She thought that if a man who takes her out for dinner doesn't sleep with her that night—something's wrong with her. When George was making *All About Eve* in San Francisco, we had a suite and next to us Marilyn Monroe had a room. George made a thing out of it and said, 'Let's see how many men are going to go into her room tonight!' I'd seen about *four*. That's a terrible thing to say about somebody who the whole country admires."

※

Marilyn Monroe was defined by Harry Brand in his second biography of her, to be released to the press each time she was in a new Twentieth Century-Fox release. The bio, dated February 7, 1951, was more complete than his first of her, written five years earlier. It was also equally inaccurate, though in different ways from its predecessor. Now she was being groomed for larger roles, and it was important for him to write something that could be used by a magazine with a lazy reporter or a magazine on the East Coast that would run a pre-written story rather than going to the expense of sending someone cross country. He wrote:

> One night not long ago Marilyn Monroe, beautifully groomed and dressed in expensive good taste, was escorted to a premiere at the Circle Theatre on El Centro Street in Hollywood by Charles Chaplin Jr.
>
> As they neared the theatre someone in the party called attention to a severe frame building sitting back from the street.
>
> "That's the Los Angeles Orphanage," someone said. "You know, where they keep the kids that nobody wants."
>
> Marilyn kept right on walking. She makes no effort to conceal the fact that her early life was spent in a series of private homes and in the orphanage as a ward of Los Angeles County, but this period of her life she prefers to forget. Her eyes are on a bright future in the make-believe world of the films, where anything can come true, and where it really is coming true for Marilyn. At twenty-two, she ranks as one of the cinema's most promising newcomers and her studio, 20th Century-Fox, is building her into a top-bracket star.
>
> Big, sprawling Los Angeles County did the best it could for Marilyn but it's a pretty impersonal sort of father and mother, and even though the various families who kept the little girl in their homes were good to her, she learned early in life to be self-sufficient and to make the best of whatever environment in which she found herself. Perhaps that accounts for the equanimity with which she faced the early disappointment of her Hollywood career after being "discovered" by a studio and then being dropped to await discovery all over again. [Note: This unnamed studio that "discovered" Marilyn then dropped her was Twentieth Century-Fox, the employer of both Brand and, at that moment, Monroe.]
>
> Marilyn's real name was Norma Jean Baker [sic] and her mother was a helpless invalid and her father was killed in an automobile accident shortly after her birth. Marilyn has never known either. She spent her childhood in

a series of private homes as a ward of the County, and even now she finds it a trifle confusing to remember all of them. [Brand's previous bio said she was Norma Jean Dougherty and also mentioned the Goddards.]

The first home with which she was placed was in Hawthorne, California. She remembers little about them as the family moved east when she was five and Marilyn was placed with a family of British actors who had emigrated to Hollywood and were playing bits in pictures. Marilyn picked up a decided British accent and got her first lessons in knife-throwing, juggling Indian clubs and other vaudeville specialties which might prove valuable in after [sic] life.

At seven-and-a-half she moved in with a Hollywood studio worker and his wife and shed the British accent. They lived in a big house on a hill and were kind to her but there were no children around, so she found herself relying for companionship on a collection of exotic birds.

They, too, could not keep her and at nine Marilyn was taken to the Los Angeles orphan's home. The superintendent, a Mrs. Dewey, was "wonderful and sweet" but there were so many children to care for that the matrons found it impossible to give any of them the affection children need. Here Marilyn had her first job—helping in the pantry and setting tables at five cents a month. These nickels were carefully hoarded by the kids so that at Christmas time they could cross the street to the drugstore and buy gifts for each other of writing tablets, pencils, etc. After serving in the pantry at five cents a month, Marilyn later had her salary doubled. She was promoted to washing dishes in the kitchen at ten cents a month. It was during this period, at the age of nine, that Marilyn and other youngsters from the orphanage were Christmas guests of RKO studios. They were shown a movie on the lot and were given a string of imitation pearls as a gift. Marilyn says this was one of the great thrills of her childhood and it may have whetted her appetite for the movies.

Before she was ten, Marilyn was again placed as a boarder with a Los Angeles family, this time in the San Fernando Valley. Then there was another move, this time to a family made up entirely of women: a great grandmother, grandmother, mother and three young daughters. She stayed there but a short time.

Then came a move which was to have its most import effect upon Marilyn. She was taken in by Mrs. E. Anna [sic] Lower, of West Los Angeles, whom Marilyn still thinks of as "Aunt Anna." Mrs. Lower was the nearest thing to "family" that Marilyn has ever known. This wonderful woman, who has since died, treated Marilyn like a daughter and within the limits of her ability provided her with things she needed, plus an abundance of love and affections.

She was with "Aunt Anna" for two years and lived in what was then called the Sawtelle District, regarded by the more favored youngsters from Bel Air, and Brentwood as the "wrong side of the tracks."

While living with Mrs. Lower she began to emerge from her shell and spend more time with other children. She took an interest in the school plays and being a lanky girl found herself playing boy's parts both in the school plays and in the out-of-school activities such as the little "radio" shows which she and her Sawtelle friends improvised. It was her fate to play the young prince when such productions as Jack and the Beanstalk were undertaken.

During one period of Mrs. Lower's illness, Marilyn lived for a time with a lawyer and his wife in Westwood, and at another period lived with a family which included three other children in the San Fernando Valley. However, "Aunt Anna's" home remained her real base until the death of that fine woman.

At fifteen and in high school, Marilyn experienced a short-lived marriage which she prefers to forget. Both were immature youngsters, the thing didn't work out, and the boy is now happily married and has a family.

After completing her schooling at Van Nuys High School in the San Fernando Valley, Marilyn went to work for the Radio Plane Co. inspecting parachutes for target planes. The firm was owned by Reginald Denny.

While working at the plant she augmented her income by modeling and one month had her picture on four magazine covers. Howard Hughes, then convalescing from an airplane accident, saw them and became interested in her but before he could arrange a screen test, 20th Century-Fox had given her a color test and signed her for a year.

The biography continues with a relatively accurate account of her first pictures. Then, as though appearing on the big screen brings peace to a troubled soul, it ends with:

"Now, with a big studio behind her, a comfortable apartment, nice clothes and a world of friends, she is able to forget the early hardships.

"Hollywood which is often the scene of heartbreak, has been the scene of her success. It hasn't been easy, but at twenty-two Marilyn has little to complain about."

Thirty

Begging for Work

Despite *The Asphalt Jungle*, Johnny Hyde was unable to get Monroe the work she needed, so he talked with actor Mickey Rooney about getting her a part in his latest film, *The Fireball*. As Rooney explained in his autobiography *Life Is Too Short*, *The Fireball* was a rollerdrome melodrama that he was making for United Artists. This was a period when roller skating was a popular activity. There were roller derbies in which teams of men or women competed in endurance races that were often almost as violent as professional wrestling, yet totally unscripted. There were roller rinks where families could enjoy skating together, and couples could come for an evening of dancing on their skates. Low-budget movies involving teens and roller skates regularly made money because of the popularity of the sport. However, no one, including Mickey Rooney at this stage in his career, was paid very much money.

Rooney's name was familiar because he had been an extremely successful child star in movies such as the Andy Hardy series. However, he was no longer a teenager, and after finishing his military service in World War II, he found that almost no one thought he still had box-office appeal. Without money and with little future in the industry, he took whatever parts he could get, usually in low-budget pictures. *Fireball* was typical.

The absurd story line has Rooney (almost thirty years old in real life) playing the teenage Johnny Casar, who runs away from Father O'Hara's St. Luke's Home for Boys. He manages to get a job washing dishes at a restaurant and bar owned by Bruno Crystal, as well as finding a pair of roller skates that just happen to be in his size.

The police find Johnny, but Father O'Hara is comfortable with Johnny working for Crystal, taking free roller skating lessons (under the tutelage of the evil Mack Miller), and hanging out at the Palamar Rollerbowl where he is properly trained by Mary Reeves, Mack's kind and beautiful skating partner.

Ultimately Johnny becomes a TV skating star destined for a showdown competition race against Mack. The rest of the less-than-believable story has Mack beating Johnny, Johnny fighting back and becoming "Athlete of the Year" after he joins the professional U.S. National Bears roller skating team. But there is far more. Johnny and Mack become teammates on the Bears, but Johnny destroys their chances of winning a race by deliberately knocking down Mack, whom he hates. Then Johnny gets polio, drops out of skating, and is emotionally supported by Mary and Father O'Hara.

Of course Johnny recovers, though it means two years of intense work. He returns to international competition with his old team, but now he is a better person. Given a chance to star or help a rookie who has just reached the big time, Johnny helps the rookie and goodness triumphs, as it must.

As for Marilyn, she puts in a brief appearance as one of Johnny's groupies. It was nothing memorable, but it was work and a paycheck, both of which she needed in the worst way.

Thirty-one

All About Eve

It was in early April when Hyde, using Schenck to smooth the way, had Marilyn meet with Joseph L. Mankiewicz, the writer/director of a film called *Best Performance*. Mankiewicz was greatly in demand, his previous screenplay, *A Letter to Three Wives*, having won an Academy Award. This time he would be working for Darryl Zanuck at Fox.

Best Performance, a movie whose title was later changed to *All About Eve*, was an insider story about show business. It told of Eve, a top stage actress played by Anne Baxter, and her aggressive rise to stardom. The woman was ruthless, willing to do anything for—or against—anyone else in order to get to the top. It was vicious, funny, and a major film for Fox. In addition to Baxter, the film had Bette Davis, George Sanders, Celeste Holm, Gary Merrill, Hugh Marlowe, and Thelma Ritter, all known as A-list talents, the first to be sought to make a film a success.

The movie began as a short story called "The Wisdom of Eve" that was published in the May 1946 issue of *Cosmopolitan* magazine. Neither the George Sanders nor the Marilyn Monroe characters are used in the story that is actually based on actress Elisabeth Bergner (the Margo Channing character, played by Davis) who was married to Clement Howell from England. The story ultimately made a profit of $1.5 million in the first-run release and would later be adapted to the Broadway stage as the play *Applause*.

Although he may not have remembered the incident, George Sanders first met Marilyn at a Hollywood party where, so drunk that he fell asleep minutes later, he proposed marriage to her. By the time Marilyn saw him again, he was married to a woman she described as "a blonde with a funny accent." The wife was Zsa Zsa Gabor, and if Sanders remembered his "proposal," he gave no indication of it.

There was no question that Marilyn was the appropriate actress to play "Miss Casswell," the dim-witted girlfriend of drama critic Addison DeWitt (George Sanders). She claimed to be an actress who was "a graduate of the Copacabana School of Dramatic Art." However, the character was perceptive about others, sensing the personality they sometimes tried to hide from the world, such as when Miss Casswell comments about producers, "Why do they always look like unhappy rabbits?" Later, Addison DeWitt puts her down with the line, "You have a point. An idiotic one, but a point."

Miss Casswell was a loner, never having meaningful friends, and provided a contrast to Eve, a highly aggressive woman, new to the theater, not very talented, but willing to do anything with a man who could help her. Eve would sleep with the producer or with a drama critic if that was what it took to get better parts and build her reputation.

Working on the film led to the awareness of a trait Monroe revealed to her fellow cast members and the crew, but not to the general public. It was noticed when everyone went to San Francisco for a location shot in the lobby of the Curran Theater. The shot should have been a quick one, but there were repeated takes and delays because of ambient street noise. Eventually it was determined that voices would have to be overdubbed because the ambient sound could not be overcome by the recording equipment. But while they were shooting and reshooting, the majority of the cast and crew spent their down time together, seemingly becoming close. They ate together. They drank together. And they watched Marilyn—always prompt, friendly, helpful, respectful, and hardworking on the set—drift off to be alone. It seemed to some of those who discussed it later that she was not shunning them. Instead, they perceived her to be totally focused on the work, on her effort to become a star. She was seemingly unaware of all else taking place around her.

This time the truth was more nuanced. When actress Celeste Holm (Karen Richards in the film) discussed the production with author Richard Bruskin she commented that the cast worked well together but did not personally get along. She specifically cited Bette Davis who she considered to always be rude no matter what she was doing. It is possible that Marilyn simply did not want to be a part of infighting and sniping by actors who were well enough established that they did not care if they alienated a co-worker so long as they were professional on the set.

Whatever else was taking place, the work was brilliant. It was nominated for eleven Oscars at the Academy Awards and took six: Best Supporting Actor (George Sanders), Best Black and White Costume Design, Best Picture, Best Sound Recording, Best Director, and Best Screenplay.

Marilyn's part in *All About Eve* was a small one, a sophisticated version of the Angela character she had played in *The Asphalt Jungle*. This time she would be "Miss Casswell," the name she would use when calling some of her long-term friends such as Sid Skolsky. The pay was to be five hundred dollars per week, the scenes so limited that they would only provide a single week's work. However, difficulties with shooting on location resulted in her being involved for two months, the most money she had ever earned.

Marilyn also revealed another side of herself with Joe Mankiewicz during this time. They had finished their work in San Francisco and were back in the studio, shooting a complicated party scene. To the writer's surprise, Marilyn appeared with a copy of *Letters to a Young Poet* by the late German writer Rainer Maria Rilke. She was reading the work whenever she had a break. It was so unusual a choice that he asked about it.

Mankiewicz said that Marilyn replied, "You see, in my whole life I haven't read hardly anything at all. I don't know where to begin. So what I do is, every now and then I go into the Pickwick [book shop] and just look around. I leaf through some books, and when I read something that interests me—so last night I bought this one."

Marilyn was embarrassed, according to Mankiewicz, but he encouraged her. He told her that her approach to selecting a book to read was the best way to do it. Touched by his kindness, the next day she sent him a copy of the book as a present.

The film was a success in more ways than Johnny had hoped. On July 18, 1950, before the release of *All About Eve*, William Randolph Hearst's Hollywood columnist, Louella Parsons, wrote:

Marilyn Monroe, who packs the same punch Lana Turner did in her early days, gets her first starring role in *Cold Shoulder* with Vic Mature and Richard Conte. Marilyn, who hasn't a relative in the world and who was brought up in any orphanage, is one of the nicest girls in this town and everybody is plugging for her to succeed. She must be proud that she is clicking big in 20th, the studio which once let her go. Marilyn didn't have a big role in *Asphalt Jungle*, but what she did was so punchy that 20th brought her back home at many times what she had received before. I'm told she is excellent in *All About Eve*, which is whispered to be a honey.

Ironically, *Cold Shoulder*, the movie the columnist was starting to plug, would never get made. Darryl Zanuck had been planning the picture that would have Richard Conte and Victor Mature as costars. Natasha Lytess was working with Marilyn to prepare her for a screen test as a gangster's moll. She was remembered as having an impressive test but with a script that was not good on almost any level. In addition, there were rumors that Zanuck found Marilyn's screen test wanting, his only interest in using her coming from a desire to capitalize on the press attention she was getting.

Johnny was now able to go further for Marilyn. He arranged for her to be interviewed by a writer for *Photoplay* and to make a television commercial promoting Union Oil Company of California. The commercial had her talking about Royal Triton Gasoline, a nerve-wracking experience much like her stage work. She would only make two other live television appearances during her life, though that was not unusual. Just as there was a disconnect between the actors who started on the stage and those who started in the movies, so there was a disconnect between working live television and movies.

The *Photoplay* interview was apparently equally upsetting. Writer Fredda Dudley described her as looking "as wild and terrified as a deer."

৪৯

It was in the fall of 1950 that Marilyn moved into the West Hollywood apartment Natasha rented on Harper Avenue near Fountain. Marilyn had a daybed in the living room, shared the care of Natasha's daughter, and enjoyed the companionship of Josefa, a female Chihuahua given to her by Schenck as a twenty-fourth birthday present. (Always a dog-lover, though unwilling to train her animals, she would eventually be given "Maf," a present from Frank Sinatra and a name chosen as being short for "Mafia," a joke about the singer's mob friends.)

The dog caused the first major split with Natasha, as well as affecting other relationships, especially with Peter Lawford. As determined as Marilyn was to be a star, she was undisciplined in her care of the pet. She never took the time and trouble to housebreak the animal. There was no effort to establish a schedule for walks. The dog was always adored, doted on, and given special meals, yet she would never go so far as to make it the pleasant companion housebreaking would have allowed. Instead, the Chihuahua relieved itself wherever it happened to be in the house.

Marilyn was disgusted by the messes the animal made in the apartment and in the subsequent home in which she lived, but she never did anything about them. Everything was left uncleaned for someone else to handle. When she lived with Lytess, it was Natasha's problem, a fact made more upsetting for the older woman because of the health danger to her child.

A year later, in 1951, actor Peter Lawford discovered the problem when he asked Marilyn for a date. He and his best friend, Joe Naar, were double-dating, Naar taking out actress Barbara Darrow.

The public image Marilyn tried to foster was of no interest to Peter as he expressed in an interview where he commented, "There are many girls with long blonde hair and sexy figures whom men consider beautiful. But I don't. To me a girl with a well-groomed look, not the flamboyant type, but a quiet beauty who radiates health and vitality is the greatest beauty of them all. I go for the typical college type, not movie sirens."

What drew Peter to Marilyn was the private woman, the physical-fitness buff who loved to jog and lift weights. This quieter side appealed to the British actor who was an expert surfer despite having had a childhood accident that left him with only one functioning hand. He was turned off by the tight dresses and low-cut blouses, but so long as the woman he was dating was Marilyn-the-quiet-fitness-buff, he could overlook the Hollywood flamboyance of an actress on the make. What he could not stand was the way she let the dog make its mess wherever it wanted.

Lawford was one of a number of young actors who dated one another, partied together, and worked among the various studios, sometimes under contract and sometimes on loan. The friends ranged from Judy Garland and Elizabeth Taylor to Joe Naar, a man who became a producer.

The one and only night that Peter had an actual date with Marilyn she was not ready to leave when he arrived. She had Peter wait in the living room where he played with her dog, discovering almost immediately that the animal was not housebroken. Worse, there were small piles of excrement in various corners of the floor, some obviously older and some fairly fresh. There was no sign that Marilyn had tried to clean them.

Peter, disgusted by the sight and what it told him about Marilyn's values, went into the kitchen and opened cupboard doors until he found cleaning supplies and paper towels. Then he spent part of the time waiting for her to finish putting on makeup cleaning what never should have been visible. Although he and the other friends had a casual attitude toward sex, Peter never tried to bed Marilyn. He worried that her personal hygiene was as negligent as her cleaning up after the dog she had not trained.

That night Peter and Marilyn double dated with his longtime friend Joe Naar and Naar's date, a woman named Barbara Darrow. Peter remained so shaken that he asked Joe to take Marilyn home and he took Barbara back to where she lived. From then on, though he, Marilyn, and their other young actor friends spent time together, it would always be at anyone's home other than Marilyn's.

(Note: Various authors have quoted various individuals, including Marilyn herself, about the relationship with Lawford. A November 1952 issue of *American Weekly* magazine quoted Marilyn as saying, "I never have had a date with Peter. We were at the same table at a nightclub (one of my few appearances at a nightclub. I don't care for them) and I may have danced with him, but that hardly constitutes a date, and certainly not a romance." And at least one author claims that Peter said he fell for her but she did not respond. The one area of agreement is that they were not lovers.)

Marilyn and some of her friends would wonder why Peter never came on to her sexually. Sometimes Marilyn would wonder if she had done something wrong, never thinking about the dog mess. Usually they assumed that there was something wrong with Peter.

Only Johnny Hyde did not have to contend with the dog. When Marilyn was dating him or living in his home, the dog was not around.

Johnny also did not see much of Marilyn in the last few months of 1950. She was keeping her distance from him, wooing Joe Schenck, trying to do whatever she could for her career. Natasha was outraged, knowing Johnny was too important for Marilyn's career to be ignored. She insisted Marilyn keep contact, if only by telephone. She knew that Hyde was increasingly bedridden, calling studio personnel by telephone, determined to be of value to Marilyn to the end, hoping she would marry him before he died. He also ensured that Marilyn would be his agency's legacy.

Marilyn, constantly demeaned by Natasha and Johnny like a beloved puppy dog that keeps getting swatted with papers as he makes mess after mess, decided to improve her mind as much as her fitness routine helped her body. The University of California at Los Angeles (UCLA) offered non-credit ten-week courses in a variety of subjects. Marilyn chose world litera-ture taught by Claire Seay. She attended faithfully and dressed modestly, the only unusual aspect of her appearance being the jeans she wore instead of the more popular skirts and dresses.

There were also acting lessons from Natasha, both formally and during daily living as the two women and Natasha's daughter occasionally shared an apartment. Since neither woman was certain of the types of roles Marilyn might be given, they developed a method for planning and executing parts that would anger nearly every director Marilyn had while still working with Natasha.

First, there was the intellectual preparation for a role. There are many theories about the best way to become the character being played on the screen. Probably none of them is terrible, though most are not as good as their promoters claim. And in some instances, an actor becomes associated with a style of acting based on training he or she never received.

Marilyn was an intensely introspective woman when she began reading a screenplay. She was determined to succeed and terrified that she might not. She worried about how well she would do. She worried about what others thought of each of her scenes, instead of being concerned with con-veying the reality of the character to the movie audience. To have her do more thinking and more planning was to create problems for the directors whose job involved guiding the actors, not getting involved with the desires of an acting coach.

To make matters worse, Natasha convinced Monroe that unless the actress did what Lytess wanted, the scenes would not go well. They created a conspiracy meant to guarantee that whatever Natasha wanted from Marilyn, Natasha got. Each action, each line of dialogue, would be evaluated by Lytess as it took place on the soundstage, then changes would be signaled by subtle looks, hand gestures, or whatever else might work.

For example, Marilyn was not supposed to make a turn without having proper motivation for her speed, body position, or hand movements. If Lytess felt she was not thinking before the move, she would signal Marilyn to do it again. Likewise, if the move came too soon for Lytess's satisfaction, Marilyn would also be signaled. The actress would not continue working until the correction had been made with the scene shot over. It did not matter that the scene was perfect in the director's eye. It did not matter if the other actors had been so flawless that Marilyn's missing a beat was not noticed. It did not matter that each unnecessary retake added to the production cost of a film, especially if the time factor forced everyone into overtime pay. Marilyn was going to be a star, and that required her yielding totally to the acting coach.

On December 5, Johnny arranged for Marilyn to sign a three-year contract with the William Morris Agency, considered the most important and influential in the industry, for exclusive representation. This was so important a step in an actor's career, Marilyn would not have become a William Morris Agency client without Johnny Hyde's intervention. She was not yet adequately skilled. However, with the three-year agreement, Johnny thought he was securing her future.

It was less than a week after the signing that Johnny had been able to arrange for the screen test for *Cold Shoulder*. The movie was never made, but Marilyn passed the screen test, and Hyde's arrangement with Fox was that if Marilyn passed, she would be given a new seven-year contract for more money than in the past, though still with no assurances after six months.

Fox decided against producing *Cold Shoulder*, but Johnny was offered a small role for Marilyn in a forthcoming production of *As Young as You Feel*. She would play a secretary this time, not a moll, but the role was not large. Still, Johnny accepted it. By the time the year was over, Marilyn would have six films in release for 1950, including two from Metro where she had done limited work—*Hometown Story* and *Right Cross*, the latter with June Allyson and William Powell. While they were all small parts, the producers, the directors, the actors, and/or the type of roles combined to ensure that Marilyn would have a basis for moving up in her career.

Arrangements had been made for *Life* magazine to run a photo of Marilyn. It was scheduled for January 1, 1951, a time when fluff and hype were encouraged. The caption under the smiling actress referred to her as "a busty Bernhardt who at twenty-two seems to have her future assured." It mentioned her roles in *Asphalt Jungle* and *All About Eve*, proof that Johnny's strategy for bringing her to public attention had worked. It also commented that "Twentieth Century-Fox is convinced she will be a fine dramatic actress too." The story mentioned her new seven-year contract and the fact that the Paddy Chayefsky screenplay *As Young as You Feel* would be her next film. Again, the part was small, but in this case Chayefsky was so respected as a writer that having his name attached assured strong publicity.

Johnny also paid for Marilyn to get minor plastic surgery that December since there was time to recover before shooting her new movie. Her chin was modified and a small amount of her nose was reshaped to make her body perfect in his eyes. She recuperated in Johnny's Palm Drive home, spending ten days with her would-be lover, the longest she had been with him in weeks. He was constantly solicitous of her, as determined to convince her to marry him as ever. He was also, very obviously, extremely ill.

Johnny may have been short, but his years as an acrobat had kept him a powerful man almost to the end. His doctor had told him to stop climbing stairs, and because his weight was dropping rapidly, his chauffeur had no difficulty carrying him to the master bedroom each day.

Marilyn had great compassion for Johnny. Just as she occasionally favored men with sex when it was clear they desired her, now she favored Johnny with a promise to marry him.

The alleged commitment was known only to three men—Johnny, his brother Alex, and his business manager, Sam Berke. Alex was on the music staff of MGM and knew Marilyn's reputation. He did not mind his brother having a last fling with an aggressive young actress. He did fear that the marriage was Marilyn's way of gaining money and whatever prestige might come from being Mrs. Hyde.

The question that must be asked, though, is why Marilyn said she'd marry Johnny and whether she expected him to die before a wedding might take place. Marilyn had too long been adamant that she would not let herself get in a position where the marriage would ruin her future, and it seems that it would unquestionably have done so. Most likely Marilyn was being kind, knowing nothing would come of the relationship beyond what they already enjoyed. This probability was reinforced by Johnny's condition while Marilyn was staying in his home. He experienced such severe pain that he went to Cedars of Lebanon Hospital where he had been treated in the past.

On December 10 the doctors determined that Johnny had another heart blockage. His body could stand little more, and after four days in the hospital, he went home with plans for a vacation in Palm Springs. He said he would take Dona Hollaway, his secretary, with him so he could work.

The trip was strictly business, the rest at the Palm Springs Racquet Club where he stayed being scheduled in ways he would not allow at home. However, Dona could not spend more than four days with Johnny. She was married to a physician whose busy schedule made it important for her to be running their home. Without Dona, Johnny would have no one from whom to seek help when in crisis.

Heart disease was little understood in 1950. Today, everything from open-heart surgery to valve replacements and the clearing of blockages is common. The heart is understood as a muscle that needs exercising, and most heart patients are taught how to appropriately increase their activity, change their diets, and strengthen what is left of the muscle so they can live many more years. Standard advice in Johnny Hyde's day was to get rest and take medication for the pain, a treatment that led to consistent decline and early death.

Dona Holloway had to return to her family, if only for a couple of days, and realized that Johnny could not be left alone. There was a painful sensation in his fingers, a more intense version of the way a foot feels when the circulation is beginning to be restored after it has "fallen asleep." He was often confused, as though the blood flow to his brain was not always adequate. He also had extreme anxiety, though neither he nor anyone else around him understood why.

Marilyn agreed to drive down to Palm Springs, though she was extremely busy with the costume fittings for the movie in which Johnny had helped her get a role. She reached Palm Springs on December 15, and the following day Johnny suffered a massive heart attack and had to be carried back to his room.

Marilyn called Johnny's physician, who wanted him immediately transported back to Cedars of Lebanon Hospital. The ambulance came and Marilyn drove behind it back to Los Angeles. She was allowed to stay in his room with him that night, Dona also being summoned because he had hours to live at the most.

Later, speaking of that night, Marilyn said, "He used to tell me that if he ever got really sick and I heard of it, I should go to him and hold him in my arms, and I'd bring life back to him. I tried it, but it didn't work. I was in the hospital corridor that last night, and he was in an oxygen tent in a room with his family. After a while a doctor came out and told me Johnny was dead. I ran into the room and took him in my arms. His sons and relatives were there, but I didn't care. I held him in my arms, and after about twenty minutes, his face grew cold as ice. Then I let him go. It was too late."

Johnny had talked of changing his will to benefit Marilyn even if she didn't marry him. He and his business manager worked out an arrangement where she would receive one-third of his estate. Johnny wanted a house to be included, but both he and his business manager felt that she would not be able to handle property ownership at that stage in her life. The will was to be drawn up during the Palm Springs stay, something aborted because of the death. Knowing this, Johnny got Dona alone and told her to be certain that Marilyn was treated as a family member when he died.

The last wishes were to be denied. Johnny died on December 18, never recognizing the hurt he had caused his family by flaunting his affair with Marilyn at the end of his life. They would be embarrassed no more, immediately ordering her to leave the Palm Drive house. They had no right to force her to leave, but Marilyn did not care to fight the family. Overcome with grief, she secluded herself in Natasha's apartment.

The family also asked Marilyn to not attend the funeral service at Forest Lawn because it would upset Johnny's son, Jimmy. This time she ignored them, sitting with Dona and her husband. Later, Jimmy Hyde recalled the graveside service saying, "All I can recall clearly is Marilyn screaming my father's name over and over again. It shook everyone."

෯෨

Natasha Lytess was concerned that Marilyn kept to her room in the apartment she shared with Lytess and her daughter. The day she came home, allegedly five hours earlier than expected, she found a note on the door telling Natasha to not let four-year-old Barbara inside. Assuming a suicide attempt, Lytess opened the door and later described the scene of what would arguably be either her first known suicide attempt or her first known cry for attention.

> I grasped Marilyn's limp shoulders and shook her. "What have you done?" Then I saw an ooze of purplish paste in her lip-corners, and forced my fingers into her mouth.
>
> It was crammed full of this purplish paste—there must have been about 30 Nembutal [pentobarbital] capsules wadded in her mouth. Enough to kill five people.
>
> She hadn't swallowed them irretrievably only because her throat had dried up in terror the instant she'd got them into her mouth.
>
> And she'd been lying there, waiting for them to melt and trickle down, to destroy her life.
>
> She hadn't expected me back in the apartment for another five hours.

There is no reason to question Lytess's accuracy about what she observed. What needs to be questioned is the conclusion to which she came.

Lytess had no way of knowing just what Marilyn had stuffed in her mouth. She almost certainly did not know how much Nembutal Marilyn had in the pharmacy container when she stuffed her mouth, nor did she mention seeing an empty container. There is also the fact that Marilyn was accustomed to taking the sleeping medication that was always consumed with either water or, if it caused a stomach upset, with milk. Equally important when questioning what really took place was the fact that Marilyn had been alone in the apartment. If she had wanted to commit suicide by sleeping pills, and if her mouth had been too dry to swallow them, she could easily have gotten up, gotten a glass of water, and finished the job.

Natasha was convinced that this was a suicide attempt because she was not expected back for several hours, but that is all the more reason Marilyn should have been expected to get a drink and really kill herself. It is quite possible that Marilyn waited to stuff her mouth with the medicine until she heard someone coming, assuring that she would gain sympathy, attention, and a rescue. Close friends of Marilyn would talk about her "rescue me" actions in which she'd deliberately take an overdose of one or another medication, then call for help immediately so she could have her stomach pumped and everyone worried about her. Peter Lawford used to derisively call the actions "phone-dangling time with Marilyn."

The idea that Marilyn, alone in an apartment, would seriously try to commit suicide by stuffing pills into her dry mouth, then laying down while they slowly melted in her mouth, trickled down her throat, and gradually entered her bloodstream is nonsense.

❦

Both at the time of his death and later in her career, Marilyn realized that, without Johnny Hyde's obsessive belief in her star quality and genius at career building, she would have been just another pretty face, another willing body. Because of Johnny, she would achieve everything she ever imagined experiencing. She would be a star. She would be a legend. She would be a cult figure. It would be his legacy, his love offering. And if he could view what happened to his handiwork as she rocketed to stardom, perhaps she would also be his eternal regret.

Norma Jean may have understood Johnny's importance and deeply grieved his loss, but Marilyn being Marilyn, she had to embellish the truth, even with one of her lovers. Years after Hyde's death, Elia Kazan wrote of what he knew about Marilyn and Johnny's family:

> When he died, it became clear how fierce his [Johnny Hyde] family's hatred for Marilyn had been. I believe her devotion to little Johnny was as pure as it was for anyone the rest of her life, not mercenary as the family chose to believe. She was at his side when he died, but the body was quickly taken away and she was forbidden to come near it. She learned that Johnny was "lying in state" in his home and that some of the family were staying there with the body. Late at night, she used her keys to enter the place. Whoever was guarding the corpse had gone to bed; the candles had burned low. Marilyn told me she climbed on Johnny and lay on him. In still, silent love she stayed there until she heard the first stirring of the family members in the morning. Then she slipped out of the house—alone in the world.

It was a touching story, a metaphor on stardom eloquent in the sadness it brings to the soul. It showed Marilyn to be something more than a tragic heroine of a troubled life and ultimately premature death. It showed her to be what she was—a fraud.

The story Marilyn tearfully told a deeply moved Elia Kazan never happened.

Thirty-two

Not an Actress but a Star

No matter how limited as an actress the studio heads may have viewed Monroe, and no matter how little exposure she had had on screen, the films *The Asphalt Jungle* and *All About Eve* created an unanticipated interest in Monroe. She began receiving two thousand fan letters a week, a remarkable amount considering that her onscreen time had generally been either limited or was in low-budget films such as *The Fireball, Right Cross, Hometown Story, As Young as You Feel*, and *Love Nest*.

It is most likely that Marilyn had inadvertently created the excitement herself. She loved modeling for artists and still photographers. Any week she wasn't under contract she was pursuing magazine cover and advertising photography work. Even when she did have a role, she often found time to oblige photographers who were willing to adapt to her schedule. It was almost impossible to go to a newsstand of any size without finding one or more photos of Marilyn in one type of publication or another. She was famous enough to pose for *Life* and aggressive enough to have her image in many of the same publications to which David Conover had first submitted pictures.

Marilyn was also a studio publicist's delight. She was always ready with a touching story about her childhood, a humorous quip, and a ready smile. She might be exhausted from several weeks of twelve-hour days because of makeup, hair styling, wardrobe, rehearsals and filming but she would agree to personal appearances and handling publicity for the films. This was most obvious with *Love Happy*, which seemed to build an entire advertising campaign around thirty-eight seconds of walking and talking. But the more popular Marilyn became, the more creative were the studios.

For example, there was the 1952 movie *We're Not Married*, a film that told the stories of five couples who had marriage ceremonies performed by justice of the peace Melvin Bush (Victor Moore) several days before his license became valid. Two-and-a-half years have passed when the mistake is finally discovered. Each of the couples has built a life together based on their assumption that they are married, and when letters arrive explaining what took place, the stories unfold individually.

Marilyn's segment involves a housewife named Annabel Norris, winner of the Mrs. Mississippi contest and now an entrant in the Mrs. America contest. David Wayne, who plays her husband, Jeff, is upset with his wife's success because it interferes with the time she used to be able to spend with him, their baby, and their housework. He is pleased to learn that she is no longer eligible to retain the Mrs. Mississippi title or to compete in the Mrs. America pageant.

Annabel refuses to be defeated by a technicality. She enters and wins the *Miss* Mississippi contest and wins while her husband, holding their baby, watches. Each is delighted with the outcome, and their segment of the movie ends with a second (legal) marriage.

&

Screenwriter Nunnally Johnson was both the writer and producer for *We're Not Married* and was extremely troubled by Marilyn Monroe. He did not find her to be a beauty when he met her in the company of Johnny Hyde, and he was concerned by the fact that she remained silent. She didn't say a word. Johnson felt that she was just another of Hyde's girlfriends and was more impressed with the fact that Hyde went to his death promoting the potential of Monroe.

What made the biggest impression on Johnson was Monroe's coldness. In an interview quoted by author Tom Stempel, he discussed the scene at the end of Monroe's segment in *We're Not Married*. It involves a baby that she is holding as she goes through the wedding ceremony a second time.

"There she was with this baby in her arms. It was crying like hell, and Marilyn didn't even look down at it. I said to Eddie Goulding, the director,

'Now look, don't you think that that's a little unbelievable? Unless she's a complete idiot, a mother would look at her crying baby and show some consideration for it.' "

Johnson said that Goulding went over to Marilyn and reminded her that the baby was supposed to be her child, that it was crying, and that she should be trying to comfort it during the scene. But Johnson remained horrified by and hostile to Monroe. He could not comprehend a woman, married or single, a mother or childless, who did not respond at all to a crying baby in her arms, no matter whose it was.

Johnson also found Marilyn boring. Over the years, there were endless stories of Marilyn carrying one book or another to work, sitting by herself and reading whatever volume she had chosen. Johnson just assumed that she recognized her lack of education and, in his mind, lack of intellect. She was working her way through what he called "Dr. Eliot's Five-Foot Shelf of Books" to try to compensate, though he felt she neither could nor did.

❧

This time Marilyn comes through adequately. Alton Cook of the *New York World-Telegram and Sun* was delighted with her beauty on the screen, and the *New York Daily News*' Kate Cameron was pleased with her performance. The backhanded compliments some of the critics had been using on Monroe were unleashed by Cameron on Zsa Zsa Gabor, the star of another of the five segments. "Zsa Zsa Gabor," Cameron wrote, "has little to do as the scheming wife but look attractive, and that she does to perfection."

What happened next was anticipated by the show business trade journal *Variety*, in which the reviewer commented, "The Monroe-Wayne sequence is pretty lightweight, but shows off the Monroe form to full advantage in a bathing suit, offering certain exploitation for film." Exploitation was exactly what Twentieth Century-Fox had in mind. This time there was no interest in something as mundane as a multi-city tour. This time the studio publicists created a series of activities with which the theaters showing the film could try to gain attention and increase box-office sales. For example, in the film Monroe played a beauty queen contestant, so one of the promotion ideas suggested by Fox was for theater owners to stage a Bathing Beauty Contest in conjunction with local beaches and/or swimming pools. Real lifeguards and swim instructors were to be the judges. As the press release to the theater managers suggested, "Approach to the girls should be along these lines: 'Do You Look Like Marilyn Monroe? Enter the WE'RE NOT MARRIED Bathing Beauty Contest.'"

A longer release sent to local businesses wherever the film was playing was headlined: EXPLOIT ALL STARS WITH MERCHANDISING TIE-INS! The release read:

There are a dozen or more favorite stars in "We're Not Married." Exploit the fact that you have a screenful of stars in one of the year's happiest and frankest entertainments on your main approach. But also be sure to break your exploitation down into separate units, so that you cash in on each of the stars in more than one way. Here are some of the directions suggested:

1. Fashion tie-ups can best be affected with glamorous Ginger Rogers, who is bedecked in a variety of breathtaking costumes in "We're Not Married!"

2. Beach wear and lingerie tie-ins can be worked with Marilyn Monroe, hottest new star on the Hollywood horizon. To connect with your summer play dates of the film and the bathing beauty contest suggested elsewhere on this page, note the special art of Miss Monroe in a bathing suit on this page in this Campaign Book devoted to her.

Beauty parlor promotions can be effected with Zsa Zsa Gabor in particular, or your local hairdresser may prefer to combine all four blondes in the film—Misses Rogers, Monroe, Arden and Gabor—and red-headed Mitzi Gaynor to display a variety of coiffeur styles and colors.

FOR ALL OF THE ABOVE, USE STILLS AND MATS AVAILABLE TO YOU (INCLUDING THOSE SHOWN ON OTHER PAGES OF CAMPAIGN BOOK), AND SUPPLEMENT WITH AD ART AND PLAYDATE CREDIT IN ALL NEWSPAPER ADS AND WINDOW AND IN-STORE DISPLAYS! [Emphasis in the original promotion piece.]

In addition to the picture's stars, its theme can be effectively utilized in merchandising tie-ins with:

Trousseau requirements for brides

Wedding gifts

Jewelers featuring wedding and engagement diamond rings

The ad and display theme for all these should follow this motif:

"WE'RE NOT MARRIED yet, but we will be soon, etc."

※

The promotion buildups and contests were not used just for *We're Not Married*. That same year Marilyn appeared in the film *Monkey Business*, in which she played Lois Laurel, Cary Grant's secretary. There were two suggested contests created by the Fox publicity department for this picture:

EXPLOITATION EXTRAS!
Secretary Contest

Marilyn Monroe is Cary Grant's blonde secretary in "Monkey Business." Run a contest for secretaries on your theatre stage to determine the local secretary closest to Marilyn's qualifications: height 5'5-1/2″, weight 118, hair blonde, eyes blue, bust 36, waist 25. Side-by-side photos of Miss Monroe and the winner good for a photo break in the local papers; interview with the winner's local boss a sure fire newspaper feature.

LAUGHING RECORD

To emphasize the laughing-room-only aspect of your "Monkey Business" play date, keep your theatre front lively with a continuous playing laugh record hooked up to your house front public address system.

※

The film *Monkey Business* would prove important to Marilyn, but first she had to transition her mentor from the late, "vertically challenged" Johnny Hyde to the even shorter columnist Sid Skolsky, a man Leon Schwab joked was 4 feet 5 inches tall, though he probably did reach 5 feet—in shoes.

Thirty-three

Sid Skolsky and the "Schwabadero"

Sid Skolsky was one of the most successful Hollywood columnists of the day. He worked for the *New York Daily News* and the *New York Post,* providing a daily column for the latter. He worked for the *Hollywood Citizen-News* and was syndicated around the country through United Features. Yet despite—or perhaps because of—his success, Skolsky never drove a car. He had people drive him wherever he needed to go, and Marilyn eventually came to be his frequent chauffeur.

Skolsky, like the other columnists of his day, created his own language. Marilyn he called "the Girl with the Horizontal Walk." The drugstore where he hung out became that glamorous location "the Schwabadero," a takeoff on the popular nightclub the Trocadero.

Skolsky was twenty-eight years old and new to Hollywood in 1933 when he first began going to Schwab's. Because he didn't drive, he would arrange interviews with actors, actresses, and writers so that they would meet at Schwab's. He could get there easily and everyone knew the place. The interview would be conducted at the counter, then they usually had dinner together there.

Skolsky was a regular contributor to the fan magazine *Photoplay* which would carry the heading "Sidney Skolsky Sounds Off" and the subheading "From a Stool at Schwab's." He also encouraged what he later said was a myth: that actress Lana Turner had been discovered there.

The "true" story Skolsky revealed in his book *Don't Get Me Wrong—I*

Love Hollywood, told of a bored Lana Turner, then sixteen, deciding to play hooky from Hollywood High School. Turner, often called "The Sweater Girl" because of the way she fit into her clinging outfits, walked across the street to the Top Hat Malt Shop at the corner of Sunset Boulevard and Highland Avenue. She ordered a strawberry malt and was sipping it when Billy Wilkerson walked in. Wilkerson was the publisher and editor of the *Hollywood Reporter*, a man who knew everyone important in the film industry. He recognized that Turner had the look to be a major star and arranged for her to meet the right men to build a career. However, people often confused the Top Hat Malt Shop for Schwab's, and Skolsky encouraged such thinking. Or such was the "official" story.

Leon Schwab contradicted Skolsky's book. He said that Lana Turner *was* discovered in Schwab's, not the Top Hat Malt Shop. The story that was told concerning Wilkerson was true, just not the location. The reason Skolsky made the "correction" in his book was to keep his friendship with Lana Turner.

According to Leon, the actress was livid that Schwab's seemed to always be receiving top billing. She would not tolerate this, and so, in the interest of friendship, Skolsky used his book to "correct" what had been said and make Turner happy.

Skolsky's most humorous story about all this was of having another teenager come in and ask if he knew on which counter stool Lana Turner had been sitting when she was discovered. There was only one empty seat so Skolsky declared that the seat was the same one on which the actress had been sitting before she became a star.

The girl was thrilled. She knew that Schwab's lunch counter was her key to fame and fortune. She ordered a strawberry ice cream soda, apparently not liking malteds but wanting to keep the flavor the same, and waited. Skolsky later said that she found him a few days later and was irate.

"Where did you get this stuff about Lana Turner?" she complained. "I've been sitting on that stool having ice-cream sodas from two to five every afternoon for a week and a half. I haven't met a single talent agent or casting director. The only thing that's happened to me is I've gained six pounds."

Leon Schwab later laughed about Skolsky's turning the drugstore into his office. Skolsky ran up a food and coffee tab, which he never paid. Skolsky also purchased gifts there, again not paying. Yet the columnist at some point spent enough time with his wife to have two daughters who were barred from Schwab's by their father. He knew they would make demands similar to his own, and he was certain that the combination of his greed and their own would end the hospitality. He was too selfish to let anyone get in his way.

All the Schwab brothers realized that they were getting good publicity worth more than the cost of the food and other items. They eventually gave the columnist an office above the pharmacy area, where he regularly received his mail as well as celebrity callers. Leon felt that Sid was rather cheap, another Hollywood character on the make—but an important one and worth supporting.

Skolsky may have been a freeloader, but he cared about the same people the Schwab brothers were concerned about—rising young talent. He worked to boost them in his column. He worked to get them jobs if he thought they were appropriate for a part. And as they began to succeed, he was a major booster of their careers. In an era of racial and sexual discrimination, Skolsky was responsible for helping entertainers as diverse as Clark Gable and Diahann Carroll. He never wanted credit. He never wanted thanks. He just liked writing about the stars of the present and the young men and women who might be the stars of the future—like Marilyn.

Skolsky was arguably the most important Hollywood columnist in the business, but his real skill was in spotting talent. No one ever understood what he saw in an actor who was still an unproven, out-of-work kid. Somehow he had an eye for inner potential, for seeing in someone who had no track record that spark which, in a few years, a few months, or occasionally in their first picture, would lead to national acclaim.

It was Skolsky who had an instinct for Monroe's potential when others did not see it. Some stories about the two of them have him encountering her at a drinking fountain in the Twentieth Century-Fox administration building. He joked with her about taking in water like a camel, then talked with her in depth.

A second story, probably more accurate, has Marilyn seeking out Skolsky at Schwab's. Either way, they eventually became the closest of friends, Marilyn regularly stopping by Schwab's to talk with Sidney, sometimes in his office and sometimes at the counter or a table. They were frequently joined by Leon and, occasionally, by Fred Otash.

Skolsky saw the drive for acting success in Marilyn. She knew she had to train in her profession, to educate herself, and to work intensely at the studio, all of which she was willing to do. All the problems she had later— the overwhelming drug and alcohol abuse, the chronic lateness, the insecurity—they came after she was a star. Skolsky met a woman who may not have been as good-looking or as skilled as most of the actresses of her day, but with a willingness to do whatever it took to succeed. He became the shepherd of her talent.

Leon Schwab later mentioned that Skolsky's actions in helping were not unique with Marilyn. Many people have imagined that his involvement was sexual, that he was being paid back in the way Marilyn often rewarded friendship. But Leon said that Skolsky helped many new talents whose potential he recognized early in their careers. He pointed out that when the columnist met the young, as-yet-little-known Barbra Streisand, Skolsky became just as involved. Leon said that Barbra even brought Skolsky to Las Vegas when she was first singing there, and the columnist was glad to lend his support. He genuinely liked helping young talent succeed where he could give their careers a boost.

Skolsky's influence though important, was limited. He could not order a producer to use Marilyn, as some of the big-money mobsters were allegedly able to do for Frank Sinatra when he was cast in *From Here to Eternity*. His skill involved guiding Marilyn through the industry he so thoroughly understood.

Skolsky's involvement with Marilyn's career came late in 1951 when the film *Clash by Night* was being cast. The story was originally a play by Clifford Odets. It told of a woman who returns to the fishing village where she was raised. It was a melodrama that follows the familiar theme of the good woman always being hurt because of her attraction to the wrong kind of man.

One reason the film was important was because of its producer: Harriet Parsons, daughter of Louella Parsons, the nationally known columnist for the Hearst newspapers. This meant that the picture would be heavily supported in much of the media, and any actress who had even a small part would have a boost to her career. However, Harriet did not have the final word on the casting.

Sid Skolsky arranged for Marilyn to have lunch with Jerry Wald, second in command to Norman Krasna at RKO, the studio for which Harriet Parsons was making *Clash by Night*. Skolsky had Monroe bring the one thing he knew would get her the role—her sexuality. He told her what to wear: black-and-white checkered pedal pushers that were as tight as she could handle while still being able to sit down, and a white shirtwaist blouse that had the top three buttons undone with a rose protruding from her cleavage. The lunch was a success, though Marilyn never said whether Wald ever saw her face.

Marilyn was under contract to Fox, but arrangements were made to have her loaned out. It was ironic since RKO was actually the first studio to have any interest in signing her, though that was because of Howard Hughes, not because of her talent.

The film was helped by Marilyn's breaking the story of her picture on the nude calendar just before its release, but box-office success was matched by contradictory reactions to Marilyn. The *New Yorker* was probably the most accurate: it mentioned the lovers in the film, played by Keith Andes and Marilyn Monroe. "Both are quite handsome," the writer stated, "But neither can act."

The Hearst-controlled *Los Angeles Examiner* was more flattering. The movie was about adultery and the tragic wages of sin. But the acting. . . . The reviewer commented, "As for Miss Pash-pie of 1952, otherwise Marilyn Monroe, the calendar girl, clad in dungarees, she proves she can also act and can hold her own with top performers."

All of the films, all of the incrementally larger roles, all the mixed reviews and public fascination, would come to a head when Marilyn was cast in *Monkey Business* and a publicity stunt led to a mismatched love affair that would be the basis for myth for decades to come.

Thirty-four

DiMaggio, the Greatest Romantic the Publicists Ever Created

The problem with telling the story of the brief marriage of Marilyn Monroe and Joe DiMaggio is that they were such towering icons in their respected professions that simply relating the facts appears to slander one or the other.

Joe was not only arguably the greatest baseball player of his day; he was also considered the greatest athlete, as well as a simple man of utmost integrity. The fact that he would seemingly sell his soul if the paycheck was large enough was never discussed. He gained a second round of fame as the spokesperson for the Mr. Coffee line of home coffeemakers, though he had stopped drinking coffee and never tasted the results of the machine he sold to make it. Also rarely discussed is the fact that his idea of remaining faithful following the unwanted divorce from each of his ex-wives was to date and bed showgirls from whom he did not want a long-term relationship. A romantic, he was not.

As for Marilyn, there was no question that she was delighted to marry Joe and her pleasure was witnessed by men such as Elia Kazan to whom she first broke the news—in his bed. He described being awakened at three thirty in the morning, two hours after he had gone to bed, alone. He had left the door to his home open for Marilyn, who often kept unusual hours. She awakened him getting into bed. "All excited and very happy, she announced her engagement," he later related in his autobiography, *A Life*.

" 'A hell of a time to tell me,' I said. 'It's three-thirty in the morning.'

'I wanted to tell you first,' she said, 'because now I'm not going to see you again.'

'Sounds real this time,' I said.

'He comes all the way down from San Francisco just to have dinner with me,' she said, 'and we haven't even done it yet!' She sounded astonished."

Kazan said that Marilyn was impressed with how different, how dignified Joe was compared with the men she knew in the film industry, presumably her present company excepted. He ended his story by saying, "It was nice to see someone so happy and so hopeful. We made love; congratulations and farewell."

It could be argued that coming naked to bed with a lover to announce marriage plans concerning a man who believed in total commitment from the women he fancied himself loving was an aberration or a fantasy. However, when she and Joe returned from their honeymoon, she delightedly stopped by Schwab's Drug Store to tell Sid Skolsky, Leon Schwab, and Fred Otash of her plans to marry playwright Arthur Miller. Skolsky wrote of the incident after Marilyn's death. Leon Schwab and Fred Otash were separately interviewed before their deaths and gave essentially the same account.

Perhaps the one point on which both Joe and Marilyn might have concurred was Joe's sexual prowess. She had been to bed with men who she later said gave her great pleasure, most prominently Fred Karger. But she constantly mentioned that no one was better than Joe, and that was the one part of their relationship in which she would continue to periodically indulge after the marriage ended.

The cynical Fred Otash, a friend to Marilyn as well as Lucille Ryman, John Carroll, and others who were directly involved with the actress, later commented,

The two years Marilyn and DiMaggio dated before their rather meaningless marriage, the publicists created a romance meant to help Marilyn's career. The ball player dropped onto the set of the movie *Monkey Business* where Marilyn had a relatively minor part compared with the true stars of the day—Cary Grant, Ginger Rogers, and Charles Coburn. The director did not want him there, nor was he pleased with Marilyn's underwhelming performance. [After the movie's release, the male critics noted that Marilyn's most appealing side was her rear view.] But he recognized that DiMaggio could help the picture, and his stars were happy to play along, thinking the film would benefit. However, the publicist was thinking of Marilyn, not the movie.

Cary Grant willingly posed for photos with Monroe and DiMaggio, never realizing that DiMaggio was considered a potentially bigger box-office draw. The movie had nothing to do with Marilyn or a romance, but if potential viewers thought they would get a glimpse of famous lovers, they would turn out in greater numbers. Thus, in the darkroom, after the photos were developed, Cary Grant's image was carefully removed. What was left was a bubbly Marilyn along with DiMaggio looking as comfortable as a gangster being arrested in a sting operation. The picture of the two committed "lovers" was used everywhere in the world where there might be interest in Monroe.

DiMaggio may genuinely have been in love with Marilyn, despite his discomfort with publicity pictures. Marilyn was not. Affairs, often quite intense, were enjoyed with at least four other men during this period.

ॐ

So if much of the story of the love affair of the century is myth—or, in the case of Marilyn, a studio publicist's "spin"—what really took place?

ॐ

Joltin' Joe, The Yankee Clipper

The taciturn baseball player Joe DiMaggio was much like his father: Giuseppe, the son, grandson, and great-grandson of fishermen originally from the Sicilian community of Isola del Femmine. Both men were strong, proud, willful, and silent. Both men were so intensely focused on their work that they were socially isolated, in Joe's case never coming to truly know either his lovers or his teammates. Giuseppe braved the ocean's unpredictable turbulence. Joe seemed equally stoic standing alone at the plate, facing the "storms" of Yankee Stadium.

The emotional isolation actually added to DiMaggio's appeal. Since almost no one knew him, the fans seemed to embrace him as they might a contemporary Ken doll, dressing him in their fantasies. Tall, powerful, dominating a game that truly was the American pastime in the early 1950s, DiMaggio on the playing field seemed like Hercules—half man, half god.

(It is interesting to note that those who knew both DiMaggio and Arthur Miller said that if the two men were across a room, identically dressed and facing away, one could not tell which was which.)

They never saw the boring, semiliterate individual whose ideal home life consisted of television, comic books, beer, and a stay-at-home woman who would care for his needs. They never saw the man who was complacent about the current woman in his life and obsessive only when the love was lost. Yet to fully understand Joe requires an understanding of his heritage and his family.

Giuseppe DiMaggio the fisherman was not a Hemingway hero any more than the thousands of other immigrants who had to care for their families through intense physical labor. Sons followed their fathers' careers in the old country because that was what they knew, and those who emigrated often tried to ply the same skills in a new land. Such was the case with Giuseppe DiMaggio, who emigrated to the United States in 1902, working until he could send for his wife, Rosalie, and their baby, Nellie. Eventually Giuseppe was an independent fisherman with his own boat (named after his wife) and eight more children born in the United States—Mamie, Thomas, Marie, Michael, Frances, Vincent, Joseph, and Dominic. Only Michael would follow his father to sea, and he paid the price for such dangerous work. He was forty-four years old when he died after falling overboard in turbulent waters.

The DiMaggios lived in a rented house at 2047 Taylor Street in the North Beach section. Giuseppe's fishing boat, the *Rosalie*, was in a wharf a quarter-mile from the home.

Giuseppe discovered that fishing for a living in America was more competitive than in Sicily, with a daily race to be first to bring one's catch to shore. There were from forty to fifty commercial fishing boats working from the same wharf where the *Rosalie* was docked, and a single channel through which they all left and returned each day.

At first, the competition did not matter much. The catch was always plentiful in the early 1900s. There was crab and salmon, and the men were able to support their often-large families from the daily sales—if they got to shore first.

Each day Giuseppe would race to be the first through the channel. The fierce competition caused sabotage and fighting. Gasoline might be poured on a rival's catch, forcing the fisherman to destroy the contaminated fish. Death threats delivered to a rival's home were not uncommon; and beatings, including an occasional fatality, were the price paid for working the boats.

All the boys were expected to work from the time they were young, though in America there was no longer pressure to stay with the business of one's father, just to succeed at whatever made his sons happy. Ultimately, the family would have a restaurant managed by Tom, the business expert in the family. Tom was also a union official and helped Joe with his New York Yankees' contracts. However, when young the boys sold newspapers and did whatever work they could find. They also became interested in baseball: Vince, Joe, and Dom all turned professional.

Joe's baseball skills were considered by sportswriters to be superior to the skills of his brothers. His image as something more than another lug who was good with a ball, bat, and glove came, in part, because he played in America's biggest city and in part because of his courtship and eventual marriage to Marilyn Monroe. However, in Boston, Dominic was the feted ballplayer, a hero of the Red Sox and subject of a song set to the music of "Maryland, My Maryland" that the crowds would sing at least once during every home game:

Oh, Dominic DiMaggio!
He's better than his brother, Joe.

There was truth to the Boston claim, though only sports purists and people who didn't root for the Yankees had a sense of why. Dom was probably superior to Joe in every defensive skill; but then, as now, batting could make a player a star, and Dom DiMaggio was only adequate as a batter. Joe was brilliant at both defense—though second to his brother—and offense, where he was perceived as second to none.

Vince, by contrast, was the odd man out. He moved among four National League teams. He was good enough to play professionally, but was never a star. He was simply a solid player who delighted in being able to earn his living with the game he loved.

There was one other difference between Joe and his brothers. All the boys except Joe developed an intense respect for learning. Giuseppe and Rosalie had always stressed that the boys had to find ways to make a living and support families of their own. They did not care how the boys achieved this end, and when they were young, good jobs could be found where one learned the field as one worked. This was why the family was unconcerned when Joe dropped out of Galileo High School, though Giuseppe *was* concerned at first when he learned that three of his sons were going to play professional baseball. Then he saw their contracts. The lowest-paid of the three was earning more than Giuseppe earned in a truly good year. That was when he understood that his boys were in a business, not spending their time in some frivolous diversion. The knowledge made him proud.

To get a sense of DiMaggio's skill, after dropping out of high school he joined the San Francisco Seals of the Pacific Coast League at age seventeen. The year was 1932, and DiMaggio only played in three games in what, for the Seals, was a losing season. The following year, at eighteen, the minor leaguer showed major league talent. He played 187 games, hit safely in sixty-one consecutive games (a Pacific Coast League record), including 29 home runs and 169 runs batted in, and hit .340. There was no finer minor league player in the United States. His fame was so great that all sixteen major league teams sent scouts to watch him in preparation for offering him a contract.

Tom DiMaggio began looking out for Joe's interest. He knew that the Seals could sell their contract with Joe to a major league team, pocketing a large profit because Joe would have to play out his old contract at what would undoubtedly be a low salary. Tom arranged for the minor league salary to rise to $6,500 and demanded that the sale price for his brother be $75,000. The latter seemed unrealistic, especially after Joe sustained a knee injury; but in November 1934, the Seals sold Joe to the New York Yankees for $25,000 with the understanding that he would stay in San Francisco through the 1935 season. He had become the West Coast's biggest draw for fans, and the Pacific Coast League wanted to profit from him for one more season. With a .395 batting average that season, he disappointed no one. By the time he reached the Yankees, just shy of his twenty-first birthday, the New York press was already calling him the replacement for Babe Ruth.

New York was where legends were made, and when Joe joined the Yankees, sportswriters felt that his consummate skill in all aspects of the game made him the finest player the city had seen since Ruth. He was also handsomer than Ruth, leaner and more muscled. His skills drew the fans and his looks drew the women, whether or not they cared about baseball.

Dominic, by contrast, was just 5 feet 9 inches tall, four inches shorter than his brother Joe's 6 foot 1, wore glasses, and was nicknamed "The Little Professor." That was another reason Dom attracted little attention outside of the city where he played.

DiMaggio's rookie year in New York saw him rise in salary to $8,500 for the season, instantly making him a financial success. A luxury six-room apartment on Manhattan's East Side, including free recreation area and private park, rented for $190 a month. If he chose to buy one of the most expensive cars on the road, it cost less than $1,200. A meal in a working-class restaurant ran thirty cents. There were rising corporate executives who were considered well paid who did not earn the money young DiMaggio received.

Joe realized that he loved both baseball and money, and though he was well off, he wanted more income, which he realized he could earn from endorsements. Since he was a heavy coffee drinker and loved Camel cigarettes (three packs a day, including cigarettes sneaked in the dugout *during* ball games), he arranged to endorse his smoking habit. (By the time Joe DiMaggio was hired to be the spokesman for the Mr. Coffee Company's products for a fee reportedly in excess of $100,000 per year, he had abandoned coffee entirely. He had developed a stomach ulcer and limited himself to tea.) He would eventually contract untreatable lung cancer from the cigarettes, but that came much later in life and, for now, he was pleased to get paid to smoke.

The ads read, "Heavy-hitting baseball star Joe DiMaggio feels the same way about Camels as so many millions of smokers do. Says Joe: 'When I need a "lift" in energy, Camels is the cigarette for me. I stick to Camels. They don't irritate my throat or get my nerves jumpy. Ball players really go for Camels in a big way.'"

What truly made Joe DiMaggio great was the way he was able to quietly inspire, work with, and lead any team for which he played. The only contemporary athletes with similar reputations have been basketball players Michael Jordan in Chicago and LeBron James in Cleveland.

Just as contemporary sportswriters have felt that the team skills and ability to help win under pressure that made Jordan and James the keys to some of their teams' success, a similar reputation was held by DiMaggio. In the years prior to World War II, sportswriters felt that there were four equally skilled baseball teams: the Yankees, the Red Sox, the Indians, and the Tigers. The only difference in who would win the Pennant was who had DiMaggio.

During the first four years DiMaggio played for New York, the Yankees won more than one hundred games in each of three years, and they won ninety-nine games in 1939, considered their "off" season. In all four years, they took the American League pennant by more than ten games, an unprecedented record experts attributed to DiMaggio's dual skills as an individual athlete and as a team player. But it was the 1936 rookie season with New York that won Joe the hearts of Yankees fans. DiMaggio dominated the World Series play, including making a spectacular catch of the Giants' Hank Leiber's 460-foot line drive. Franklin Roosevelt was in attendance, and as he was driven through the center field gate, he congratulated Joe. DiMaggio also received a bonus of $6,430.55, bringing his income for the year to more than $15,000. Some of the money went into high living. Some of it paid for Joe DiMaggio's Grotto, a highly profitable San Francisco restaurant he bought for his brother Tom to manage.

Whether Joe was humble about all this is hard to say. He rarely talked with reporters, and that intense shyness was presumed to be humility. His mother, Rosalie, however, was in attendance, and her words, spoken through an interpreter, delighted the fans. When she was asked if her son looked like the best player of the Yankees, she commented, "I couldn't say that. All the Yankees looked very good. And the Giants looked good, too. I feel sorry for them, playing so hard and losing."

And so Joe began to know the thrill of being cheered by more than sixty thousand adoring fans every game. He lived in the Concourse Plaza near Yankee Stadium, spending his free time with girls, reading comic books and an occasional Western, drinking beer, and listening to the radio. He also agreed to "write" his autobiography for the *World Telegram*, which assigned writer Dan M. Daniel to "help" with the six-part series. The proof that Joe neither wrote nor read what was supposedly his own book came as quickly as reading the first sentence in which he states: "My name is Joseph Peter DiMaggio." It was an innocuous lead. It was also incorrect. Joe's middle name was Paul, a fact he hopefully knew and would have corrected if he ever had seen the manuscript at any stage prior to publication.

৯৯

THE FIRST MRS. DIMAGGIO

Dorothy Arnold was everything Joe claimed to want in a wife. She was an actress and entertainer from a background that ultimately stressed marriage and family over career, a concept with which she agreed. She also understood that if she could break into the studio system of the day, she could make more money than she would in any other job for which she was qualified. She would also meet high-profile men who wanted to marry a woman for her looks and image, enabling her to transition to housewife and mother before she became just another minimally talented starlet with an unrenewed contract.

Much of Dorothy Arnold's values and character were shaped by where and how she was raised, just as Marilyn's had been. Marilyn was a child of Hollywood and the movie industry. Dorothy was one of four sisters raised by a railroad company official and his wife in Duluth, Minnesota. She studied singing, dancing, elocution, and sports. The first three were routine for a middle-class young lady. The last was rare, for she was skilled in everything from tennis to softball. She, like Joe, left high school early, in her case to join a musical comedy company working the Balaban and Katz theater circuit. She was fifteen years old, yet her parents were unusual in tolerating a career that most families considered a road to harlotry or worse.

Dorothy moved from one touring company to another, loving the stage and hating the road. She expected glamour, not boardinghouse accommodations, shared dressing rooms, and just enough food to stave off hunger. She returned briefly to Duluth, living at home while working in little theater and various clubs in the area, then took a job in summer stock in New England before moving to New York City.

It was in New York that Dorothy became a professional singer, taking every available job as a way to get noticed. She appeared on radio. She sang with dance orchestras. She worked in nightclubs, and at age nineteen was signed by Universal Pictures in New York. It was the same stock contract Marilyn would sign a few years later, and Dorothy's first picture (with an uncredited appearance) was the 1937 production *Manhattan Merry-Go-Round* in which Joe DiMaggio appeared.

What made the movie unusual was that it included a small role for Joe DiMaggio. He had discovered that he could use his rookie year fame to go backstage wherever there were actresses, entertainers, or showgirls who interested him. Thus he was pleased, but not surprised, when the producers of *Manhattan Merry-Go-Round* offered him a small role in the musical that was filmed in the Astoria Studio in Queens, New York. The appeal for Joe was all the showgirls, but for Dorothy, this was a chance to work not only with actors but also with such major entertainers as Louis Prima, Kay Thompson, Leo Carillo, Phil Regan, Gene Autry, Jack Benny, Ted Lewis, and Cab Calloway, among others. The addition of DiMaggio's name was meant to further enhance the box-office appeal, and when he agreed, the writers had him just be himself, delivering a monologue on baseball.

The publicity about Joe may have helped the box office but his performance did not help the film. His acting range started at wooden and ended with stiff. It was the same problem Joe had years later when the Yankees hired him to be a television commentator. He knew baseball as well or better than anyone alive, but his social isolation, lack of interests, and few, if any, genuine friends made it seemingly impossible to work with such media.

Joe had been looking for a woman to take to bed more than once or twice, and Dorothy was willing to abandon her career for marriage to the right man. The couple was instantly attracted to one another, and by the end of the production schedule, Joe had Dorothy's telephone number and assurances that she would date him when he called.

For both Joe and Dorothy the relationship came to seem a dream come true. The San Francisco fisherman's son was desired by a Hollywood actress, the type of beautiful woman he once could meet only vicariously in a darkened movie theater. Dorothy, the studio actress with little future beyond the chorus line, was desired by the most popular sports figure of the day.

In a sense, Joe had achieved the stardom that many studio starlets and chorus girls sought, though usually in vain. A popular star's name on a movie theater marquee was believed to boost attendance. Sports entrepreneurs were convinced that Joe's name was a saleable commodity, not just his baseball playing. They decided to make him a year-round star, approaching him with the offer to try his hand at professional basketball whose season, in those days, did not start until after baseball was over.

The contract Joe was offered was enormous. He would receive a base of five hundred dollars per game if he just suited up and was kept on the bench. For every minute he was actually playing the game, he would receive fifty dollars. The problem was that basketball had more physical contact and greater risks of injury than baseball and the Yankees would not let Joe sign, fearing he would be out for the season. Ironically, several decades later Michael Jordan, one of the athletes on a par with DiMaggio, wanted to leave basketball when he was still at his peak and try his hand at professional baseball.

Joe, once settled in New York during the early years of his career, settled into a pattern for how he liked to spend his free time when he wasn't home or in a woman's bedroom. His "office," such as it was, was Toots Shor's, one of the most popular saloons in New York. Shor was a man who had run a speakeasy during Prohibition, worked as a bouncer, and ran a joint where sportswriters, columnists, sports figures, and tough guys all hung out. The place was always jammed, or as baseball great Yogi Berra famously said, "Toots Shor's is so crowded, nobody goes there anymore."

Shor wanted to have a place where men could gather to drink hard liquor. He had steaks as the joint's one specialty food because Toots loved them. The rest of the food was mediocre because Shor saw eating as little more than a necessary interruption from drinking. Women were not desired by Shor but they were tolerated because, without them, men like DiMaggio would find another place to hang out, receive his fans, and talk baseball with men who idolized him, including such top, normally objective columnists as Bob Considine and Jimmy Cannon. When the latter wrote about him, they gave him the image of someone handsome, invincible, and capable of superhuman feats.

Joe's skills, all power to some observers, were poetic to others. Radio broadcaster Arch McDonald, watching DiMaggio play, said that his smooth movements reminded him of the sailing ships that once plied the North Atlantic. He nicknamed DiMaggio the "Yankee Clipper," a nickname other writers quickly began using.

For Dorothy, marrying Joe would be a coup greater than becoming the leading movie star of her day. And while she was just one of hundreds of bit players with studio contracts, she was unique in having caught Joe's eye.

In the spring of 1939, Joe asked Dorothy Arnold to marry him. She agreed, and what happened next was an important clue to subsequent actions Joe would take allegedly in the name of love.

Dorothy Arnold was thrilled to be marrying Joe. He was famous, his income was high, and she would be leading a more glamorous life than if she, herself, had achieved stardom. But as both should have expected, professional athletics being as much a part of the entertainment business as movies, Universal Pictures recognized a time for promotion. The studio publicists arranged for a press conference on April 25, 1939, during which Dorothy stated that she and Joe would be married that summer. They would honeymoon after baseball season was over.

The reporters asked to see the ring Joe had given her, but Dorothy explained that they had not had time to get one. That did not matter, though, because the summer marriage was a certainty.

Joe had either not been warned that Universal Studios had arranged for a press conference or he did not expect the sudden rush of reporters seeking more information. "We may be married next winter or even the following winter," he was angrily quoted as telling the reporters who tracked him down after Dorothy's conference. "The wedding definitely will not take place while the baseball season is on."

The anger on DiMaggio's part was clear because he understood that he was being used to sell movies. Dorothy was a second-rate actress, adequate but without a hint of star quality. She was brought to Hollywood to appear in a series of lower budget "B" movies and serials that were a staple of Saturday afternoon children's matinees. Her greatest success was playing one of the leads in the highly forgettable *The Phantom Creeps*. However, once she was about to become Mrs. Joe DiMaggio, Universal Pictures knew it had to exploit her to whatever degree was possible including getting her to pose for *Life* magazine, not as an actress but rather as DiMaggio's fiancée. So long as she was working for Universal and the studio was always mentioned, the publicity department did not care what it took to get her face in newspapers and magazines.

Joe had his way concerning when and where the marriage took place. It was November 19, 1939, six days before he turned twenty-five years old,

Teenaged Norma Jean poses during her early career as a model. Judging from the ring on her left hand, she was still married to Jim Dougherty when this photo was taken. (CMG Worldwide)

Top: Many thought that Marilyn Monroe was the natural successor to actress Jean Harlow, who died in 1937. (Cleveland State University Library, Cleveland Press Collection)

Left: Actress Marilyn Miller, whose alliterative moniker was the inspiration for that of Marilyn Monroe. (Cleveland State University Library, Cleveland Press Collection)

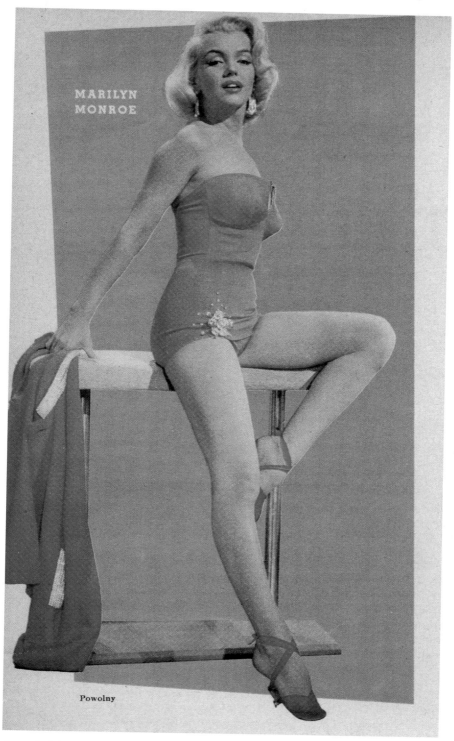

An early "cheesecake" pose. (CMG Worldwide)

A classic Marilyn look from 1953. (CMG Worldwide)

Mr. and Mrs. Arthur Miller. (CMG Worldwide)

Mr. and Mrs. Joe DiMaggio. (CMG Worldwide)

Top: Arthur Miller leaving
the hospital following
Marilyn's miscarriage in
December 1959.
(CMG Worldwide)

Left: Clark Gable relaxing
on the set of *The Misfits*.
It would be the last film
for both Gable and
Marilyn Monroe.
(Cleveland State University
Library, Cleveland Press
Collection)

Peter Lawford, shown here with his wife, Patricia, was instrumental in covering up many of Marilyn's liaisons with the Kennedys. (Cleveland State University Library, Cleveland Press Collection)

President John F. Kennedy at the infamous birthday gala where Marilyn serenaded him with "Happy Birthday." (Cleveland State University Library, Cleveland Press Collection)

and the ceremony was held in San Francisco. Playing season was over and Joe had been named that year's Most Valuable Player in the American League by the Baseball Writers Association. Dorothy, a Protestant, had prepared herself for the Catholic wedding by taking instruction in the church from Father F. Parolin of St. Peter and St. Paul Church, then formally converting to Catholicism.

The wedding day was a major news event. San Francisco Mayor Angelo Rossi was invited, as were immigrant fishermen friends of the family. There were ball players, police officers (including "The Singing Cop," Officer George Stinson who sang "Vesti la Giubba" from Pagliacci), and numerous others. The eight hundred invited guests downed $1,500 worth of food and liquor. Another twelve hundred people managed to crash the ceremony while ten thousand curiosity-seekers showed up outside, pressing against the church doors to such a degree that the two o'clock ceremony had to be delayed thirty minutes while a flying squad of police officers helped Dorothy Arnold and her family get inside. Joe, looking handsome in a full cutaway coat, seemed embarrassed by all the fuss his fame had brought the couple and their families.

Years later, Joe's obsession with Marilyn caused most observers to forget there had been a first wife, also an actress, and also the object of both his obsession and his lifestyle demands.

Joe treated Dorothy the same way he would eventually treat Marilyn. The romantics who looked at DiMaggio's seeming lifelong obsession with Monroe and wondered at their breakup never looked at his first marriage.

Joe was self-indulgent, a boy who grew into manhood with money, adulation, and fans who would never say "no" to any request. He may or may not have been faithful to Dorothy when on the road or living apart from her, but unfaithfulness would never be revealed by the press. Dorothy also might have turned a blind eye to what many baseball player wives assumed was inevitable. The problem she faced was that her husband did not know the difference between a steady date with sleeping privileges and a wife. He expected Dorothy to live in San Francisco, caring for the house, meeting his needs, and tolerating his travels. He kept a hotel room in New York, but it was clear that during the baseball season she was not welcome. He would be in the city and on the road. She would be alone in San

Francisco where his family lived but she knew no one. And Dorothy was also forbidden to return to show business, even in little theater productions or small clubs.

Dorothy did not mind sacrificing a career she always knew would be short lived. What she did mind was being shunted aside. She was Mrs. Joe DiMaggio and proud of it. She demanded that Joe start including her in his life whenever he did not have to travel with the team.

Joe agreed to move Dorothy and his primary residence from the Beach Street house in San Francisco to an apartment in Manhattan. The couple first lived on West End Avenue, then switched to the more expensive 241 Central Park West. Unfortunately for Dorothy, Joe maintained his old life-style, coming to their apartment to sleep and change clothes. He spent all his spare time with friends, hanging out at Toots Shor's, coming and going as he chose. Dorothy saw no more of him than when they dated. The only difference was that when Joe wanted sex, he returned home to Dorothy.

Perhaps to strengthen the marriage, perhaps because she always liked children and Joe came from a large family, Dorothy decided they should have a child. Joe was amenable, but Dorothy's pregnancy and the birth of their son, named Joe Jr., did not change DiMaggio's lifestyle.

In fairness, Joe had known little of life that others might consider normal since joining the minor leagues. A ballplayer was constantly on the road. From spring training to exhibition games, traveling to other ballparks, practice, and the like, home was wherever the suitcases happened to come to rest. He traveled by train, leaving behind everything except the game and the adoring fans who could be found everywhere. The world was one of men. Relaxation meant cigarettes, coffee, and later, alcohol. Strangers would buy him food and drink. Sportswriters treated his few words about the game of baseball with the respect philosophers hold for the world's greatest minds. It was heady stuff for a shy, undereducated, not-very-bright young man barely out of adolescence. It was death to a marriage.

Joe was brilliant in his field, the key to his team's success. But Joe would be ruined if his marriage ended. As Dorothy Arnold DiMaggio quickly learned, baseball players did not get divorced. They could play single. They could play married. They could play widowed. They could enjoy a few hours with what the ball clubs called "camp followers"—the 1930s equivalent of the rock star "groupie"—and know they would never be disciplined;

their actions, if discovered by the press, would never be revealed by the sportswriters. The fantasy about the heroes of America's pastime was that they were heroes to be emulated, and that meant that a married ballplayer stayed a married ballplayer until the end of his career.

Dorothy repeatedly sought a divorce, then let Joe or the Yankees management talk her into staying. The issue was not about cheating. Dorothy understood about the time a ballplayer had to be away from home and his likely yielding to the temptation of a one-night stand. She only wanted Joe to put her ahead of Toots Shor's, the fans, and the casual nightclub lifestyle he enjoyed both off season and when the Yankees were in New York.

Further pressures on DiMaggio came with the bombing of Pearl Harbor and the entrance of the United States into World War II. The California/Oregon/Washington coast was considered a primary enemy target since the first attack against the United States had been against Hawaii. Any person living in the area who was of Japanese, German, or Italian descent was classified as an "enemy alien." This did not mean that they were considered a danger. Instead, the war hysteria led some people to imagine that anyone who was not an American citizen might feel a greater loyalty to his or her country of origin than the United States. If that country of origin had become the designated enemy, it did not matter how long the immigrant had been in America. He or she was a risk and must be banned from areas of strategic importance, such as the waterfront wharf in San Francisco where Joe DiMaggio owned his restaurant.

To the shock of both Joe and the sportswriters, Giuseppe DiMaggio found himself banned from his son's restaurant. He was sixty-seven years old, loyal to his adopted country, and the father of an American icon—but had never bothered to apply for citizenship papers. They had seemed unimportant and unnecessary for the pursuit of his livelihood, and the majority of his children were American by birth. It was only the intense adverse publicity about the banning of Joe DiMaggio's father that allowed Giuseppe to return to the wharf.

Joe DiMaggio's feelings about the war are unknown. The greatest sports figures in the nation, if they were single, were being drafted. Joe, being married and with a child Dorothy still thought might help her husband change his ways, was 3-A, a lower priority than the 1-A single men. A prolonged war would mean he would be called to duty. If the fighting ended quickly—and at that time no one knew how long the war would last—he could continue living his life.

Many Japanese-American youth, legal citizens whose parents faced the same problems as Giuseppe DiMaggio, entered the military to prove their family's loyalty even as their parents and siblings were placed in internment camps in Arizona and elsewhere. Joe might have considered entering the military as a way to show the patriotism of the DiMaggio family; but if that had been a consideration when he decided to enlist, it was not one he discussed with sportswriters or friends. And, like the Universal Pictures celebration of the Dorothy Arnold/Joe DiMaggio engagement, Joe was livid when word leaked that he would be leaving baseball long enough to fight in the war. And as matters turned out, though Joe did enlist, it was only a matter of leaving professional ball.

On February 17, 1943, Joe DiMaggio entered the Monterey, California, reception center where he was processed and made a member of the special services unit. His orders were essentially to be a ballplayer. He would travel and play exhibition games, have a sports column (written by another GI) that would appear in the various military publications (including some that would have Norma Jean Dougherty's picture prominently displayed), and show off his hitting skills. He was stationed at the Santa Ana Army Air Field near Los Angeles where Dorothy and Joe Jr. moved to be closer to him.

Once again, Joe promised to be more involved with his family. However, even in the army, Joe could not change. He was almost a dandy, taking his military uniforms to a tailor to have them altered to perfectly match the contours of his body. And the brass so nurtured him that he never left the region consisting of California and Hawaii.

The only person who openly commented on Joe's ego and special treatment was Dorothy. She also realized that the army had different rules for husbands and wives than did professional baseball. DiMaggio, playing for the Yankees, could not divorce her. DiMaggio, playing for the Army, was fair game. On October 11, 1943, Dorothy filed for what would prove to be an uncontested divorce on the grounds of cruelty.

While Dorothy was working to rid herself of a man who had never fully committed to another person, even in marriage, DiMaggio was promoted to staff sergeant. He was given orders to move to the Seventh Air Force team in the Pacific theater where there was already a large number of former major league baseball players, assigned to keep the baseball diamonds safe from foreign invaders by playing as many games as possible. Joe was back in his element, maintaining his batting and fielding skills in anticipation of the war's end: the only problem was a paycheck meant for the ordinary GI, not the high-living DiMaggio. Apparently being treated like everyone else, if only in the amount of money he received, was too much of an emotional stress for Joe. He quickly developed stomach ulcers. Fortunately, his health was improved by a September 14, 1945, discharge from the army and a return to New York, with accompanying high pay and high living.

The importance of the relationship with Dorothy, as limited as it proved to be, is rarely discussed. The myth of Joe DiMaggio is that Marilyn Monroe was the one great love of his life. Fans know about the flowers he left on her grave over the years. They are aware that during Marilyn's troubled last months, DiMaggio would always be available to help her. They know of his obsessive desire to remarry her. What they don't realize is that this was a pattern of Joe's, first evident with Dorothy.

Joe DiMaggio hated to lose anything. He hated to lose ball games, a fact that helped make him a consummate team player at the same time that he was honing his own hitting and fielding skills. He hated to lose money, the reason he endorsed Mr. Coffee machines years after he stopped drinking coffee. And he hated to lose a wife. As soon as he was signed to play for the 1946 season (for his pre-war salary of $43,750), he began courting Dorothy anew. They regularly saw each other whenever he went to spend time with his son. He regretted the divorce. He loved Dorothy. He wanted her to be his wife. He would do anything to get her back. She was the only woman for him.

Dorothy delighted in the attention she had not received during their marriage. However, she was not about to risk being ignored once again. She accepted his advances but led an independent life, eventually marrying, then divorcing, a stockbroker.

DiMaggio struck out with Dorothy, both before and after her second marriage, because she knew that if she agreed to go back to him, their home life would be the same. He was also having trouble on the playing field, though this came—as it did for all the top pros who took two or more years from the sport to serve in the military—from being away from the game.

There were also issues of aging for Joe. He had had to wear ankle braces from the time he was six years old until he was eight in an attempt to correct a congenital weakness. Then, in 1949, Joe had to have heel surgery. He seemed to recognize that his best playing days were in the past and he became extremely depressed. The public and even the Yankees' management were not certain whether he could recapture enough of his skills to continue playing at all, though some spectacular hitting against the Boston Red Sox dispelled all doubts. During the 1950 season, he played in 139 games, hit three home runs in a single game, and brought his batting average up to .370 for the last six weeks of the season, among other accomplishments. He was considered a great sports hero even by those who had never seen him play, never had an interest in the game itself, but recognized what he had overcome.

The success did not mean he was well, though. He had heel spurs. He had arthritis. The ulcer he assumed would be cured when he was able to indulge in the hedonistic pleasures of a wealthy civilian had not been cured at all. There were calcium deposits on his throwing elbow, and he had become very much a loner, not trusting men or women enough to develop friends. He assumed that everyone wanted something from his friendship and so he seldom tried to befriend anyone new.

Joe also realized that the Yankees were undergoing transitions in ownership, management style, and players. Younger men were being developed to be tomorrow's stars, and some of them might prove to be what he had been. He understood that he remained a major draw for the team, but he could see the time was coming to retire. Still, his last years were spectacular. He helped the club destroy the Dodgers in the 1949 World Series, and the following year, when he hit 32 home runs, they took the Series from the Philadelphia Phillies.

It was 1951 when DiMaggio realized he had played his last season. His salary was $100,000, a figure that would be matched with a broadcasting contract the following year. His lifetime batting average was .325, and that included 361 home runs, 2,214 hits, and 1,537 RBIs achieved in 1,736 games. He played in ten World Series championship games, a feat matched only by Babe Ruth.

On December 11, 1951, not long after his thirty-seventh birthday, Joe DiMaggio announced, "I have reached a stage where I can no longer produce for my ball club, my manager, my teammates, and my fans the sort of baseball their loyalty to me deserves." The Yankee Clipper had retired.

The adoration of DiMaggio was boundless. He would make the Baseball Hall of Fame in 1955, a record two years after he became eligible for consideration. He would become the subject of songs and literature. And even his detractors admired him, as was the case with a Spring 1952 *Life* magazine article in which retired baseball great Ty Cobb wrote of DiMaggio that he "made a name for himself without even scratching the surface of his talents. He was perhaps the outstanding example of how modern baseball players neglect to train and keep themselves in condition. He hated physical exertion and as far as I know he never took a lick of exercise from October until March. Naturally he went to spring training with his muscles weakened and soft; naturally he got hurt a lot."

It is doubtful that Joe cared. He was pursuing new careers, new relationships. Even while he was wooing his ex-wife, he had affairs. The most publicized occurred during spring training in Panama his first year back in the game following the war. He was fined fifty dollars for breaking curfew, and the reason was a woman named Jade Rhodora. She was an exotic dancer he met in a nightclub, unfortunately during a time when reporters were also present. He remained relatively discreet that first day, no one seeing the couple outside a booth in the club. The next night—when he was fined the fifty dollars—a more intimate sharing was a part of his entertainment.

Retirement brought new concerns. Joe had always been a man who sought privacy. He disliked talking with fellow players or fans except in Toots Shor's. He tried to avoid the mobs, except for the heady rush when he was on the playing field and thousands were cheering for him. He often delayed leaving Yankee Stadium until the police had cleared the crowds from the grounds.

Suddenly, the old world ended. For twenty years, the man had been a star. People still knew him, still approached for autographs, still bought him drinks. But the cheering had stopped.

Joe was financially set from investments. He might never get rich by the standards of the most popular contemporary athletes, but he could still take all his meals in restaurants, hang out at Toots Shor's, and squire as many beautiful women to nightclubs and bedrooms as he was able.

But Joe was also yesterday's news, a historic figure from the past to kids just starting to learn the game. With each passing year, he would become nothing more than a legend boys heard about from their fathers, not someone they could witness firsthand in the stadium. The sudden lack of fame was as disconcerting to Joe as the extreme adulation had been.

And always there was the roar of the crowds, a sound he knew would only be a memory.

Thirty-five

The Soon-to-Be Mrs. DiMaggio

> She's a plain kid. She'd give up the business if I asked her. She'd quit the movies in a minute. It means nothing to her.
>
> —Joe DiMaggio speaking to his friend,
> syndicated columnist Jimmy Cannon, concerning his
> new love, Marilyn Monroe

Joe knew of Marilyn Monroe. He was naive, but he was not dead. He knew of the infamous nude photo, had probably seen one of the calendar images. It was certainly not a major concern for him except, perhaps, to whet his interest in yet another blonde actress who would let him touch what other men were only allowed to fantasize about. However, there was a myth that circulated after the couple began dating that Joe had seen a photograph of her taken during the Chicago White Sox spring training in Pasadena that led him to say, "Who's that blonde?"

The photograph in question was a picture of Chicago White Sox players Joe Dobson and Gus Zernial with Marilyn in the usual tight top and white shorts, holding a bat. The caption of the publicity photo, meant to promote both Marilyn and the White Sox, read, "White Sox pitcher Joe Dobson checks over film starlet Marilyn Monroe as outfielder Gus Zernial does the catching."

It was in the early months of 1952 that Joe decided he wanted to meet

Marilyn Monroe. He learned she was doing publicity photographs with ballplayer Gus Zernial, then an outfielder for the Philadelphia Athletics. She was wearing perhaps the sexiest baseball outfit ever designed; Gus supposedly teaching her how to hit a ball. When Joe saw the published pictures, he called Zernial and learned that everything had been arranged by a press agent named Dave March. When March learned of Joe's interest, he set up a date at the Villa Nova Restaurant on the Sunset Strip as a publicity stunt.

Everything gets a little fuzzy after the basic story of his seeing the Zernial picture and, possibly, calling him for the lead. Most stories about this meeting stress that Joe thought Marilyn loved baseball or would not have been in the picture. That is possible, even probable, because as famous as Joe was, he had also been isolated since a teenager, his life revolving around baseball and Toots Shor's. Some writers have claimed all Marilyn knew was that it was played with a stick and a bat, that she knew nothing of DiMaggio, and when the Yankee was compared to Babe Ruth as a way of helping her put him in perspective, she knew nothing of Ruth.

This aspect of the story ignores the fact that Marilyn not only played softball at the orphanage, she also periodically was involved with pick-up games during down times when filming a movie on location. Cast and crew used softball as a way of passing the time in places where the only alternatives were booze and sex. She simply wasn't a fan of professional sports, but she knew Joe DiMaggio's name for the same reason DiMaggio knew hers (though he may never have seen one of her films).

In another story, DiMaggio was dining with attorney Edward Bennett Williams in Long Island when he saw Marilyn, later described as "this beautiful blonde with big eyes and big bosoms." Williams knew the actress, and DiMaggio remembered seeing the photograph with Zernial. They then all had dinner at Toots Shor's the following night, and Marilyn found herself liking Joe seemingly against her will. She later explained that she had been tired, had changed into casual clothes, and didn't want to be bothered meeting some ballplayer. "I was afraid when I heard he was a ballplayer and part of the sports crowd, he might have slick black hair and wear flashy clothes, but he was very conservative. Like a bank vice president or something. His hair had a touch of gray in it [he was thirty-seven; she was twenty-five]. I liked that. And I could see he was as shy as I was. No jokes that I can remember. Not then. Not even any compliments. My exhaustion left me all of a sudden."

Joe DiMaggio was allegedly left waiting with David March for two hours, a statement that has been questioned by people who knew DiMaggio personally later in his life. They talked of a man of great impatience who would not have waited an hour or two for anyone. Whether the story is false, or waiting for Monroe was different in Joe's mind, or he had more patience in those days than he did when the friends knew him much later in his life is unknown.

What seems to be certain was that Marilyn had a date with Joe in Los Angeles, though whether they had earlier eaten together in New York is uncertain. It was also a dinner that proved rather boring, thanks to the presence of Mickey Rooney. The actor was an odd person to interfere with someone's date. He was known for his love of women, was constantly having affairs, and would marry and divorce with great frequency over the years. But he was also a baseball fan, and that was the problem. He stopped by the table to speak to his friend, Marilyn, then recognized DiMaggio. Instead of speaking briefly and then leaving, he sat at their table and proceeded to talk baseball.

The evening went nowhere. Some stories say that Marilyn refused to ask Joe to her place after they left the restaurant. Others have her chauffeuring him back to his hotel where he offered to show her his trophies, the most original line she claimed to have heard. Some say they had sex, which would not have been unlike Marilyn in those days; others say she bragged about denying him time in bed with her (one friend said Marilyn laughingly told her that the great DiMaggio had "struck out"). Whatever the truth, he was interested enough in her to call the next day. She turned him down.

DiMaggio began a daily round of calls, though it took a week before Marilyn agreed to a second date. She quickly realized that DiMaggio would not be right for her, something her friends also stressed. She liked successful older men, one point in the ballplayer's favor. But Marilyn thrived on publicity, which Joe abhorred. She loved the phoniness of Hollywood: she recognized it as theater, which could be painful on the way up but would make you a star if you survived. She also knew that Joe was taken more seriously by the public than she was, and she could use his declining career to bolster her rising one.

Joe felt the need to assume a protector role with Marilyn. He was convinced that he understood Hollywood, the phonies, the leeches, and those who would rob others of their money under the guise of helping them. Marilyn's drama coach, Natasha Lytess, was among those he held in disdain, a feeling that was mutual. Lytess saw Joe as an ignorant man who had gotten lucky because of baseball but had probably never so much as read a real book in his life.

The few friends to whom Marilyn introduced Joe who met with his approval were usually blue-collar workers or behind-the-scenes individuals who had long-term, positive relationships with the actress. He liked Whitey Snyder, Marilyn's makeup man at Fox and a longtime friend. He liked the Kargers, a family quite similar to the one in which he had been raised.

Joe was rigid in ways it is likely Monroe did not understand. This would not have been unusual for a couple falling in love. Most people feel that the few things they dislike about the person they are dating will change with the marriage. When they don't, the spouse either becomes tolerant of the annoyance or what was once seen as "minor" suddenly is a major rift.

Joe, raised in small spaces with numerous siblings and having spent many years living out of suitcases in hotel rooms, was neat and orderly. He found dignity in an extensive, conservative wardrobe kept clean, pressed, and tailored to suit his impressive physique. Marilyn was a slob, not only in the way she ignored her dog's need to be housebroken but also in the way she kept her house.

Joe expected a woman to be housewife and mother, an ideal Marilyn seemed to share. She was introduced to Joe's son, by then twelve years old, and delighted in the boy. Marilyn had always liked kids, and she understood the tensions with Dorothy. She never tried to become Joe Jr.'s mother, nor did she use the boy to impress his father. She even agreed with Joe that the ideal situation was family, something she had never experienced in the manner Joe had known. What she did not say was that family would not come before her career at the moment. Unlike Dorothy, who knew her talent meant she could aspire to no greater success in films than what little she had already achieved, Marilyn felt certain of stardom. She was driven in ways that may have mirrored Joe's ambitions during those few months between the end of his minor league career and his first season with New York.

Joe believed in modesty in public and when friends were over. Marilyn was flamboyant: this was evident in everything from how she delivered a song from the stage to her penchant for going naked at home. And when it came to their expectations about marriage, Joe's were not keys to long-term success. Joe expected a beautiful, sensual wife who was the envy of every man he knew yet who understood her place and was willing to please her husband, care for the children, and find satisfaction in his happiness. The problem was that Joe also loved being popular. He liked being a celebrity. He liked being seen as a man's man, approachable by anyone who loved baseball and wanted, like Mickey Rooney, to talk about Joe's achievements. He could no more stay at home for Marilyn than she could be a housewife for Joe, though neither of them seemed to understand this reality.

The subtle confrontations between Joe and Marilyn began during their courtship period. The first item of contention was Natasha Lytess. Joe was spending more and more time at Marilyn's apartment, answering her telephone and speaking for "Miss Monroe." He told Natasha, and presumably other formerly close associates, that Marilyn had to be reached through her agent. They could not keep bothering her at home.

Marilyn did not confront Joe about all this. She worked around him. She was under contract to Fox, working at the time on the film *Monkey Business*, and had gained enough clout to request that Natasha be placed on the payroll. The acting coach was given a two-year contract so the women could continue to work together closely, albeit away from Joe.

Monkey Business starred Cary Grant, Charles Coburn, and Ginger Rogers. Monroe, playing the last minor character of her career, was Coburn's secretary, Lois Laurel. Coburn is Charles Oxley, the head of Oxley Chemical Company where Barnaby Fulton (Cary Grant) is a research chemist. He is using a chimpanzee for testing, but when Barnaby leaves the lab, the chimp gets out, mixes what proves to be a youth serum, and dumps it in the water cooler.

The story is one of sex, greed, and slapstick, a comedy that never quite lived up to the quality of the cast, especially Grant and Rogers (playing Edwina Fulton, Barnaby's wife). Monroe was still cast as an old man's lover/play-toy, a point made clear, if anyone missed it, when Oxley tells his secretary he needs help with what the audience would know was a basic secretarial skill of the day, along with shorthand for dictation. Oxley says, "Miss Laurel, find someone to type this."

She responds, "Oh, Mr. Oxley, can't I try again?"

And he answers, "No, it's very important. Better to find someone to type it for you."

One of the high points of the film comes when Barnaby and Edwina (Grant and Rogers) drink the youth serum just before taking the same honeymoon suite they used when they got married. By the time they get inside, they have regressed to the point where she sends him into another room so he doesn't see her undress. Edwina then starts to cry, scared and missing her mother, before picking a schoolyard-type fight with her husband. He leaves, she forgets about him, and he spends the night in the hotel laundry room. The script was adapted first from the short story *The Fountain of Youth* by Harry Segal; then a revision in the characters in a new script by I. A. L. Diamond (now called *Darling—I Am Growing Younger*) added the chimpanzee. The final script, approved on January 11, 1952, was touched up by Ben Hecht, who stressed the bimbo angle for the secretary and added the lines about typing.

Marilyn was still a relative unknown whose work was watched closely by Grant. He later commented,

> I had no idea she would become a big star. If she had something different from any other actress, it wasn't apparent at the time. She seemed very shy and quiet. There was something sad about her. She came to the set early, went into her room, and read. She would stay there until we called her. When the studio workers whistled at her and made remarks that I certainly did not want to hear, it would embarrass her a lot. People don't realize how distressing that sort of thing is. I'm sure they don't or they wouldn't do it. She was a victim of the Hollywood system. It's difficult for a girl to get used to being chased around all the time by the press. They never really leave you alone.

Grant also commented that during the filming of *Monkey Business*, comedian Charles Coburn taught Grant how to upstage, an actor's trick for drawing attention away from another actor, usually one of the stars, without being obvious about what is happening. One trick would be to accidentally spill something during a scene in a kitchen, the spill minor enough so the filming continues. Then the actor who did the spill moves to clean it, again an action so natural that the film still rolls. However, for those few extra seconds, all eyes are on the second actor, not the star.

Coburn loved to use a cigar to gain attention. This was 1951 and smoking was so common, no one thought anything of someone puffing on a cigar in a scene. It was also not unusual for an actor to blow a smoke ring or two, puffing the second immediately after the first so it went in the center of it. Both actions would likely be ignored.

Coburn took all this one step further. He learned, when the wind was right, to puff first one smoke ring and then a second, then prepare his mouth for an unexpected third. The ring would be puffed and all eyes would follow it to see if it entered its target. Again, it was nothing that hurt the scene, nor was it so obvious that the director would stop the action and reshoot. But Coburn briefly took the attention from the star, and that was what it was all about.

According to Cary Grant, when speaking to author Nancy Nelson, Coburn used Monroe as what amounted to a prop to take attention away from Grant. Grant said,

> When we were filming *Monkey Business*, he [Charles Coburn] had to chase and squirt Marilyn Monroe with a siphon of soda, a moment he approached with glee. Any seeming reluctance, he later explained, was only his indecision about *where* on Marilyn's . . . um . . . *ample* proportions to *squirt* the soda. Miss Monroe seemed to present so many inviting parts. Everyone on the set awaited the moment with goggling eyes. You could have heard a pin drop. Eventually Charles gave it a healthy squirt, and missing Miss Monroe, he hit me full in the puss, thereby completely obliterating me from a scene again.

Monroe was later criticized for her chronic lateness by Rogers, who grudgingly admitted that the young actress knew all her lines. What was not mentioned was that Monroe was suffering from severe appendicitis during the March shooting. She arranged to have an antibiotic regimen during a week spent in Cedars of Lebanon Hospital, then returned to work with the knowledge that she would not get worse for a few weeks. She finished the movie, then went to the hospital in April.

Joe was invited to visit Marilyn on the set of the movie and Cary Grant graciously encouraged the publicity department to photograph the three of them together. He did not realize that eventually the photo would be published with Grant's picture carefully removed. The studio understood that Grant had been working less and was less popular than he had been before World War II. Marilyn's star was on the rise, and Joe was so recently retired that his fame still eclipsed that of Grant. The photo of Marilyn and Joe on the set of *Monkey Business* was used to promote Marilyn both for the film and for future work. Joe went along with it, though presumably he was not told that he would be the primary focus when Grant's image was retouched.

Thirty-six

Courtship

DiMaggio's courtship of Marilyn during their early months together was frequently exaggerated by studio publicists and columnists looking for a story when there wasn't one. Louella Parsons suggested that DiMaggio was the right man for Marilyn, though she admitted that Marilyn only "sometimes" talked about him on what Parsons said were daily visits to the columnist's home.

DiMaggio actually was uncomfortable with the type of dating most couples would consider normal. He had no women friends. He did not like to include women in the bars and restaurants he favored. His idea of appropriate intimacy with a woman began and ended in the bedroom, a fact that had helped destroy his first marriage with Dorothy.

Even Marilyn understood the importance of trying to find mutual interests. She went fishing with Joe, having enjoyed the activity when married to Jim Dougherty. She also provided him with a stack of books, from popular novels to some of the classics. She assumed that, just as she was willing to spend hours away from Hollywood glamour fishing with the son of a fisherman, so he would try to improve his mind in the same manner as she was doing. Joe was too self-centered to try.

Joe's one close male friend during this period was the ultimate groupie, a man named George Solotaire who ran the Adelphi Theater Ticket Agency. Solotaire had a wife and child in Bronxville, yet his nights and days were often filled with doing favors for DiMaggio. He played golf with the retired

345

ballplayer. He ran errands for him. He acted as valet and, on many a night, roommate.

George and Joe were constant companions at the Stage Delicatessen and at Toots Shor's. The Stage Deli was a welcoming place for everyone, from actors eating after their performances on Broadway, to theater patrons, to locals who walked from their apartments and resident hotels. Toots Shor, on the other hand, would always be a male bastion where insistent women were seated and provided with excellent service yet always understood they were not truly wanted.

Joe recognized that one of the reasons his marriage to Dorothy had failed was because he had not included her on his evenings out. He wanted to do better by Marilyn, and began taking her with him to Toots Shor's, not anticipating the reaction of the other men. Suddenly Marilyn was the center of attention, a not difficult phenomenon. In that almost all-male environment, even a rather plain woman might seem attractive. Marilyn Monroe stood out like the beacon of a lighthouse on an otherwise black night. Joe was jealous and quickly returned to his mostly "boys' night out" attitude.

Joe may have been a quiet man, but he was vain and determined to be the best at what he did. He had mastered the baseball diamond, his movements as graceful and refined as those of a carefully choreographed classical dancer. When he was given his own television show for the Yankees after retirement, he had it thoroughly scripted. There was even an opening cue card which he used show after show, apparently never memorizing the words. That card, the first one he saw, always read the same: "Hi, I'm Joe DiMaggio. Welcome to *The Joe DiMaggio Show*." Yet it has been told that on the one occasion the card was mislaid, he panicked about the possibility of opening without it. Because it was found in time, no one learned whether Joe was superstitious and determined to get everything right, or if he was simply not bright enough to remember the standard greeting.

Joe seemed to want to feel as much in control off the ball field as he felt he had been on it, from his physical appearance to his activities throughout the days and nights. This level of control was impossible to achieve, and as new players joined the Yankees' team roster, even the greatest of former players stopped being news.

Marilyn, by contrast, was still on the rise. She was about to become the most popular actress in America despite how seemingly little she had developed her talents by then. Where once Marilyn had benefited from Joe's popularity, seeming more a beautiful appendage than someone important in her own right, during their courtship the roles were reversed. Joe increasingly became irrelevant. He was no longer playing baseball, so there were new players to write about, to photograph. Suddenly he was the man on the arm of Marilyn Monroe: a celebrity appendage, just as she had been. His ego did not tolerate it; yet seemingly neither Joe nor Marilyn understood the implications of their courtship at this time in their careers.

Hedda Hopper column for May 4, 1952: "Blowtorch Blondes are Hollywood's specialty, and Marilyn Monroe who has zoomed to stardom after a three-year stretch as a cheesecake queen is easily the most delectable dish of the day. . . . She is fast supplanting Sam Goldwyn as a source of anecdotes and every producer at Twentieth is bidding for her as box office insurance."

There was another stress, again a foretaste of the future. This resulted from Marilyn's taking singing lessons. All the studio contract players had voice lessons as part of their training. All learned how to carry a tune, though obviously there were many whose skills were too limited to use in films.

Marilyn proved to be a competent singer under the tutelage of Fox's Hal Schaefer, a man Joe would later come to believe was having an affair with her. Her vocal skills were such that she could go before an audience without embarrassing herself. What made her special during those occasions when she traveled as a celebrity entertainer was her acting ability. Marilyn had learned how to play the seductive innocent, a character that would fully blossom when she eventually made the film *The Seven Year Itch*. She knew how to project virginity and desire in a way that made a man feel not only wanted, but that this beautiful, voluptuous woman had been saving herself just for him.

As a singer, Marilyn took the character she had created for the films in which she was cast and applied it to her live stage performance. It was an act, of course—another role in the Monroe persona—but she used it in ways that shocked Joe.

The first time Joe became aware of what, to him, was the embarrassingly public side of Marilyn was when she was asked to be part of a show taking place at Camp Pendleton, the military base south of Los Angeles. While World War II was over, the military was increasingly tense, and enlistees knew that they could be called to battle at any time. Russia was not only aggressively pursuing nuclear weapons, it was also clamping down on countries that were becoming too independent within the Soviet bloc. North Korea had been engaged in a war with South Korea, and France was having problems in Indo-China. An attack against the United States was seen as a likelihood, and civil defense programs were being considered in cities around the country. The thousands of men stationed at Camp Pendleton were keenly aware of what was taking place, and they embraced the relief Hollywood entertainers brought them with emotions that came close to those felt by soldiers stationed in remote regions of the world during the World War II traveling USO shows.

There was more to the Camp Pendleton appearance than a simple entertainment program. Marilyn wanted to use her appearance as an audition for Twentieth Century-Fox. The Anita Loos novel *Gentlemen Prefer Blondes* was first serialized in six issues of *Harper's Bazaar* during 1925, then turned into a 1928 silent film starring Alice White and Ruth Taylor. The story again resonated strongly with audiences after World War II, and Loos, along with Joseph Fields, was hired to adapt it for the Broadway stage. This was a major musical starring Carol Channing as Lorelei Lee, and the show had eighteen songs written by Leo Robyn and Jule Stein. The show opened in 1949 and was a major box-office success, leading Channing to think that this could be her chance to star in films. Several companies bid on the project, most of them looking at house stars for the role. Channing had no box-office recognition outside New York. Others, such as Judy Holliday who had just won an Oscar for *Born Yesterday,* were taken more seriously. Holliday was under contract to Columbia and her studio was willing to buy the rights to the play, whatever the cost, if she wanted to star. She did not.

Channing's chances ended when Twentieth Century-Fox won the bidding war for the movie rights. Neither Darryl Zanuck nor the producer assigned to the new project, Sol Siegel, wanted someone who was not assured of filling seats in a movie theater. That was why they first thought of Betty Grable, an experienced singer, dancer, and the "house blonde" for almost twenty years. Marilyn had been a toddler when Grable was a starlet, and Grable, though getting older than would be ideal for the character in the movie, was almost perfect for the part. The one problem was her salary. Her contract called for her to be paid $150,000 per film. This was the same fee that would be paid for Jane Russell, the brunette best friend, who was playing Dorothy. However, Russell was a proven star with both the talent and the body for the role.

Marilyn, probably with the advice of Sid Skolsky, knew she had to indirectly audition for the part of Lorelei Lee. She had the box-office recognition, the magazine publicity, and a fan base that had her receiving as many as twenty-five thousand letters a week. She was also a professional blonde, a fact that guaranteed Zanuck could not ignore her because of his preference for dark-haired women.

Twentieth Century-Fox hired Charles Lederer to write the Technicolor musical, which was changed from the play in a number of ways. The most important change was made because the musical, according to Lederer, had no book (story line). It was actually a musical revue, and revues could not translate to the screen. He had to make up a story line so that there were fewer songs and a cohesive beginning, middle, and end. He also had to change some of the songs he kept in the show (only three of the original eighteen) because the lyrics were risqué. Broadway might have families attending, but the audience knew the shows were sophisticated and not meant for children. Movie theater audiences could include entire families. That was why in the title song Lederer removed the original second verse that said, "Some girls find/Some peace of mind/In a trust fund that banks recommend/But if you are busty/Your trustee gets lusty/But diamonds are a girl's best friend."

Lionel Newman was to be the musical director and choreographer Jack Cole would handle the dance numbers, including "Diamonds Are a Girl's Best Friend" in which whoever was cast as the blonde would be passing dozens of men she ignores as she sings of the erotic delights of the major jewelers—Tiffany's, Cartier's, and Harry Winston's. It was to be a parody of materialism as sex, and it was not a song for someone with limited abilities. Marilyn Monroe, who had to be considered for the Lorelei part since she was both under contract to Fox and only had to be paid $750 a week ($9,000 for the production schedule of December 1952 through February 1953), did not seem capable. It was for this reason that she decided to go to Camp Pendleton, turning her performance for the troops into an audition for Darryl Zanuck.

Thirty-seven

Niagara and Robert Slatzer

Perhaps it was because Marilyn Monroe lied so frequently and about so many aspects of her life that a cottage industry of pretenders has gained national attention through telling the dirty little secrets of her existence. With the exception of the mail fraud photograph scam, few, if any, occurred during her lifetime. It would have been too easy to denounce them as fraudulent and have Marilyn prove their lies. After her death, the people in the know dismissed such individuals and those who had no knowledge bought into the most interesting stories. Then the Internet added its own mythology support center because anyone with the right skills, or the money to hire someone with the right skills, can create a web site that, if well designed, seems to be factual. Worse, frequently the great-looking web sites with the seemingly factual information are carefully annotated and cross-referenced to sources that include or began with Robert Slatzer. Thus there is the appearance of a scholarly confirmation.

Slatzer's later "career" as friend of Marilyn, keeper of secrets, and writer of books about their supposed time and conversations together came after her death but began with the one legitimate moment they shared—a fraction of a second when she posed for a photograph with him as she did with any fan who asked. Others, mentioned at the end of this book, emerged after her death. Some are colorful, such as the woman who has found success as the reincarnated Marilyn. Others are real neighbors who depended on the mutual friends who knew that the two never had a relationship to either be dead and silent or simply not bother to contradict them to the writers conducting interviews.

But in Slatzer's case, he seemed to believe that he was the love who dared not speak its name. Marilyn would not have recognized it.

❦

The story Robert Slatzer told—long enough after Marilyn's death so it would not be challenged by the one person who intimately knew it—was nonsense, and came about because of the movie *Niagara*. The couple met in Niagara Falls and Slatzer had a photo of the two of them to prove it. Also according to Slatzer, on the weekend of October 3–6, 1952, he and Marilyn were in Tijuana, Mexico, getting married, honeymooning, and getting an annulment. This was not only a truly rushed marriage, it was also a miraculous occurrence: for Marilyn had been seen by friends and co-workers in Los Angeles during this period (without Slatzer), and spent money there, for which author Donald Spoto found undisputed receipts. The one witness to the Mexican nuptials was Noble Chissell, a friend of the "groom" who later admitted to lying about the incident.

The real story of *Niagara* was a simple one, though it did involve Slatzer, Joe DiMaggio, and Darryl Zanuck, each in differing importance.

DiMaggio had learned little from his marriage to Dorothy Arnold. She had given up her career for him, though she did not have much of a career to abandon. Arnold was like a dancer in a chorus line. She could dance on the stage, one of perhaps dozens of other women all dressed and moving alike, for many years until she began to stand out not for her talent, but for her age. She would need more makeup, have to do more stretching to avoid muscle and joint problems, and no longer be able to rehearse and do several shows a day without napping.

Marilyn was the lead dancer in such a scenario, the dancer around whom the chorus was choreographed. She stood out in the front and had all eyes riveted on her movements. Her career would be as a featured performer, and since no one ever knew how long they might star, she wanted to grasp every moment of it. Dorothy Arnold was as different from Marilyn Monroe as Joe DiMaggio was from a baseball player in the Little League.

Joe also did not recognize that his bias often had to do with his last, desperate clinging to fame. The cheering throngs were a thing of the past.

He wanted privacy, but he also wanted attention. It was a joke among the Yankees that, following a game, Joe would linger in the locker room, staring into a mirror at his pomade-covered hair. He would carefully groom himself, making certain that everything was perfect before emerging to the fans and the sportswriters.

Joe might not like to have strangers approach him when he was enjoying his friends in a place like Toots Shor's, but friends would tell stories of his stopping by such locations as the Stage Delicatessen for a sandwich. This was one of the popular spots in the theater district where, after a show, one could see celebrities, many of whom had just starred on the stage. Most received a glance from the tourists and locals stopping by on their way home. When Joe started eating, it was not unusual for almost everyone in the place to stop what they were doing and watch him chew his food. He was a step removed from mortals, and he was gradually aware that Marilyn was becoming a step removed from him.

The other problem with the relationship was the fact that Marilyn had fame without obvious talent, while Joe's fame resulted from his having proven his talent. Joe thought Marilyn would never succeed and saw no reason for her to continue taking a series of sex-focused roles. The fact that she had been a caricature in *Don't Bother to Knock* added to his feeling that she should quit the studio, marry him, and be a housewife catering to his wishes.

Joe certainly understood the potential for embarrassment in all this since his one serious effort at show business—having a television show for the Yankees after he retired as a player—had bombed. He was out of control and out of his element. He saw Marilyn heading in the same direction and frequently criticized her work. He dismissed her growing popularity as the result of her undeniable sex appeal. But sex appeal was not good enough for a career; and even if it was, Joe did not want men lusting after his wife's body. She should leave the business and settle down with him. He had no sense that her drive to be a star, her willingness to risk failing every time she was given a slightly more demanding role, easily matched the drive that had driven him to succeed in baseball.

Marilyn saw Joe as someone to be respected. He wasn't part of Hollywood. He wasn't part of the motion picture industry. Her salary under contract was peaking at seventy-five thousand dollars a year, while he earned close to a hundred thousand *before* payment for television, endorsements, and the like. He owned a restaurant, and though he had little to do with running it, that fact still made him a businessman. She decided she could trust him because he had nothing to gain from her success. Neither realized that what he wanted from Marilyn required her failure. Thus his praise mattered to her, and his criticism was taken far more seriously than it warranted.

Darryl Zanuck also had his doubts. *Don't Bother to Knock* had been a wake-up call for everyone. Marilyn's fan mail increased during the movie's release, but the box-office receipts were down. It appeared that some portion of her core fans went to see the film, then told their friends it was not worth viewing. This did not change their love for her, their clipping her photographs from magazines, and their requesting her autograph. In a preview of what would take place with the celebrity fascination a half-century later, Marilyn the celebrity was more popular than Marilyn the actress.

Director Howard Hawks viewed what was happening with a broader understanding of the film medium than Zanuck. Marilyn Monroe was a contract employee of Twentieth Century-Fox. As such, she was placed in any movie the studio desired. It did not matter where her skills might lie. She could be in a Western one week, a horror movie the next, a romance after that, and then a comedy. It was only when a contract employee began to show there was a strong audience for a certain type of movie that more consideration was given to skill.

Hawks understood that Monroe was not a dramatic actress. Her childhood had been relatively isolated. Her schooling was limited. Her stage experience was nonexistent. She had never lived the life created for her (and re-created, and re-created) in her studio biographies. Norma Jean had never thought through who this Marilyn Monroe persona needed to be in order to go the next step to stardom. What she did do well was a kind of over-the-top performance more exaggerated than even Natasha Lytess's lessons. She needed to forget trying to be realistic and start exaggerating as appropriate for the film. The two of them applied this thinking to the character she would be playing in *Niagara*, a film both recognized was being cast in a way that made Zanuck uncomfortable.

It was the summer of 1952 when Marilyn began working in Niagara Falls. She had been cast as Rose Loomis, working with Joseph Cotten (as

353

George Loomis), Jean Peters (Polly Cutler), and Casey Adams, the name used by actor Max Showalter for the film's credits (Ray Cutler), Richard Allan (Ted Patrick), and others. The film was a dark drama about adultery, murder, and revenge, with Rose Loomis manipulating and destroying two men: one her husband and the other her lover.

The story had Ray and Polly Cutler arriving at a motel on the Canadian side of Niagara Falls for their honeymoon. George and Rose Loomis are also at the motel, and Polly spots Rose kissing Ted Patrick. The two are lovers plotting the death of George Loomis, but Polly remains silent about what she's seen even when George admits to her that he thinks his wife is cheating on him.

The plot has numerous twists. George Loomis disappears, a body is found, and when Rose, who reported her husband missing, is asked to identify it, the body proves to be that of Ted. Rose is overwhelmed with shock and grief, and is hospitalized under sedation. It is later learned that George killed him, allegedly in self-defense.

George becomes involved with Polly, who he hopes will help him just disappear. She does not tell what she knows and has seen, believing George. However, when Rose eventually leaves the hospital, George sees her, chases her into a tower, and strangles her. Finally George and Polly are on a boat heading for the falls after the two accidentally meet while he is running from the police and she, not knowing he was there, was getting supplies for herself and her husband.

At the end of the movie, Loomis saves Polly as the boat approaches the Falls. He puts her on a ledge by the river and she climbs to safety. A helicopter in pursuit saves Polly as Loomis's boat is carried over the Falls.

The movie was Marilyn's eighteenth film and her second dramatic starring role. The quality of the performance was mixed and Monroe knew it. Otis L. Guernsey Jr. of the *New York Herald Tribune*, in his review of the movie, wrote two sentences that seemed to sum up all the positive reviews she received around the country. "Miss Monroe plays the kind of wife whose dress, in the words of the script, 'is cut so low you can see her knees.' The dress is red; the actress has very nice knees, and under Hathaway's direction she gives the kind of serpentine performance that makes the audience hate her while admiring her, which is proper for the story."

Howard Hawks's instincts had been correct, and fortunately they were shared by Henry Hathaway, the director of the film, and Joe MacDonald, the cinematographer. The script was worked and reworked, and as it took shape, so did the character originally slated to be played by Anne Francis or Maureen Stapleton. Francis was also being considered, along with Jeanne Crain, for the character eventually named Polly. Darryl Zanuck had his own preference for Rose—Constance Smith. Always they had in mind that the first draft of the script called the adulterous wife Rose Bayford and described her as "a lusty slut who used to be a manicurist in Duluth." They were thinking of the adulterous wife as being dark, not a blonde.

Prior to Marilyn being cast, the character of Polly Cutler was to be the lead. Anne Baxter loved the part and agreed to take it, but before contracts could be signed, the decision was made to give Monroe the role of Rose. This was not because of the quality of her acting but because she would go along with a change in the marketing of the film that also meant a change in how her part would be handled. There were to be billboards of Marilyn in what looked like painted-on clothing standing in front of the Falls. The image is supposed to be an allusion to the Greek mythical Sirens whose song was so beautiful that no passing fisherman or other sailor could resist going to see the women whose voices carried over the water. The men would risk, and lose, their lives going to hear them. That is why, in the story of Jason and the Argonauts, Jason has his crew tie him to the mast so he cannot break away and jump into the water. Then he has them plug their ears so they hear nothing. Finally they plot their course to go past the Sirens: Jason is able to hear the song and going almost mad with the desire to be with them but the restraints protect him from an otherwise deadly fate.

However, if Greek mythology was too obscure in 1952, the promotion refers to Monroe as a siren who "sang of love just as she lived for love, like a Lorelei flaunting her charms as she lured men on and on to their eternal destruction." One of the film's posters has the line: "Marilyn Monroe and *Niagara:* A raging torrent of emotion that even nature can't control!" She is also given lead credit, followed in same-size type by Joseph Cotten and Jean Peters.

Director Henry Hathaway and cinematographer Joe MacDonald worked to carefully plan the framing and action of each scene in which Monroe appeared. They were fortunate to have Marilyn's experience as a still photography model for so many years. She understood how to lower her head so she would have a half-lidded gaze, her lips carefully made up so the Technicolor film would linger on the moist redness as she kept them slightly parted. Marilyn had long since learned the advertising trick of using red to draw the eye.

Color advertising photos of the 1950s would frequently either be selling a product or selling the results of using that product. Color ads in which a model is holding expensive bath towels will have the towels in warm colors—red, orange, yellow—and the model dressed in cool tones—blues, greens—with subdued makeup. But ads meant to sell makeup that would make the buyer physically desired by the special man in her life would have bright red lipstick and often a red ribbon or other adornment in her hair. Her earrings would be a warm color and the combination would draw the eye to her face. Then the photographer would focus most sharply on her lips for sensuality and most sharply on her eyes for intimacy.

Cinematographer MacDonald, the hairdresser who further whitened Marilyn's artificially blonde hair, Whitey Snyder, her personal makeup artist, and the costumer worked together to create the same impact in a moving picture that advertising photographers used with still. Then, in one scene, Marilyn had to walk 116 feet in a manner that would tell the audience everything it needed to know to understand Ted's obsession. The costumer designed a black skirt with a red top that was literally sewn onto her body prior to the walk. Then Hathaway had the camera positioned behind her, ordering MacDonald to focus on her rear. It was an image that was shocking in its day, changing the focus of the film to Marilyn and further downgrading the role of Polly. Jean Peters later explained that she thought the script change that had caused Anne Francis to refuse the Polly role had simply left the two women characters as equal. This appears to be the case when the script is read. However, in addition to the shot of the walk, Monroe's look was designed to call attention to herself. Her hair was treated so it was an even lighter blonde than usual; that, combined with the choice of lipstick and gloss on her mouth, would result in the audience unknowingly being led directly to her lips, enhancing the sensuality of both the actress and everything taking place around her. It was a subconscious reaction, but one that had been used for years as photographers focused on the lips of models they wanted to appear sexual to the viewer. It was the same view someone would have as he leaned in for a kiss.

Monroe's sexuality may have worked on the screen, but her personal habits were troublesome to cast and crew. First, there were the living arrangements. Cast and crew were housed at the General Brock Hotel. Darryl Zanuck insisted that Max Showalter, the actor playing Ray Cutler (credited on the screen as Casey Adams), have a room next to Marilyn's. There were two doors between them so that they could be shut and locked for absolute privacy within each separate room, or unlocked and opened to create an instant suite. Marilyn insisted that they be unlocked except when Joe DiMaggio came to visit the set. Then, on the first night before she was to be filmed, Showalter said that Marilyn, naked, came into his room, climbed into his bed, and asked to be held because she was frightened of how the next day's shooting might go. She wanted him to help her with her lines, then she returned to her own room. There was no sex involved, and Showalter was to later learn that nudity was either enjoyed by Marilyn ("I like to feel blonde all over," she was once quoted as telling a columnist) or was part of an exhibitionist streak designed to get attention.

For example, at the end of each day's filming, Joseph Cotten opened his room to the rest of the cast so they could talk, drink, and relax. Marilyn did not join them. She apparently went to her room and, on at least one occasion, took off her clothes. The story, as related by Max Showalter to author Richard Buskin, has the naked Marilyn calling to the actor in the next room because she is troubled by men standing on the street, looking up at her hotel room window. She seemed to think that they had an inordinate curiosity about her and was genuinely surprised at Showalter's suggestion: that they might be looking, he said, because "you haven't got a stitch of clothing on."

There was a scene in the film where Marilyn also was more revealing than others desired. This came during the two days it took to film her singing the song *Kiss*, a production number handled back in the studio at the end of June.

The final draft of the screenplay had a scene in which Marilyn was to sing Cole Porter's "Night and Day," a lush love song that would be sung in front of Ray Cutler. It was Rose's favorite song in the film. However, for reasons that are unclear, the song "Kiss," recently written by Lionel Newman and Haven Gillespie, was substituted. Then Rose, wearing the red dress that Ray describes as "cut down so low in front you could see her knees" proceeds to move as seductively as she can. The costume, the movements, and the camera position were all such that it was obvious Marilyn was not wearing any undergarments. Worse, the crew needed to film the singing over and over again, getting long shots to close-ups for cutting when the final edit was made. Each take seemed to cause her already short dress to ride higher, revealing her intimate nakedness. They finally found a horse blanket and covered her from her waist down as they filmed the close-ups of her face.

The exhibitionism was not a naïve act. There were other scenes where Marilyn worked to achieve what amounted to too much reality. At one point she was taking a shower and the curtain was translucent, letting light and form through so that her nakedness could be seen when she stood against the shower. Director Henry Hathaway told her to move back in the stall. Even a few inches ensured that nothing more than shadow would be visible. Each time Monroe agreed. Each time Monroe returned so she was flush against the material, her nakedness showing through. And because she was constantly being told what to do, it was obvious she knew the effect she was having.

Finally Hathaway stopped correcting Marilyn and wasting money with yet another take. The shower scene was crucial so he had the special effects people darken each frame so he would have the effect he originally sought to achieve.

Sid Skolsky deliberately increased interest in Monroe during the filming. He visited her on the set, a visit that required the approval of the Fox publicists, who undoubtedly understood that whatever the two friends had devised would likely help the movie. There was an interview in which Sid gave Marilyn the straight line, asking her what she wore to bed and she gave her reply: that all she wore was Chanel No. 5.

All the effort was futile. The movie was dark, shocking, dramatic, and ultimately unsuccessful. John McCarten, reviewing the movie for *The New Yorker*, wrote:

"Marilyn Monroe, whom Hollywood has been ballyhooing as a new-day Lillian Russell, takes a fling at big-league melodrama in 'Niagara' and demonstrates a wide assortment of curves and a tendency to read her lines as if they were written in a tongue she is not entirely familiar with."

The awareness of the speech problem was more discerning than he realized. During one scene in which Max Showalter is on a beach photographing Jean Peters, Marilyn comes over to him and says the line, "I'm sorry, but have you seen my husband?" It was nothing major, yet Monroe did not look at the other actor; she looked past him and he found it disconcerting. She was supposed to be looking at him, and when she didn't, he complained. Marilyn refused to acknowledge what she was doing; Henry Hathaway, unconcerned, was willing to let her play it any way she wanted.

Showalter was not convinced that Marilyn was actually working with him to make the scene effective. He glanced over his shoulder and saw Natasha Lytess standing where Marilyn could see her but where the camera would not record her. Natasha mouthed the words Marilyn was to say, and Marilyn pronounced them aloud exactly the same way. She was only satisfied when Lytess was satisfied. The director was superfluous. The result sounded as though English was Monroe's second language.

But McCarten did not place all the blame for the film's weaknesses on Marilyn. "In addition to this lingual difficulty, Miss Monroe is handicapped by the whimsical direction of Henry Hathaway, who runs an admiring camera alternately over the contours of his star and the contours of Niagara Falls. However admirably constructed Miss Monroe may be, she is hardly up to competing visually with one of the wonders of this continent, and the cataract keeps stealing scenes from her."

And as for the script: ". . . the actors in 'Niagara' try hard to make some sense of their implausible situations. None of them succeed."

Years later, director Hathaway was interviewed by author John Kobal. He discussed how he viewed Marilyn after their work together in *Niagara* and what he would have liked to have done with her as an actress.

I wanted to do *Of Human Bondage* with Marilyn and Jimmy Dean way back then, because after I did that picture with her I found her marvelous to work with, very easy to direct and marvelously, terrifically ambitious to do better. And bright, really bright learning. She may not have had an education, but she was just naturally bright. But always being trampled on. You talk of Rita [Hayworth] being trampled on by men. This little thing was trampled on by bums! I don't think anyone ever treated her on her own level. To most men she was, I won't say a bum, but something that they were a little bit ashamed of, to put it bluntly—even Joe DiMaggio. If she had been allowed to do this picture, it would have put her in another category. I think she would have been absolutely marvelous doing it. But Darryl said, "Jesus Christ, how can you think of it! How can I say I'm putting Marilyn in a very sensitive Bette Davis-style play? We'd get lampooned before we started. There would be a problem with her work, and meantime I'd lose three to four million dollars on the films I could be making with her being Marilyn Monroe."

༄

It was in the midst of all this that Marilyn posed for a photograph with the twenty-five-year-old Robert Slatzer, a fan who was to prove an opportunist greater than Beebe Goddard. It was an action repeated many times, and sometimes many times a day when Marilyn was making publicity appearances. She was one of the most accessible actresses in a time when entertainers were still expected to be generous to their fans. However, Slatzer claimed this was the start of a relationship, one that proved to be so secret not even Marilyn Monroe knew it was happening.

Slatzer planted an item with columnist Dorothy Kilgallen that was used in her column on August 16, 1952. Kilgallen wrote: "A dark horse in the Marilyn Monroe romance derby is Bob Slatzer, former Columbus, Ohio literary critic. He's been wooing her by phone and mail, and improving her mind with gifts of the world's greatest books." The column was never substantiated by a check with Monroe or even the studio publicists. It was pure Slatzer, and, as such, not credible.

Kilgallen also let Slatzer write (or have the credit for writing) an item for her September 12 "Voice of Broadway" column. He said that he was supplying Marilyn with literature to improve her mind. Slatzer was later quoted in *Confidential* magazine, discussing why Marilyn probably would not marry DiMaggio, explaining that DiMaggio's jealousy was overwhelming.

It was 1972 when Slatzer teamed up with Will Fowler to write the "truth" about his relationship with Monroe that he had not discussed when she was alive. At first Slatzer supplied the journalist with an article he had

360

written, which he hoped Fowler could flesh out and sell. The article claimed that Monroe's death was part of a political conspiracy (one of many theories that would become popular long after she died). Fowler did not feel there was a potential for such a book until Slatzer decided to claim that he had briefly been married to her. This eventually led to the publication of *The Life and Curious Death of Marilyn Monroe*, a book that included the story of the wild October weekend when the alleged marriage and annulment took place. Fowler was not dishonest with the work he did for Slatzer. He simply told the story as Slatzer fabricated it, receiving confirmation from characters such as Noble Chissell, a friend of Slatzer who originally claimed to have met the couple in Tijuana, then later admitted he had lied.

Slatzer's work has long been seen by those who did not thoroughly check out the man as a definitive study of missing information in Marilyn's life. The trouble was that there was absolutely no corroboration in the form of records, letters, or anything else. Except for the single photograph, all "proof" of the long-term friendship, the marriage, and the rest of the intimate relationship was nonexistent. Slatzer briefly married Kay Eicher in 1954, but when she was interviewed years later, she talked of his using the photograph—the kind that any fan with a camera and someone to snap the picture could have, and often did, take—to "prove" a story that was pure fantasy.

Slatzer later added such information as the story of her "murder" and the involvement of the Kennedy brothers. He also sold photographs from her last film, the unfinished *Something's Got to Give*, claiming credit for work actually taken by James Mitchell. (Mitchell was a still photographer on the Fox payroll who took the images as part of his job.)

Slatzer would later claim that the fast annulment came because Marilyn was afraid of Joe DiMaggio. In truth, the delay in reporting the "marriage" came because Slatzer was afraid of Marilyn. She would have denied the ridiculous story had it come out during her lifetime.

(In speaking with one of his publishers, the publisher admitted that he knew Slatzer was lying. However, he spoke about matters no one could confirm or deny. He also said that Slatzer brought with him "witnesses" who were the type of friends who would agree to anything Slatzer said, enjoying the ruses. The tragedy is that otherwise good biographies have often relied on Slatzer and similar opportunists, creating a new "truth" about something that never occurred.)

Director Henry Hathaway was among the first of the men and women who worked closely with Monroe to realize the intensity of her drive for success and the health problems that could result. The Slatzer photo was not unusual during location filming. Every interview request was granted, regardless of the size or readership of the publication. This meant that, no matter how long a day she had to put in, more time would be spent posing and talking, further limiting her chance to rest.

Other actors faced similar requests but had their agents and/or managers and/or studio publicists screen the requests, evaluating them in relation to the free time that could be devoted to such interview meetings. This assured adequate rest breaks and appearances in the most important publications. The problem for Marilyn was that when Johnny Hyde died, the William Morris Agency failed to follow normal procedures in such matters. The agency should have assigned a go-between to handle such requests, but without Hyde's presence, no one was interested in her. They took their percentage, guaranteed by contract, and let the Fox publicity department handle the rest, even though she was on the brink of exhaustion from the demands.

Hathaway, regardless of his desires for Marilyn, knew that no matter what the critical reaction to *Niagara*, Marilyn had made a breakthrough. She was about to get the star treatment in ways she never dreamed of. There were going to be business pressures, and he urged her to seek professional help in the industry.

Marilyn talked with Joe DiMaggio about all this, either unaware of or ignoring the fact that Joe wanted her to leave the business. She respected Joe's business sense and wanted his view on the problems she was facing. Finally, after listening to everyone and personally looking at her own situation, she had her lawyer fire the William Morris Agency. Then she began working with Charlie Feldman of the Famous Artists Agency, an agent who had been courting her business for many months. He had long recognized that William Morris had been in a bind with Marilyn when Johnny died. The clients of the heads of the agency were supposed to pass to other high-powered executives when the earlier agent died or retired. But Marilyn was still seen as the old man's mistress and no one seemed to look beyond that.

Feldman had none of the pressures, constraints, or embarrassments of William Morris. He was also willing to woo her, offering to do extensive work without charge to show Marilyn how she could benefit from his skills. As a result, Marilyn was not only protected from the excesses resulting from her own intense drive; she also discovered the one strong point in Joe DiMaggio that would be enough for her to risk marriage. He understood the stress she was under as a rising celebrity, the way management tried to get the most work for the least money, and the tremendous exploitation of anyone famous in show business, in its various forms. The fact that he was a decade older, had been through intense public adoration and fascination, and could speak about the business from experience made him seem the ideal next husband.

Joe saw that the film industry was the same as baseball. Team promotions were like movie and star promotions. Radio endorsements and the perquisites of stardom were the same in both fields. Marilyn was one of the biggest box-office draws in the world, regardless of the quality of the films she was in or the size of her parts. He wanted to have her manipulate the studio heads the way an athlete might exploit his fan appeal at contract negotiation time. Helping Marilyn aroused his competitive spirit, and he seemed to ignore the fact that in doing so, he would also be encouraging her to stay in an industry that he, personally, hated.

Joe had tremendous insight and maturity on the one hand, and a fantasy life about "happily ever after" on his terms on the other. Knowing Marilyn was unhappy with the way her career was going, he thought she should consider leaving the business. He still did not understand her obsession and the fact that her way of coping with depression over her treatment by the studio involved throwing herself into her work. This meant taking any role requested by the studio, even if she did not like the script.

At that moment, taking any role meant accepting the part of a nightclub singer/dancer for the 1953 film *Gentlemen Prefer Blondes*. She entered into the work with an intensity not seen when she was happy with her career and her love life. She even went so far as to make certain she reported to work exactly on time, or even early. She was never late during the filming, a signature act of disdain when she was feeling good about herself.

Gentlemen Prefer Blondes was a story about love, gold diggers, a concerned father, a private detective, and a cruise ship. It was typical of the story line of many films of the day—a vehicle for displaying songs, dances, and good-looking women. Marilyn co-starred with Jane Russell, a brunette who had the looks and maturity to appeal to every man in the audience who was uninterested in unnatural blondes. As Otis Guernsey Jr. wrote in the *New York Herald Tribune* when the movie was previewed: "Putting these two buxom pin-up girls in the same movie is merely giving two-to-one odds on a sure thing, and the payoff is big in a rousing musical number. . . ." He also commented: "Singing, dancing or just staring at diamonds, these girls are irresistible and their musical is as lively as a string of firecrackers on the Fourth of July."

Gentlemen Prefer Blondes was escapist entertainment, but it was escapist for Marilyn as well. She threw herself into every aspect of the part. She would stand uncomplaining for costume fittings, makeup sessions, and the altering of her hair, a routine situation for her. The unnatural blonde would gradually become lighter and lighter as each new director decided that her appeal was, in part, measured by the closer her hair changed toward platinum.

Marilyn knew that the audience was coming to see sex, something proven by many of the costumes. Indeed, the *New York Post* review by Archer Winsten commented that "the girls wear form-fitting thises and thats, revealing native talents celebrated in pin-ups, traveling compartment conversations, and legend of the cinema world." However, she also knew that she wanted to give them something more. She wanted to entertain them as a singer, for which she had long been taking lessons, and a dancer, her weak point at the time.

Jack Cole choreographed the dancing, neither he nor Marilyn having any illusions about her abilities. Jane Russell was far more competent. Though a professional, she willingly rehearsed with Marilyn until exhaustion forced her to stop. Marilyn drove herself further, however, working until Cole left, then working on her own. She would never be a great dancer. She would never be more than another competent hoofer trained by the studio system. But the performance she gave represented the best of which she was capable, something a less driven actress would not have done.

Marilyn was determined to win the part of Lorelei even though she still had a poor relationship with studio head Darryl Zanuck. She worked intensely on her singing, lowering her voice even though when her character (Lorelei Lee) was talking, Monroe used a higher-pitched, whispery style of speaking. She also worked on the choreography, including after she got the Lorelei role. She and choreographer Jack Cole would work after the shooting was over, the cast was out of makeup, and almost everyone had gone home for the night.

Cole understood not only how much the role meant to Marilyn—though no one realized how successful the movie would be for all involved—but also the fact that she was not a dancer. Some starlets had natural talent. Others traveled in musicals, gradually mastering dancing through hard work. Marilyn probably worked harder than anyone else, but her understanding that she lacked technique, that she would have to master what she was shown by others because she brought little dance ability to the set, terrified her.

Marilyn also worked on her singing, including with Hal Schaefer, the vocal coach for the film. This was an area of professional competence often unrecognized. Monroe had little experience singing for the movies because a starlet was mostly seen and not heard. Songs called attention to an actress, so her work was often chorus, such as in *A Ticket to Tomahawk*. In addition, some of the early actresses whose singing impressed theater audiences had performed in nightclubs and cabarets while working their way up in show business.

Fred Karger had been the first person to nurture Marilyn's innate ability as a professional singer, and by the time Schaefer was through with her, she could hold her own. The problem was that no one knew it, the reason she was so anxious to sing at Camp Pendleton. She knew she would be watched by people who mattered in the industry, and if she wanted to star with Russell, she had to prove she could grab an audience and make it her own.

Marilyn sang "Do It Again," a song little known outside musical theater buffs. It came from a collaboration between lyricist B. G. DeSylva and composer George Gershwin for their 1922 show *The French Doll*. The times were rebellious. Young adults were throwing off the strictures of the Victorian era. Alcohol consumption had risen because of Prohibition, and sex had become the focus of the young. There was even a professor who suggested that the country institute trial marriages, a two-ceremony approach to wedlock. A couple would commit for a year, during which they would be legally married with all the rights and privileges of any other couple. Then, at the end of twelve months, they would either go through a second ceremony that would establish the permanence of their relationship or they would go their separate ways. There would be no alimony, no recriminations, and they would have enjoyed a year of sex and cohabitation without anyone considering them to have "lived in sin." In such an environment, the naughty lyrics of "Do It Again" were a delight to the audience. The implication was one of a woman asking a man for sex, not just once but repeatedly, the type of song which would have been deemed inappropriate during and immediately after the war years. As it was, in the conservative days of the early 1950s, the words were stretching the boundaries of propriety in much the manner of Marilyn's nude calendar or the soon-to-be-issued first *Playboy* magazine.

Marilyn worked the song for all its sexuality. Her flawlessly controlled breathing included moans of pleasure and desire. And the reaction was one that would be repeated over and over again whenever she went on tour. First there was the hushed silence, then thunderous applause, the soldiers stomping, whistling, and, in several instances, rushing toward the stage.

Using the sense of humor that may have been original and may have been supplied by either Sid Skolsky or the Fox publicity department, Marilyn accepted the master of ceremonies' compliment on her tight sweater and high skirt looking so attractive. Then she said, "I don't know why you boys are always getting so excited about sweater girls. Take away their sweaters—and what have they got?"

The Marines exploded as she fled backstage, delighted by a performance she knew would sway Zanuck. She was right. He was sent a recording of her singing and agreed to use her as the blonde. The fact that she would cost him a maximum of $9,000 compared with the $150,000 of Betty Grable was also a factor, though not one he publicly stressed. Instead, the Fox publicity machine announced that this second movie version of *Gentlemen Prefer Blondes* was obtained specifically as a starring vehicle for Monroe.

The lavish Technicolor musical tells the story of two showgirls, best friends, who are going to France together. Lorelei is engaged to Gus Esmond, a wealthy young man she and Dorothy will be meeting in Paris.

Gus's father thinks Lorelei just wants her son's money and hires a private detective, Malone, to find out the truth. Dorothy, in turn, falls in love with Malone, to Lorelei's disgust. She does not care about his job; she is concerned because Malone has no money and Lorelei sees no sense in marrying just for love.

Hoping to save Dorothy from the fate of true romance without financial benefits, Lorelei arranges a date for Dorothy with the wealthy Henry Spofford III, someone she has heard about but never seen. When he appears for his date, Lorelei and Dorothy learn that Spofford is a child.

The story gets more complex with the theft of a tiara, blackmail, and Malone thinking that Dorothy actually hates him. Eventually, after several musical numbers by such greats as Hoagy Carmichael, Jule Styne, and others, Lorelei marries the wealthy Gus and Dorothy gets her Malone.

Marilyn wanted *Gentlemen Prefer Blondes* to be her breakout picture. She also knew that she was nobody's first choice and would have to fight both to keep the part and to prove she was ready for lead roles in comedy musicals, where most observers felt she had strength as a performer. This would be her seventh comic role, including the thirty-eight-second scene with Groucho Marx, and they had always proven to be better than her more dramatic appearances during the same period. However, though she had become a competent singer and had learned how to deliver a song so the listener took the lyrics personally, she was not much of a dancer. But that problem would be corrected when rehearsals began and Marilyn worked overtime with choreographer Jack Cole to master every move.

Joe DiMaggio was not happy with the new movie, the costumes, the songs, and the dancing. He was always drawn to showgirls and starlets. His first awareness of such women often came when he saw them on the stage or on the screen. Yet it was as though each one was putting on a private performance for him, dancing for him, dressing for him. Once they started dating, he was routinely upset with the general public seeing the same women in the same manner that he had. Marriage meant the end of their careers, and a serious relationship was one in which the woman would stop dressing erotically in a play or movie. It was a double standard totally unrealistic and impossible to maintain.

No matter how upset Joe might have been learning about *Gentlemen*

Prefer Blondes and the production numbers that would boost Marilyn's popularity, he would have been livid had he understood the way Marilyn separated sex from love. Joe routinely bedded whatever woman interested him; yet he apparently could not tolerate the idea that a woman might have the same interests and appetite as a man.

The truth Joe never learned was that Marilyn saw no reason to be faithful to a man until she decided to marry him. Before Marilyn openly admitted going to bed with Joe, she continued having sex with her friend, director Elia Kazan. Her role in his life was a confused one—not quite a mistress, yet available sexually to him when she felt he had a need. For his part, Kazan truly believed in Monroe's potential as an actress. He regularly tried to find roles for her, arguing with producers and casting directors that her talent was greater than was appreciated in Hollywood. That was why she routinely went to see him, becoming so intimate that she would occasionally stop by in the middle of the night, sharing whatever was troubling or exciting her, then "thanking" the director with sex. This private relationship continued even as she was regularly seeing Joe DiMaggio, and she could not comprehend that it might upset the ballplayer.

Thirty-eight

Gladys Returns

The last person Marilyn expected to return aggressively to her life was her mother.

Gladys Baker was never the madwoman many biographers imagined her to be. She was psychologically troubled from her physical problems, but the biggest problem she had was having adapted to life in an institution.

All long-term care facilities are closed societies in which the rules of behavior are clear to everyone and the patients are rewarded for behaving as the staff desires. Individuality must be suppressed. Extremes of emotions, whether joyous or severely depressed, are not tolerated, even though the behavior may stem from an experience that makes it appropriate to anyone on the outside.

Some long-term residential patients who had led troubled lives but were never mentally ill learn to look and act like those who are mentally ill. The misdiagnosis means that they have had to adapt to looking like the mentally ill with whom they have been living and to develop those behaviors and gestures that win approval from the caretaking staff. They may sit quietly for hours. They may carefully protect their food at meals, eating hurriedly and sitting so their arms surround whatever they have been served, because other patients steal what is not guarded. They may walk with their heads down, perhaps their hands clasped behind their backs, moving silently up and down the halls. Inside the institution this is normal. These same actions on the outside are eccentric and perhaps a little frightening. Unfortunately, the eccentricities often make people who have only lived on the outside uncomfortable, which will limit the former patient's chance for normal social interaction.

Gladys was a typical example of this. She would remain extremely eccentric because those had been rewarded survival behaviors for so long. Marilyn discussed this fact about her mother a few years earlier when Gladys lived briefly with her before moving to Oregon and becoming involved with salesman John Stewart Eley, whom she eventually married. Marilyn told her half-sister Berneice Miracle, "I keep telling myself that Mother will act better when she has been on the outside longer. I still feel as if we're strangers. I'm still trying to get acquainted with her. When I went to see her in Portland, I drove up there thinking it would be a joyful occasion—all those years I had waited and wished . . . but then she was so cold. I felt so let down."

Marilyn avoided all contact with her mother, even when the woman and her new husband, John Eley, were living near Pasadena, California. Gladys, as eccentric and withdrawn as ever, had learned to work as a private nursing home aide at Homestead Lodge. By all accounts, Gladys did her job well. The problem was that as she, herself, had been "institutionalized," her mannerisms seemed odd to the staff and too in tune with those of the patients.

Perhaps all this might have continued without any more problems than Gladys being the subject of stares and amusement for the staff had it not been for the death of Eley on April 23, 1952. Gladys was extremely upset, apparently bothered by the passage of the years, and wanted a reunion with her daughter Marilyn, if only by mail. She sent a letter reading,

> Dear Marilyn,
>   Please dear child, I'd like to receive a letter from you. Things are very annoying around here and I'd like to move away as soon as possible. I'd like to have my child's love instead of hatred.
>   Love,
>
>   "Mother"

Marilyn was shaken by the contact. She had no relationship with Gladys and did not want one. A few months earlier she had hired Inez Melson to be her business manager and, eventually, Gladys Baker's guardian. Melson took the responsibility seriously and was sensitive to all parties in the relationship. Long after Marilyn's death, when Gladys was confined in Rockhaven, a private sanitarium, Inez dutifully visited the woman at least once a month for the rest of her life.

On April 18, just before the letter came, Twentieth Century-Fox renewed its option for Marilyn's contract, paying her $750 per week—a bargain, given her new status. And just after the letter, on April 28, she had her appendix removed by Dr. Marcus Rabwin at Cedars of Lebanon Hospital.

The appendix removal was a major concern for Monroe because she desperately wanted to be able to have a baby at some time in the future. The father would probably not be DiMaggio, though the publicists promoting the relationship for Marilyn's career benefit would never say such a thing. Instead there was talk about how she wanted six children while he still wanted one. There were stories about Joe Jr., DiMaggio's son by his first wife, with whom Marilyn truly was close.

Pregnancy would become a driving force in Monroe's life shortly before she made the movie *Some Like It Hot*, but that was in the future. Her only concern right then was making sure that the surgeon removing her appendix did no damage to her reproductive organs. She even went so far as to tape a note to her abdomen for her surgeon, Dr. Mark Rabwin. It was marked "*most important* to read before operation!" and it read:

> *Cut as little* as possible. I know it seems vain but that doesn't really enter into it. The fact that I'm a *woman* is important and means much to me.
> Save please (I can't ask you enough) what you can—I'm in your hands. You have children and you must know *what* it means—*please Dr. Rabwin*—I know somehow *you will! Thank you—thank you—thank you.* For Gods sake Dear Doctor *No ovaries* removed—please again do whatever you can to prevent large *scars*,
> Thanking you with all my *heart*.
> Marilyn Monroe.

Dr. Rabwin was moved by the plea. He arranged to have Dr. Leon Krohn, a gynecologist, present during the surgery in case there were any complications or problems, but everything went well. Marilyn was so pleased that she utilized Dr. Krohn as her gynecologist for the rest of her life.

The pressures on Monroe were overwhelming. The surgery was physically minor but of great emotional concern. She had been lying for years about the reality of her mother, when suddenly Gladys was attempting to get back in her life. She had five films being released that fall and a relationship with Joe DiMaggio that regularly made headlines. Because of the advice of her mentor Sid Skolsky, she was giving interviews to almost anyone who asked, and willingly posed for publicity photos that landed her on a variety of magazine covers three to four times a week.

There was no way to compare what was happening to Monroe with other actresses, but it is probably accurate to say that no other actress in the world was receiving so much publicity for so very limited a career. Fans who bought everything they could find about the actress came to think that they knew her and most had memorized the tragic stories she mentioned in her many interviews. When her supposedly "dead" mother re-entered her life, Marilyn faced another publicity crisis.

Thirty-nine

The Industry Loves Her—Mostly

Marilyn Monroe had become a rapidly rising celebrity. Joe DiMaggio was a fading sports star. And Charlie Feldman was a man who worked with celebrities to maximize their exposure and income.

While all this was going on, Joe and Charlie Feldman were talking with Marilyn about the business of being a celebrity. Joe DiMaggio had never been money-hungry in his early years. His first concern had always been to play the best baseball he could, and for his achievements he was handsomely rewarded. However, he realized that the way he played ball had great value to whatever team he was on. He could not only help the team win games, his skills helped make the game exciting. That led to greater box-office receipts, strong radio interest, and an appeal to sponsors. Joe felt that the ultimate result of that proven value to the team owner should be an increase in his own pay and/or bonuses and/or money for sponsorships, appearances, and the like.

Joe used this same thinking when analyzing Hollywood. He recognized the unfairness of the studio system. He saw that the person who brought movie viewers to theater seats should be paid appropriately. Instead, Marilyn was making $750 a week, a great income in those days, but nowhere near enough for someone of Marilyn's caliber. Even worse, she actually only took home half that amount, the rest of the money paying for acting, singing, and dancing lessons. She had moved into a suite of rooms at the Beverly Hills Hotel, where the rent just about matched her take-home pay. She was a star, yet it looked as though she would be able to eat only if she returned to standing on Hollywood Boulevard until a man bought her breakfast. While she worked on *Gentlemen Prefer Blondes*, Feldman and DiMaggio began plotting a strategy to improve her finances.

The hard work Marilyn did to get the Lorelei Lee role carried over during the filming as she became something of a perfectionist. For example, she insisted upon working with the orchestra that would provide the backing for the songs she would sing in the movie. Normally there would be two separate recording sessions and an overdubbing session.

Marilyn went to music director Lionel Newman and insisted that she and the orchestra record together. She felt the results would be far superior, and she knew exactly the style, delivery, and sound she hoped to achieve. Ultimately the song "Diamonds Are a Girl's Best Friend" required eleven takes with the orchestra before she was satisfied, but the general consensus of the Fox executives who watched the takes was that she was right. This became a signature song for both Marilyn and the movie. Equally important, Marilyn was so respectful of the orchestra, always showing up on time completely prepared to work, that they felt she was being professional, not obstinate. She was also courteous and friendly with the musicians in a way her shyness did not allow her to be with the actors.

Joe DiMaggio did not relate Marilyn's intensity as an actress to his own as an athlete. He was more concerned with the way she was appearing in public, especially when he learned about the dress she planned to wear on the night of February 9, 1953.

Photoplay magazine was one of the most powerful publications in the motion picture industry. The studios were always delighted when some of their talent could be featured and they always allowed starlets to appear in created stories.

Photoplay magazine held an annual awards ceremony, and in 1953 it was held on February 9. Each year the magazine awarded a gold medal to the fastest rising star of the previous year. Marilyn was the publication's choice for 1952, and the prestigious honor was presented during a dinner in the Crystal Room of the Beverly Hills Hotel. There were between three and four hundred movie industry leaders, as well as numerous top stars, among them Joan Crawford who had been a major star when Marilyn was born. Crawford had "adopted" Monroe, having her to her home on occasion and giving her advice about how she needed to appear in public. Crawford also enjoyed some early upstaging at the banquet by deliberately arriving five minutes late. She knew that it was enough time for the photographers from the newspapers and magazines covering the dinner to have gotten inside and staked out their positions for shooting pictures. Her timing assured that all lenses would be trained on her as she made her way to her table. She did not expect to be overshadowed by an upstart.

The appearance of a motion picture actress attending a major awards ceremony has gradually evolved in the last fifty years. There was always a glamorous element to the clothing the women wore, and often the dresses were supplied by a major designer. However, what was considered acceptable formal glamour in 1953 was quite different from today. Today it is expected that many young (and not-so-young) actresses will attend events such as the Academy Awards ceremony in outrageous clothing. See-through material, gowns that look like they are barely covering the "virtue" of the wearer during an attempted seduction, and colorful arrays of strategically placed jewels and trim are normal. But in 1953, women did not flaunt their bodies at such ceremonies, at least no more than they might at a formal cocktail party.

Marilyn, by contrast, defied convention by wearing the gold lame' dress used in *Gentlemen Prefer Blondes*.

The costume choice was outrageous, especially since it was never intended as street wear. Designer Billy Travilla was not concerned with creating something to be worn in public. He designed the dress for a movie fantasy, the fabric clinging to Marilyn in a way that would be both sensual and natural under the harsh movie lights. Her appearance was then further altered by the type of film used in the motion picture camera, the type, intensity, and placement of the lighting, colored gels, and her movements within a carefully defined set. The material was for Technicolor, not *Photoplay*.

Marilyn was not to be deterred. She had been warned that the gold lame' dress might rip or otherwise come apart as she moved about at the ceremony. She was told that the nature of the material would make her appear to be naked, her body covered with paint. She wouldn't be able to comfortably eat, drink, or do much moving about. What Travilla did not realize was that she had no intention of truly participating in the meal and all the events of the evening. She just wanted to get her award.

Joe DiMaggio was outraged over Marilyn's plans and refused to accompany her to the ceremony. Instead, Sid Skolsky took her to the awards, delighted to have the beautiful young woman to escort and knowing that anything outrageous she might do would be great for his column.

There was no way Marilyn could attend the festivities from the start. She had to come late (two hours, as it turned out), not to make an entrance as Joan Crawford had done; rather, she literally had to have the gown sewn on her body while Skolsky waited for her in the lobby. By the time she had to be downstairs to accept the award, the gown had the desired effect, especially from behind. As Associated Press writer Jim Bacon cattily, but accurately, referred to his view of Marilyn moving to the stage to take her award, her rear looked like "two puppies fighting under a silk sheet." Comedian Jerry Lewis, the master of ceremonies for the event, jumped on a table and began howling when he saw her. Naturally the photographers mobbed her, turning the "newcomer" into the only star who mattered that night. (The *Photoplay* staff was not horrified. They honored her the following year, giving her the 1953 "Best Actress" award for her work in both *Gentlemen Prefer Blondes* and a second movie later that year, *How to Marry a Millionaire.*)

Joe DiMaggio was obviously livid over what Marilyn did, though the event was for the industry, not the public. However, one member of the industry, Marilyn's former friend and occasional mentor Joan Crawford, was outraged. She had more than been upstaged. She had seen the future, and it did not include herself.

Crawford's anger was shocking to those who did not know her. Crawford (originally Lucille Fay Le Sueur) was one of a number of sexual libertines in her early years in Hollywood. She was also a viciously abusive mother who had beaten her children with clothes hangers and eventually was nicknamed "Mommie Dearest." But in 1953, Crawford pretended to be a lady. She also had Bob Thomas to do her fighting in his syndicated Hollywood column in much the manner that Sid Skolsky and Louella Parsons were Monroe's knights errant. Thomas quoted Crawford—poor, scandalized, upstaged Crawford—as saying:

It was like a burlesque show. The audience yelled and shouted, and Jerry Lewis got up on the table and whistled. But those of us in the industry just shuddered . . . Sex plays a tremendously important part in every person's life. People are interested in it, intrigued with it. But they don't like to see it flaunted in their faces . . . The publicity has gone too far. She is making the mistake of believing her publicity. Someone should make her see the light. She should be told that the public likes provocative feminine personalities; but it also likes to know that underneath it all, the actresses are ladies.

Monroe, as quoted by Louella and probably scripted by Sid, returned fire:

Although I don't know Miss Crawford very well, she was a symbol to me of kindness and understanding to those who need help. At first, all I could think of was WHY should she select me to blast? She is a great star. I'm just starting. And then, when the first hurt began to die down, I told myself she must have spoken to Mr. Thomas impulsively, without thinking . . .

The feud was real and never-ending. When many in the industry hosted a party for Marilyn at Mike Romanoff's restaurant in November 1954, a year when she had achieved all that Johnny Hyde had hoped for her, Crawford was deliberately not invited. However, she did have the ultimate victory. She had become a star when Marilyn was born, and she was still enjoying success in 1962, the year Monroe died.

Marilyn may have put on a show in the way she dressed to accept her *Photoplay* magazine award, but the appearance was more difficult than anyone, other than Joe, realized. She had been dealing with concerns about her mother's living arrangements for several days prior to the event honoring her, and on the morning of the event, Gladys was moved to Rockhaven Sanitarium.

Gladys, troubled and "institutionalized" but lucid and emotionally stable, had been watching her daughter and reading the publicity. She was horrified when the stories went from being about strangers she had seen in miniature as she cut and spliced the movies being edited, or larger-than-life on the screen, or as local neighbors shopping in the stores, to her own daughter. There was no glamour in what Norma Jean was doing. There was nothing healthy that could come from being like her namesake, Jean Harlow. And because Gladys had increasingly turned to extreme religious theology for comfort, she felt compelled to denounce her daughter as a slut, a whore, an evil woman. She made clear to her daughter that she did not approve of the career path Marilyn Monroe had chosen.

All of this went on before Marilyn dressed for the awards ceremony, and there are those who feel she may have had her mother in mind when she requested the flamboyant dress she wore to accept her medal. By this thinking, the actions were simultaneously a declaration of independence from her mother's influence and an act of defiance: in a sense, "flipping her off." And such feelings certainly added to her anger against Joan Crawford.

The ruckus at the awards banquet had its impact on Darryl Zanuck as well. He suddenly was concerned with how Monroe would look singing *Diamonds Are a Girl's Best Friend*. The dress Marilyn wore to the banquet was shocking when she walked past the attendees, but with the lighting and staging planned for the film, it would look far more conservative on the screen.

Zanuck was shown another possible outfit, a surprisingly conservative creation on which diamonds had been sewn on a leotard. The problem was that, while in person the costume was not a problem, when blown up on the movie screen it suddenly appeared intensely sexually suggestive.

Eventually the matter was settled with Marilyn dressed in a bright pink gown deliberately fitted to be very loose. She looked beautiful and sensual, but there would be no backlash concerning going too far.

Charlie Feldman, still working without compensation and still not knowing if Marilyn would sign with his Famous Artists agency for representation, began tackling each issue that affected Marilyn's financial well-being. He wanted to so prove his value that she would use him for a standard percentage.

Natasha Lytess wanted more money from Marilyn. She knew that the relationship between the two of them was becoming more frequently stressful and that they were becoming estranged, but she also recognized that Marilyn was still emotionally dependent on her. She said that the $175 per week she was being paid was inadequate. She wanted an immediate raise from either Fox, Marilyn, or both, or she would leave the set of *Gentlemen Prefer Blondes* before filming was complete.

Darryl Zanuck knew that Marilyn would panic and could not be replaced without re-shooting the entire film with someone else; and other than Betty Grable, who undoubtedly would reject the idea of being second choice, there was no one. Worse, Marilyn was the least expensive actress who was a solid box-office draw. He let Feldman know that he would go as high as a thousand dollars a week for Natasha—more than Marilyn was making—if that was what it took to keep from losing her prematurely.

Feldman was livid. He went to Natasha, letting her try to blackmail him over Marilyn, finally "reluctantly" telling her he could get as much as five hundred dollars a week for her from Zanuck. Lytess, triumphant, accepted the deal. Zanuck was equally pleased that the agent had guaranteed the completion of the film for half what might otherwise have had to be paid.

Ironically, director Howard Hawks was so fed up with Marilyn following Natasha's directions instead of his own that he ordered Lytess off the set. She stayed on the payroll. She continued to work with Marilyn. But when the cameras were about to roll each day, Natasha had to be off the set and out of sight. It did not matter what Marilyn desired, her acting coach made clear that the new way of working together was best. She did not say that it was the only way she could build some savings for the day she was banned from both the studio and Marilyn's life: a day she knew would soon be at hand.

Marilyn was oblivious to all the machinations and jealousies as she took advantage of all possible publicity, including having a chance to appear on the Jack Benny radio show.

Forty

~

The Jack Benny Program

It is hard to fully appreciate the importance and popularity of Jack Benny today. He was a serious classical musician who played the violin well enough to make appearances with symphony orchestras, yet for his radio and, eventually, television show, his playing was always deliberately bad and meant for comic effect. He was a comedian who developed a style of humor—self-deprecating, utilizing the sounds of words for laughs, and using the repetition of subtle physical and verbal actions (for example, touching his chin with his right hand while holding the right elbow with his left hand as though contemplating something serious, then saying only, "Well," as though too disgusted to know what else to do) to get a laugh. He was not only one of the genuinely nice men of Hollywood—that eccentric oddball who loved his wife, was faithful throughout their marriage, and used comic material that never was offensive—he was also a quiet pioneer in challenging racial hatred in the United States. At a time when black men were so demeaned and classed as worthless that they were called "boys" even on national radio, Benny developed what might be called a reverse relationship with Rochester Van Jones (actor Eddie Anderson). This was an era when there was so much bigotry against blacks that the most popular radio show about blacks, *Amos and Andy*, actually used two white men to play the roles of Harlem cab drivers.

Not only did Benny change the role of Anderson's character Rochester from that of a street hustler (one of only three acceptable stereotypes for

380

black males; the others being either violent criminals or slow-talking, slow-witted, slow-moving comic relief), he turned himself into the comic foil. The relationship between the two men evolved to the point where Rochester was the wise, helpful straight man and Benny the ultimate self-obsessed miser. (Radio skit: Robber to Benny, "Your money or your life." A prolonged silence, a rare occurrence in radio. Then Benny, annoyed at being rushed to make a decision, says, "I'm thinking. I'm thinking.") Benny's persona also had an ego that refused to admit he was aging, balding, and less handsome than he had been in his youth—when, even then, he hadn't been all that good looking. Another of his running jokes was that he was thirty-nine years old. He had obviously long passed that youthful figure, but Benny's age was forever frozen at thirty-nine.

Jack had starred in movies and radio before moving on to television where his show, a visual version of what he had done for years on radio, played to large audiences. The staff of *The Jack Benny Program* realized that Marilyn and Jack could play off each other. The show was scripted, but relied upon another established aspect of Benny's character—he believed himself to be irresistibly handsome to women.

Marilyn was the first guest of the new season for 1953 and 1954. Benny understood that Monroe's contract was such that the studio would not let her be paid for her appearances. Any cash that might be arranged would go to the studio, not the star. It was unfair, but Benny deliberately got around the proscription by arranging for Marilyn to be "gifted" with a black Cadillac convertible with red interior. It was the top-of-the-line car, fully equipped: a car worth far more than she would have been paid had a payment been allowed.

The show, a series of interrelated skits set on a set that looked like the deck of a luxury cruise ship, was aired live from the Shrine Auditorium in Los Angeles. This was the season premiere for 1953–1954 and it was about Jack's vacation in Hawaii. He falls asleep on a deck chair while sitting next to a large, obnoxious blonde who is thoroughly unattractive. Benny is thinking about the movie *Gentlemen Prefer Blondes*, so while he is dreaming, he begins chasing the oversized blonde. The two go behind a large funnel, and when they emerge, it is Marilyn Monroe, not the unattractive woman, who is there. She admits that she has been running away from Jack, "Because I can't trust myself with you. You're so strong and I'm so weak,

and when you look at me with those big blue eyes, I just . . . I just . . ."
Benny looks deadpan at the audience and, with a combination of compassion and wistfulness, obviously sensitive to her plight, he says, "I understand."

There are several jokes related to her movies, and then Jack proposes to Marilyn, who explains that she is troubled by the disparity in their ages. "There isn't that much difference," says Benny. "You're twenty-five and I'm thirty-nine." (Benny was born February 4, 1894. He was fifty-seven when the show was aired.)

Monroe has obviously bought into Benny's exaggerations, agreeing with him, yet still worried. As she explains, "But what about twenty-five years from now, when *I'm* fifty and you're thirty-nine?"

Eventually Marilyn sings "Bye, Bye, Baby," the song ending with a passionate kiss. They agree to meet for dinner and Marilyn goes back behind the funnel. Emerging from the other side, Benny's dream obviously over, is the heavyset woman who had been replaced by Marilyn at the start of the skit. Jack, now awakening, grabs the woman in what will soon be a moment of passion, then is shocked by the reality. "Hey, wait a minute, you're not Marilyn Monroe," says Benny, to which the indignant woman replies, "Well, you ain't no Errol Flynn!"

The sketch was a delight, well written and well acted by two comic professionals, only one of whom, Benny, getting credit for his talent. It also provided free advertising for Fox, expanding Marilyn awareness to television. However, the medium was so uncomfortable for her—especially since it was much like the stage where one goes on, performs, and leaves with no chance for a retake—that it made her uncomfortable. She never again appeared on live television.

The one benefit Monroe did receive was the black Cadillac convertible. The high-end luxury car was considered one of a half-dozen vehicles stars were expected to drive. It was the ideal gift, for it symbolized to Marilyn that one star—Benny—had recognized her as also being a star.

Forty-one

How to Marry a Millionaire

Marilyn made one more movie in 1953, after which she married Joe. This was *How to Marry a Millionaire*, and the writer was Nunnally Johnson. Despite thoroughly disliking the actress as a person, he wanted to write for her.

There were major differences in the ways movies were written among the studios during the 1940s as Monroe entered the system, eventually settling at Fox where Johnson was doing some of his work. Darryl Zanuck was cheap. He wanted to make movies without being locked into star vehicles for his most expensive talent. His idea was to have a movie tell a solid story, then cast the actors who could best interrelate in a believable manner on the screen.

Warner Brothers and MGM were headed by men who had, in some cases, been involved with theater ownership. They had watched how their box-office income varied with the star. People would come to see a movie with a star they liked, sometimes returning two or three times during the film's run, more than they would come to a critically acclaimed film with stars who were simply competent professionals.

A screenwriter for MGM or Warner Brothers was expected to know the actor or actress in the lead of a movie, to understand the person's strengths and weaknesses as an actor, singer, dancer, or comedian, then write a story playing to those strengths. The approach worked well enough that by the early 1950s, Twentieth Century-Fox executives had to admit that they needed to change to boost revenues.

Nunnally Johnson recognized that, while Monroe was not an actress who could carry a story-type film, she was physically riveting on the big screen, very much the "star" Hyde had seen in her while at the same time mocking her acting skills. He wanted the challenge of writing for her in the style of the MGM and Warner Brothers films. *How to Marry a Millionaire* would give him that chance.

There was another advantage for the film. It was going to be the first film ever made in CinemaScope (the second film, after *The Robe*, to actually be released in that process). The new process allowed an ultra-wide image to be shown on the screen. It required special equipment and there were questions raised at the time about studio extortion and who might have benefited from forcing theaters to adapt.

The basics of storytelling would not change, but the cinematographer had both new challenges and new opportunities with the new medium because the image was so much wider. However, at least one person, not understanding the difference, asked Nunnally how he would write for the new process. He explained that he would insert the paper into his typewriter sideways. He never said whether the person got the joke.

How to Marry a Millionaire was a story stimulated by the work of other writers and filmed in a manner that would show off the new CinemaScope process. There were many images of the New York City skyline meant to captivate the audience rather than to move along the plot. The basic story—three women trying to marry money—was the same as a play by Zoe Akins that was filmed in the 1930s called *The Greeks Had a Word for It*. But the characters he created were mixed, including Betty Grable's character, the semiliterate Loco Dempsey, who was based on a now obscure play called *Loco*.

The story is simple. Three models move into an expensive apartment in New York City which they can only afford by pooling their money, and even then they can only afford it for a short time. They are determined to cold-bloodedly find themselves three wealthy men who will enable them to live in the manner to which almost no one is accustomed. The problem comes when two of the friends take advantage of chances to leave town, presumably having a chance to succeed in their goal. The third remains behind and is pressured financially.

Polaire "Pola" Debevoise was Marilyn Monroe's character and the one that most interested Johnson since he was writing for the way she would come across on the screen. The other two were simple. Lauren Bacall was Schatze Page, the tough leader of the friends, a woman so intent on marrying wealth that she eventually agrees to marry J. D. Hanley (played by William Powell), a very nice, very rich man Schatze does not love. Naturally she also meets, then dismisses, Tom Brookman (Cameron Mitchell) who is introduced to Schatze by Loco (Betty Grable) after Tom helps Loco with her groceries. Tom then falls in love with Schatze who, if forced to admit the truth, is also in love with him. However, she does not face the reality of her emotions until she finds the courage to break off with Hanley and marry solely for love. And as was typical of the fantasy happy endings of so many musicals of this period, it is only then that she learns that she found love and got her wish because Tom truly is a millionaire.

Loco goes off with a married millionaire whom she thinks is taking her to a convention in Maine. Instead he takes her to a lodge, obviously planning to have his way with her. She decides to return to New York while she still has some control over what happens. Before she can do so, however, she comes down with measles, which forces her to stay; eventually she meets a forest ranger named Eben (played by Rory Calhoun), with whom she falls in love despite his lack of funds.

Monroe's character was the most difficult. Marilyn was not a good actress and was still using Lytess to coach her with each line in every scene. The result was that Monroe looked dazed and unfocused at the best of times.

There was no way Monroe would be dismissed from the movie and her part recast. She was enormously popular at the box office and her contract made her the least expensive draw in the film. No one receiving her salary could demand the public's attention. Johnson was forced to write around her weaknesses, something he actually enjoyed doing as a personal challenge.

The solution he found (supposedly following a suggestion by his friend, producer Sol Siegel) was to make Marilyn's character dumb, vain, and so extremely nearsighted that all of life was a blur when she refused to wear her glasses, and she refused to wear her glasses when she was around men. The concept made Marilyn vulnerable, rather than a caricature, and made strengths of her weaknesses.

Marilyn hated the role of Pola at first. She thought she looked terrible in glasses and wanted Betty Grable to switch roles so she could play Loco and Grable could play Pola. Given Natasha's misguided directing and Monroe's rather dazed reaction to her acting coach, her director, her producer, and her costars, any change in casting would not have worked.

The gimmick advances the plot by letting Pola be completely lost. The vagueness that was so frustrating for the director was perfect on film, Marilyn looking as though it was impossible to see the people into whom she kept bumping. By the time she was seated on the wrong plane, about to fly off with the wrong man, the audience could readily accept the story line as believable because Pola seemed so real.

And so the audience is rooting for her when she sits next to an eye-glasses-wearing stranger who convinces Pola that she looks better in glasses. His acceptance and enthusiasm for how she looks in the glasses she so desperately needs result in their falling in love.

The success of *How to Marry a Millionaire* was due not only to the quality of the script but the fact that Johnson convinced his director, Jean Negulesco, to let him rehearse the cast before each scene. Johnson knew his talent and what he wanted each of them to do. Negalesco tended to let his stars work through their parts, and his earlier work was frequently the subject of complaints by the men and women who acted in it. They wanted more guidance, and the director was pleased to let the writer/producer take over a portion of that task.

Because of the perceived egos of the three stars, the media was spreading rumors about possible feuds on the set. The truth was quite different. Johnson would later comment in a letter to Thornton Delehanty: "The two Bettys have gone out of their way to help, and make friends with Marilyn, but Miss Monroe is generally something of a zombie . . . . Talking to her is like taking to somebody underwater. She's very honest and ambitious and is either studying her lines or her face during all of her working hours, and there is nothing whatever to be said against her, but she's not material for warm friendship. Except, of course, for DiMag."

Lauren "Betty" Bacall commented to Nora Johnson, the producer's daughter who was an actress, screenwriter, and author in her own right,

> She was really terrified—shaky—she was late all the time. During *Millionaire*, Nunnally was very sweet to her, he made all those jokes about him and Marilyn, but she didn't have tremendous humor. She wasn't easy to act with because she never looked at you, she didn't react to what you'd say. She'd rehearse, she had a coach, she'd gone through the scene with the coach and the coach had told her how to do it and screw what anyone else did, which was great for her because she had a magic on film, but it wasn't terrific for the rest of us poor slobs. And then at the end she would never look at Negulesco [Jean Negulesco, the director] she would look right past him at the coach . . . she was really very selfish but she was so sad you couldn't dislike her. You just had to feel sorry for her, her whole life was a fuck-up. She just happened to have this great thing and she made a connection with the camera . . . she ended up being very good in the movie, though she was not an actress.

The film would not be easy for Marilyn for more reasons than the skills involved. Work began four days after *Gentlemen Prefer Blondes* was finished filming. She was still emotionally upset about her mother, extremely overtired, yet so determined to succeed that she had been spending many a late night working with Natasha. The long hours left her little time to rest. Desperate for sleep, she began taking sleeping pills to rest.

The sleeping pills were not well understood when Marilyn was using them. They were thought to be harmless, providing rest for people who had trouble going to sleep. Many entertainers liked to use them, not just when they were making late-night appearances headlining shows in places such as Las Vegas, but also when they had late-night evenings with friends. Marilyn felt that it was all right to take the pills any time she had a period for rest. She used them not only to sleep after working with Natasha but also to sleep when she had a couple of free hours for a nap. Not only was she using too many, she was using them in a psychologically addicting manner. Even worse, because the pills rendered the user unconscious, not in the depths of natural sleep where full rest occurs, she was always tired.

Charlie Feldman recognized that Monroe's problems went beyond the areas of concern of her fellow actresses, but did not realize how much was physically wrong with her. He did know that she seemed genuinely over-stressed, and he also knew that the two men who headed Fox—Darryl Zanuck and his boss, studio president Spyros Skouras—were in rare agreement about Marilyn. Zanuck thought Skouras was a fool when it came to understanding the creative side of the business. However, they were in agreement about the introduction of CinemaScope, the musical *How to Marry a Millionaire*, and the importance of Monroe to the eventual success of the picture. They were willing to listen to Feldman and do what he thought best, and the director, Jean Negulesco, understood that his future required him to go along with the man the studio bosses respected.

Privately Charlie worried that Marilyn, if placed under too much pressure, would become mentally ill. She had told him the myth of her mother's problems and her own fears of ending up institutionalized. He never questioned the truth, even when it was revealed that Monroe had lied about her mother being alive, because he had long been a friend of actress Vivien Leigh, a woman who—little known to the viewing public—was a manic/depressive with mood swings that occasionally left her suicidal.

It turned out that Charlie had reason for concern, though not about Marilyn's mental health. The exhaustion from overwork led to a virus that caused her to collapse. She was rushed to a hospital where the enforced rest helped her quickly recover from what otherwise would have led to pneumonia.

There was conflict over how to handle Monroe's illness among the lower-level executives involved with production. The ideal would have been for Marilyn to drive herself to finish the film, and then enter the hospital: an impossibility. Skouras and Zanuck might accept delays, but ultimately the other executives would be called to account for the cost of each day's lost filming. Actors had to be paid to be available the moment Monroe returned to the set, and there was no way of predicting from day to day when that would be. Sets had to be fully prepared, all technical people in place, the cinematographer ready to film, and makeup artists, dressers, and the myriad others who work on a movie essentially being paid for being ready, not for working.

The publicity department felt that they could make everyone happy by turning the hospital stay into a photo opportunity. They wanted to send a hairdresser and makeup artist to her hospital room, have her camera-ready and smiling sensuously, then let photographers record her "suffering" in images that would be published throughout the country. Then they waited until the photographers had been sent to Cedars of Lebanon Hospital before calling her to tell her to be ready.

Monroe was livid. She was far sicker than anyone realized, having already pushed herself so far that even with the hospital stay, it would be a full year before she recovered from the aftermath of the virus. Feldman, equally angry, stopped the publicity department's plans, though he did not argue when Marilyn returned to the movie set sooner than her doctors desired. This was still a business where another blonde was always waiting to step into the spotlight, as they were forcefully reminded by Betty Grable. She was thirty-six, an aged has-been by studio standards, and she knew that no matter what her future, this would be her last role for Fox. She earlier had explained to Marilyn that it was Monroe's turn to run with the opportunity, but Marilyn knew that no matter how young and increasingly successful she might be, there was another starlet waiting to take her place as the Twentieth Century-Fox designated blonde.

By mid-July 1953, everything was right and everything was wrong. *Gentlemen Prefer Blondes* opened to excellent reviews and solid box-office success. Monroe had created a type of character who could be repeated again and again in different ways. She would be like the young Betty Grable, who had been placed in the same type of movie over and over again for a decade. The public flocked to see her. Men who had used her picture as the most popular pin-up of World War II lusted after her. She gained ever-larger contracts, becoming wealthy without ever being given a chance to prove the range of her acting ability. And then, at the age of thirty-six, Grable was suddenly boring, too old to continue the career she had enjoyed, too old to prove that she could do more than be the sexy blonde in musicals.

Monroe wanted the success that Grable indicated would soon be hers, but she also did not want to be typecast. She tried to explain this to the two men in her life with whom she trusted the business of the image she had created. Neither understood. Charlie Feldman was thrilled that she might have Grable's success, since his focus was getting his hoped-for client the largest amount of money she could earn as her studio contract expired and a new one had to be negotiated. He did not care what roles she had so long as she was treated—both personally and in her paycheck—as a star.

The other man, Joe DiMaggio, saw Marilyn's frustration as yet another reason for her to leave the business and just be his wife. He had no idea that, although Marilyn enjoyed having sex with him, and though she found him to be a gentleman who was kind to her, she told her intimate friends that he was boring. His world was baseball, even in retirement, and she could not stand listening to talk that revolved solely around the game. Worse, she recognized that Joe was constantly rejecting her in his refusal to escort her to events that honored her, complaining that her physical appearance was embarrassing or too sexual. He either did not understand or did not care that the theatricality of her appearance was part of the Marilyn Monroe mystique, part of the publicity surrounding the event.

DiMaggio was constantly giving Monroe mixed messages. He made clear that he did not want her to be an actress. He also made clear that he and Charlie, whose business sense he respected, should be protecting her from the phonies in the business. It was an odd attitude, at once overprotective and yet keeping her working in ways that he criticized her for accepting.

The first concern for everyone except Marilyn was her income. She had reached the level of $1,250 a week for each week that she worked following the filming of *How to Marry a Millionaire*. Charlie Feldman had watched an early screening of *Gentlemen Prefer Blondes* and saw how her presence dominated a scene. Standing still she could draw every eye in the theater, regardless of who else was on the screen with her. Johnny Hyde had been right about her star quality, and she was also turning into a better actress than originally expected. The public loved her, the fan mail was growing daily, and it was time to renegotiate her contract.

ॐ

The five thousand-seat Fox Wilshire Theater at the corner of Wilshire Boulevard and La Cienega Avenue was the scene of the November 4, 1953, premiere of the $2.5 million movie that would go on to earn $12 million by the end of its run. (Note: the dollar figures represented the results of the movie being shown at the time of release and for however many weeks afterwards it circulated. More money would be earned later from television showings, and still later from the invention and sale of videotape and DVDs. Monroe was one of many stars who would have an estate earning more money per year than the star earned while alive.) Joe was outraged by the film and refused to attend the premiere, flying to New York instead so he could claim his absence was for business reasons.

The night of the premiere Marilyn drove from her home on Pico Boulevard to the Fox studio where Alan "Whitey" Snyder was on makeup, Gladys Rasmussen was working hair, and Los Angeles *Mirror-News* columnist (Candid Kandis) Kandis Rochlen was the official observer of Marilyn's hair being bleached and tinted, her fingernails and toenails covered with platinum polish, and makeup skillfully applied. The studio provided everything, including diamond earrings for the evening, along with a high-waisted white lace dress embroidered with sequins and cut to curve under her breasts. She had a gold belt with white velvet train and white gloves that went all the way up her arms. Marilyn's only personal items were a white fox-fur muff and stole, and her panties.

The premiere was a major production in which nothing was left to chance. Monroe's preparations by the studio personnel took six hours and twenty minutes, though the crowd outside the theater would think she was so glamorous she had simply gone into her closet at home and put on whatever outfit seemed appropriate for the occasion. Every limousine driver, and those rare participants who drove themselves, had to show an invitation to the police. Only five thousand would be inside for the movie. Outside there were five blocks of barriers, and behind them were bleachers that held far more than the theater so the public could watch everyone's arrival. Eventually even those seats were filled, forcing the police to try to find standing room.

The night sky was lit by searchlights, and with each arriving celebrity, the mob screamed the person's name. This moment—not just having a name on the marquee—was the reason Norma Jean Mortenson had done everything she felt was necessary to become a star. She had demeaned herself as a playmate for anyone who would buy her breakfast. She had been a willing starlet adding color and sexual relief at producers' parties. She had taken acting lessons, elocution lessons, created a life that had never been her own, and done anything else she could to achieve this moment. And then, with the new television cameras broadcasting her every move and with reporters' microphones thrust toward her as she walked the theater's red carpet, she entered the theater alone.

Earlier in the day Norma Jean had been sick, nauseated from fear. She tried taking orange juice and gelatin for what would pass as nourishment. She tried taking pills to stop the pain. But everything had been vomited up. Finally she bathed and left for the studio to become Marilyn Monroe.

That night, when the movie was finished and the crowd had dispersed—the observers to their homes and the stars to private parties—Marilyn entered her limousine and was driven back to the Fox studios. It was after midnight, and though she was too much of a star to be forced back to living among the cinders, her coach once again a pumpkin, her horses once again mice, she could not retain the trappings of a star. Aided by a single wardrobe woman working overtime, Marilyn's clothing was carefully removed, checked in, and left to be prepared for the next wearing. Finally, she put on her own slacks, loafers, and sport shirt, put the furs into their two respective boxes, tossed them in the back seat of her convertible, and went home to bed. Marilyn Monroe was over for the night.

Feldman chose a business game he had used in the past to benefit his clients in negotiations with the studio. Marilyn's contract had to be allowed to expire without negotiations in order for a new one being completed, or she would have little leverage. At the same time, if she was seen as deliberately avoiding signing, everyone would know she was fighting for more money—and even a star like Marilyn could be destroyed by the studio heads if they so chose. That was why Charlie followed a path clearly defined by the Internal Revenue Service so there would be a third party—a *government* third party at that—on whom everyone could place the blame.

Charlie told Marilyn that she was to buy the screen rights to any novel she liked that was available for purchase. She would pay a few thousand dollars for the rights, then another few thousand dollars to hire a screenwriter to develop a script written so it was obviously a starring vehicle for her. Then she would not renegotiate her contract with Fox for six months, the minimum time she had to hold the option on the book in order to have a tax deduction, a standard business tactic the studio would not question. Finally, as part of Monroe's new contract, Darryl Zanuck would have to agree to buy the book option and the screenplay from Monroe for a sum Feldman felt would be enough to give her at least two hundred thousand dollars profit. If the studio failed to make the picture, it did not matter. Marilyn would have a bonus in addition to whatever weekly salary was negotiated.

Both DiMaggio and Marilyn's lawyer liked Charlie Feldman's idea. (He was still not under contract, still not making a percentage for the work he was doing. Instead, with Johnny Hyde's contract still in effect, the various percentages assigned as agent's commission went to William Morris and would continue to do so until her studio contract ran out. Only then would Feldman and his Famous Artists agency benefit from any further income from the project, including the sale of rights to Fox.) In order to help other clients of his agency, Feldman ordered his staff to send over ten different novels. Among them was *Horns of the Devil*, and to Marilyn's surprise, it was Joe who picked it.

The finalization of the purchase of rights to *Horns of the Devil* occurred at the end of the first week of August 1953. Then, between August and February of 1954, Marilyn, Charlie, and Joe would decide what income, benefits, and the like they would insist upon in her new contract with Fox. In the meantime, she had at least two films to make under the old contract. The first, confirmed with Otto Preminger directing, was *River of No Return*, in which Marilyn would be a cabaret entertainer on the Canadian frontier. The second, not yet confirmed, was to be the same type of sex, comedy, singing, dancing role she had experienced in her earlier musicals. It was called *The Girl in Pink Tights*, or just *Pink Tights*, and it was actually the second movie considered for Marilyn, though the first pushed by Zanuck.

Nunnally Johnson was so pleased with the final results of *How to Marry a Millionaire* that he began looking for a way to create a new story from two plays he felt had aspects of an effective film. One was *Sleep It Off*, a comedy about a college's effort to have a wealthy alumnus give a large sum of money. In the play a bubble dancer, popular on some burlesque circuits, was sent to the campus to be with the alumnus, "entertaining" him. However, before she can achieve the school's desired results, one of the students accidentally hypnotizes her, leaving her to perform most of the play in a daze (much like the Pola character).

The second play, elements of which would be blended into a script that would be original in the final writing, was *She Loves Me Not*. This play takes place in a dormitory at Princeton University. A chorus girl is used rather than the bubble dancer, and she has to hide from a killer after witnessing a murder.

Johnson's script was eventually called *How to Be Very, Very Popular.* The story had two koochy dancers witnessing a murder, then hiding out on a college campus where students are allowed to stay for years after others have long since graduated. There are mistaken identities based on the fact that the older males—bad guys, academics, fathers, etc.—are all bald and thus supposedly look alike.

A character named Curly was created for Monroe, but she explained to Johnson that she was not interested. The studio was not demanding she be in it based on her contract and so she declined in favor of pursuing more serious roles. As Betty Grable had predicted, she was one of two actresses hired to star; the other was Sheree North, a young dancer. Grable's pay remained high, but her character, "Stormy Tornado," was the type of lesser movie role she knew was her future. North, the new kid on the block, had an obvious lack of developed talent when she took the Curly Flagg role originally conceived for Monroe. She was undertrained and trying her hardest, but several years from achieving well-earned stardom. As for Marilyn, she was being sent to Canada to star in the film *River of No Return* to be directed by Otto Preminger.

Marilyn's role in this new film—a cabaret performer—would require acting as well as singing four songs. It was not a role she desired, but it was also not a film to argue about. There were more important fights to win, including Zanuck's telling her that he wanted the film that would follow *River of No Return* to be *Pink Tights.* The latter was another sensual musical, one that would contribute to typecasting her. She was livid, but Charlie Feldman saw the film as a vehicle for asserting her independence. She could validly argue that she was exhausted from so much work. She had already been in the hospital with the virus that left her weakened for months. In addition, Feldman could argue that Monroe was being overexposed, risking a reduction at the box office if too many movies came too fast.

The arguments were probably valid, but they were all meant to buy time until the contract ran out and serious new negotiations could begin. Feldman saw his client as being in the power position, especially if she refused to report to work for *Pink Tights* after returning from Canada. Marilyn saw the possibility of being suspended by the studio, an action Zanuck could legally invoke, thus ending her career. That would render meaningless everything she had worked so hard to achieve, and the idea terrified her.

Forty-two

River of No Return

The relationship with Joe DiMaggio was far less than the myth the publicists and columnists wanted it to be. Joe was a true friend, though his judgment was colored by his own feelings, circumstances, and ideas about what retirement from baseball should be like. He had long dated starlets and chorus girls. He liked beautiful women from the world of glamour and show business. He hated the attention Marilyn received from other men, yet liked being able to advise her about the financial aspects of a career he kept telling her to leave. His idea of a perfect evening at home involved television, comic books, and food. Most of the time he preferred the saloon atmosphere where men talked sports and praised their idea of the country's greatest player—Joe DiMaggio. He was a walking ego with little interest in the greater world around him.

Marilyn seemed to feel safe with Joe, though over the years her primary comments were about his sexual prowess. She respected his achievements to the degree that she understood them, and recognized that they were equally driven in their respected fields. However, his career was all downhill and on the periphery of what he had done in the past. Her career was still rising, and if she ever got a contract that matched her box-office success, she would earn more than he had in his prime.

River of No Return was a period Western set in 1875, a wilderness survival story of greed, betrayal, determination, and selfless love. The movie should have given Monroe the kind of exposure as a dramatic actress that she craved, but Preminger treated her as though she had worked her way through life at a "gentleman's club," a 1950s equivalent of Hooter's.

Monroe played a saloon singer named Kay whose costumes while performing stressed what many claimed were her best assets. And lest the viewer not get the message that here was an actress to watch, even if she could sing and play a character, Preminger had her wear tight-fitting, wet, clinging jeans while fighting the elements along with an ex-convict widower named Matt Calder (Robert Mitchum) and his son Mark (Tommy Rettig). The still shots of the jeans worn in the film were so provocative that more than three decades after her death they were used in an advertisement for Levi Strauss jeans. The advertising image shows a still of a standing Marilyn in tight blouse and jeans, looking into the camera, her face rather hard. The caption reads: "Our models can beat up their models."

But that was in the future. At the time of the movie, Marilyn found herself increasingly powerful as an actress. The growing fan mail, the public reaction to her romance—already of mythic proportions—with Joe DiMaggio, and the desires of a growing number of directors to work with her despite her idiosyncrasies, all meant that she could begin making demands of her own. However, first she had to endure (and, in one instance, survive) Otto Preminger.

Otto Preminger was a director whose successful films had been sophisticated stories such as *Laura*. Even the film that led to the idea for *River of No Return*, Vittorio De Sica's Italian film *The Bicycle Thief*, was more in line with Preminger's sensibilities. That story, about a man who relies on a bicycle to get to work each day and how his life is radically changed after his bicycle is stolen, was moved to the frontier and centers on Matt Calder, whose indispensible horse and gun are stolen after he is released from jail. But *River of No Return* is a far rougher story involving Matt's relationship with his son, Mark, a singer named Kay (Monroe), and her gambler "husband" Harry. These were rough people in rough times, finding love and reconciliation as they fight the elements and one another.

Twentieth Century-Fox publicists would try to put a positive spin on the use of Preminger in a film for which he was obviously unsuited, but the truth was less complicated. Otto Preminger was play-or-pay for one movie in 1953 and this was all they had to offer. The public rarely hears of play-

or-pay, and the studios have tried to reduce or eliminate the concept even as it continues into television production.

Play-or-pay is an arrangement with a producer, writer, director, or actor in which the person is placed on the payroll for a set number of projects (or hours of television) each year. This is usually done for motion pictures or made-for-television movies.

The idea is that the name of the person has a drawing power, and the studio does not want a rival using that person. These are men and women not on the regular studio payroll; instead, the studios have whatever the contracted time might be—usually one year—in which the person can pro-duce/direct/act/write. Projects assigned early in the year have the greatest chance of using the individual's skills in an appropriate manner; these show the person's skills at their best and the money paid is well worth the cost. However, as the year is coming to a close, the studio heads panic. They know they have to pay full salary even if the person under contract does nothing. Thus it is easier to let someone "play," even when the project is inappropriate, than to do the year's projects with appropriate people and still have to "pay" the person with this agreement. Otto Preminger was used because he had to be. Otherwise he would be paid for doing nothing.

Not only was the movie inappropriate for Preminger's sensibilities, he was a bully who liked to tell those whom he considered the weaker actors— including Monroe and boy actor Tommy Rettig, who played Mark Cal-der—what he thought of them. Natasha Lytess interceded and managed to coach Monroe into achieving a melodrama where none should have existed. She overemoted everything, from being angry to being emotionally shattered. There was also too little attention paid to details, the result of which is that even Monroe's hair extension becomes visible at one point, further destroying the critical suspension of disbelief expected of the audi-ence.

୫ର

Robert Mitchum speaking to *Time* magazine writer Ezra Goodman:

> Marilyn was reading a dictionary of Freudian terms. I asked her why she was reading it and she said, "I feel one should know how to discuss oneself." I said: "What chapter are you up to now?" She said: "Anal eroticism." I said: "That's charming and do you think that will come up in a discussion?" She

went back to reading and looked up after a while and said, "What's eroticism?" I explained. A minute or two later she looked up from the book again and said, "What's anal?" My stand-in, Tim, who was working on a scratch sheet nearby, couldn't stand it any longer and butted in: "That's the keester," he said.

ℬ

The weakness of the script for *River of No Return* did not help Marilyn's frustrations, though it was not as bad she later claimed. There was some accuracy to her comment that the final film was "a grade-Z cowboy movie in which the acting finished second to the scenery and the CinemaScope process."

The basic story told of Matt Calder, an ex-con cowboy, seeking his son and finding him in the care of a cabaret singer. She has a gambler boyfriend—her alleged "husband"—but he leaves Kay, Matt, and Mark and forces them to travel a perilous river replete with rapids, Indians, fortune hunters, and even a bobcat. None of it works well, a fact Zanuck anticipated in a memo dated April 22, 1953, when the script was ready but no one had been cast.

Darryl Zanuck's memo explained that the movie would only work if they could get a cast that included Robert Mitchum, Monroe, and Rory Calhoun (all three were in the film). He stressed that the story was a character story, ignoring the plot he never cared about. He expected to see sexual tension and explosive fireworks as the main characters fight each other, romance each other, and try to survive together.

"The next star in the picture is the rapids. If the rapids do not really come off as something spectacular to the *n*th degree, then we really are licked. The episodes of the raft going down the river have got to stand an audience on its ear. It has got to be the Cinerama equivalent of the rollercoaster," Zanuck stressed. The roller-coaster reference was to another new process called Cinerama. Again using special equipment for filming and playback, Cinerama was a moderately successful effort to create a 3-D experience without the need for the polarizing lenses audience members had to wear to watch 3-D. The introduction to the medium, *This Is Cinerama*, was filmed so that one dramatic scene gave the audience the visual sense of sitting in a roller-coaster car as it raced around the track. Audience members screamed in fear and delight during the "ride" even though their seats did not move.

૭ૐ

The script was not a difficult one for an actress, but making the movie was difficult. First there was the incongruous costuming. The tight jeans and blouse, the flawless makeup, all in the middle of mountainous terrain and Indians on the warpath, were ridiculous. Worse, Marilyn had to experience multiple retakes of scenes on the raft, some of which were in the wilderness, some of which were done in the studio, all of which required many gallons of water being thrown on her.

There was also a moment of unexpected danger. Otto Preminger wanted to film a section of the river on which Marilyn, Robert Mitchum, and Tommy Rettig would be viewed in close-up, albeit by a camera with a telephoto lens so the cinematographer could maintain his physical distance. The water was unusually dangerous, and two boats, each with lifeguards, traveled just out of camera range in case of danger. There were also ropes attached to the raft to guide it in the rapids.

Preminger was right in thinking that the image would be dramatic and show the danger the three were in while pursuing the man who had left them. What he did not bother telling either of the adults or the mother of Tommy Rettig, who had to approve her son's participation, was that the reason stunt doubles were not being used was that they had refused to ride the raft. Stunt performers are not daredevils. They are highly trained athletes who carefully plan each stunt to ensure their safety. They examined the stretch of water, the rapids, and the equipment that would be used and told the director it was too dangerous. That scene should not be shot, and if he wanted to do it, he would have to do it with the actors.

Preminger never told the cast what was taking place, but he did learn why the stuntmen were leery of the shot. One of the ropes working the raft broke, as did one of the boats carrying lifeguards. Everything started going out of control; Mitchum was thrown from the raft and traveled several hundred yards downstream before he could be rescued. Monroe and Rettig were luckier, clinging together as they rode the raft until it could be stopped.

Marilyn never complained about what she had to do, despite coming to hate Preminger. There were times when she insisted on even more retakes than he did, knowing that she was shifting the power balance and subtly telling Preminger that what he thought was "perfect" could be improved. Whether or not she believed the extra work was needed is unknown. Most observers suspected she wanted to control him.

Preminger's disdain was understandable. There was the fight over Natasha, an issue that upset all Marilyn's directors. But perhaps more important, Preminger was a regular at Sam Spiegel's house. He remembered Marilyn as one of the girls available to any man who chose to enjoy a break from the card games and fine dining. He knew what talents had helped her get started in the film business, and they weren't the ones that would help her in front of his cameras.

Marilyn had her own vengeance, creating problems that could not be challenged. For example, there was one scene Preminger wanted to shoot with the last vestiges of daylight that would be recordable in a manner unique in each twenty-four-hour period. For approximately five minutes, given the sensitivity of the film, the sky gave a hint of night yet was bright enough so a shot of the actors would also show in the distance light only a painter could duplicate.

Preminger worked from early afternoon with Marilyn and co-star Robert Mitchum, who would be locked in an embrace during the brief, beautiful scene. Everything was carefully planned, and all equipment was set in place. Then the technical people began watching a light meter as it showed the setting sun. The moment the needle registered enough light remaining for the scene at the same time the night sky reached the right illumination, it would be filmed. Any delay and they would have to wait another twenty-four hours.

Monroe said nothing. She and Mitchum prepared themselves as directed, and when the light meter read the anticipated amount of light, the camera started rolling the film. Marilyn, after pausing for a moment, left Mitchum and walked to Preminger.

"What is it, Marilyn?" he asked, livid.

"You'll have to excuse me," she said, innocently. "I have to go to the bathroom."

Another time, when Preminger was trying to get thirty seconds of critical dialogue, Marilyn kept missing her lines. Such a problem was not unusual for any actor. There were days when nothing seemed to go right, words were mispronounced, a scene to be filled with anguish left the actor laughing, and any number of other problems occurred. This was different, though. This was another Monroe revenge.

Preminger stopped filming after several retakes, called for a ten-minute break, then walked over to Marilyn to assure her everything was all right. She should relax a few minutes and then she would be fine.

Marilyn looked at Preminger with complete innocence, as though she had no idea what he was saying, and asked, "Why? Is anything the matter?"

The war between Preminger and Monroe escalated on August 19, 1953, when Marilyn accidentally twisted her ankle while trying to move across a shallow section of water in Jasper National Park. The cast was rehearsing a scene and Marilyn was wearing high boots to protect her costume. She had been told that the rocks were slippery and the current could be a problem, but she had ignored the warning. Her left leg went down, tearing tendons and ligaments. The local doctor thought she might be crippled for life if she didn't let it heal. However, when she called Joe, he came up to see her, bringing a more experienced doctor who declared the injury painful and needing rest, but minor in nature. Her leg had to be in a cast and there was a loss of time on the set.

Marilyn milked the injury for all the sympathy she could get. She talked with reporters, making clear how hard she had been working to be perfect. The subtle message was that she had given her all for Preminger, so how dare he be in any way critical of her efforts? In the end, however, Marilyn flew back to Los Angeles, stopping briefly in San Francisco, to finish the film in the studio.

ૐ

It was during this brief time that Marilyn saw a side of DiMaggio that moved her deeply. She knew he was obsessive, and though she delighted in his rushing to her side, others had done the same, albeit for many different reasons. Instead, it was an incident that occurred in San Francisco that changed her image of Joe.

Joe's brother, Michael, had gone fishing in Bodega Bay when a storm came up, throwing him off his boat and killing him. Joe turned to Marilyn for comfort as he grieved, a side of him she had never witnessed. Had she been asked before it occurred, she probably would have predicted that he would turn only to one of the men in his life. That he could be vulnerable to a woman moved her to the point where she was willing to agree to marry him. Only later would she begin to feel it was about the only sensitivity he had toward her and her life.

৪৯

The end result of the film was as bad as everyone feared. The respected trade journal *Hollywood Reporter* provided an unfortunately objective review. "If *River* proves anything at all, it is that Marilyn Monroe should stick to musicals and the type of entertainment that made her such a box office lure. If the film fails to bring in smash returns, 20th-Fox can attribute it to Marilyn's inability to handle a heavy acting role. Most of her genuine values are lost here."

If there was any irony to the highly flawed movie, it was the fact that it showcased Monroe's singing ability in ways that went unnoticed until long after her death. She sang four songs in the film—"River of No Return," "I'm Gonna File My Claim," "One Silver Dollar," and "Down In the Meadow," the latter sung to Mark Calder, the Tommy Rettig character who was in the care of Monroe's character, Kay, while his father was in jail. There were too few songs to make a record, and it would only be many years later that they would be included in a retrospective of her music and reveal how much she had learned.

During the time in Canada, Joe stayed where the cast and crew were housed. He was in Becker's Bungalows when they were in Jasper, Alberta, and in the Mount Royal Hotel in Banff when the company moved there. He and Marilyn were quite open about living together during the filming, something they could not do back in the States.

Joe spent his days hunting and fishing, resenting the way Marilyn liked to spend their evenings. He wanted quiet, intimate time with Marilyn. Marilyn—unlike the past, when she had seemed to prefer time to herself—wanted to unwind with some of the cast and crew. Perhaps as a result of her growing estrangement from Joe, her idea of relaxing on location was a bit of partying, which upset the very quiet DiMaggio.

The press interviewed DiMaggio, who was far more candid than he had

403

been in Los Angeles. Southern California and its media were unknowns to Joe. The New York press would cover the couple, stressing their dates, photographing them in nightspots, but not discussing the open secret that their nights were frequently spent together. The Los Angeles–based press corps had a similar attitude; not out of hero worship for Joe but to assure they did not incur the displeasure of the studios, whose greatest weapon was to deny access to the stars. If this were to happen, columnists would have no access and no perks since the most powerful among them received thousands of dollars in Christmas presents each year.

Joe told the Canadian press that he was visiting his girl, and the reporters left it at that. Then they discussed the trout streams, and when Marilyn had her leg in a cast, he acted as though it was a major catastrophe, reinforcing her statements to the press. His only indiscretion, if it could be called that, was to challenge the Canadian medical community by angrily saying that if the local doctors could not fix the leg, he would find someone who could. That wasn't much of a challenge, since the injury was minor and she was both young and athletic enough that the healing was going swiftly.

By the end of the film, Marilyn was feeling powerful. She had Joe DiMaggio's love. She had the attention of the press. She had a massive and growing fan base, and she was fed up with movie scripts, the bulk of which were variations on the musicals. "I was put into these movies without being consulted at all, much against my wishes. I had no choice in the matter. Is that fair? I work hard, I take pride in my work, and I'm a human being like the rest of them. If I keep on with parts like the ones [Fox] has been giving me, the public will soon tire of me," Monroe related, and she was probably correct. Certainly that had been an issue with her modeling career. She had been warned repeatedly that the public liked a variety of faces on magazine covers and in advertising. Her agent and some of the photographers wanted her to say no occasionally, or at least to slow the volume before she became the face of yesterday.

There had been fewer possible ramifications in the magazine field because the magazines targeted often radically different audiences. The images were spread among publications read by different demographic groups. The movies, by contrast, were aimed at identical audiences each time, so her concern about being typecast (in the manner of her predecessor blonde, Betty Grable) was valid.

Marilyn, encouraged by Charlie and Joe, returned the screenplay for *The Girl in Pink Tights* to the Fox executives, announcing it was too "lousy" for her to be in.

⅋ꙮ

It was much worse even than I had been afraid it would be. Movie musicals usually had dull stories. This one was way below dullness. It was silly—even for a movie about the 1890s.

I had to play the character of a prim, angrily virtuous school-teacher who decided to become a sort of hooch-koochy dancer in a Bowery dive so as to earn enough money to put her fiancé through medical college. The fiancé is high up in society with a dowager ma, but they are shy on money. This dreary cliché-spouting bore in pink tights was the cheapest character I had ever read in a script.

What's the use of being a star if you have to play something you're ashamed of? When I thought of Joe or any of my friends seeing me on the screen as this rear-wiggling schoolteacher doing bumps and grinds in the great cause of medicine I blushed to my toes.

Pink Tights didn't even get to marry the Society Man for whose sake she unveiled herself to wiggle in a Bowery Dive. She married instead the owner of the Dive—a man of rough appearance but with a heart of gold (or mush) underneath!

—Marilyn Monroe with Ben Hecht in *My Story*

⅋ꙮ

(Note: There is some question about when Marilyn actually had a script to read. Marilyn had been telling the Fox executives that she wanted script approval. This was allegedly the issue as she finished filming in Canada and back in the states. However, many sources indicate she was sent the script while finishing *River of No Return*, the implication being that she read it. Equally reliable sources, however, say that she did not read it until after returning from her honeymoon with DiMaggio in January 1954. Either way, when she finally rejected the role, one of the objections was that she hated the writing.)

Marilyn genuinely did not like the film, though the rejection was actually part of a larger strategy on her part. Joe and Charlie, in addition to being concerned about financial issues for Marilyn, recognized a negotiating strategy Fox was quietly creating. Marilyn was given back-to-back films that would not have immediate release. This was giving the studio a backlog of films to release as they chose, should Marilyn refuse to work. The audience was clamoring to see Monroe on the screen, something that would stop if the studio's production was merely current. Having a backlog of movies would assure that the studio would face no backlash from Marilyn's fan base while the executives played hardball concerning the terms for the contract renewal.

Turning down the next movie and having a screenplay in development specifically to be used as a starring vehicle would give her the leverage Joe and Charlie felt she needed. This was why Joe and Marilyn optioned *Horns of the Devil*, and this was why Charlie loaned Marilyn the five-thousand-dollar option fee to make the deal.

Twentieth Century-Fox was livid over what was taking place. The studio system had been built on the idea that the stars were owned by the moguls, their lives dictated by the moguls, their indiscretions made to disappear by the moguls, and that they would accept fame and fortune in exchange for doing whatever the moguls desired. But by the early 1950s, the studio system was ending. Television was an unknown that everyone had to consider. And the moguls wanted to either avoid change or control its pace. If Marilyn won her fight, the trades would cover the story and other actors and agents would also make challenges. That was the reason Monroe was told she would be suspended by the studio if she didn't agree to the new film. It was the right tactic to use on a woman who had been living from paycheck to paycheck, fearing income loss and an end to her career.

Joe was at his finest in supporting Marilyn, though he was fighting the seductive lure of yet another potential bonus for Monroe. *The Girl in Pink Tights* was a remake of the 1943 Betty Grable picture *Coney Island*. Marilyn would have the Grable role, and Frank Sinatra, moving from being "boy singer" for the big bands and then an entertainer in his own right, was being paid five thousand dollars to be the male lead. Monroe's contract called for her to receive less than a third of that amount to play a schoolteacher who becomes a music hall singer. However, she would receive equal star billing, she and Sinatra being equally popular draws for the viewing public.

Charlie Feldman had arranged for Marilyn to option *Horns of the Devil* so she could hold out until February, at which time she would have the greatest power. Nervously Monroe agreed, refusing to show up for work on *The Girl in Pink Tights*. She thought she was just in breach of contract as explained by Charlie and Joe. She thought she could get married, have a honeymoon, and avoid going to work until February. She did not understand the character of Darryl Zanuck and what movies meant to him.

Zanuck loved screenplays of all types in much the same way that a top book editor loves literature. He not only appreciated the skill of the writer, he also saw his job to be the provider of the final polish to a story that was a gem in the rough. Just as an editor will make often-extensive suggestions to the novelist, so Zanuck delighted in taking the time to make notes for the screenwriters whose work he wanted to buy for Fox.

Zanuck had read the basic screenplay for *The Girl in Pink Tights*, enjoying the story line and adding notes for the screenwriter to follow for the next, more polished draft. Some writers objected, but the truth was that Zanuck often caught the subtleties that needed changing in order to truly improve the story.

Once the film was being shot, Zanuck would take a hands-on approach to the editing process. He knew that the screenplay was the structure for the movie. However, the emotions of a story were conveyed by more than just the effective interaction of the actors. The length of a scene, the camera angles, close-ups, long shots, and numerous other factors that had to be judged after viewing the raw film all would have an impact on the audience. Zanuck felt his involvement had to carry through the cutting and editing process.

Zanuck's work ethic was admirable. His skills were mixed. Some films were so badly slashed that the story, as shown in the theaters, did not make sense. Other films were vastly improved over what anyone else involved with the film might have been able to accomplish.

Most important, Zanuck did not try to demean the people who worked for him. A successful film, even if mostly the result of his efforts, was credited to the original writer, cinematographers, actors, editors, and others. When the film failed to work as hoped, Zanuck accepted the full blame.

While such an attitude came naturally to the producer, he expected it to be respected. Actors were to follow his wishes because he knew better than they did how the picture had to come together. Monroe, without realizing it, had committed several "sins." She criticized a script Zanuck had approved, then refused to act in a movie Zanuck would be refining in the editing process. He was truly hurt by her actions, and could not comprehend why she was being difficult when he knew how much effort he would be making to assure the final film was an effective showcase for the stars. He saw the action as disrespectful toward himself, his skills, and his efforts, and that disrespect was of greater concern to him than contract discussions.

Zanuck understood that the studio needed films featuring Monroe and that it was important to get her to fulfill his request to appear in the movie. The only other picture being shot in the same time period would be an even more personal project, a movie entitled *The Egyptian*, whose female lead would be a character named Nefer. Marilyn further aroused Zanuck's anger by suggesting that instead of appearing in *The Girl in Pink Tights*, she audition to play Nefer and someone else do the role initially proposed for her. She did not realize that Zanuck was saving the role of Nefer for his mistress. This fact was common gossip in Hollywood, so it was assumed— not necessarily correctly—that Monroe was aware of that fact. Her suggestion of herself for the role of Nefer would seem to imply that she knew quality better than the studio head and that she was a better actress than his mistress.

Marilyn returned to Los Angeles. Zanuck was determined to have Marilyn in *The Girl in Pink Tights*, and he was going to do it with flattery. But first he needed to get her on the Fox lot, away from the close control of Feldman and DiMaggio.

To this end, a letter was written to Marilyn—indirectly. It was on Zanuck's stationery and addressed to the film's director and casting director. It discussed, in glowing terms, Marilyn Monroe and her skills, and extolled the many virtues she would bring to the role he wanted for her in the movie she hated. The recipients understood that they were to share this good news with Monroe. Zanuck would be "surprised" and then delighted when she relented and took the part—not because of contract pressure, but because she was so respected by him.

While the letter was being "surreptitiously" sent on to Monroe, Zanuck attempted to get her away physically from her comfort zone by having her come to the Fox lot. He claimed that he needed her to record a song for *River of No Return*. All the work had been done in Canada, but he felt there was one song that needed to be redone and then dubbed into the film over the footage of her performing. It was a not unusual request, but she, along with the rest of the cast, knew that between the work in the studio and the work on location, the film had wrapped with no more work to be done except the editing. There was no overdub necessary.

Marilyn and Joe recognized that the demand for post-production work was just a ploy. She had a strong enough sense of the quality of her work that she felt she did not have to return. Although she was correct, refusing was a dangerous move, since it would have hurt her had the dub actually been necessary.

Zanuck also went after Natasha, the more vulnerable of the two women. Lytess was making more money than ever before in her life, but it was only because Marilyn had insisted she be hired for every picture. Few directors liked the woman, and some made clear that she could not work on the sets of their films. Lytess understood that if she could not convince Marilyn to appear in the new picture, there was no reason for the studio to pay for her time, for any picture, for any actor. Her life would be radically changed, and that was a concept she could not face. She went to Monroe and tried to talk her into making the movie.

Marilyn was horrified. She had never understood how self-centered the acting coach could be. Lytess had frequently made Marilyn look like a caricature of an actress with her exaggerated pronunciation and often awkward body movements. But Marilyn was insecure enough that, if she recognized the work was not good, she blamed herself—not her coach. This time Marilyn realized that Lytess was betraying her. They had discussed the contract negotiations and Marilyn's desire to take on more challenging roles. It was obvious that Natasha had capitulated to the studio pressure.

Joe, livid, went to Natasha and informed her that from then on, any contact she wished to make with Monroe would have to be through the actress's agent. Their relationship was not over, but it would never be the same.

The battle with Fox continued. There were legal maneuvers, the sending of messengers, demands, and counter-demands, but Marilyn held firm, allowing Joe and Charlie's strategy to work. More important, Marilyn saw Joe as truly caring for the first time. She knew he was not happy with her career; yet the fight with Zanuck seemed to electrify him. He used his competitive instincts, no longer challenged on the playing field, in order to help Marilyn triumph over the studio. It was like being in the World Series of Hollywood with the corporate office replacing the ball diamond, and Joe's advice the equivalent of a batting coach. Winning became more important than any feelings about what it meant for Marilyn to be a star.

Marilyn, always delighting in men who were obsessed with her, reveled in the changed DiMaggio. He had stopped talking about the games he played. He had stopped trying to spend most of his time with other men. It was as though the care and handling of the Monroe contract renewal with Fox was the new sport of the moment, and Joe was going to be the master.

While this was taking place, several other relationships were influencing her actions and her future. One of the relationships would be with Milton Greenholtz, who had taken the name Milton Greene when he became a photographer, making a reputation for himself as one of the young, new, extremely talented fashion and celebrity photographers working after World War II. He was twenty-seven when he first met Marilyn in 1949. Johnny Hyde had arranged for her to go to the home of Rupert Allan and Frank McCarthy to meet several New York photographers who were in Hollywood to do a photo essay on the new starlets. Monroe saw Greene's portfolio and thought the images were brilliant.

Hyde had gone on a week's vacation, during which Marilyn had a rather curious relationship with Greene. She was not one of the starlets he was assigned to photograph before returning to New York, and though Marilyn wanted him to take her picture, he never did on that trip. Instead, they allegedly spent extensive time in his room at the Chateau Marmont Hotel. Exactly what happened is unknown, though on September 14, 1949, Milton "Hot Shutter" Greene received a less-than-brilliant telegram reading,

Milton Greene, I love you dearly
And not for your "house" and hospitality merely,
It's that I think you are superb—
And that, my dear, is not just a blurb.

It was signed "Love, Marilyn."

No matter how intense the week together, Greene had been out of Monroe's life until he returned to see her after having achieved the personal status of being one of the highest-paid magazine photographers in the country. The reunion occurred in late 1953, when Milton had been sent back to Hollywood to photograph Marilyn for a cover story for *Look* magazine. By then he was thirty-two and married to his second wife, Amy Greene, a New York fashion model. That marriage seemed strong, a sharing of each other's dreams of success, and those would eventually include helping Marilyn.

Still photographers like Greene were nearing the end of having a personal importance little understood in the contemporary era, when television news crews seem to be able to cover any crisis within minutes or hours of its taking place. We think of news as a live experience, a thought reinforced by satellite broadcasting and networks such as CNN. But in the 1950s it was the still photographer who brought the images that defined the world for most Americans. And the medium most respected was the news and feature magazine. Among them were the two leaders—*Life* and *Look*. The former was originally the picture magazine illustrating stories told in the sister publication *Time*. The latter featured top photojournalism, combining general interest reading with in-depth features.

Look magazine, *Life*'s rival, had Greene on the then-enormous salary of fifty thousand dollars a year at the end of 1953 when he was sent to photograph Marilyn. He was making more than most movie actors: an ironic fact given that photographing the stars of stage and screen had become his specialty.

The November 17, 1953, issue of *Look* magazine reveals why Marilyn was so impressed with Milton, and also why Joe was not jealous. One full-page image was a brilliant design concept in which Greene used a solid black background, had Marilyn wear a black dress, and then lit her so that all the viewer sees are her head, hands, and legs. Another dozen, smaller images showed her in a thick knit sweater, plucking the strings of a mandolin.

What mattered most to the two of them was that they saw Norma Jean and Marilyn Monroe in the same way. Norma Jean came across as a sweet young woman, almost virginal, as she poses for the camera. This was not the aggressive movie star wannabe who would do almost anything with almost anyone to get ahead. This was a girl grown into womanhood, pleasant to be around, attractive, someone who might be a neighbor.

The images capturing Marilyn Monroe are those of someone almost playing movie star. They are fun, as though she is making fun of the image that made her a success. Greene saw the woman in the same manner in which she saw the best of herself.

Greene and Marilyn, reuniting as success stories four years after they first met, talked about their mutual ambitions at a party given by actor/dancer/choreographer Gene Kelly when Marilyn returned from the location shooting for her film *River of No Return*. They discussed a possible partnership, a business arrangement that would ultimately result in the creation of Marilyn Monroe Productions, Inc. at the end of 1954.

But first Marilyn had to get married.

Forty-three

Bed and Bored

Everything came to a head with the studio when Marilyn was notified at the end of December 1953 that *The Girl in Pink Tights* would begin filming on January 4, 1954. She was to be ready to work, the script memorized, or there could be a lawsuit against her.

Marilyn had no intention of showing up, something Charlie Feldman related to Spyros Skouras in New York. The action brought the crisis to a head, Marilyn laying low while Skouras flew to Los Angeles to plot strategy with Zanuck. When it became obvious that the studio was going to suspend Marilyn's contract, Joe asked Marilyn to marry him. The date was January 12, Tom DiMaggio's birthday and one day after Marilyn was told her pay was going to be stopped from Fox. Having nothing to lose, everything to gain from the publicity, and the belief that maybe she and Joe could succeed as a married couple given his intense interest in her business, she agreed.

Two days later, at 12:30 in the afternoon, Marilyn called Fox publicist Harry Brand and told him she was getting married.

Brand was stunned. Marilyn explained that the ceremony would be that afternoon. Municipal Court Judge Charles Peery agreed to leave a lunch he was attending for the local Bar Association, return to City Hall, and perform the ceremony that afternoon.

DiMaggio had wanted a big church wedding with San Francisco Archbishop John J. Mitty presiding. However, the Catholic Church did not recognize Joe's divorce from his first wife, a fact that made him a married man in the eyes of the Archbishop. The ceremony he undertook with Marilyn would be legal only in the eyes of the secular law, and the moment it was performed, Joe was excommunicated .

Excommunication meant little to Joe. He would still be allowed to attend all services of the Catholic Church. However, he would be denied access to the rites of confession and communion. This—a serious spiritual matter for a devout Roman Catholic during those conservative times—was of little consequence to Joe. He had rarely attended his family parish of St. Peter and St. Paul, nor had he been attending elsewhere.

Reporters and photographers met the wedding party, which consisted of Joe's brother Tom and Tom's wife, Reno Barsocchini; the manager of Joe's restaurant and his wife; and Lefty O'Doul, Joe's former manager from his Pacific Coast League playing days, along with his wife. There were also reporters and photographers present, probably the result of Harry Brand's frantic telephone calls in order to milk the event for all he could. Marilyn might be suspended from her contract, but Harry knew he needed to keep her before the public eye in order to assure box-office success when she went back before the cameras.

The *New York Daily Mirror* gushed about the ceremony, which lasted no more than three minutes, saying:

> Marilyn and the fabulous DiMag pressed their way through a swarm of newsmen who raced to the entrance of City Hall when word of their marriage plans spread through San Francisco like wildfire. As Joe and Marilyn were pronounced man and wife by Municipal Court Judge Charles Peery, he took her into his arms and kissed her. Newsreel men and photographers asked him to do it again. Joe did a repeat, then another and another. Nothing like a record of batting safely in 56 games, but close.

News of the wedding forced Darryl Zanuck to lift Marilyn's suspension. He ordered her to return to work by January 25, still too early a date for Feldman to make the deal he wanted. Fortunately Marilyn and Joe decided to leave town, gaining so much notoriety that Fox would have to make major changes.

The marriage had been consummated long before the ceremony, so Marilyn and Joe settled for privacy as the ideal initial escape. The day of the marriage they drove to Paso Robles, stopping at the Clifton Motel. They arrived at 8:00 P.M., checking out at 1:00 P.M. the next day. However, the reality of what would prove to be a very short-term marriage was obvious from Joe's one known request upon checking in. He wanted to be certain that the room had a television set, something that was never a certainty in those years. Other men would have fantasized about spending their hours either making love to Marilyn or recovering their energy so they could return to love making. Joe wanted to see if he was going to be inducted in the Baseball Hall of Fame in Cooperstown, something that was being announced that day. (It was his first year of eligibility, and he would not be elected until the following year.) He also wanted to make certain he didn't miss his favorite television shows.

The rest of the honeymoon involved staying in a house in the mountain area of Idyllwild, approximately fifty miles from Palm Springs, for the next ten days. It was isolated, though a caretaker and his wife were on the grounds to see to the couple's needs. To Joe's credit, there was no television set, and no one knew how to reach them by telephone. To enhance their sense of isolation, snow was falling almost daily.

The couple truly talked for the first time. They played billiards. They took long walks. They shared a relationship in a manner they had never done before. Marilyn got to know Joe in ways that were impossible when they were either hounded by the press or choreographed by the studio. It was also a type of intimacy that they would not share again in the weeks that followed. Marilyn found Joe boring.

Returning January 24, 1954, one day before Marilyn was to report to work, the couple found a copy of the screenplay for *The Girl in Pink Tights* waiting at their gate. This time Marilyn became aggressive. On January 25, her lawyer told the press that she had read the script and did not intend to do the movie.

Zanuck was livid, but there was nothing he could do. Joe DiMaggio had to briefly go to New York to handle some of his broadcast duties for the Yankees. Then he was taking Marilyn on what amounted to a second honeymoon, albeit a working one. Lefty O'Doul was beloved in Japan, a country that had aggressively adopted the game of baseball following World War II. O'Doul had been regularly traveling to Japan to put on exhibition games and stage clinics. This time he asked Joe to accompany him so Marilyn could spend her time with Lefty's wife.

Contemporary baseball players consider the signing of autographs at sports and sports memorabilia shows to be a way to make extra cash from their past fame on the field. In the 1950s both the players and the fans would have been horrified at the idea that they should charge money for an autograph. Instead, they picked up extra cash through product endorsements, often unrelated to sports, being a radio commentator for the team that was usually the last one for which they played, and through baseball clinics. The latter were sophisticated training camps where athletes of proven ability trained younger men eager to master the game. In addition, the clinics allowed the athletes, many of whom were small-town kids who had only seen the cities in which they played ball, to experience the world at large.

The trip would not be what Joe or Marilyn anticipated. Even if the marriage should never have taken place originally, the trip to Asia guaranteed there would be a divorce.

DiMaggio expected to be treated as the star when the couple reached Japan. The cheering for him had diminished even faster than it was rising for Marilyn, and he was convinced that being abroad would change that. He and Lefty would talk about the mechanics of baseball to awestruck young men. Joe would show how a player needed to position himself in the field when playing defense, how to throw, and how to hit the ball. He would be in his element, and he presumably pictured Marilyn as the adoring wife, either sitting in the stands with Lefty's wife or perhaps going shopping in the stores.

Joe's first shock was when the plane landed in Hawaii at the end of the initial leg of their trip. They would only be on the island long enough to change planes like every other traveler flying to Asia from the West Coast. Yet despite this fact, thousands of people turned out to cheer them.

There were security forces on the ground after the Pan Am plane landed, but the crowd surged against them and broke free, mobbing the field. There was no way to keep the people back as they shouted the couple's names.

The most frightening portion of the arrival was when people began pulling at Monroe's hair. They had never seen anything of that color (nor had nature, of course). Many reached out to touch it and a few wrapped strands around their fingers, pulling it from her head.

Finally, concerned about not only Joe and Marilyn's safety but also the possibility that one of the fans could be crushed, the security forces encircled the newlyweds and slowly made their way to the airport lounge where they could await their next flight.

Japan was to prove even more astounding for both Joe and Marilyn. The couple had been invited to Asia because of Joe's fame. The country had fallen in love with baseball, and he was one of the great players. Marilyn, like Joe, felt her role would be that of adoring wife, always letting him be the center of attention. Neither of them comprehended what had recently happened with Marilyn's career.

There were two cuts to many motion pictures: one for the American audience and one for overseas. The latter was often more erotic, including scenes and dialogue that had been cut from the domestic version because the censors felt they violated standards of decency established for the motion picture industry.

Neither Monroe nor DiMaggio paid attention to the foreign distribution of her films, and she probably did not see the cuts made for the overseas market. Marilyn was on straight salary with the studio. She made the same money if the movie played in one theater domestically before disappearing from view, or ten thousand theaters internationally and run again and again in the years that followed. Television had begun to be a medium for movies and stage plays, but there were no special arrangements to pay her or most actors when, or if, a film was shown in this manner.

Joe and Marilyn were unaware that Asia had become a major market for her work. This was a region of the world where blondes—natural or otherwise—were unfamiliar sights. The sensual American actress appearing on screens throughout the region had developed a massive fan base about which she knew nothing. She seemed to assume that she would be the anonymous person traveling with DiMaggio, her role strictly that of the doting wife who would look lovingly at Joe when they were together, focusing her eyes solely on her husband as she presumed everyone else would be doing. She was wrong, and both were caught by surprise.

Thousands of movie fans had mobbed the airport in Japan. Airport security was just able to maintain the crowd while the doors to the passenger plane were shut, but they recognized that the moment Monroe emerged, the crowd would rush to the walkway and be unstoppable. To prevent injuries and probably deaths, they positioned themselves as though they were about to open the doors. Then, as the crowd stood, barely in control, the luggage hold was opened and Marilyn, hidden from view, was taken off the plane as though she had just been another suitcase.

Away from the mob, Marilyn and Joe were taken to the safest and one of the most beautiful hotels in earthquake-prone Tokyo. This was the Imperial Hotel, designed by American architect Frank Lloyd Wright, who created a floating base for the hotel that imitated a waiter's hand when holding a tray of dishes. Just as the waiter's fingers support the tray while the hand constantly makes subtle adjustments to the shifting balance, so the hotel was meant to stay erect by adjusting to the shifts of the earth during a quake.

Everyone in Tokyo knew the Imperial Hotel, and many were aware that Joe and Marilyn were staying there. Once again there were mobs waiting for them, and this time two hundred police officers were assigned to get the couple through the crowds and safely to their rooms.

As Mr. and Mrs. DiMaggio made their way upstairs, the mob was not so much out of control as it was overwhelming too small a space for so many people. Men and women pushed each other into fish ponds, were jammed in revolving doors, and broke plate glass in the hall; and their weight, when they stood close together to see the couple, broke the boulders on which they tried to stand together in the rock garden. Yet the fans also viewed Monroe with bemusement concerning her outrageous dress and walk. As *Time* magazine reported in its February 15, 1954, issue, a Tokyo radio commentator said, "The Japanese will probably not discard their underwear as a result of the visit of the Honorable Buttocks-Swinging Actress because it is much too cold. But because our people are quick to adopt fads, I'm sure that they will soon start swinging their buttocks."

⁓

Yoko Hazama, a Tokyo movie fan who managed to talk his way into getting an interview with Monroe, transcribed his interview as best he could—his English was limited—and mailed it to his favorite magazine, *Modern Screen*. Among his questions and the answers as he understood them were:

"What is your opinion about your famous Monroe Walk?"

"I had been walking since I was six months old and couldn't stopped yet. It naturally come to me."

"Is it true you didn't wear any underwear clothes, whether or not?"

"I'm planning to buy a Japanese kimono and I'm wearing underclothes like this lace slip."

❦

Joe DiMaggio, the king of New York baseball, had no royal standing in Tokyo, Japan. The mob gathered outside the hotel where they could look up at the couple's room. The police and management asked them to leave, but none would go until Marilyn stepped onto the balcony to greet them. "King" Joe had become a trivia question for baseball buffs. Marilyn was the new royalty, her stardom coming from a film career that remained on the rise.

Worse for a man of DiMaggio's ego was the fact that Monroe was the most recognized woman in Tokyo. Joe frequently walked about Manhattan either unrecognized or undisturbed. His fame did not deprive him of normal activity. The public asked for autographs or just for a chance to look at her. The press trailed her, recording the public reaction and asking her questions wherever she went.

To be fair, a blonde was a rare sight in Japan, and it was impossible to mistake Monroe for any other woman. She would have been a curiosity had she just been another tourist. Being blonde and a movie star assured attention on a scale Joe could not have imagined. And because of her movies and her walk, the reporters began adopting the radio commentator's description, the papers filled with articles about "the honorable buttocks-swinging madam."

It was not just the Japanese who were interested in Marilyn. She and Joe attended a cocktail party where an army officer present asked if she would be willing to take a little time from her honeymoon to do something for the military. He wanted her to fly to Korea to entertain the troops. She would be gone no more than four days, during which time Joe would be almost constantly involved with the baseball clinics.

Marilyn was certain Joe would not mind the trip; and even if he did,

419

she had no intention of *not* going to entertain the troops. She also knew that one reason for being present was to spend time with Jean O'Doul, Lefty's wife, since the clinics would be as boring for her as for Marilyn. She asked Jean to accompany her on the trip, and though Joe was livid, there was no way to stop Marilyn.

The military was in Korea as an occupying force, the war between the North and the South recently having ended with a truce that could be broken at any time. The tension was so high between the two Koreas that a formal peace treaty had not been signed even decades later.

Monroe started her tour traveling by helicopter to the various military bases where the soldiers and Marines remained on constant alert. The first men she was to entertain were members of the First Marine Division located in the mountains. The area was isolated, and she had no idea what type of reception she would receive as the troops came into view from her vantage point in the helicopter.

There were two Marilyn Monroes, as became obvious when she went onto the makeshift stage from which she would be performing. She was the creation of a girl with a vivid imagination and little training as an actress. She knew that the screen persona was a work in progress, probably the reason she did not formally change her name to Marilyn Monroe until March 12, 1956, a time when she had a good understanding of the character she had created over the years. Yet Marilyn was also an exhibitionist with an ego that dominated all else in her life. She craved attention, adoration, and obsession. She dressed to arouse desire in men, and women were often shocked and angry with her for flaunting her body in ways inappropriate for the circumstances. Put her in front of a still camera and she would seduce the lens. Place her in the midst of a group of reporters and she would titillate them with risqué quotes just polite enough to be quotable, yet obvious enough to be naughty. And put her on a stage in front of an audience of men and she understood how to project an intimacy that could make each member of a crowd feel she was talking to and singing for him alone.

The Marines were even more appreciative because Marilyn was known to them all. For the previous several years, photographs of Monroe were the most popular of all the movie stars. Like Betty Grable's pictures a decade earlier, Monroe's images were in tents, on bulletin boards, in airplanes, mess halls, and anywhere else the men lived and worked. Some were still photos meant to advertise her movies. Some were head shots provided by fan mail services. Some were torn from newspapers and magazines. The fantasy had warmed and delighted them in a land that could be colder than any terrain they had previously encountered in their young lives. Now Marilyn was present in the flesh, and they roared their appreciation and delight.

Excited by what she was seeing below, Marilyn had the men in the helicopter open the door, hold her legs, and let her dangle out as the aircraft swooped low over the heads of the Marines. She blew them kisses and responded to their cheers, whistles, and applause.

Marilyn had worn proper protective clothing for the flight—a combat jacket that would protect her from flak if any shooting started, combat boots, and a shirt and trousers, all issued by the military. Once she landed, though, she quickly changed into a skin-tight sheath, a dress that showed her figure to full advantage. She had to be nearly frozen from the cold, but she did not care. With her seemingly painted-on sequined gown cut low enough to heat up the men far from home and most female companionship, bright red lipstick, and bleached blonde hair, she had the men screaming for her as she stepped to the microphone and started singing. She sang "Diamonds Are a Girl's Best Friend" so suggestively as to cause a near riot. She also sang "Do It Again," the song that had been so popular at Camp Pendleton. However, she was forced to change the words to "Kiss Me Again" because one of the colonels on the first base where she performed thought that the Gershwin lyrics were too suggestive.

Marilyn gave ten performances for one hundred thousand soldiers over four days' time. The first show was the largest—between thirteen thousand and seventeen thousand men in the audience, depending upon which estimate you read—and she entertained more than thirty thousand in the first three shows. The enthusiasm of her first audience was the most exciting for her, though, and she was still exhilarated that night when she had dinner with fifty Marine officers, followed by a telephone call to DiMaggio in Japan that had been arranged by the Signal Corps.

Marilyn was told that the equipment used for the call would keep the conversation with DiMaggio from being private. Anyone near her would hear both sides of what they were saying. It was a situation that delighted her.

Joe DiMaggio was a very private man, uncomfortable with public displays of affection. He was horrified by the idea that anything he felt should be part of his personal life might become public knowledge. That was why Marilyn decided to have fun with him during the call, asking Joe, "Do you still love me, Joe?" and "Do you miss me?" He answered positively, though without enthusiasm, knowing what she was doing to him.

Joe DiMaggio was never known to have discussed with Marilyn what it was like to be a famous ballplayer. He had never mentioned the roar of the crowd the moment he ran onto the field, the adulation of the fans wherever he traveled. He seemed to assume that Marilyn would know who he was, what he had done, and what the reaction had been. She did not, nor did she care. He had his career from which he had retired. She had her career which had suddenly reached the level Johnny Hyde predicted was inevitable for her. She later told Amy Greene, the wife of future business partner Milton Greene, "I never felt like a star before in my heart. It was so wonderful to look down and see a fellow smiling at me."

As for Joe, Marilyn excitedly spoke of the seas of soldiers responding to each performance. A portion of what each of them said to the other has been quoted so often that most biographers think the partial quote is accurate. Marilyn said, "You've never heard such cheering."

Then Joe is quoted as saying, "Yes, I have." Just those three words alone make for a rather sad commentary about a man no longer in the spotlight. The possible implication of those words was that the cheering had just begun for Marilyn and she was not going to leave show business as Dorothy had done for him. And implied in all this was the idea that he could not stand the idea that he might fall under her shadow: "Mr. Monroe" taking the place of "Mrs. DiMaggio" in the public eye.

However, that was not the full quote. The real exchange, allegedly provided independently to biographer Maurice Zolotow, among others, was:

"It was so wonderful, Joe. You should have heard such cheering."

"Yes, I have. Don't let it go to your head. Just miss the ball once. You'll see they can boo as loud as they can cheer."

The full quote puts quite a different spin on the exchange.

Had the Korean War still been a shooting war, probably none of the reporters present would have done more than mention that Marilyn had brought the troops a much-needed respite from the death and destruction. Any seemingly inappropriate behavior by the soldiers or Monroe would either have been ignored by the reporters or credited to the release of almost overwhelming stress. Certainly this was the case during World War II with the USO tours and the individual performers who managed to travel to war zones to entertain the soldiers in the trenches. But in Korea there was a cease-fire, and the press corps had no battle news to cover. They were present for Monroe's performances, and since her appearances provided the only events that passed for news, they created a major negative story out of a minor incident. During two separate performances by Monroe, some of the soldiers rushed the stage. One instance was minor and easily handled, but when members of the U.S. Fortieth Infantry Division rushed the stage in a separate incident, they nearly trampled the men providing security before order was restored.

Hanson Baldwin of the *New York Times* dispatched a story that was carried in the paper's February 17 edition, then spread nationally by the wire services. He wrote, in part: "On two occasions troops rioted wildly and behaved like bobby-soxers in Times Square, not like soldiers proud of their uniform."

A week later, on Wednesday, February 24, 1954, *Weekly Variety*, the show business publication, carried a follow-up to the Hanson concerns.

"*N.Y. Times*" on Army Morale

    Hanson W. Baldwin, the *N.Y. Times*' military expert, in his Sunday feature, "McCarthy and the Army," pointed up and paired "Senators Inquiry and Marilyn Monroe's Visit to Korea Show Service's Weakness."

    Bypassing as politics, Baldwin's diatribe against the Wisconsin senator's meddling into Army protocol, and his (McCarthy's) attack on Secretary of the Army Robert T. Stevens, show business will be guided by the part about Miss Monroe:

    It is completely true, as Senator McCarthy said, though not in the way he meant it, that "we witnessed a disgraceful performance [last week], and I think it is up to Secretary Stevens to correct it quickly."

    It is also up to Mr. Stevens, and especially to General Ridgeway, to correct the weaknesses in service morale epitomized by the visit of Miss [Marilyn] Monroe to Korea. On two occasions during the visit of the motion picture actress, troops rioted mildly and behaved like bobbysoxers in Times Square, not like soldiers proud of their uniform.

Their conduct must have delighted the Communists and all who hope for signs of degradation and decline in the United States. Their poor discipline, it is true, merely reflects some of the softness on the "home front." But the Army cannot tolerate this if it is to remain an Army.

Mr. Stevens might well ascertain why Miss Monroe was in Korea anyway. Sweater girls and young ladies scantily clad in ermine-trimmed bathing suits have nothing to do with military morale; tours by such as these are not the stuff of discipline and pride and toughness.

The Army Special Services officer charged with trying to provide recreation for the troops, too often has usurped the functions of command instead of implementing them.

The Army needs fewer McCarthys and Monroes, less demagogues (sic) and less Hollywood and more leadership and moral fiber from the top down. It is up to Secretary Stevens and his immediate superiors and subordinates in the Defense Department to restore the soul of the Army.

The seemingly minor incident and seeming overreaction foreshadowed a hostile political climate that would soon have an impact on Hollywood. However, Marilyn was oblivious to all this. Her first concern was marriage—not the one to Joe DiMaggio from which she had just come back from their honeymoon—but to Arthur Miller, a playwright she had met briefly in 1950, who was also married.

The lifelong love affair of Marilyn Monroe and Joe DiMaggio has always been a wonderful story that might be considered part of American show business mythology. Few women, if any, would tolerate Joe DiMaggio as a husband for very long, something Joe only minimally understood. The closest he came to explaining himself was when he talked with syndicated columnist Jimmy Cannon, saying,

> My life is dull. I never interfere in Marilyn's work. She goes to the studio and I don't go with her anymore. It's the same stuff all the time. They do a scene and then they hang around a long time waiting to look at it.
>
> I don't resent her fame. She was working long before she met me. And for what? What has she got after all these years? She works like a dog. When she's working, she's up at five or six in the morning and doesn't get through until seven at night. We eat dinner, watch a little television, and go to bed.

Marilyn was harsher. United Press columnist Aline Mosby had written a story about Marilyn's purchase of an eight-foot bed for herself and Joe after their marriage. In Pete Martin's book *Will Acting Spoil Marilyn Monroe?*, she was quoted as saying,

> People say it's very chic to have separate bedrooms. That way a man can have a place for his fishing equipment and guns as well as for sleeping, and a woman can have a fluffy, ruffly place with rows of perfume bottles clinking against each other. But the way I feel, they ought to share the same bedroom. With a separate bedroom deal, if you happen to think of something you want to say to the other one, it means you have to go traipsing down the hall, and you may be tired. For that matter, you may forget what you started out to say. Besides, separate bedrooms are lonely. I think people need human warmth even when they're asleep and unconscious.
>
> For a man and a wife to live intimately together is no easy thing at best. If it's not just exactly right in every way it's practically impossible. However, I'm still optimistic.

Then, Martin wrote, she added a line that strongly reinforced her feelings immediately following the return from Japan when she met with Sid Skolsky, Leon Schwab, and Fred Otash in Skolsky's office above the pharmacy in Schwab's Drug Store. "However, I think TV sets should be taken out of the bedroom."

Joe DiMaggio loved television and comic books. Monroe was never an intellectual, though she firmly believed in trying to better herself. She read a variety of books, sometimes reading them all the way through, sometimes reading enough so that she convinced herself she understood the gist of what the author was saying. Regardless of whether she was right or just had pretensions about herself, she tried to improve herself both as an actress and intellectually. Joe was great in bed, but eventually the couple had to talk with each other, and Joe had nothing to say.

Still, there was something troubling about Marilyn's announcement to her friends that she was going to marry Arthur Miller. Skolsky, who had died before interviews were begun for this book, left his memories in *Don't Get Me Wrong—I Love Hollywood.* He wrote, "Joe DiMaggio bored Marilyn Monroe. His life-style added up to beer, TV, and the old lady. The wife who ran third to *Gunsmoke* or *The Late Show* and a can of beer, night after night after night. She couldn't settle for that—not even with an All-American hero."

There were rumors from Marilyn's friends that DiMaggio, an extremely obsessive man, often became physically and/or emotionally abusive during the courtship and presumably the brief marriage. The details will never be known. All that is certain is that Marilyn never had any intention of being faithful to DiMaggio. Fred Otash later commented that on reflection:

> She probably married the guy because he wanted her and the publicity was good for her career. Or maybe she didn't know how to get out of it after all the build-up. Certainly she bragged to Skolsky and other friends about how happy she was, though even with Sid, she spoke of her happiness in one breath and her determination to divorce the former ballplayer in her next one. This was not the great love affair of the century.

As Marilyn commented when she finally went to divorce court in October 1954, "He didn't talk to me. He was cold. He was indifferent to me as a human being and an artist. He didn't want me to have friends of my own. He didn't want me to do my work. He watched television instead of talking to me."

But first, before the marriage could end, there were the movies, including the infamous *Seven Year Itch*.

Forty-four

There's No Business . . .

In his book *We Thought We Could Do Anything*, Henry Ephron later told the story of the writing of the final screenplay for *There's No Business Like Show Business* in a way far more interesting than the movie itself in any of its incarnations. The idea was a simple one. Darryl Zanuck had paid Irving Berlin $600,000 for the right to use a number of the composer's songs, including the classic show business song that was the title of the film. Some sort of connecting story line would be needed, though the story was not important. This was to be a musical where as many Irving Berlin tunes were used as possible. Everything else was secondary, and originally it was thought that Berlin would handle voice-over narration.

The writing of the film was assigned to Lamarr Trotti, a man versatile enough to write the highly acclaimed drama *The Ox-Bow Incident* as well as a series of highly forgettable Fox musicals such as *Mother Wore Tights*. He understood what Darryl Zanuck desired for the studio, and the first draft of his screenplay turned in to the studio on June 12, 1952, succeeded in having room for between twenty-five and thirty Irving Berlin songs. The story revolved around a show business family so that the songs could be used during the various scenes that showed them performing over the years.

The story as eventually developed, following several drafts by three different writers, told the story of Terry and Molly Donahue, a song-and-dance team performing just after World War I. They have a two-year-old son, Steve, and soon have two other children, Tim and Katy. Everyone is part of the act until Molly worries that an education on the road, in railroad cars, hotel rooms, and the theater is no education at all. She sends them to a boarding school while she and Terry continue performing. The children are miserable, so they eventually reunite and perform happily as the five Donahues until trouble besets the troupe. There are clichéd scenes in which one son pursues women and booze and the other son decides he would rather be a priest. Katy stays with the act, though she does fall in love.

The backstage story was more interesting than the film. The original screenwriter died unexpectedly of a heart attack on August 28, 1952, at the age of fifty-one. Immediately I. A. L. Diamond was handed the job of rewriting the screenplay, a decision producer Sol Siegel shot down. He did not feel Diamond was ready for such a rewrite, but Zanuck let him try.

By this time a decision had been reached to hire Robert Wagner as Tim (ultimately the part went to Donald O'Connor), then the young actor was given the odd role of singing the song "Heat Wave" before entering the military and dying in World War II. Not only was the idea of even the most skilled male singing the erotically charged "Heat Wave" a ridiculous one, the movie required a happy ending, if only for the last moment on screen. No one could die; all the characters had to go their separate ways, find the lives they wished to lead, and then return for a stirring show business finale.

Zanuck telephoned Henry and Phoebe Ephron, skilled writers who thought the story idea was terrible and did not particularly care for Zanuck, but were delighted to do the rewrite, since that was how they earned their living. What they did not expect was that Irving Berlin was a Monroe groupie, and his lusts required a change in plans.

Henry Ephron quoted Zanuck as saying, "This is a crazy story, but I'll cut it as much as I can. It gives me a headache to tell it. Berlin had dinner at Joe Schenck's, and on Schenck's piano is the calendar picture of Marilyn, and Berlin has a hard-on for Marilyn. Excuse me, Phoebe. He wants her in the picture."

Zanuck explained that he realized that there was no way Marilyn Monroe would look like the fourth child of Dan Dailey and Ethel Merman, so he decided that the writers should make her Donald O'Connor's girl friend, of whom the family doesn't approve. He then added ". . . and Berlin wants her to sing 'Heat Wave.' I don't want to be around when Merman hears that news."

That afternoon the couple who would prepare the final screenplay met with Marilyn in what was called a musician's bungalow on the Fox lot. It was equipped with a couch and a piano so the musician could work alone, with a singer, or with a songwriter. However, as Henry Ephron described it in his book *We Thought We Could Do Anything*, "The place looked like a cubicle in a whore house. Marilyn's sweater was pinned, a few buttons were missing. Her shirt could have stood a trip to the cleaners, her hair, a trip to the beauty parlor. She didn't even bother with 'Hello.' She just said, 'Don't make me Donald O'Connor's girl. I could eat him for breakfast.'"

Henry explained that, as currently considered, the relationship would not work out. The character would use O'Connor to get into show business and they break up after he helps her. However, nothing else was certain, because they had just learned of the change.

"That crazy Schenck called me at two in the morning," Marilyn told the Ephrons. "And then he put Berlin on the phone. Berlin wants me to sing 'Heat Wave.'"

With Marilyn added and the script undergoing radical change, the casting resulted in performances that ranged from the bizarre to the sublime. Steve was played by Johnnie Ray, a popular singer of the day who was apparently cast to guarantee that his fans would turn out. Ray had the appearance of a man with a dazzling smile on a face so perpetually happy that it seemed to have been the result of anything from drugs to a clunk on the head with a soft mallet. His specialty was ballads, given the unique sound that came from his working his lower jaw from left to right as though it had been hinged incorrectly. He never seems to be a part of the family as the story unfolded on the screen, and his quitting the family act to study for the priesthood (the story, ending during World War II, finds him a chaplain) seems no more unlikely than the idea that he had been a traveling performer.

The other two children in the troupe are played by Mitzi Gaynor and Donald O'Connor, two brilliant singer/dancers who, along with their "mother," Ethel Merman, dominate the screen whenever they perform. O'Connor's character, Tim, leaves the act in search of women and booze, eventually falling in love with Vicky, a rising young singer/dancer played by Marilyn Monroe, the character having been added to the script by the

Ephrons in order to placate Irving Berlin. Ultimately Tim, Katy, and Vicky form an act together, Katy also falling in love with singer/songwriter Charley Gibbs (Hugh O'Brien). The act causes an estrangement among Tim, Molly, and Vicky, who seems to be stealing Molly's material, such as the production number "Heat Wave." Tim joins the Navy; Katy unites Molly and Vicky; and Terry (well played by Dan Dailey), who quits the act while Katy and Molly work together, finds a reunited family gathered at the old Hippodrome Theater, where they are part of a benefit for the Actors' Fund. Naturally the entire family, including Vicky, sings the title song, "There's No Business Like Show Business."

Perhaps there would have been a more positive reaction to the film had the Vicky character not been added. Marilyn Monroe was given four songs: "After You Get What You Want You Don't Want It"; "Heat Wave" (which she performs in a strapless bikini top over an open flared skirt and wearing an exotic headdress); "A Man Chooses a Girl"; and "Lazy," along with the title production number. It was *Lazy* that revealed the tremendous limitations Monroe had as a singer/dancer, since she performed with O'Connor and Gaynor, among the most brilliant performers of their generation.

The filming for "Lazy" was scheduled for nine o'clock in the morning, a time when everyone would be fresh and able to tackle a physically demanding choreography. Although Monroe's part required her to pose on the couch while Gaynor and O'Connor dance all around, then get up and say just two words—"Wrong number"—she could not drag herself to the set until six hours later. There were a reported fifty failed takes with the only mistakes made by Monroe. Then director Walter Lang who, with his cinematographer Leon Shamroy, had given Monroe the screen test that earned her her first contract with Fox, no longer had compassion for the nervousness of a now-experienced actress. Fortunately they also understood her oddities. She was told that the way to look at the scene they were shooting was to think of herself as a bubble which, when she rises from the couch to do her line, simply bursts. Two takes later the number was perfect and they could finally stop.

While the dancing was weak, the singing was actually far superior to what anyone had expected, so much so that there were rumors that Marilyn had a voice double. That rumor was reinforced when Decca Records released a cast album in 1954 with all of Marilyn's songs from the film performed by Dolores Gray, a Broadway star. It was assumed that Gray had also handled the singing for the film, but the truth was that Marilyn had just signed a contract with RCA prior to the decision to make the Decca release. There would be an album with Marilyn singing all the songs as well as "You'd Be Surprised," sung by Dan Dailey in the movie.

The problem of Marilyn's arriving late was more significant than anyone realized. Some biographers have believed her critics in the industry who felt she either was intensely shy, with an extreme performance anxiety, or, as Marilyn seemed to believe, was seeking to show the power that Norma Jean had previously been denied when growing up. The truth was much more disconcerting. The sleeping pills and occasional other drugs she took regularly were having adverse reactions. She had great difficulty getting out of bed on time to prepare for work, and even more difficulty getting her mind focused. Had the times been different, had the studio heads not looked upon pharmaceuticals as the answers to their desire to work from dawn to dusk while keeping the talent and support personnel rested, and had addiction been fully understood, Marilyn and many others would have been placed in rehab. They would have been weaned from the medication, given a more rational shooting schedule, and ultimately proven productive. Instead, Marilyn was already starting the decline that would eventually culminate in her death.

"Heat Wave," a song that would become as closely associated with Marilyn as "Diamonds Are a Girl's Best Friend," involved elaborate choreography handled by Jack Cole, whom Marilyn personally requested for the number. Robert Alton was the choreographer for the rest of the movie and the credited choreographer on the film. He was also the original choreographer for "Heat Wave," developing the number over a month-long period when he gathered the four male dancers who would work with Monroe, along with a stand-in for her. They practiced on a large rehearsal studio on the Fox lot, and when it was exactly the way Alton desired, Monroe was brought in to watch.

Monroe liked the number but did not like the choreography. She wanted something edgier, an "in-your-face" approach she had enjoyed from Cole. The studio agreed to her request to use Cole for the number, and those involved later felt she was right about the switch. The problem was that Cole liked to insert commentary and stretch the limits of propriety, a fact that made Joe DiMaggio livid.

Bosley Crowther of the *New York Times* made the most pointed comment: "When it comes to spreading talent, Miss Gaynor has the jump on Miss Monroe, whose wriggling and squirming to 'Heat Wave' and 'Lazy' are embarrassing to behold."

Also problematic was that Cole liked to add small asides that gave a number sexual innuendo not in the original script. This was certainly the case with "Heat Wave." Marilyn, moving her hands around her breasts, notes that "Moderately high barometric pressure will cover the, er, north, east and . . ." Then the four dancers ask, "Where else?"

Marilyn jerks her body forward in an obviously sexual gesture and says, "The Deep South!" And if anyone doesn't understand, she pushes her skirt between her legs that are spread apart and says, "Hot and humid nights can be expected."

Joe was visiting the set when Marilyn practiced the number, and he was furious with what she was doing. His wife was going to appear on the screen, larger than life, challenging every movie-going man in America to have sex with her.

The action, though shocking for the day, was as ridiculous as Crowther found it. In addition, the stress between the DiMaggios was as much about Joe as any actions of Marilyn's.

Marilyn had taken Phoebe Ephron aside after they met. She explained that every night when she went home, the house was loaded with men. They were playing cards, smoking, calling their bookies, and drinking. She said that Joe would greet her with a kiss on the cheek and then return to the card game.

Phoebe said that she should walk in the house, pull down Joe's zipper, climb on his lap, and shout to the men that everyone had to clear out of the house. It is not known how serious either woman might have been about the "solution" to Joe's inappropriate socializing, but Marilyn responded that she couldn't shout. She might hurt her singing voice. (Phoebe had no idea that the couple would soon be living on separate floors as they raced toward divorce. For the moment, the marriage was obviously strained and far from the storybook romance the press portrayed.)

None of this mattered to Marilyn's career. She had been promised the lead in the film version of the successful Broadway show about adultery, *The Seven Year Itch*, as a compromise in the fight over the rejected *The Girl in Pink Tights*. Irving Berlin may have wanted her in *There's No Business Like Show Business*, but her acceptance was part of the negotiations when her contract had been up for renewal. She was also to be given a signing bonus for the film of $100,000, though the money was never fully delivered.

It was also during the period of intense turmoil in April 1954 that Marilyn agreed to write her life story, or at least to create a life story for the press and public. This was not tied directly to her Fox negotiations or the back-to-back movies she would be making for them.

Celebrity autobiographies were popular in the 1950s, and with Marilyn being one of the biggest box-office attractions in the world, it was thought hers could be quite successful. She knew the life she had lived, and Sid Skolsky knew the life she needed to claim she had lived in order to make a more dramatic telling. However, ultimately the work completed by Hecht and the work credited to Hecht were not entirely the same.

The Newberry Library in Chicago has Ben Hecht's archives, and the Hecht writing they have in their collection is different from the material released in serial form in 1954 and in its first book form twenty years later after both Hecht and Monroe were dead. As near as can be determined, Hecht worked with Marilyn, preparing a first draft of her autobiography in April. She was allegedly deeply moved by the writing and felt it represented her story. However, what eventually was released as *My Story*, appearing in different editions—most recently in one with Milton Greene photographs that have been brilliantly restored by his son, Josh—seems to be an amalgam.

The book may be what was eventually written by Ben Hecht. Successful writers rewrite many times, often changing details as they find mistakes or have mistakes pointed out to them before the final pre-publication edit. It may also have been a combination of Hecht material along with material prepared by Sid Skolsky, working with Marilyn to help her career. There may also have been some unauthorized rewriting, probably by Hecht's agent, Jacques Chamburn.

The material for the book was created between 1951 and 1952, though the period of the interviews with Hecht was only a matter of days. Then the autobiography was sold to the *Empire News* of London, England, which serialized and syndicated it from May to August of 1954. None of this was done with the advance knowledge or approval of either Hecht or Monroe, and neither party read what was used prior to its appearance.

The book as it appeared is largely the Norma Jean/Marilyn Monroe-myth that has dominated stories about her over the years. It has been alleged that she actually was ready to tell most of the truth about her life. She called people truly familiar with her past, such as Lucille Ryman Carroll, and told them to be free with information about her past when Ben Hecht called. Presumably this included the days during which she prostituted herself on Hollywood and Sunset boulevards.

The fact that Marilyn wanted Hecht to have access to her past did not mean that she expected to have her past revealed. If anything, the knowledge would give the writer a better understanding of the full dynamic of his subject, even though the final work might be incomplete.

The times were different in the early 1950s. It was one thing to know the "dirty little secrets" of a high-profile entertainer, politician, or other individual in the public eye. It was quite a different matter to reveal it to the public.

The unwritten code of conduct for members of the media lasted until Richard Nixon's presidency, when the press realized that the man holding the highest office in the nation was also dishonest. Prior to that time, the media wanted access so the reporters and photographers could enhance their careers with their "exclusive" and "intimate" stories. If they had to ignore the fact that the "joyous" marriage of a popular pair of movie stars had been ordered by the studio heads to keep anyone from realizing that one or both had a same-sex orientation, so be it. Reporters knew not only that Franklin Roosevelt had a mistress, but that she was present at his death and had to be whisked out of the house before Eleanor was brought to see her husband. Walter Winchell discovered a rising Democratic senator sneaking out of a single woman's apartment during a Los Angeles convention, but when he called in the item to his New York editor, he was told, "We can't print that. Senator [Jack] Kennedy's a married man!"

(AP reporter and columnist Jim Bacon, an acquaintance of both Monroe and Jack Kennedy, later joked that it was only when the president was doing to the country what Jack Kennedy did to women that the members of the media felt they had to start covering the stories.)

The most important aspect of the story of the Hecht book is that it was deemed a legitimate project in the first place. The hiring of the author was validation of everything Marilyn had achieved. More important, as mixed as the reaction to *There's No Business Like Show Business* might have been, when she took over the role of "The Girl" (no name was ever used) in the screen adaptation of *The Seven Year Itch*, she was about to prove her skills as a comedienne—as well as her indifference to the desires of her soon-to-be ex-husband.

Forty-five

The Seven Year Itch

Marilyn Monroe is what most people remember about *The Seven Year Itch*. She was not the kind of girl you would bring home to your wife.

Marilyn told me right away that she didn't ever wear a brassiere. She needn't have mentioned it. I had no personal or professional objection.

—Director Billy Wilder, as quoted
in *Nobody's Perfect*

⚘

Marilyn had been sick since she returned from Korea. She had picked up a virus and then suffered from bronchitis. She was chronically fatigued, and the combination of sleeping pills and stimulants to assure a full night's sleep and a full day's work was proving destructive. She was getting no rest, only unconsciousness. She was often confused on the set, late from the inability to function, and certain, like most abusers, that more drugs could solve the problem. The fact that she was far from unique—Judy Garland would die from a similar regimen, and numerous studio employees, from actors to crew members to the heads of the studios, were plagued with problems from similar abuse—did not make her actions acceptable.

Marilyn and Joe were at odds, but Marilyn attempted to be professional, ignoring her domestic situation as much as she could and working with Natasha at night to master her lines. This meant more stress, less rest, and temporary loss of short-term memory. She could master her lines with Natasha only to have them gone from memory by morning.

Marilyn was reported to have collapsed three separate times during the filming of *There's No Business Like Show Business*, creating delays that ultimately caused the picture to be too expensive to break even during its first American run. Some thought she was faking illness to further control her contract. Others recognized she was ill from something, but felt there was too much money invested in her to not go ahead with the next picture, *The Seven Year Itch*, and demand that she work like everyone else.

Marilyn may have been at odds with Darryl Zanuck and Fox, but she recognized that her career needed a hit movie. The filming was to start in August 1954 with a planned release for the following year: two years after her last hit movie, and the longest period between movie releases since her career had begun. This also meant that there was a chance that her fan base, one that had grown steadily from the time she had electrified the screen with her presence in her first minor roles, might dwindle. Just as she had replaced Betty Grable, there was always a resident blonde waiting to be the next big star. There were also more serious issues of concern that are rarely discussed, and they had to do with Charles Feldman's ambitions apart from his desire to represent Monroe.

To understand the shock over the success of George Axelrod's Broadway play *The Seven Year Itch*, one must understand the times in which it was first mounted. World War II ended with a combination of celebratory glee, radical social change, and great fear. Hundreds of thousands of men exchanged their military uniforms for tuxedos, taking advantage of the GI Bill to get married, get an education, and buy what was often a low-priced tract home in a new suburban development. Women had gained independence over the social strictures of the pre-war era. They had been earning high incomes in war plants often so far from home that they routinely rented their own apartments, no longer feeling they had to live with their parents until marriage. Maternity ward demand exploded and cities began planning for building new schools as the baby boom of 1946 heralded an unprecedented number of births.

The rise in labor unions, the conversion from wartime manufacturing to the making and selling of products ranging from new cars to kitchen appliances, the demand for steel and rubber, and even a new era of pharmaceutical treatment gave Americans the highest standard of living in the world. At the same time, there was a fear of the little-understood and rarely well-defined Communist menace. Russia seemed to be growing ever more powerful, crushing revolts in Hungary and other Soviet-bloc countries. Even the atomic bomb, which briefly made the U.S. government the world's most feared, was soon being tested by the Soviet Union.

The idea that another war might be inevitable, this time affecting mainland United States, led to the creation of a civil defense program. The reinforced basements of theaters, civic buildings, and other locations deemed effective were filled with food, water, cots, blankets, first aid kits, and other survival needs. Communities installed air raid sirens, which they tested once a week. Construction companies and do-it-yourselfers began installing home bomb shelters the way some people installed in-ground swimming pools. Elementary school children debated the ethics of allowing neighbors to come into the shelter during a time of crisis vs. leaving them outside, reinforcing the family's survival by stocking .22-caliber rifles with extra ammunition in the shelters. And everywhere there was duck and cover, a concept developed by government officials trying to avert public panic during an attack.

Duck and cover as a defense against nuclear attack was so patently ridiculous that it shows the public's desperation for any sense of safety. The idea was simple and actually a variation of a technique for surviving the tornados prevalent in the Midwest. First the air raid siren would sound (or some sort of irritating warning alarm within the schools). Children fortunate enough to be near a solid wall away from glass windows, doors, and skylights, would kneel down facing the wall. Other children would hurry under their desks. Then they would kneel, duck their heads, and cover their necks with their arms—duck and cover.

As would be explained both verbally and in a number of ridiculously humorous (in hindsight) public service television messages, the bomb would explode and everyone caught outside—or, presumably, still sitting upright at one's desk—would be killed or vaporized or whatever horror of the damned would occur. Those who were kneeling beneath their desks, heads down, arms over their neck, would live to triumph over the Communist Menace. More important, Russian schoolchildren did not know about duck and cover, assuring their destruction by the bombs our military would be sending in retaliation.

Even the development of the interstate highway system, a project started by President Dwight D. Eisenhower, the war hero general who succeeded Harry Truman in 1952, was meant for war footing. The ease of travel increased car sales, brought regional music to the nation, and changed housing patterns, yet its original and primary purpose was the rapid transport of soldiers and supplies from one coast to the other.

Religious bigotry was extensive during this era. Each denomination had proponents who were convinced that their theology was the only true theology. The popular magazines of the day, such as *Reader's Digest*, ran articles on "Why I Am Proud to Be a Baptist" or "Why I Am Proud to Be a Lutheran" or "Why I Am Proud to Be a Catholic." It was an era of "my God can beat your God," and in many parts of the nation the schism was broken down further by language and race within a particular faith.

But always the family—or at least the white, middle-income family with working father commuting by light rail, bus, or car; stay-at-home mother; and two to four children—was what mattered. They were the backbone of American society, linked lovingly through all the rites of passage: marriage, birth, adulthood, new generations, and death.

So what was one of the most successful plays of the season about? Adultery! And this was a play that would run three years and make large sums of money for playwright George Axelrod and the show's backers in a time of rising conservatism and "family values." It was no wonder it was eyed for a screen adaptation, even though great care had to be taken to avoid offending middle America.

The story is simple. It is summer in New York. Air conditioning, though not new, is expensive, and not found in every building, or even in every office or living quarters within a particular building. Families regularly escape to the beaches both in New York and nearby New England states. Richard Sherman, who lives with his wife, Helen, and son, Ricky, in an air-conditioned Manhattan apartment, sends his family to the cooler clime of Maine for a two-week vacation. The apartment is a rather odd one in that it had originally had larger units. One of the building owners had divided the existing apartments so there would be more tenants, but some of the suites, including the one in which the Shermans live, have a sealed access door that once led to other rooms. Now the other rooms are smaller apartments, the reason the access has been sealed.

Richard Sherman is a man who leads a rather odd, lonely existence under normal circumstances. He works for a paperback book publishing company where he designs lurid covers for classic literature. His imagination is always focused on sex and violence as it can be used to create yet another cover.

Adding to Richard's problems is the "seven year itch," a condition that (according to the play and, later, the film) afflicts all men in the seventh year of married life. This is when a normal, healthy man, regardless of how happily married he may be, biologically has to stray. And to help along this fact of life is The Girl (she is never otherwise named in the play or the movie, for the reason that George Axelrod could never think of a name he felt was right), a model, an actress in commercials, and the tenant of an apartment immediately above Richard's. The Girl not only lacks air conditioning, she finds a way to open the previously sealed access door so she can walk down into the Sherman apartment whenever she wishes. She is naïve, sexy, too hot to want to sleep without air conditioning (she cools her undergarments in the refrigerator so they are more comfortable to wear), and desiring companionship. He is suddenly alone and faced with a younger, very attractive woman who seems to be a bit of a libertine.

The appeal of The Girl is not just that she is young and single. Youth alone would not be enough to arouse the seven year itch. Instead, she is a sharp contrast to Sherman's wife and bratty son: a wacky free spirit who has a naïve sophistication, such as when she recognizes that the music Richard enjoys is classical "because there's no vocal." She is a type of young woman he never dated when single, who probably never considered guys like him, and suddenly he is the available older sophisticate in whom she is interested.

The play's story line can be summed up as: Richard Sherman meets The Girl. Richard Sherman beds The Girl after a series of clumsy seduction efforts. Richard Sherman feels overwhelming guilt for cheating on his wife. Richard Sherman lets The Girl have the use of his suite while he flees to Maine to spend the rest of the vacation time with Helen and his son.

From opening night—when the wealthy, sophisticated audience laughed continuously despite the pseudo-sophistication that normally caused them to have a reserved demeanor noted by the critics—until Holly-

440

wood knocked on the playwright's door, a play about adultery dominated Broadway. The problem was that Broadway was a medium for the sophisticated, and a play was only performed in theaters, where there was a large draw of individuals who would not be offended. A movie was presumably family fare. Movies could be filled with violence, with sex, with foul language—but there could not be a comedy in which the hero commits adultery. It just wasn't done.

Charles Feldman had fallen in love with *The Seven Year Itch*, in part because he was certain Marilyn Monroe would be perfect as The Girl. Tom Ewell (as Richard Sherman) and Vanessa Brown (The Girl) starred on Broadway, but only Ewell, then a rising comic actor, would reprise his role in the movie.

Feldman believed he needed several parts to create an effective package. He wanted Monroe to star and he wanted Billy Wilder to co-produce with him, as well as direct and co-write the screenplay. This meant he needed Twentieth Century-Fox as the production company, despite the fact that Skouras was initially hostile to the project. He eventually got what he desired, though he was paid less money for putting the package together than he would have been had he gone to Warner's or one of the other studios, using one of their contract actresses.

Monroe had extremely mixed feelings about *The Seven Year Itch*. This was another sexy blonde role, at a time when she had made clear that she wanted to broaden her experience by taking radically different parts. She also was aware of the potential conflict of interest that existed with Feldman acting as both her manager and the producer. She did not know what would happen if there were a situation in which the best interests of the actress and the producer were in opposition. Would he stand up for his client before defending his career interest? And did she want to be in a position where she might learn the potentially unwelcome answer to that question?

Marilyn tried to discuss her concerns with DiMaggio, but Joe was of no help. He saw that Feldman had given Marilyn opportunities, a script, and a fee that were among the best she had received to date. Feldman might be advancing his own career, but he did not seem to be doing so at his client's expense.

The problem for Monroe was that, to Joe, everything came down to money. Acting was like playing in a sport. You played for whoever gave you the most money, and you did so wherever they wanted you. You might want to play third base, but if the person signing your paycheck wanted you on first, that's where you went. Dreams were secondary in the fleeting fields of sports (or entertainment) stardom. You performed for the highest bidder for your talents.

Marilyn stopped arguing. It was a good script, and would be a funny movie. Besides, she knew that the business she was developing with Milton Greene would eventually change her working life.

The one seeming eccentricity Monroe had developed during this time was to look upon "Marilyn Monroe" as an almost fully realized person, though apart from her "real" self, Norma Jean. She was known to look at a script and talk about what Marilyn Monroe would do and what would be inappropriate for Marilyn Monroe to do. Yet even as she defined the actress she had created, her work on the set made some co-workers, especially Billy Wilder, uncomfortable. As Wilder later told Maurice Zolotow,

> She can't remember a line. She never hits the groove the first time. I've directed many pictures, and when you say "Action" an actor will do some-thing—anything—even if it's the wrong thing, it's instinctive with an actor to do this. Not Marilyn. It takes her twenty seconds to say a line or make a move, the first two or three lines, sometimes, she can go on and on, even if it's a long speech. She doesn't seem to get tired. She'll do take after take. She poops out the other actors. But Marilyn blooms as the day goes on, and she's at her best in the late afternoon when the other actors are dropping like flies.

The Motion Picture Production Code made clear that self-censoring was critical. In the case of *The Seven Year Itch*, Billy Wilder decided to write the script so that, while Richard Sherman never goes to bed with The Girl, he feels intense guilt for even thinking about it.

Wilder later told of Axelrod's frustration during an interview with Charlotte Chandler: "Axelrod couldn't believe what was happening to his play. On Broadway, the guy has an affair with the girl upstairs, but in the picture, he only gets to imagine how it would be to go to bed with Marilyn Monroe. And just the *idea* of going to bed with her has to terrify him, or it won't get past the censors."

George Axelrod talked with Marilyn about how she viewed his script, and she told him the part that reflected her own feelings. It comes near the end of Scene 85 where Richard says, "Let's face it—no pretty girl in her right mind wants me. She wants Gregory Peck . . ." To which Marilyn, as The Girl, replies:

> How do you know what a pretty girl wants? . . . You think every pretty girl is a dope. You think that a girl goes to a party and there is some guy—a great big hunk in a fancy striped vest, strutting around like a tiger—giving you that "I'm so handsome, you can't resist me" look—and from this she is supposed to fall flat on her face. Well, she doesn't fall flat on her face. But there's another guy in the room . . . way over in the corner . . . maybe he's kind of nervous and shy and perspiring a little . . . First you look past him, but then you sort of sense that he is gentle and kind and worried, that he'll be tender with you and nice and sweet, and that's what's really exciting!

The basic structure for both the movie and the play has Richard Sherman sending his wife, Helen, and son, Ricky, to Maine to escape New York's heat. This is viewed as typical, hundreds of husbands doing the same thing, all of them vowing to behave, neither drinking, nor smoking, nor chasing women during the separation. But Richard Sherman is different, his imagination stoked by his work as the designer of lurid covers, he begins having Walter Mitty–type fantasy adventures from the moment he invites his new neighbor, The Girl, for a drink.

The action quickly moves to sophisticated slapstick and failed seduction. Sherman wants to bed the twenty-two-year-old model and attributes to her a sophistication that she does not truly possess. He makes martinis, puts on a recording of Rachmaninoff's *Second Piano Concerto*, and shares her gift of champagne and potato chips. Then they move to the piano in his apartment where they play *Chopsticks* and he makes a pass so clumsy that they fall off the bench; however, neither mentions what has happened. (Allegedly the choice of music was not the result of how the play was written but Wilder's desire to emulate a part of David Lean's film *Brief Encounter* that utilized the same piece.)

The guilt leads to a dream sequence in which The Girl is wearing a dress that reveals every curve of her figure and Sherman is a sophisticate who plays the Rachmaninoff piece himself while she says, "It shakes me, it quakes me, it makes me feel goose-pimply all over," at which time he stops playing and announces, "Now I'm going to take you in my arms and kiss you, very quickly and very hard."

The comic sensibility of Tom Ewell, the Broadway star, did not impress director Wilder. Ewell was just coming into his own as an actor, and the skills needed for Broadway—which did not yet have sophisticated sound equipment—included an overly loud, exaggerated speaking style coupled with often bold gestures that seemed natural to the distant audience but looked and sounded ridiculous on film. There was a question in Wilder's mind as to whether the stage actor could learn to convey emotion through subtlety of expression in a nuanced comedy of this type.

ℰ

Wilder's concerns seemed justified, at least to the reviewer for the Los Angeles *Examiner*, who wrote, "*The Seven Year Itch* is as merry a romp as ever screened—up to a point. Never has Marilyn the Marvelous been so well photographed, wonderfully dressed, nor presented as such an understanding young comedienne. She truly is a knockout. And that's the trouble, even as in the film. Because, excellent and funny actor though he is, Tom Ewell, next to her, presents all the sex appeal of a wet sandwich."

ℰ

Billy Wilder wanted to use a then-little known actor for the film role of Richard Sherman. The actor he desired had the deadpan face of a hound dog, excellent comic timing, and would have been quite believable as an Everyman with an overactive imagination who has a chance at the first, and probably last, true romantic adventure of his life. This was Walter Matthau who, working with actress Gena Rowlands, did a black-and-white screen test on June 15, 1954. Wilder, working from the unfinished screenplay, had Matthau do the scene in which The Girl first comes into his apartment. (Wilder liked to start filming when the script was approximately two-thirds complete so he could fine-tune the ending based on how the actors developed their characters in the early part of the movie.) Matthau was brilliant. However, Twentieth Century-Fox executives did not want to take a chance on an unknown, fearing he would lack box-office draw no matter how brilliantly he might perform on the screen. A decade later Wilder cast Mat-

444

thau opposite Jack Lemmon in *The Fortune Cookie,* and Matthau was a major star the rest of his career.

Ewell was a second choice, a man who knew the part and had name recognition but lacked the skills for the screen. Billy Wilder later commented during an interview with author Cameron Crowe, "He wasn't a bad actor. He was Tom Ewell. But the wrong casting, the wrong actor . . . Plus I didn't have the scene I *wanted.* All I needed was a hairpin . . . second act, third act . . . the maid finds the pin in Tom Ewell's bed. And you know then that they have committed the act."

The overall plot follows Richard Sherman going to his office and discovering that his feelings for The Girl are normal. He reads about the "urge curve" that afflicts middle-aged men (he is thirty-eight), an estimated 91.8 percent of all married men developing the seven year itch during the summer months. This leads to The Girl, who experienced his clumsy attempt at lecherous behavior, telling the nation from her influential position as the Dazzledent Toothpaste girl.

Richard Sherman tries to stay away from his neighbor, but then convinces himself that Helen is having her own affair with Tom MacKenzie, a writer who was also on the train Helen and Ricky took to Maine. MacKenzie routinely takes the train between Manhattan and Maine, and Sherman is certain that Tom will be spending his visits to Maine with Helen.

Sherman takes The Girl to see the movie *The Creature from the Black Lagoon.* They kiss briefly outside the theater, then return for the night to his air-conditioned apartment. She sleeps in his bed; he sleeps on the couch. For the film, nothing else happens, though Sherman dreams that his wife comes home, discovers him with The Girl, and shoots him for having an affair.

The next morning The Girl tells Sherman that, though he might be a dull man unlike his fantasies, she thinks his kindness makes him more exciting than vain, handsome men. Sherman takes heart. When the object of one of his fantasies, writer Tom MacKenzie, comes by the apartment as a favor for Ricky (Sherman's son has left a beloved toy paddle behind, and since Richard is staying in the city and Tom is commuting, he asks to take the toy back to Helen and Ricky in Maine), an enraged Richard slugs him, then leaves The Girl in the apartment and goes to be with his family.

The plot was simple. The fantasies were what made the movie both challenging and a delight to see. Some were left in the film. Some were cut. For example, there is a scene in Richard's fantasy when he and The Girl have returned from the movie. She had shown Richard how she presented her Dazzledent Toothpaste ad on television (this was an era when the commercials were done live so the model could change what she said, as she did in the fantasy sequences) and told him about a time when she got her toe caught in a bathtub faucet. Thinking about The Girl, naked with her toe caught, Richard's fantasy evolves into a scene in which she is in the bathtub and an elderly plumber is in the room trying to free her. She says to him, "Then suddenly he turned on me, his eyes bulging. He was frothing at the mouth, just like the Creature from the Black Lagoon!"

A longer version of the scene was actually shot and shown in Europe, but fear of censors kept it from the American version. The scene continues with the plumber, startled by what he is hearing, dropping his wrench in the water between her legs. He immediately starts groping for it, saying, "I'm sorry" as he appears to have accidentally touched her in an intimate manner. She is unfazed, saying, "That's all right."

The next scene that was shot has the plumber riding the subway and telling another rider that Richard Sherman molested The Girl. Then, when Sherman enters a vegetarian restaurant, two of the servers start talking about him.

The story (in Sherman's fantasy) is spread both on television, by The Girl, and by the rumor mill throughout New York. The next scene is at Yankee Stadium where filming was done during a game using a long lens so no one would notice. Then close-ups and dialogue were added in New York. The scene looks typical of what is viewed at many games, where there is a discussion of what type of pitch the catcher wants to use to strike out the batter. This time, the pitcher, Eddie Lopat, throws a ball to catcher Yogi Berra, who calls time, walks to the mound, takes off his mask, and begins telling Lopat about Richard Sherman "attacking" The Girl when they were on the piano bench together. Lopat is not surprised: "The guy's got the seven year itch."

The umpire walks to the mound and says he heard about the incident when riding the subway. He wants to know who the girl is. Berra replies, "I don't know her name, but she's on the Dazzledent program. The one with the teeth . . . on television."

The most memorable aspect of *The Seven Year Itch* was not the innuendo or the delightful fantasy scenes. Instead it was a photograph taken by Sam Shaw, a man previously unconnected with Monroe.

The studios, including Fox, used staff and freelance still photographers to take pictures during the making of a movie. These stills were used in a variety of ways. Some were provided to each movie theater along with posters when they were advertising and showing the movie being promoted. The theaters all had outside display cases in which the poster would be placed, surrounded by stills, sometimes in small frames beneath the poster and sometimes tacked to the board holding the poster. They were a popular way to draw customers in to the theater to see the film.

Some photographs were included in press kits sent to newspapers throughout the country in hopes that they would accompany reviews and/ or be used as stand-alone images with a caption related to the actors. They also might be used in carefully placed stories telling about the behind-the-scenes making of the movie and the enthusiasm of the cast for the picture.

Sam Shaw wanted to create one image that would help sell the concept of the movie. The image had to have a lighthearted sexual flavor to it, and the only moment when that was evident was one that took place as Sherman and The Girl were walking back to their apartment building after seeing the movie *The Creature from the Black Lagoon*. The Girl walks across a sidewalk grate under which a subway train is roaring through. It is a hot night, and, though the reality of subway grates is that any air that might have risen up from below would have been hot, for the movie it was supposed to be a cool breeze.

The breeze catches The Girl's skirt, blowing it up and cooling her off. The incident delights Sherman, who enjoys the view as The Girl laughingly says, "Don't you wish you could wear skirts? I feel sorry for you men in your hot pants."

The scene was retained though not the dialogue. The movie censors felt the double entendre was inappropriate for the audience. The scene was also perfect for Shaw's idea for a single photo to draw a viewing audience, a photo Billy Wilder came to call his two-panty shot.

The two-panty shot was originally supposed to be handled quietly, with only the cast and crew present. The exterior of the Trans-Lux Theater was used for the movie house Richard and The Girl were exiting, and as they approached the intersection of Lexington Avenue and Fifty-Second Street, there was a grating over a subway tunnel. Each time one of the trains went by, a blast of air hit the street and would cause her dress to billow.

The original photograph was to be taken straight—no special effects, no audience, nothing but an early-morning shoot with Marilyn walking over a real subway grate. The technology available for location shooting did not allow for the camera crew to try to have a controllable blast of wind. However, there seemed no concern because the unit production manager had walked the same area at two o'clock in the morning and found it deserted. He contacted the manager of the Trans-Lux and explained that they wanted to shoot a scene near the theater, showing the front, and that they would do it at the same early-morning hour since no one would be around.

Billy Wilder was pleased with the location choice and left word with everyone involved with the scene to keep the location quiet. Instead, it was leaked to all the news media. The end result was an odd mix of chaos and, at the time, underused publicity.

First there were the fans. The Twentieth Century-Fox publicists claimed that ten thousand people were present for the shooting, though the police department, which was handling crowd control, stated that the number of spectators did not exceed two thousand.

Next came the newspaper and magazine photographers—between two and three hundred from throughout the world. New York not only had numerous English and foreign language daily and weekly newspapers, it was also the headquarters for many news and feature magazines, the U.S. base for much of the overseas press, and the location of stock agencies that syndicated images throughout the world. The majority of the cameras were large and used 4 × 5 inch film. Each had a holder attached for the flash bulb, an object that looked like a household 100-watt bulb and was either set into a reflector base or screwed into it. The light was brief but could illuminate the side of a building. There were also amateur photographers with either similar equipment or twin lens reflex cameras using roll film that was 2-1/4 × 2-1/4 inches.

The exploding flashbulbs gave off a tremendous amount of heat. The moment they were used, they had to be removed by hand and either tossed on the street, in a trashcan, or in the oversized gadget bag the photographers carried with them.

It was the lighting that resulted in the need for the precaution of two panties. The flash equipment illuminated the street, but Marilyn was concerned with the extremely bright arc lights that were needed for the cinematography. They were so powerful that Marilyn decided to check and see how her panties would look in the glare when she walked over the grate and her skirt blew up. She realized that they became translucent and everyone would see through them. The image was supposed to be risqué, but what Marilyn realized could be seen would result in the censors ordering the shot removed from the picture. That was when she put on a second pair of panties: Wilder's "two-panty shot."

Marilyn's efforts were genuine but the results were not what she expected. The moment she stood at a certain angle to the powerful arc lights, the viewer could see through *both* pairs of panties. Fortunately the scene was reshot in the studio so lighting and costume could be controlled. The potentially offending footage was cut and supposed to be stored with other material that had been cut. Instead, it was stolen by someone with access to the footage and is believed to still be in private hands.

ℰ∂

I was so stupid because we were looking for a representative ad. And it did not occur to me that this thing, where she's kind of trying to keep the dress down, that this is it! They copied it. They made little figurines and sold it. We had some noninteresting ad for the movie.

—Billy Wilder speaking to Cameron Crowe

ℰ∂

The noise was almost overwhelming as Wilder and his crew prepared for the scene. Marilyn stayed in the theater, the film started to roll, Marilyn and Tom walked out onto the sidewalk, and the crowd surged forward. There were barricades and police, but there were too many people for them to handle.

Surprisingly, the mob respected director Wilder, who had made an arrangement with the crowd. First, everyone had to stay behind the barricades, the credentialed press corps helping to keep the amateurs back as well. Then Wilder would shoot the scene with Tom and Marilyn on the subway grate. When he was done, the camera would be moved back, Marilyn would stay on the grate, and the amateurs would be allowed to step forward and take as many pictures as they desired. Everyone was happy, and Wilder got the scene he hoped to achieve, though not the way he wanted it.

A review of the film showed that the actors were obviously distracted by the fans. The sound equipment recorded whistles and cheers as well as the subway noise, and it was obvious that the dialogue was lost.

Today Wilder would probably arrange for the dialogue to be dubbed onto the film. This was not possible back then, both because the equipment was limited to duplicate the sound of the scene and also because Monroe did a terrible job of staying in character when dubbing only a few lines. The entire image would have to be reshot.

Careful notes, photographs, and sketches had been made of what the Trans-Lux looked like. Then the exterior, the subway grating, the stores, and the street were all duplicated at the studio. The subway was actually a stage over a wind tunnel, and there was a sliding top that was removed each time the wind from the passing subway train supposedly blew Marilyn's skirt. Marilyn wore tight panties, and the men who handled the technical arrangements each sought to work the top under the grate, enabling them to look straight up.

Adding to the sexual nature of the photograph was the costume designed for the scene. It was a fully pleated halter dress that had been specially prepared to imply The Girl's sexual excitement.

Costume designer William Travilla had studied Monroe's body shape and realized that the way her breasts hung allowed him to cut her tops lower than for other stars. The censors would not allow cleavage to be shown, but the ability to show some of her chest implied more than it revealed. Then he furthered the illusion by taking what was called a half-button ball and sewing it where the viewer would expect her nipples to be. This was a ball cut in half, then, in Marilyn's case, attached to the inside of her blouse or the top of her dress. Study the screen image closely and it is "obvious" that her nipples are hard, presumably from a constant state of sexual arousal. The truth was that the audience was seeing the effect of inside out buttons.

The full history of both the creation of the famous skirt-blowing scene for *The Seven Year Itch* and the beginning of the end of Marilyn's second marriage started on September 8, 1954, when Marilyn kissed Joe DiMaggio goodbye and took a night flight to Manhattan. He had no idea what was awaiting her or how the press was being manipulated. He did know that Natasha Lytess was going to be involved with the work and the publicity, and he was no longer tolerant of her presence. Joe made clear to Marilyn that if Natasha traveled with her, he was staying home.

Neither Monroe nor DiMaggio was telling the truth. Marilyn did take Lytess because she wanted her advice and because Marilyn was planning to make New York her base. She and Milton Greene would leave Hollywood behind. Greene originally planned on taking a book of photographs of Marilyn, but then she broached the issue of his being her producer and business partner.

Joe had no intention of staying in California without Marilyn if she would be doing something he might find embarrassing or inappropriate. Columnist Walter Winchell understood this about his friend, also realizing that Joe still wanted to maintain a low profile. However, Winchell's first loyalty was to his readers who would delight in a good story about the couple. That was why he telephoned DiMaggio, convincing him to meet the columnist in Toots Shor's. From there they would go to the subway location and Winchell would have the exclusive concerning any personal drama that unfolded.

Marilyn's New York trip was as much about publicity as it was getting the necessary scenes for Billy Wilder. She was first told to change the style of clothing she would wear when first arriving in New York.

Marilyn was keenly aware of fashion, and not the flamboyant outfits the studio used to sell her as a sex symbol. Any time she flew with Joe or went by herself to an event where she did not need to be the center of attention, she wore the latest style created by designer Christian Dior. During this period the designs were loose-fitting, downplaying the bustline. The expensive clothing was attractive, though neither sexy nor sensual. It was enormously popular with women like Marilyn who had the money and the need to be wearing the latest styles.

Twentieth Century-Fox had told Marilyn to leave Dior behind and wear a form-fitting woolen dress that clung to her body, revealing every curve. It was neither low-cut nor slightly outrageous in the manner of some of the outfits she wore when still posing for cheesecake images. The sensuality of the dress was subtle, yet no reporter seeing Marilyn could take his or her eyes off her. Once again, it was the type of publicity gimmick that Joe understood—and hated.

Marilyn arrived in New York for her first meeting with reporters and photographers at eight fifteen in the morning. She wore the dress the publicity department had approved, one of a style no one would suspect was not specifically chosen for comfort while traveling.

Newspapers were printed throughout the day in that era, the news being updated as often as every hour or two, depending upon the specific paper and any breaking story. Each edition would be noted in some way, often with stars added with each change (the features such as opinion columns, crosswords, and comics remained the same for the entire day). The one-star edition might feature overnight stories, while the five-star edition might have the closing stock market report. Publicity stunts were planned so they would get into as many editions and in as prominent a position in each edition as possible.

For example, to achieve prominence in Monday's first edition, a staged "event" would be held on a Sunday afternoon, a trick politicians often use to get front-page attention for an announcement that would otherwise be buried inside. A publicity stunt held early on a weekday morning would appear in papers before noon the same day, the images often continuing to be used through the evening finals. The ideal day had enough breaking news to warrant several editions, though always with enough newspaper space to keep repeating the stories and/or photos the publicist had orchestrated.

Harry Brand, director of publicity for Fox, was a master of the game. He knew that no matter how popular a box-office draw someone might be, most people, though more than willing to go to a movie in their free time, would not turn out to catch a glimpse of a star first thing in the morning on a work day.

The moment Marilyn's plane landed and she disembarked, everything was as choreographed as possible. As many as five hundred men and women who worked at Idlewild Airport formed what allegedly was a paid presence, a technique used by publicists for several years. (For example, Manhattan's Paramount Theater always had a contingent of professional teenage "swooners" in the crowd when the young Frank Sinatra appeared in the 1940s.) The truth about the numbers is uncertain and the pay was unnecessary. Every mechanic normally making certain that the aircraft were in top mechanical form before departing quietly left where they were working to see Marilyn. All flights into and out of Idlewild at that time ended up being delayed for an hour from the curiosity seekers alone. (This was not unusual. Most airport workers had a code to alert one another to the presence of a beautiful woman, whether movie star or "civilian." In Washington DC, for example, the seemingly innocent cry of "ramp check!" followed by a specific location, once, meant that the airport workers should check out a passing young woman.)

Adding to the Idlewild confusion were the other passengers on the various planes, family members and friends who wandered freely in those days of limited security concerns. Marilyn received extensive attention from people who were neither paid nor knew she would be arriving.

The 8:15 press conference was the first of six separate events throughout the first few hours that Monroe was in New York. Each corresponded to the news deadlines for various starred editions, wire service releases going across the country and throughout the world, radio, and television. The latter often relied upon still photographs as much or more than the motion picture film still in use. There might also be a movie clip of the event included in Pathé and other newsreels shown in movie theaters throughout the country over the next several days.

The multiple press conferences and photo sessions served a dual purpose. Not only were changing editions considered, Brand also knew that most reporters and their editors liked the idea of having exclusive information to offer their readers in a highly competitive market. New York City alone had dozens of newspapers in several different languages. By having a half dozen conferences, everyone got to ask a unique question of interest to their readers. It was also possible to have new material for each edition if a reporter chose to hang around for more than one conference. And if there was a breaking story that dominated a reporter's time, there would presumably be enough hours for him or her to return to also cover Marilyn.

The other reason for having Marilyn meet the press and pose for photographs was that it was free advertising. It would cost hundreds of thousands of dollars to place advertisements equal in physical space to the pages of pictures and text that were run as news stories. The reporters liked access because it helped them with their employers. The publicity department provided access because it assured coverage they could not afford to buy. The New York *Herald Tribune*, for example, ran front-page stories with both art (a photograph) and text each day for five days, a feat never previously accomplished by any entertainer. One of the columnists said that if the Russians sent a plane to buzz the landing area, it could drop to just five hundred feet above ground and none of the reporters would have bothered to look up.

Marilyn delighted in the mob scene, and though the bulk of the people present were just doing a job, they were also fans, and she was arguably the most glamorous actress of her day. They were thrilled as she talked with everyone while she was slowly being escorted to a waiting limousine. Then she talked more throughout the press conferences with newspaper reporters, a working luncheon with magazine writers and editors free to ask questions, and a final press conference held in the *New York Daily News*, the city's most popular tabloid and one of the largest-circulation daily newspapers in America. Its readership was mostly blue-collar, and attending movies was their primary recreation. Market studies had found that a story in the *Daily News* could fill as many theater seats as stories placed in all the other New York papers combined. Every studio thus felt it necessary to give this paper's staff special attention.

Ultimately, though, it was neither the arrival of Marilyn nor the shooting schedule in New York that mattered for either the press or DiMaggio. Instead it was the image that was to be taken at two-thirty in the morning of September 15.

Advance publicity assured a massive turnout of spectators and professional photographers. The street had been scouted to ensure it was quiet, that almost no one would happen by. Instead, there were almost two thousand people gathered to watch, and several hundred more with cameras. Many represented news services; others were amateurs fascinated with

Monroe. Almost no one was certain exactly what they were going to see that night, but if it involved Marilyn, they wanted to be there.

There were a few in the know, thanks to Harry Brand, and one of these was syndicated columnist Walter Winchell, the man who had convinced DiMaggio to come to New York. He was well aware of Joe's determination to guard his wife's modesty while she was working for a studio that exploited her sensuality.

The drama DiMaggio created seems ridiculous in hindsight. This was a man who was neither naïve about life nor lacking experience with the women who fought for stardom in show business. His first wife was an actress who gained his attention with her sexuality on and off the screen, yet when she was willing to take on the role of demure housewife and available lover, it had been Joe who lost interest. It had been Joe who chose to hang out with his friends, to play poker, to talk baseball—the same circumstances in which Marilyn now found herself.

Joe—when single—preferred showgirls to women in "proper" fields. He would delight in a scantily clad chorus girl who was somehow also supposed to represent his ideal, isolated, mothering, cooking, nurturing, silently enduring wife, yet he would not date a sales clerk, waitress, or businesswoman whose desires for a husband and family matched his own. And though Marilyn always maintained that the best sex she ever had was with Joe, she also indicated that Joe's obsession with watching television in the bedroom made their intimate times less frequent than with her other husbands and lovers.

Joe lied to himself and others, the studio taking advantage of the public fantasy of what was taking place between Joe and Marilyn. It was the reason why, long after friends and longtime acquaintances had tried to tell the press the truth, the media was still writing about the "love affair of the century."

DiMaggio had no idea what Marilyn would have to do at the early-morning filming on Lexington, though he assumed it was nothing that would interest him. He felt it was best to avoid being bored by staying in the St. Regis Hotel, where he had a room, instead of going on the street. Winchell would have none of that, though. He found his friend in the bar and convinced him to walk over to Lexington Avenue.

The scene was being recorded at the Trans-Lux Theater on Lexington Avenue at Fifty-Second Street. Paul Wurtzel, in charge of special effects, had arranged to have a powerful fan directly under a subway grating. Gloria Mosolino, Marilyn's slightly better endowed (37–24–36) stand-in for the picture, was present to earn her twenty dollars per day pay. And Marilyn was there, dressed carefully in nothing but a white dress and white panties. Proper dress for a young woman of her age at that time would have included either a full- or half-slip, a girdle, and stockings. However, the half-slip and the girdle would have resulted in a less risqué image.

Gloria Mosolino posed first, standing on the grate while Paul Wurtzel worked his makeshift wind machine. Once he was certain they could achieve the special effect he desired, Marilyn came over.

To Joe's horror, he watched Marilyn's dress fly up, revealing her panties as she laughed and tried to keep the dress down. The action was much too revealing for the Breen Office, the Legion of Decency, or even the theater audiences who would be paying to see the film. It was naughty in ways they dared not use. Instead it was meant to be cheap publicity: a far more modest shot was taken, under controlled studio conditions, for both the film and the publicity sent around the country when the movie was being shown.

Marilyn was her usual aggressive self that night. So long as a camera's shutter was clicking, she smiled and posed happily. She became tired and extremely chilled from the night air and the wind machine, but she never complained. An agreement had been reached with the public and the press that first the "official" images would be taken for the movie. Then the Fox crew would step aside and let everyone photograph her for so long as they wished. Marilyn, as always, acted as though she was thrilled, requesting only two short breaks while she went into the theater for cups of coffee.

Despite all the attention and the endless photographs, Marilyn was still a created character. Amy and Milton Greene met her when she finished the shoot. She had changed into clothing that would not attract attention and the three rode in a taxi to the hotel. So different did Marilyn look and sound that when they arrived that, as Marilyn was leaving the cab, the driver excitedly alerted his passengers to the fact that a famous celebrity was inside that hotel "right now." And who was the celebrity? "Marilyn Monroe." He never recognized his passenger.

By the time Marilyn reached the hotel room where Joe was staying, he was livid. He beat her, striking her shoulders hard enough to leave bruises that had to be hidden with makeup. The marriage, such as it was, was over. Marilyn would file for divorce two weeks later.

Marilyn was physically ill after the New York episode. Exhaustion and the cold had taken its toll. By the time she flew back to Los Angeles, she had to see a doctor, who diagnosed pneumonia and ordered her to bed for at least two weeks.

Monroe may have been chronically late on the set; yet in her own way she was a professional. She understood that the film cost money with each delay. Billy Wilder wanted a thirty-five-day shooting schedule, and while she could not prevent his losing a total of thirteen days during which she could not leave her bed, she did show up on the set for several days between when she returned and October 1. For once in her career, she was being solidly professional within the very real limits of her physical ability as she recovered from her illness.

Forty-six

The Divorce

On October 2, Marilyn arranged for Joe to be barred from the Fox lot. She also discussed the divorce with him for the first time, a divorce he did not believe she would seriously pursue. He moved to the downstairs den of their home, assuming she needed time alone to come to her senses. Instead there was a noisy, apparently physical, fight as Joe came to realize the marriage was over. (The issue of Joe's beatings is uncertain. It is known that he became physical with Marilyn on more than one occasion, but his motivation—an angry outburst that surprised him as well, and/or a deliberate beating, and/or something else—has never been discussed. The fans of both have long been uncomfortable discussing this aspect of their relationship, though each Joe and Marilyn admitted to close friends that there had been violence.)

Marilyn hired Jerry Geisler, Hollywood's most famous criminal defense attorney, to act as her divorce lawyer. She knew that he had expertise in dealing with the media and would be able to do whatever was necessary to see that the divorce was handled discreetly. She also contacted Harry Brand so he could coordinate the appropriate publicity.

Brand understood that the Monroe image had to be maintained at all costs, and that meant publicly being nice to Joe. There would be no stories of his quick temper and violence. Instead, Joe would be treated like a man who was overextended in life. He was so involved with numerous business enterprises stemming from his career as America's most famous athlete, and

Marilyn so involved with her career as one of America's most famous movie stars, that they could not spend the time needed to build a strong marriage. The announcement of the divorce said that the couple was splitting "because of incompatibility resulting from the conflicting demands of their careers."

The entire Fox publicity staff was focused on the divorce announcement. All the news media were called, and because there were seven publicists working together, the first seven Los Angeles area papers called were each told they had exclusives. It was a bit of trickery meant to get the biggest possible stories from each paper, and when the editors complained after the stories ran, the publicists were in the clear. Each had truly been given a single exclusive, a readily checked fact. No one thought the department would cheat by using multiple publicists at the same time.

On October 5, as Jerry Geisler was preparing the divorce statement discussing Joe's abusiveness for the court's awareness, the attorney told the press that everything was amicable. Although Marilyn was alone, sedated by her physician, the attorney created the fiction that Joe was tenderly preparing her soup. Later she would make clear to the press that there was no other man in her life, dispelling rumors that perhaps an affair had broken up the marriage. By the time Marilyn was free to talk and the divorce petition was public record, it was too late to hurt Marilyn's career.

Marilyn went before the judge in the Santa Monica Courthouse on October 27. She was determined to put on what became the show of her life. She provided a glimpse of Joe DiMaggio that was no more real than her own actress persona.

Ultimately the failed relationship resulted in large measure from the fact that Joe was a moody, self-centered, boring man. Marilyn's intelligence has always been a matter of conjecture, but she had at least pretensions of intellect, taking acting lessons and trying to read books she thought were important. Marilyn was self-centered and needed a man to be obsessed with her, something Joe only managed when he was courting a woman or after he lost her. Worse, when pushed to change, Joe would become violent. He might have been an exciting man in bed, but sex with bruises became old fast. Unfortunately, in October 1954, the second wife of Joe DiMaggio could not say such things. Instead, she combined truth with fiction:

Your Honor, my husband would get in moods where he wouldn't speak to me for five to seven days at a time—sometimes longer, ten days. I would ask him what was wrong. He wouldn't answer, or he would say, "Stop nagging me!" I was permitted to have visitors no more than three times in the nine months we were married. On one occasion, it was when I was sick. Then he did allow someone to come and see me.

It was all true and elicited sympathy because the idea of the beautiful and desirable Marilyn being kept in isolation was a fan's nightmare. However, she softened her statement by lying about her efforts to preserve the marriage. She claimed that she was willing to give up her career, though Joe did not want her to. It was a touching performance, enhanced by her wearing a demure black dress, white gloves, a black hat, and white pearls.

It took eight minutes for the judge to decide in Marilyn's favor. The divorce was effective immediately, but would not be finalized for a year. There would be no alimony, no argument over property.

Forty-seven

The Wrong Door Raid

Marilyn may have thought that the DiMaggio stress was over and that she would be free to pursue the very married Arthur Miller, the man she told friends would be her next husband. She did not realize that the obsessed DiMaggio had other plans. Never an ardent spouse, he seemed to become obsessed with a woman only when he was an ex-husband. His first wife knew that, and now Marilyn was about to endure the same problem.

DiMaggio, for reasons never explained, hired private detective Barney Ruditsky to follow Marilyn and make note of everywhere she went. One of the more frequent stops was at 8122 Waring Avenue, and she went there dressed in what Ruditsky described as a disguise.

There were several questions raised by the report, one of the more important being what Ruditsky, who did not know Monroe or her habits when avoiding fans, considered a "disguise." Marilyn had become so well known for her distinctive walk that she learned that she could become virtually invisible with a few simple changes. Whenever she wanted to be left alone by fans, she would put on sunglasses, a scarf over her head, and shoes that enabled her to walk without the bounce for which she was known. Numerous friends have told of Marilyn's showing off in cities such as Manhattan. She would walk down the street for several blocks, keeping her head covered, her sunglasses on, and her walk controlled. Then, without removing the glasses or head covering, she would return to the walk for which she was famous, a dip enhanced by keeping the heel of one shoe shaved slightly shorter than the heel on the other shoe. Almost instantly she would be recognized, passersby approaching her for her autograph.

Another question was whom she was seeing. Hal Schaefer was a close friend and resident of the building. Some say she and Hal had become lovers; others say that he was gay and had no physical interest in her. The truth will probably never be known for sure, though whether Marilyn was even visiting Hal is uncertain. Another tenant in the building was longtime friend Sheila Stewart, an actress and a fellow student of Hal Schaefer.

Marilyn and Sheila were both concerned about Schaefer. He had been extremely troubled that summer, eventually becoming so despondent that, in July, he allegedly took a large but unknown quantity of pills and washed them down with typewriter-cleaning fluid. He was rushed to Santa Monica Hospital for treatment, during which time Marilyn visited him. She also got the studio to agree to delay her going into the recording studio to record a song needed for the film until after Schaefer's recovery, so he could accompany her.

The implication that there was a love affair was a not-unusual allegation, and one that was often true—though probably not with Schaeffer. He was her singing coach for *Gentlemen Prefer Blondes*, *River of No Return*, and *There's No Business Like Show Business*. He worked with her on individual songs, trying to convince her that she had natural ability as a singer. He wanted her to develop how she delivered a song and he provided her with Ella Fitzgerald recordings to study since he felt Ella was one of the great singers performing at the time.

Marilyn never worked at her singing in the same way she did her acting. This may have been laziness. It may have been that she thought she was being complimented to win her favor but had too weak a delivery. And it may have been the result of the people she kept close at hand, such as Natasha Lytess, each of whom had a stake in her succeeding as an actress, not a singer.

Schaeffer worked with Monroe for a number of recordings, and Marilyn insisted that his traditionally anonymous credit status be changed. She wanted his name on the recordings where he worked with her.

The result of all this was a friendship, not a love affair. However, in the world of 1954—and, more specifically, in the beliefs of naïve men like DiMaggio and Ruditsky—a man could never have a female friend unless he was gay or secretly bedding her. Joe considered both possibilities with Schaeffer. The only way to be certain was to catch Monroe in the act of . . . . whatever it was she was supposed to be doing.

DiMaggio, Ruditsky, Phil Irwin (another private investigator), and Frank Sinatra (whose presence added a curious twist to the plans), gathered together on the night of November 5, 1954. Their rendezvous was the corner of Warning Avenue and Kilkea.

The timing of the raid reflected the poor judgment of what amounted to an assault by a group of sexist fraternity boys either defending or attacking someone's honor: they weren't sure.

The men knew that Marilyn was being watched by the celebrity-obsessed public, who were aware that the night before was a highly publicized private dinner at Romanoff's Restaurant celebrating the final filming of *The Seven Year Itch*. The film industry trade journals were also covering the challenge to Twentieth Century-Fox. The corporate lawyers were engaged with negotiations with Marilyn's lawyers so she could end her contract and work with Milton Greene in their Marilyn Monroe Productions partnership.

The studio was afraid of a challenge to its authority. If she could do what she planned, she would make a higher salary and have a tax break that would put her thousands of dollars ahead of where she had been. It might also set a precedent for other actors under studio contracts, the reason the negotiations were important industry news.

Finally, Marilyn was switching agents, changing from Feldman to the members of Music Corporation of America (MCA).

It was the party at Romanoff's that should have alerted Joe to back off on his mission. She wore a red gown borrowed from the studio, and when she made her entrance in the midst of other dinner guests—including Humphrey Bogart, Claudette Colbert, Loretta Young, Gary Cooper, Billy Wilder, Susan Hayward, Clark Gable, and others—all heads turned to look at her. Sid Skolsky was also invited, using the gathering for many days of columns, announcing to the world that Marilyn Monroe had arrived: a star, without question.

For DiMaggio to choose the following night for the assault on the apartment where he was convinced his ex-wife was having an affair guaranteed he could not win. As it was, the incident would come to haunt him for three years.

There are many versions of what happened, but the most accurate, later confirmed during an investigation by the State of California, was told by Fred Otash. As he later explained during an interview: "DiMaggio was convinced that Marilyn was having an affair, and he wanted Ruditsky to prove that fact. Later Phil Irwin said that the ballplayer thought Marilyn might be involved with Hal Schaeffer, her voice coach. Irwin was convinced that Schaeffer was gay, and that Marilyn's attentiveness was the result of a caring friendship, nothing more."

In his book *Goddess*, author Anthony Summers's research indicated that Marilyn probably did have an affair with Schaeffer, but if she did, it was typical Marilyn. There was no emotional commitment on either person's part. Sex was the recreation of friendship as well as a business tool, a form of coercion, and that most unlikely of Hollywood activities: an aspect of marital fidelity. Certainly Schaeffer was not the cause of the breakup with her husband. The marriage to DiMaggio had been a ritual commitment in name only.

Otash noted that

> the one thing Marilyn was doing, according to the surveillance reports of Irwin, was drugs. She was occasionally partying in the Solimar Beach area just past Ventura on the way to Santa Barbara. The drugs were Demerol and Hexadril (sic), both available by prescription and popular with drug users who had doctors willing to give them legitimate prescriptions. [Otash may have meant Hexadrol or a similar-sounding drug.] The pharmacists would provide the medication without questioning the need, and the doctors who cooperated were well paid. It was one of Hollywood's hidden secrets, and the cooperation of the medical community led to more than one actor's premature death by accidental overdose or unexpected allergic reaction.

The drug abuse that evolved naturally from the studio supplied and required sedatives and stimulants, the physical abuse by DiMaggio, and the carefully hidden sexual orientation of some of Hollywood's most famous male and female lovers were all among Hollywood's dirty little secrets. Marilyn was the sensual blonde girl next door, a Cinderella story with the prince an athlete pure of heart and dedicated to the woman he loved. An incident like what came to be known as the Wrong Door Raid was a serious public relations problem, especially since the motivation of the famous men involved did not match their image.

The private investigators Joe DiMaggio hired to follow Marilyn had the bigoted mentality of their day. The baseball hero was the epitome of maleness, and the idea that any woman could stray from his arms had to mean that she was at least bisexual and probably a lesbian. Otherwise a woman would not have close female friends.

The investigators identified Sheila Stewart, a longtime friend and fellow actress, as the almost "certain" lover Marilyn was seeing. Sheila lived in an apartment at Kilkea Drive and Waring Avenue in West Hollywood where Marilyn was visiting the night of November 5.

The less-than-brilliant investigators overlooked several factors. First, the friendship between the two women was a business friendship. They were both working on their singing with the help of their mutual friend Hal Schaeffer, yet their careers and audience appeal were quite different, so there was no competition between them. Their shared interests and career concerns were the reason they enjoyed each other's company.

Second, Hal Schaeffer had gone to Stewart's apartment with Marilyn. The investigators were convinced both that Schaeffer was gay (though there never was any indication of such orientation), and that Monroe had been having an affair with Natasha Lytess prior to her affair with Sheila Stewart. Had any of the nonsense been true, whatever bedroom scene these private Keystone Kops thought they would encounter would have been among the more unusual sexcapades in Hollywood history. The men certainly did not expect to come across a quiet dinner shared by three friends.

Otash talked extensively with the investigators involved, in part because of their friendship and in part because the story made all the media, including *Confidential* magazine for which Otash was the lead investigator. However, the story would first be broken in full in the September 1955 issue (Vol. 3, no. 4) of *Confidential*. Otash explained.

Phil Irwin later claimed that there was no surveillance on Marilyn's place that night. Instead, he and his first wife, Dorothy, then six months pregnant, went for a drive. They happened to pass Sheila Stewart's apartment and noticed Marilyn Monroe's black Cadillac convertible parked a half block down Kilkea. Since his job had been to try and learn who Marilyn was seeing, he stopped by a telephone booth and called Ruditsky.

Ruditsky, who had been having dinner with his wife and a man named Larry Kopak at Larry Finley's My Own Place, came over with his wife to join what was then to be a stake-out. After leaving Irwin and the women to watch the apartment, he left to try and find DiMaggio who, according to Irwin's account, was driving around the area, looking for his ex-wife's car.

The situation deteriorated from the moment DiMaggio was located, and the cast of characters became an unusual one. Joe had been drinking, probably the reason he decided to prowl the streets looking for his ex-wife's car. Although the press would characterize him as being hopelessly in love with Marilyn, that night he decided to go to Stewart's apartment and kill either Marilyn, Sheila, or both. Apparently he felt he would decide once he was inside and caught them in the act of whatever they were supposedly doing.

Irwin kept DiMaggio from entering the apartment building until Barney Ruditsky could take over "athlete-sitting." Then, for reasons never explained, Irwin left to call Frank Sinatra, who was having dinner at Patsy D'Amore's Villa Capri Restaurant. Fifteen minutes later, according to what Irwin, then twenty-four years old, told Otash, Sinatra, Patsy D'Amore, Hank Sanicola, who served as both manager and occasional bodyguard for Sinatra, and Billy Curran, the Villa Capri's maitre d' showed up.

Whatever the preliminary, DiMaggio was convinced that if the men charged into the apartment, they would catch Marilyn and Sheila engaged in a lesbian act.

The apartment was actually one of three suites created from a house. According to Irwin, the seven men went upstairs to the apartment that had been identified as Sheila's. Ruditsky kicked in the door and they rushed inside, raced through the dark living room, and into the bedroom where Irwin began taking flash pictures. All anyone saw was someone on the bed until Sinatra turned on a table lamp, revealing the fifty-year-old Mrs. Florence Katz (Irwin's spelling. Her name was actually Kotz), wearing a nightie and holding up a sheet to hide her breasts.

Panicked, the men fled. Sinatra and DiMaggio drove to the Villa Capri, and the Irwins and Ruditzkys drove to Barney's office. Eventually DiMaggio went to Marilyn's house on DeLongpre to which she had returned after everyone left Stewart's building. The two of them spent the rest of the night together.

A second story, initially presumed to be more accurate, was provided by columnist Jim Bacon. He was dining at the Villa Capri that night and spotted Frank Sinatra and Joe DiMaggio together, along with several friends, including Hank Sanicola.

According to Bacon, Irwin, cruising, spotted Marilyn's car, called Ruditsky, and Ruditsky called the Villa Capri. Both DiMaggio and Sinatra were notified, leaving together, though in separate cars so Sinatra could take along the three men already mentioned

Eventually the incident was investigated by the California State Senate. When Sinatra was put under oath, the following dialogue took place:

༄

Investigator Lloyd Harris interrogating Sinatra for the State Senate committee on February 26, 1957:

Q. Were you in the vicinity of 8122 Waring St. on November 5, 1954?

A. I was.

Q. Will you tell the circumstances?

A. Well, I drove Mr. DiMaggio to the general area.

Q. Mr. Joe DiMaggio?

A. That's the only one I know.

Q. There is a brother.

A. He's the hottest one.

(Courtroom laughter)

Q. Do you know a Philip Irwin?

A. No, I don't think so.

Q. Do you know a Barney Ruditsky?

A. Yes.

Q. What restaurant did you and Mr. DiMaggio dine in that night?

A. Villa Capri in Hollywood. He got a telephone call, came back to the table and asked me to drive him someplace.

Q. You went in your car?

A. My car.

[Sinatra said that DiMaggio directed him to the general location.]

A. I parked my car and Mr. DiMaggio was met by Mr. Ruditsky and a man with a camera. They went around the corner and a few minutes later came back.

Q. How many minutes?

A. Two, three, five minutes.

Q. Did you hear a disturbance in that two, three, five minutes?

A. I did not.

Q. You were not present at all when the entrance was made?

A. I was not.

[Sinatra continued, saying that when the men went back to the car, they returned to the Villa Capri where he had coffee, then went home. He said that he was with DiMaggio, Henry Sanicola, and Bill Karen, one of DiMaggio's friends.]

Q. Did you read a story in *Confidential* magazine, September 1955?

A. I'll put it this way. I don't have time to read that type of trash.

Q. Were you told about it?

A. I heard about it.

Q. Did you at any time authorize anyone to release a report of that incident?

A. No, sir.

[The question was based on rumors that Sinatra had arranged for the release of information concerning the Wrong Door Raid in order to generate publicity for himself. His career was back on track, yet the question was a valid one. He was both intensely private and very much in favor of keeping in the news. This approach went as far back in his career as when he appeared at the Paramount Theater in New York with paid Bobby-Soxers outside who swooned on cue to generate excitement among the teenagers present. It was never resolved as to who alerted the press initially when the investigator's questions returned to the issue at hand.]

Q. Did anyone make any reference to it [the raid]?

A. When they all returned to the car I heard someone say we went into the wrong door.

[Sinatra claimed he stood outside by the car, smoking a cigarette.]

Q. Did you ask whose door?

A. No. It was none of my business.

Q. Was there a reference about a picture being taken?

A. Karen said it should be a very strange picture.

Q. Were you satisfied that they had broken in?

A. I was not satisfied or dissatisfied. I was not interested. I had no connection.

[Sinatra then discussed what DiMaggio had said to him while directing him to the general area of the building. He explained that DiMaggio told him his wife was visiting someone and he wanted to go see her.]

Q. Have you met Marilyn Monroe?

A. Delightfully, yes.

ക്ക

The next witness to the raid was Virginia Blasgen, the landlady, who spotted Sinatra and DiMaggio walking around outside. This was around 10:15 P.M., and the Wrong Door Raid took place approximately an hour later. She did not see the men enter, though she positively placed Sinatra at the scene.

"It was definitely Sinatra," she had earlier told reporter James Denver of the *Los Angeles Mirror-News*. "He was laughing and standing next to another exquisitely dressed man across the street just before it happened.

"About 11:15, I heard a crash, like thunder. I grabbed the phone to call the police and looked out my kitchen window. I saw four of them rush out the back to Waring Avenue."

The case was more complicated than the obvious actions of the people involved. The police looked upon the incident as an attempted burglary. It was then left as an open case, which could result in criminal prosecution for everyone—including DiMaggio and Sinatra—should there ever be adequate facts for arrests.

Phil Irwin was the first to discuss the fact that Sinatra had been lying in his testimony, though he would not provide many details because he feared being beaten. The story of the Wrong Door Raid was originally broken in *Confidential* magazine, and Sinatra believed that Irwin had been the leak. The private investigator thought that it was Sinatra who had arranged for him to be beaten, an incident confirmed by state investigator James J. Callahan, who said: "Irwin had a black eye. I don't think his nose was broken, but it was very badly bruised. He had severe welts from his shoulder to the belt line. His arms and legs had been kicked. He was pretty thoroughly worked over."

Although Irwin was circumspect through the time of the state investigation, he had talked with investigators for the popular tabloid, the forerunner to the contemporary *National Enquirer* and *People*, and they had started running stories on the incident. Eventually, after his mistreatment, Irwin was given a chance to relate the story under his own byline.

Ruditsky later admitted that there was no mistake in the actions he took. He had followed Monroe, making careful note of the exact suite she visited. He looked for all possible entrances and exits from both the building and the suite. He also checked for windows. However, he also realized that he was working for a hothead and that it was best for everyone involved that he not reveal the full information.

Ruditsky deliberately had the men break down the door to the wrong apartment. He knew exactly where Monroe was visiting. He had her under surveillance and was too good to not identify the exact suite, its entrances, exits, and windows. He also either saw guns or believed that some of the men, including Sinatra, were armed. He was certain that someone was going to get shot, maybe killed, if he went in to where Marilyn was having dinner with her two friends.

Marilyn later told friends that she had watched all the excitement. She heard the noise, but was smart enough to go on Sheila's balcony to look out. She spotted the cars and the people. She knew who was there and why. And she watched them flee in terror after surprising Mrs. Kotz. She found the scene hilarious.

Sheila Stewart told James Denver of the *Mirror-News*, "I heard the commotion and went out on the landing to see what was happening.

"Down below, I saw four or five men falling all over themselves trying to get out, and then running down the street.

"Marilyn did not get out in time to see them but we looked at the shambles they had made of the door before she left."

Sheila also told the reporter that a few days earlier, her brother-in-law had seen a man watching the house. When confronted, the man said his name was Barney Ruditsky of the City Detective and Guard Service. "I gave the information to a state investigator who was working on revoking the agency's detective license," said Stewart.

"The raid was typical of Joe's jealousy, which was the reason she divorced him. I think he pulled the stunt because Frank needled him into it.

"None of them even had the decency to pay for the broken door, even anonymously. That was the least they could have done."

The real question was what DiMaggio hoped to gain from the raid. Several of the men involved believed that the ballplayer wanted to have proof of Marilyn's infidelities. He was certain that the affair he imagined she was having had begun before their divorce was final. He was equally certain it was with a woman, the two "facts" combining to give him everything he needed to blackmail the actress.

Joe seemed to think that if Marilyn felt he had evidence of her being in severe violation of the morals clause in her studio contract, she would do anything to keep the information from being made public. Her career was all-important to her and the "facts" would be reason for the studio to eliminate Marilyn Monroe and return her to being scared little Norma Jean. DiMaggio would remain silent so long as she returned to being his loving, docile, obedient wife.

The incident and the subsequent publicity led to a hearing that was part of what was officially called the "Kraft Interim Committee Hearings on Private Investigators and Car Repossessors, Insurance Companies," where Irwin again told his story. Sinatra was questioned and claimed under oath that he had stood out by the car, smoking cigarettes, waiting for the issue to be resolved by DiMaggio and the others who had gone inside the apartment.

By March 1957, a grand jury investigation into the Wrong Door Raid was making headlines nationally. There was a question as to whether Sinatra had committed perjury when he testified before the state senate committee, and that led to a rather eclectic defense team. Sinatra's Los Angeles lawyers were Martin Gang and Mickey Rudin of Gang, Kopp & Tyre. Rudin, in turn, called private investigator Fred Otash to help. In addition, Sinatra called Sidney Korshak in Chicago. Korshak was the mob lawyer and famous for being able to fix the problems of seemingly guilty men with just one or two telephone calls.

The problem was a simple one. The truth had to be determined, then everyone had to agree upon a consistent story so that, wherever truth might lead to a perjury conviction for Sinatra, everyone made the same misstatements.

Phil Irwin was the easiest to discredit. He had been beaten, and it was certain that either Sinatra or some of his friends had arranged the violence. However, the beating took place under awkward circumstances for the investigator. He should have been on a stakeout for a client that night. Instead he had sneaked off to be with his girlfriend. The beating may have been related to the Wrong Door Raid, but the fact that he was cheating on his wife did not sit well with the jury.

Otash was able to show that the witnesses to the incident would not have been able to see with certainty that Sinatra was inside the apartment. There was also a witness willing to testify that Sinatra was "too yellow" to enter the building, that he had stayed outside by the cars instead. The latter was important because those closest to Sinatra knew he liked to play at being a gangster and a thug but was actually a rather weak man. He might start fights, but he knew that his trusted bodyguard would settle them. He was more talk and tough-guy fantasy than the pseudo-mobster he pretended to be.

Ruditsky said that he would testify under oath that Sinatra was not inside. However, not only was he sick at the time, he also needed the money Sinatra paid him for his work. He would lie for a client.

The end result was a frustrating one for the prosecution. There was no question that the statements of men under oath were inaccurate at best. There was also no question that there was inadequate evidence to assure a successful perjury conviction. Worse for the entertainers who tried to discredit *Confidential*'s methods and report, the March 2, 1957, edition of *The New York Times* noted that the writers and editors handling the Wrong Door Raid *Confidential* story were "quite zealous in checking out and documenting their reports to the public. . . ." The article also noted that the private investigators looking into the case had handled everything properly. As for Florence Kotz, she was paid $7,500 by the celebrity "burglars."

The respect Marilyn had for Hal Schaeffer also resulted in her first stand against the racism that was prevalent throughout the United States. She had never considered herself a social activist. Certainly her sexual behavior reflected an acceptance of studio executives who made women a commodity. However, as she rebelled against the studio contract and the impotence of actors when trying to select the type of role they would have, she seemed to generalize her anger to everyone who would limit an entertainer's performing life. This led to her challenging the bigotry of Hollywood nightclubs.

The world of Hollywood nightclubs was an oddly white one. New York's clubs often had black entertainers, though they restricted their clientele to whites only. There were also "black-and-tan clubs" where whites and blacks could mingle in the audience. But in Hollywood the clubs were strictly segregated. Black entertainers did not perform.

Marilyn, like all Hollywood actors, had attended the various high-level nightclubs, sometimes to see an act, sometimes specifically to be seen, often as part of studio publicity. Arguably the most famous was the Mocambo, and Marilyn was a desired guest.

That was why she was shocked to learn that Ella Fitzgerald, the singer whose work Hal Schaeffer had been having her study, was denied the opportunity to perform in the Mocambo, solely because she was black.

Livid, Marilyn called the owner of the Mocambo and demanded that Fitzgerald be allowed to sing immediately. She insisted that the engagement be identical to that of any white performer of equal star caliber, and she explained that she, Monroe, would take a front-row table every night of the engagement.

Two things were not said in all this. The first was that because Marilyn was at the peak of public interest in her life, her work, and her activities, the press would swarm over the club every night that Marilyn was there. Photographs would be in newspapers throughout the country, and stories would provide positive publicity so great that the club could never afford to pay for the equivalent advertising.

The second was the unspoken threat that if Ella was not given a contract, the press would hear about it. There was no choice. The owner hired Fitzgerald immediately and Marilyn attended every performance.

Forty-eight

Hey, Girl, Do You Want to Make a Movie?

Norma Jean and Milton Greene were a couple of kids so outside their areas of expertise that they thought they were in control. He was thirty-two. She was twenty-eight. He was one of the most brilliant photographers in the United States, his celebrity portraits capturing aspects of his subjects' personalities missed by other professionals. She was one of the greatest box-office draws in the movie industry, playing to perfection the sexy/ditzy/comic/singer/sometime dancer. There was a large moviegoing audience who wanted to see any film starring the Marilyn Monroe character she had created and almost understood (she was a little over a year from legally taking that name). Each had conquered a mountain that, for some in their respective professions, was considered the epitome of achievement. But each had greater ambition than the success already achieved. What they did not realize was how complex the movie industry could be and how little knowledge they had of how it operated off camera.

The first act of independence was the firing of Charles Feldman, a man who might have had Marilyn's interests at heart but was also a close friend of Darryl Zanuck. Given that Feldman's agency had several clients, there was a valid risk that he would not always put Marilyn and her career before friendship and other clients. She also agreed to repay Feldman the money he had advanced her, a total of more than $23,000.

Greene selected MCA as the agency to handle Marilyn since it had representatives on both coasts who could guide them on any endeavor. Lew Wasserman was the West Coast head and considered the most powerful agent in Hollywood for his business-changing deals. Years earlier the William Morris Agency had brokered deals that led to actors being paid for work sold to new media, such as television, then in its infancy. MCA's Wasserman introduced the idea that an actor's salary would be reduced for a picture in exchange for that actor receiving a percentage of a film's profits. The percentage deal offered extensive opportunity for cheating talent if a studio so desired, but it also allowed for reducing production costs that came out of a studio's pockets. Once profits were being made, the money paid to the talent essentially came from the box-office returns. Since most of the studios were honest about their earnings, the actors fought for such contracts, effectively breaking the old studio system.

(Among the methods used to cheat actors, writers, and others receiving percentage deals was creating wholly owned subsidiaries that were not part of the deal. For example, one screenwriter had a percentage deal with a major studio that guaranteed him 10 percent of the production company's profits. The film cost $7 million to make, and when *Variety* reported that it had earned $77 million, the writer went to get his check. Instead he was told that the production company had yet to break even, and his contract was with the production company. The distribution company, by contrast, had made a $70 million profit. The "distribution company" was a wholly owned subsidiary of the production company, but it was not part of the profit-sharing deal. The percentage deal the writer thought would make him rich ended costing him a few thousand dollars that he would have been paid had he accepted a standard work for hire contract.)

Twentieth Century-Fox wanted to do more than stop Marilyn from breaking her contract; they wanted to destroy her if she would not return to their fold. This could be done by both ruining her reputation and replacing her with an actress the studio heads hoped would be the new Marilyn Monroe, in the same manner that Norma Jean had become the new Betty Grable. The choice for the change was Sheree North, an actress who agreed to star in one of the films Marilyn rejected (*How to Be Very, Very Popular*). The screenplay was written by Nunnally Johnson, the writer of *How to Marry a Millionaire*, a man whose work Marilyn liked. However, the film never came together. Monroe had been right about not taking the role, and Sheree North did not suddenly sing and dance her way into fame.

The studio also tried defaming Marilyn's character. They issued a press release meant to make Fox look like the victim in the labor war. "No one can handle her," stated a release sent to the press. "No one can give her advice. She has always decided everything for herself. We're getting two hundred letters a day demanding we get rid of her, but we have $2,000,000 tied up in this picture [*The Seven Year Itch*], and we're trying to protect that."

The studio enlisted Hedda Hopper to help them, and the columnist was more than happy to oblige, given that the studio provided her access to their talent and her column would fail without that access. Hedda wrote a column in which she used an anonymous source, a supposed stockholder at Fox, for a quote that read, "It's disgusting. She's had four or five years' training—enough to produce ten competent actresses—and she still can't act."

But Marilyn had an unusual popularity and a base of support that was different from that of most stars. Usually a star's biography contained stories of a happy childhood, learning to sing and dance in a hometown studio, maybe having an after-school job or working to help the family, and eventually making his or her way to Hollywood. Sometimes there was theater work along the way, the stage being the base for breaking into film. At others times the actor came out, gained some small roles, and gradually worked his or her way to the top with a boost from the publicity department. Then the image as a person—rugged, sensual, shrewish, tender, etc.—comes from the type of roles performed.

Marilyn's appeal came because she mostly played the types of roles on the screen that matched her created biography. She was the slightly emotionally battered, ever-hopeful, slightly zany girl with ambition for success while looking for love. It was an image the audiences wanted to see in the different parts she played.

It was not the image she wanted for her entire career.

Marilyn left Hollywood at the end of 1954, planning to take time to study her craft through watching Broadway plays and working with Lee Strasberg at the Actors Studio. Sometimes she lived in Manhattan. At other times she stayed in a guest room in the Greenes' home in Weston, Connecticut. It was a country place, the main part of the house originally serving as a stable that had gradually been converted and enlarged. Greene used it both as an escape from his work and as a peaceful location for photography, maintaining a full studio in one section. Then, throughout 1955, Greene's lawyers would negotiate with Fox on Marilyn's behalf.

Milton and Marilyn decided that she would make a public declaration of her new independence on Friday, January 7, 1955. Milton arranged for his attorney, Frank Delaney, to host a gathering of eighty people in his East Sixty-Fourth Street home. Potential investors were present, as well as a variety of journalists from all media, the only exceptions among the major players being both Dorothy Kilgallen and Walter Winchell. They were deliberately not invited because they were perceived as being biased against Monroe.

Delaney's involvement and his confidence that Norma Jean was within her rights with her declaration of independence from Fox came from a visit Marilyn had paid to Fox attorney Frank Ferguson several days after finishing her work on *The Seven Year Itch*. She claimed that her divorce from Joe had left her without the various contracts and agreements with the studio. They were all in safe storage but she could not get to them immediately. She was provided copies, and it was from these documents that Delaney determined Fox had inadvertently broken her contract and she was free to start her own company.

At the announcement party, Norma Jean arrived as yet another version of her screen persona. She borrowed a white ermine coat, wore it over a white satin dress, and had her hair color changed yet again so it tended toward platinum. It was a Jean Harlow look, though Marilyn never said what the purpose of such an appearance might be. Milton's wife, Amy, was later quoted as saying that Monroe always believed she was destined to be a star and die young—very much like Harlow, who also had problems with both romance and her mother. However, that explanation seems unlikely for that night.

❧

From *Variety* for January 12, 1955:

> Miss Monroe told a mob of jostling reporters that in mid-December she had formed her own producing company, Marilyn Monroe Productions, Inc. Purpose of the new outfit, she explained rather vaguely, was to make "better pictures" and also to spread her talents into other media, primarily television.
>
> Apart from that, the actress, whose entire career has been at 20th and whose popularity is based to a large part on her sexy portrayals, said she was looking for roles more apt to bring out her talents as a dramatic performer. Toward that end, in any new contract with 20th, she'd want director and script approval, she insisted.

❧

Monroe said nothing about her relationship with Fox, but Delaney, the following Monday, January 10, talked with *Variety* reporter Fred Hift who had been at the Friday evening gathering with Marilyn. Delaney explained that

> 20th picked up its '54–'55 option, but the letter informing Miss Monroe of that fact included a reference to the two pix—"Showbusiness" and "Itch"—as coming under the "new" contract which at last time, was in the negotiation stage. Eventually, Miss Monroe repudiated the new document, and it was never signed.
>
> It's Delaney's contention that the studio's letter represented an admission on the part of the studio that it considered the old contract invalid. He claimed that 20th had subsequently agreed that the star had made her last two films for the studio without any contract, a contention that is strenuously denied by 20th execs.

The implication was that Marilyn Monroe Productions, Inc. could do whatever it wanted with whatever production company wanted to work with them.

The year in New York was a complex one as Marilyn was working among several concerns. She had to have legal protection from Fox through an official change in residency, so she obtained a Connecticut driver's license and registered to vote, the two actions that, in many states, qualified her as a resident. She also had a suite leased in the Gladstone Hotel at Lexington Avenue and East Fifty-Second Street, not far from Greene's studio at 480 Lexington. This assured that she was available for posing for Greene's cameras, having business meetings, and, it has been alleged, having an affair with Greene. The latter has never been fully documented, though given Monroe's erotic attachment to the camera and, by extension, to every photographer who had ever wanted multiple posing sessions with her, it seems plausible.

What is certain is that one of the highest-paid photographers in the United States was in business with a partner without money but who would, in today's jargon, be considered "high maintenance." Greene used savings, a mortgage on his home, and other resources to pay for a press secretary and press agent for Marilyn (both legitimate business expenses) and one hundred dollars a week for the care of her mother, Gladys (an emotional choice). The Arthur P. Jacobs Company, with staff in both New York and Los Angeles, handled her publicity. Among those who worked the account with Jacobs were staff members Patricia Newcomb (who would later form complex relationships with Marilyn and the Kennedy family), Rupert Allan, John Springer, and Lois Weber.

Even in this early stage of the partnership, Milton's lack of business sense was obvious. Marilyn owned 51 of the 101 shares of stock in MMP and needed only to star in movies chosen and produced by MMP. Milton arranged for Marilyn's living in New York, at first either in a hotel or with his family, to keep her from the studio. He paid for her classes, her psychoanalysis, and just about everything else, MMP actually being the bank of Milton's savings. They were quickly twenty thousand dollars in debt, but that was of little concern at first.

Worse, while there were necessary expenses, Milton approved Marilyn's living for several weeks in the Waldorf-Astoria Towers apartment at a cost of a thousand dollars a week. There was another fifty dollars a week for perfume and five hundred dollars for "beautification"—whatever that meant. And finally an additional cost of $125 a week when Greene convinced her to go into psychoanalysis. Total cost for the first year, all without financial return, was an estimated fifty thousand dollars, the salary he left behind with *Look* to start the business. When he sold his share in MMP in 1958—a little over two years after having formed the company—for reasons that, in hindsight, made little sense, he was paid $85,000 for his stock.

It was not sex or business that was of greatest concern to Marilyn. Nor was it Joe DiMaggio, who still followed her occasionally and with whom she occasionally spent intimate time, despite both the divorce and her certainty she could never again be married to the man. Instead, Marilyn decided that she would become an actress of greater depth and breadth by studying with Lee Strasberg. It was a decision that would affect her in more ways than on the screen, though she had an incomplete understanding of who he was and how he had been viewed in the past. What she knew was his fame: the credit some actors gave him for his help, and the credit he took for others (some of whom felt he was considerably less of an influence than the legend). She also had met his wife, Paula, and daughter, Susan, when they visited in Hollywood. But Lee and the political ramifications of being connected with the Actors Studio, much like Norma Jean's understanding of different types of show business, were unknowns.

Stage and screen actors were quite different in the demands put upon them. Stage actors stood in front of an audience, living out a story from the playwright's imagination. They had to learn to whisper so that people thirty rows back could hear them while also believing that someone onstage across from the whisperer could not make out what was being said. They had to use exaggerated gestures that, from the audience, seemed subtle nuances. And they had to learn to re-create a character in a manner that made the people in the seats feel they were witnessing a real time period in that person's life. This meant not just memorizing the entire play, but letting the character grow and change as the story unfolded before the audience.

Screen actors had to look good on the screen. Their speech was natural because microphones were just out of camera range to allow them to be heard. Their facial expressions were the same they would use in everyday interaction. The ability to memorize an entire screenplay or maintain a character for ninety minutes to two hours or more was unnecessary; what was essential was the ability to draw all eyes when appearing on the screen. Some of this was learned. Some of this was enhanced through makeup, wardrobe, lighting, hair styling, and camera angle. But ultimately it came down to being born with "star quality," the chance physical appearance that was riveting to watch when sitting in a movie theater, staring up at the screen.

Marilyn Monroe was a movie star, and though she worked hard to improve her performances, to be effective on the screen, and to learn to play characters, she would always be a second-rate actress on the stage.

Perhaps, had Marilyn gone to a different acting school, one created to help the students develop their skills in whatever ways most effective for them, at least part of the New York experience might have been different. Unfortunately, she chose to work with Lee Strasberg, who knew that having a movie star come to his classes was the greatest free advertising possible. All he had to do was convince Monroe that whatever failings she might have were her own fault, and any success or even positive change as an actress occurred solely through Lee's efforts. She was being positioned for failure and did not realize that fact.

Broadway stars had egos, of course. They could be pompous, bombastic, and self-absorbed, but most were little known outside of Broadway. By contrast, because they appeared larger-than-life on movie screens throughout the country, movie stars were much like spoiled brats, the type of individuals who could become flatulent and know that everyone around them would say "excuse me" so they would not be embarrassed by their own bodily functions.

Billy Wilkerson, the publisher of *Hollywood Reporter*, probably put the situation best in his angry response to Marilyn's announcement about her new company, her new independence, and the future she planned outside the studio system despite having been offered $100,000 per picture by Fox. He commented in his "Trade Views" column for January 10, 1955,

Marilyn Monroe is a stupid girl and is being fed some stupid advice. . . . Marilyn Monroe is the most publicized individual in the world. Unquestionably, she is a big box-office draw, a top money attraction. Much of this has been due to her handling by Twentieth, and the pictures she has been given, the talent she has been surrounded with to bring her up to the spot she now occupies. For her to ignore this, taking her case to the nation's press, is a stupid move, based on stupid advice, and we rather think she will gain nothing from it because when the public is told that her new deal would have brought her better than a quarter of a million a year there will be no sympathetic reaction and some of her attractiveness will have been lost.

For a year, as Marilyn worked with Lee Strasberg, she was taken into his home for private lessons, sent to see his and Milton Greene's approved analyst, and generally treated with affection not experienced by his wife or children. The praise Marilyn received was lavish. Other students liked her because she was down to earth, never claiming to be better than anyone else, seriously trying to learn to improve her skills. Most had less money than Marilyn, yet income and fame were never an issue. Norma Jean attended the classes wearing jeans and sweaters chosen for comfort rather than to provide a beacon for her breasts. And always Lee told her how well she was doing, what ability she had, how far she had come . . . and other lies.

The truth was that this was a year of losers and fools. Lee Strasberg was one of the finest acting teachers in the nation with a highly respected list of former students. Just ask him. After all, hadn't Brando learned everything he knew from Strasberg? That was what Lee said, and Lee would never lie—except when he did.

The harsh realities of Norma Jean, Marilyn Monroe, and whatever persona existed in between came quickly in 1955. By the end of January, Milton Greene had failed to get the financial backing the new production company should have had in place before announcing its formation. Everything was financed from Greene's income, savings, and marketable holdings, which, though substantial for a magazine photographer, were inadequate for an entertainment business. Marilyn had fantasized that the announcement of her actions would cause reporters to take her more seriously, to look at her in new ways as a maturing artist. Instead, newspaper reporters were bemused and trade journal reporters were mocking in their coverage.

The only positive experience in Marilyn's mind was meeting Cheryl Crawford, who had formed the Actors Studio with Elia Kazan and Robert Lewis. She was a producer who used the Actors Studio, an offshoot of the earlier Group Theater, in order to give actors a private workshop to develop beyond their current skills. In theory, it was a nonjudgmental arena since the work was not open to the public. Crawford acted as administrator both when producing plays and for the Actors Studio, handling the bills, interviewing actors, attending rehearsals, meeting with agents, and nurturing talent. She was, in a very real sense, the boss of the Strasbergs, encouraging Lee's work and thwarting Paula's constant demands for a pay raise for Lee.

The actors who trained in the Actors Studio bought into both Lee's version of the Method and the idea that only Lee could train them. He was often called the Rabbi, the Teacher. Some followers believed he knew more about acting than any person alive. He was not only charismatic, he seemed so comfortable with himself, so sure of what he said, that even though he often spoke in such convoluted sentences that even his wife and his daughter could not be certain they understood, no one challenged his supposed brilliance.

Strasberg secured his status by playing off the insecurities of his students. He routinely ignored them when they were not working together. He would pass them in the hall or on the street and either not see them or stare through them, as though they were no more important in his daily life than a pigeon in the park. Yet during the sessions, when working to help the actor improve, he would ask intensely personal questions that often seemed to have nothing to do with the work at hand.

Lee also hated Hollywood, declaring that its commercialism destroyed actors. This fit nicely into Marilyn's belief that she had been misjudged, mishandled, and inadequately challenged. Lee also reinforced the idea that Marilyn would not be taken seriously until she learned to be a serious stage performer, taking on great roles. He knew she was capable of such achievement. He related her to "other" serious actors of the past, focusing on the stage instead of mentioning her real predecessors such as Jean Harlow and Betty Grable. There would be no more designated blonde; no more working-class bimbo. Marilyn was destined to achieve greatness through developing her underlying personality.

It was all nonsense. Lee Strasberg did not care whether Marilyn became a great actress. He did not care if her career remained in Hollywood or moved to the Broadway stage. Marilyn Monroe was a movie star. Marilyn Monroe the movie star was about to become a student of Lee Strasberg. And Marilyn Monroe, student of Lee Strasberg, provided the best free advertising for his services that anyone could want. He was going to use her for his own ends, though he probably was also serious about helping her develop her talents along the way. The better she did, the better he would look: and as the myth of Marlon Brando's career seemed to generally go unchallenged (other than by Brando, who kept praising Adler and damning Strasberg when his false biography was quoted), Lee knew he could take credit for any success Marilyn might have after they started working together.

But Marilyn was not an actress in the manner expected of someone in the profession. Susan Strasberg, Lee's daughter, was outraged by Marilyn's behavior and her father's condoning it. "She wasn't professional," Susan later wrote. "She was late. She popped pills and drank excessively. She lost contact with reality. She was unpredictable, explosive, impulsive, easily distracted. He didn't yell at her. He totally accepted her. No matter what she did, he constantly validated her."

Lee Strasberg told Marilyn that her acting skills would develop faster if she had a psychoanalyst who could help her get in touch with her life and feelings in much the way he was having her do during classes. Strasberg said, "To the actor, something that is a problem for somebody else becomes a creative force for him. It serves as the material that he transmits, that he transmutes, that he somehow shares."

The problem was that Norma Jean's Marilyn character had pushed her into a corner from which she could not extricate herself. Marilyn Monroe was to seek understanding of self. Marilyn Monroe was expected to find emotions deeply buried within. But Marilyn Monroe did not exist, and Norma Jean's childhood had little to do with the well-publicized fictional experiences that had been presented as fact to the media and the public. And even though Norma Jean was author of the Marilyn Monroe story, she would not feel comfortable enough with the character she created to legally change her name until the following year.

It was Milton Greene who brought Marilyn Monroe to see Dr. Margaret Hohenberg, a logical choice for helping Marilyn as an actress and a person—if only Marilyn existed as a full person. Dr. Hohenberg had worked with Milton for several years and he trusted her implicitly with this new, most important woman in his business life. He was already paying for Marilyn to live in the Gladstone Hotel, so covering the expenses of psychoanalytic sessions (two morning and three afternoon visits a week), the timing planned around her work with Lee Strasberg, was a natural extension of the groundwork for developing the key component of Marilyn Monroe Productions.

Dr. Hohenberg was an unusual character. She was born in 1898 and raised in Hungary, eventually studying in Budapest, Prague, and Vienna. She had worked in insane asylums—hospitals for the hopelessly mentally ill where little could be done and straitjackets had to serve as restraints because psychotropic medication had not yet been developed. She was also one of the practitioners of the psychoanalytic movement, now largely discredited, that required years of discussing every experience to assure good mental health.

Dr. Hohenberg was known as a psychotherapist, an interesting title because there was no specific educational requirement for licensing psycho-therapists in New York. Different psychotherapists used different approaches: some positive; some bizarre; and some, like Dr. Hohenberg's following the psychoanalytical route, creating an intimate form of what critics called "navel-gazing" that beautifully dovetailed into Lee Strasberg's Method.

Forty-nine

Beginning the Downward Spiral

Marilyn may have felt herself in control of her life, but she was actually busier than when she worked for the studio. At least during a production there were long periods when, though in costume and makeup, she could rest between takes. In New York her days were filled with acting lessons—some in regular classes, some in private classes, and some in the Strasberg apartment, where Lee was emotionally distant around his wife and daughter but not Marilyn. The actual time working as a private student came to four hours, two of which were devoted to getting in touch with sensory memory and two to working on scenes. She had five psychoanalysis sessions a week. And she had to work with Milton and the lawyers concerning her Fox contract. There was also the periodic presence of Joe DiMaggio and an effort to once again read books in which she was either interested or felt she should be reading to better herself. Every minute seemed taken up by what she felt she should do or what she had to do, and the result was stress that led her to seek relief from pharmaceuticals.

In 1955, the pharmaceutical industry was still unaware of what drugs could do, what dangers they posed, and what addiction could mean. There was an understanding of the dangers of street drugs such as heroin, and the 1955 movie *The Man with the Golden Arm* furthered the respect Frank Sinatra had gained as an actor when he starred in it. However, few people were looking at the possible dangers of dependency on stimulants and sleeping pills. Their use as a means to function more effectively in a busy lifestyle was routinely accepted.

There was also little monitoring of medication. A pharmacy might keep a list of medicines a customer routinely ordered, though it was unlikely. Files seemed unnecessary and took up space that could be used for more practical purposes. Even more than a decade later, when prescription narcotics began to be more controlled, pharmacists simply maintained a list for each controlled substance. A customer ordering one of the drugs would sign the appropriate list. Then, as time permitted, an inspector would stop by and glance at the list to see if anything was out of line. There was no effort to compare the list for codeine from one pharmacy, for example, with the list for the same drug sold at a pharmacy a couple of miles away, unless there was an investigation into deliberate fraud. The inspections that mattered were usually in reaction to suspicion of criminal abuse, and only then would the records of different, targeted stores be compared.

The drug abuse among Hollywood actors and even technical people required to work long hours was never intentional. Doctors saw no reason to talk with one another about which patients might be seeing more than one physician for the same medication; nor did they discuss with the patient other physicians he or she might be seeing. There was no sense of the necessity of having a primary care physician keep track of everyone a patient saw, every drug a patient was taking, and how many prescriptions he or she might have at any time.

There were any number of people in Hollywood being hurt by their drug abuse, and director John Huston was aware that it was destroying Monroe. He tried to warn Arthur Miller, but there was little help available. Most professionals thought there was nothing inherently troubling about someone taking prescription medication, any more than they were troubled by an individual taking a glass of wine with the evening meal. Alcoholics Anonymous existed, but that was often viewed as a support group for degenerates and those with little self-control. Drug addicts were heroin users and, depending upon the social circle of the critic, pot-smokers. Some men couldn't hold their liquor, and the effect of alcohol on the inhibitions of a starlet were well known, such seductions a long practiced art. But sleeping pills and stimulants? What was the harm?

Later there would be stories from everyone close to Monroe, not only about the drugs she "legitimately" took because they were prescribed for her (washing them down with champagne whenever possible) but also those she would take from the Strasbergs's medicine cabinet. Milton Greene's brother was a doctor, and he provided both Marilyn and Milton with the samples the pharmaceutical companies handed out.

Susan Strasberg, who had befriended Marilyn and often spent nights talking with her after Susan herself finished performing in a show on Broadway, was asked by Milton Greene to keep Marilyn from a bottle of sleeping pills she had obtained. Susan was happy to help, but when Marilyn came near to violence over this "help," Milton relented.

The problem was exacerbated by Lee's constantly asking her to probe her innermost being and the psychoanalyst having her review her past in great detail, exploring the pain that had mostly been Beebe Goddard's. It was all madness. Marilyn's health deteriorated dramatically, even though she claimed to feel free and in charge of her life.

Fifty

Nobody Understands Me

Marilyn Monroe celebrated her twenty-ninth birthday the same day that *The Seven Year Itch* opened in Manhattan movie theaters. The reviews were positive, but Marilyn sadly said to Susan Strasberg, daughter of her new drama coach, "I hope it's the last of those kinds of parts I'll have to play. If I thought I had to keep on wiggling in crummy movies, I wouldn't want to work in movies anymore. I could go back to working in a factory if I had to. It wasn't so bad, sort of fun . . . pretty boring." Then, as Strasberg wrote in her autobiographical *Marilyn and Me*, Marilyn went on, "It's a good thing I wasn't a Method actress then [when making *The Seven Year Itch*]. Imagine living that part, a dopy blonde? I've had my moments, but never that bad. Of course, Lady Macbeth wouldn't be so great to live, either."

The year's hiatus took Marilyn in several directions apart from the premier of *The Seven Year Itch* and the continued volatile relationship with her by-then-ex-husband, Joe DiMaggio. There was the dismantling of her former support group, from Natasha Lytess to agents and lawyers, and the creation of a new group, including Milton Greene and Paula Strasberg. She also became a more serious reader than in the past, reading not just books that she thought would improve herself, but also volumes she purchased just to enjoy, including *Gertrude Lawrence as "Mrs. Q,"* by Lawrence's husband, Richard Aldrich, and James Joyce's *Ulysses*. She bought several books of

489

poetry, a longtime interest. She also met and began spending time with poet Norman Rosten and his wife—as well as renewing her friendship with Arthur Miller, who had been Norman's college classmate.

Miller had never experienced a lover quite like Monroe. There was no more instant magic between them than she seemed to reveal with any of her husbands or longer-term lovers. He was tall, a year younger than DiMaggio, athletic, and an intellectual with a seemingly limited ability to put the world—whether his own life, the nation's, or the international scene—into appropriate perspective. As was mentioned, when other writers were running from any support of Stalin's ideology and the American Communist movement, Miller was still embracing causes that seemed to indicate freedom for the masses. He was horrified to learn of the anti-Semitism, the censorship, and the other denials of human liberties that existed in the Soviet Union. He tended to have the same black-and-white attitude toward politics as the early immigrants from the countries being taken over by Adolf Hitler before World War II, who had supported Communism because it seemed the only viable alternative to the extremes of Nazism. Miller supported Communist front groups because he found aspects of the changes in the way the American government allowed its citizens to be treated increasingly offensive.

Monroe understood that the House Un-American Activities Committee seemed to feel that Miller was somehow a threat to the government. Certainly there were right-wing extremists who felt his plays should not continue to be produced and he should not be allowed to keep writing. She realized that Miller was frightened and considered himself to be alone, though neither she nor Miller seemed to remember that his wife, Mary Grace Slattery, was still a part of his world. In addition, Monroe remained good friends with Elia Kazan, acting as volunteer usher at the March 9 premiere of his film *East of Eden*. She worked the aisles with Marlon Brando, another friendship that allegedly involved occasional intimacy. Then, two weeks later, she attended the opening of Tennessee Williams's *Cat on a Hot Tin Roof*, the play, a premiere, having been directed by Kazan.

The one escape from men and politics came on March 30, when the Ringling Brothers Circus, appearing at the Madison Square Garden, held a benefit for the Arthritis Foundation using various stars to draw a capacity crowd of eighty thousand. Monroe was placed in a tight outfit covered with spangles and feathers, a costume somewhat reminiscent, at least in its fit, of what she wore during the "Heat Wave" number in *There's No Business Like Show Business*.

The Greenes and Marilyn also achieved national publicity through what Milton seemed to think was the high point of that first year of MMP. On April 8, 1955, the three appeared on Edward R. Murrow's Friday evening CBS television show *Person to Person*. The importance of the program is difficult to imagine today, but in 1955, with television just beginning to become a primary form of affordable entertainment for most Americans, *Person to Person* was a live, supposedly spontaneous equivalent of a serious fan magazine.

Edward R. Murrow himself was a lean, intensely curious former war correspondent who in 1935 entered the news business, where he was a pioneer in leading the crossover from radio to television. His voice, style, courage, and knowledge were most evident in 1939 when he stood on a London rooftop broadcasting to America during the Battle of Britain. The impact of how he described what he was witnessing provided the first intense understanding of the danger of Nazi Germany and the Axis powers.

Twenty years later, when Norma Jean, Milton, and Amy were to be featured on *Person to Person*, the show was so popular that Murrow had won one of his eventual five Emmys for being the Most Outstanding Personality in all of television in the show's 1953 inaugural year.

Person to Person was a thirty-minute show broadcast at 10:30 P.M. and divided into two segments of fifteen minutes each. There would be two celebrities, one for each segment, and often located in different parts of the country. Each would be interviewed by Murrow, who was sitting comfortably in the New York studio of CBS.

The show was extraordinarily complex. Television cameras were massive at the time, and the cables attached to them were thick and unwieldy. Several days before each broadcast, a technical crew would arrive at the home of the person to be interviewed. Cables were laid throughout the house, almost like a miniature railroad freight yard, then carefully concealed.

Usually the subject would be seated in the living room when first welcoming Murrow, then would offer to show him around. There was an intimacy to the show, as though Murrow had just shown up; the lens would, in effect, be another guest. As the celebrity showed Murrow different rooms throughout the segment, the viewer would be made to feel he or she were also present, unseen but all-seeing.

The producer of the show, Fred Friendly of CBS News, explained to Marilyn that she needn't worry about the viewing audience. He understood that she was not accustomed to television, where a show like *Person to Person* was carefully planned but unscripted, a prisoner of time constraints where mistakes, if made, could not be corrected. There were no retakes, the reason Marilyn Monroe made only two appearances.

There are numerous questions about what the broadcast actually meant. Norma Jean decided, apparently with the encouragement of MMP junior partner Milton Greene, that she would not use her Marilyn Monroe persona during the show. She would wear a simple skirt and blouse along with basic makeup—very much like the girl next door, not a cover girl or movie star. This was a serious actress and businesswoman at home, not some sexually flighty movie star. This was the woman who succeeded Marilyn Monroe once Norma Jean was able to flee the confines of her Hollywood contract. And this was the woman Milton placed next to his young, model wife Amy, a woman Marilyn never trusted because she felt that Amy was using Milton's success and contacts for her own ends.

There were several problems with the interview. The first was that Milton wanted to control how it proceeded, starting with the opening shot of the outside of their home. Normally Murrow, Fred Friendly, or a field producer would handle how the segment was run, but Milton felt he should be in control, and Marilyn guaranteed a large audience so Murrow did not object.

Norma Jean thus went on *Person to Person* in an odd state. She refused to be the ditzy, sexy, rather vacuous Marilyn Monroe; however, the persona she considered the "real" Norma Jean was too far in the past to be resurrected. No one was certain who was in between, so Amy Greene decided to dominate the conversation.

The show began with Monroe and the Greenes, the second half devoted to showing conductor Sir Thomas Beecham and his wife in their New York home. First the Greene home was shown from the outside, then Milton took the camera through his studio where there were framed cover photos from the magazines for which he had worked. Finally there were Marilyn and Amy sitting at a kitchen table as though having taken a break from some womanly activity in order to greet their guest, Murrow.

Marilyn first discusses a little of her modeling career, and then Murrow seems to shift to where Marilyn is not present but an object to be discussed. He asks Amy such things as "Does Marilyn know her way around the kitchen? Is she very much help around the house?"

Amy reacts positively. "She's sort of an ideal guest. She's not trouble to anyone, and she picks up after herself, and . . . she's just fine. You don't even know she's around."

The conversation sounds like one two mothers might have after a weekend sleepover when the mother of the girl who is the guest comes to pick up her daughter. It continues with Amy explaining that Marilyn cleans her own room, makes her bed, and helps babysit the Greene's one-year-old son.

Norma Jean/Marilyn Monroe was almost thirty years old, an actress whose pictures had grossed millions of dollars for Twentieth Century-Fox, a woman who had had two husbands, many lovers, and traveled the United States. She was president of her own production company. Her holdout against the studio, if she truly broke the studio contract system, had ramifications for the entire industry. And the questions initially asked were demeaning.

Amy next takes over the show by guiding Ed into the den, where Milton talks about MMP considering numerous movie and television projects in the United States and abroad, as well as the optioning of books. Then Marilyn gets a chance to answer a question, this time why the corporation was formed.

"Primarily to contribute to help making good pictures," she replies.

Finally Murrow, actually talking to Monroe again, gives her a chance to expound on her statement. "Well, would it be fair to say that you got rather tired of playing the same kind of roles all the time and wanted to try something different?"

Monroe, not willing to risk any further problems, responds, "It's not that I object to doing musicals or comedies. In fact, I rather enjoy it, but I would like to do some dramatic parts." She also mentions that among her best work, as she sees it, is *The Asphalt Jungle* and *The Seven Year Itch*.

Murrow asks about Marilyn's smallest role but she forgets, and Amy reminds her of *Scudda Hoo! Scudda Hay!* This is followed by a question concerning those who have been most helpful with her career, a question that is answered without naming Johnny Hyde, though John Huston is mentioned. It seems almost as though she only wants to mention those who can still be of value to her.

Murrow asks if Monroe tries to please her directors, a question that may reveal more preparation on Murrow's part than he had shown with the other questions. However, instead of telling the truth—that her past has been one of trying to please her drama coach rather than her director, as most directors have believed—she claims she does. "The story is very important, but personally, more important to me than the story is the director, because . . . a good director usually has a good story . . . A director, I think, can contribute a lot because . . . he's really with you every moment, everything you do, I think it's very important. It has been to me."

There was more, including questions about how she liked New York, but the overall interview went very poorly for Marilyn. It was more than the seeming condescension of many of the questions. Watching the interview you see that neither Milton nor Amy are comfortable when the attention is on Marilyn. She is asked about her best part and Milton becomes restless, getting up to take out a pipe while Amy obviously looks everywhere but at Marilyn who is talking. They are clearly uncomfortable with the show, either anticipating Marilyn saying or doing something that makes them ill at ease, or simply bored.

The Hollywood reaction to Marilyn's appearance was all negative. However, much was changing. Darryl Zanuck was leaving Twentieth Century-Fox to become an independent producer and would be replaced by Buddy Adler. Actresses placed in what would have been Marilyn Monroe roles either failed or had their pictures earn at least a million dollars less than predictably would have been the box-office receipts for Monroe.

Monroe was given much less than the hype and much more than she had earned in the past. She would only have to make four films in the next seven years, though she could make more if she so desired. She would be paid a flat rate of $100,000 per film and expenses of five hundred dollars per week. She would be able to approve the storyline, the director, and the cinematographer. She could make records and appear on radio as often as she chose, but she was limited to no more than six television appearances a year. The latter was not a hardship because she hated television. She also could make one film for another studio for each film she made for Fox.

There was other money made available to Monroe, including $142,500 as a compensation payment for *The Seven Year Itch* and another $200,000 for the rights to the screenplay for the novel *Horns for the Devil*, which MMP owned.

Money was arranged for both Marilyn and Milton through their corporation to reduce their tax burden. In all, it was an excellent deal, yet still below what some other actors with similar box-office success were receiving. Elizabeth Taylor, for example—a younger, brunette version of Marilyn (including scandals and problems caused by sex, drugs, and illness)—was rapidly heading toward a salary of a million dollars a picture, yet her popularity did not exceed Monroe's.

Marilyn had spent a year in New York, studying with Lee Strasberg and preparing to utilize Paula in place of Natasha. She had been dating Arthur Miller, reading extensively, becoming absorbed with poetry—and using an increasing number of prescription drugs, both those meant for her and those taken from friends when she went through their medicine cabinets. The relationship with Milton seemed to have been beneficial to both, but in reality they were becoming estranged and he had lost extensive sums of money.

But none of that mattered to the moviegoing public. Marilyn was going to make her first picture under her new contract, a movie of William Inge's Broadway success *Bus Stop*. This would be followed by her independent film *The Prince and the Showgirl*, which would be produced by Marilyn Monroe Productions and released in 1957.

Fifty-one

Dirty Little Secrets

Sid Skolsky was the first "civilian" to know Marilyn was missing from the set of *Bus Stop*, the first movie she was making for Fox under her new contract. Not that Fox head Buddy Adler wanted the columnist to know the studio's problem—not when Marilyn had a history of showing up hours or days late, not when her disappearance could be covered by claiming she was having health problems. This time was different, though. This time she was neither at home nor with any known friend or lover. This time the studio was at risk of having to shut down the movie for an unknown amount of time, incurring what might be hundreds of thousands of dollars in expenses that could never be recovered.

Sid had already noticed Marilyn's absence. She routinely stopped by to see him, Leon Schwab, and other regulars at Schwab's Drug Store, but had not done so in several days. Sid, especially, had been a part of her life for several years and Buddy Adler, the new head of Fox, knew he could trust the columnist to act as a go-between with a private investigator needed to look into the matter. Not only had Skolsky helped create the myth that was Monroe, he needed access to both top talent and rising stars in order to continue his column. Doing the favor meant either Marilyn or Buddy Adler would owe him in ways far more profitable than a single scoop.

Skolsky met the investigator in Schwab's, telling him just enough to get a commitment that the investigator would meet with Adler.

It was 9:00 A.M. on a Saturday when the investigator arrived at Nate and Al's Delicatessen in Beverly Hills to meet with Buddy Adler. The investigator sat with his back to the wall. Adler took a position where the entrance door was behind him, a situation that made him extremely uncomfortable.

It was not unusual for studios to use private investigators. Questions arose from time to time about an actor's private life, about potential for blackmail, about prostitution and extortion. A private investigator could learn the truth, and if there was a problem, he or she could handle it in ways that might be outside the law. Everyone understood the reality: a more sophisticated approach than in the past when the studios had the police chief on the payroll, and a combination of money and a few words to the right person could turn a murder—such as that of Jean Harlow's husband, Paul Bern—into a suicide.

Adler was still nervous. At the very least, he feared being overheard, though he was the one who had suggested the meeting place.

The discussion was circumspect. Adler talked about the fact that everyone knew Marilyn had not been well, admitting that, had he known the problems she would have, he would not have cast her for the film. The public would be told only that Marilyn had to take a few days off for the treatment of bronchitis. The movie was going to lose thousands of dollars under the best of circumstances. The star returning to the set could regain at least some of the shooting momentum. The star reported "sick" but actually in a drug stupor would cost everything.

The filming of *Bus Stop* began in March 1956 using two location cities—Phoenix, Arizona, and Sun Valley, Idaho. Phoenix was hot and dry as expected for that month. The days were long and filming conditions were excellent. Sun Valley, by contrast, required the use of both mountains and the desert valley. A short ride could force the actors to adjust to two extremes of weather, and it was this unavoidable circumstance that allegedly resulted in Norma Jean's bronchitis and subsequent hospitalization in April.

Joshua Logan was the director for the film, one of sixteen directors the new contract named as being acceptable to Marilyn Monroe. He was not happy about taking the job, and even Monroe had wanted John Huston, hoping to repeat the quality of onscreen work she felt she had achieved under Huston's direction in *Asphalt Jungle*. Huston had other commitments,

497

however, and Logan was that rare Hollywood individual who, once committed to work on a film, never let the cast know what he really thought of them. He handled each actor in a manner that made the person feel Logan believed only he or she was ever right for the part. Thus, no matter how much he ordered a scene be reshot, no matter what his criticism and the changes he demanded, the actor always felt that, even with the problems, no one could have been better.

The basic plot was a simple one. Bo Decker is a twenty-one-year-old Montana cowboy traveling to Phoenix to compete in the rodeo. He has lived in relative isolation on the ranch and reached a time in his life when, as he puts it, he wants to "find me an angel" to marry, a decision encouraged by his guardian, Virgil.

Also in Phoenix during that time is Cherie, a singer from the Ozarks with pretensions of a career in Hollywood. She performs in the Blue Dragon Café, singing "That Old Black Magic" when Bo arrives. He is instantly in love with the girl he calls Cherry and has decided is a great "chantoose." The two kiss, a not unusual situation for Cherie but a first, at least in the intense emotions it triggers, for Bo. He decides that Cherie will be marrying him and returning with him to Montana.

The next day Cherie decides to attend the rodeo, going there with Vera, a waitress from the café. Cherie is certain that Bo is crazy: he has already given her an engagement ring and a wedding ring and he has had her sign the license. The slightly out-of-order circumstances are about to be corrected, Cherie learns, when she discovers that Bo has both a wedding cake and a preacher.

Virgil realizes that Bo has gone too far. While Bo is winning his events in the rodeo, he and Vera provide money and help as Cherie packs her few possessions and boards a bus to Hollywood. Bo, determined to keep his lady love, chases after her with his lasso, kidnapping her and placing her on the bus to Montana. He takes the seat next to her, but, exhausted from the competition and the chase, falls asleep. He remains asleep when the bus stops at Grace's Diner during the start of a blizzard.

Cherie leaves the bus as Bo continues to sleep. However, there is no escape from the storm's isolation. Bo awakens, enters the diner, grabs Cherie and throws her over his shoulder, determined to find any preacher in the immediate area.

This time the bus driver comes to Cherie's rescue. He challenges Bo to a fight, then batters the younger man, who is as embarrassed as he is sore. Virgil has come and told him to apologize to everyone he has upset in the past couple days. Then Cherie tries to add to his discomfiture by explaining that she is not some virginal lover: she has been with many men in the past.

Bo is not upset by Cherie's confession. He does not care how many men she has been with. He loves her, and in his mind, that is all that matters.

Cherie, long used and abused, is shocked. She realizes that Bo truly loves her, and because he is contrite instead of continuing to be so aggressive, she accepts Bo's marriage proposal and leaves with him for Montana.

This would be one of the first films in which the critics consistently praised Marilyn Monroe's performance. They saw her become the rather battered, lost, would-be singer of limited talent who was vulnerable to life. They credited her studies in New York—an idea that Lee Strasberg was quick to confirm since it made him and Paula, who was working on the set for the unheard of fee of $1,500 a week, look like heroes.

The shooting was more difficult than the final film appears. For example, there was a scene in which Cherie, Vera (the actress Eileen Heckart) and Virgil (played by Arthur O'Connell) are together. There was nothing difficult about it, yet Marilyn could not seem to get it right. Five takes became ten. Ten takes became fifteen. Each time the scene would be replayed, Marilyn's nervousness would cause her to forget her lines or otherwise make a mistake. By the time they had done thirty-seven takes, Logan's patience was almost at an end. Finally, two takes later, they had what they needed.

Later Don Murray, who played Bo, would reflect on the experience of working with Marilyn. He actually had the greatest insight into what was happening, though he did not realize it. He felt that Marilyn was unable to stay focused. She would say a few lines, then seem to drift. However, when it was realized that she was getting different parts of a scene right on different takes, the actors had to try to be perfect each time so that Logan could splice together footage from several different takes in order to get a successful scene.

Marilyn also followed the Strasberg technique of taking a moment to reflect; only the other actors felt she was trying to remember her lines. Whatever the case, while she was facing an actor, the camera off her face, her eyes would drift, she would lick her lips, and otherwise ignore the fact that the other person was trying to play off her as might occur when two people talk in real life.

Eventually Josh Logan realized that Marilyn made the greatest number of mistakes when he stopped a scene and restarted it. He told the cinematographer to keep the film rolling no matter what happened or how often Marilyn blew some portion of a scene. The filming was only to stop when Logan shouted "cut," and he tried not to do that until he was certain Marilyn had effectively completed all parts of a scene. It was easier for her to stay in character, though she still had basic problems, such as staying within camera range by moving from set mark to mark.

Marilyn was also becoming increasingly demanding and seemingly jealous. Hope Lange, a natural blonde, had been cast as Elma, one of the owners of the diner. Marilyn did not want Lange to have attention, and insisted that she have her hair dyed a darker shade of blonde so Marilyn's own would stand out by contrast.

Marilyn also relied intensely on Paula Strasberg; or Paula made it seem as though she did. Marilyn was distracted to such a degree during the filming that it made sense for Paula to insist that Marilyn always talk in the Oklahoma accent developed for the character of Cherie. She said that if Marilyn stopped, and only Paula encouraged her, then she would not be consistent during the filming. The statement was possibly fact, possibly nonsense; but with Marilyn missing from the set with the alleged bronchitis (a cover story no one would question, when in fact she was sickened from the drugs she was taking), being unfocused when her face was not on camera, and needing retake after retake, no one was willing to challenge Paula too much.

Buddy Adler regretted the use of Monroe for *Bus Stop* because too much film had been shot to scrap the project. The director was angry, the actors were upset, and the crew was frustrated. Some work could be done without Monroe but the schedule was off, the board of directors would be outraged, and Adler would likely lose his newly won job.

Not that Adler was willing to go down without a fight. He allegedly told the investigator, "If the studio takes a hit on this picture, Marilyn will see her career go to hell. Her problem is listening to advisers that know absolutely nothing about filmmaking."

Part of the problem was the period in history. This was a time when movie stars were expected to lead lives that were modest, wholesome, and without personal scandal. A woman might have several lovers and/or husbands, but the studio publicists knew how to spin the story so it did not come back to haunt her. A man might be a homosexual playing intensely heterosexual roles, such as Rock Hudson whose screen name alone indicated "straight" masculinity, but the studio would make certain no one suspected, even if they had to arrange for a marriage.

Drugs were pervasive because of the studio distribution of uppers and downers, but drug addiction was not allowed to exist in Hollywood. The idea that someone could become so dependent on drugs that they were unreliable was the death of an actor's career. There was no forgiveness, no acceptance, no understanding at all. And it was drug abuse that was the cause of Marilyn's failure to show on the set.

The cover story, that Marilyn was hospitalized with bronchitis, was already in place. What was needed was someone to find her before the reality of her disappearance might become known.

The investigator asked about all personal relationships that might be connected. The first one who came to mind from Adler was Hal Schaefer, the musician and voice coach. Adler had heard that Monroe was having an affair with him, including when married to DiMaggio. Oddly, Adler was more sympathetic toward Schaefer, the unwitting subject of the Wrong Door Raid, than Monroe. Adler was certain Hal had been seduced by Marilyn, putting him in danger from her then-husband.

The investigator did not think that Schaefer was the logical choice for someone who would endanger his own career, a movie, and Monroe's future for a few days of sex. Instead, he began looking through his personal files from past cases. He also contacted a friend who worked for Chief Bill Parker, one of a series of Los Angeles police chiefs who kept personal files.

Parker, who ironically was being considered as a possible replacement for FBI Director J. Edgar Hoover if a way could be found to force Hoover to retire, liked to keep files in a manner similar to that of the FBI director. These contained information on politicians, movie stars, and others whose past actions made them vulnerable to outside influence. The files were not so much illegal as unknown by legislators who would have made such actions illegal, if only to protect their own reputations.

In going through the files, one name appeared related to a past divorce case. One of the witnesses was a heroin addict with no connection with the film industry or the medications routinely prescribed by studio doctors. He had suggested that he was "very cozy with Marilyn Monroe," according to the notes from the case. However, there was nothing about Monroe that related to the divorce case, and though the information seemed irrelevant, it was retained.

The same man's name appeared in a couple of other incidents and it became a curiosity. The contact in Chief Parker's office was again called and he agreed to see what he could find. It took just twenty minutes.

The man had a record of arrests for being a junkie. He frequently bought and sold at Western and Hollywood Boulevard where he was arrested. The police files indicated his drug of choice was heroin and that he was mainlining, his arms loaded with needle marks.

Barney Ruditsky, an investigator working for the agency and who had been involved with the Wrong Door Raid, was assigned to check out the junkie and Monroe. He found that Marilyn was considered an abuser and probable addict only known to use uppers, downers, and alcohol. She had no history with using hard drugs like heroin, yet there was no question that there were records of the two of them having been caught together at least twice. There was also a police photo of the man, which was shared with investigators Norm Placey and Barney Ruditsky.

Another investigator began doing the legwork needed to trace whether or not Monroe was booked in a hotel. Both columnists and investigators working with the movie studios developed contacts at the travel agencies, hotels, train stations, airports, bus terminals, and the like during that era. The actors who were important to the studios had the money to travel anywhere they wished and buy anything or almost anyone they desired. There were established trysting places, such as resorts in the Tucson and Oak Creek Canyon regions of Arizona, that were expensive enough to assure privacy and close enough to Hollywood to be able to take the train back in time for a movie shooting. There were also spur-of-the-moment decisions about where to go and what to do that could be embarrassing. What mattered was that the studio heads could keep track of the talent, controlling lives they felt were out of control. Toward this end, the private investigators that they hired paid travel agents, booking agents, room clerks, reservation clerks, and similar individuals to be on the lookout for talent of interest. Additional money was paid when they were able to supply needed information to the investigators.

Gossip columnists spread a similar but much wider net. They bribed hospital clerks and other support staff. They bribed divorce attorneys, estate planners, real estate sales people, and the like. They made certain that no matter what circumstances a star might be in—a new and better contract, overwhelming gambling debts, a divorce in the planning stage, and the like—someone would call in and be rewarded for that information.

The problem for Barney Ruditsky and his firm was that, though they had the contacts, they could not call them and ask if Marilyn Monroe had booked a reservation somewhere through them. If they did, the person providing it would get paid and then call whichever columnist he or she found most accommodating, gaining double pay for the same information. Instead, Ruditsky and the others called and paid for all bookings for the previous few weeks. Since all the actors tended to use the same agencies, there was a limited number to acquire.

Marilyn Monroe was not on any list; nor was Norma Jean. There was no Dougherty. There was no DiMaggio. There seemed to be no connection whatever; yet it was assumed that if Norma Jean had used an agency to book wherever she was hiding, the name she would use would somehow be connected with her own. Otherwise she might forget under which name the reservations had been booked.

The list was reviewed again and again, and gradually one name—Pearl Baker—seemed familiar. The name was not in the telephone book; it was not that of an actor. Yet something about it was worth checking with the one person who both could be trusted during the investigation and who knew most, perhaps, all of Norma Jean's real history. This was Sid Skolsky, the go-between Buddy Adler had originally used.

Skolsky was not fully to be trusted. The investigators asked him if he knew a Pearl Baker but did not say where they had found the name. Sid said he did, but that they did not have the full name: it was *Gladys* Pearl Baker, and she was the mother of Marilyn Monroe.

There was no way to determine if Pearl Baker was Marilyn Monroe, and though the investigator assumed it had to be, the reservation on the list was an odd one. It was for a second-rate motel near Santa Barbara, one it was doubtful Marilyn Monroe would have known about.

Barney Ruditsky and Norm Placey drove to the motel. Ruditsky asked in which room Pearl Baker was booked, slipping the room clerk enough cash so the man would ignore whatever happened next.

The investigators drove their car to the front of the unit, then tried to decide what to do next. Ruditsky was already in trouble for the Wrong Door Raid. A second mistake could result in a complaint that would cost him his license and probably get him jail time. He had no reason to think Pearl Baker was Monroe other than what Sid had said about her mother, and there was every reason to suspect whoever was inside was a prostitute, perhaps with her john.

Ruditsky knocked on the motel unit door. He wasn't certain what he and his partner would or should do, but the first thing he had to do was see who was inside.

There was no answer.

Barney knocked again and this time a man inside said, "Just a minute." His voice registered neither alarm nor curiosity.

A few moments later the latch was unhooked and the door slowly opened. A man stood in his jockey shorts, still unconcerned about the men he was facing.

Ruditsky and Placey recognized the man as the heroin addict who had been the divorce case witness claiming to know Marilyn and having the contacts with Chief Parker's office. They assumed Marilyn was with him; however, even if they had made another mistake, he wouldn't be bringing a lawsuit. With his record, he wouldn't dare.

Ruditsky rushed the man, catching him off guard and sending him back against the wall, sprawling on the floor. The investigators saw then that his arm was bleeding. He had been giving himself a fix when they knocked.

Placey grabbed the syringe so it couldn't be used as a weapon and Ruditsky hurried to the double bed on which a naked, unconscious Marilyn Monroe lay in a fetal position. They checked her breathing to be certain it was steady, checked her pulse and the pupils of her eyes, and then examined her for track marks: one of the most common signs of a heroin junkie. There were none, but she did have a fresh needle mark, indicating she had used heroin sometime before they arrived. However, her vital signs were good, and they determined there was no need for her to go to a hospital.

Buddy Adler's office was contacted and a private ambulance was dispatched by Fox to the motel. The office clerk was paid two hundred dollars to give the investigators the ledger page that would prove Marilyn was there. The junkie was given fifty dollars and taken to the south entrance to the Pacific Coast Highway so he could hitchhike anywhere else. Then the room was cleaned of everything that could be found—syringes, needles, even blonde hairs. It was all placed in a plastic bag and eventually locked in a cabinet.

Marilyn was covered, and when the ambulance arrived, she was taken to a private clinic in Hollywood, the official story being the relapse of the bronchitis. A few days later she was back on the set.

The change in drug use was a shock to everyone involved with Norma Jean. No one was taken aback by the drug and alcohol abuse. There were too many others involved with the same self-destructive activities. There was even the fantasy among her friends that she knew so much about stimulants and depressants, she was better than any doctor in determining what would have a desired effect and what might be a problem. Her self-confidence was unwarranted and her body was slowly deteriorating, but the reality was kept from the press so the public never realized what was happening. And in the case of *Bus Stop*, the devastation of the heroin left her looking as if she had brilliantly prepared herself for the role of Cherie.

Why did Monroe suddenly try heroin? There is no way of knowing. This may have been a onetime activity since there was no indication of earlier use and she apparently did not try it thereafter.

One possibility was that she was having sex with a junkie who goaded her into trying what he enjoyed. She may have thought it would make the sex better. She may have wanted to forget about the movie she was making. She may have had no other drugs. She may have been curious or wanted something that would work better than the chloral hydrate that seemed to have lost its potency with her.

In hindsight, what is certain is that with the new contract, Norma Jean was rapidly deteriorating physically and mentally as a result of the drugs. She should have been placed in a rehab center and given help in freeing herself from the medication that dominated her life. However, she would not admit to a problem, the men in her life wanted to keep her as their fantasy (whatever that meant for each of them), and the studio did not want to risk losing the millions of dollars her films were making. *Bus Stop*, for example, would gross more than $4.25 million after production expenses of $2.2 million, and that was in its initial run. It would later earn more through television, where it was shown both as *Bus Stop* and with its alternate title, *The Wrong Kind of Girl*.

As for Marilyn, the ravaged look she achieved (through acting skill, according to Paula Strasberg and Milton Greene, both of whom were involved with everything, from how she said her lines to how she was made up and lighted; or through her heroin adventure, according to the handful who knew the dirty little secret) resulted in the *Hollywood Reporter* commenting: "There has been a good deal of comment and some knowing laughter about Miss Monroe's attempts to broaden her native talents by working at her acting. It should be some satisfaction to the lady that she now has the last and very triumphant laugh." The review went on to say that she had achieved ". . . a sensitivity, a poignancy, and an apparent understanding that Miss Monroe did not display before."

Joshua Logan was also lavish in his praise, though his reaction is somewhat suspect. Having taken the director's job with great reservations, noting to Buddy Adler that Norma Jean "can't act," he did his best to assure the filming went as smoothly as possible when his star was on the set. He had long known Paula Strasberg and was comfortable telling her to not interfere with his work on the set. The fact that he had actually studied *with* Stanislavsky at the Moscow Art Theater instead of just knowing *about* him was an intimidating factor with which she could not argue.

The financial costs of the film were a concern for both Logan and Adler, though nothing could be done about them while investigators were searching for Monroe. Logan also had to deal with Marilyn's assertiveness on the set, something that upset the other actors who showed up each day and gave excellent performances. Thus it was probably an act of career and film protection when, after the movie was released and Logan's early reservations became public knowledge, he stated, "I could gargle with salt and vinegar even now as I say that [she can't act], because I found her to be one of the greatest talents of all time."

Fifty-two

HUAC/Kazan/Miller and the World Outside Hollywood

Trying to accurately piece together the story of Marilyn Monroe during her yearlong hiatus from Hollywood is like assembling a group of adult Barbie doll enthusiasts, all strangers to one another, who share the hobby of creating adult worlds for their dolls. Each clutches what, to you, is an identical looking Barbie doll.

One at a time you take each person just far enough from the others so they cannot overhear your conversation. Then you ask each in turn to tell you the life story of Barbie. One Barbie helps the homeless and the sick; another runs through husbands and boyfriends, grabbing all the "bling" she can get. One is an astronaut, another a movie star, and a third seems to hang out at the beach, living on unknown but obviously adequate resources. Barbie might have siblings, but the idea of experiencing her own childhood or even who might have been her parents will be vague concepts. Yet no matter how these identical-looking Barbies differ in the eyes of the enthusiasts who cling to their fantasies well past childhood, each is certain he or she has told you the 100-percent true story of the beloved plastic friend.

Barbie might have been Marilyn Monroe in the eyes of director Billy Wilder, long disgusted with the actress's antics despite appreciating the way she came across on the screen. He commented, "The question is whether Marilyn is a person at all or one of the greatest Dupont products ever invented. She has breasts like granite and a brain like Swiss cheese, full of holes. She defies gravity. She hasn't the vaguest conception of the time of the day. She arrives late and tells you she couldn't find the studio and she's been working there for years."

A quite different Barbie doll was beginning to intrigue the New York editors of *Time* magazine. They had decided that, between Marilyn Monroe's film career and her strike against the studio system, she was an important enough representative of the times to warrant their cover. This was an honor shared with heads of state, Nobel Prize winners, scientists of note, and other societal achievers. A Marilyn cover would be pandering to popular culture, but it was also felt to be richly deserved within her sphere of influence. And toward this end, an extremely experienced Hollywood writer, Ezra Goodman, was assigned to reveal the woman who was the person behind the movie star.

Time magazine cover stories were believed to be intensely researched, carefully balanced, and totally accurate, a reputation that was generally deserved. They were the longest and most important stories in each issue, and two issues a year were devoted to Hollywood. The problem for Goodman, when he was told the story on which he would be working for a 1956 cover, was that the New York editorial office had celebrity fans making the final decisions. These were men and women who had come to believe the hype with which the actress had been sold over the years. Truth would be whatever Goodman found that backed the most recently accepted studio/personal biography. Although they did not tell this to the reporter, perhaps did not recognize their personal bias as they edited Goodman's raw copy, there was no way the truth was going to be reported.

The Los Angeles–based writers for *Time* had been covering the film industry for many years. Some served as film critics as well. They lived among the actors. They knew the support personnel—electricians, makeup artists, cinematographers, and the like. They often enjoyed the industry, but they had no illusions. They saw the need to be as thorough and accurate when handling what would become a cover story as did European-based reporters when handling a serious news story.

The New York editors were different. While hard-core fans and star worshippers like many in America, they also held the industry in disdain. It was an inefficient business model with too many people contributing too little to assure profits. Costs were often out of line because expenses were sometimes incurred when paying bonuses, such as guaranteeing a producer transportation to and from location—a legitimate expense—then buying the producer a Rolls-Royce, paid for out of budget, which he could keep or sell back to the dealer when production was over. And actors not under studio contract were rewarded based on box-office returns for previous work instead of being allowed to share in the profits for each picture made, which would be a greater incentive for constantly improving their work.

Goodman was a longtime professional who understood all this, and, as was shown earlier, he tracked down everyone he could find who had been a part of Norma Jean's life both before her career began and since she had become a star. Many people spoke to him, and all were honest about both specifics of which they had direct knowledge and their personal feelings. The story he sent to New York shattered the myth of Marilyn Monroe, revealing the woman and the childhood she led. The story that appeared became a validation of all the lies she had been telling, *Time*'s New York editors choosing to change what did not coincide with myth.

During the same period that Ezra Goodman was on the trail of Marilyn Monroe, HUAC investigators were on the trail of Arthur Miller. He was being asked to testify in the same way his former friend, Elia Kazan, had been asked to reveal his past. It was a demand that had been several years in coming.

⁂

HUAC: The Back Story

Norma Jean was working primarily as a pin-up model for artist Earl Moran when Mississippi congressman John L. Rankin decided to have the House Un-American Activities Committee investigate Hollywood. He was convinced that there was a plot to overthrow the U.S. government and that it was centered in Hollywood, where the motion picture industry was actually the propaganda arm of Moscow. The American public was being seduced into accepting Communism, and if any further proof was needed, the anti-Semitic Rankin pointed to the fact that there were Jews among the studio heads, writers, actors, and directors. If they were also liberal, the connection was "obvious" to the congressman.

The fact that there was nothing illegal about being a Communist or joining a Communist organization meant nothing in those early Cold War years. Rankin ignored the reality that the Communist Party USA could legitimately have candidates running for the office of President of the United States, for senator, or anything else provided they received enough signatures in a state to get on the ballot. He also ignored the fact that most of the Hollywood professionals who had participated in activities related to the Communist Party, Communist front organizations, and/or left-wing organizations related to the arts were doing so when there seemed no other alternative to fascism. President Roosevelt had not announced any effort to stop the growing power of Germany, Italy, and the other Axis powers. Refugees from the violence in Europe talked of ghettos, censorship, isolation, and even arrests related to their efforts to continue in film and on stage. No one wanted to overthrow the U.S. government. They just wanted to support whatever might stop what would become the Holocaust. The fact that most left even before they learned that Russia's Stalin was an anti-Semite who censored those in the arts did not matter. Rankin had made up his mind and did not want facts to confuse him.

There were several Hollywood hearings, the first beginning on October 20, 1947. It was covered by reporters for newspapers, magazines, and radio. One local television station also sent a crew to record the proceedings. There was also a large audience of spectators, though neither the media nor the people who showed up—mostly middle-aged women—cared about being duped by Communists making movies; they were there to see movie stars. To their disappointment, however, Jack L. Warner, the head of Warner Brothers, was the first person to testify.

Warner played to the congressional subcommittee. He was determined to prove his patriotism, his loyalty to the nation, and his skill at ferreting out Communists. He told the committee that he fired every writer he thought was a Communist, though within his list of "fired" names were at least two—Clifford Odets and Irwin Shaw—who were still on the payroll. These were extremely popular writers, and a study of those accused finds that over the years both HUAC and the cooperating witnesses were careful never to name anyone very popular with the American public.

Warner could not have been more helpful in assuring that he and his brothers were willing to establish a fund to pay the expenses of anyone in

Hollywood so displeased with the American system that they wanted to go to Russia. Gary Cooper, then one of the biggest stars in Hollywood, testified, proving his patriotism by announcing that whenever he received an un-American script, he rejected it immediately. Not that he could recall any particular script, writer, or studio that had upset him. In fact, when asked to define Communism, he had no idea what it was. He did assure the committee that his ignorance did not matter. "From what I hear, I don't like it because it isn't on the level."

Ginger Rogers's mother made an appearance to tell of how she saved her daughter from being involved in films that were Communist propaganda. She even named a Communist writer based on "something" she remembered reading in "someone's" column "somewhere," and the "proof" of the vaguely remembered allegation was that she could not remember reading that the person protested.

The Screen Writers Guild was frequently declared to have Communists as members. A few of the members, such as Elia Kazan, had belonged to leftist groups, and some may have liked Communism. But the scripts they wrote that were made into films were never seen as a problem, and the criticism was almost exclusively from less successful writers in the Guild.

The big news story at the time was about the Hollywood Ten, part of a group of nineteen unfriendly witnesses. There were a dozen writers, five directors, one producer, and one actor, and ten of them took the Fifth Amendment, refusing to testify.

Reading the testimony given by some of the unfriendly witnesses, it is often hard to tell whether the committee members or some of the witnesses were the greatest fools. John Howard Lawson, an active Communist, told committee chairman J. Parnell Thomas, "I am not on trial here, Mr. Chairman. This committee is on trial before the American people. Let us get that straight." Then he tried to read a statement denouncing the committee, though Thomas refused to allow it and threatened the writer with contempt. "You are using the old technique, which was used in Hitler's Germany, in order to create a scare here!" Lawson shouted before being removed while defending his Americanism.

One month after the start of the HUAC hearings on November 25, 1947, the most powerful producers in Hollywood took a stand for political morality. These were men whose movies reflected middle-American morality. The scripts they selected frequently lauded the honest American "Everyman" who, when called upon, would defend the flag while standing against the powerfully corrupt who thought they could fool or intimidate "Joe Average." The heroes fell in love, got married, had sex (though never on screen), raised children, and lived to an honorable old age.

And since this was Hollywood, these were men whose private lives were, in many instances, practically a 180-degree reversal of their films. Adultery was common, and sexual extortion was a routine part of casting. Illegal high-stakes gambling, tacit approval of the prostituting of starlets provided to out-of-town investors, union-busting with the help of organized crime, and disdain for blue-collar employees who were the backbone of film production—all were a part of many of their lives.

The men were scoundrels, and as the cliché suggests, patriotism was their last refuge. This was why, on November 25, 1947, the producers proposed, and later adopted, the ruling that no current or former member of the Communist Party could work in the film industry unless they recanted that affiliation.

The producers' decision, which would become known as the Hollywood Blacklist, has often been blamed on the men and women who chose to testify before HUAC. The truth was quite different. The blacklist was an accomplished fact, regardless of whether or not someone named names.

During the early 1950s, when Russia had the atomic bomb, many Americans thought they were going to be invaded at any time. Fear was everywhere, and programs about atomic bombs, atomic radiation, and the Cold War frequently were on television. They were frequently inaccurate, and the nation lived in terror of everything from a Russian invasion to the results of atomic mutations.

The fear was spread even more by the new science fiction movies that told the "reality" of the atomic bomb. There were massive mutant ants, giant caterpillars, and even a fifty-foot woman created by problems with radiation.

Oddly, some of the films were perceived by Hollywood critics as propaganda pictures, either against Russia or against HUAC itself, though both ideas were difficult for a rational person to comprehend. That the suspicions were true, the writers telling of their actions years after the fact, made the period even more ridiculous because the supposedly important messages were so obscure. Certainly if true, they were as ineffective in that way as the rantings of the unfriendly witnesses. For example, *Invasion of the Body Snatchers* was meant to carry the hidden message that Communists could take control of people without their knowing it. And *High Noon*, where a retired gun fighter must stand alone against a bad guy, was supposed to be a subtle way of telling the public about the fight against the bad guys of HUAC and others who thought like the committee members. The hidden meanings the writers thought they had cleverly planted were *so* hidden that the public saw the movies as innocuous, enjoyable, escapist stories.

Even the admitted Communists among the writers would never meet Russia's ideals. Dalton Trumbo, a brilliant writer who had become rich writing movies such as *Thirty Seconds over Tokyo*, lived in splendor on an income of more than $100,000 a year. He had a social conscience, but he never let it get in the way of high pay and even higher living. When Ring Lardner Jr., admitted he was a Communist party member in an article he wrote in 1948 for the *Saturday Evening Post*, he made clear that he had been a thoroughly undependable one.

Mostly the writers held fund-raising cocktail parties, marched at protest rallies, and wrote articles critical of whatever they were against at the moment. They had no interest in overthrowing the U.S. government. And they really did not want to get directly involved with the poor and disenfranchised. They also admitted that the movie industry was a terrible place to try to influence public opinion. For example, Albert Maltz, an admitted Communist who was part of the unfriendly witnesses, told about the critical reaction to Lillian Hellman's play *Watch on the Rhine* when the production was reviewed in the American Communist party publication *New Masses*. The review declared it a terrible play because it was anti-Nazi at a time when Russia's Joseph Stalin was working in seeming close friendship with Adolf Hitler. Two years later, Germany invaded Russia, breaking all treaties. Again a reviewer for *New Masses* went to see *Watch on the Rhine* and this time, because the party line had changed, the anti-Nazi play was greatly praised. Other than international politics, nothing else had changed.

Additional HUAC hearings were held through 1952, and eventually ten of the unfriendly witnesses went to jail for contempt of Congress. Most of the ten were writers, because the Committee figured that the writers were in the perfect position to be subversive in their influence. That no crime had been committed, that the once active members had mostly seen the meetings as a farce, did not matter. The reality—such as when one actor honestly admitted that he had joined a Marxist study group because a friend had said, "Get to know this stuff, and you will make out more with the dames"—was not publicized by reporters.

The studio owners, lacking the courage to admit they were refusing people jobs for fear of government retaliation, denied that they had created a blacklist or that anyone was denied a chance to work. They said that they were just taking actions necessary to keep Communist propaganda from being spread in their pictures.

The truth was always that the money people controlled the screenplays. The studios did not have to produce anything subversive. The American public would not be interested in seeing propaganda as entertainment: something Elia Kazan realized when he decided that the Detroit-based instructors for his cell did not know what they were talking about.

The truth was harsh. Blacklisted writers, directors, and others could not get work in Hollywood under their own names, though they could work with New York theater companies. Unlike Elia Kazan, who could move between both coasts to do the work he loved, the blacklisted artists were men and women whose lives involved the film industry and nothing else. Some took other jobs, some left the country, and many wrote under assumed names for far less money than they had earned before the blacklist. For example, "Robert Rich" won the 1956 Oscar for Best Motion Picture Story for the film *The Brave One*. "Robert Rich" was actually the name the blacklisted Dalton Trumbo was using. And in 1957, when Sam Spiegel's movie *The Bridge on the River Kwai* won the Oscar for best screenplay, the French writer Pierre Boule got the credit, despite the fact that he could not write in English. It wasn't until 1985 that it was learned that the actual writers were the blacklisted Carl Foreman and Michael Wilson.

Norma Jean was never connected with the blacklist, nor was she personally a target of any hearings, but some of the men in her life were, and the effects of the blacklist lasted until well after her death. There was also no appealing what was taking place—because, legally, it should not have been taking place.

Congress had neither demanded that a blacklist be created nor author-ized the necessary change in the Constitution to make it legal. The nation was living in fear a Communism they could not define, an impending attack that never happened, and the belief that the foundation of American society could somehow be subverted by a handful of often-unnamed individuals.

It was in the midst of this that Elia Kazan was called to testify about his Communist past.

Ironically, while Kazan (Norma Jean's lover) and Arthur Miller (the play-wright who would become her third husband) would be professionally challenged by the studio attitude, Norma Jean (by then known as Marilyn Monroe) was helped. Sex appeal and sensuality provided the allowable plea-sures in movies that were increasingly limited in approved content. Serious films that might be misinterpreted as having political undertones—and it seemed as though almost every serious film could be construed in that man-ner—were not going to be made. The studio heads were too frightened. Musicals, comedies, and the like were safe. Using a woman like Norma Jean, known for her body and not her intellect, was also safe. What no one expected was how she would react when her former occasional lover, Kazan, and her soon-to-be third husband were caught in the political fallout from HUAC's investigations.

This is not to say that Marilyn's movies weren't scrutinized. The Catho-lic Church was conducting its own form of moral purification through an organization known as the Legion of Decency. The Legion of Decency members watched the final cuts of movies, then decided how to rate them. Changes might be demanded or the films might be given the ultimate kiss of death: a "C" (Condemned) rating. Although Norma Jean did not realize it, before *The Seven Year Itch* film script was shown to her, it had been changed in accordance with the demands of the Legion of Decency. The play included actual adultery; in the movie, the protagonist is never seduced away from his family, despite strong temptation.

Elia Kazan was already having trouble with the Legion of Decency for the film he made of Tennessee Williams's *A Streetcar Named Desire*. He later likened their rigidity in what they would approve to that of the postwar Communist Party.

As this was taking place, Jack Warner was doing his best to ingratiate himself with HUAC. When asked about the stage work of the two young men who were being looked upon as among the best American playwrights and directors, he said, "Arthur Miller and Elia Kazan worked on Broadway where they practiced some sort of subversion." He offered few more specifics than did Ginger Rogers's mother.

To further win both the government and the various censors' favor, Warner arranged for David Weisbart, a film cutter, to go to New York City without Kazan's knowledge. The first showing of the film of *Streetcar* was to be in Radio City Music Hall, and Warner had no intention of the film being condemned by anyone. Weisbart was to secretly edit the film under the direction of Jack Vizzard, a man connected with the Catholic Legion of Decency and a conservative who had once trained for the priesthood.

The aggressive action by the studio heads anxious to prove their patriotism was reinforced by the newsletter *Counterattack*, which was sent to all the film industry executives. *Counterattack* printed the names of all the actors who either talked to HUAC or refused to speak. It was also the publication in which an actor, writer, director, or producer was expected to file an anti-Communist statement if he or she had previously been involved with the Communist Party or a Communist front group.

The mood in Hollywood was one of fear. Norma Jean, who periodically was used for relaxation by Kazan during this period, felt herself immune from the politics. She did not realize that her increasingly high profile as an actress and in connection with first Joe DiMaggio and then Arthur Miller would eventually create problems for her.

Subpoenaed to appear before HUAC, Kazan arrived in Washington on January 14, 1952. He had decided that he would not name names. Instead, he would explain that he had been a member of the Communist Party for eighteen months before quitting in disgust. He was in the Communist cell of the Group Theatre and had tried to take control of it. However, none of the members of the cell ever had any influence and nothing happened.

This first interview was handled gently by the committee's research director, Raphael Nixon. Kazan was told the names of some of the actors in whom the committee had an interest. The director was also given copies of the testimony of such already-friendly Hollywood professionals as Budd Schulberg, Eddie Dmytryk, and Richard Collins.

The meeting planned for that day was to be a private executive session.

This would not be with the full committee. That would come later. Kazan was told he should go to lunch, be back at two, and be ready for what presumably would be questioning as friendly as that by Nixon.

To Kazan's surprise, the executive committee session was handled in a room he might have used in a play where the main character was to be intimidated as much by the setting as the men around him. The room was a raised, open-end rectangle with chairs along the rim above. Kazan and Nixon were seated at either end of a table in the pit. The executive committee sat above them, looking down. It was a setting he felt guaranteed his personal humiliation no matter how he answered.

Kazan's testimony that first day was simple and direct. The Group Theatre was not a Communist front and the three director/founders were unaware of the Communist cell within. He said he had not been recruited by any of the big names the Committee wanted to publicize, which included John Garfield and Clifford Odets.

Seemingly satisfied with what Kazan had done, he was dismissed for the moment. There would be a second appearance before the entire committee, though, and it was that appearance that would leave lingering anger in the industry for the next almost fifty years.

The pressure began building on Kazan almost immediately. First there was the discovery that the supposedly secret executive session was anything but secret. Committee members made certain there were leaks of information to news media they felt appropriate. Illinois congressional representative Harold Velde contacted Billy Wilkerson, publisher of the *Hollywood Reporter*, with information about the Kazan testimony. As a result, the next issue ran the gossip column item: "Elia Kazan, subpoenaed for the Un-American Activities Committee session, confessed Commie membership but refused to supply any new evidence on his old pals from the Group Theatre days, among them, John Garfield."

Next came a leak from HUAC member New York representative Bernard Kearney. He passed on all the minutes of the "confidential" meeting so that George Sokolsky could write a public affairs column on the testimony for the *New York Journal-American*. The column carried both what was said and the full details of Kazan's past.

At the same time, Molly Kazan, Elia's wife, was livid. She had been the assistant editor of *New Theatre* magazine, working with editor-in-chief Herb Klein, back in the days when Elia was with the Group Theatre. The magazine published plays and criticism, their circulation reaching 35,000 copies a month. There was little advertising and Klein was paid a survival wage of fifteen dollars per week.

Some of the staff people of the *New Theatre* were involved with Communism under the direction of V. J. Jerome, who guided the Communist Party's activities in the arts from his Twelfth Street office in New York. The *New Theatre* was a left-wing monthly, but it was too liberal for Comrade Jerome's taste. When he learned that Herb Klein, Molly's boss, planned to publish Archibald MacLeish's play *Panic*, he was livid.

There was nothing about *Panic* that bothered him; rather, it was that MacLeish worked for *Fortune* magazine, which somehow made him a tool of Wall Street. He was also concerned that Molly Kazan saw nothing wrong with publishing the play, a fact that made Jerome want her dismissed.

Herb Klein refused to fire Molly or change the way he selected plays for publication. This led to a power play because Comrade Jerome, as he was known, had influence over many of the key newsstands where *New Theatre* was sold. He could effectively ruin the circulation of the publication, ending its appeal to advertisers and putting it out of business. Instead, he arranged for the temporary closing of the magazine, a time when Klein went to Russia for a few weeks.

Herb Klein's trip was not about politics but to study the work of a director named Meyerhold. Klein came to the conclusion that Meyerhold was the best director he had ever seen and was well worth a major feature article. That was when he was quietly informed that the Communist Party in the U.S.S.R. disagreed with his assessment. The director was not acting appropriately in the eyes of the Communists. It was necessary to put an end to his career—by killing him.

Upon returning to the United States, shocked and disturbed by what had happened in Russia, Klein was bullied by playwright John Howard Lawson, perhaps the most successful of the party members owing allegiance to Jerome. There were further threats about hurting distribution, which angered the editor. He was struggling to do good work for fifteen dollars a week while Lawson was taking home a thousand dollars a week, his plays commercial successes despite his Communist involvement.

The pressure proved too much for Klein, who resigned and went to Spain. Molly Kazan also resigned and stayed with her husband, and the magazine folded two issues later. The experience colored her feeling toward Communists and Communism forever after.

On February 16, 1952, the House Un-American Activities Committee demanded that Congress enact a law to make espionage against the United States, whether in peacetime or in war, punishable by death or a mandatory life sentence. The committee also criticized the motion picture industry for failing to do more with "sufficient firmness to weed out Communists" and said that Hollywood was "the Communists' greatest financial angels." In truth, by the time of the Korean War, the largest source of dues income for the Communist Party U.S.A. came from undercover special agents and civilian informants on the FBI payroll.

Elia Kazan relied upon two women to help him deal with his personal turmoil during this period. He used Norma Jean as an escape from all pressures. They would talk about aspects of the film business unrelated to HUAC, her involvement with DiMaggio, and her career in general. And then they would have sex. This continued until shortly before Kazan had to make his second appearance before HUAC, a time when Marilyn was so close to marrying Joe that any further sex seemed inappropriate. A man could have his mistresses, but a woman getting married owed it to her fiancé to become monogamous just before the ceremony.

The other woman on whom Kazan relied was his wife, Molly. Sexual fidelity had nothing to do with his respect for her opinions, especially since she had been a victim of Communist excesses during the same time that he was a member of the Communist cell within the Group Theatre.

Molly Kazan hated the Committee's tactics but had reached a point where she said, " . . . it's the duty of this Congress to find out all there is to find out about the Party and what they're up to and to ask people like you what you know. I hope you tell them the truth."

Molly's feelings carried over to her reaction to Arthur Miller's anger. He wanted to write a play that would attack the mentality that led to the creation of HUAC. Toward this end, he had done research that led him to discover a book entitled *The Devil in Massachusetts* by Marion Starkey. He brought the book over to the Kazans' house in hopes that Elia would read it. Eventually, when he finished the play, to be entitled *The Crucible*, he wanted Kazan to direct it.

Molly Kazan read the book first. She was outraged by Miller's wanting to compare the search for Communists, whose prewar tactics she had experienced firsthand, with a witch hunt. She told her husband,

> What's going on here and now is not to be compared with the witch trials of that time. Those witches did not exist. Communists do. Here, and everywhere in the world. It's a false parallel. Witch hunt! The phrase would indicate that there are no Communists in the government, none in the big trade unions, none in the press, none in the arts, none sending money from Hollywood to Twelfth Street. No one who was in the Party and left uses that phrase. They know better.

Kazan later said,

> When I thought about it, I agreed with Molly. I believed it was the duty of the government to investigate the Communist movement in our country. I couldn't behave as if my old "comrades" didn't exist and didn't have an active political program. There was no way I could go along with their crap that the CP was nothing but another political party, like the Republicans and the Democrats. I knew very well what it was, a thoroughly organized worldwide conspiracy. This conviction separated me from many of my old friends.

What has been mostly overlooked in the lingering anger against Kazan is that before he named names, he spoke to each member of the Communist cell in the Group Theatre, discussing his forthcoming testimony. All their names were known. None of them were against his telling who they were. Thus he did no damage that had not already been done, and he acted with the approval of the people involved. However, everyone who testified was looked upon with equal contempt. It was felt that if there somehow had been a united front, with no one in Hollywood testifying, the committee would have been stymied. They would have looked like fools and Hollywood would have won. What went unsaid was that many of the witnesses were friendly, willing to admit they had made a mistake and proud to help the fight against Communism. In Kazan's case, he recognized that Russia had become an imperialist power very different from what it had been seventeen years earlier. Kazan would later write,

> Why didn't all of us in the Group now name each other? Wouldn't that clear the air, if everyone admitted everything? If we were open about our membership at last, wouldn't that reduce the issue of Communists in the Group Theatre to its proper scale? Why had no one suggested that?
>
> I knew very well why not. Party discipline.
>
> Cornered and angry, I wanted to name everybody, break open the secrecy, not only of those in our cell but of everyone else I knew to be "in," at any time; anywhere and everywhere, starting with those who'd given Molly a bad time at *New Theatre* magazine and everyone who'd continued after I'd quit in '35 and snake-danced their way through the political postures that followed and who still believed. I was against them all. I wanted to hit the Party's elite especially hard; pull them down into the muck with me. I knew damned well they weren't good for the country.

The day after Kazan's statement was issued to the House Un-American Activities Committee, it was rushed to the *New York Times*. Kazan could not read it. He felt embarrassed and ashamed because the statement didn't represent his true feelings, which were confused and contradictory. He felt he had done something wrong by testifying, yet would have done something worse by remaining silent.

Molly prepared a carefully worded explanation of her husband's feelings (or perhaps her own feelings, with which her husband concurred). The two then paid to have it printed in the *New York Times* as a clearer explanation of what he had done when he chose to testify fully.

Kazan's secretary resigned. Actors, including some he had trained and who had worshipped him for his skills, avoided facing him. He got hate mail, some of the letters pointing out the actors who were losing roles in plays because of him. The Communist Party called meetings to isolate him for attack because of his testimony and because of the advertisement in the *New York Times*. The others who named names—such as Burl Ives, choreographer Jerome Robbins, and Budd Schulberg—were not attacked, probably because they did not add the public explanation in the *Times*.

* polo*

Newsweek magazine, April 21, 1952:

> Out of the Red: Elia Kazan, stage and film director of "A Streetcar Named Desire," admitted that he was a member of the Communist Party for eighteen months in the mid '30s when there was "no clear opposition" between the United States and Russia, the House Un-American Activities Committee disclosed. Kazan testified he joined the party in 1934 and quit. . . . later with a "deep and abiding hatred" of Red philosophy. On Saturday, Kazan took a two-column ad in *The New York Times* to explain his stand.

ℐℇ

In addition, Arthur Miller stopped speaking to his longtime friend. When the two had talked before Kazan testified, he felt Miller had assured him that whatever his decision, it would be all right. Kazan thought Miller backed him for his convictions, even if Miller chose a different route for himself. Instead, Miller hated Kazan, a fact that would become deeply troublesome for Norma Jean when she began pursuing the playwright as her third husband.

Kazan—applauded and reviled, certainly misunderstood—continued working, often with people who held his politics in contempt. For example, Marlon Brando was hostile to Kazan's actions but willingly took the lead role in the 1954 film *On the Waterfront*. Ironically, the film, written with Budd Schulberg, who had also chosen to name names when called before HUAC, was a justification for what Kazan felt he had done when testifying. The film is the story of Terry Malloy, a former boxer working as a longshoreman who discovers that his union's leadership is both corrupt and deadly. He heroically goes before a government crime commission and tells them everything he knows. Brando illogically later would claim, "I did not realize then . . . that *On the Waterfront* was really a metaphorical argument to justify finking on their [Kazan and Schulberg] friends." Since the Malloy character either reveals what he knows or gets murdered, he is *literally* fighting for his life by going before the committee: a very different situation than Brando stated.

   By contrast, writer Lillian Hellman was livid with Kazan and offered to testify about anything the Committee requested, so long as she was not asked about other people from the past.

> I am not willing, now or in the future, to bring bad trouble to people who, in my past associations with them, were completely innocent of any talk or any action that was disloyal or subversive. I do not like subversion or disloyalty in any form and if I had ever seen any I would have considered it my duty to have reported it to the proper authorities. But to hurt innocent people whom I knew many years ago in order to save myself is, to me, inhuman and indecent and dishonorable. I cannot and will not cut my conscience to fit this year's fashions, even though I long ago came to the conclusion that I was not a political person and could have no comfortable place in any group.

Kazan's actions had a strong impact on playwright Arthur Miller. The two friends had also worked together: for example, Kazan had directed Miller's 1947 play *All My Sons*, a play concerned with business corruption and war. It tells the story of a manufacturer of airplane parts who knowingly ships faulty parts for assembly into warplanes. Many lives are lost, including that of one of his sons. Also appearing that year was *Death of a Salesman*, a play that tells of a man who pursues the American dream of success through hard work, only to find that it is a hollow premise. The play won the Pulitzer Prize and gained long-term acclaim. However, in the years immediately following World War II, when corporate life was the ideal for white male ambitions (although General, and later President, Dwight D. Eisenhower warned of the dangers of the military/industrial complex, and cartoonist Al Capp skewered the General Motors Corporation's arrogance in announcing that "what's good for General Motors is good for the U.S.A."), plays that implied American business ideals might not match the myth of their value became suspect. The fact that Arthur Miller had previously attended meetings of Communist writers, was a well-known liberal, and also dismissed his past as being unimportant in the present, made him realize that he likely was in for trouble. He also understood Kazan's situation, for as he wrote in his autobiography *Timebends*, Miller grew frightened listening to Kazan's justification.

> There was a certain gloomy logic in what he was saying: unless he came clean he could never hope, in the height of his creative powers, to make

another film in America, and he would probably not be given a passport to work abroad either. If the theatre remained open to him, it was not his primary interest anymore; he wanted to deepen his film life, that was where his heart lay, and he had been told in so many words by his old boss and friend Spyros Skouras, president of Twentieth Century-Fox, that the company would not employ him unless he satisfied the committee.

In 1953, Arthur Miller's play *The Crucible* was first produced. Exactly what it was about has been the subject of much controversy. On the surface it is the story of the Salem witch trials of 1692 written to contrast with McCarthyism. Miller would later write in the June 17, 2000, *The Guardian/ The Observer* (online):

> Anyone standing up in the Salem of 1692 and denying that witches existed would have faced immediate arrest, the hardest interrogation and possibly the rope. Every authority not only confirmed the existence of witches but never questioned the necessity of executing them. It became obvious that to dismiss witchcraft was to forgo any understanding of how it came to pass that tens of thousands had been murdered as witches in Europe. To dismiss any relation between that episode and the hunt for subversives was to shut down an insight not only the similar emotion but also the identical practices of both officials and victims.
>
> There were witches, if not to most of us then certainly to everyone in Salem; and there were Communists, but what was the content of their menace? That to me became the issue. Having been deeply influenced as a student by a Marxist approach to society, and having known Marxists and sympathizers, I could simply not accept that these people were spies or even prepared to do the will of the Soviets in some future crisis.

And as to HUAC, "Part of the surreality of the anti-left sweep was that it picked up people for disgrace who had already turned away from a pro-Soviet past but had no stomach for naming others who had merely shared their illusions."

There allegedly was more to all this, at least in the eyes of some of Miller's friends and close acquaintances, and it related to his sexual behavior. Miller long claimed that he worked out aspects of his life in his plays, not being able to write an effective story if he knew from the start how it would resolve itself. He had also never been the quiet intellectual he has frequently been portrayed as being. He loved partying, had a wicked sense of humor, and took his marriage vows far less seriously than did his wife, Mary Slattery Miller. As a young man he had played football and baseball, and had long enjoyed hunting and fishing. He liked to relate to the laboring class, taking a physically demanding job every year to get a feel for what the working man experienced.

Mary Miller, by contrast, was quiet, often disapproving of her husband's antics, though whether her stern appearance was because of her nature or because she knew her husband seemed to be seeking a sexual adventure is uncertain. The fact that they were often separated when he was working in the theaters putting on some of his plays assured he would be able to enjoy any woman who attracted him.

Miller's other problem was that he was *not* an intellectual when it came to truly studying what was happening in the world at large. He was familiar with life in the theater and the impact of government investigations, but he supported governments whose actions he would have condemned had he bothered to investigate. This was why he was aggressively involved with various world peace, arts, and youth gatherings involving countries whose repressive governments censored the artists and were anti-Semitic. He simply did not bother to acquaint himself with the full history, through neither reading about the countries nor talking with friends who had dropped such support a decade or more earlier.

ℰᴂ

To understand Arthur Miller's place in Marilyn's life, one must go back to 1950, when both the nation and the film industry were shocked by HUAC investigations and she was still mourning the loss of Johnny Hyde. Marilyn was working on the set of *As Young as You Feel*. She had no enthusiasm, doing her scenes but obviously devastated by her loss.

Actor Cameron Mitchell, who had been in both the play and the movie versions of *Death of a Salesman*, brought Elia Kazan and Arthur Miller, both visitors to the set, to where Miller could meet the actress between scenes. Kazan and Marilyn had once had dinner together, along with Hyde and Johnny's William Morris Agency partner, Abe Lastfogel. However, this was the first time she had met the playwright.

Mourning did not last long for Marilyn. This was when she began spending more and more time with Kazan, who was both casting the John Steinbeck film *Viva Zapata!* and living, along with Miller, in Charlie Feldman's home while he was in New York. She recognized that not only was Kazan interested in her, he was also in a position to boost her career, perhaps even more than Johnny Hyde.

During the first part of January 1950, Marilyn made her move on Kazan, with whom she frequently spent the night while also accompanying him during the day when she had no studio work to do. Miller was also there, allegedly so aroused by Marilyn that he began swimming extra laps in Feldman's pool. The fact that she was an obvious opportunist and he a married man did not matter.

On Sunday, January 21, Charlie Feldman returned home and immediately understood the dynamics. He planned a dinner party to honor Miller on the following Friday night, having it catered by the Hillcrest Country Club. It was to be what amounted to a stag affair—men and women would be present but the men's wives would not be there (Miller's was in Brooklyn and Kazan's was also in the east). Instead, the usual starlets would be utilized, Marilyn simply considered Kazan's girl.

Kazan was capable of being the type of philanderer even Hollywood executives did not respect. Adultery might be the sign of a normal marriage, but a decent man never cheated on his mistress. In this case, he did not quite go that far. Marilyn was his official date for the evening, but Marilyn was a known bedmate, and another opportunity with a different woman presented itself. He decided to cheat on Marilyn, with whom he was cheating on his wife. He explained to Monroe that he had a business meeting, arranged for Arthur Miller to be her escort to the Feldman party and left to enjoy a different woman.

Neither Miller nor Monroe had any illusions about her situation. She knew Kazan expected to spend the entire night with her; she also understood that when a new escort was arranged, she would be bedding that man. The only aspect of the evening that was unusual for Monroe was Miller's insistence upon picking her up. He seemed to be treating her as a date, though he allegedly had enjoyed the favors of other women when attending similar parties. Whether or not he thought about having casual sex that night is unknown. Apparently he had enough feeling for the actress that he became uncomfortable with his own emotions.

Others have described what happened that night, as Miller's autobiographical writing focuses more on the relationship that began when he and Mary were headed for divorce approximately five years later. Actress Evelyn Keyes, a friend of both Feldman and Joe Schenck, had also been invited to the party specifically to meet Miller, though solely because Feldman thought they would enjoy talking with each other. She was recently divorced from John Huston and a woman considered extremely intelligent, with interests ranging far afield from just acting. Instead of meeting Miller, she found herself a fascinated observer of the playwright and Monroe, later mentioning her bemusement that Marilyn's dress showed her breasts in a manner that made her look like "the prow of a ship."

Kazan returned early from his other date and went to Feldman's home, but did not try to reclaim Monroe after noticing the way she and Miller were dancing together. Miller, either feeling guilty or desiring a seduction without secrets, talked about Mary and the fact that his marriage was essentially over, though never mentioning his personal actions that guaranteed such an end. The truth was that he and Mary were building a home that she believed they would be sharing in the years to come. Miller eventually would write about the issue of his betrayal of the woman who was not only his wife and the mother of his children but who also had stood behind him as he mastered his craft. He would not say that he lacked the courage to be honest with her, pursuing activities that would assure her they had a future. At best, he lacked the courage to admit the truth, except a few years later when he tried to work out the feelings of adultery by making it a major theme of two of his plays—*The Crucible* and *A View from the Bridge*. The former, assumed by the viewing audience to be an allegory about the House Un-American Activities Committee, has an equally important story detailing John Proctor's adultery with a teenager who was helping his wife, Elizabeth, until her anger with John for ending the relationship led her to accuse Elizabeth of witchcraft. *A View from the Bridge* included a more blatant look at the results of one man's secret: inappropriate yet extremely intense sexual desire for his niece.

As for Marilyn, she talked of her feelings with Natasha Lytess, who later quoted the actress as saying about the tall, athletic Miller, "It was like running into a tree! You know—like a cool drink when you've got a fever. You see my toe—this toe? Well, he sat and held my toe and we just looked into each other's eyes almost all evening."

Miller returned to New York, and while he seemingly had nothing better to do, he and Marilyn exchanged a number of letters and talked by telephone. Perhaps embarrassed by the relationship they almost started, Miller took upon himself the role of older (by eleven years), more experienced friend. He told her of the Marilyn Monroe persona she, Norma Jean, was still developing for the public, "Bewitch them with this image they ask for, but I hope and almost pray you won't be hurt in this game, nor ever change. . . ." Once he started working on a new project, the correspondence ended. The marriage to Mary Slattery also had emotionally ended, though the legal "death" would not take place until 1956. Miller treated all his wives the same, in that he seemed to like to have a new woman fully committed to him before he broke off with the previous one.

Arthur Miller was the next logical move for Marilyn. He was a man who had won both the New York Drama Critics Circle Award for the 1947 *All My Sons* and two years later, the Pulitzer Prize for *Death of a Salesman*. He was at least as successful in his own career as Marilyn had become in hers. He was a man who the critics were certain would have even greater success, the same goal Marilyn sought to achieve with her time of training with Strasberg in New York. And Miller was respected for his achievements, an accomplishment Marilyn had yet to realize for herself.

Having a love affair with the married Miller, who began secretly dating Marilyn when he learned she was conveniently living in New York for at least the next several months, provided her with self-respect. Some came from the knowledge that she was wanted by a man nationally respected for his intellect. The fact that much of their relationship was sexual did not matter. She told herself and others that he would not seek a committed relationship with someone he could not respect. "If I were nothing but a dumb blonde," she explained after the couple was married, "he wouldn't have married me."

No matter what the reason for the relationship with Arthur Miller, the affair was one she chose to use personally but not publicly. New friends, such as poet Norman Rosten who was also close with Miller, were aware of what was taking place. However, everything was done to ensure privacy. The couple used bicycles for dates, going to areas such as Coney Island where, if seen, it would be assumed that they were just locals. There were occasional group parties where Miller and Monroe were known to be present, but these were always larger gatherings where everyone was in theater and nothing happened that indicated a more intimate arrangement.

The dates seemed to follow a fairly consistent pattern. They might go out to eat in locations where they could have privacy, and sex was certainly an aspect of their time together. But Marilyn felt she could learn about philosophy and history from Miller, a man she thought was better read than she was. Certainly she felt herself learning from him, that he was someone to whom she could turn for information she lacked.

In a rather humorous twist, Monroe felt herself forced to make clear that there was more to her attraction to the playwright than his intellectual prowess. "I'm in love with the man, not his mind. The Arthur Miller who attracted me was a man of warmth and friendliness. Arthur has helped me adjust myself. I've always been unsure of myself. Arthur has helped me overcome this feeling."

For his part, Miller seemed fascinated by Monroe, ascribing characteristics to her that he fantasized she had. For example, in a *Time* magazine interview with reporter Robert Ajemian, Miller claimed that, though Monroe had enjoyed intimacy with a number of men, each relationship was meaningful to her. She used it in the hope of change, of bettering her life. He then added that he knew social workers with a more checkered history.

The fact that Marilyn had a history of using men seemed to be ignored by Miller. Marilyn maintained to friends such as Fred Otash and Leon Schwab that she liked the idea of fulfilling a man's fantasy. If he thought it would be wonderful to have sex with Marilyn Monroe, she would often oblige.

Miller also believed that Marilyn was a totally honest woman. She was incapable of not telling the truth. The fact that everything about her—from the publicity relating to her childhood to the characters she played on the screen—was a lie, making it certain that either Miller was too in love to see the truth or Marilyn had convinced him that the public story was the private reality.

Both Miller and Monroe also seemed to have unspoken expectations of the other as they reached a stage where he was willing to seek a divorce from Mary. Miller would come to make notes about Marilyn Monroe when he married her. The writing would be a factor in his preparation for creating the play *After the Fall* that was staged following her death.

For her part, Marilyn was most revealing after the marriage. In 1959, while working on the Paramount lot for the movie *Some Like It Hot*, she chanced to speak briefly to her former director, Henry Hathaway. As he later recalled in an interview with John Kobal, he found Marilyn walking up and down outside the stage, crying, and when he asked her what was wrong, she revealed her own fantasies at the time she committed to the man she fantasized about.

> All my life I've played Marilyn Monroe, Marilyn Monroe, Marilyn Monroe . . . . I've tried to do a little better and find myself doing an imitation of Edie Adams doing an imitation of me. I try to do a little better, but then I do an exaggeration of myself doing the same thing. I want to do something different. That was one of the things that attracted me to Miller when he said he was attracted to me. When I married Miller, one of the fantasies I had in my mind was that I could get out of Marilyn Monroe through him.

While Marilyn worked on *Bus Stop*, Arthur had gone to Reno, Nevada, and obtained a divorce from Mary Slattery. Then both returned to New York where Marilyn was preparing to appear in *The Prince and the Showgirl*, the film version of the Terence Rattigan play *The Sleeping Prince*, which Milton Greene had purchased. The play had starred Sir Laurence Olivier, one of England's most lauded actors, and the movie would both star Olivier and have him act as producer and director. Marilyn would play the role of Elsie, the same role that actress Vivien Leigh had played on the British stage.

The arrangement should have been a simple one; but nothing was simple with Monroe, Greene, and Miller, even aside from Arthur's problems with HUAC. No one argued with the choice of Olivier as actor/director/producer, and he was initially delighted to work with the woman who had come off a starring role in *Bus Stop*. Only later would he realize that he was in the midst of a power struggle between Arthur Miller, who did not want his wife singing in the film though she was playing a chorus girl, and Milton

Greene, who wanted her singing more than the single number that became their compromise. The latter also served as Marilyn's supplier of uppers and downers. In addition, they were all stuck with the presence of Paula Strasberg, who had agreed to accept $25,000 plus overtime and expenses (another $13,000), then served as an emotional crutch for Marilyn, who brought her coach onto the set whenever she had to appear. The only relief for Olivier came when Paula flew back to New York, replaced by Marilyn's analyst who lacked industry background, and thus lacked the courage to intrude.

There were two stories playing out simultaneously. While Marilyn prepared to fly to London to work on her new movie, Arthur Miller was trying to accompany her after having had his passport invalidated in 1954. The 1954 timing of the initial HUAC investigation into Miller belied his angry fantasy that it was only because of his love affair with Marilyn and the attendant publicity that he was called to testify before Congress. There had been no love affair in 1954, and though Miller's marriage may have been in emotional shambles, no one, including Miller himself, thought there might eventually be a relationship with the actress.

Not that Arthur looked at the dates of his experience. As he later wrote for the June 17, 2000, edition of *The Guardian/The Observer*:

> In 1956, the House Un-American Activities committee (HUAC) subpoenaed me—I was cited for contempt of Congress for refusing to identify writers I had met at one of the two Communist writers' meetings I had attended many years before. By then, the time was going out for HUAC and it was finding it more difficult to make front pages. However, the news of my forthcoming marriage to Marilyn Monroe was too tempting to be passed. That our marriage had some connection with my being subpoenaed was confirmed when Chairman Walters of the HUAC sent word to Joseph Rauh, my lawyer, that he would be inclined to cancel my hearing if Miss Monroe would consent to have a picture taken with him.
>
> The offer having been declined, the good chairman, as my hearing came to an end, entreated me to write less tragically about our country.

The testimony before Congress occurred on June 21, 1956, ten days after Miller's divorce, with the new Marilyn Monroe—she had legally changed her name from Norma Jean on March 12, 1956—quietly present behind the scenes. Earlier, when it was known that Marilyn was going to marry Arthur, a Fox executive (believed to be Spyros Skouras) told her to convince Arthur to cooperate fully with HUAC. He had underestimated Marilyn's sophistication and her courage. She explained to the executive that she fully agreed with Arthur's thinking and with his reasons for refusing to name names. She was told that her career could be ended, the implication being that the studio would work to destroy her, rather than that the public would care; but the words meant nothing. At that point she was strong enough both to back her future husband and to consider her career less important than a principle.

The exact date of the planned marriage was uncertain other than it had to be before July 16 when Marilyn would fly to London to start her new picture—as, she explained, Mrs. Arthur Miller. The press began following the couple wherever they moved about New York City. Each paper tried to get more information, but Arthur explained during an impromptu meeting with several of the reporters, "It's your job versus my privacy. That's a remorseless conflict."

Soon, wherever Miller and Monroe walked or drove, alone or together, members of the press were in pursuit. They fled from Marilyn's Manhattan apartment to Miller's home in Roxbury, Connecticut, trailed by members of the press who then staked out the property. They left only when Miller promised he would hold a news conference at the end of the week. The date would be June 29, and Miller planned to be married that day—a fact he withheld by having his attorney, Samuel Slavitt, make plans to get the license for a civil ceremony issued on the same day for which it was applied, a variation from the normal procedure.

Among the hundreds of reporters and photographers sent to cover the marriage was Mara Scherbatoff, the New York bureau chief for *Paris-Match*, a news and picture magazine that was France's equivalent of the American *Life*. She had been assigned a teenager to drive her as they pursued Arthur and Marilyn.

The roads surrounding Miller's home were quite different from the streets on which the teenager had driven in New York. He drove as rapidly as he could so his passenger could stay close to the action and get her story. But the youth was not accustomed to the twists and turns in the area and he lost control, slamming into a tree. Arthur and Marilyn were ahead of the crash and apparently did not hear it. By the time everyone knew what had happened, Scherbatoff was being rushed to an area hospital, where she died.

Rumors circulated later that the marriage was immediately rushed to prevent further tragedy. That was probably not the case, but that evening the couple drove just over the border to White Plains, New York, for the civil ceremony. Two days later, on July 1, 1956, there was a religious ceremony at the home of Miller's agent, Miller's father and mother, Isadore and Augusta, in attendance and Paula Strasberg giving the bride away.

The Jewish ceremony was Marilyn's decision, not Arthur's, and it caught him by surprise. She loved Isadore Miller, and long after her marriage to Arthur was over, she and Isadore talked regularly, missing each other only on the day she died, though a message from Isadore had been left for her that afternoon. It is also a little-known fact that when Marilyn sang "Happy Birthday" to Jack Kennedy, her escort for the event was her ex-husband's father, Isadore. Augusta Miller died on March 8, 1961, and Marilyn attended her funeral.

Arthur, somewhat bemused by all that took place between his parents and his bride, later said, "Until recently, I took my family for granted. But Marilyn never had one, and she made me appreciate what that means. When you see how much a family matters to her and you understand the depth of that feeling, you'd have to be an ox not to respond." And it could be argued that when they eventually got a divorce, it was Marilyn who was granted "custody" of Arthur's father.

The first MMP production was promoted for maximum publicity even before the Millers flew to England. A press conference had been held in New York in February 1956, Olivier flying in to stand by his co-star, who appeared wearing a black velvet dress. As approximately two hundred reporters began asking questions and taking pictures, one of Marilyn's dress straps broke. It was a typical publicity stunt of a type befitting the sexy starlet image she claimed to have wanted to leave behind. It also caused Olivier to realize that there would be more to the relationship than he might desire.

Olivier consulted with Joshua Logan concerning how to work with Marilyn. He was not accustomed to the types of delays and repeated takes that were normal with Monroe. Logan explained what seemed to succeed and what caused Monroe to lose self-confidence.

The warnings struck Olivier as strange for someone of Monroe's presumed caliber. She had several years' experience and he expected her to respond to both direction and her fellow actors in much the manner that he did: Pay attention to the director and follow his suggestions or discuss an alternative. Pay attention to fellow performers, playing off them as two people would do in real life, if real life could have scripted dialogue.

The basic story was not particularly exciting. Olivier, as Grand Duke Charles, the widower Regent of Carpathia, arrives in London with his sixteen-year-old, pro-German son, King Nicolas VIII (Jeremy Spenser), and his mother-in-law, the queen dowager. It is 1911 and they are present to attend the next day's coronation of King George V and Queen Mary. Nicolas will be taking control of Carpathia from the regent in eighteen months, and it is important to keep him happy. This task is assigned to Northbrook, deputy head of the Foreign Office's eastern branch.

The youth and his father are taken to see *The Coconut Girl*, a musical in which Elsie Marina (Monroe) has a small part. Grand Duke Charles has Elsie invited to a late-night dinner at the embassy, but when she arrives, she realizes that the grand duke has eaten and is waiting to seduce her.

Elsie handles the grand duke easily; the two argue, but then he decides to make one more effort, during which she falls asleep from drinking too much vodka and champagne.

The next morning, after an argument between the grand duke and his son, King Nicolas, concerning the treatment of political opponents back home in Carpathia, the regent tells Northbrook that the previous night was a failure. The showgirl, by contrast, has fallen in love with the grand duke and the queen dowager (Sybil Thorndike) helps her have a chance at him by making Elsie her lady-in-waiting for the coronation at Westminster Abbey.

Elsie is present to overhear King Nicolas's plans to overthrow his father and take control of Carpathia immediately. She works out a deal in which he will back off and wait his turn in exchange for free elections and a motorbike. Naturally the regent and the showgirl fall in love, but they part still single, planning to return to one another in eighteen months when he will have turned over the reins of power and she will be through with her contractual obligation to *The Coconut Girl*.

What was never said was that the original story was about adultery. The regent was married, not a widower, and it is his wife he leaves when he goes to seduce Elsie. However, American censors would not tolerate such a story, especially one told with so many well-known and highly respected actors.

The reviews were as tepid as the plot. *The New York Times'* Bosley Crowther had praise for Sybil Thorndike's dowager queen, Jeremy Spenser as the son, and Richard Wattis as Thorndike. However, "The main trouble with 'The Prince and the Showgirl,' when you come right down to it, is that both characters are essentially dull. And incidentally, the scene shown in advertisements of Sir Laurence kissing Miss Monroe's shoulder does not appear in the film."

Olivier almost did not care about the reviews. He had been as frustrated as every director in recent years. He tolerated her nightly sleeping pills. He said nothing publicly about her drinking gin for breakfast. However, he tended privately to call her a "troublesome bitch" (an opinion allegedly shared by her new husband), especially for the problem Olivier had when she walked away from him in the middle of a sentence as he was telling her how to play the next scene.

Marilyn rarely remembered her lines, no matter how simple they were. Eventually Olivier was reduced to not trying to get a scene right in one take. Rather, he kept track of what she did during each take, eventually taking bits and pieces of her best work and splicing it together.

Paula Strasberg, though present for only approximately half the production, created many of the problems by having Marilyn take a moment to decide how to handle a scene. Olivier would talk to the actress and explain motivation. Then Paula would say something such as "just think of Frank Sinatra and Coca-Cola," the statement a serious one and not the joke the others on the set first believed. Monroe, receiving conflicting and rather odd directions, would then go off in a daze and blow her lines.

The film was finally finished on November 17, 1956, the co-stars barely on speaking terms. Later it would be reported that when the cast and crew assembled after the wrap, Marilyn apologized. She said she had been sick throughout the picture.

There was more to the story than anyone wanted to discuss. Marilyn had become estranged from Milton Greene, and after the film was released with Milton listed as Executive Producer, all subsequent prints had his name removed. Olivier felt Milton had not done his job and Marilyn did not object. But other factors existed in all this.

Marilyn Monroe had gotten pregnant sometime in August, her daily regimen of highly addictive pills and gin (alcohol content 40 percent: roughly ten times or more the alcohol content in beer) continuing even after she learned she was carrying the baby she claimed she wanted. The miscarriage she suffered at the end of the first or start of the second trimester could easily have been caused by her destructive habits. In any case, had she been able to bring the baby to term, it is almost certain that the infant would have suffered from fetal alcohol damage and would probably have been born addicted to drugs.

(Note: Some sources say that Marilyn did not learn she was pregnant until she and Arthur returned from England following the shooting of *The Prince and the Showgirl*, the miscarriage handled at Doctor's Hospital in New York City. Allegedly, this was when Arthur Miller decided to gift his wife with a story that would become the movie *The Misfits*. He had already used her as his inspiration for a short story called *Please Don't Kill Anything*.)

The Miller marriage was deteriorating rapidly, though the couple gave the impression that they were happily seeking a quieter existence alternating between an apartment they had on East Fifty-Seventh Street and Miller's farm retreat in Roxbury, Connecticut. They only went out to Hollywood for a prolonged period so Marilyn could make the films *Some Like It Hot* and *Let's Make Love* in 1958 and 1960, respectively.

Fifty-three

Some Like It Hot

In 2000, the American Film Institute's members voted *Some Like It Hot* to be the "Best Comedy of All Time." It is the one Monroe film in which no one is overly critical of her performance, because the lunacy of the film, and the believability of it once one accepts what is taking place, leaves audiences laughing literally with the last line.

The story, which had the working title of *Not Tonight Josephine!* is deceptively simple. Tony Curtis and Jack Lemmon are Joe and Jerry, musicians who can't seem to find steady work anywhere in Chicago when they chance to witness the 1929 St. Valentine's Day Massacre. The mob's hit is successful, but the idea of surviving witnesses is so dangerous that soon the chase is on.

Not knowing what else to do, Curtis and Lemmon dress as women in order to join the one group of musicians who can get them out of town without anyone being the wiser: Sweet Sue and Her Society Syncopators, an all-girl jazz orchestra with a booking in Miami. Once there, the complications arise in a way that is almost logical.

First Joe (Josephine) falls in love with the ukulele-playing singer, Sugar Kowalczyk (Marilyn Monroe), who uses the stage name Sugar Kane. He can't tell her he's a man, especially when Josephine becomes Sugar's friend and confidante, so his only hope is to become the man she thinks she could love. This means that the musician impersonates a woman impersonating a man . . . yes, it's convoluted, but it does work out. The man meets all of

Sugar's criteria—a fondness for bootleg liquor, a fondness for sax players, and a fondness for men who wear glasses. Joe adds his own touch by pretending to be "Junior," the heir to the Shell Oil fortune who "proves" his wealth by taking her on *The New Caledonia*, a yacht actually owned by millionaire playboy Osgood Fielding III (played by Joe E. Brown): "The *Old* Caledonia went down during a wild party off Cape Hatteras." Eventually Joe and Sugar are double-dating with Osgood and Jerry in his guise as Daphne.

This convoluted love story/crime story/mob story/whatever has flappers and playboys, gangsters, and fish-out-of-water type experiences (such as when the mob chases Joe and Jerry through a hotel holding the convention for "Friends of Italian Opera"). But the genius of both director Billy Wilder and of Jack Lemmon is what allows Daphne to transcend the man-in-drag type of joke.

There have been reports that Frank Sinatra was supposed to take the role of Daphne. According to the stories, Sinatra missed the meeting with director Billy Wilder and the director, incensed, gave the part to Lemmon.

Lemmon starts with the obvious—he can't get comfortable walking in heels. He is chilled wearing a dress instead of long pants. Gradually, though, he more than slips into character; he discovers his feminine side, and by the end of the movie he is totally comfortable living as a woman. Even his flat chest is not a problem because this is 1929, when clothing was meant to flatten, and Sugar Kane is jealous since her chest has too many bulges.

A female impersonator named Barbette had been hired to help the men better refine their actions. For example, they were to walk by placing one foot in front of the other, each crossing the previous, and their hips would swivel, but Jerry (Lemmon) could not maintain any comfort. The impersonator, frustrated, left after two days and Jerry found his own way to be effective.

In the film, Jerry has to date Osgood Fielding III, an aging lecher who has married so many showgirls that only his mother is able to keep track of them. Daphne is obviously his next target, and on one fateful evening, Osgood and Jerry/Daphne dance until dawn. Jerry returns to the room he shares with Joe shaking the maracas used during their wild hours doing the tango and happily announces, "I'm engaged."

Joe, amazed, says, "Why would a guy want to marry a guy?"

Jerry calmly replies, "Security."

The maracas formed another inspired moment by Wilder. He wanted to milk the laughs in the script so he had Lemmon shake them after each joke's punch line, giving the audience a moment to appreciate the humor and laugh without losing the next line. Lemmon thought the director was wrong, but when he watched the film, he realized that he, along with everyone in the audience, loved the timing without realizing it was a gimmick.

(The scenes leading up to that moment are carefully planned and counterpointed for humor. Brown and Lemmon have no problem with the tango, including the dips and the rose in the teeth. But the scene on the yacht where Curtis is playing Mr. Shell was brilliantly changed. There was no question that he and Sugar had to have sex, but Wilder later explained in an interview with Cameron Crowe—"Conversations with Billy," *Vanity Fair* October 1999: "This is no good, this is expected. But what we will do is that he plays it impotent! And she suggests the sex. And she fucks him— that has to be better. It must be better to be subdued, seduced, and screwed by Marilyn Monroe—what could be better?")

At the end of the movie, the mobster who has been chasing them is murdered by a rival gang and the two entertainers are finally able to reveal their true identities. Sugar Kane is delighted. She loves Joe in any form and wants to marry him.

Jerry likewise shows Osgood that he's actually a man, to which the still-quite-happy Osgood says, "Nobody's perfect."

The brilliance of the movie gave no indication of the behind-the-scenes problems with Monroe. The drug abuse affected her ability to report on time and seemed to be a factor in her inability at times to remember even the simplest of lines. But there was also her ego, something that seemed to have increased as a result of the new contract.

For example, Marilyn Monroe movies were all to be shot in color. This was still a time of transition when color was not only far more expensive than black-and-white, but audiences did not demand color movies to entertain them.

Some Like It Hot was filmed in black and white, a fact Marilyn did not know until she saw the first of the rushes. Wilder, in a 1994 interview, told author Richard Buskin,

> At that time I was against color. I also had the feeling that since it was a period picture we should do it in black-and-white, but when Marilyn saw the rushes she was very unhappy. So my wife and I had to tell her that she looked very beautiful, and that black-and-white is much more interesting and more difficult to use than color film. After all, any cameraman will tell you that with grey, black, and white shades the effects have to be much subtler, whereas with Technicolor almost anybody is a very good camera-man. Then I also told her that the two actors who were playing female musicians, you would be able to see through the makeup where they had shaved their faces. Now, I don't know if that was true or not, but it satisfied her.

There was a hostility during the making of the film that was of uncertain origin. Some of the anger was over the fact that she had agreed to do the film. This was another ditzy blonde role, the type she felt she should not do, would not do again. She had taken the job in order to help pay Arthur Miller's legal bills from fighting the HUAC appearances and the contempt citation. But, as Henry Hathaway had learned, she also had counted on marriage to Miller to free her from the necessity of such roles, if only by having him create more serious properties for her.

Some of the anger seemed to be a growing emotional volatility caused by the drugs to which she was at least psychologically addicted. Also problematic was that a common side effect of any mood-altering drug is an increase in the symptoms for which the drug was originally prescribed. This was a distinct possibility for Monroe. There was no one monitoring what she was taking, no single physician or pharmacist keeping track of what she was using. No one could tell her of the risks or even recognize she might be in crisis.

Marilyn was also an alcoholic, though whether anyone was willing to admit this is unknown. What is certain is that she kept a red Thermos just off the set. Each time Wilder would yell "Cut!" an assistant would bring Monroe the Thermos so she could take a few sips to soothe her throat. She pretended it was coffee, and everyone agreed to the fantasy. It was actually vermouth.

Whatever the cause, she became vicious. For example, there was the day she had retreated to her dressing room to read *The Rights of Man* by Thomas Paine. The selection was typical Monroe, and she was serious about studying the ideas contained therein. But although her first responsibility was—or should have been—to the production, when an assistant director knocked on her door to tell her they were ready for her on the set, she shouted "Go fuck yourself," then continued reading until she decided to appear.

Another pregnancy further complicated matters on the set. She had apparently deliberately gotten pregnant before the filming started, and it was later alleged that she had done so as a way of backing out of the film if she decided she did not want to do it. She had spent her off time in part with Arthur Miller's children and he seemed comfortable with a child by Marilyn, but questions remained that would never be answered.

Marilyn was sick for approximately two weeks, and lateness on the set placed shooting back another week. This time there was a doctor who understood the problem. Her gynecologist warned her that if she continued taking drugs, she would likely miscarry with so much as a single alcoholic drink.

The red Thermos remained on the set, and one night, when Marilyn needed to get to sleep quickly despite not having eaten in several hours, she took four Amytal sleeping tablets, washing them down with sherry, then panicking that she may have killed her baby.

Jack Lemmon noticed another trait that created problems. He said that she thought she could feel whether or not a scene had worked. If she felt it hadn't, she'd insist upon doing it again until she sensed it was right. He was unable to see any difference in the two takes, but he accepted the fact that this was the reality of working with Marilyn.

Marilyn was not comfortable with the film that helped convince film critics that she was a brilliant comedienne. She thought she looked fat on the screen, yet Wilder had made every effort to show her in the best way possible. He did not position her so she would be viewed next to Lemmon or Curtis when they were in drag, knowing how awkward she might appear. There were no cheap laughs, but Marilyn did not feel she was respected. Again, the mild paranoia was likely linked to the drugs, the alcohol, and the pregnancy.

Ultimately the experience of working on the film that would be universally praised following its release was summed up with a remark Billy Wilder made following the November 6, 1958, wrap: "I am eating better. I have been able to sleep for the first time in months. I can look at my wife without wanting to hit her because she's a woman."

Tony Curtis was also asked to comment: in his case, on the experience of kissing Marilyn Monroe. "You want to know how it was?" he said—much to his regret, when the remark was seemingly endlessly repeated in the media. "Okay, I'll tell you. It was like kissing Hitler."

And Wilder had the final word when he was later asked if he would work with Marilyn a third time: "I have discussed this project with my doctor and my psychiatrist, and they tell me I'm too old and too rich to go through this again."

Arthur Miller was furious, and Wilder's name was removed from her approved director list, saving him the trouble of ever having to say no.

Marilyn's personal problems were increasing on November 8, when she was rushed to Cedars of Lebanon Hospital, convinced that she was about to miscarry. The baby was in danger, and Marilyn, who decided that she was carrying a girl, suddenly stopped the self-destructive behavior. She checked into the Bel Air Hotel to spend a week resting, then went to the airport in an ambulance so she could fly back to New York. There she again returned to bed.

It was Sunday, December 14, that Marilyn screamed in agony and was rushed to Polyclinic Hospital where she miscarried her baby.

As for *Some Like It Hot*, the film was released a half million dollars over budget, the total cost being $2.8 million. By the end of 1959 it was the third-highest grossing film of the year, bringing Wilder approximately seven million dollars. At least for the studio, all the hassles had been worth the effort.

Fifty-four

~

Let's Make Love

Reality was in the eye of the beholder by the time Marilyn Monroe was facing her next Twentieth Century-Fox film as per the terms of her new contract. *Some Like It Hot* had been done for Paramount. Now the studio was back in control for her next picture, a script Elia Kazan wanted to direct called *Time and Tide*, a story of the Tennessee Valley Authority. However, there were many concerns coming into play, from Arthur Miller's hostility toward his former friend to Kazan's discomfort with using Monroe. In addition, only the lawyers had been checking contracts and a vehicle had to be found quickly or Fox would have no right to Marilyn's immediate services. This meant returning to the type of comedic blonde loser/winner who had become the stock Marilyn Monroe character in so many of her past films, a character that, with each new film, she greeted off-set with an increase in her intake of alcohol and drugs.

In addition, there was Arthur Miller's perceived masterpiece, a story that would be her last completed film, a story reuniting her with her first major director, John Huston. This was the screen adaptation of a short story Arthur Miller had written for *Esquire* magazine back in 1957: *The Misfits*. He had the idea for the story when he was in Nevada to divorce Mary. It was based on cowboys he met who captured wild mustangs, then shipped them in trucks to companies that turned them into animal feed.

The expanded story was little different. Roslyn Taber, in Reno for a divorce, and her landlady, Isabelle Steers, meet Gay Langford, a cowboy who works wherever the mood strikes him, doing whatever is needed to get food and shelter. Eventually Gay, an auto mechanic named Guido, and an alcoholic rodeo rider, Perce Howland, decide to engage in the same wild horse roundup that Miller learned about. Roslyn is disgusted by the men and their actions, and Guido says they'll stop—if Roslyn will have sex with him. Ultimately the only one of the men who seems to share Roslyn's principles is Perce, and with him she is able to set free the captive horses.

Gay goes after the horses, rounding them up in defiance of Roslyn. However, it is obvious that he has fallen in love with her. He sets the horses free, determined to get a real job so they can start a family.

There are many problems with the story. The ending has undeveloped motivation for Roslyn, who is supposed to see herself as a hunted woman who relates to the wild horses Gay is pursuing; and the script fails to develop the conflict between Gay and Guido. It is as though Miller, afraid to explore those relationships that are similar enough to how he perceives his life and Marilyn's, cannot face whatever truth may lie buried.

Arthur wanted John Huston to direct the film, and Huston worked with Miller on ways to improve the screenplay. Miller was completely out of his element as a screenwriter, a fact that seemed to upset Marilyn. She had seen him as an intellectual and great storyteller, but instead of writing a stage play for her—something that had already won him great acclaim—he went into her medium. Marilyn, a product of Hollywood, had spent more than a decade mastering her craft and familiarizing herself with all aspects of production. As such, she recognized Miller's script as second-rate. Additionally, she knew she was supposed to be Roslyn, an idealized woman of little depth despite a somewhat sad backstory. What was upsetting was realizing that Rosalyn's dialogue had come from comments Marilyn had made during private conversations with her husband.

In 1957 and 1958, when Arthur was turning the short story into a screenplay he considered a valentine for his wife, she was in the midst of a battle that would end MMP as it had been known. Marilyn, Arthur, and Milton all seemed to think that there were plots to undermine the authority of one or the other partners. The fact that the company had a single asset—the acting of Marilyn Monroe—added to the tension. Worse for Marilyn, there were many in the entertainment industry who wanted her services but dismissed her importance as a factor in any decisions made. They had gone to Greene in the past and now went to Miller, but in all circumstances she was bypassed: a product more than a person.

Milton Greene could take no more of the hassles. He had been offered a half million dollars for his minority share of Marilyn Monroe Productions when she was between husbands. In April 1958, he was offered approximately $85,000, which he took. The company was essentially worthless, no further films being made. However, the buyout assured that Marilyn would not have to share future income with Greene. It also meant that Miller would be working directly with Kazan, a situation that still rankled the playwright.

Ultimately, instead of *Time and Tide*, Marilyn was placed under contract for yet another version of her primary screen persona in *Let's Make Love*. She would co-star with Yves Montand, a pairing meant to guarantee an audience. It was also filled with such clichés as the mistaken identity of one of the soon-to-be lovers—a concept probably considered overdone in Shakespeare's time, and he had been dead for several centuries before *Let's Make Love* met a well-deserved demise.

The original screenplay, written by Norman Krasna, was called *The Billionaire*. The story had been purchased in November 1958 and the first-draft screenplay was finished in February 1959. It would be a grand, international story set in New York, Europe, and the West Indies. The film was budgeted at almost $3 million and the casting would be similar to *Around the World in 80 Days*, an international movie with numerous cameo appearances by famous actors being released in 1959. *The Billionaire* would have cameos from at least twenty major stars including Groucho Marx, Gwen Verdon, Jimmy Durante, Dinah Shore, Danny Thomas, Jack Benny, and others. Gregory Peck was to play the man then known as Mark Clemens (Jean-Marc came with the casting of the French Yves Montand, since his accent was too thick to be pure American) and Billy Wilder was to direct. Wilder, knowing when to keep his mouth shut, explained how happy he was to be asked, and how much he wanted to work again with Marilyn Monroe; but alas, he was directing *The Apartment* with Jack Lemmon and would not be available.

Marilyn, though committed by contract to do the movie for Fox, still had influence over the script, which she abhorred. Amanda Dell, the character she would play in the movie, did not have the biggest part, so no matter how good the script might be, she would not tolerate what amounted to a vehicle for another actor.

Monroe was deemed more important than Peck, so Hal Kanter was hired to rewrite the script to assure it was practically all Marilyn, all the time. She found this appropriate and signed to appear on September 30, 1959. However, the changes being made were deemed not adequate by Monroe so Arthur Miller was hired to see what he could do.

The reason for hiring Miller is unclear. He was not a screenwriter, though he was Marilyn Monroe's husband and it might have been presumed that she would be amenable to a script that he wrote. He had been doing little that was new to generate income since his marriage to Marilyn and may have felt he would regain her respect. Or he may have thought that he could benefit his wife. Whatever the case, his main contributions seemed to be the changing of the male lead's name to Mark Bruester, reducing the male lead's part in the film while simultaneously giving more screen time to Amanda Dell, and eliminating whatever had been in the script that Peck found amusing.

Gregory Peck, livid about the changes, had the nerve to go directly to Miller and tell him that the revised screenplay had become "about as funny as pushing Grandma down the stairs in a wheelchair." He would not make the film.

Next came Rock Hudson, who was under contract to Universal, but that studio refused to loan him to Fox. Cary Grant was next, and while he was turning down the role, Norman Krasna was asked for another rewrite, this time calling the film *Let's Make Love* and trying to restore the earlier quality of the script—such as it was.

Charlton Heston was shown the script and said "No." Then came Yul Brynner, William Holden, James Stewart, and probably a few others. Finally, remembering that whoever the male lead might be, and no matter how large his part, he would need to be able to both act and sing. That reality led everyone to look at a performer Arthur Miller first met when he was cast in the French version of Miller's play *The Crucible*. The French termed the play, and the movie that followed, *Les Sorcières de Salem*; and the combination formed the breakthrough to success for an Italian Jewish actor named Yves Montand. (Despite his name, Montand was born in Italy to a Jewish peasant family that fled Benito Mussolini's rule. Montand was two years old when the family reached Marseilles where he was raised, the reason he spoke flawless French. It was also a background that made him an ardent supporter of the Communist Party, since he perceived it as the opposite of everything his family had fled.) In addition to Miller's play, he had performed a one-man show on Broadway, proving his skills as a singer and dancer.

Yves Montand ultimately got the starring male role because he was available. He was affordable. He was willing to practice his English with coaches ranging from studio professionals to his actress wife Simone Signoret. Krasna, assisted by Hal Kanter, brought a French angle to the story and created the final male character of Jean-Marc Clement.

The script was weak. On that, everyone agreed. Still, filming was started on January 18, 1960, the screenplay being rewritten in sections as they shot. The effort seemed to be improving the script to some degree, but the production was racing against the impending Writers Guild strike. The union's members wanted to be paid whenever movies they had written were shown on the new medium of television. The production companies balked, and a strike was called in early March. Any writer who did not stop working on every film project he or she had been writing would be blacklisted when the strike was over.

Arthur Miller was supposed to be an ardent supporter of the union, but $15,000 for his work and a guarantee of anonymity was enough for him to compromise his principles. The action troubled Monroe, who, by then, was seemingly troubled by almost everything her husband did.

The story was simple. Yves Montand played Jean-Marc Clement, a French-American billionaire who is sexier and more serious than Osgood Fielding III had been in *Some Like It Hot*, but is still a playboy worthy of ridicule. And ridicule comes. A play is being mounted off-Broadway, and while it is still in the casting stage, Clement is told by his lawyer, John Wales, to sue to protect his image.

Clement, curious, goes to a rehearsal using the name Alexander Dumas, another supposedly amusing twist since Dumas was one of France's best-known writers. Not that anyone notices. In fact, Clement shows such style that he is immediately cast in the part of the wealthy playboy—life becoming art becoming life. . . . Or something.

Among the cast members are Tony Danton and Amanda Dell, not quite lovers but becoming seriously fond of one another. This relationship is interrupted by "Alex," who is impressed with the maturity and comments of Amanda as she criticizes the superficial lifestyle of Jean-Marc Clement, the butt of the satire in the play.

The plot twists become a little like a bedroom farce without the sex. Clement's attorney pretends to be a man of wealth who likes to back theatrical productions otherwise likely to fail for want of money. He buys 51 percent of the theater company, giving him the right to interfere with casting.

Tony Danton may be Clement's unknowing rival for Amanda, but Clement is determined to earn his way into her heart through hard work. He hires Milton Berle, Bing Crosby, and Gene Kelly, each playing himself, to teach him to sing, dance, and tell jokes. The movie also uses impersonators to include lookalikes/soundalikes for opera singer Maria Callas, pianist Van Cliburn, and singer Elvis Presley.

Amanda, perhaps in deference to the new, "serious-sided" Marilyn Monroe, spends her spare time knitting and taking evening classes to improve her mind.

Clement does well enough to earn the lead in the show, greatly upsetting Tony Danton. Amanda, feeling sorry for the actor, goes on a date with "Alexander Dumas" so that, hopefully, Tony can get time alone with the producers so he can convince them he is the better entertainer. Of course he isn't, and she comes to realize that what she feels for Tony is sympathy and not love.

Alex now tells Amanda of his love for her. He explains that he really is Jean-Marc Clement, a confession that infuriates her. She will love a man for himself and not because he pretends to be rich. After all, she is not a gold digger (though Marilyn has played them in earlier movies).

All seems lost, so the lawyer/"investor" John Wales sadly explains that Jean-Marc Clement has taken out an injunction to stop the show. "Alex" tells Amanda that perhaps if she visits the billionaire she can convince him to let the show continue.

Once Amanda is in Clement's home, the staff is able to convince her that their billionaire boss and Alexander Dumas are one and the same. She is furious. She has been misled. She cannot be treated in such a cavalier manner. But, this being Hollywood, Marilyn Monroe, and a sexy French star, she realizes that she is so madly in love with him that she must have him forever.

There was a more dramatic story than just the movie, as seemed to be true for everything with which Monroe was involved. Yves Montand and his wife, and Marilyn Monroe and her husband, each moved into adjoining bungalows at the Beverly Hills Hotel. They became friends, Marilyn and Simone going so far as to practice the cooking skills they rarely used and had little developed in order to make the men a spaghetti dinner. Then, in April, Arthur had to travel to Ireland to continue working on *The Misfits* for John Huston, and Simone was filming her own project in Italy.

Marilyn was deteriorating rapidly. Instead of the Thermos she was using champagne as her major source of alcohol, but between the champagne and the wide range of pills she was taking, she had reached a point that she could no longer remember her lines. She became frightened and insecure, but director George Cukor had anticipated such difficulties. He did whatever was necessary to help her, from shooting scenes in very short segments to taking advantage of a restaurant setting to place her lines on the menu where she could read them and seem to be having a regular conversation.

He also recognized that, even though Marilyn had done a scene correctly, there were days when she refused to believe it couldn't be better. When she would beg repeatedly for just one more take, Cukor—rather than have her fall apart on him or verbally attack him the way she had Billy Wilder—simply had the cinematographer continue shooting with no film in the camera. When Marilyn was satisfied, Cukor pretended to stop the filming. Then, when Marilyn saw the rushes, she was thrilled because, in her mind, Cukor had listened to her until he got the perfect take.

But of all the work that went into the film, the only part that seemed to have life was the love scenes filmed in the absence of the spouses. This was because Montand, notorious for having affairs, recognized that Monroe's marriage was essentially over and that she was vulnerable to seduction. They had frequent sex in their bungalows even as they feigned sex for the screen.

The only problem the two faced was the eventual discovery of the affair and the subsequent publicity (possibly encouraged by the Fox public relations division). Simone was outraged but accepted the fact that, in her husband's mind, sex was quite apart from love.

As for Montand, on August 28, the day after Marilyn (by then working on *The Misfits* in Reno) had to be hospitalized for dehydration and exhaustion caused by the heat, alcohol consumption in the desert, and too many pills, he arranged to talk with Hedda Hopper. The agreement was surprising. Hopper hated the Montands' left-wing politics and they disliked her hostility. But Yves knew that he was perfect gossip for Hopper and that no matter what she wrote at that point could only help the movie and his career.

Montand dismissed the idea that there was a love affair. Instead he claimed that, at most, Marilyn had a schoolgirl crush on him, thus creating a misunderstanding about their relationship.

Hopper, angry, said to him, "You deliberately made love to this girl. You knew she wasn't sophisticated. Was that right?"

And Montand's answer, printed in Hopper's September 1 column, was vicious. "Had Marilyn been sophisticated, none of this ever would have happened. I did everything I could for her when I realized that mine was a very small part. The only thing that could stand out in my performance were my love scenes. So, naturally, I did everything I could to make them good."

No matter what Marilyn's feelings about Montand, she had believed he had desired her as a woman, perhaps as his next wife. She had not realized that she was being used. The truth was emotionally shattering, though there was no time to absorb it all. She was in the midst of her next picture, her next drug binge, and her next complete breakdown.

Fifty-five

~

Reality Check

The ongoing myth of Marilyn Monroe is that she was somehow tossed from man to man, a helpless waif worn down by verbal, emotional, and/or physical violence. Sometimes the stories even tell of her being used by the Central Intelligence Agency to seduce heads of state in order to obtain pillow talk that would help national security. This makes her at once a noble individual, a patriotic whore, and a woman with high ideals and low morality. It is also nonsense. Sometimes the stories tell of her desperate need for love, the tragedy of her having been an orphan, the difficulties she faced and the ways in which she was willing to behave in order to be approved. Sometimes she is a manipulating bitch, determined to be in control, playing the diva who can cost a studio thousands of dollars by her coming in late when she should be working or perhaps not coming in at all.

On the other hand, some stories describe Marilyn wanting nothing more than to be loved for herself, Norma Jean—wanting to have a baby, to live in a small house with a man who loves her, to have a family that could be the subject of a Norman Rockwell cover for the *Saturday Evening Post*, to be the ideal suburban white housewife targeted by the editors of the *Ladies' Home Journal*. This version of Marilyn wanted to be Everywoman but just happened to be a movie star, just happened to make hundreds of thousands of dollars, just happened to be in a position to have affairs with wealthy and powerful men. She was really just the simple girl next door who shared the values of middle America during the height of the Cold War.

The stories go on and on, one or more of them cropping up in books that have been published over the years. Sometimes they are in otherwise well-researched biographies. Sometimes, as would be the case with Norman Mailer, they are done by a famous fan. Often an academic weighs in, using Marilyn as an example of a white woman who has touched the hearts of blacks, or a feminist in slut's clothing, or whatever the flavor of the month might be in that part of the world of university ivory towers.

Fact: As we reach the start of what will be the last movie Marilyn Monroe completes, she is dying. Her body has been ravaged by booze and drugs, taken with abandon. The handful of people who seem to genuinely care about her are not in a position to help or make her stop, and those who are in a position to intervene will not do so. Most simply don't give a damn—a crude condemnation that, tragically, matches the reality of their interwoven lives. Some just want Marilyn to be happy, and if that means helping her get a good night's rest, what's wrong with that? Some know she is a cash cow and are milking her for every extra million dollars her pictures can earn while she is still at the height of her popularity, apparently telling themselves that they will get her help after the next picture . . . or the next . . . or. . . . Some don't want to lose Marilyn's friendship. They genuinely like her. They find her funny, smart, insightful, sexy, and a great woman to be around; so why mess up a perfectly good relationship by pointing out that she is an addict so over the top it is amazing she is still alive? That's just Marilyn. And some are justifying their own outrageous behavior by pretending that Marilyn is okay because their lives are not all that different.

Truth? Let's start with the drugs Marilyn Monroe is *regularly using* as she prepares to star in *The Misfits*. In alphabetical order they are known to consist of at least (there may be others that have not been documented; certainly she liked to raid friends' medicine cabinets when visiting, taking a little of this or that if she thought it would help her sleep, or be better on the set, or feel good, or whatever was going through her mind at the time): Amytal, antihistamines, Benzedrine, champagne, chloral hydrate, codeine, Demerol, Dexamyl, Dexedrine, gin (40 percent alcohol—80 proof), Librium, methamphetamines, morphine, Nembutal, Percodan, Phenobarbital, Seconal, sherry, sodium pentothol, sulfathalidine, vermouth, and 100 proof

(50 percent alcohol) vodka. If all was going well, Marilyn would take a nighttime cocktail consisting of a half tumbler of champagne, a Nembutal capsule opened so the drug would enter her system faster, and a chloral hydrate tablet. When working on her last movie she would sometimes have a dinner that consisted of three ounces of steak, one Librium, one chloral hydrate, one Nembutal, and two glasses of Dom Perignon. In addition, there were methamphetamine shots she received at Twentieth Century-Fox.

※

John Huston, speaking about Marilyn on the first day of filming of *The Misfits*: "She got some sleeping pills from a doctor in town. I first noticed her condition when we started production. She was *very* late, and as time went on her condition worsened. Often she would not even know where she was. Her eyes had a strange look. She was definitely under the influence. She had apparently been on narcotics for a very long time. I spoke to Arthur about it . . . it seemed so hopeless."

※

Whitey Snyder, her longtime friend and frequent makeup artist, said that Marilyn Monroe's work habits contributed to her problems. She would get off work at the studio, go home, and go to bed. This was frequently very early in the evening—seven or eight o'clock. She had usually not wound down from the day's work and would have fallen asleep easier and deeper had she stayed awake another couple hours. Instead, she took her sleep medication, either alone or in the "cocktail" listed above. She would then give the medication no more than an hour, which was seldom long enough. Today it is known that one side effect of mood-altering medication is an increase in the problem for which it was taken. It is also known that there are drugs to which a regular user can develop a tolerance, requiring them to either increase the dosage (a potentially dangerous but common approach), switch to another drug, or detox their system over several days or weeks, then try the original dose again. Marilyn chose the first approach, taking more medication around ten and still more as late as midnight. At that point, everything would take effect, and she could not be readily roused in the morning.

Snyder often had to do makeup while Marilyn was still in bed, and starting times for filming were pushed back by one or more hours to accommodate what was happening.

The drugs sought by Marilyn Monroe were provided by doctors and pharmacists. These were not street drugs; they were not smuggled into her home and forced into her body as she slept. This was her daily choice for living, for working, for dealing with almost everything, good or bad. She was a junkie. She was an alcoholic. She was a woman ravaging her body, her heart, and her brain.

To better understand what Marilyn was doing to her body, it is important to understand two concerns—drug half-life and drug interaction. Half-life refers for the number of hours or days it takes for half the medication to leave a person's body. It is not a figure routinely mentioned to the patient. For example, if a drug has a half-life of twenty-five hours, from the time the patient stops taking the drug, its effect in his or her body will be reduced by half in twenty-five hours. Then that half will be reduced by half again in another twenty-five hours, and so on. The effect of the drug will be lessened, but not ended, if the user takes nothing else. If the user chooses to drink alcohol, as Marilyn did daily, and to take other drugs or other doses of the same drug—again, as Marilyn did daily—the impact is a combination of the drugs that may not be safe, even though each drug, by itself, was not dangerous.

Marilyn, by her relentless abuse and consistent use of drugs and alcohol, was in constant danger of death. Not that the manufacturer's warnings necessarily explained this. Usually there was a notice about central nervous system (CNS) depressants. Without worrying about the exact medical terms, this means that the wrong combination of the wrong drugs results in the user's death. Almost all of the medications Marilyn took to try to sleep were potentially deadly when combined with alcohol, and she had been using the combination since at least some time before the making of *Bus Stop*. That she would die young was not a surprise. Rather, the surprise was that she lived as long as she did.

Then there was the sex.

From the time Norma Jean began modeling, she understood that certain jobs, such as with André de Dienes, involved activities where sex could be anticipated. Traveling with the photographer did not have sharing a bed as a requirement, but models understood that young women of equal abilities willing to reduce the photographer's expenses by sharing a hotel room would get more jobs.

Norma Jean knew that she did not have to attend the card parties and other primarily stag events held in the homes of various producers, but that young women who did attend made important contacts. You couldn't sleep your way to fame and fortune, but you were assured of getting a small part or even the first-level studio contract. True, you could get the same work without such actions—though maybe not so quickly—especially if you had a pretty face, great figure, and minimal talent. Allowing yourself to be bedded speeded the process.

Norma Jean was never raped. She was never kidnapped, never held hostage, never ordered to have sex in order to get a part in a movie. She spread her legs with frequency because it was the way she chose to achieve some of her career goals, the way to reward an occasional fan, the way she could say "thank you" knowing that any real or perceived debt had been paid.

Norma Jean married, divorced, gave "birth" to Marilyn Monroe who also married in addition to having serious affairs in a calculating manner. Each person was able to help Marilyn achieve her goals, and each was obsessed enough with her that she felt herself in control of what she felt they had to offer. When Marilyn Monroe had sex with Yves Montand, *she* was choosing to commit adultery.

Yes, Montand has always been seen as the "designated bastard" for cheating on his wife and demeaning Marilyn when their "love affair" was revealed. And yes, he was rotten. But Marilyn said yes because her husband was out of the country and she would not get caught. Maybe she fell in love with the man. However, it is doubtful that she and Montand discussed the idea of divorcing their spouses, changing the locations of their careers, and developing an actor-and-actor marriage before hopping into bed. He made clear he wanted to have sex, and she agreed with his desires. The first time, at least, was cold-blooded on both their parts. Presumably they enjoyed it every time, and it is certain that neither coerced the other.

So let's have a reality check. It is 1960. Marilyn Monroe is the female lead in a movie that has one of the greatest casts of its time, a director of international fame, a writer lauded for his plays (though barely competent when creating film scripts), and a desert location that is hot and dry in ways most of the crew has never before experienced. Marilyn is an alcoholic and a prescription drug addict who often appears to be just one or two more pills away from death. She is exhausted. She is sickly. And she has suffered miscarriages almost certainly caused by the damage from her self-destructive ingesting of more drugs than food.

It is extremely doubtful that she was mentally ill. Certainly mental illness *never* ran in her family, though a number of her ancestors had illnesses that created behaviors that looked like mental illness.

What Marilyn *was* was brain-addled from drugs and exhaustion. She probably had not been truly sober at any time on the set, only sober enough to feel she could work even though the quality was often poor, lines were forgotten, and she was functioning a little like a beginner with stage fright. Most of her co-workers, friends, and lovers recognized this truth to one degree or another.

The full extent of Marilyn Monroe's self-destructive actions may not have been known, but she was in such serious condition that John Huston talked with Arthur Miller about getting help. No one told the actress to stop. No one forced her to be hospitalized. No one confronted her. No one did anything, and that is the crime.

The tragedy was not that Monroe was a drunken, drug-addled slut—though those terms were as valid as those lauding her for her beauty, her comic skills, and the personality she conveyed on the big screen. The tragedy was that no one in the film industry who knew Monroe had the courage and the love to force her to stop when she made the choices that would soon take her life. And if the men who claimed to love her were users and emotional abusers, they had simply met their mirror twin in Monroe.

And now *The Misfits*.

Fifty-six

The Misfits

If Norma Jean could have imagined the ideal movie in which to star during her yearlong stay in New York, it would have been *The Misfits*. John Huston, the man who had directed her first success, agreed to direct the picture. Frank Taylor, a friend for several years, was producer. And Arthur Miller, the beloved intellectual lover—or so he had once seemed—was the screenwriter.

Then there was the cast. Clark Gable was one of the male leads, and Clark Gable was the claimed fantasy father in Norma Jean's life. Sometimes she said she had once believed him to be her father; sometimes she claimed that he was a father figure. Certainly she was an adoring fan who kept a framed photo of the actor.

Others in the cast were such brilliant performers as Eli Wallach, Montgomery Clift, and Thelma Ritter, among others.

The timing of the movie location was originally carefully planned to avoid the intense summer head of Reno, Nevada. Cast and crew were to begin shooting on March 3, 1960, but a strike by members of the Screen Actors Guild (a strike that had followed that of the Writers Guild) meant that the start of filming was delayed. It also meant that there were delays in completing *Let's Make Love* and Marilyn would have to go from one movie set to the next without a break. Her health was bad from exhaustion, pills, and alcohol, and the heat in Reno, when she arrived in the third week of

July was unlike anything most of the cast and crew had ever encountered. The dry heat reached 110 degrees.

Reno was not the only desert location used by the film industry for location work. Southern Arizona was also popular, and the Sonoran Desert outside of Tucson could easily reach over 120 degrees. However, most studios using locations had learned not to film in the heat of the summer. There was no choice for *The Misfits*, however. The only concession to the weather was a shooting schedule often handled at night: massive portable lights and reflectors created artificial daylight whenever possible, letting the crews experience "cooler" temperatures that could still reach 100 degrees.

Adding to the problem was a reality of desert activity. It was critical for everyone out in the sun to drink large quantities of water *before* they felt thirsty. They also needed to avoid diuretics (for example, caffeinated and alcoholic beverages) when out in the sun. Monroe's drinking on the set, in combination with the pills and the heat, resulted in regular periods when she was "indisposed," in the room she and Arthur had in Reno's Mapes Hotel—or in a hospital. On August 27, she had to be flown to Los Angeles' Westside Hospital for a week, forcing the complete stoppage of the filming. Marilyn was off the set even after her return, acting only for the week of September 5–12 before being away from the set for another week.

Adding to Marilyn's problems was the constant rewriting of the screenplay. Marilyn would work all day, then return to the hotel (approximately sixty miles from the location) and be handed freshly typed pages from Miller. It would all have to be memorized before the next day's shooting.

Clark Gable seemed to have the best handle on the original script. He would likely be doing only one or two more films before retiring due to his own declining health. The character of Gay Langland was unusual because the character had so much respect for all life, such an intensity of feeling; yet there was not enough to the role to understand the man. Perhaps it was Gable's own insecurity that led him to accept the role, admitting to friends that he didn't truly understand the part but felt the movie could be a great one.

Script doctors are not unusual in Hollywood. There are writers who are called in to make changes when a screenplay isn't working. They create new dialogue and perhaps new scenes the cast must learn. It is usually a onetime correction and then it is over.

Miller came from the theater where there are endless ways to learn what works and what doesn't. There are readings with professional actors. There are staged readings where the actors either stand still while holding the scripts or move about as directed. There are rehearsals and theatrical productions done out of town, or even in a small amateur or professional theater, happy to work with a playwright for a future Broadway production.

Each performance, no matter how elaborate, has the playwright present, listening to what happens when real people say dialogue aloud instead of just hearing it either in the mind or reading it aloud him- or herself. Are there laughs in the right places? Does the tension build where it should? Are the interactions of the performers believable? Does the audience suspend disbelief and become the fourth wall?

The experience of seeing and hearing the work in development leads to rewriting, often several times. And even during rehearsals for Broadway, it is not unusual to have changes because that cast, different from previous casts, interacts in a unique way.

Movie people do not have to work all day and then go to a hotel to learn new material for the following day. Movie people (in what some felt was the location from hell) do not have to return to their hotels exhausted, then master dialogue, think of new ways to perform, and only then, overtired—and, in Marilyn's case, overmedicated—try to sleep.

The drug dependence was obvious to everyone. Angela Allen, Huston's script supervisor, was later quoted as feeling that Marilyn was late in part as a way to get back at Miller. However, what concerned her more was the constant consuming of pills, to which Allen believed she had built up a tolerance. She also explained that despite all the problems, the lateness was tolerated because of the image Marilyn projected from the screen.

The reality of the destruction of the Miller marriage was increasingly noticeable. Miller felt obligated to get his wife to the set each day; yet that often meant that he, himself, would get to bed late, awaken early, and be obviously exhausted as he tried to be screenplay rewriter, nursemaid, cheerleader, and whatever else was necessary.

There was one slight change in Marilyn's abuse of medication, and that came when the doctor working for the production company faced what no one else had the courage to admit. He could not legitimately provide any more medication because of what it was doing to her. He said that he would quit before providing her with any more prescriptions.

Marilyn immediately switched to a doctor in Reno, claiming that she needed the barbiturates to tolerate being in the same hotel suite with her husband. However, it was clear that production would have to be stopped fairly soon. She was deteriorating so rapidly that the cinematographer noticed that her eyes were no longer focusing. Finally on Saturday, August 27, Huston arranged for Marilyn to be flown in a private plane to the West-side Hospital to be detoxed and get some rest. She entered under the name Mrs. Miller and was accompanied by Paula Strasberg and her secretary, May Reis. After that she was placed in the care of a psychiatrist, Dr. Ralph Greenson, and his associate, internist Dr. Hyman Engelberg, with whom Huston had to consult in order to see if the picture could be finished. Dr. Engelberg handled the press inquiries, explaining that Marilyn was suffering from acute exhaustion.

What went unsaid was that movies are insured so that if an actor doesn't complete the film for some reason, the production company does not take a financial loss. There is another story about this hiatus. Marilyn needed treatment but the production needed money. Huston had been losing thousands of dollars in the casinos, working out an arrangement to have the money come from the production budget. United Artists eventually had to use Marilyn's hospitalization as an excuse to collect enough money from the insurance company covering the completion of the film to replace the money misused by Huston.

No matter what Huston's motives, Dr. Greenson, to his credit, recognized that Marilyn was a drug addict. He cut her off from almost everything except small amounts of chloral hydrate, Placidyl, and Librium while supplementing her diet with vitamin B-12 shots and liver. He was able to begin strengthening her, though he could do nothing about the emotional pain caused by Yves Montand's remarks to Hedda Hopper during this time.

Marilyn was allowed to return to work on September 5. Studio publicists, knowing the airstrip would be watched by reporters, erected a large sign saying WELCOME MARILYN. The reporters felt they were in the midst of a loving reunion with an actress everyone cared about. They did not realize they were being subtly directed away from the real stories, from the drug overdose, to the affair with Montand and its aftermath, to the tension on the set.

The stress on Clark Gable during this period would one day be the subject of speculation and myth. He had been told that when Marilyn was a child she had kept his photograph and pretended he was her father. He did not know what about her past was true, but he could see how serious her problems were. He began treating her more like a father than a co-worker and discovered that, to some degree, she responded favorably. He also made certain that his wife, Kay, saw Monroe and what was happening so that she would be understanding of his efforts and not think he was having an affair.

Later there would be stories of Gable taking advantage of Monroe, of the two of them having a three-week sexual romp prior to starting the picture, of Gable being so upset about Marilyn's lateness and failure to show that it led to what would be a fatal heart attack. None of it was true. He was calm, controlled, and understanding. One friend, an electrician on the set who had known Gable since childhood, said that the stress came from the intense heat, the long hours, and working the animals against the advice of everyone around him. He was comfortable with Marilyn's quirks and occasional madness.

In one instance, Gable proved to be Marilyn's savior. By the time the movie was partially complete, the anger on the set concerning Marilyn's behavior had led to the creation of factions: for Marilyn and the original movie; or, in the case of a conspiracy among Arthur Miller, John Huston, and Eli Wallach, against Marilyn. The latter conspired to change the script, presumably to build Wallach's ego and hurt Monroe. Instead of the original story in which Guido (Wallach) offers to free a captured colt and mare that the three men were going to sell to a slaughterhouse for money, but only if Roslyn (Monroe) has sex with him, Wallach becomes the hero. He is the one who finds compassion and respect for life, instead of Gay Langland (Gable), as was in the script to which all the actors originally committed.

The changes were more extreme than just making Guido the hero. Langland would be an alcoholic ne'er do well and Roslyn's background would be changed to that of prostitute. There would be no sympathy for Monroe's character and the script would demean the character of Gable, the man who had been her childhood idol. The changes did not improve the movie; they only changed the story in a manner that had to be meant to hurt the people Huston and Miller could no longer tolerate beyond the working arrangement in which they found themselves.

The psychological aspects of the rewrite involved more than just script changes. It was believed by most of the people involved with the screenplay that Arthur Miller was using himself and Marilyn as the models for Gay and Roslyn. The idea was that he was writing the ending he wanted in real life; but if that was true, the change in script was a slap in Marilyn's face. What the change meant for Arthur is anyone's guess, but if he had written the original with the two of them in mind, he may have been willing to "sacrifice" his character in order to demean the woman who had dared to cheat on him—presumably before he could cheat on her.

Many months later, after Marilyn's death, the depth of Arthur Miller's hatred for his former wife, or perhaps his cold-blooded observational attitude, led him to create the play *After the Fall*. It is a vicious attack on Monroe, though Miller tried to pretend (perhaps even to himself) that it had nothing to do with her. Yet reading the dialogue, it is obvious he was working from their life together. It would also be learned that he took notes on what Marilyn said and did during their marriage, making the actress a character in a future play without her knowledge.

Why John Huston allowed the effort to change the script is an unanswered question, because Huston and Wallach knew Gable had script approval. This radical a change had to be acceptable to the actor or it could not be made, and there was no way Gable would tolerate what was being planned. As it was, Gable called John Asher, his agent, to alert him that he was quitting the set and not finishing the picture.

Huston was notified that the movie was about to be shut down because Gable was quitting, an act well within his rights given the contract to which they had agreed. The director spent two hours trying to persuade Gable to accept changes that were to improve the script, though both men knew it was nonsense. In addition, Huston had spent extensive free time shooting craps in the Nevada casinos, and had gambling debts. His ultimate losses during the filming have been pegged at fifty thousand dollars. The personal financial repercussions from having the movie ended over an unneeded script revision would have been devastating.

The performance bond was not enough to help Huston with his gambling debts. He agreed that his next movie would be *Freud*, and while he was directing *The Misfits* he took a break to go to San Francisco to collect a $25,000 advance for that project. Despite his need for Marilyn's cooperation, Huston returned to the desert and began shooting a scene in which Gay (Gable) awakens Roslyn (Monroe) as she sleeps naked under a sheet, at which point she sits up. The scene was repeatedly shot until finally Marilyn decided to impress Huston by going a step farther than agreed. She sat up, letting the sheet drop to reveal her breasts.

Instead of pleasing him, Huston found Marilyn's act pathetic. He commented that he had seen breasts before. The scene required two more takes, both with her upper body covered by the sheet.

The ultimate redemption for Monroe, in the eyes of her director, came on September 25, during one of the longest dialogue scenes in the movie. Roslyn and Perce Howland (Montgomery Clift) have a five-minute conversation which she had been able to neither remember nor act effectively the first time they tried it. Huston had given them a few days' break, then tried again on that Friday. To everyone's surprise, including Marilyn's, the scene went perfectly. It was the best performance of the film and probably one of the best scenes of her career, if such instances can be viewed out of context. Huston, who had grown disgusted with Monroe, was so impressed that he offered her the female lead in his next movie. She would play Cecily, a patient of Sigmund Freud. Freud would be acted by Montgomery Clift, with whom she had just worked so well. However, this would be shot down by Dr. Greenson, who convinced her to not take the role because Anna Freud, Sigmund's daughter, did not want the film made.

Proud of what she had accomplished but estranged from Arthur, Marilyn moved into the Holiday Inn where Paula was staying. Perhaps Strasberg was incapable of recognizing that Monroe was an addict and that to continue any of the medication she had been taking in the past could kill her; or perhaps she just didn't care. Regardless, there was no question that Monroe was in trouble when Huston and Miller went to see her after she had been off for a couple of days. Her hair was matted. Her nightgown had obviously not been changed and she looked and smelled as though she had not had a shower.

Paula also let Marilyn see doctors who would give her drugs. At one point Miller entered the suite and found Marilyn being injected with Amytal. She kept the doctor in her suite, but kicked out her husband.

Eventually Huston took the cast and crew back to Paramount Studios' Stage 2 in order to try to finish the picture in a controlled environment. Marilyn and Arthur stayed together in the Beverly Hills Hotel while she apparently deteriorated psychologically and physically. She no longer trusted or wanted her husband, and in the end sent him to a different hotel.

John Huston arranged to work around Marilyn's health. The craft unions agreed to change the working schedule, so they shot from noon to 6:00 P.M. in deference to Marilyn's lateness. The one time there was a change, it involved a *Life* magazine photographer sent to the set to record Marilyn after six, but Gable interceded, refusing to allow her to be used in that way even though she had applied makeup and changed clothes for the session. (The still photography would have involved working an unspecified number of hours posing after a long day of filming: an extremely tiring situation, even for someone in better health than Monroe.)

There was also a second photographer on the set: Inge Morath, who worked through the Magnum photo agency. As always seemed to be the case with Miller, though his marriage was over, he needed a new companion before the divorce. Inge, whom he would meet again in New York and begin dating, would soon be his third wife.

Marilyn knew nothing about Inge Morath until the end, but during the filming she was convinced Arthur was having an affair with Angela Allen, Huston's script assistant. Her suspicions were unfounded. A bemused Allen told her that she was pleased to learn about a relationship she did not even realize she was having.

The end result of *The Misfits* was nowhere near to the quality of the talent being paid to be in the film, but Clark Gable refused to reshoot scenes on location that had been completed in the studio. He had been a sick man at least since the start of World War II, but he liked the idea of working despite the stress. The nature of the scenes in which his character was fighting with a wild horse were of such intense physicality that a wrangler on the set could have, and should have, handled them. But Gable insisted on doing the work himself, just as he insisted in smoking cigarettes almost constantly and drinking excessively.

This is not to say that Gable was as foolish as Monroe. He tried to follow a reasonable lifestyle while working, at least to the degree possible in the heat. He arranged for his contract to assure that he would walk off the set at five o'clock each day, no matter what work John Huston had hoped to do. He understood Marilyn and was never upset by her lateness, in part because he knew his work day would end at the same time whether she showed an hour late or five hours late. Kay Gable was pregnant and he was looking forward to the birth. But his own past heavy alcohol and tobacco use, coupled with stress and his longtime heart condition, made it no medical surprise when he suffered a heart attack on November 5. His health never seemed so precarious that his wife wanted to be with him as he worked, but his condition was deteriorating at an unknown rate prior to that first heart attack. In the next eleven days Gable's health seemed to be improving, but his medical history was such that there was little hope of adequate recovery for him to ever resume the life he had led. A second heart attack on November 16 killed him.

Marilyn was inconsolable. The death was so unexpected that even Kay Gable was not with him at the time. The person who notified Monroe of the death was not a friend but a reporter calling from the West Coast.

Desperate for help, Marilyn eventually called Joe DiMaggio that night and he came over to comfort her. More in control, Marilyn called the Associated Press to explain, "I'm sorry I couldn't talk last night. All I can say about Clark is I'm very sorry."

The press was intolerable. They headlined her breakup with Arthur Miller. They questioned her about the pressures on the set of *The Misfits* and how they might have affected Clark Gable. They wanted to know why she wasn't going to the funeral. (She couldn't explain that she was so sick she was likely to collapse at the funeral and that would not be fair to Kay Gable.)

Simone Signoret was approached by the press to learn if the breakup with Miller was the result of the affair with her husband, Yves Montand. She responded,

If Marilyn Monroe is in love with my husband, it proves she has good taste for I am in love with him, too . . . Marilyn is a warm, delightful person. I lived with her three months while Yves was filming *Let's Make Love*, but this business could spoil our friendship. It's strange, you know, people go to the theater or the movies and they laugh and cry as lovers on the screen. But when those same stars are living real-life heartbreak, the same public becomes cruel. I'm not going to play the heartbroken wife as some people would have me. I'm no Joan of Arc, politically or personally.

The attention given *The Misfits* while it was being made, the coverage of the Arthur Miller/Marilyn Monroe marriage disintegration, and the Clark Gable heart attacks brought extensive news coverage, but the movie simply wasn't very good. Worse, with all the changes, the gambling debts, and Marilyn's deterioration, the movie was so over budget—$3,955,000, the most expensive black-and-white movie ever made up to that time—that profit was impossible. The first-run box office was $55,000 under cost.

Fifty-seven

Something's Got to Give, Jack

It is easy to forget that Marilyn Monroe, when young, was a physical fitness buff. She loved to run and worked to keep the figure that was securing her modeling jobs while she tried to get more than one or two words of dialogue from ending on the cutting room floor. And it was while running that she met the handsome, athletic young actor Peter Lawford, a man who ran and surfed (and who also ultimately was overcome by drug addiction).

Peter Lawford first met Jack Kennedy at Gary Cooper's house. Jack's father, Joseph P. Kennedy Sr., had been active as a producer in Hollywood in the years before the Depression, and was notorious for dating and bedding a number of movie actresses, the most famous being Gloria Swanson. This affair was so blatant that he took her to the Kennedy family home in Hyannis Port, and later he and his wife, Rose, traveled to England with Swanson and her husband. It was also a time when the teenage Jack came to understand both his father's philandering and his mother's acceptance. When Joe took Gloria sailing (an excuse to get away from the family home in order to have sex), Jack sneaked on board and hid. When he popped out at the wrong time, he was so shocked that he leaped in the water and started swimming to shore. Because of his congenital bad back, he was not a very strong a swimmer, and his father had to leap in and bring him back to the boat. Father and son came to some sort of an understanding, never publicly discussed; but the adult Jack seemed inspired, perhaps by his father, to enjoy the services of as many starlets as possible.

The meeting at Gary Cooper's house came when Jack was recovering from injuries sustained when the PT boat he was commanding in the South Pacific was inadvertently rammed by a Japanese vessel. The boat was sunk; two crewmen were killed and Jack managed to save the life of a third. The full story involved dereliction of duty and failure to obey the plans made to save the lives of anyone caught in enemy territory, as were the surviving crew members. But the mistakes Jack made were covered up by Joe calling in favors from both J. Edgar Hoover and Franklin Roosevelt. The respected writer John Hersey was hired to write an inaccurate, heroic account of the event, and the truth was suppressed (documents are in the navy archives). Regardless of who was to blame, however, Kennedy was badly hurt, and the handsome young war veteran with a penchant for bedding women was welcomed in the movie colony.

Peter was impressed with Kennedy, commenting, "My immediate reaction was that there was no bullshit with him. He was very straightforward and had a marvelous sense of humor. I knew there was a force in the room when I shook his hand. I felt that he was a rather extraordinary fellow."

Kennedy was impressed with Peter because Peter was an actor. The fact that his movies were often second-rate did not matter. He was a man who could sing, dance, and act with major stars, and that, for the young man who would be entering politics after he began to heal, put Lawford in a special category. "He had an affinity for Hollywood and its personalities that I think came from his father," said Lawford. "He would read weekly *Variety* voraciously. After he was president, he would sometimes ring up and tell me what the grosses were on new films. He was that kind of fellow."

It was 1952 that Lawford and the Kennedys would come together in a meaningful way that would ultimately include Marilyn. Peter had become friends with a number of wealthy, influential businessmen. One of them, Henry Ford, invited Peter to the 1952 Republican presidential convention where Ford was a delegate.

Pat Kennedy, Jack's sister, was also at the 1952 convention. The two began talking, started dating, and soon were engaged. They were married on April 25, 1954.

The relationship that developed among Jack Kennedy, his brother-in-law Peter Lawford, and Peter's friends and acquaintances in the entertainment field—including Marilyn Monroe—must be placed in the context of the times.

The idea that the media had standards when it came to reporting the affairs of the rich, famous, and powerful seems ridiculous today. Men and women make their living uncovering, recording, and reporting sex scandals, lifestyle excesses, and generally outrageous personal behavior among people who have more money, influence, and glamour than the average person can imagine. Drug abuse, anorexia, promiscuity, infidelity, wrinkles (from aging), no wrinkles (from Botox to fight aging), and all the other weaknesses and character flaws of politicians, singers, dancers, actors, and television personalities are the fodder of supermarket tabloids and respected news magazines alike.

This was not the case in the 1950s, however. Yes, powerful men and women engaged in activities that in hindsight raise eyebrows but at the time often went unreported despite numerous media witnesses. Nan Britton had President Warren Harding's "love child." President Franklin Roosevelt's lover, Lucy Mercer Rutherfurd, had to be sneaked from the president's side when he died in her presence. And many presidents had affairs in their backgrounds, such as Dwight Eisenhower's relationship with his driver, Kay Summersby, during World War II. Always the media was present at one time or another. Always the media ignored what was taking place.

Jim Bacon, Hollywood columnist and author, was one of the deans of the West Coast reporters in the 1950s. He always knew who was dating whom, who was cheating on whom, and the private, dirty little secrets of public officials who came out to Hollywood to play with some of the most beautiful (and aggressively ambitious) women in America. Referring to the man who became president, he said, "I used to always cover JFK when he came west to Palm Springs. We knew all about his girlfriends, but the press in those days was a little different than they are now. Everything changed after Watergate. We always looked upon Kennedy's affairs with girls as a hobby, just like Eisenhower's golf. And then when Nixon came and did to the country what Kennedy was doing to the girls, it made it different."

Bacon was not joking. The first person to try to break the media code of silence about sexual trysts was the extremely powerful columnist Walter Winchell, a man with close connections to both mobsters and the director of the FBI. In 1958, after encountering then-Senator Jack Kennedy sneaking out of a woman's apartment while attending a political gathering in Los Angeles, Winchell called his editor in New York. The Massachusetts senator, considered a lightweight in his home state, was viewed on the West Coast as a "comer" who was also movie-star handsome. Winchell felt that the story would be a good one for his syndicated column, but he was not allowed to use it on the grounds that Kennedy was a married man, a fact that fifty years later only heightens public interest.

The private lives of the rich, famous, and powerful are now presumed to be less than honorable; the exceptions are lauded by some but their principled behavior makes no real difference in their success or failure. In recent years the most dramatic example was when President Bill Clinton had an affair with intern Monica Lewinsky during his second term in office. There was physical evidence to support the allegations and an impeachment attempt that, though failed, resulted in much titillation concerning the thong she wore and how the president handled his cigar in a manner alleged to be sexual. Late-night comics delighted in what was taking place, and numerous columnists had months of material no matter who they supported. Yet when Clinton left office, he was praised for everything from how he handled the economy to his involvement with international crises to his post-president office rented in Harlem. When his wife, Senator Hillary Rodham Clinton, an accomplished politician in her own right, decided to run for president, Bill Clinton was discussed for his political savvy and the role he might play in his wife's administration—not his past, which included several instances of adultery dating back to his days as Arkansas governor.

The 2008 presidential primaries had candidates from both parties with multiple marriages, at least one sexual harassment incident related to alcohol abuse a few years earlier, serial adultery, and even misuse of government funds to pay for a mistress's protection. Yet during the primary campaigns, these issues were not raised when the press presented how they and, presumably, the electorate viewed the qualifications for the nation's highest elected office.

Marilyn Monroe and Jack Kennedy had their affair during a time when members of the media would have been horrified to have to reveal the truth about a politician's personal life. The president, whoever he might be, was held in awe the moment he assumed the highest office. Any activity that deviated from the idealized image of the president at home was fodder for gossip in private, but not appropriate for newspaper and magazine coverage.

Jack Kennedy *was* a married man. He also had sex with as many women as possible and had been doing so since 1942 when the FBI recorded his affair with Inga Arvad, a newspaper columnist, friend of Jack's sister Kathleen, and falsely presumed Nazi spy. Marriage made Jack more discreet, often forcing him to use the bedroom and bathroom of Pat and Peter Lawford's Santa Monica home. (The bathroom was the result of his congenital back problem exacerbated by wartime injuries in the Pacific when his PT boat was sunk. He found that he often was most comfortable lying on his back in the bathtub with the woman on top.)

The press was never privy to the intimate moments but they did witness lunch dates, travel dates, and other activities that could only be understood as affairs. Jim Bacon later talked about when several of Pat and Peter Lawford's friends gathered by the ocean and he held Marilyn's sweater while she frolicked with Jack Kennedy and others. However, nothing was said at the time. Nothing was said until the revelations of corruption and criminal acts led to President Richard Nixon's resignation.

This is not to say that Kennedy's actions were ignored by everyone. This was a period of political blackmail among rival politicians, often using FBI director J. Edgar Hoover and his resources. Assistant FBI director William C. Sullivan, writing in his memoir *The Bureau: My Thirty Years in Hoover's FBI*, made clear the behind-the-scenes machinations in regard to both Jack and his brother Bobby. He wanted to add to his files whatever information could be used for blackmail that would assure his retaining his job as FBI bureau chief at a time when he knew that Jack hoped to replace him with Los Angeles police chief William Parker. Sullivan wrote,

> Although Hoover was desperately trying to catch Bobby Kennedy red-handed at anything, he never did. Kennedy was almost a Puritan. We used to watch him at parties, where he would order one glass of Scotch and still be sipping from the same glass two hours later. The stories about Bobby Kennedy and Marilyn Monroe were just stories. The original story was

invented by a so-called journalist, a right-wing zealot who had a history of spinning wild yarns. It spread like wildfire, of course, and J. Edgar Hoover was right there, gleefully fanning the flames.

Lyndon Johnson, who would become Jack Kennedy's running mate and eventually inherit the White House following Kennedy's assassination, was a neighbor of Hoover and often shared information. Teamster president Jimmy Hoffa, Howard Hughes, and other men who disliked the Kennedys also gathered background material, as did Chief Parker of the Los Angeles Police Department. Parker did so in order to protect them, however: Bobby had been named his brother's attorney general and Parker did not want to lose the opportunity to replace Hoover if that option arose. He made certain that there were members of the attorney general's staff who alerted him each time Bobby came to Los Angeles, either to see Pat and Peter or for other business. There were to be no surprises, no leaks to the media, but full awareness of whatever was taking place both publicly and privately.

Marilyn Monroe fit nicely into that place and that time. She was physically, mentally, and emotionally exhausted. On November 11, 1960, three days after Jack Kennedy won the presidency by 150,000 votes, Marilyn announced that she and Arthur Miller were separating. "She has more guts than a slaughterhouse," Miller told a reporter for *Time* magazine a few days later. "Being with her, people want not to die. She's all woman, the most womanly woman in the world."

The emotions revealed as the couple met separately with members of the media did not alter the fact that he would marry Inge Morath as soon as the divorce was finalized and that she was involved with Jack Kennedy, Frank Sinatra, and their friends.

The Sinatra relationship was an odd one. They had originally met when the onetime teen singing idol was to appear opposite Marilyn in the 1954 movie *The Girl in Pink Tights* (ultimately never made). This was the time when she was also divorcing DiMaggio, a friend of Sinatra's, though not so close a friend that either felt guilty when she stayed in Sinatra's home following her divorce. Sinatra had also been part of the "Wrong Door Raid" for which he had to go to court in February 1957.

Sinatra and Monroe began dating following her divorce from Arthur Miller, moving into his Coldwater Canyon home for a short period, then to her Doheny Drive apartment where Sinatra was a neighbor. Neither was particularly faithful: Sinatra was involved with dancer Juliet Prowse at the time and Marilyn with Jack Kennedy.

The story of Marilyn Monroe has too often been told with the emphasis on the last couple years of her life when she had access to the White House, was sleeping with the president, and had trysts with Jack's brother, Bobby. There has been speculation that Jack was only interested in showing up his father, whose history included not only dating numerous starlets when he was a Hollywood producer himself, but also the dramatic affair with screen star Gloria Swanson. Some say that Jack Kennedy told Marilyn he was going to marry her. Others say that when Jack was shown to be callous and not committed to any woman—most certainly not his wife—Bobby convinced her that he would divorce his wife and marry her after Jack's re-election, an action the by-then estranged Lawfords had quietly told friends they would be taking. The fact that Bobby had presidential ambitions and could no more divorce Ethel than Jack could Jacqueline was never said, and Monroe presumably understood that fact of political life.

As near as can be determined, Marilyn truly believed in Jack as a leader for the nation. Her understanding of the necessity to keep the relationship quiet until re-election was such that she would not jeopardize his retaining power. The idea that she could become second-term first lady was no more implausible than her having been married to the man considered by many to be the nation's greatest athlete or the man considered to be the greatest intellectual playwright. She would happily wait.

This situation, if true—and it certainly seems to be—means there was no danger that the affair would be exposed or could interfere with the marriage. This being the case, Marilyn Monroe was not a threat to Jack Kennedy.

The greatest mystery posed by many writers is why Marilyn Monroe died at this time. The truth was that, with her history of self-medication and alcohol abuse, had she acted in the exact same manner but been a sales clerk, the server in a restaurant, or otherwise held a low-profile job, one would marvel that she was as healthy as she was.

For Marilyn, there was the added strain of a new movie contract that had to be fulfilled for Fox before she could make the movie in which she was looking forward to starring.

All biographers discuss *Something's Got to Give*, a film that also starred Dean Martin, Cyd Charisse, Wally Cox, Phil Silvers (Sinatra's friend and co-writer of Frank's early signature song "Nancy with the Laughing Face"), and others of equal professionalism. What they ignore is *The Jean Harlow Story*, a movie in the production planning stage by Marilyn's friend Sid Skolsky. He had produced the 1946 Oscar-nominated success *The Al Jolson Story* and loved the field known as "bio pics." His second film, all while writing his column, was the 1953 *Eddie Cantor Story*. That was why, when he talked with Marilyn about starring in *The Jean Harlow Story*, she knew he would pull together all aspects of the production for her. He had proven his ability in ways Milton Greene had only imagined.

But first Marilyn was committed to her third Fox film under her post–New York contract, *Something's Got to Give*.

Something's Got to Give was slightly risqué for 1962. Nick Arden (Dean Martin) is a lawyer whose photographer wife, Ellen (Monroe), was swept overboard while covering a trans-Pacific yacht race five years earlier. She is presumed dead, and Nick has gotten on with his life, raising the children he had with Ellen and falling in love with Bianca Russell Arden (Cyd Charise). Immediately after the judge declares Ellen legally dead so Nick can remarry, the judge performs a wedding for Nick and Bianca.

Of course, Ellen is not dead. She managed to reach a desert island where she survived all those years before being picked up by a submarine whose captain is kind enough to take her to Hawaii, the place where she and Nick honeymooned. She calls her home from Honolulu, only to find out from her children that Nick has gone off with their new mommy. And of course, Nick chooses the same place for his honeymoon with his new wife.

Morals being what they were in 1962, the marriage to Bianca will not be consummated. Nick listens to the story of what Ellen has endured, takes her in his arms, and realizes that she is the woman he loves and desires. He starts to make love to her but she refuses until he tells Bianca what happened.

Nick is a coward and, without Bianca understanding what has happened, he and his new wife end up in different suites, the marriage never going past the kissing stage. Ellen is outraged by Nick's spinelessness and returns to Los Angeles and the children, who do not recognize her.

Disguising herself as Ingrid Tic, a Swedish nanny, Ellen goes to war against Bianca. Before anything can be resolved, the plot is complicated by an insurance investigator who has learned that a woman was rescued who matches one seen in Los Angeles, and that woman may be the one on whose life Nick collected insurance. He also mentions having heard that she was rescued along with a man named Stephen Burkett (Tom Tryon) who also had been stranded, the two of them calling themselves Adam and Eve when they boarded the submarine.

The story plays out with Bianca seeking help from analyst Dr. Herman Schlick (Steve Allen); Nick learns of the existence of "Adam," and to allay his fears Ellen tries to get a meek shoe salesman (Wally Cox) to impersonate the man known as Adam, since Burkett—the real Adam—is muscular, handsome, and reason for Nick's concern.

Naturally, matters get worse. Nick is arrested for bigamy. Adam proposes marriage to Ellen, offering to take her and the children back to the desert island where they can live happily away from the world. Ellen only wants Nick, who realizes he truly loves only Ellen. He then stands up to Bianca, who finds love and happiness with Dr. Schlick.

The rather convoluted comedy was a bedroom farce that remade the 1940 film *My Favorite Wife*, a starring vehicle for Cary Grant and Irene Dunne; the script, written by Sam and Bella Spewack, was adapted from *Enoch Arden*, a poem by Alfred Lord Tennyson. David Brown, previously a story editor and executive vice president of Fox, was going to produce the picture to be written by Arnold Schulman and directed by Frank Tashlin.

Schulman's idea for a script outraged Marilyn, who had to approve of the writing. He created a thoroughly unlikable woman who, after being seduced by her husband's boss, tries to flee to the Far East. She gets to Honolulu, misses her connection, and the plane she should have been on crashes into the Pacific, killing all on board.

Ellen suddenly has the chance for a new life. She stays in Honolulu, meets another man, falls in love again, and five years later, realizing that the affair is over and with no reason to stay in Hawaii, heads home. She has knowingly misled the husband who loved and mourned her. She has had two affairs while married. And Monroe knew the character would be hated by the audiences, no matter how much they might like the film.

Not only did Marilyn demand the screenwriter be replaced, she also refused to work with the director. He had not been on her approved list, and the poor-quality storyline was proof to her that he had bad judgment concerning writers.

George Cukor, with whom Marilyn had been impressed when they worked on *Let's Make Love*, took over as director. He assigned story editor Ted Strauss and the art director/associate producer Gene Allen to rework the script to make Ellen more sympathetic. Marilyn trusted Cukor but wanted other eyes on the script, so she met privately with Nunnally Johnson, apparently never telling Cukor.

The script took shape, but other factors kept changing even as locations were scouted in Honolulu and shooting permissions were obtained. Vittorio De Sica, originally conceived as the actor to play Nick, withdrew from the movie, as did David Brown. James Garner was brought in for Nick, but he, too, would not be right. Worse, it was January 10, 1962, as all this unfolded and the filming was to have started five days earlier.

Changes came rapidly. James Garner demanded $200,000 to do the movie, but Fox thought he was a $150,000-a-picture actor and would pay him no more. He quit. Then, in the convoluted thinking of Hollywood, the new producer, a man named Henry Weinstein, turned to Dean Martin that March, paying Martin double what Fox had wanted to give Garner. Martin also ran Claude Productions, and the contract called for Martin's company to co-produce the film. The budget would be $3,254,000, Cukor would still be the director (an exact replica of his Beverly Hills home was built for the set), and Marilyn received and approved the Nunnally Johnson script on March 30. In addition, Walter Bernstein, a friend of Cukor and a writer the director respected, was brought in to improve the dialogue in the Johnson script. As with Arthur Miller's work on *The Misfits*, Bernstein rewrote continually during the filming.

There were several factors taking place simultaneously with *Something's Got to Give*, none showing the people around Marilyn in a good light. First, there was the fact that Fox was desperate for this movie to be made at low cost in order that the profit expected from a Marilyn Monroe picture would be high. During this same period, the studio was bogged down in an overwhelmingly expensive film starring Elizabeth Taylor and Richard Burton. All period costume epics are expensive, *Cleopatra* especially so since work had to be done in both Rome and London. The original cost was slated to be two million dollars, half of that sum going to Taylor. However, she became seriously, nearly fatally, ill when the movie was started, and the set had to be shut down while the actress fought for her life. Then the married Burton fell in love with the married Taylor, and the two carried over the onscreen romance with an offscreen passion that brought photographers from several countries.

While Elizabeth Taylor's illness and love affair were widely reported, what was not said was that when she became sick, Fox was told by Lloyd's of London to switch Marilyn to the Cleopatra role. Lloyd's of London was a consortium of insurance companies sharing high-risk, potentially high-profit insurance, including movies. Everything from accidents to the loss of a star can result in a setback or the end of a film. The insurance diminishes ultimate risk, and Lloyd's did not want to have a delay that could cost them hundreds of thousands of dollars. Substituting Marilyn for Elizabeth made excellent financial sense, not only in eliminating delays but also in reducing base salary.

Producer Walter Wanger (and later Elizabeth herself when she learned what had taken place) was livid. Elizabeth Taylor was a skilled dramatic actress who had been making successful films since she was a teenager. Just as she would be ineffective in the rather ditzy/comic/glamour roles in which Marilyn excelled, so Marilyn would likely be unable to handle the Cleopatra role.

How much Elizabeth disliked Marilyn would be shown after Marilyn's death when writer Max Lerner was chastised by Elizabeth for daring to write, "Elizabeth Taylor was a legend, but Marilyn Monroe was a myth."

Lerner said that an angry Taylor telephoned him saying, "You have a nerve saying that Marilyn was a 'myth' and I'm just a lousy 'legend.' I'm much more beautiful than Marilyn Monroe ever was, and I'm certainly a much better actress. What the hell do I have to do to be a myth? Die young and at my own hand?"

Exactly what was done and when in regard to *Cleopatra* is hard to tell. The first director spent $7 million and could not determine where the money had gone. The second director was fired during the editing of the film, then rehired because there was no one to replace him. The screening showed a movie so flawed that Elizabeth Taylor purportedly became nauseated and vomited as she watched. Worse, it ran six hours in length, an impossibly long story.

The eventual American cut, lasting approximately four hours, contains an opening session with Caesar (Rex Harrison) that was tightly made and told an effective story. The rest was boring. Since the movie ultimately cost the unheard of figure of $44 million (approximately one-third of a billion dollars in today's buying power), Fox was in serious trouble if something didn't bail them out. The only project at the time was *Something's Got to Give*, and that was not starting out well.

Although the public was not aware of the intensity of emotions of Elizabeth Taylor and Marilyn Monroe, the two women hated one another. It is no exaggeration to say that Marilyn was aging in an industry where thirty seemed the right age for a man to play a sophisticated young lover while a woman might be considered for the role of that actor's grandmother. Marilyn was the older of the two actresses, yet both were considered beauties and both were occasionally under consideration for the same parts. More important in the minds of the Twentieth Century-Fox executives was the fact that Elizabeth Taylor's pay for *Cleopatra* was one million dollars. Marilyn, seemingly an equal draw at the box office, only had to be paid one hundred thousand dollars each under her contract.

There were no changes, however. Fox was in trouble from which it would not emerge without having to break up some of its holdings. Even if *Something's Got to Give* was a major success because of Marilyn Monroe's drawing power, it would not make an adequate dent in the cost of *Cleopatra*.

The pressure placed on Henry Weinstein, the producer, came from several fronts. There was the need to provide Fox with a financially successful picture using their most bankable star. Marilyn had lost twenty pounds since she appeared in *The Misfits* and seemed to be in the best shape of her life. He did not realize that she was continuing to drug herself, until he made the mistake of going to see her at 6:00 A.M. when she was theoretically getting ready for the shooting. He found her in what he decided was a "barbiturate coma," though it was something others had seen many times. The studio executives played along with the fantasy that she was fine when she worked, and if she needed an extra hour to get ready in the morning, that was not a problem. Weinstein, by contrast, wanted to stop the picture. He soon learned, however, that not only did Monroe seem to get out of the stupor within a couple of hours, no one wanted her to change so long as they profited. This seemed to include the increasingly unorthodox Dr. Greenson.

Ralph Greenson, M.D. treated Marilyn when she was in the Westside Hospital. He was also the brother-in-law of Milton Rudin, the Los Angeles attorney whose services were used by both Marilyn and her occasional lover, Frank Sinatra.

Starting in 1961, when Marilyn returned to Los Angeles, she began having thrice-weekly sessions with Dr. Greenson in his home. The relationship seemed an odd one from the start, especially when it was discovered that his nickname was Romeo. Many doctors have an office in their homes, but Greenson began integrating Marilyn into his family life in sometimes cordial and sometimes unusual ways. For example, Dan Greenson, Ralph's son, worked with Marilyn when she wanted to impress Robert Kennedy. He helped her write out a series of political questions for him to answer when they were together at a party at the Lawfords. And Greenson's daughter, Joan, was treated by Marilyn as a younger sister. Marilyn helped her with her walk and her makeup, giving her pointers on sexiness.

Once again, Marilyn seemed to want to be independent while totally directed by a man, much as had occurred with DiMaggio, Miller, and Greene. In this case, she looked to Greenson to guide her on everything from her medication to her living arrangements. It was Greenson who had Marilyn hire Eunice Murray, whose role and psychiatric experience remains uncertain to this day, and it was Greenson's home she imitated in the interior design of her own house. And it was Greenson who was supposed to be Marilyn's savior—just as, previously, DiMaggio was supposed to guide her through the business side of her career, Greene was supposed to help Norma Jean break out of the Marilyn Monroe persona and movie, and Arthur Miller was supposed to write her into being a dramatic actress.

Greenson worked to control Marilyn, though not in ways that made sense. What was wrong with her was plain to see: she was cross-addicted to alcohol and prescription drugs, and she was physically and emotionally exhausted. Perhaps there were more problems, especially coming from a family in which heart problems appeared to be prevalent, if not genetic. But until weeks or months could be spent detoxing and rebuilding her health, there would be no way of knowing.

Greenson was as determined to be important to Marilyn, to be the person on whom she depended, as were the Fox executives, Paula and Lee Strasberg, and too many others she respected—or was simply too tired to contradict. A healthy Marilyn Monroe—perhaps leaving the film industry forever, perhaps truly creating a business—would cost the users in her life millions of dollars, as well as fame, influence, and prestige.

Greenson's controls never seemed to bother Marilyn, but they bothered others in her life. Joe DiMaggio came by the Greenson home when Marilyn was upstairs. He wanted to see how she was doing, but Greenson wanted Marilyn to remain where she was and for Joe to stay downstairs with the psychiatrist. Marilyn, who had remained a friend of Joe's long after the marriage was over, called for him to come up. DiMaggio, disgusted with the doctor, went upstairs. Never recognizing that he had been controlling, Greenson used the incident as an example of Marilyn Monroe being a narcissistic personality, always insisting on having things her way.

Henry Weinstein was an acceptable part of the Greenson/Monroe "family" relationship since he was paid to produce her picture and thus create a demand that she work even though she was not healthy enough to do so. This led to his being given "privileged" information about Greenson's patient including the "fact" that, like many girls, Marilyn wanted to go to bed with her father. The actress had never made such a statement. She had never even tried to have an affair with Clark Gable, the actor who had long been a fantasy parent. Greenson seemed to be projecting his own feelings onto his patient.

Ultimately it was found that part of Greenson's efforts to treat Monroe were based on his belief that she was either schizophrenic or had a "mental illness" which could be treated in the same manner as schizophrenia. The idea came from psychoanalyst Milton Wexler, whose real claim to fame came after watching his wife, brothers-in-law, and father-in-law die of the genetic disorder Huntington's disease. He created the Hereditary Disease Foundation in 1968 after his wife's diagnosis and the knowledge that his two daughters each had a fifty percent chance of dying from the same illness. But prior to what became the focus of his life's work, one that ultimately led to the identification of the gene that causes Huntington's, Wexler looked at schizophrenia and decided it was best treated in a home environment. The idea was that if the patient was living in the doctor's home (or if the doctor was present in a group or individual home), anxiety would be reduced. There would be a rhythm to both life and treatment that would prevent abandonment issues, a concern because there was also some belief that schizophrenia may be partially caused by the lack of appropriate relationships in childhood.

It is not known why Greenson assumed Marilyn was schizophrenic, though it might have been because she had gotten in the habit of referring to her movie character as Marilyn Monroe while many of her friends called her Norma Jean. This was especially true when Walter Bernstein was still involved with the rewrites for *Something's Got to Give*. He discussed how he would bring his work to Monroe's house for her to read the screenplay revisions. She was gracious and professional; however, she would discuss the actions of "Marilyn Monroe," indirectly reminding the writer that he was working with a developed character. The situation was a little like the famous comment Cary Grant once made as he tried to explain his own shyness and lack of real-life sophistication: "All my life I've wanted to be Cary Grant." Marilyn Monroe was just the opposite. She wanted to be herself, not her onscreen persona.

Adding to Marilyn's concerns was the fact that no matter what the final script, no matter how *Something's Got to Give* eventually came together, the studio would be selling her sexuality, the same appeal as Elizabeth Taylor's screen image. Perhaps the most famous of the images, especially since it has survived and is shown both in documentaries and in snippets on such Internet sites as YouTube, is the scene in which she swims naked in the Arden family pool. In another scene she falls into the swimming pool while fully clothed, then removes everything while under a bed sheet, though in the presence of both her husband and the man with whom she spent five years on the desert island. She also shoots a scene in which Nick comes to her hotel room and finds her standing in a negligee.

There were delays beyond the script writing. Marilyn had acute sinusitis when she flew into Los Angeles to start filming on Monday, April 23. She had spent the previous few days in New York, working on her dialogue with Paula Strasberg. The passenger cabin was typical of flights of the day and essentially recycled the air, causing many flyers to develop minor ailments after they landed. The change in pressure during the flights, the weather differences, and similar factors struck Marilyn in the same manner as they did other business passengers in that era. However, the possibility of Marilyn's becoming mildly ill or some other key actor having a problem was built into the schedule. The first few days when Marilyn did not feel well were spent, among other ways, in recording what were considered point-of-view images in which the camera replaced the actor and the audience saw what the actor supposedly was seeing.

When international visitors were being shown the United States, Twentieth Century-Fox and the other studios were used in the manner of amusement parks. Marilyn was asked to be on the set that Tuesday because the Shah of Iran would be there for a visit. Marilyn explained to Henry Weinstein that she would be too sick to be present, even though no work would be expected. She said that she had converted to Judaism during the time she was married to Arthur Miller and she could not tolerate the Shah's stated anti-Semitism and failure to support the young state of Israel. It was one absence that Weinstein understood.

A week after Marilyn was supposed to begin work, she arrived on the set for a difficult emotional scene that actually was enhanced by the fact that she had a 101-degree fever and sore throat. The scene was the one in which Ellen comes home to a house she has not seen in five years and to children playing in the pool who are hers yet who she has never seen at their present ages. She is elated, saddened, and generally overwhelmed at the emotional experience, a fact she has to convey with facial expressions and body language. And because of a number of different set changes and movement changes during the scene, six different set-ups had to be made during the course of the day. By 4:00 P.M., when Monroe was not certain she could continue any longer, there had been twenty-seven takes and, as determined by her doctor the following day, the sinus infection was again raging through her body.

In an effort to keep moving, the shooting schedule was changed so that for another few days the cast could do work that did not require the Ellen character. However, the script changes were still brought to her each evening and she was expected to memorize the work.

Marilyn fought to do her best but was genuinely sick, this time from something other than the drugs and alcohol. She started to pass out under a hair dryer on May 7 as she prepared to work, then had to be sent home after a half hour of preparation and no filming. She would not return to the set until May 14, at which time seemingly all the work that could be done without her had been completed. This time everything went well—for two days. By that time, the movie was five-and-a-half days behind production schedule.

It was at this point that matters changed in ways that would temporarily cost Marilyn her job.

Twentieth Century-Fox had been facing the cost problem with *Cleopatra* since 1960 when the budget was expected to be $6 million. Marilyn's illness came about when the budget had exceeded $30 million and was climbing, forcing the studio to lay off almost two-thirds of the people who worked there. The commissary, which each large studio maintained as a popular way to get an inexpensive meal, share the room with everyone from "suits" to crew, and to see and be seen, was closed. And a deal was made to sell 260 acres of West Los Angeles property to a developer, who turned 185 acres into what is now called Century City. The remaining 75 were leased back to Fox for continued use in making movies.

It was in the midst of these problems, on May 17, 1962, that Marilyn Monroe stopped by the Fox lot long enough for Peter Lawford to fly in by helicopter. At approximately 11:30 A.M., Lawford, Monroe, and her press secretary, Pat Newcomb, flew to Los Angeles International Airport where they caught a plane to New York City. Marilyn had asked for—but not received—permission to take a couple days off for the trip. It was the birthday of President Jack Kennedy, and she was to be part of the gala bash in Madison Square Garden.

The event itself was on May 19, and though Marilyn was scheduled to briefly perform, this was a fund-raiser where she, along with such celebrities as Mike Nichols, Elaine May, Maria Callas, Ella Fitzgerald, Jack Benny, Harry Belafonte, Henry Fonda, Peggy Lee, Jimmy Durante, and other show business headliners, each paid one thousand dollars to be there (tickets, depending upon seating location, ran from one hundred to one thousand dollars). The problem was that she had other obligations that could affect her contract and her future—as Fox production chief Peter Levathes explained to attorney Mickey Rudin on Friday, May 11.

Kennedy's forty-fifth birthday party was actually a fund-raiser to pay off campaign debts. More important, the same night that Levathes had talked with Rudin, a gala White House dinner honoring French minister of culture André Malraux included the newly rehabilitated Arthur Miller. His presence, and his being placed near the president (Jacqueline handled the seating arrangements and understood that the positioning was the equivalent of showing that the HUAC influence was over), was noted in the news. In light of this, Marilyn felt she had to go: perhaps to thank the Kennedys, perhaps to be near her lover, perhaps to stand up for her ex-husband. She also arranged to take her dear friend Isadore Miller, Arthur's father. She and the elder Miller truly were close, but she certainly knew that Arthur would be shocked.

Marilyn prepared for her performance by practicing singing "Happy Birthday" into a tape recorder, then playing it back. She wanted to find a stylized way to sing, something clips of that performance clearly show she accomplished. She made certain that she gave the studio full measure of her time, actually coming early to makeup that Monday. She also was insistent that she should not work past noon on Thursday so she would have plenty of time to travel.

Marilyn's focus was the Kennedy gala and the movie she was shooting. Spyros Skouras, the head of Fox, would also be in New York though he had to be there that Wednesday. The annual stockholders' meeting was being held and there were approximately three hundred men and women in attendance, all aware that their holdings were rapidly losing value. They were savvy enough to understand that between Marilyn's missing shooting days and Elizabeth Taylor's affair that interfered with the completion of *Cleopatra*, Skouras had failed to stop a severe drain on studio resources. Taylor's movie especially was bankrupting the studio, and not only was he responsible, the people attending the meeting knew that, with Marilyn reported to be coming for the Kennedy gala, yet more time would be lost.

Marilyn understood some of the risks. She had known about the birthday gala the previous February and had received tentative approval to attend. Henry Weinstein was amenable because shooting had not begun and there was no way to know the problems that would result from delaying production. By the time Marilyn was preparing to go to New York, the film was ten days behind schedule, which cost thousands of dollars over budget. Frank Ferguson, one of Fox's lawyers trying to stop the excess spending and help Skouras appease the stockholders, sent Marilyn, Milton Rudin, and Dr. Ralph Greenson identical telegrams. Each stressed that if Monroe failed to appear on the set to work on May 17 and 18, she would be fired and a lawsuit would follow.

The threat was effective. Marilyn and Jack had been planning her appearance as somewhat of a joke. He had her sing to him on the telephone, suggesting she use the voice she had adopted for some of her earlier Marilyn Monroe movies, the president understanding that she had created a persona apart from the woman she had become. He also had advised her about the gown she planned to wear, a twelve-thousand-dollar creation by designer Jean Louis. She wanted a dress that Norma Jean would never put on, a dress right only for Marilyn Monroe. However, she did not explain to the designer where she planned to wear it, nor did it matter. Jean Louis got the assignment in Beverly Hills and Marilyn would be fitted by Elizabeth Courtney, who worked Rodeo Drive, arguably the most expensive shopping area in the nation.

Jean Louis studied photos of Marilyn from her early pictures, then developed a nude dress, the fabric known as silk soufflé being created with an extraordinarily delicate thread. Sequins and beading would help focus on her figure without the gown seeming obscene.

The fitting was also different. She was draped, then the contours of her body marked for the creation of the pattern. Panels of soufflé—one report indicated as many as twenty carefully shaped and sewn together for her breasts alone—were strategically placed to cover the genitals and nipples because Marilyn refused to wear undergarments. Everything was carefully planned, measured, cut, and fitted so that when the dress was worn, it was so skin tight that it looked as though she was naked with beads on her skin.

The cost of the dress was from not only the expensive fabric but also the staff needed to construct it. Eighteen seamstresses were hired, and they were given only a week to accomplish the task. At the same time, Marilyn was polishing the song she would sing, working with Fox musical director Lionel Newman.

Pearl Porterfield, the hair colorist who had worked with Marilyn on her movies and for various special appearances, designed a color that *Vogue* magazine's writers called pillow-slip white. Whether deliberate or by chance, the color was the exact opposite of Jacqueline Kennedy's black hair.

Richard Adler, the composer and director, was handling the talent portion of the birthday fund-raiser. He scheduled Marilyn for last, not realizing that having her at all could be a problem because of the affair. Jacqueline knew what was happening and refused to go to the party, though the media had no idea why. Adler became more sensitive to the behind-the-scenes machinations as the event drew near, warning Marilyn that he expected an absolutely straight rendition of "Happy Birthday."

Marilyn kept her word—sort of—because she planned to sing the song her way, then have all those attending join her in the traditional melody. She lied only about what she had said she would wear: a high-necked black Norell gown.

Adler learned the truth about Marilyn's plans when he heard her rehearse the song the night of May 18. The following morning he planned to fire Monroe during the technical rehearsal. Adler discussed his plan with Jack Benny, one of the people who would be performing, and Benny was livid. He understood what was going on and was outraged that Adler had asked Marilyn to sing in the first place.

Shirley MacLaine was another star who would be appearing, and Adler had worked with her when she appeared in his musical *The Pajama Game*. MacLaine understood all the ramifications of what was happening and thought Adler was overreacting when he asked if she would be willing to take over. She explained that it was a long evening, the place was filled with top talent, and Marilyn was a minor part of it all.

Not knowing where else to go, and concerned for what might happen, Adler called Jack Kennedy at the White House and was referred to the suite the president was using in the Carlyle Hotel. Robert Kennedy had previously been contacted and asked to try to calm Fox so that Marilyn would not be fired, since it was obvious she was not going to back down. Both brothers felt there would be no problem with Marilyn's plans.

The day of the gala, the gown had to literally be sewn on. There were tiny stitches under the arms of the dress, down a breast panel, and up the side of the dress. Walking was possible because a small slit at the bottom of the dress enabled her to take tiny steps without losing her balance. However, she could not take stairs, and when she arrived at Madison Square

Garden, Secret Service agents carefully held her so they were, in effect, carrying her down the two flights of stairs needed to get where she could make her entrance.

Marilyn made a dramatic entrance, her hair white, her dress looking almost like she was wearing nothing but the beads that adorned the fabric. She clasped an ermine wrap in such a way that the impact of the dress was delayed. Then she moved in an odd sort of dance step through the lights, finally pausing by Peter Lawford where she shook her shoulders and let the ermine drop into his hands.

The show had been going on for quite some time, Jack Benny acting as master of ceremonies and singers, comics, and other entertainers performing. Marilyn did not arrive on time, and musicians filled the gap between when she was scheduled and when she showed. The crowd knew she was missing, and at the suggestion of one of the comedians, when Marilyn finally arrived, Peter Lawford announced, "This lovely lady is not only pulchritudinous but punctual. Mr. President, Marilyn Monroe." He gestures and nothing happens. The spotlighted stage area is empty. Then, with the spot out, Lawford turns back to the audience, and says, "But I'll give her an introduction anyway." The light goes on but Lawford is supposedly unaware as Marilyn steps into the spot. "Mr. President, because in the history of show business there has been no one female who has meant so much, who has done more, who . . ." Marilyn pauses for the crowd to see her, then starts walking rapidly, though with tiny steps, toward the podium where Peter is standing. She pauses again, pulling her ermine tight around her shoulders, hiding her upper body, then releases it into Peter's waiting hands as he says, "Ladies and gentlemen, the *late* Marilyn Monroe."

There were between fifteen and twenty thousand people attending the gala, depending upon the report. There were still and movie cameras present, recording the event. It was like a small-town gathering where everyone knows everyone else and there are no secrets—a fact that will soon be important to remember.

Monroe goes to the microphone she is to use, a different one than Peter was using, and as the audience applauds, she flicks her finger against it to be certain it is live. Then, with her right hand lightly touching just above her right breast, her voice slightly deep and throaty, her phrasing just different enough to demand attention, she begins singing:

Happy . . . birthday . . . to you,
Happy birthday to you.
Happy birthday Mr. Pres . . . i . . . dent.
Happy birthday to you.

Then, after the applause, she sings to the tune of "Thanks for the Memory":

Thanks, Mr. President,
For all the things you've done,
The battles that you've won,
The way you deal with U.S. Steel,
And our problems by the ton,
We thank you . . . so much.

When Monroe begins the line about U.S. Steel, she begins to make a subdued form of the gesture she has used, seemingly automatically, in all the movies in which she has had to sing a song that is sensual in nature (e.g., "Diamonds Are a Girl's Best Friend," "Heat Wave," "After You Get What You Want," etc.). Her right hand slowly glides up her right side, following the contours of her body until it reaches her right breast, then her hand lifts away and is flung outward so she is openly gesturing to the crowd as she leads them in singing the more traditional *Happy Birthday*. A five-foot cake is carried out by several waiters and Jack Kennedy makes his way to the podium where he says, "I can now retire from politics after having 'Happy Birthday' sung to me in such a sweet, wholesome way."

Fifty-eight

A Moment for Reflection

It is not spoiling the story to say that, by the time she sings to the president, Marilyn Monroe only has a short time to live. The question better addressed at this point in her life is not how she died, but why.

Americans have always loved a bit of fantasy when looking at their history, their idols, and the people living lives of glamour, wealth, and excitement. Some of this is the natural "spin" of history written by the winners—and other self-interested parties. That is why George Washington is a traitor to the British and a hero to the Americans. That is also why we don't read of George, a man with a wandering eye and a heart that did not belong to the widowed Martha Custis (who came financially well-endowed from her late husband's estate) but rather to his neighbor's wife, Sally Fairfax. Thanks to Parson Mason Locke Weems, author of an idealized pseudo-biography (the source of the chopping-down-the-cherry-tree story, the tossing-of-the-coin-across-the-Potomac, and other fabricated events), we celebrate that idealized portion of Washington's life that makes us comfortable.

Abraham Lincoln's actions during the Civil War are viewed in three ways: the Confederate version, in which he destroys the South's economy and way of life; the idealized northern version, in which he hated slavery, hated what was done to blacks, and fought against pure evil; and reality, in which many of his feelings are unknown from looking at his papers and the legal cases he handled before running for president, but it is clear that saving the Union was critical in his mind, no matter what the consequences.

Entire industries revolve around maintaining the myths of our entertainers. Public relations specialists, advertising account executives, magazine editors and writers, gossip columnists, tabloid papers, and the like provide us with the person we want to be our hero. Rock Hudson, a gay male who enjoyed being the aggressor in sadomasochistic sex, played virile, heterosexual leading men. He married on orders of the studio, proving he was straight, loving, and the ideal spouse/lover seen on the screen with such professional virgins as Doris Day. Most recently, a young rock star—apparently with bipolar disorder, which led to violent outbursts—was endangering her children, destroying her marriage, and making her home a regular stop for law enforcement. Her sister—too young, sweet, and innocent for more than a chaste kiss on television—was "surprised" to find herself pregnant. And their mother was writing a book on how even the mother of celebrities can raise healthy, stable, moral children.

So now we have Marilyn and all the people around her, from reporters to columnists, dealing with a secretly cross-addicted film star whose ability to make money for a studio was determined by her physical appearance, not her acting ability. She had come to the set of *Something's Got to Give* twenty pounds lighter than when she appeared in *The Misfits*, a fact that seemed to indicate she was healthy. Certainly her skin lacked the lines and wrinkles that might otherwise betray the fact that she was getting older (though she did note in an interview that eventually gravity caught up with every woman). She would be making *The Jean Harlow Story*, a movie that would please her mother and others in her life. Minimum profit per picture seemed to be $1 million; and the industry was just beginning to see the possibility of showing their feature films on television, another source of revenue and one from which almost no actor would profit under the contracts in force when the films were made. And even more important, Marilyn was not the only star in the Hollywood universe. Some were older, some were younger, and some were just beginning to catch on with the movie audience. All needed to be written about in order to become better known (and to promote their films). But all of the newspeople needed access to prove to their editors that they should keep their jobs.

Between fifteen and twenty thousand men and women, including police, secret service, and the Madison Square Garden support staff, were all aware that Jack Kennedy was having an affair with Marilyn. They knew that his wife, Jacqueline, was also aware of this fact, and had refused to come to Madison Square Garden unless she could coordinate the event to ensure Marilyn would not be present. They knew that the public would be shocked. And they knew that none of them was going to say anything. Otherwise there was no way that Bobby Kennedy—who handled uncomfortable problems for his older brother—and the president's advisers would have allowed such a scene. (Again, note that both men had been called and both approved this very public show of affection.)

All the details of Marilyn's last days and the machinations of what, to the nation, were far more important concerns, such as the attempts since 1959 to kill Cuban leader Fidel Castro, are too involved for a book that must cover so much of her life. A number of writers have tried narrowing their attention to this time period, with varying degrees of accuracy. However, there are some details that must be noted.

1. U.S. president Jack Kennedy and Chicago crime boss Sam "Momo" Giancana were both having sex with Judith Campbell Exner, who was acting as a go-between, delivering personal messages related to organized crime activities on behalf of the U.S. government. She knew about the assassination attempt against Castro. She presumably knew about the rigging of the 1960 election in at least Illinois. (That Illinois, West Virginia, and New Jersey had vote counts that would not equate with the number of living voters turning out at the polls did not mean one side was dirty and the other clean. At the time, when the approximately 150,000-vote win by Kennedy was a statistical anomaly that could have been reversed with a recount, Richard Nixon magnanimously accepted the results and bided his time until he could be elected in the future. Later knowledge indicates that both individuals, and/or members of their party, and/or independent supporters undoubtedly rigged the elections in a number of areas. An investigation would have shown that both sides were dirty.) And most important of all, Exner was the living proof that the president of the United States was working directly with one of the most violent, amoral leaders of the Mafia.

What happened to Judith Campbell Exner? She died of cancer on September 25, 1999, many years after both Kennedy brothers and Monroe. If anyone could have exposed illicit or dishonorable behavior on the part of the Kennedys, it was Exner, making her, not Monroe, the most dangerous woman alive at the time.

2. Marita Lorenz, still alive and healthy at this writing, was the female assassin chosen to poison Fidel Castro with capsules concealed inside a cold cream jar for transport to Havana. She knew everything taking place but fell in love with her target, eventually giving birth to one of his sons. If Monroe was considered too dangerous to live, would not Lorenz—so intimate with a national secret—have been even more so?

3. Marilyn Monroe was cross-addicted, a fact that would have made the staging of an auto accident the easiest and safest (for any would-be murderers). Since the publicity mill had hidden the horrendous amount of drugs Marilyn took and the way they had ravaged her body, just finding her cache of medication would be shocking. Instead of realizing that her addiction and deterioration had been concealed, the unexpected find would convince some observers that she had been murdered, then the pill bottles strewn about to imply an accident that had not happened. However, the truth was that the death was accidental, the only question being how she had managed to physically survive the abuse of the pills.

4. And always when looking at this moment in Marilyn's life, it must be remembered that in any crowd of more than fifteen thousand people there are going to be those who talk. Celebrities, as curious and malicious as their fans, love to gossip about one another. If anyone in the government had feared Marilyn, she never would have gone to Madison Square Garden to sing "Happy Birthday" ". . . in such a sweet, wholesome way."

And now back to Hollywood.

Fifty-nine

Countdown to Overdosing

Dr. Greenson, increasingly the villain in the destruction of Marilyn's health, was a questionable "benefactor" in other ways as well. He knew that Marilyn received "vitamin" shots from Twentieth Century-Fox staff physician Lee Seigel, M.D., an experience the actors and crew never questioned.

Dr. Seigel was the West Coast equivalent of New York's Dr. Max Jacobson, a renegade physician generally known as "Dr. Feelgood," and whose client list included Jack Kennedy. He, too, specialized in "vitamin" shots and all who experienced the treatment went away feeling better. This was because the "vitamins" were amphetamines and other prescription drugs, perhaps combined with vitamins, perhaps not. No one was familiar with the full range of contents, but Dr. Greenson had to know what was happening.

In addition to Seigel, Dr. Hyman Engelberg, Marilyn's internist, provided similar shots on a frequent basis, ultimately giving her twenty-nine shots in the period from June 28 through August 3, 1962. He also provided her with twenty-five Nembutal capsules, which he arranged for her to pick up in Brentwood's San Vicente Pharmacy on August 3, 1962, two days before her death.

The controlling side of Greenson and his delusions about his own importance seems most evident in a comment he made that was later quoted by author Donald Spoto.

> When I left for a five-week vacation, I felt it was indicated to leave her some medication which she might take when she felt depressed and agi-

tated. [Note: Marilyn is still under the care of Dr. Hyman Engelberg and the studio doctor. No matter what their competence or contributions to Marilyn's drug abuse, they were valid doctors who could easily serve as back-ups if needed. They seem to have not existed in Greenson's planning.] I prescribed a drug which is a quick-acting anti-depressant in combination with a sedative—Dexamyl. I also hoped she would be benefited by having something from me to depend on. [Note: This sounds like a pharmaceutical teddy bear or security blanket.] I can condense the situation by saying that, at the time of my vacation, I felt that she would be unable to bear the depressive anxieties of being alone. The administering of the pill was an attempt to give her something of me to swallow, to take in, so that she could overcome the sense of terrible emptiness that would depress and infuriate her. [Note: The doctor's wording sounds as though he is having his patient perform a ritual little different from the way some Christian traditions view communion.]

Dexamyl (the brand name of the combination of dextroamphetamine and amobarbital) was not considered a problem drug at the time Greenson prescribed it for Monroe. The idea behind the drug seemed a logical one—until the problems emerged (though, admittedly, this was only after Marilyn was given the drug). There was an amphetamine for stimulation and a barbiturate to counter the extreme stimulation of the amphetamine. When it worked, it seemed to be an effective way to fight depression and help with weight reduction/weight control. When it did not work, it could increase depression. Either way, the drug was highly addictive over time, though when someone would become dependent was uncertain, since it seemed to vary according to unpredictable factors.

The problem in Greenson's case is the sick use of the drug. Marilyn was an active addict. He knew at least some of the medication she was on, and he knew it was far too much. Why he would leave her drugs on top of the drugs she was already taking raises as serious questions about his dependency on her and on keeping her in his life as it does about her dependency on him and the drugs he prescribed. Likewise, the use of alcohol when taking the medication added to the danger. The idea that they were sharing a special pill between them, a pill that would be as seemingly symbolic as the bread and wine of communion, was a perversion of the therapist/patient relationship.

And all of this would be ignored as Marilyn raced toward her premature death.

There were other players in the last act of this scenario. Marilyn, on Dr. Greenson's recommendation, employed Eunice Murray, whose exact function—other than helping Marilyn get from day to day and following the doctor's orders—remains unclear even after she wrote a book (*Marilyn: The Last Months* with Rose Shade) about this period of her life.

Eunice Murray had been hired to work in Marilyn's home in November 1961 and she would be there through August 5, 1962. In her book, Murray states that her role in Marilyn's life was a little like that of a butler, social secretary, companion, and interior decorator, with other chores handled as needed. Some of her self-described skills may have come from the fact that when Marilyn bought a small, one-story home in Brentwood in February, Eunice assisted Marilyn with the purchase of Mexican furnishings and the remaking of the interior. Beyond that, there was the rather odd comment she would make in mid-August 1962 to the *Los Angeles Herald-Examiner:* "Dr. Greenson gave me certain instructions about Marilyn, but I can't say what they were."

The real question is who or what Murray was other than, perhaps, self-important and scared by events. It is known that she was born in Chicago in 1902, moving to Los Angeles where she lived in a Mexican-style house. In 1948, well before anyone knew Marilyn Monroe as a screen star, Murray sold her house to Greenson. Why they stayed in touch after that time is not known, though Shade wrote of Murray, "She was drawn to psychology, feeling a need to work with people and their problems. Eunice read and studied, and when an opportunity came to care for a psychiatric case in the patient's home, Eunice was prepared with enough knowledge and understanding to work under the guidance of a psychiatrist as his aide, helping in any kind of therapy that seemed indicated. She worked with many kinds of patients."

(Note: Murray's book, the most complete resource available, raises more questions than it answers because Murray seems to have little to say. Most as-told-to autobiographies—the category into which her book falls—is written, as much as possible, in the first person. The book is, after all, the subject's story of his or her life. *Marilyn: The Last Months* reads like a book written by an author who could not get her subject to open up about herself; or, equally likely, a book about a woman who had almost nothing to say. Murray was not a nurse, nor did Marilyn need or want one in her home. If she was Greenson's spy, as many have alleged, then she was fully aware that Monroe was disintegrating in her care. More important is the fact that Eunice Murray's stories changed with the telling, a common trait among those who succeeded in profiting from Marilyn's life and/or death.)

Marilyn Monroe had no reason to know she was being targeted as the scapegoat for Elizabeth Taylor's excesses on *Cleopatra*. That movie was so ridiculously over budget that even if it was a major success, it was doubtful that the costs could have been recouped. In addition, Taylor had her own problems with health, including meningitis and pneumonia. However, the script was complete, the sets built, the costuming done, and a large portion of the movie had already been filmed. Shutting it down would accomplish nothing and might make matters worse—or so the Fox executives thought. It was easier to focus on the problems and potential of *Something's Got to Give*, except. . . .

It was May 22 when Dean Martin arrived on the set with a cold. Marilyn was back from New York and looking to work, but exhausted and—according to her doctor—susceptible to getting sick if she worked with Dean while he was likely still contagious. He ended up going home and not returning until May 25. Although this was a setback for production, they had picked up two-and-a-half days prior to that time so the filming had gone from ten days behind schedule to just seven-and-a-half days, time that could probably again be regained.

Marilyn reported to work while Dean was off, producing the most famous scene to survive the early filming. This was the nude pool scene that was both filmed and recorded by three staff photographers. Marilyn was given a flesh-colored bodysuit to wear, but she saw no need for false modesty. She removed the suit and did the scene naked. The still images became among the most reproduced pictures from a motion picture, used on more than thirty magazine covers internationally within the next few months, and gracing more covers and inside stories after that. This was also the first time a major American film star had gone nude in a movie, adding to the interest.

The real concern was the script. It was being rewritten so often that there was no ending. In a sense, the film had been started prematurely, though it was not all that unusual for a movie to be started before the script was finished.

Much of the criticism came from the producer and director. The crew enjoyed working with Marilyn because she was helpful and willing to do anything they requested, and her desire to rework scenes until she felt they were right also meant she would work with the crew when they needed retakes. At the same time, there was a sense that Marilyn was not comfortable with the film, that she wanted an out.

Whatever the truth to Marilyn's feelings, she worked daily and well from the moment Dean returned on May 25 even though she had an ear infection. On Friday, June 1—Marilyn's birthday—there was a scene successfully shot with the diminutive Wally Cox, the shoe salesman claiming to be the Adam with whom Ellen spent five years on the island. When the work was done, director George Cukor allowed Marilyn's stand-in, Evelyn Moriarity, to bring in a birthday cake for a small celebration. Everyone was cordial, but it was clear that Marilyn resented the way she had been treated by the Fox top brass. As a result, Marilyn called in "sick" on Monday, and by 4:00 P.M., outraged by the backbiting and problems created by the executives, Dean Martin walked off the set. All work that still needed to be done involved Dean, Marilyn, or both; their absence effectively shut down the set.

On Tuesday, June 5, Marilyn was told to report to work or face a lawsuit, and Cukor upped the pressure by "secretly" alerting Hedda Hopper to what was happening. Two days later, there was a "leak" that said Marilyn had been fired, the movie was continuing, and the streets were being scoured for replacement actresses.

George Cukor had his columnist and Henry Weinstein had his, Sheilah Graham. He told Graham that Marilyn was not sick because there was no medical report; instead, she was simply not coming to work. He claimed that there had been thirty-three scheduled shooting days and Marilyn had shown for twelve of them; then she refused to do more than one page of script a day. (If true, that meant an average of one minute a day had been filmed, perhaps twelve minutes in all.) He said that she was no longer wanted by the studio and that he suspected she was in willful breach of contract. That same day the studio brought suit against Marilyn for $500,000.

On June 8, after Fox was turned down by Shirley MacLaine and Kim Novak to replace Marilyn, Lee Remick agreed to take the suddenly controversial role of Ellen. Dean Martin reminded Fox that he had costar approval and would only work with Marilyn. This led to a possibly frivolous lawsuit against *him* for $500,000.

That night, concerned with the relationships she might be breaking by her actions, Marilyn telegrammed director George Cukor concerning her firing: "Please believe me it was not my doing. I had so looked forward to working with you."

Three days later, production officially stopped on *Something's Got to Give* and Martin was sued for an additional $14,000, this time by Cyd Charisse, the dollar amount apparently what she would have been paid for the remaining filming. Seemingly not to be outdone by its cast, Fox added another $250,000 in its demand against Marilyn. Ultimately, in what amounted to little more than saber-rattling (since each dropped the suit against the other a year after they were announced), Fox sued Martin for $3,339,000 for lost production costs, even though their attorneys had agreed to give Martin the power to choose with whom he worked. Naturally he countersued, approximately doubling what had been requested of him.

June 13 saw Marilyn bemused as much as scared by what was taking place with the film. Robert and Ethel Kennedy were planning a party for the Lawfords and wanted Marilyn to attend. She declined, saying, "Unfortunately I am involved in a freedom ride protesting the loss of minority rights belonging to the few remaining earthbound stars. All we demanded was our right to twinkle."

Again Marilyn's life seemed to be taking a downward spiral, the reason she supposedly would soon be contemplating suicide. Again, this was not the case.

Darryl Zanuck, one of the Fox shareholders, forcefully encouraged Spyros Skouras to retire. At the same time, efforts were made to get an outside production company to take over *Something's Got to Give*. United Artists offered to turn it over to Filmways Productions after paying Fox $1 million. However, Fox demanded too large a completion bond—the contract that guarantees the movie will be finished on time and at or under budget.

Filmways, on its own, offered a $500,000 completion bond (the money to be paid if the movie was not on time and at or under budget) with Filmways receiving 5 percent of the gross take for the movie. When this was turned down by Fox, the company offered to pay for everything with the agreement that Filmways' president, Martin Ransohoff, would receive a producer's fee and bonus. Still no deal.

Marilyn also talked with Filmways. Fox had overspent for the project, whose cost at the time of the shutdown was estimated to be $2 million. It only made sense to reinvolve her with the movie—providing, she made clear, that there would be a new script.

Hal Kanter rewrote the script that would no longer be directed by George Cukor, whose contract time had expired. Then Peter Levathes hand-delivered the script to Marilyn's Brentwood home.

Again the facts are important. Marilyn Monroe was *rehired* to star not only in *Something's Got to Give*, for a salary of $200,000, but also in an unnamed second picture for which she would be paid $750,000. She approved a new director, Jean Negulesco, and agreed to keep Paula Strasberg away from the set the entire time they were filming. Production would resume in October. This was all in addition to Sid Skolsky's *The Jean Harlow Story* which, though not yet financed or written, was being coordinated by a longtime friend with a proven track record of keeping his word.

Norma Jean's creation, Marilyn Monroe, having reached her thirty-sixth year, was on top of the entertainment world. She was happier than she had ever been—though still an addict, still drinking too much, still in deteriorating health.

Sixty

~

And Then She Died

Every biographer of every person who has led a fascinating life, experiencing events both varied and comprehensive in their retelling, ultimately has to make a decision about where to put the emphasis if the book is to be of manageable size. Some writers focus on the high points of a career, such as the movies that were made. Some writers focus on the social implications of the person's work. Some come to their writing with preconceived notions and the determination to focus solely on what backs their opinions. At least one pair of writers focused on her last movie, presenting her life and death in the context of that film. Some, like Robert Slatzer, focus on the secrets that are secret precisely because the author created them in the first place. And some, especially those writing about the lives of presidents, in which personal life differs greatly from the public life, ultimately write multiple volumes covering different years.

I made the decision when starting this book that I would not go beyond a single volume in telling her story, though that volume might be long. I also made the decision to eventually house all research material in my archives at Arizona State University, where recordings of interviews used for previous books, such as *The Peter Lawford Story* written with his widow, Patricia S. Lawford, are housed. In addition, locations such as the Margaret Herrick Library in Beverly Hills, the UCLA library, the Beverly Hills Public Library, and others have original documents and interviews with people who truly interacted with individuals such as Monroe. Thus if my emphasis proves wrong, others can get the full details. And if my statements and conclusions are challenged, anyone can learn on what they are based. That is why I feel justified in making the statements I have made about the Kennedys, the media in those times, Marilyn herself, pretenders such as Slatzer, and the like. That is also why this chapter may seem to skip important details about conspiracies and the role of the Mafia, CIA, the Kennedy brothers, and even little green men. (Among the conspiracy theorists is one that tells of her having to be murdered because she was going to reveal the truth about what Jack Kennedy said concerning a crashed UFO and the dead bodies found therein.)

There are also personally important people in Marilyn's life who were ongoing friends, though not involved with the machinations of the movie industry or her drug abuse. These include poet Norman Rosten and his wife, Hedda, who acted as a companion and personal secretary during the first part of the London filming of *The Prince and the Showgirl* before a conflict with Sir Laurence Olivier resulted in her returning to New York.

It has already been shown that Jack Kennedy was a womanizer even when in the White House. Bobby Kennedy was Jack's fixer, keeping as much information from going public as possible and ignoring incidents such as the birthday party, where the nature of the media was such that it would not get reported (the birthday was filmed for television but it was never broadcast; fortunately, clips were saved). Peter Lawford was Jack's pimp and the brothers' sycophant, and Frank Sinatra liked to share with his friends. The idea that Marilyn was killed to protect Jack is nonsense, if only because there was no reason for Marilyn to even consider destroying her own future plans with her lover by talking about her affair before he won his second term in office. The idea of murder also ignores the fact that there were women like Judith Campbell Exner who were far more dangerous to his career.

Judith Campbell Exner had met Frank Sinatra when she, actress Angie Dickinson (another of Jack's girlfriends), and Nick Sevano (Sinatra's one-time manager and longtime friend) happened to be in the same club at the same time. A beauty in the manner of Jacqueline Kennedy, Exner caught Frank's eye, but she dated him only briefly. Sinatra had reached a point in sexual experimentation where he wanted more from her than she was willing to give—in her later writing she said he brought another woman into bed with them, something she could not abide. However, they remained friends.

Later, through Frank, she was invited to go to Las Vegas in 1960 where Frank, Peter Lawford, Joey Bishop, Dean Martin, and Sammy Davis Jr. were filming the movie *Ocean's 11*. Jack Kennedy was also there, having just announced that he would be running for president. Jacqueline was not present, and he and Judith began an affair without her realizing he was married.

Sinatra also introduced Judith to "Sam Flood," a man she later learned was the powerful Chicago Outfit head Sam "Momo" Giancana. She began having sex with both men, and soon Jack asked Judith to be a go-between with Giancana. He wanted help with the election, and Giancana wanted to influence the White House. Eventually Judith's role was almost that of a secretary (with bed expectations) and she periodically called the White House from Giancana's home.

It has also been shown that Marilyn was a drug addict and alcoholic; and that, no matter how toned her body on the outside, inside she was falling apart. She had had numerous hospitalizations, a gall bladder operation, an appendix operation, two miscarriages, and other problems. Worse, the studio never gave her time to recover, and her friends, husbands, lovers, and employers were more concerned with her being on the set and making a profitable movie than if she lived even into middle age.

Another problem is that seemingly everyone who really did know Marilyn had their own stories often involving one another without matching one another. Worse, coroner Thomas Noguchi was so convinced that she accidentally overdosed that he did not bother with writing as complete a report as he would have done had there been the slightest suspicion of foul play. As a result, years later he made an effort to explain what had happened and to suggest the case might be looked at anew: *not* to find a killer, but for completeness that would set the subject to rest.

Finally, there were the people who were, if not liars, in possession of too little information for understanding. For example, those connected with law enforcement in Los Angeles, with friends who had been sent to the death scene, talked about such matters as the ambulance that came for Marilyn, took her partway to the hospital, then returned her to the house and reset the death scene. The reporting "experts" weren't present, but the details are etched in the minds of their friends forever . . . or some such nonsense.

During the research, one of the comments made by the people trained in death—homicide, accidental, and natural causes—first on the scene was that "Marilyn was in full *livor mortis*." No, this is not a typo. It is a medical term referring to how the blood pools in the tissues following death and does not break up in any way *if the body is not moved*. Move the corpse—such as into an ambulance for an aborted hospital ride—and there will be no livor mortis. Rigor mortis (a stiffening of the body followed by a relaxing of the body a few hours later) does change. But livor mortis will only be found when the body is discovered where death occurred.

And the issue of livor mortis is only one of many that points to a death that was not a murder. So what did happen to Marilyn?

Jack Kennedy had been vulnerable to blackmail and political ruin since 1942, when FBI agents taped him having sex with journalist Inga Arvad, a friend of his sister Kathleen and a woman believed by J. Edgar Hoover to be a Nazi spy. His womanizing, both as a bachelor and as a married man, were notorious and widely known among members of the media. But by the time Jack was involved with Marilyn, the greatest danger to him came from the possible revelation of his involvement with Judith Campbell, later known as Judith Campbell Exner.

Marilyn Monroe was in a somewhat different circumstance from that of Exner. She, too, had sex with Sinatra, Giancana, and Jack Kennedy; she, too, was caught on wiretaps and in-home listening devices. However, her relationship with Jack had nothing to do with politics. Judith was aware of events being planned, including the attempted assassination of Fidel Castro: an effort that involved yet another woman, Marita Lorenz, though not one who knew Kennedy. Monroe was simply a sexual pleasure and sometime friend. She was not a mistress. She certainly was not loved. And she was aware that there was nothing exclusive about her being bedded by Jack, other than the fact that their affair lasted well over a year (Jack joked with his brother-in-law Lawford that he liked to have women three different ways and then be done with them).

The problem with the story of Kennedy's love affairs is that they occurred in a media transition period. The publicity from the White House kept the nation enchanted by the young president, his son, his daughter, the tragic loss of a second son at birth, his glamorous, bilingual wife, and the sophistication of the White House parties where the entertainment was often some of the world's finest musicians. Kennedy was a war veteran, a war hero in the myth of PT-109 created by journalist John Hersey; a Harvard graduate; and movie-star handsome. The idea that Jack Kennedy could cheat on his wife was considered impossible. The photos of Jack, his siblings, and most of their spouses playing touch football "proved" his vigor, though his back was so bad it could lock up on him at a moment's notice. The fact that the White House physician frequently followed him just far enough back to not be photographed was unknown at the time.

For her part of the myth, Marilyn Monroe was the abused orphan, the glamorous movie star who wanted nothing more than true love, a house with a picket fence, children, and a normal life. She knew the rich and the famous. She was a friend of Kennedy's sister and brother-in-law. But she would never involve herself with a married man.

The truth was simpler. Jack Kennedy used the glamour of wealth and power to seduce anyone he desired. He was no different from the studio moguls from Marilyn's past.

Marilyn enjoyed the romantic intrigue, the fantasy of sneaking around with a man covered by more media even than she was. She was sometimes angered, sometimes bemused by the dark brown wig, the thick glasses, and the drab clothing that Peter had her wear as she clutched a stenographer's notebook and pen, making notes.

A mere secretary was invisible, especially when everyone around her had an aura of glamour and excitement. Peter would take his "assistant" onto Air Force One and the photographers would take only his picture.

Not that the secret was 100 percent secure. There were many journalists who recognized Marilyn and understood what was happening. But as Jim Bacon discussed, this was not something they would publicize.

If anything reinforced Marilyn's certainty that there was a future with Jack Kennedy, it was her eventually being given the private family telephone number, which rang directly into the quarters shared by Jack and Jacqueline. This was not a hotline-type number. Government affairs were never discussed. This was a line for family and close friends, and Jacqueline often answered the telephone when Marilyn called Jack. More important for what Marilyn believed about the second term, Jacqueline would hand the telephone to Jack and he would talk, presumably freely, while she was in the room.

Sid Skolsky, writing in *Don't Get Me Wrong—I Love Hollywood*, stated:

> Marilyn Monroe's last newsworthy romance never got reported while it was going on. In a society that boasts of freedom of the press no reporter, including myself, dared to write about Marilyn Monroe's affair with John F. Kennedy, president of the United States. In retrospect, we can argue that good taste, discretion, even national security prohibited the few reporters who knew the facts from reporting them. The truth, I believe, is that freedom of press, like other freedoms, is more dangerously fragile than we care to confront. I accept my share of the blame. I also confess that I still find it grim to speculate on what might have happened to me if I had tried to write about this romance in my column when it first came to my attention in 1962.

Later, after Marilyn's death, there would be allegations that Bobby Kennedy had an affair of his own with the actress. Assistant FBI director William Sullivan did not believe Bobby acted in that manner, though enough people close to him think he occasionally strayed that they assume he did, indeed, have sex with her. They discount the stories that he told Marilyn that, unlike Jack, he was willing to leave his own wife, Ethel, to marry Marilyn. She knew his political ambitions and was savvy enough to know that even if Bobby did love her and would be using her as his mistress, he had his own run for the presidency to make before he could change wives.

Into this mix was Frank Sinatra, a man trying to be a friend to the president and a friend to the mob. All of them shared women, including Marilyn, but what that meant for the woman varied with the incident and the player.

What is certain is that Marilyn was an occasional guest at the Cal-Neva Lodge at Lake Tahoe on the California/Nevada border. The lodge was owned by several men: the most famous was Frank Sinatra; the most infamous was a silent partner, Sam Giancana. The latter could not legally invest in a casino because of his criminal record, but he was a regular guest (though officially banned from such locations). The last weekend in July, Marilyn went to hear Sinatra sing at the Cal-Neva, traveling as a guest of the Lawfords. There were stories that she had violent sex with Giancana during the stay. There were stories that she called the hotel operator for treatment of an overdose. However, what can be confirmed was that she had a pleasant weekend, and that either she had a quiet dinner with Giancana present or Giancana was nowhere around. (The confusion seems to stem from the fact that his presence was so low-key that if he was there, he called almost no attention to himself.)

Anyone who has worked extensively in the field of organized crime has run across Mafia myth. This is the tendency to take a true incident and change it slightly so as to either give a member of organized crime more credit than perhaps he deserves or demean an enemy of the mob. For example, at the start of the twentieth century a New York police officer was upset to witness the result of a mob hit. He found the victim dead, his penis cut off and placed in his mouth as a warning to others to never talk. The officer was so angered by this outrage that he arranged to travel to Sicily to view the mob in what he thought was its native land.

The true story is that the officer traveled to Sicily, disembarked from the boat, and walked into town. The mob knew he was coming and killed him. The Mafia myth has the officer still on the boat prior to landing. He is sitting on the toilet, his pants down, when the Mafia assassin shoots him. Either way, the officer is dead, but the Mafia myth creates a scenario that humiliates an enemy at death. It is believed that Sam Giancana sometimes told stories in a way that was traditional Mafia myth, and that includes the idea that he had violent sex with Marilyn in the Cal-Neva that weekend at the end of July.

It is also known that Marilyn would sometimes take what she claimed was an overdose of one or another medications, then call for help so she could have her stomach pumped. No one ever confirmed what she was doing, and no one in the hospitals recommended treatment for depression. Her overdoses were as likely accidental, the result of repeated doses taken too close together when she felt the medication was not working, as a means to seek attention. This is the behavior referred to by her "friends" as Marilyn's "phone-dangling" time.

At the same time, there were several perceived real attempts by Monroe, starting with the odd overdose of sleeping pills left to dissolve in her mouth after Johnny Hyde's death. She also allegedly overdosed on sleeping pills before her marriage to Joe DiMaggio and during her marriage to Arthur Miller. Again, given the massive quantities of drugs and alcohol she was ingesting, it is likely that the overdoses were not deliberate, but caused by mental confusion from what was in her system that she felt was not yet working.

There was one humorous incident in all this. During the filming of *The Misfits*, a 4:30 A.M. telephone call alerted press agent Harry Mines to a wire service report that Marilyn had committed suicide. The wire service sought confirmation before notifying its clients. Mines summed up Marilyn and the people around her beautifully when he said, "Why, that's impossible! She has to be on the set at 7:30 A.M.! Besides, Paula Strasberg would never stand for it."

So how did Marilyn Monroe die?

ℐฉ

The listening device was called a Stephens Tru-Sonic Transmitter, actually a low-powered FM radio that could broadcast three to four blocks from where it was placed, everything heard recorded on a receiver and wire recorder. It was originally developed for the theater. The device would be worn with a tiny microphone built into a tie tack, lapel pin, or whatever the costume allowed. Then, no matter where the actor moved about the stage, his or her voice would remain at the same level throughout the theater. Prior to its use, microphones were hung from above and/or placed in props on the set. The closer they were to the actors, the better the sound, but if the actors failed to take their marks during a show, and if the mikes were suspended over those marks, voices would fade in and out.

It was only natural that the Tru-Sonic would be adapted for surveillance. The Stephens units were both battery-powered and capable of being plugged into someone's home wiring system. There was even a variation that could be placed inside a table lamp or other electrical device. The Stephens was hidden in the base, then what looked like a normal power cord came out. Actually, it was a replacement power cord containing three wires instead of the normal two; the third wire was part of the transmitter. Plugged into the normal power line, the Stephens could broadcast for days, weeks, or months. The recorder could be hidden inside a car trunk, the situation in which Marilyn died, in an adjoining apartment, or anywhere else. If it could be kept in its location indefinitely, a voice activator would be used so the recording would take place whenever anyone talked near the hidden mike.

There was also a way of switching the telephone, again using a power booster to avoid detection, so that it became open all the time. The person could use it normally to make telephone calls. But when the receiver was replaced on the cradle, the unit would keep transmitting.

In August 1962 there were a number of these devices in place wherever Jack Kennedy was likely to visit. The Peter Lawford home had been wired, as had Marilyn's new house and other locations regularly visited by the president. Information about what he was doing and what he was saying was desired by Teamster leader Jimmy Hoffa, Howard Hughes, J. Edgar Hoover, and others. Each had a reason to hate one or both of the Kennedy brothers.

Thirty years after Marilyn Monroe's death, four different types of long unused listening devices were found in Marilyn's house. It was safer to abandon such devices when the client no longer needed the information that could be obtained by them than try to return to the house.

The Los Angeles Police Department had no known listening devices, but Chief Parker did have contacts within the attorney general's office to alert him whenever Robert Kennedy would be in Los Angeles. The chief was in line to take over the FBI and wanted to make certain that nothing bad happened to the man who would become his boss if that event occurred. There never was a time when Bobby Kennedy sneaked into Los Angeles after Jack became president. It was always known when he came in, where he stayed, where he went, and when and how he left town.

The attorney general of the United States had security concerns much like those of the president, though without the same massive protection afforded by the Secret Service. He developed a habit of going someplace near to where he ultimately needed or wanted to be, acting in a highly visible manner. Then he would quietly slip away from wherever he was staying, get into a waiting car or helicopter, and go to his intended destination, keeping a low profile while there. On August 4, 1962, while supposedly with his family in San Francisco, Bobby slipped down to Los Angeles to see his sister, brother-in-law, Marilyn, and other friends. The police had a loose tail on him from the moment he arrived. (Darryl Gates, who succeeded Parker as Chief in Los Angeles, confirmed all this in his autobiography.) In addition, the various private investigators activated the listening devices they maintained in both Marilyn's home and in the Lawford home.

Of the Kennedy brothers, it was Bobby who was most likely to arrange for Marilyn to meet him or Jack by flying her to Palm Springs and other locations. While it seems certain that Bobby and Marilyn shared a degree of intimacy, Marilyn seemed to be fixated on Jack and the future she was certain they would have after his re-election. Peter Lawford also handled the transportation of Marilyn for Jack, but he did it as a friend to both.

Press agent Pat Newcomb had slept over in Marilyn's house and awakened around noon that Saturday. Private investigator Fred Otash, working for Jimmy Hoffa, among others, remembered years later Bobby and Peter having stopped by in the morning. Since the tapes and any notes no longer exist, what is known is that, in the course of the day, the following occurred.

Robert Kennedy started August 4 in the San Francisco Bay area, where he visted friends and allowed himself to be seen before going to Los Angeles, in part to see what had been described as a depressed Monroe. She had stayed in Chalet 52 of the Cal-Neva Lodge three weeks before her death, listening to Sinatra and overdosing on medicine (more likely the result of her increased drug use than a deliberate suicide attempt). She had been discovered by the housekeeping staff before her body had absorbed enough to kill her.

There were also rumors that Marilyn had had "another" abortion. The story was that Marilyn was pregnant, probably by Jack or Bobby, though possibly by a casual lover. It was said that she had found a California doctor skilled at performing abortions and had gone with him across the border into Tijuana, Mexico, where he was allowed to operate. The operation occurred in the early part of the first trimester, and the only reason for going to Mexico was that abortion was legal there and was not legal in the United

States. The problem for biographers—as with so much about Marilyn's life and relationships at this time—is that the constant repetition of such stories has created "truth." But Marilyn's gynecologist, Dr. Leon "Red" Krohn who knew her body better than anyone, said she had never had an abortion. She had been pregnant three times. The first two times she lost the baby through miscarriage, the natural result of the massive amount of drugs and alcohol she "shared" with the fetuses. The third was an ectopic pregnancy during her marriage with Miller that required emergency termination, a very different situation from an abortion. (This pregnancy was almost unknown, meaning either the termination was not a major psychological trauma, occurring so early in the pregnancy that neither parent had had time to think of the fetus as a growing child; or it was a dirty little secret in the manner of the mildly retarded son Miller conceived with his last wife, Inge Morath.)

Marilyn had been trying to reach Bobby in Washington that week in August, and when she couldn't get him, she called Peter to see what he could do. Bobby did not like the way Marilyn was behaving, though there was no indication that he feared anything she might say to the press. His father, Joseph P. Kennedy Sr., was upset with Jack's relationship and the way Marilyn had been used at the birthday bash. Most evidence seems to indicate the brothers wanted her to stop bothering them. She had become another sexual conquest and nothing more serious, something they wanted her to understand.

Bobby asked Peter to get Marilyn away from her house to some place they could talk privately. That Saturday, Peter decided to have a casual party to which they would invite Marilyn, along with friends who were familiar with the relationship.

Years after Marilyn's death, when all known recordings had apparently been destroyed or become illegible with age, one of the investigators, Fred Otash, discussed with biographer Anthony Summers his electronic surveillance on behalf of Jimmy Hoffa and (allegedly) one or more members of the Mafia. He also talked with this author and allowed access to the files he had retained during what proved to be the last year of his life. According to Otash, during the early part of August 4, Peter talked with Marilyn about joining him, Pat, and some mutual friends at the beach. "I'm having a party this evening, Marilyn," he allegedly said. "Come on down. It'll do you good to get out of the house. You won't have to drive. I'll pick you up."

"Who will be there?" she asked.

"People you know."

"What people?"

"Warren Beatty."

"Who else?"

"Some others."

"What others?"

"Bobby. Isn't that what you want to hear?"

"Who else?" Otash felt that her attitude was one of interrogation more than casual questioning. He thought she was aware that Peter was trying to manipulate her.

Peter gave Marilyn several other names, including several starlets she thought were the same type of women she had been—Hollywood hookers earning more from prostitution than bit parts in movies. The knowledge that they would be there must have reminded her of the cavalier attitude of the Kennedy brothers. Whatever the case, she told him "Go to hell!" and hung up.

The time at which Bobby Kennedy arrived at Marilyn's home is uncertain. Fred Otash remembered that it may have been late morning, around 11:00 A.M., but if Pat Newcomb was right about when she awakened, it was probably some time after noon. In any case, there was an argument during which Marilyn stressed her frustration with the relationships. She had had both pills and alcohol; allegedly, she had sex with Bobby as she calmed down. He would return later that afternoon with Lawford. They were the only two people there at the time and Bobby made some calls from her phone. The telephone bug was not working properly so only Bobby's side of the conversation was heard. This was not a problem since the client (believed to be Jimmy Hoffa) only wanted to know what Bobby was saying.

Marilyn allegedly began screaming at Bobby, telling him how much she had lost for him. She threatened to tell the world the truth about the Kennedy brothers, whatever that meant to her at the time. However, such outbursts were by then fairly common with Marilyn. She would take so many pills, washed down with so much liquor, that she would scream, cry, and carry on, always away from the public and always saying similar things to the same people. Those who isolate the anger from the broader context of the drunk and overly self-medicated woman see it as a motive to kill her. The reality was that, by then, such a scene was just Marilyn being Marilyn. It was a repeat of what had occurred with her several times before.

Otash, purportedly the most credible of the private investigators interviewed by a number of the more respected biographers, described Peter trying to calm Marilyn, telling her she should come for dinner, that they were having takeout Chinese, a common feature of their parties.

Marilyn was still screaming like an out-of-control, overtired child having a temper tantrum. There was no camera in the house, but from the sounds being heard, it was believed that Peter or Bobby grabbed her arms and pushed her on her back on the bed, an action that would have thrown her against the hard frame and left bruises on her arms and back. Then one of them apparently covered her face with a pillow just long enough to quiet her. Otash couldn't tell if the pillow scared her or simply stopped the hysteria in the manner of someone breathing into a paper bag when hyperventilating. Whatever the objective with the pillow, Marilyn, though still angry, was more calm.

At this point the credibility of the Otash commentary must be questioned. It would be expected that the marks left by the struggle he describes would remain for enough hours to be visible at death. They should have been noted in the autopsy report, even though the bruising would be obviously from a different time of the day. There was no such bruising in the autopsy report.

Twenty years later, when Coroner Thomas Noguchi, M.D. was interviewed about Marilyn's death on KABC Television, he mentioned the same bruising that Otash had described. It was consistent with what he thought he had heard on the monitor. The problem was that it was twenty years later: the discovery had never been mentioned before, and Noguchi could not explain why he had waited so long.

Lawford kept trying to calm the now less volatile Monroe, explaining that she should come to dinner at his place. Bobby would be there. Friends would be there. They would order out for the Chinese food they all loved.

"Lookit, Marilyn," Otash remembered Bobby saying. "You're hysterical. You're having problems. You've been drinking, evidently. There's something going on with you. I came here at great risk to sit here and try to give you comfort and understanding. I hear that you're having some problems, and I'm here to do what I can to give you the comfort you need."

Annoyed with Marilyn's drug-fueled hostility, Bobby got her a glass of water and told her to take a pill and get some sleep. It is believed that she was handed one of the pills she routinely used—and this is where the problem arises.

Peter was a drug addict, though not yet to the degree to which it was obviously endangering his life. He occasionally was known to carry his prescription with him, and it was believed that Bobby did the same. Both Bobby and Peter had prescriptions for the same sedative Marilyn used, at the same dosage that Marilyn had, and it was quite possible that the pill she took came from one of their bottles.

California law in 1962 concerned itself, in part, with death from accidental overdose. If the overdose of a prescription drug was the provable result of medication the deceased had legitimately purchased by prescription, the death was ruled accidental or possibly a suicide. If the overdose included a prescribed medication but in a quantity prescribed for another person, the person who had handed the victim the drug from the container not belonging to the victim could be tried for murder. There was no death penalty. It was not considered anything other than it was: an accidental death at the hand of the user. But there would be jail time for the one who handed the other the medication, a situation no different than contemporary laws by which a bartender or liquor dealer can go to jail for providing alcohol to an already intoxicated individual who obviously cannot make sensible choices and who then hurts him- or herself or others after leaving the establishment.

Marilyn apparently wasn't through talking according to Otash. (Note: Peter Lawford's widow, Patricia Seaton Lawford, the person who was with Peter longer than his other three wives, including Pat Kennedy, independently told some of the same stories as Otash. These were related by her late husband and had never been discussed by her with Otash. Other comments about that afternoon could not be corroborated because the three participants died before Otash recounted what had been said.)

Several details are certain regarding that night. Several are speculation.

And some are obvious fantasy created by people who did not want to confront the truth about rich, famous, cross-addicted personalities.

Bobby Kennedy decided against going to Peter's party. It would be a private affair with no one present who did not know about Marilyn and Jack. Bobby, whether having had sex with Marilyn or just continuing his role as his brother's protector, was also known to spend extensive time with Marilyn, and anyone who read the news for the day was aware that he was believed to have been in San Francisco. However, if she continued to drink and take pills—something she was doing on movie sets so there was no reason to think she would do otherwise during time off from work—she was likely to get belligerent, or maudlin, or both. He didn't want the hassle, so he went to his waiting helicopter and flew back to be with his family. Again, the Los Angeles Police Department tracked his every move, so the visits to Los Angeles, to Peter, to Marilyn, to Peter, and back to San Francisco have never been in doubt.

Peter Lawford was handsome, friendly, well liked, and a competent song-and-dance man. He was also weak, an addict, and refused to use common sense when that might result in his having to behave like a responsible adult. As he later admitted to his closest friends, he was about to kill Marilyn through indifference, though he did not realize that fact until it was too late.

Lawford was a junkie in his own right. He started on sleeping pills when he and his first wife, Pat Kennedy Lawford, enjoyed playing late-night card games with friends then had to be on the set for a movie or television show early the next day. Excited from the pleasures of the evening, they found the easiest way to ensure adequate sleep time was to take a sleeping pill. Eventually many added stimulants to their breakfast menu so they could come alert as quickly as possible. And then, with time, they increased their dosage and/or supplemented with alcohol. To admit that Marilyn was dangerously out of control was to be forced to admit that he was as well.

Several years ago I worked with Patricia S. Lawford on the biography of her late husband, at which time I interviewed numerous individuals connected with his life and work, from actors to producers, directors, friends, and even mobsters who liked him more than he was sometimes comfortable experiencing. When someone died—like Jimmy Durante, his occasional partner in a Las Vegas act—I interviewed the widow whenever possible.

Each interview was taped and notes were made; the vast majority of the records were transferred to the Ted Schwarz and Peter Lawford Archives, both in Arizona State University's Hayden Library Special Collections Division.

Then other writers, presumably equally careful about their research and, in some cases, also leaving records with one or another libraries, interviewed many of the same people. To my surprise, the stories were different. "Facts" were changed. However, when comparing what was said in Patricia's and my book and what was told interviewers who spoke with the same source following my book's release, it seems that the changes were meant to save embarrassment. There was a callous indifference toward Marilyn by people who had grown tired of her meaningless dramatics and had no idea how close her drug-taking had brought her body to, with the addition of only a few more drugs, simply ceasing to function.

According to the most accurate information (the times are approximate: this was a normal night for everyone who received a telephone call, and no one felt the need to check and note the exact hour and minute), Peter talked with Marilyn around 5:00 P.M., asking her to come. Joe Naar, one of the guests that night, explained that Peter said that Marilyn claimed to be tired and wanted to stay home. Given that she had been drinking and taking pills during the day, Peter's quoting of Marilyn was probably accurate.

At 7:30 P.M. a telephone call from Marilyn, which became serious after the fact. She reportedly said to Peter, "Say good-bye to Jack, say good-bye to Pat, and say good-bye to yourself, because you're a nice guy."

In hindsight, Marilyn had just announced a forthcoming suicide. But had she?

First, Marilyn, Peter, and several others were actors. There was always a bit of drama to their lives even if, like Frank Sinatra, there had to be an entourage that was sometimes paid to sit around in public so that the singer could look a little like one of the godfathers. Marilyn was perceived as melodramatic. Peter was cowardly enough to want her to be melodramatic so he wouldn't have to take action. And the truth was that no one at the party cared for Marilyn very much of late. They didn't want to be seen as a supporting player in her drama of the week, or so it seemed at the time.

Peter held the telephone receiver by the cord and said, "It's phone-dangling time again."

Marilyn Revealed

Some friends were not as dismissive as Peter. Joe Naar, for example, wanted to stop by Marilyn's house to check on her, but he had not talked with her; Peter, who had, said there was no reason for concern. Joe should stay at the party.

Peter called Marilyn back a few times, though there is no record of exactly when or how often. Always the line was busy, not a warning sign because there was no voice mail at the time, no way to leave a message when someone was talking unless they also used an answering service, which Marilyn did not. She could have been dying, the phone dropped to the floor. She could have been calling others, reminding them why they had stopped giving a damn about the actress's dramatic flair when it came to her love life.

Never, apparently, did Peter consider trying to go the four miles to the house of the woman who was supposedly a friend. It would have taken ten minutes—if driving was unusually slow.

Eventually Peter did realize that maybe someone should check on Marilyn. The simplest approach would be to call the police. There wasn't a Kennedy in town except his wife, so Marilyn was not going to be caught in bed with a politician. But she might be in some sort of trouble, and the police were the logical people to call to break in.

Peter did not call them.

Marilyn had at least three doctors she saw with regularity. The gynecologist might not be appropriate, but Peter knew that her internist, Dr. Hyman Engelberg, would have knowledge of her health, the medications she was taking, and possible problems. He was also at least one of the people who provided her with a prescription for the Nembutal she was using (or, more accurately, abusing) on what proved to be the day she died.

Nembutal is not meant for long-term use. Some studies have shown that after two weeks the drug loses its effectiveness to induce and maintain sleep. However, it does not lose its ability to depress the central nervous system. It also has a half-life that can be as much as fifty hours, meaning that daily or more frequent use adds fresh medication to existing medication still functioning within the user. A safe dose for once a day, for only a few days as needed, can become a toxic dose when used too soon after the same medication, taken hours earlier. Thanks to Engelberg, who knew Marilyn was not using medication in a safe manner, Marilyn overdosed in pursuit of sleep—and that was with just one of the drugs she was taking.

But Peter did not call Dr. Engelberg.

This was Hollywood. This was a land where ordinary people with extraordinary luck felt themselves elevated above human status to where, if they were flatulent, a minion would apologize and act embarrassed. There were personal assistants, managers, dressers, agents, chauffeurs, housekeepers, and even arranged marriages when it would help a career. Peter understood this, having been in the industry for more than two decades. One of the most famous stars of the moment might be in trouble. He might possibly be the last person to talk with her. She was having sex with his brother-in-law, the president of the United States. And she might be in trouble. Thinking quickly, determined to save the woman who—it bears repeating—might be in trouble, Peter called . . . his manager, Milt Ebbins.

And Milt Ebbins, using the same Hollywood logic, called Marilyn's lawyer, Mickey Rudin.

While all this was taking place, Joe Naar and his wife went home shortly before eleven. The couple lived within easy walking distance of Marilyn, and Peter seemed to realize that fact. He called Joe and asked him to walk over to check on Monroe.

Joe, who had been getting undressed, was happy to go, and put his clothes back on. However, Peter had second thoughts based on Milt Ebbins's advice. He called back just as Joe was leaving and told him not to bother. Joe, assuming Peter had everything under control, stayed home.

Sixty-one

A Pause for Confusion

LAPD interview report with Mrs. Eunice Murray, 933 Ocean Avenue, Apt. #11, Santa Monica. The report, dated 8-10-62, several days after the death, was taken at 8:30 A.M. by a detective working in the West Los Angeles Detective Division.

Mrs. Murray stated that she had worked for Marilyn Monroe since November 1961, that on the evening of 8-4-62 Miss Monroe had received a collect call from a Joe DiMaggio Jr. at about 7:30P. Mrs. Murray said that at the time of this call coming in, Miss Monroe was in bed and possibly had been asleep. She took the call and after talking to Joe DiMaggio Jr., she then made a call to Dr. Greenson and Mrs. Murray overheard her say, "Joe Jr. is not getting married, I'm so happy about this." Mrs. Murray states that from the tone of Miss Monroe's voice, she believed her to be in very good spirits. At about 9P, Mrs. Murray received a call from Mr. Rudin who inquired about Miss Monroe.

Mr. Rudin did not talk to Miss Monroe. Mrs. Murray states that these are the only phone calls that she recalls receiving on this date.

It is officers opinion that Mrs. Murray was vague and possibly evasive in answering questions pertaining to the activities of Miss Monroe during this time. It is not known whether this is, or is not, intentional. During the interrogation of Joe DiMaggio, Jr., he indicated he had made three phone calls to the Monroe home, only one of which Mrs. Murray mentioned.

October 16, 1975, Los Angeles Police Department interview with Peter Lawford, a follow-up investigation to the death because of so much publicity in the more than a decade that followed the discovery of her corpse:

> Mr. Lawford stated that most of what has been written by various authors, such as Slatzer, [Anthony] Scaduto, [Norman] Mailer, and others regarding the last days in the life of Marilyn Monroe is "pure fantasy." He states that Miss Monroe was a regular weekend guest at his beachfront home in Santa Monica those last weeks before she died.
>
> On August 4, 1962, Mr. Lawford telephoned Marilyn Monroe at approximately 5:00 P.M., to ask her if she was coming to his house that weekend. She sounded despondent over her loss of contract with 20th Century-Fox Studios and some other personal matters [presumably the romance with Robert Kennedy]. Lawford tried to convince her to forget about her problems and join him and his wife, Pat, for dinner that evening. She replied that she would consider joining them.
>
> At approximately 7:30 or 8:00 P.M., Lawford telephoned her a second time to ascertain why she hadn't as yet arrived at his home . . . Lawford stated Miss Monroe was still very despondent and her manner of speech was slurred. She stated she was tired and would not be coming. Her voice became less and less audible and Lawford began to yell at her in an attempt to revive her. [He described it as a verbal slap in the face.] Then she stated, "Say goodbye to Pat, say goodbye to Jack [JFK] and say goodbye to yourself, because you're a nice guy." When the phone went dead, Lawford, assuming she had hung up, tried several times to redial her number and received a busy signal each time.
>
> Lawford then told [Milton] Ebbins [his agent and dinner guest] he was going to Marilyn's house. Ebbins recommended against it, "You know how agents are," and suggested that he [Ebbins] would call her doctor or lawyer. Eventually, Ebbins was able to reach her attorney.
>
> Lawford stated he often talked to Marilyn on the phone while she was under the effect of downers, and her voice on this evening sounded about the same. For some reason, however, he had a "gut" feeling that something was wrong. He states he still blames himself for not going to her home himself.
>
> Approximately three weeks prior to this event, on a weekend, Lawford states Marilyn was a guest of the Lawfords at the Cal-Neva Lodge in Lake

Tahoe where Frank Sinatra was headlining. When Lawford awoke one morning, his wife told him Marilyn had overdosed the evening prior. She was discovered when she fell out of bed and was able to be revived without professional medical assistance.

Regarding Robert F. Kennedy, Lawford is adamant that the attorney general was not in the Los Angeles area on August 4 or 5. He states that whenever RFK came to town he would come to the Lawfords' home and swim in the pool. Lawford states he has no knowledge of RFK's stay in San Francisco, as alluded to in the article.

That was one of Peter's official stories. Another was told to columnist Earl Wilson, a man who had known Marilyn, Peter, Frank Sinatra, and the other show business leaders. Wilson wrote of Marilyn's death in his 1971 book *The Show Business Nobody Knows*. In that story, Marilyn's friend and a press agent and onetime Kennedy family employee Pat Newcomb had stayed overnight with Marilyn, leaving early Saturday.

Newcomb, who had a cold, had an argument with Marilyn. However, either late Friday night or early Saturday, Lawford invited both women to dinner at his house Saturday night, and Marilyn accepted, agreeing to arrive by seven o'clock.

Marilyn did not show when expected, according to Peter's account to Wilson, so he called her at eight. Her voice was supposedly "fuzzy," as though she had been asleep or was going to sleep. Her speech was slurred, typical of the way Peter had heard Marilyn when she was drunk or on pills.

Peter quoted the line "Say goodbye to Pat, say goodbye to the president, and say goodbye to yourself, because you're a nice guy." This was the one accurate and consistent statement in all of Lawford's accounts.

According to Wilson, and based on his interview with Peter, the actor realized she was talking about something "terminal," so he telephoned his manager, Milt Ebbins, to see if he would go with him to Marilyn's house. (Note: There are contradictory reports as to whether or not Milt Ebbins had dinner with Peter that night. Otash believed that Ebbins was at home. When Ted Schwarz interviewed some of the guests, Ebbins was not remembered there. Yet other writers, seemingly equally credible, put Ebbins at dinner at the house. The 1975 statement in the LAPD files is unclear whether Ebbins was physically present or telephoned.)

Wilson quoted Lawford as saying that Ebbins told him, "You can't go over there! You're the brother-in-law of the president of the United States. Your wife's away. Let me get in touch with her lawyer or doctor. They should be the ones to go over."

Peter was quoted as having claimed to argue with Ebbins. His agent thought that Marilyn was attempting to gain sympathy as she had before. Peter was more concerned, and because he had talked with her, thought he should go over to the home. However, Ebbins said he wanted to call her lawyer or doctor, despite Peter explaining that the telephone was no longer on the hook and Marilyn might be dying.

Ebbins, according to Lawford's statements to Wilson, phoned both Marilyn's lawyer and her psychiatrist. Mrs. Eunice Murray was telephoned on her separate line, and she reported checking on Marilyn, saying that everything seemed all right. However, the truth appeared to be that Mrs. Murray never saw Marilyn. The bedroom door was closed and the assumption was made that Marilyn wanted privacy. It was not until 3:30 A.M. that the corpse was finally found, and Peter blamed himself for not having gone over to check on her.

Dr. Theodore J. Curphey, chief medical examiner-coroner for Los Angeles County, made the following official statement after reviewing the Psychiatric Investigative Team report on Marilyn's death:

> Miss Monroe had suffered from psychiatric disturbance for a long time. She experienced severe fears and frequent depressions. Mood changes were abrupt and unpredictable. Among symptoms of disorganization, sleep disturbance was prominent, for which she had been taking sedative drugs for many years. She was thus familiar with and experienced in the use of sedative drugs and well aware of their dangers.
>
> Recently, one of the main objectives of her psychiatric treatment had been the reduction of her intake of drugs. This has been partially successful during the last two months. She was reported to be following doctor's orders in her use of the drugs; and the amount of drugs found in her home at the time of her death was not unusual.
>
> In our investigation, we have learned that Miss Monroe had often expressed wishes to give up, to withdraw, and even to die. On more than

one occasion in the past, when disappointed and depressed, she had made a suicide attempt using sedative drugs. On these occasions, she had called for help and had been rescued.

From the information collected about the events of the evening of August 4, it is our opinion that the same pattern was repeated except for the rescue. It has been our practice with similar information collected in other cases in the past to recommend a certification for such deaths as probable suicide.

℘

Dr. Robert Thomas Noguchi, the coroner who performed the autopsy, said that his findings were consistent with the accidental death (or suicide) of the true addict who is used to ingesting certain types of pills. Where the pills leave residue in the body of the casual user, the addict's body moves them quickly through, with no trace left in the stomach. His report stated, in part:

> The esophagus has a longitudinal folding mucosa. The stomach is almost completely empty. The volume is estimated to be no more than 20 cc. No residue of the pills is noted. A smear made from the gastric contents examined under the polarized microscope shows no refractile crystals. The mucosa shows marked congestion and submucosal petechial hemorrhage diffusely. The duodenum shows no ulcer. The contents of the duodenum are also examined under the polarized microscope and show no refractile crystals. The remainder of the small intestine shows no gross abnormality. The colon shows marked congestion and purplish discoloration.

In lay terms, a normal expectation for an addict who overdoses. There were no indications of anything in the autopsy that could even hint at murder.

Sixty-two

~

What Went Wrong

The first clue of a conspiracy to destroy Marilyn Monroe—for those who believe in conspiracies—was that there was no crime scene. No one secured Monroe's home, put up a barrier, posted officers, or otherwise handled the obvious murder case. Marilyn Monroe had been planning to shoot off her big mouth about the Kennedys, the Mafia, the little green men, the. . . . No matter what the fantasy, it was the reason for thinking maybe the death was from either natural causes or the result of an accidental or deliberate overdose.

But there was no murder. There was a housekeeper who found her employer's body when she finally agreed to open the bedroom door. There was a corpse, an empty glass on the floor near her body, and empty pill bottles. The corpse was in full livor mortis. The pills were those to which she was known to be addicted. There was no forced entry. There was no sign of a struggle. She was known to suffer from depression and was believed to have a history of suicide attempts. Whatever had happened did not involve bad guys, at least if one ignores the doctors who supplied her with drugs, the producers and directors who cared only that she showed up to work when they wanted her, and the friends who didn't have the guts to try to help her stop.

There was a bit of a panic, of course. No one knew if Marilyn kept souvenirs of the men she bedded. And most biographers indicate that Fred Otash was contacted that night, making his comments probably credible.

As he explained, it was around midnight when his telephone rang. He had two phones at home: one was an extension of his office line and the other was his unlisted personal number shared with close friends, key clients, and anyone else he wanted to be able to reach him at all hours. However, he made clear that the calls must be important because there was an occasional abuse of access to that line. The night of Marilyn's death he answered the midnight call with the words, "The office is closed. Talk to my secretary tomorrow." That was when the caller identified himself as Peter Lawford.

Otash was not happy to hear from Peter. Lawford was a friend, not a client, and friends knew to never call after ten o'clock at night. The fact that Peter was scared and said he was in big trouble, needing to talk with Otash immediately, did not matter. Otash knew that Lawford was a drug and alcohol abuser, a fact that made the urgency questionable.

Otash refused to see Lawford that night but Peter hung up on him and drove over anyway. After the hang-up, Otash made note of the time, confirming it was midnight. Later he said that Milt Ebbins claimed Peter had called Fred from his beach house at one-thirty in the morning. Otash, paid to be accurate and to know times and dates of events, was certain that his memory was the accurate one.

When Peter arrived, Otash remembered, he "looked like hell, trembling in the manner of a junkie going through cold turkey withdrawal. He was drunk, stoned, and an emotional basket case. I had picked guys up off the street looking like that when I was a beat cop, guys I took to a hospital to detox. This was the first time I had encountered a supposedly sober person [who looked like that]."

Peter, terrified, said that he thought Marilyn was dead, but Otash explained that he hadn't heard anything on the news.

"I mean she is . . . I mean . . . she was . . ." He started to sob. "Oh, God, what'll we do?"

Lawford was asked if he was talking about an accident of some sort.

"Oh, God, I don't know. I need a drink."

The discussion was confusing. Peter talked about Marilyn, saying she was going to get even for the way the men were treating her. It was a comment Otash had heard many times before. Not even Marilyn believed that she would ever actually try to do anything that would hurt the men in her life. It certainly wasn't a threat that was taken seriously.

Lawford knew Marilyn was drunk when she made such threats. He berated himself for not taking her seriously since he concluded that, this time, she might actually mean to kill herself.

Otash remembered noting the contradictory way Peter was talking, so he said to him, "You just told me you didn't know if she was dead. Is she or isn't she?"

"I guess she is. Her housekeeper is there with her. It's all my fault. But she was always threatening suicide. I never took it seriously. You know, she was just blowing off emotional steam. I was used to that. I'll bet there hasn't been a week all summer that she hasn't called me up and swore she was about to take her life. Tired of living, she said."

That was when, under continued questioning, Lawford admitted that he had no idea what had happened. He wasn't there.

None of this made sense to Otash. There was no way Marilyn could have been obviously suicidal if the attorney general of the United States stayed in town most of the day. Bobby would have run back to San Francisco, establishing as airtight an alibi for the day as he could.

And the threats Peter said Marilyn had been making were the same she made with some frequency; none had meant anything. However, what really mattered was that when Otash asked Peter about what the police were saying, Lawford admitted that, so far as he knew, they had not been called.

Otash remembered Peter looking panic-stricken as he said, "Jesus, Fred, I couldn't call the police. I came right over here."

"Who else is at the house?"

"Just Mrs. Murray, the housekeeper."

"Didn't she call the police, for Christ's sake?" Marilyn was either dead or dying, yet it seemed everyone was chiefly interested in saving his own ass. Otash had always known Lawford was weak, but to do nothing to help a so-called friend he thought might still be alive . . .

"Maybe," said Peter. "I don't think so. I don't know. She said to let Marilyn alone. Let her sleep."

Peter's biggest fear seemed to be that there might be something left in the house or something Marilyn retained that would implicate the president in the love affair that was long common gossip but would not be nationally publicized until years after his death.

625

Otash was concerned that someone on the scene act appropriately and call the police. He was disgusted by what was taking place. Lawford's concern was keeping the president and his brother from being embarrassed. He did not even know if Marilyn was dead or alive. He did not seem to consider that, if she was alive, immediate intervention might save her life.

Otash hoped that Eunice Murray would do what Lawford was unwilling to do—assuming she was on the premises. And if she did do what was right, it would mean that the coroner's investigator, an ambulance, detectives, and others would be swarming over the house. Otash pushing his way into the house would likely result in his arrest.

Otash said that Peter begged him, saying, "But you've got to help me. We're not talking about Peter Lawford here. We're talking about a presidential scandal. You're an ex-Marine, for Christ's sake. You want to dishonor your president?"

Disgusted, all Otash could think was that the president had dishonored himself.

&

From the *New York Times*, August 6, 1962:

Hollywood, Calif., Aug. 5—Marilyn Monroe, one of the most famous stars in Hollywood's history, was found dead early today in the bedroom of her home in the Brentwood section of Los Angeles. She was 36 years old.

Beside the bed was an empty bottle that had contained sleeping pills. Fourteen other bottles of medicines and tablets were on the nightstand.

HOUSEKEEPER LAST TO SEE HER

The last person to see her alive was her housekeeper, Mrs. Eunice Murray, who had lived with her. Mrs. Murray told the police that Miss Monroe retired to her bedroom about 8:00 P.M. yesterday.

About 3:25 A.M. today, the housekeeper noticed a light under Miss Monroe's door. She called to the actress, but received no answer. She tried the bedroom door. It was locked.

Mrs. Murray went outside and peered into the bedroom through the closed French windows. Miss Monroe, she later told the police, looked "peculiar." An arm was stretched across the bed and a hand hung limp on a telephone, she said.

The housekeeper rushed back into the house and telephoned Miss Monroe's analyst, Dr. Ralph R. Greenson. When he arrived a short time later, he broke a pane of the French window and opened it.

He quickly examined the star. She was dead. He phoned Miss Monroe's personal physician, Dr. Hyman Engelberg. After his arrival, the police were called. This was at 4:20, almost an hour after the housekeeper had called Dr. Greenson.

Inspector Edward Walker of the Los Angeles police was asked if he regarded such a delay in calling the police as unusual. He said he did not think so.

"So far as the doctors were concerned, there was no evidence of crime, and the first doctor already knew she was dead," he said. "I have no criticism to make of them."

Two radio patrolmen and a sergeant were the first policemen to arrive in the tree-lined neighborhood. Shortly afterward the case was taken over by Detective Sgt. R. E. Byron.

Room Simply Furnished

Sergeant Byron said Miss Monroe's bedroom was neat, but sparsely furnished. He estimated it at fifteen feet square.

"All she had in the room, so far as I can recall, was the bed, a little dressing table and the night table. And the telephone that she pulled on the bed."

After the police had completed their investigation, Miss Monroe's body was removed to the Westwood Village Mortuary. The house was sealed and placed under guard.

The body was later taken to the county morgue for the autopsy, which was performed by Dr. Tsunetomi ["Thomas"] Noguchi, a pathologist.

Sixty-three

~

Immediate Aftermath

Retired CBS newsman Walter Cronkite said it best during a discussion of obituaries of the famous on the April 26, 2006, edition of National Public Radio's *All Things Considered*. When someone dies too young, he said,

> the obituaries can only ask why? The first instinct was to assume some one or some thing was to blame. Even the Russians sat in judgment, calling her [Marilyn] a victim of Hollywood. In Hollywood a team of doctors and psychologists are trying to determine exactly what she was a victim of, her own hand or an accident. But the coroner's inquest can only tell us how Marilyn Monroe died, not why. Why, with everything to live for, with fame and fortune in their grasp, are so many of our movie queens so desperately unhappy?

Joe DiMaggio arranged for Marilyn Monroe's funeral, asking her half sister, Berneice Miracle, and her business manager, Inez Melson, to help. He restricted access, refusing to let the Kennedys, Frank Sinatra, or any of her friends from Hollywood attend. He felt that they were all responsible for the death of the woman he claimed he still loved, the woman he had planned to remarry. (In fact, Joe DiMaggio had a more intense relationship in the retelling after her death than he had in the months leading up to it. He was also one of the people who claimed that he truly cared about her yet did nothing to intervene to stop her drug addiction and alcoholism.)

The service, at 1:00 P.M. on August 8, 1962, at the Westwood Village

Mortuary Chapel on the grounds of the Westwood Memorial Cemetery, was odd for several reasons. The first was the fact that the service was conducted by Reverend A. J. Soldan, a Lutheran minister from the Village Church of Westwood, even though Marilyn had converted to Judaism (in large measure for her father-in-law, Isadore Miller, whom she had loved to the end).

The other oddity was the preparation of the body so the casket could be partially opened. Normally the damage from the autopsy would have led survivors to go with closed-casket service, to keep the memory of her beauty, rather than the reality of her disfigurement, in the minds of those attending. But once the partially open casket decision had been made, the Abbott & Hast funeral home prepared the body, assisted by her hairdresser, Sydney Guilaroff, and Allan "Whitey" Snyder, her longtime makeup man.

The autopsy had damaged her skull and so a wig was used, the style similar to the hairstyle she wore in *Something's Got to Give*. Marilyn's neck was swollen, so the embalmer had cut away some of her hair and made an incision on the back of her neck to relieve the swelling before sewing the flesh back together.

Mary Hamrock, a mortuary partner, obtained a chartreuse Pucci dress from Florence, Italy, for Marilyn to wear. The dress did not fit right, the autopsy having left Marilyn flat-chested. Berneice brought some of Marilyn's breast enhancers ("falsies") to add bulk, but they did not create the right effect. Mary Hamrock took out the falsies and fashioned her own from cotton, the end result looking exactly like the way the public had last seen Marilyn's figure when she was alive.

The eulogy was given by Lee Strasberg:

In her own lifetime she created a myth of what a poor girl from a deprived background could attain. For the entire world she became a symbol of the eternal feminine.

But I have no words to describe the myth and the legend. I did not know this Marilyn Monroe.

We gathered here today, knew only Marilyn—a warm human being, impulsive and shy, sensitive and in fear of rejection, yet ever avid for life and reaching out for fulfillment. I will not insult the privacy of your memory of her—a privacy she sought and treasured—by trying to describe her whom you knew to you who knew her. In our memories of her she remains alive, not only a shadow on the screen or a glamorous personality.

For us Marilyn was a devoted and loyal friend, a colleague constantly reaching for perfection. We shared her pain and difficulties and some of her joys. She was a member of our family. It is difficult to accept the fact that her zest for life has been ended by this dreadful accident.

Despite the heights and brilliance she attained on the screen, she was planning for the future; she was looking forward to participating in the many exciting things which she planned. In her eyes and in mine her career was just beginning. The dream of her talent, which she had nurtured as a child, was not a mirage. When she first came to me I was amazed at the startling sensitivity which she possessed and which had remained fresh and undimmed, struggling to express itself despite the life to which she had been subjected. Others were as physically beautiful as she was, but there was obviously something more in her, something that people saw and recognized in her performances and with which they identified. She had a luminous quality—a combination of wistfulness, radiance, yearning—to set her apart and yet make everyone wish to be a part of it, to share in the childish naiveté which was so shy and yet so vibrant.

This quality was even more evident when she was in the stage. I am truly sorry that the public who loved her did not have the opportunity to see her as we did, in many of the roles that foreshadowed what she would have become. Without a doubt she would have been one of the really great actresses of the stage.

Now it is at an end. I hope her death will stir sympathy and understanding for a sensitive artist and a woman who brought joy and pleasure to the world.

I cannot say goodbye. Marilyn never liked goodbyes, but in the peculiar way she had of turning things around so that they faced reality—I will say *au revoir*. For the country to which she has gone, we must all someday visit.

It should have ended there, but when the most famous film star of the day dies prematurely, a woman created by her own hand, with the help of the studio's publicity mill and friends such as Sid Skolsky, no one can let her rest in peace.

Death was the great enabler for those who wanted to reinforce their own role in Marilyn's life, seek revenge (though possibly subconsciously), or capitalize on what no one could disprove. The longer she was dead, the more such people seemed to appear, and the greater the distance from her life, the more exaggerated the stories.

Perhaps the most ironic situation was that of Beebe Goddard. Marilyn had stolen Beebe's childhood from hell, appropriating much of it as her own. Marilyn did, indeed, give her gifts during their adult lives, but Beebe made at least part of her income selling "authentic" Marilyn Monroe gifts, some of which had not even been made until after Marilyn's death.

To be fair, there have been other collectors of Marilyn Monroe memorabilia who eventually put their "authentic" items on display and up for sale. Many, if not most, of the items came into existence after her death.

Then there were people who had met Marilyn, perhaps even hung out with some of the same friends, but who were never close to her . . . until *after* Monroe's death. Robert Slatzer was the most outrageous. He claimed to have married Monroe during a wild weekend in Mexico; he provided stories about his lifelong relationship with her; he described how the Kennedy brothers had her murdered—and on and on.

Sam Giancana, who had dined with Marilyn, was a friend of her friends (or at least a working acquaintance), and had enjoyed sex with her, discussed how she had been "hit" because of her relationship with the White House and the danger to very important people. Not only was this Mafia myth but no professional would have murdered Monroe with a suppository, an injection under her fingernails, or any of the other bizarre methods ultimately described.

Interviews with members of top organized crime families who were earning respect for their skills in eliminating enemies during the early sixties talked of the training they received, especially those who went to an assassination school in Milan. They explained that there were three ways to kill that were common, safe for the killer, and would not fail: the most likely choices for a real mob hit. One was straight assassination involving a revolver held at the nape of the neck and fired upwards into the skull. It was usually a .22 or slightly larger caliber so the bullet would break up and destroy the brain. The second involved creating an accident, an easy arrangement in the winding hills of Southern California. And the third, the easiest of all, was the injection of potassium. Hospitals had found that a leading cause of death resulting from treatment came when an IV had the wrong amount of potassium. Too much potassium causes a heart attack, and the key to hiding an assassin's deed is the fact that when a heart attack occurs—natural or otherwise—the body is flooded with potassium. A professional wanting to kill Marilyn without leaving a trail could simply inject her with potassium. The resulting heart attack, combined with what was known about her long-term drug abuse, would assure any investigator that she had died of her own foolish actions, not a murder.

Seemingly credible individuals came forward with stories such as the transportation of the body to the hospital and back, never realizing that she had been found in full livor mortis and how that fact belied their assertions. And some thought that if they waited long enough to bring forth "the truth," no one could discredit them. This apparently was the case with long-retired Los Angeles prosecutor John W. Miner, who was head of the District Attorney's medical-legal section when Marilyn Monroe was killed.

Miner's claim to fame occurred in 2005 when he disclosed that Dr. Ralph Greenson had let him hear tapes Monroe had recorded in her home for use by the psychiatrist between their sessions. Miner said he put together a transcript of the tapes, though his description was not of a transcription but of notes made after he listened to the tapes. Either way they are dramatic and prove that she was undoubtedly murdered—and are absolute nonsense. They contain only information that seems titillating to the public and do not reflect the type of personal concerns that would be normal for work done with a psychiatrist. In addition, they go against the sessions she was used to having starting back when she first entered psychoanalysis in New York. Her comments, if real, seem to have been made for a tabloid audience, not a trusted doctor.

The "transcripts" include much biographical information about various relationships. But Marilyn is not new to this doctor/patient relationship. Dr. Greenson would have known these details; she would not have wasted her time providing them at this stage.

Much of Marilyn's so-called phrasing makes no sense when it comes to everyday speech. They seem to be included as "proof" of her intelligence and literary acumen. For example, "Little shrimp: is that redundant or tautological? I always get them mixed up." And "I was everything to him: wife, mother, sister, daughter, mistress." Or proof of her political leanings: "[JFK] is going to change our country. No child will go hungry. No person will sleep in the street and get his meals from garbage cans. People who can't afford it will get good medical care."

The "transcript" is also riddled with errors. For example, in one of the creepier sections she discusses her relationship with Mae West, providing such intimate details as "She is given an enema every day and she has at least one orgasm a day . . . Mae says her enemas and orgasms will keep her young until she is a hundred." Titillating, but Mae West said she never met Monroe.

There was also the supposed sexual liaison with actress Joan Crawford. She gave Crawford "a gigantic orgasm" that caused Joan to shriek "like a maniac." One trip to the bedroom was enough for Marilyn, though. When Crawford wanted an encore performance later in their relationship, Marilyn explained that she was not only straight, she had not personally enjoyed what had brought Crawford such pleasure. This story was also nonsense.

And there have been others, too many others. Jean Carmen, a beautiful blonde actress, good-time girl, and delightful raconteur, talked about Marilyn's love life with Bobby Kennedy, her "murder," and other fascinating details shared in frequent personal conversations. The fact that she was Marilyn's neighbor added to her credibility. However, people who truly had been friends with Marilyn maintained that she did not know Jean Carmen as anything more than a fellow celebrity. Jean also did not come forward with tales of the friendship until Marilyn was long dead and buried.

June DiMaggio, Joe's niece and Marilyn's supposed best friend, wrote a book providing details about which she is either mistaken or has no proof. These range from Marilyn's reaction to having sex with studio bosses early in her career: long showers, self-loathing, and other reactions that correspond with some rape-victim behavior. However, Marilyn never saw herself in that manner, never had such problems, other than when she had to exaggerate how good the man might be when they were in bed. One allegation is that the DiMaggio "niece" is actually someone named June E. Elpine. Whatever the truth of the relationship, friends of Marilyn never mentioned this "best friend" any more than they did Jean Carmen or Robert Slatzer. In addition, a close look at the claims made by June are too silly to be taken seriously, such as her bringing an anchovy pizza to her "best friend's" home on August 4, returning after her body was found and the police were still keeping the house closed to outsiders. Neither Eunice Murray nor Pat

Newcomb ever mentioned June, there was no way she would have been allowed inside immediately after the death, and the autopsy found no food in Marilyn's stomach (see Appendix 1).

There is even walking "proof" that Marilyn Monroe did not exactly die. Sherrie Lea Laird, a singer whose story seems to be everywhere on the Internet, has discovered—through the help of her doctor—that she is the reincarnation of Marilyn Monroe. This is different from the story of Elvis Presley living in Michigan and seen at a shopping mall, having faked his own death. Sherrie Lea knows Marilyn died. She was simply reincarnated, and Sherrie is frequently asked to discuss "her" relationship with Jack Kennedy and her feelings about Joe DiMaggio and others.

I won't take time to discuss Sherrie Lea's supposed past. She certainly seems honest about believing what she is saying (which does not make it true). However, credibility must be challenged with any allegedly reincarnated soul when they answer the questions that reveal dirty little secrets to which there were no witnesses, but do not discuss the mundane. For example, can she describe the suite in which Marilyn lived in the Waldorf Astoria Towers apartment, including the furnishings and their placement? Can she describe in detail the dressing rooms and living quarters when Marilyn was in studio and on location for the various movies? Can she describe her favorite casual places to eat, what they had on the menu, and what she liked to order? We never forget the little, everyday details of our lives; so if the reincarnated Marilyn remembers conversations, certainly she should remember the places she spent so many hours, weeks, and months of her life. So far, Sherrie Lea has not revealed them.

Ultimately the question must be asked: why does Norma Jean's creation, Marilyn Monroe, fascinate us so much? I began writing with the expectation that the book would be half this length, and even then I worried that it might not be interesting. Now I find myself with the same dilemma as the other serious biographers who have looked at her career. There are important people and incidents I have had to either omit or gloss over for lack of space. I have tried to ensure that the most important individuals and events at least are mentioned, and I have tried to present stories from her life that have not been discussed elsewhere. Still, even at this length, the book seems too short, despite the fact that the woman was just thirty-six years old when she died.

Perhaps the fascination lies in the fact that Marilyn belongs to a different era, a time when the movies had a designated blonde. She was the successor to Betty Grable and, it might be argued, predecessor to Goldie Hawn and Farrah Fawcett, who worked in both motion pictures and television (such as Hawn starring in *Laugh-In* along with Dan Rowan and Dick Martin— Rowan ironically being the father of Peter Lawford's second wife—and Fawcett starring in *Charlie's Angels*). But the number of blondes on the big and small screen increased, casting for women became more diverse, and the time when a woman could become a star because she was a publicity-created icon representing the ditzy, beautiful, funny, endearing, and intensely desirable girl next door passed from the industry.

Or the fascination might have to do with the men in her life. Even her blue-collar "nobody" of a first husband gained fame in his law enforcement career for creating what we now call the police SWAT team. She had the greatest athlete of the day, the leading intellectual heterosexual playwright, and the most handsome and successful actors. Ultimately, the president of the United States gave her a mystique unmatched today. Princess Diana was heralded as a lowly kindergarten teacher who gained the love of a prince before mutual adultery, divorce, a wealthy lover, and premature death ended her great, albeit tragic, Cinderella story. But Diana's conquests were limited, and the notoriety lingers in part because of ongoing lawsuits involving the royal family.

Marilyn Monroe, by contrast, the woman who excited a nation yet never really existed, is like one of the goddesses of ancient times: a cursed seductress who died an accidental death by her own hand, aided and abetted by friends, minions, lovers, employers, doctors, and fools. Perhaps the reason writers have worked so hard to find a conspiracy, to declare her a murder victim, to condemn this or that famous man is because, to see her for what she was—an intensely driven woman who became a junkie and alcoholic, an individual either of limited talent or one whose life was cut short before she could fully blossom—makes her richly human and intensely pathetic.

Or as *Time* magazine writer Ezra Goodman said of Marilyn, after being both angered and bemused by his publication's 1956 cover story being changed to match the Monroe myth rather than the facts he had uncovered: "her best acting is reserved for real life."

Appendix One

Marilyn's Autopsy

Coroner Thomas Noguchi conducted the operation. He was assisted by Eddy Day.

External examination: The unembalmed body is that of a thirty-six-year-old, well-developed, well-nourished Caucasian female weighing 117 pounds and measuring 65-1/2 inches in length. The scalp is covered with bleached blond hair. The eyes are blue. The fixed lividity is noted in the face, neck, chest, upper portions of arms, and the right side of the abdomen. The faint lividity which disappears upon pressure is noted in the back and posterior aspect of the arms and legs. A slight ecchymotic area is noted in the left hip and left side of lower back. The breast shows no significant lesion. There is a horizontal 3-inch long surgical scar in the right upper quadrant of the abdomen. A suprapubic surgical scar measuring 5 inches in length is noted. The conjunctivae are markedly congested; however, no ecehymosis or petechiae are noted. The nose shows no evidence of fracture. The external auditory canals are not remarkable: No evidence of trauma is noted in the scalp, forehead, cheeks, lips, or chin. The neck shows no evidence of trauma. Examination of the hands and nails shows no defects. The lower extremities show no evidence of trauma.

Body cavity: The usual Y-shaped incision is made to open the thoracic and abdominal cavities. The pleural and abdominal cavities contain no excess of fluid or blood. The mediastinum shows no shifting or widening. The diaphragm is within normal limits. The lower edge of the liver is within the costal margin. The organs are in normal position and relationship.

Cardiovascular system: The heart weighs 300 grams. The pericardial cavity contains no excess of fluid. The epicardium and pericardium are smooth and glistening. The left ventricular wall measures 1.1 cm. and the right 0.2 cm. The papillary muscles are not hypertrophic. The chordae tendinea are not thickened or shortened. The valves have the usual number of leaflets which are thin and pliable. The tricuspid valve measures 10 cm, the pulmonary valve 6.5 cm, mitral valve 9.5 cm, and aortic valve 7 cm in circumference. There is no septal defect. The foramen ovale is closed. The coronary arteries arise from their usual location and are distributed in normal fashion. Multiple sections of the anterior descending branch of the left coronary artery with a 5 mm interial demonstrate a patent lumen throughout. The circumflex branch and the right coronary artery also demonstrate a patent lumen. The pulmonary artery contains no thrombus. The aorta has a bright yellow smooth intima.

Respiratory system: The right lung weighs 465 grams and the left 420 grams. Both lungs are moderately congested with some edema. The surface is dark and red with mottling. The posterior portion of the lungs show severe congestion. The tracheobronchial tree contains no aspirated material or blood. Multiple sections of the lungs show congestion and edematous fluid exuding from the cut surface. No consolidation or suppuration is noted. The mucosa of the larynx is grayish white.

Liver and biliary system: The liver weighs 1890 grams. The surface is dark brown and smooth. There are marked adhesions through the omentum and abdominal wall in the lower portion of the liver as the gallbladder has been removed. The common duct is widely patent. No calculus or obstructive material is found. Multiple sections of the liver show slight accentuation of the lobular pattern; however, no hemorrhage or tumor is found.

Hemic and lymphatic system: The spleen weighs 190 grams. The surface is dark red and smooth. Section shows dark red homogeneous firm cut surface.

The Malpighian bodies are not clearly identified. There is no evidence of lymphadenopathy. The bone marrow is dark red in color. Endocrine system: The adrenal glands have the usual architectural cortex and medulla. The thyroid glands are of normal size, color, and consistency. Urinary system: The kidneys together weigh 350 grams. Their capsules can be stripped without difficulty. Dissection shows a moderately congested parenchyma. The cortical surface is smooth. The pelves and ureters are not dilated or stenosed. The urinary bladder contains approximately 150 cc of clear straw-colored fluid. The mucosa is not altered.

Genital system: The external genitalia shows no gross abnormality. Distribution of the pubic hair is of female pattern. The uterus is of the usual size. Multiple sections of the uterus show the usual thickness of the uterine wall without tumor nodules. The endometrium is grayish yellow, measuring up to 0.2 cm in thickness. No polyp or tumor is found. The cervix is clear, showing no nabothian cysts. The tubes are intact. The right ovary demonstrates recent corpus luteum haemorrhagicum. The left ovary shows corpora lutea and albicantia. A vaginal smear is taken. Digestive system: The esophagus has a longitudinal folding mucosa. The stomach is almost completely empty. The contents is brownish mucoid fluid. The volume is estimated to be no more than 20 cc. No residue of the pills is noted. A smear made from the gastric contents and examined under the polarized microscope shows no refractile crystals. The mucosa shows marked congestion and submucosal petechial hemorrhage diffusely. The duodenum shows no ulcer. The contents of the duodenum is also examined under polarized microscope and shows no refractile crystals. The remainder of the small intestine shows no gross abnormality. The appendix is absent. The colon shows marked congestion and purplish discoloration. The pancreas has a tan lobular architecture. Multiple sections shows a patent duct.

Skeletomuscular system: The clavicle, ribs, vertebrae and pelvic bones show fracture lines. All bones of the extremities are examined by palpation showing no evidence of fracture.

Head and central nervous system: The brain weighs 1440 grams. Upon reflection of the scalp there is no evidence of contusion or hemorrhage. The temporal muscles are intact. Upon removal of the dura mater the cerebro-spinal fluid is clear. The superficial vessels are slightly congested. The convolutions of the brain are not flattened. The contour of the brain is not distorted. No blood is found in the epidural, subdural, or subarachnoid spaces. Multiple sections of the brain show the usual symmetrical ventricles and basal ganglia. Examination of the cerebellum and brain stem shows no gross abnormality. Following removal of the dura mater from the base of the skull and calvarium no skull fracture is demonstrated.

Liver temperature taken at 10:30 A.M. registered 89 F.

Specimen: Unembalmed blood is taken for alcohol and barbiturate examination. Liver, kidney, stomach and contents, urine, and intestine are saved for further toxicological study. A vaginal smear is made.

T. NOGUCHI, M.D.
DEPUTY MEDICAL EXAMINER 8-13-62

Appendix Two

~

Last Will and Testament

I, MARILYN MONROE, do make, publish and declare this to be my Last Will and Testament.

FIRST: I hereby revoke all former Wills and Codicils by me made.

SECOND: I direct my Executor, hereinafter named, to pay all of my just debts, funeral expenses and testamentary charges as soon after my death as can conveniently be done.

THIRD: I direct that all succession, estate or inheritance taxes which may be levied against my estate and/or against any legacies and/or devises here-inafter set forth shall be paid out of my residuary estate.

FOURTH: (a) I give and bequeath to BERNICE MIRACLE, should she survive me, the sum of $10,000.00.

(b) I give and bequeath to MAY REIS, should she survive me, the sum of $10,000.00.

(c) I give and bequeath to NORMAN and HEDDA ROSTEN, or to the survivor of them, or if they should both predecease me, then to their daughter, PATRICIA ROSTEN, the sum of $5,000.00, it being my wish that such sum be used for the education of PATRICIA ROSTEN.

(d) I give and bequeath all of my personal effects and clothing to LEE STRASBERG, or if he should predecease me, then to my Executor herein-after named, it being my desire that he distribute these, in his sole discretion, among my friends, colleagues and those to whom I am devoted.

FIFTH; I give and bequeath to my Trustee, hereinafter named, the sum of $100,000.00, in Trust, for the following uses and purposes:

(a) To hold, manage, invest and reinvest the said property and to receive and collect the income therefrom.

(b) To pay the net income therefrom, together with such amounts of principal as shall be necessary to provide $5,000.00 per annum, in equal quarterly installments, for the maintenance and support of my mother, GLADYS BAKER, during her lifetime.

(c) To pay the net income therefrom, together with such amounts of principal as shall be necessary to provide $2,500.00 per annum, in equal quarterly installments, for the maintenance and support of MRS. MICHAEL CHEKHOV during her lifetime.

(d) Upon the death of the survivor between my mother, GLADYS BAKER, and MRS. MICHAEL CHEKHOV to pay over the principal remaining in the Trust, together with any accumulated income, to DR. MARIANNE KRIS to be used by her for the furtherance of the work of such psychiatric institutions or groups as she shall elect.

SIXTH: All the rest, residue and remainder of my estate, both real and personal, of whatsoever nature and wheresoever situate, of which I shall die seized or possessed or to which I shall be in any way entitled, or over which I shall possess any power of appointment by Will at the time of my death, including any lapsed legacies, I give, devise and bequeath as follows:

(a) to MAY REIS the sum of $40,000.00 or 25% of the total remainder of my estate, whichever shall be the lesser,

(b) To DR. MARIANNE KRIS 25% of the balance thereof, to be used by her as set forth in ARTICLE FIFTH (d) of this my Last Will and Testament.

(c) To LEE STRASBERG the entire remaining balance.

SEVENTH: I nominate, constitute and appoint AARON R. FROSCH Executor of this my Last Will and Testament. In the event that he should die or fail to qualify, or resign or for any other reason be unable to act, I nominate, constitute and appoint L. ARNOLD WEISSBERGER in his place and stead.

EIGHTH: I nominate, constitute and appoint AARON R. FROSCH Trustee under this my Last Will and Testament. In the event he should die or fail to qualify, or resign or for any other reason be unable to act, I nominate, constitute and appoint L. Arnold Weissberger in his place and stead.

Marilyn Monroe (L.S.)
SIGNED, SEALED, PUBLISHED and DECLARED by MARILYN
MONROE, the Testatrix above named, as and for her Last Will and Testa-
ment, in our presence and we, at her request and in her presence and in the
presence of each other, have hereunto subscribed our names as witnesses
this 14th day of January, One Thousand Nine Hundred Sixty-One
Aaron R. Frosch residing at 10 West 86th St. NYC
Louise H. White residing at 709 E. 56 St., New York, NY

Postscript

~

The Reinvestigation Twenty Years
after Her Death

Twenty years after Marilyn Monroe's death, the Los Angeles District Attorney's Office reinvestigated the circumstances of the night in question, ultimately validating the work of coroner Thomas Noguchi, M.D.

Conspiracy theories abounded after two decades. Some long alleged, for example, that Marilyn had drugs administered to her at the home of Frank Sinatra and was then flown from Palm Springs to Brentwood, where she was placed in her own bedroom. And in his 1984 book *Coroner*, Dr. Noguchi mentioned listening to his car radio as an announcer said, "James Hall, who was an ambulance attendant in 1962, says that Marilyn Monroe was murdered right before his eyes. In an exclusive story in the newspaper the *Globe*, he was quoted as stating that he was actually reviving Monroe when he was pushed aside by a 'doctor' who injected a mysterious fluid directly into her heart and killed her."

There were many other theories, but the reinvestigation report noted, "Her murder would have required a massive, in-place conspiracy covering all of the principals at the death scene on August 4 and 5, 1962; the actual killer or killers; the Chief Medical Examiner-Coroner; the autopsy surgeon to whom the case was fortuitously assigned, and almost all of the police officers assigned to the case, as well as their superiors in the LAPD . . . our inquiries and document examination uncovered no credible evidence supporting a murder theory." And going unsaid in the report, perhaps not

645

even considered by the investigators, was the fact that Marilyn was not worth a conspiracy. Of all the people involved with the dark side of the Kennedy brothers, she was too well known to have her relationship be seen as threatening.

The reinvestigation had validity in that much had changed in scientific procedure in the last twenty years. Testing devices were far more sophisticated and capable of occasionally revealing previously overlooked causes of death. However, Dr. Boyd G. Stephens, Chief Medical Examiner/Coroner in San Francisco, was asked as an independent expert to review the twenty-year-old autopsy, after which he concluded that "even the application of more advanced—1982—state-of-the-art procedures would not, in all reasonable probability, change the ultimate conclusions reached by Dr. Noguchi in 1962."

The official report, prepared by unbiased investigators, was a relief to Dr. Noguchi, who had always maintained that he had performed an accurate autopsy. Over the years, there were numerous "experts" who claimed that Monroe died from an injection, not drugs she herself had consumed. Norman Mailer, the highly respected author of numerous bestsellers, was seemingly infatuated with the idea of Monroe, writing about her in the manner of a fan who had read her biographies instead of working as a journalist interviewing those who knew and had worked with her. Among other quotes in his book on her life was, "The word was out to keep this thing a suicide, not to make it a murder. . . . If you're the coroner and you feel the official mood is to find evidence of a suicide, you wouldn't particularly want to come in with murder."

Robert Slatzer, the author who turned a brief meeting and single photograph into a moneymaking second career, claimed that sources within the Los Angeles Police Department said Dr. Noguchi did prepare an accurate autopsy report—which was suppressed and replaced with a fake one, also written by the doctor.

It was too late for Dr. Noguchi to correct the misunderstandings of the people who were his harshest critics. He wrote in his autopsy that Monroe's stomach was "almost completely empty," but he also felt she had consumed a large quantity of pills. The critics did not realize that a drug addict's stomach develops along the lines of food routinely consumed. The body has no trouble digesting routinely taken drugs or food, sending them into the intestinal tract. It is only with unfamiliar drugs or food that indigestion occurs, leaving traces. Dr. Noguchi felt that the lack of evidence of pills confirms the addiction: the addict, in this case, being Monroe.

One writer, George Carpozi Jr., quoted Dr. Sidney B. Weinberg, then chief medical examiner of Suffolk County, New York, in his evaluation of the Noguchi autopsy, raising such issues as: "With such a massive dose of barbiturates in her system, you must expect to find at least some partially digested capsules or tablets in the stomach, . . . some powdery material adhering to the stomach lining, and oftentimes—as in this case—you would expect a corrosive or raw, red appearance on the stomach lining."

Noguchi did not dispute Weinberg's conclusions but merely noted that his report stated that the "mucosa shows petechial hemorrhage diffusely." The layperson was looking for mention of redness, not understanding the technical terms used by Dr. Noguchi. Beneath the mucosa (stomach lining) there was "widespread pinpoint hemorrhaging—the raw, red appearance Dr. Weinberg suggested."

Noguchi also addressed the fantasies of laypeople who thought they had expertise. Monroe used large quantities of Nembutal, a drug commonly used for suicide. He had seen the results often, and though the pill is yellow, and amateurs imagined that it should have stained the inner linings of the throat and stomach, reality was different. "I pointed out that if you take a yellow Nembutal and touch it to your lips to moisten it, then rub your finger over the wet pill, you'll find that the yellow color does not rub off." The capsule was made with a color that did not run.

Finally, the former coroner discussed the fact that he said in the original autopsy that there were no visible needle marks—and he examined the skin with a magnifying glass—even though it was known the actress had been injected with drugs by Dr. Greenson. Again, this was a layperson's question. Dr. Noguchi explained that whenever a surgical needle is injected in the skin, the puncture mark made by the fine point heals within hours. Greenson's injection had been almost forty-eight hours prior to the autopsy. By then it, or any similar injection, would be invisible.

Ultimately, despite the "experts" who created emotional books based on reading, supposition, and/or outright misstatements of fact, Dr. Noguchi's original work was validated. The only question that remained was whether or not Monroe committed suicide, especially since she had been laughing on the telephone with Joe DiMaggio Jr. at 7:30 P.M. Yet that call came *after* the call with Peter Lawford that indicated she knew she had overdosed. And there was the bruise on Marilyn's hip, though that was explained by the early visit with which Noguchi was unfamiliar.

The end result, twenty years later, was the conclusion that Marilyn Monroe had committed suicide, a term that must be used to indicate death by her own hand. Was it an accidental overdose? Was it a deliberate overdose? And did it have anything to do with her life circumstances?

Thomas Noguchi, at the end of his chapter on Monroe in *Coroner*, states the obvious: "The remaining questions will go unanswered, and no one will ever be able to say definitely what went on that evening which, in only thirty minutes, transformed Marilyn Monroe from a beautiful and talented actress, laughing and talking cheerfully on the telephone, to a dying movie star—and an undying legend."

Quite apart from the conspiracy theorists, the answer seems to be with the cause of death itself. Professionally there was no reason for Monroe's death. She was going to return to work on *Something's Got to Give*. She was going to play the lead in *The Jean Harlow Story*. And the problems she was having with the lovers of the moment were no different than those she had experienced in the past, even if one of them was the president of the United States.

Personally, matters were different. She was on an emotional roller-coaster ride with the alcohol and drugs that had been destroying her for years. Her moods shifted with the drugs, as she ingested them and later, while they were still in her bloodstream, even as she thought she needed more.

The depressant alcohol typically shows a familiar pattern for the person overindulging. First, there is a loss of inhibition that can make the mildly intoxicated person the "life of the party," especially to others in the same state of inebriation. Then speech becomes loud, and the person may become angry or belligerent over something that would normally not cause such emotions. Finally, the person becomes quiet, perhaps falling asleep, as the full depressant takes over.

Marilyn likely experienced something similar, her mood swings being normal for what she had ingested. She may have deliberately taken too many drugs when she went from the uninhibited high with Joe DiMaggio

Jr. on the telephone to the state of unconsciousness and death. Or she may have felt, as she often did, that she would not be able to sleep after her happy conversation with Joe Jr. and so took more. The decisions she made and the thoughts that were factors in her making them had nothing to do with a conspiracy or with a sudden, overwhelming urge to die. Marilyn Monroe had been taking too many drugs for too long a period, gradually destroying her body as other actors had done and would continue to do. It was that, and not the CIA, the FBI, the Mafia, the president, or any other real or perceived bad guy that killed her. This was true when she died. It was proven again twenty years after her death. And it remains true today.

SELECTED BIBLIOGRAPHY

Andrews, Suzanna. "Arthur Miller's Missing Act." *Vanity Fair* 565 (September 2007): 252.

Bailey, Margaret J. *Those Glorious Glamour Years: The Great Hollywood Costume Designs of the Nineteen Thirties.* Secaucus, NJ: Citadel Press, 1982.

Barlett, Donald L., and James B. Steele. *Howard Hughes: His Life and Madness.* New York: W.W. Norton and Company, 1979.

Barris, George. *Marilyn: Her Life in Her Own Words.* New York: Citadel Press, 1995.

Beck, Carl. *Contempt of Congress—A Study of the Prosecutions Initiated by the Committee on Un-American Activities.* New Orleans: The Hauser Press, 1959.

Behlmer, Rudy, ed. *Memo from Darryl F. Zanuck: The Golden Years at Twentieth Century-Fox.* New York: Grove Press, 1993.

Brando, Marlon, with Robert Lindsey. *Brando: Songs My Mother Taught Me.* New York: Random House, 1994.

Brown, Peter Harry, and Pat H. Broeske. *Howard Hughes: The Untold Story.* New York: DaCapo Press, 1996/2004.

Buskin, Richard. *Blonde Heat: The Sizzling Screen Career of Marilyn Monroe.* New York: Billboard Books, 2001.

Calistro, Paddy, and Fred E. Basten. *Hollywood Archive: The Hidden History of Hollywood in the Golden Age.* New York: Universe Publishing division of Rizzoli International: 2000.

Carlisle, Olga, and Rose Styron. "The Art of Theatre II: Arthur Miller, an Interview." *Paris Review* 10 (1966): 61–98.

Chandler, Charlotte. *Nobody's Perfect: Billy Wilder—A Personal Biography.* New York: Simon and Schuster, 2002.

Crowe, Cameron. *Conversations with Wilder.* New York: Alfred Knopf, 1999.

Custen, George. *Twentieth Century's Fox: Darryl F. Zanuck and the Culture of Hollywood.* New York: Basic Books, 1997.

De Dienes, André. *Marilyn.* Los Angeles: Taschen America, 2004.

DiMaggio, June, as told to Mary Jane Popp. *Marilyn, Joe and Me: June DiMaggio Tells It Like It Was*. Roseville, CA: Penmarin Books, 2006.

Dougherty, Jim, as told to LC Van Savage. *To Norma Jeane with Love, Jimmie*. Chesterfield, MO: BeachHouse Books, 2001.

Eells, George. *Hedda and Louella: A Dual Biography of Hedda Hopper and Louella Parsons*. New York: G. P. Putnam's Sons, 1972.

Fraser-Cavassoni, Natasha. *Sam Spiegel*. New York: Simon & Schuster, 2003.

Friedrich, Otto. *City of Nets: A Portrait of Hollywood in the 1940s*. New York: Harper & Row, 1986.

Gilmore, John. *Inside Marilyn Monroe*. Los Angeles: Ferine Books, 2007.

Goode, James. *The Story of the Misfits*. Indianapolis: Bobbs-Merrill, 1963.

Goodman, Ezra. *The Fifty Year Decline and Fall of Hollywood*. New York: Simon & Schuster, 1961.

Griffin, Alice. *Understanding Arthur Miller*. Columbia, SC: University of South Carolina Press, 1996.

Guilaroff, Sydney, as told to Cathy Griffin. *Crowning Glory: Reflections of Hollywood's Favorite Confidant*. Santa Monica, CA: General Publishing Company, 1996.

Hack, Richard. *Hughes: The Private Diaries, Memos and Letters*. Beverly Hills: New Millennium Press, 2001.

Hersh, Burton. *Bobby and J. Edgar*. New York: Carroll & Graf Publishers, 2007.

Higham, Charles. *Howard Hughes: The Secret Life*. New York: St. Martin's Griffin, 1993/2004.

Hoyt, Edwin P. *Marilyn the Tragic Venus*. Radnor, PA: Chilton Book Company, 1965/1973.

Johnson, Nora. *Flashback: Nora Johnson on Nunnally Johnson*. Garden City, NY: Doubleday, 1979.

Kazan, Elia. *A Life*. New York: Anchor Books of Doubleday, 1988.

Kelley, Kitty. *His Way: The Unauthorized Biography of Frank Sinatra*. New York: Bantam Books, 1986.

Kidder, Clark. *Marilyn Monroe Cover to Cover*. Iola, WI: Krause Publications, 1999.

Kobal, John. *People Will Talk*. New York: Alfred Knopf, 1985.

Marill, Alvin H. *Mickey Rooney*. Jefferson, NC: McFarland and Company, 2005.

Martin, Pete. *Will Acting Spoil Marilyn Monroe?* Garden City: Doubleday, 1956.

Marx, Arthur. *The Nine Lives of Mickey Rooney*. New York: Stein and Day, 1986.

Mathison, Richard. *His Weird and Wanton Ways: The Secret Life of Howard Hughes*. New York: William Morrow & Company, 1977.

Messick, Hank. *John Edgar Hoover*. New York: David McKay, 1972.

———. *The Mob in Show Business*. New York: Pyramid Books, 1973.

Miller, Arthur. *After the Fall*. New York: Viking Press, 1964.

———. "Are You Now Or Were You Ever?" *The Guardian/The Observer* (on line): Saturday, June 17, 2000.

———. *Timebends: A Life*. New York: Grove, 1987.

Miracle, Berneice Baker, and Mona Rae Miracle. *My Sister Marilyn: A Memoir of Marilyn Monroe*. Chapel Hill, NC: Algonquin Books of Chapel Hill, 1994.

Murray, Eunice, and Rose Shade. *Marilyn: The Last Months*. New York: Pyramid, 1975.

Nelson, Nancy. *Evenings with Cary Grant: Recollections in His Own Words and by Those Who Knew Him Best*. New York: William Morrow and Company, 1991.

Nicholson, Stuart. *Ella Fitzgerald: The Complete Biography*. New York: Routledge, 2004.

Noguchi, Thomas T., M.D., with Joseph DiMona. *Coroner*. New York: Simon and Schuster, 1983.

Orten, Terry. *The Temptation of Innocence in the Dramas of Arthur Miller*. Columbia, MO: University of Missouri Press, 2002.

Parsons, Louella. *Tell It to Louella*. New York: G. P. Putnam's Sons, 1961.

Pepitone, Lena, and William Stadiem. *Marilyn Monroe Confidential*. New York: Simon & Schuster, 1979.

Porter, Darwin. *Brando Unzipped*. New York: Blood Moon Productions, 2005.

———. *Howard Hughes: Hell's Angel*. New York: Blood Moon Productions, 2005.

Rooney, Mickey. *i.e., an Autobiography*. New York: G. P. Putnam's Sons, 1965.

———. *Life Is Too Short*. New York: Villard Books, 1991.

Roudané, Matthew C. *Conversations with Arthur Miller*. Jackson, MS: University Press of Mississippi, 1987.

Rubin, Gretchen. *Forty Ways to Look at JFK*. New York: Ballantine Books, 2005.

Schickel, Richard. *Elia Kazan: A Biography*. New York: HarperCollins, 2005.

Shaw, Sam, and Norman Rosten. *Marilyn Among Friends*. New York: Henry Holt & Company, 1987.

Skolsky, Sidney. *Don't Get Me Wrong—I Love Hollywood*. New York: G. P. Putnam's Sons, 1975.

———. *Times Square Tintypes*. New York: Ives Washburn Publisher, 1930.

Solomon, Aubrey. *Twentieth Century-Fox: A Corporate and Financial History*. Metuchen, NJ: The Scarecrow Press, Inc., 1988.

Spoto, Donald. *Marilyn Monroe: The Biography*. New York: HarperCollins, 1993.

Stempel, Tom. *Screen Writer Nunnally Johnson*. San Diego: A. S. Barnes and Company, 1980.

Strasberg, Susan. *Marilyn and Me: Sisters, Rivals, Friends*. New York: Warner Books, 1992.

Sullivan, William, with Bill Brown. *The Bureau: My Thirty Years in Hoover's FBI.* New York: W. W. Norton & Company, Inc., 1979.

Summers, Anthony. *Goddess: The Secret Lives of Marilyn Monroe.* New York: Macmillan, 1985.

Thomas, Tony. *Howard Hughes in Hollywood.* Secaucus, NJ: Citadel Press, 1985.

Ward, Richard Lewis. *A History of the Hal Roach Studios.* Carbondale, IL: Southern Illinois University Press, 2005.

Wayne, Jane Ellen. *Marilyn's Men: The Private Life of Marilyn Monroe.* England: Robson Books, 1992.

Weatherby, W. J. *Conversations with Marilyn.* New York: Paragon House, 1992.

Wilkerson, Tichi and Marcia Borie. *The Hollywood Reporter: The Golden Years.* New York: Coward McCann, 1984.

Wilson, Earl. *Hot Times: True Tales of Hollywood and Broadway.* Chicago: Contemporary Books, Inc., 1984.

———. *Show Business Laid Bare.* New York: Putnam, 1974.

———. *The Show Business Nobody Knows.* Chicago: Cowles Book Company, Inc. division of Henry Regnery Co., 1971.

———. *Sinatra: An Unauthorized Biography.* New York: Bantam Books, 1963.

Zolotow, Maurice. *Marilyn Monroe.* New York: Harper & Row: 1960/1990.

The Internet web site YouTube contains extensive material related to Marilyn's life. One can, for example, watch the *Person to Person* interview, see Marilyn perform in Korea, and view clips from various news programs. Start the site search with the name Marilyn Monroe and then expand to the sites of others in her life—Joe DiMaggio, Arthur Miller, and so forth.

Extensive use was made of FBI files concerning:

Sammy Davis Jr.
Clark Gable
Sam Giancana
Hedda Hopper
Marilyn Monroe
Frank Sinatra

Among the libraries with special collections involving interviews, documents, and other resources were the Margaret Herrick Library in Beverly Hills, the John F. Kennedy Presidential Library, and the Beverly Hills Public Library.

INDEX

4/2009